# NEGOTIATION

# NEGOTIATION

**Second Edition**

**Roy J. Lewicki**
*The Ohio State University*

**Joseph A. Litterer**
*University of Massachusetts*

**John W. Minton**
*Appalachian State University*

**David M. Saunders**
*McGill University*

*IRWIN*

Chicago • Bogotá • Boston • Buenos Aires • Caracas
London • Madrid • Mexico City • Sydney • Toronto

**IRWIN**
**Concerned About Our Environment**
In recognition of the fact that our company is a large end-user of
fragile yet replenishable resources, we at IRWIN can assure you
that every effort is made to meet or exceed Environmental Protection Agency
(EPA) recommendations and requirements for a "greener" workplace.
To preserve these natural assets, a number of environmental policies, both
companywide and department-specific, have been implemented. From the
use of 50% recycled paper in our textbooks to the printing of promotional
materials with recycled stock and soy inks to our office paper recycling program, we are committed to reducing waste and replacing environmentally
unsafe products with safer alternatives.

© The McGraw-Hill Companies, Inc., 1985 and 1994

Senior sponsoring editor: Kurt L. Strand
Editorial assistant: Michele Dooley
Marketing manager: Kurt Messersmith
Project editor: Rebecca Dodson
Production manager: Laurie Kersch
Designer: Mercedes Santos
Art coordinator: Heather Burbridge
Art studio: Precision Graphic
Cover illustrator: Chris Gall
Compositor: University Graphics
Typeface: 10/12 Times Roman
Printer: R. R. Donnelley & Sons Company

**Library of Congress Cataloging-in-Publication Data**
Negotiation / by Roy J. Lewicki . . . [et al.]. — 2nd ed.
        p.   cm.
    "This textbook parallels . . . a completely revised companion
volume, Negotiation : readings, exercises and cases"—Pref.
    Includes bibliographical references and index.
    ISBN 0-256-10163-9
    1. Negotiation in business.   I. Lewicki, Roy J.
HD58.6.N437   1994
658.4—dc20                                                    93-40307

*Printed in the United States of America*
        7890  DO  10987

*To our children: Karen, Susan, Aaron and two Davids: who probably taught us more about negotiation than we ever wanted to know.*

# Preface to the Second Edition

"This book has been a long time in the making." So began the preface to the first edition of this book, published in 1985. A similar phrase would be no less appropriate for this volume: this book has been a long time in the revision.

Since the first edition was published, the world of teaching and research on negotiation has changed significantly. There are several new professional divisions (the Conflict Management Division of the Academy of Management and the International Association of Conflict Management) that have devoted themselves exclusively to facilitating research and teaching in these fields. There are several new journals *(Negotiation Journal, International Journal of Conflict Management)* that focus exclusively on academic research and writing for professional practitioners in these fields. There are new funding agencies, such as the National Institute for Dispute Resolution, whose mission has been to enhance the development of new research and training materials. Finally, through the generosity of the Hewlett Foundations, there are a number of new university centers that are devoted to enhancing the quality of teaching, research, and service in the negotiation and conflict management fields. Many, many schools now have several courses in negotiation and conflict management—in schools of business, public policy, psychology, social work, education, and natural resources. And development has occurred on the practitioner side as well. Books, seminars, and training courses on negotiation and conflict management have proliferated. And finally, mediation has become an extremely popular process as an alternative to litigation for handling divorce, community disputes, and land use conflicts. In pragmatic terms, all of this development means that as we assembled this second edition, we have had a much more diverse and rich pool of resources from which to sample. The net result for the student and instructor is a highly improved pool of teaching and research materials that has permitted us to extensively revise this text, referring to the very best and most recent work on negotiation and related topics of power, influence, and conflict management.

For the instructor who was not familiar with the first edition, a brief overview is in order. The text is organized into 14 chapters. The first chapter introduces the field of negotiation and conflict management; the second describes the basic problems in situations of interdependence with other people and managing that interdependence. The next three chapters focus on the basic dynamics of competitive (win-lose) and integrative (win-win) negotiation and the planning and strategy processes associated with each one. Chapter 6 explicitly focuses on negotiation breakdowns and ways to manage them more effectively.

The next five chapters describe and review critical subprocesses and specific dynamics of negotiation: persuasion processes, communication processes, the social context of negotiation (the role played by constituencies, audiences, and parties other than the negotiators themselves), sources of power and uses of influence, and individual differences ("personality" factors) in negotiation. Chapter 12 addresses ways that negotiators can break negotiation deadlocks through the assistance of third parties such as mediators, arbitrators, and other intermediaries. Chapter 13 specifically addresses negotiator ethics. Finally, Chapter 14 describes many of the challenges of international negotiation—that is, negotiating across international and cultural boundaries.

For those instructors who were familiar with the first edition, the most visible changes will be in the content and organization of the book, as follows:

1. The content is almost **entirely** new. Every chapter was completely revised for this second edition, and approximately 60 percent of the content is new.

2. We have reorganized the book slightly. First, as you will note, we have expanded from 13 to 14 chapters. We have explicitly recognized the importance of cross-cultural differences in negotiation by adding a new chapter on international negotiations. We have also reorganized some of the early sections by placing the chapter on planning, preparation, and strategy development slightly later in the outline, and by explicitly addressing techniques for managing negotiation breakdowns. We have also increased the focus on ethics in negotiation and expanded our coverage of individual differences among negotiators.

3. This textbook parallels the structure of a completely revised companion volume, *Negotiation: Readings, Exercises and Cases,* by Roy Lewicki, Joseph Litterer, David Saunders, and John Minton, also published by Richard D. Irwin (1993). An excellent *Instructor's Manual* is also available from the publisher. The text and readings books can be used together or separately, and we encourage instructors to contact the publisher for an examination copy.

Once again, this book could not have been completed without the assistance of many other people. We would specifically like to thank:

- Many of our colleagues in the negotiation and dispute resolution field, who adopted and gave us excellent feedback on the first edition and whose research contributions have made the growth of this field possible.
- Specific colleagues who have read and commented on our revised chapters, including Nancy J. Adler, Deborah Kolb, Debra Shapiro, and Stephen Weiss.

- Reviewers Michael Elliot of the Georgia Institute of Technology, Max H. Bazerman of Northwestern University, and Patricia Seybolt of the University of Utah for their insightful suggestions and comments.
- Tracey Hesslink of the Master of Labor and Human Resource Management Program at the Ohio State University, for her work on the Lucasville Prison Riot case.
- The excellent editorial assistance of Marcia Caton Campbell.
- The Hewlett Foundation, for their grant to the senior author, which provided financial resources that were used for background research and manuscript preparation.
- The staff of Richard D. Irwin, and particularly Kurt Strand, our editor, for his confidence in the project and his continued patience as we completed the project.
- Our families, who continue to provide us with the time and support that we require to finish this project.

Thank you one and all!

**Roy J. Lewicki**
**Joseph A. Litterer**
**John W. Minton**
**David M. Saunders**

# Contents in Brief

# Contents

**Tactical Tasks.**

*Assess Outcome Values and the Costs of Termination. Manage the Other Party's Impressions. Modify the Other Party's Perceptions. Manipulate the Actual Costs of Delay or Termination.*

**Positions Taken During Negotiation.**

*Opening Offer. Opening Stance. Initial Concessions. Role of Concessions. Pattern of Concession Making. Final Offer.*

**Commitment.**

*Tactical Considerations in Using Commitments. Establishing a Commitment. Preventing the Other Party from Committing Prematurely. Finding Ways to Abandon a Committed Position.*

**Typical Hardball Tactics.**

*Good Guy/Bad Guy. Highball/Lowball. Bogey. The Nibble. Chicken. Intimidation. Aggressive Behavior. Other Hardball Tactics.*

**Dealing with Typical Hardball Tactics.**

*Ignore Them. Discuss Them. Respond in Kind. Co-Opt the Other Party.*

**Summary.**

**Introduction.**

**An Overview of the Integrative Negotiation Process.**

*Creating a Free Flow of Information. Attempting to Understand the Other Negotiator's Real Needs and Objectives. Emphasizing the Commonalities Between the Parties and Minimizing the Differences. Searching for Solutions that Meet the Goals and Objectives of Both Sides.*

**Key Stages in the Integrative Negotiation Process.**

*Identify and Define the Problem. Understand the Problem Fully—Identify Interests and Needs. Generate Alternative Solutions. Evaluation and Selection of Alternatives.*

**Factors that Facilitate Successful Integrative Negotiation.**

*Some Common Objective or Goal. Faith in One's Own Problem-Solving Ability. A Belief in the Validity of the Other's Position. The Motivation and Commitment to Work Together. Trust. Clear and Accurate Communication. Summary.*

**Why Integrative Negotiation Is Difficult to Achieve.**

*The History of the Relationship Between the Parties. A Belief that an Issue Can Only Be Resolved Distributively. The Mixed-Motive Nature of Most Negotiating Situations.*

**Summary.**

**Strategy: An Overview.**

*Strategy, Tactics, and Planning. Types of Strategy. Plan, Ploy, Pattern, Position, or Perspective? A Choice Model of Negotiation Strategy. Summary.*

**Managing the Planning Process.**
*Many Negotiators are Not Good Planners! Defining the Issues. Assembling Issues and Defining the "Bargaining Mix". Defining your Interests. Consulting with Others. Prioritizing—Defining the Relative Importance of Our Issues. Assessing the Other's Priorities. Knowing Our Limits. Goal-Setting. Developing Supporting Arguments—Research. Analyzing the Other Party.*
**Summary.**

**Culture: A Critical Factor.**

*Power Distance.    Individualism/Collectivism.    Masculinity/Femininity. Uncertainty Avoidance. Other Approaches to Cultural Differences. How Do Cultural Differences Influence Negotiations?*

**Some Specific Country Negotiation Styles.**

*Negotiating with the Japanese. Negotiating with the Chinese. Negotiating with Koreans.*

**Culturally Responsive Negotiation Strategies.**

*Low Familiarity. Moderate Familiarity. High Familiarity.*

**Summary.**

# CHAPTER 1

# The Nature of Negotiation

Negotiating is a basic, generic human activity—a process that is often used in labor-management relations, in business deals like mergers and sales, in international affairs, and in our everyday activities. The negotiations that take place to free hostages, to keep peace between nations, or to end a labor strike dramatize the need for bargaining and its capabilities as a dispute management process. Negotiation is not a process reserved for the skilled diplomat, the top salesperson, or the ardent advocate for organized labor; it is something that we *all* do, almost on a daily basis. Although the stakes are not usually as dramatic as freeing hostages or keeping peace, everyone negotiates; sometimes on major things like a job, at other times on relatively minor issues, such as who will wash the dishes. The structure and processes of negotiation are fundamentally the same at the personal level as they are at the diplomatic and corporate levels.

Because we all negotiate about many different things in many different situations, knowledge about and skill in negotiating is essential to anyone who works with and through other people to accomplish objectives. We may fail to negotiate at times, perhaps because we do not recognize that we are in a bargaining situation. By choosing options other than negotiation, we may fail to handle our problems as well as we might like to. We may recognize the need for bargaining, but do poorly at the process because we misunderstand it and do not know the methods for negotiating. This book will teach our readers how to recognize situations that call for bargaining; what the process of bargaining involves; and how to analyze, plan, and carry out a successful negotiation.

Note that we have used the words *bargaining* and *negotiation* interchangeably. In most conversations, the words mean the same thing, but sometimes they are used as if they mean different things. For example, *bargaining* is more like the competitive haggling over price that goes on in a yard sale or flea market, whereas *negotiation* is the more formal, civilized process that occurs when parties are trying to find a mutually acceptable solution to a complex conflict. In this book, we tend to use the terms *bargaining* and *negotiation* interchangeably. In Chapters 3 and 4, when we describe the differences between two very different forms of negotiation, we will call one *bargaining* and the other *negotiation* to make the comparisons between the two clearer.

To better understand what this book is about, and the breadth and scope of negotiation in our professional and personal lives, we ask you to consider a hypothetical, but not unrealistic, situation. The case below describes a "typical" day in the life of Joe Carter, a manager who is involved in a number of negotiations. After presenting the case, we will discuss some of the incidents as they portray an array of challenges and problems in negotiation.

## THE JOE CARTER STORY

The day started early, as usual. Over breakfast, Sue Carter (Joe's wife) again raised the question of where they would go for their summer vacation. She wanted to sign up for a tour of the Far East being sponsored by her college's alumni association. However, two weeks on a guided tour with a lot of other people were not what Joe had in mind. He needed to get away from people, crowds, and schedules, and he wanted to charter a sailboat and cruise the New England coast. In addition, they were still not sure whether the kids would go with them. Both really wanted to go to camp, and Joe and Sue couldn't afford both summer camp and a vacation for the four of them. They had not argued (yet), but it was clear that they had a real problem here. Some of their friends handled problems like this by taking separate vacations. With both of them working full time, though, the one thing he and Sue did agree on was that they would take their vacation together.

As Joe drove to work, he thought about the vacation problem. What bothered Joe most was that there seemed to be no good way to manage the conflict productively. With some conflicts, they could compromise; but given what each wanted this time, compromise didn't seem possible. At other times they would flip a coin; that might work for choosing a restaurant, but it seemed unwise to use that procedure to solve this problem because spending that much money and that big a block of time on the basis of a coin flip was pretty risky. In addition, flipping a coin might be more likely to make one of them feel like a loser and the other feel guilty than to help either one feel really satisfied.

Walking through the parking lot, Joe met his company's purchasing manager, Ed Laine. Joe was the head of the engineering design group for MicroWatt, a manufacturer of small electric motors. Ed reminded Joe that they had to settle a problem created by the engineers in Joe's department: The engineers were contacting vendors directly rather than going through MicroWatt's purchasing department. Joe knew that purchasing wanted all contacts with a vendor to go through them; but he also knew that his engineers badly needed technical information for design purposes, and waiting for the information to come through purchasing slowed things considerably. Ed Laine was not unaware of Joe's views about this problem, and Joe thought the two of them could probably find some way to work this out if they really sat down to work on it. Joe and Ed were also both aware that higher management expected them (and all other managers) to settle differences among themselves; if this problem "got upstairs" to senior management, it would make both of them look bad.

Shortly after getting back to his desk, Joe received a telephone call from an automobile salesman with whom he had been talking about a new car. The salesman asked how Sue (Joe's wife) felt about the car and whether she wanted to drive it. Joe wasn't quite sure that Sue would go along with his choice; Joe had picked out a luxury import, and he expected Sue would say it cost too much money. Joe was pleased with the latest offer the salesman had made, but thought he might still get a few more concessions out of him; so he introduced Sue's concerns to put more pressure on the salesman to lower the price.

Most of Joe's afternoon was taken up by the annual budget meeting. Joe hated these meetings. The people from the finance department came in and arbitrarily cut everyone's figures by 30 percent, and then all the managers had to argue endlessly to try to get some of their new-project money reinstated. Joe had learned to work with a lot of people, some of whom he did not like very much, but these people from finance were the most arrogant and arbitrary number-crunchers imaginable. He could not understand why the top brass did not see how much harm these people were doing to the engineering group's research and development efforts. Joe considered himself a reasonable guy, but he recognized that the way these people acted made him feel like he didn't want to give them an inch. He was prepared to draw the line and fight it out as long as it took.

In the evening, Joe attended a meeting of the town Conservation Commission, which, among other things, was charged with protecting the town's streams, wetlands, and nature preserves. Joe is a member of the Conservation Commission and strongly believes in sound environmental protection and management. This evening's case involved a request by a real estate development firm to drain a swampy area and move a small creek to build a new regional shopping mall. All projections showed that the new shopping mall would attract a significant number of jobs and revenue to the area and considerably fatten the town's treasury. The new mall was badly needed to replace several others that had closed, putting a sizable number of people out of work and reducing the town's tax revenues. But the plan might also do irreparable damage to the wetlands and the wildlife in that area. The initial plan proposed by the development firm had some serious problems, and the commission had asked Joe to see if an acceptable solution could be developed. Eventually a site plan had been worked out that would have considerably more benefits than drawbacks. But now Joe was having difficulties with some members of the commission who were ardent conservationists and argued against *any* change in the wetlands on that lot. In addition, word about the application had gotten out, and even some members of the Town Council had decided to join the conservationists in the fight.

At 11:30 P.M., Joe finally got home. As he sat on the patio and listened to the crickets, he thought about his day and realized why he felt so tired.

## CHARACTERISTICS OF A NEGOTIATION OR BARGAINING SITUATION

A day in the life of Joe Carter brings out the variety of situations that can be handled by negotiation. Any of us might encounter one or more of these situations over the course of a few days or weeks. We identify them as "negotiation situations" because they have fundamentally the same characteristics as peace negotiations between countries at war, labor negotiations between management and union, or a hostage crisis involving police and a radical political group. Negotiation is a viable way of resolving a conflict when the following conditions hold true (see Rubin and Brown, 1975; Lewicki, 1992):

1. There are two or more parties—two or more individuals, groups, organizations. Although we can "negotiate" with ourselves—as when we debate whether we are going to spend the afternoon studying, playing tennis, or going to the football game—we will primarily talk about negotiation as an *interpersonal* or *intergroup* process. In the case, Joe negotiates with his wife, the purchasing manager, the auto salesman, and the Conservation Commission, among others.

2. There is a conflict of interest between two or more parties; that is, what one wants is not necessarily what the other one wants, and the parties must search for a way to resolve the conflict. In the Joe Carter case, Joe negotiates over vacations, budgets, automobiles, and company procedures.

3. The parties negotiate because they think they can use some form of influence to get a "better" deal than simply taking what the other side will voluntarily give them or let them have. Negotiation is largely a voluntary process. It is a strategy pursued by choice; seldom are we required to negotiate.

4. The parties, at least for the moment, prefer to search for agreement rather than to fight openly, have one side capitulate, permanently break off contact, or take their dispute to a higher authority to resolve it. Negotiation occurs when there is no fixed or established set of rules, procedures, or "system" for resolving the conflict, or when the parties prefer to work outside of the system to invent their own solution to the conflict. If we keep a rented videotape too long, the store will charge us a fee, but we might be able to negotiate that fee if we have a good excuse as to why the tape is being returned late. Similarly, attorneys negotiate or plea bargain for their clients because they would rather be assured of a negotiated settlement than take their chances with a judge and jury in the courtroom. In the case, Joe pursues negotiation as opposed to letting his wife decide on the vacation, accepting a fixed price for the car, accepting the budget cut without question, or letting others decide how to resolve the problem with the shopping mall (or taking it to court).

5. Finally, when we negotiate, we expect give and take. We expect that both sides will modify or give in somewhat on their opening statements, requests, or demands. Although the parties may not give in initially, arguing strenuously for what they want and pushing the other side for concessions, usually both sides must modify their positions and move toward the other. As we will discuss, however, truly creative negotiations may not require compromise because the parties can invent a solution that meets the objectives of all sides. As as we can see from the Joe Carter story, Joe is searching for the best "give and take" in all of the disputes, to find mutually acceptable solutions to the problems.

# CONFLICT

In order to discuss the topic of negotiation throughout the remainder of this book, we need to begin with some groundwork in the area of social conflict itself. The next several pages will present a broad overview of key definitions, concepts, terms, and models.

## Definitions

There are numerous ways to define conflict. Traditionally, Webster (1966) defines conflict as a "fight, battle or struggle." The definition of conflict has evolved to include events that are somewhat less physically violent and that encompass psychological terms—such as a "sharp disagreement or opposition, as of interests, ideas, etc." A third way to approach conflict is as "the perceived divergence of interest, or a belief that the parties' current aspirations cannot be achieved simultaneously" (all from Pruitt and Rubin, 1986, p. 4). Or, similarly, conflict is "the interaction of interdependent people who perceived incompatible goals and interference from each other in achieving those goals" (Hocker and Wilmot, 1985).

## Levels of Conflict

Conflict is ubiquitous—it exists everywhere. One way to classify conflicts is by *level,* and four levels of conflict are commonly identified:

**Intrapersonal or Intrapsychic Conflict.**    At this level, conflict occurs within an individual. Sources of conflict can include ideas, thoughts, emotions, values, predispositions, or drives that are in conflict with each other. We want an ice cream cone badly but we know that ice cream is very fattening. We are angry at our boss but afraid to express that anger because the boss might fire us for being insubordinate. Depending upon the source and origin of the intrapsychic conflict, this domain is traditionally studied by various fields of psychology: cognitive psychologists, personality theorists, clinical psychologists, and psychiatrists. Although we will occasionally delve into the internal states of negotiators (e.g., Chapter 6, on cognitive traps that negotiators often set for themselves), this book generally doesn't address this area.

**Interpersonal Conflict.**    A second major level of conflict, which we will call interpersonal conflict, is between individual people. Conflict that occurs between husbands and wives, bosses and subordinates, siblings, or roommates is all interpersonal conflict. Most of the negotiation theory in this book is addressed primarily toward the resolution of interpersonal conflict, although much of it can also be applied to the other levels specified below.

**Intragroup Conflict.**    A third major level of conflict is within a small group—among team and committee members and within families, classes, fraternities and sororities, and work groups. At the intragroup level, we analyze conflict as it affects the ability of the group to resolve disputes and continue to achieve its goals effectively. We address the nature of within-group negotiation in detail in Chapter 9.

**Intergroup Conflict.**    The final level of conflict is intergroup—between groups, union and management, warring nations, feuding families, or communities challenging governmental authorities. At this level, conflict is quite intricate because of the large number of people involved and possible interactions between them. Conflict can occur within groups and between groups simultaneously. Negotiations at this level are also the most complex, and we will discuss the nature of intergroup negotiations throughout the book, particularly in Chapter 9.

### Functions and Dysfunctions of Conflict

Most people's initial view of conflict is that it is primarily "bad" or dysfunctional. This notion has two aspects: first, that conflict is an indication that something is wrong or that a problem needs to be "fixed," and second, that conflict creates largely destructive consequences. Deutsch (1973) and others (Folger, Poole, and Stutman, 1993; Hocker and Wilmot, 1985) have elaborated on many of the elements that contribute to conflict's destructive image:

**Competitive Processes.**    Parties compete against each other because they believe that their goals are in opposition and that the two of them cannot both achieve their objectives. Frequently, however, goals are not actually in opposition, and the parties need not compete. In addition, as we will point out, competitive processes often have their own side effects so that the conflict that created the competition also leads to its further escalation.

**Misperception and Bias.**    As conflict intensifies, perceptions become distorted. People tend to view things consistently with their own perspective on the conflict. Hence they tend to interpret people and events as either being "on their side" or "on the other side." In addition, thinking tends to become stereotypical and biased—parties in conflict endorse people and events that support their position and reject outright those that they suspect oppose their position.

**Emotionality.**    Conflicts tend to become emotionally charged as the parties become anxious, irritated, annoyed, angry, or frustrated. Emotions tend to dominate thinking, and the parties may become more emotional and irrational as the conflict escalates.

**Decreased Communication.**    Communication declines. Parties stop communicating with those who disagree with them, and communicate more with those who agree. What communication does occur between disputing parties may be an attempt to defeat, demean, or debunk the other's view or to add additional weight to one's own prior arguments.

**Blurred Issues.**   The central issues in the dispute become blurred and less well defined. Generalizations abound. New, unrelated issues are drawn in as the conflict becomes a vortex that attracts both related issues and innocent bystanders. The parties become less clear about how the dispute started, what it is "really about," or what it will take to solve it.

**Rigid Commitments.**   The parties become locked in to positions. As they are challenged by the other side, parties become more committed to their points of view and less willing to back down from them for fear of losing face and looking foolish. Thinking processes become rigid, and the parties tend to see issues as very simple and "either/or" rather than as complex and multidimensional.

**Magnified Differences; Minimized Similarities.**   As parties lock into commitments and issues become blurred, they tend to see each other—and each other's positions—as polar opposites when they may not be. All the factors that distinguish and separate them from each other become highlighted and emphasized, while any similarities and commonalities that they share become oversimplified and minimized. This perceptual distortion leads the parties to believe they are farther apart from each other than they really may be, and hence they work harder to "win" the conflict and work less hard at finding a common ground.

**Escalation of the Conflict.**   As the above points suggest, each side becomes more entrenched in its own view, less tolerant and accepting of the other, more defensive and less communicative, and more emotional. The net result is that parties on each side attempt to win by increasing their commitment to their position, increasing the resources they are willing to put up to "win," and increasing their tenacity in holding their ground under pressure. Each side believes that by adding a little more pressure (resources, commitment, enthusiasm, energy, etc.), the other will capitulate and concede defeat. As most destructive conflicts will tell us, nothing could be further from the truth! However, escalation of the level of the conflict and commitment to winning can increase to very high levels at which the parties destroy their ability ever to deal with each other again or to resolve the dispute.

These are the processes that are commonly associated with conflict, but they are characteristic only of *destructive* conflict. In fact, as some authors have suggested (Coser, 1956; Deutsch, 1973), conflict can be productive. In Figure 1.1, Tjosvold (1988) outlines many of the more functional (productive) aspects of conflict. In this model conflict is not simply destructive or productive, it is *both*. The objective is *not to eliminate conflict but to learn how to manage it* so the destructive elements are controlled while the more productive aspects are enjoyed. Negotiation is a strategy for productively managing conflict.

## Factors that Make Conflict Difficult to Manage

Greenhalgh (1986) has suggested a number of factors that make conflicts more or less difficult to resolve. Figure 1.2 presents the most important ones.

**FIGURE 1.1**   Functions and Benefits of Conflict

- Discussing conflict makes organizational members more aware and able to cope with problems. Knowing that others are frustrated and want change creates incentives to try to solve the underlying problem.
- Conflict promises organizational change and adaptation. Procedures, assignments, budget allocations, and other organizational practices are challenged. Conflict draws attention to those issues that may interfere with and frustrate employees.
- Conflict strengthens relationships and heightens morale. Employees realize that their relationships are strong enough to withstand the test of conflict; they need not avoid frustrations and problems. They can release their tensions through discussion and problem solving.
- Conflict promotes awareness of self and others. Through conflict, people learn what makes them angry, frustrated, and frightened and also what is important to them. Knowing what we are willing to fight for tells us a lot about ourselves. Knowing what makes our colleagues unhappy helps us to understand them.
- Conflict enhances personal development. Managers find out how their style affects their subordinates through conflict. Workers learn what technical and interpersonal skills they need to upgrade themselves.
- Conflict encourages psychological development. Persons become more accurate and realistic in their self-appraisals. Through conflict, persons take others' perspectives and become less egocentric. Conflict helps persons to believe that they are powerful and capable of controlling their own lives. They do not simply need to endure hostility and frustration but can act to improve their lives.
- Conflict can be stimulating and fun. Persons feel aroused, involved, and alive in conflict, and it can be a welcome break from an easygoing pace. It invites employees to take another look and to appreciate the intricacies of their relationships.

SOURCE: Reprinted with the permission of Lexington Books, an imprint of Macmillan Publishing Company from *Working Together to Get Things Done: Managing for Organizational Productivity* by Dean Tjosvold. Copyright © 1986 by Lexington Books.

Conflicts with more of the characteristics in the middle column will be much more difficult to resolve. Those that have more characteristics in the right column will be easier to resolve. Greenhalgh's lists offer useful criteria for analyzing a dispute and determining how easy it will be to resolve.

### Approaches to Managing Conflict

**Approaches by the Parties Themselves.**   One of the most popular areas of conflict management research and practice has been to define the different ways that conflict can be managed by the parties to it. A number of different approaches to managing conflict have been suggested, and inventories have been constructed to measure these different approaches (Filley, 1975; Hall, 1969; Rahim, 1983a: Thomas, 1992; Thomas and Kilmann, 1974). Each of these approaches begins

**FIGURE 1.2** Conflict Diagnostic Model

| Dimension | Viewpoint Continuum | |
|---|---|---|
| | Difficult to Resolve | Easy to Resolve |
| Issue in question | Matter of "principle"—values, ethics, or precedent a key part of the issue | Divisible issue—issue can be easily divided into small parts, pieces, units. |
| Size of stakes—magnitude of what can be won or lost | Large—big consequences. | Small—little, insignificant consequences. |
| Interdependence of the parties—degree to which one's outcomes determine the other's outcomes | Zero sum—what one wins, the other loses. | Positive sum—both believe that **both** can do better than simply distributing current outcomes. |
| Continuity of interaction—will they be working together in the future? | Single transaction—no past or future. | Long-term relationship—expected interaction in the future. |
| Structure of the parties—how cohesive, organized they are as a group | Disorganized—uncohesive, weak leadership | Organized—cohesive, strong leadership |
| Involvement of third parties—can others get involved to help resolve the dispute? | No neutral third party available | Trusted, powerful, prestigious third party available |
| Perceived progress of the conflict—balanced (equal gains and equal harm) or unbalanced (unequal gain, unequal harm)? | Unbalanced—one party feels more harm and will want revenge and retribution whereas stronger party wants to maintain control | Balanced—both parties suffer equal harm and equal gain; both may be more willing to call it a "draw" |

Adapted from "Managing Conflict" by L. Greenhalgh, *Sloan Management Review* (Summer 1986), pp. 45–51, by permission of the publisher. Copyright 1986 by the Sloan Management Review Association.

with fundamentally the same two-dimensional framework and then applies different labels and descriptions to its five key points. We will describe these different approaches, using the descriptive framework proposed by Dean Pruitt and Jeffrey Rubin (1986).

The two-dimensional framework is represented in Figure 1.3 as the *dual concerns model.* The model postulates that individuals in conflict have two types of *independent* concerns: a *level of concern for their own outcomes* (shown on the horizontal dimension of the table) and a *level of concern for the other's outcomes* (shown on the vertical dimension of the table). These concerns can be represented at any point from none (representing very low concern) to high (representing very high concern). The vertical dimension is often referred to as the cooperativeness dimension and the horizontal dimension as the assertiveness dimension. The stronger their concern for their own outcomes, the more likely people will be to pursue strategies located on the right side of the chart, whereas the weaker their concern for their own outcomes, the more likely they will be to pursue strategies located on the left side of the chart. Similarly, the stronger their concern for permitting, encouraging, or even helping the other party achieve their outcomes, the more likely people will be to pursue strategies located at the top of the chart. The weaker their concern for the other party's outcomes, the more likely they will be to pursue strategies located at the bottom of the chart.

Although we can theoretically identify an almost infinite number of points within the two-dimensional space based upon the level of concern for pursuing one's own and the other's outcomes, five major strategies for conflict management have been commonly identified in the dual concerns model:

**Contending** (also called *competing* or *dominating*) is the strategy in the lower

**FIGURE 1.3**    The Dual Concerns Model

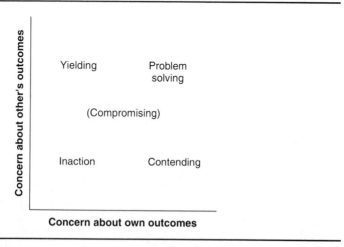

Adapted from D. Pruitt and J. Rubin, *Social Conflict: Escalation, Stalemate and Settlement* (New York: Random House, 1986). Used by permission of McGraw-Hill.

right-hand corner. Actors pursuing the Contending strategy, as its location in the space indicates, pursue their own outcomes strongly and show little concern for whether the other party obtains his desired outcomes. As Pruitt and Rubin (1986, p. 25) state, "parties who employ this strategy maintain their own aspirations and try to persuade the other party to yield." Threats, punishment, intimidation, and unilateral action are consistent with a contending approach.

**Yielding** (also called *accommodating* or *obliging*) is the strategy in the upper left-hand corner. Actors pursuing the Yielding strategy, as its location in the space indicates, show little interest or concern in whether they attain their own outcomes, but are quite interested in whether the other party attains her outcomes. Yielding involves lowering one's own aspirations to "let the other win" and gain what she wants. As we will point out, yielding may seem like a strange strategy to some, but it has its definite advantages in some disputes.

**Inaction** is the strategy in the lower left-hand corner. Actors pursuing the Inaction strategy, as its location in the space indicates, show little interest or concern in whether they attain their own outcomes, nor do they show much concern about whether the other party obtains his outcomes. Inaction is often synonymous with withdrawal or passivity; the party prefers to retreat, be silent and still, or do nothing.

**Problem Solving** (also called *collaborating* and *integrating*) is the strategy in the upper right-hand corner. Actors pursuing the Problem Solving strategy, as its location in the space indicates, show high concern for attaining their own outcomes *and* high concern for whether the other attains her outcomes. In Problem Solving, the two parties actively pursue approaches to maximize their joint outcome from the conflict, so that both sides "win."

**Compromising** is a strategy located in the middle of the chart in Figure 1.3. As a conflict management strategy, it represents a moderate effort to pursue one's own outcomes and a moderate effort to help the other party achieve his outcomes. Pruitt and Rubin do *not* identify Compromising as a viable strategy; they see it "as arising from one of two sources—either lazy problem solving involving a half-hearted attempt to satisfy the two parties' interests, or simple yielding by both parties" (1986, p. 29). However, because all the other scholars (see references above) who use versions of this model believe that compromising represents a valid strategic approach to conflict, we have inserted it in Pruitt and Rubin's framework in Figure 1.3.

The dual concerns model and its variations have become some of the most ubiquitous and durable vehicles for approaching and understanding conflict management strategies. Several of the most common themes in this research are as follows:

• Analysis of one's own "style" and preferences for particular strategies. Many of the models have produced self-assessment instruments that indicate personal preferences for tactics associated with one strategy versus another, thereby determining whether one has a stronger or weaker preference for each manner of handling conflict. Differences in strength of preferences may be traced to direct experiences of success and failure in using a particular style, instruction as a child about which styles were more or less preferred, or simply beliefs about which style might be more or less likely to work in a particular situation.

• Description of the likely level of conflict that will occur when individuals of similar or different conflict resolution styles interact with each other. If two "contenders" come into conflict with each other, each wants to win, and one can predict an intense and passionate dispute. In contrast, if a "yielder" and a "contender" come into conflict, the contender will attain her objectives while the yielder should be happy that the contender got what she wanted.

• Articulation of the conditions under which each strategy is likely to be effective. As many researchers have pointed out (see Lewicki, Weiss, and Lewin, 1992, for one summary), much of the writing on conflict—particularly the work in the 1960s and 1970s—had a strong normative value bias against conflict and toward cooperation. Although the various models and instruments suggested at least five viable strategic approaches to conflict, the same works also suggested that cooperation, collaboration, or problem solving was the distinctly *preferred* approach. Thus, these writings preached the virtues of problem solving, advocated using it, and described how it could be pursued in almost any dispute. More recent authors in the field, although still strongly committed to problem solving, have also been more careful to stress that each conflict management strategy has its advantages and disadvantages, and is *more or less appropriate given the type of conflict and situation in which the dispute occurs.* Thus, conflict research has moved from a normative, prescriptive approach advocating problem solving at any cost toward a contingency approach advocating that the strategy selected should be based upon the objectives of the parties and the nature of their dispute. Although a full-fledged contingency approach to conflict management has yet to be fully articulated and supported by research (a task well beyond the scope of this introductory chapter), tables such as Figure 1.4 reflect efforts to delineate some of the conditions under which each strategy is appropriate or inappropriate.

**Approaches by Other Parties or "the System."**   The dual concerns model and its five strategies reflect actions that the parties in conflict can take themselves to manage and resolve a dispute. However, conflicts can be resolved in other ways—either independent of the efforts of the parties themselves or by seeking outside assistance when the efforts of the parties break down. Two major mechanisms for resolving conflicts extend above and beyond the strategies of the parties themselves:

*Third Parties.*   When the parties cannot resolve a dispute on their own, they may involve a third party. Similarly, third parties may intervene independently when they believe a conflict is rapidly getting beyond the bounds of reasonable

**FIGURE 1.4** Styles of Handling Interpersonal Conflict and Situations Where They Are Appropriate or Inappropriate

| Conflict Style | Situations Where Appropriate | Situations Where Inappropriate |
|---|---|---|
| Integrating | 1. Issues are complex.<br>2. Synthesis of ideas is needed to come up with better solutions.<br>3. Commitment is needed from other parties for successful implementation.<br>4. Time is available for problem solving.<br>5. One party alone cannot solve the problem.<br>6. Resources possessed by different parties are needed to solve their common problems. | 1. Task or problem is simple.<br>2. Immediate decision is required.<br>3. Other parties are unconcerned about outcome.<br>4. Other parties do not have problem-solving skills. |
| Obliging | 1. You believe that you may be wrong.<br>2. Issue is more important to the other party.<br>3. You are willing to give up something in exchange for something from the other party in the future.<br>4. You are dealing from a position of weakness.<br>5. Preserving relationship is important. | 1. Issue is important to you.<br>2. You believe that you are right.<br>3. The other party is wrong or unethical. |
| Dominating | 1. Issue is trivial.<br>2. Speedy decision is needed.<br>3. Unpopular course of action is implemented.<br>4. Necessary to overcome assertive subordinates.<br>5. Unfavorable decision by the other party may be costly to you.<br>6. Subordinates lack expertise to make technical decisions.<br>7. Issue is important to you. | 1. Issue is complex.<br>2. Issue is not important to you.<br>3. Both parties are equally powerful.<br>4. Decision does not have to be made quickly.<br>5. Subordinates possess high degree of competence. |
| Avoiding | 1. Issue is trivial.<br>2. Potential dysfunctional effect of confronting the other party outweighs benefits of resolution.<br>3. Cooling off period is needed. | 1. Issue is important to you.<br>2. It is your responsibility to make decision.<br>3. Parties are unwilling to defer; issue must be resolved.<br>4. Prompt attention is needed. |
| Compromising | 1. Goals of parties are mutually exclusive.<br>2. Parties are equally powerful.<br>3. Consensus cannot be reached.<br>4. Integrating or dominating style is not successful.<br>5. Temporary solution to a complex problem is needed. | 1. One party is more powerful.<br>2. Problem is complex enough to need a problem-solving approach. |

SOURCE: Modified and reproduced by special permission of the Publisher, Consulting Psychologists Press, Inc., Palo Alto, CA 94303 from *Rahim Organizational Conflict Inventories: Professional Manual* by M. Afzalur Rahim. Copyright 1990 by Consulting Psychologists Press, Inc. All rights reserved. Further reproduction is prohibited without the Publishers's written consent.

and likely settlement. For example, in the first case, two managers who disagree about a policy issue might ask their boss to help them determine the appropriate thing to do. In the latter case, a parent who hears two children arguing in the family room over which TV program to watch might intervene quickly before the conflict escalates into physical confrontation.

Many different types of third parties and approaches are used to intervene in conflict. Third parties have always been popular in dealing with certain types of conflict (e.g., labor relations), and their popularity is increasing. In Chapter 12, we will specifically describe numerous third party styles and strategies.

*Dispute Resolution Systems.*   As an alternative to going to an individual third party, conflicts are also handled by taking them to a system specifically set up to hear and resolve conflicts. The civil court system (the legal system) is the most common and visible system for handling conflict in our society. Parties who have almost any type of dispute with each other—property line disputes between neighbors, marital disputes between husband and wife, patent rights disputes between two companies—can hire any attorney (advocate and legal expert) and take their dispute through a system that will assure both a thorough, fair hearing and a resolution. Smaller and more manageable systems are also available in other contexts—sometimes because the parties want to manage conflict in a simpler way, at other times because the legal system has become so big, bureaucratic, and cumbersome that the parties no longer feel that fairness is possible. Labor contracts provide grievance systems by which possible violations of the contract or ambiguities in its interpretation can be heard and resolved. Organizations provide ombudspersons to listen to employee complaints and investigate charges of unfair treatment. Universities provide tribunals and judicial committees to review infractions of student codes of conduct. Many of these systems are actually third parties that have been institutionalized and legitimized into the organization's rules, policies, and procedures. Unlike the third parties we described above, who may invoke any number of procedures to resolve the dispute on the spot (dependent on the nature of the conflict, the parties, and so on), the third parties who operate in these systems are bound to follow the procedures set out by the system, and they cannot stray very far from those procedures without endangering their own legitimacy, credibility, reputation, and ability to resolve future disputes (see Singer, 1990; and Ury, Brett, and Goldberg, 1988, for reviews of approaches to dispute resolution systems).

### Summary

In this section, we presented a brief overview of the dynamics of conflict and its management—dynamics that underlie much of what we will have to say about the negotiation process. We defined conflict and pointed out that it exists at various levels. We indicated that although many people tend to view conflict as primarily destructive, it also has many vital and productive aspects; it is important to manage conflict effectively to preserve its productive features while attempting to minimize its unproductive and destructive aspects. Finally, we examined the strategies most commonly identified for managing conflict: strategies that the parties can use themselves and strategies that the parties use by turning to others (third parties or conflict management systems) to resolve the dispute for them. As we will show, these strategies and approaches are fundamental to—and in some cases, even identical to—the strategies parties use in negotiation.

## APPROACHES TO STUDYING AND ANALYZING NEGOTIATION

Before digging into the "meat" of this book—the strategy and tactics of negotiation—we believe it is useful to provide a broader context to give some perspective on the way negotiation has been researched and studied, the way it has been written about, and the various fields in which this work has occurred.

### Major Changes in the Last Decade

In the past 10 years, since the first edition of this book was prepared, the field of negotiation—particularly in the context of organizations—has grown and changed substantially. Prior to that time, the study of negotiation was largely restricted to several small arenas where formal negotiations took place. Within organizations, the study of negotiation was limited to industrial relations and collective bargaining, and to purchasing (Douglas, 1962; Walton and McKersie, 1965). Outside organizations, negotiation had been studied in the resolution of international political disputes, and to some degree in community disputes. Because the post–World War II cold war kept America at the brink of nuclear war, a large amount of basic research on the psychology of conflict and negotiation was also done during this period (see Bazerman and Lewicki, 1985, for one review). For the most part, these research areas did not communicate with each other, nor was there significant extension and application of the knowledge to new arenas where negotiation theory had not yet been applied.

The past decade has witnessed a tremendous boom in the negotiation "industry," in several ways:

**Development of Negotiation Theory.** Extensive research has been performed in areas not previously studied, and much of this work has been integrated into this revised volume. Areas of significantly new work include an improved understanding of the process of integrative negotiation (Chapter 4), an exploration of the cognitive biases that affect the way negotiators make judgments about conflict and negotiation processes (Chapter 6), a discussion of the dynamics of multiparty or group negotiations (Chapter 9), an exploration of the key roles played by third parties, particularly mediators (Chapter 12), and a growing emphasis on the negotiation processes across different nationalities and cultures (Chapter 14).

**Cross-Fertilization of Negotiation Research and Fields of Application.** Not only has research progressed into new areas, but also researchers have increasingly taken interdisciplinary approaches to understanding, interpreting, and integrating negotiation theory and practice. These interdisciplinary efforts have occurred at two levels: across academic disciplines, and across areas of negotiation practice. The foundational disciplines of psychology, sociology, economics, anthropology, political science, and mathematics have all taken different theoretical and conceptual perspectives on negotiation. Each has its own analytical tools, models, and preferred methods of study. In the past, these fields operated as "silos," with a great deal of work going on within the field but little or no exchange across the fields. In addition, the hybrid disciplines that focus on areas of practice—decision sciences, marketing, international affairs, law, public policy, urban and regional planning, social work, natural resources management—tended to develop applications of negotiation theory without referring to comparable problems and applications in other disciplines. In recent years, however, cross-disciplinary application has increased significantly. Negotiation and dispute resolution are clearly becoming highly integrated fields of both theory and practice (see Bazerman and Lewicki, 1985, and Lewicki, Weiss, and Lewin, 1992, for two reviews; and research volumes by Lewicki, Sheppard, and Bazerman, 1986; Sheppard, Bazerman, and Lewicki, 1990; and Bazerman, Lewicki, and Sheppard, 1991).

**Development of Education Programs to Improve Negotiation Practice.**    As theory has developed, so has the application of theory to practice. Seminars in negotiation and conflict have become very popular as part of management development programs. Negotiation courses have become extremely popular in schools and colleges of business, law, and public policy. Negotiation training has become a prerequisite for managers and practitioners in many professions that require skill in influence and persuasion—law, sales, diplomacy, purchasing, financial lending, and public management. A large (and continually growing) number of negotiation how-to books are published each year.

**Development of Applications to Key Problem Areas.**    Finally, there has been a significant movement (called the Alternative Dispute Resolution movement) toward resolving disputes in settings other than the courtroom. In part, this movement has been encouraged by the court system itself as a way to deal with significant overload, backlog, and delay, but it has also been fueled in part by businesspeople, community leaders, and even attorneys as a way to resolve disputes more quickly and inexpensively, and with more direct participation by the parties involved. Mediation centers, staffed by trained volunteers or skilled practitioners, have become a popular way to resolve disputes in marriages, landlord-tenant relationships, neighborhoods, and universities. Businesses have installed internal grievance systems and ombudspersons to hear and review employee conflicts. Arbitration and its variations have become as common as taking a party to court.

## "Maps" of the Negotiation Process

Negotiation is a highly complex social process. A number of social science and practice-oriented disciplines have each taken their own unique view of what is important in negotiation, how it should be studied, and what are the most important perspectives. We will mention briefly a number of these different perspectives here and address some of them in greater detail throughout the book (see Lewicki, Weiss, and Lewin, 1992, for a comprehensive framework and review of these models).

**Models of Negotiation—Distributive, Integrative, and Contingency.**    Probably the most popular way to map the negotiation process is to describe the different strategies of negotiation. Two dominant strategies, distributive (competitive or win-lose) bargaining and integrative (collaborative or win-win) negotiation, have received the most attention. These approaches can be traced to the highly influential work of Richard Walton and Robert McKersie (1965), who first identified them in their observation of the labor management process. (Interestingly, two other processes that they identified—intraorganizational bargaining and attitudinal structuring—have been almost wholly ignored.) Although Walton and McKersie simply identified and described the approaches, more recent works have begun to specify the conditions under which the two approaches (and other, less popular strategies) should be used (e.g., see Savage, Blair, and Sorenson, 1989), clearly reflecting the application of the dual concerns model to negotiation practice.

**Descriptive versus Prescriptive.**    Much of the research on negotiation coming from the basic social science disciplines has been descriptive—that is, it has attempted to identify, describe, and document negotiation phenomena and dynamics, usually by studying it under controlled laboratory conditions. However, many of the applied disciplines, as well as the large number of how-to books, have been highly prescriptive in nature—they tell the reader exactly how to negotiate. Much of this work is not clearly based on sound research, but instead is drawn from the personal experiences of the author(s)—successful salespersons, attorneys, talent agents. The same is true for many of the management seminars and programs conducted every year. In addition, many—but not all—have a strong bias toward advocating either the win-lose or the win-win strategy under all circumstances. As we will point out, no single strategy of negotiation is either appropriate or effective under all circumstances, and hence the advice given in these books and seminars must be taken with caution.

**Stages and Phases.**    Some approaches to negotiation have viewed the negotiation process from a "time series" perspective—that is, tracking negotiation and describing the events that traditionally happen (1) as the parties prepare for negotiation, (2) as the parties begin to negotiate, (3) as the parties proceed into the "heart of negotiation," and (4) as the parties conclude negotiation. Several research works (e.g., Douglas, 1962; Zartman and Berman, 1982) and several practitioner volumes (e.g., Dawson, 1986) have addressed negotiation in this way.

**Market Transactions versus Negotiation in Relationships.**    Although negotiation has been studied in some areas where the parties continually negotiate with each other over time (e.g., labor relations), most of the research on negotiation has been done in market transactions—that is, arenas where parties do not know each other well and have neither a previous history with each other nor any expectation that they will have to "live with" the consequences of their negotiation process and outcomes. More recently, researchers have begun to explore the ways that negotiation changes as it occurs in the context of longer term relationships—such as in marriages, political systems, and communities. Works by Rubin and Rubin (1989) and Rothman (1992) are examples of this trend.

**Study of Key Variables and Processes.**    By far, the greatest amount of attention—both in research and in application to practice—has been to focus on the key variables and processes that affect negotiation outcomes because they are the easiest to study and isolate in both laboratory and field research. Like other researchers, we give many of these variables and processes our attention in this book also. They include

- Perception—how we perceive events differently.
- Cognitive processes—how we organize information and make sense of the world around us.
- Decision making—how we make decisions, and the biases and distortions that can affect this decision making.
- Communication—the factors that enhance effective communication or contribute to communication breakdowns.
- Persuasion—how parties organize and present information to change the other's position, mind, or opinion.
- Individual differences—the role played by differences in an individual's gender, personal background, personality, or style as it affects negotiation.

**Study of Differences in Social Contexts.**    Similar to the study of key variables and processes, negotiation research has also isolated key contextual factors that affect the way the parties negotiate. These factors will also be addressed more fully throughout this book, and include

- The number of other parties in the negotiation—whether negotiation is interpersonal, intragroup, or intergroup.
- The nature of the issues under dispute—how they are structured and how easily they lend themselves to win-lose or win-win solutions.
- The location and configuration of the physical space in which negotiation occurs.
- The time boundaries and deadlines placed on negotiation.
- The social context or venue in which negotiation takes place—in the family, business organization, community, or policy-making body.
- Negotiators' sources of power and the impact of differences in power on negotiation strategy, tactics, and outcomes.

- The cultural context of negotiation—primarily noticed across international boundaries and cultures, but also seen within different businesses and organizations.
- The availability of alternative ways to resolve the dispute if negotiation fails—particularly the various types of third parties and dispute resolution systems mentioned earlier.

### Summary

This list of ways to study negotiation is not meant to be exhaustive. Rather, we have simply tried to provide an overview of the complexity of negotiation as a social process, and the wealth of different ways it has been defined, described, studied, analyzed, and advocated. In picking up any book or seminar brochure on negotiation, you should have a general idea of the broad map of this field to determine how the book or program in question will describe negotiation—are the prescriptions offered based on research, personal experience, or someone else's common sense? Our effort in this text is to integrate much of the research and the common sense philosophies into a single coherent whole. We will use the remainder of this chapter to outline the terrain we hope to cover.

## OVERVIEW OF THE CHAPTERS IN THIS TEXT

Each chapter in this book can be related to the introductory scenario about Joe Carter, which incorporates many of the critical elements addressed during negotiations.

In Chapter 2, we explore interdependence, one of the core factors that determines when parties will negotiate rather than pursuing other alternatives for resolving the dispute. Each party in a negotiation is interested in achieving her own personal goals and meeting her own personal needs. As a result, negotiators—particularly inexperienced ones—tend to think only of themselves and their own goals and to treat the other parties as though they were simply "in the way," somehow blocking the achievement of that goal. In fact, the essence of most negotiations is that the parties are *interdependent,* that is, one party cannot get what he wants without taking the other party into account. When parties are interdependent in a relationship, each one is partially dependent on the other's actions; either the goals themselves or the means for achieving them are linked so that one party's ultimate achievement is in part tied to how the other behaves. This interdependence is what gives negotiation its complexity and creates much of its drama and tension. Chapter 2 addresses the fundamental characteristics of interdependent human relationships. It also explains the different forms of interdependence and describes ways that problems of interdependence have been modeled and investigated through the study of games and simple negotiation problems.

Researchers have defined several major strategies or approaches to negotiation as vehicles for dealing with conflict. For example, in Joe Carter's negotiations, he would choose one strategy to negotiate for the car: distributive, or win-lose, bargaining. Joe would use another strategy for negotiating with his wife over their vacation plans: integrative, or win-win, negotiation. Chapter 3 describes and evaluates the basic assumptions and strategies that characterize the competitive, win-lose, distributive bargaining process. In this chapter, we will also review the tactics most commonly associated with distributive strategies and evaluate the consequences of using them.

Chapter 4 describes and evaluates the basic strategy and tactics common to cooperative, win-win, integrative bargaining. The process of integrative negotiation is significantly different from distributive bargaining. Whereas distributive bargaining is usually characterized by mistrust, suspicion, and strategies designed to beat the opponent, integrative negotiation tends to be characterized by greater levels of trust and openness and by tactics designed to achieve the best possible solution for all parties involved. Integrative negotiation often resembles the process of problem solving; Chapter 4 reviews the strategy and tactics necessary to perform this process successfully in detail.

In Chapter 5, we step back from the two major approaches to negotiation to explore more broadly the nature of strategy in negotiation and the key role that planning and preparation play in making a strategy work. In the first edition of this book, we addressed the importance of planning before describing distributive and integrative processes; we have since decided that it is useful to understand the difference between the two approaches before describing the mechanisms for developing and executing a strategy. Hence this chapter first explores the broad nature and role of strategy as a process planning tool. We present a general model of strategic choice and identify the key factors that affect how a strategy is designed. We then move to the more specific elements of adequate and effective planning for negotiation. Planning and preparation are the most important steps in negotiation; yet these are the steps that many negotiators neglect or even completely ignore. (Note that Joe Carter really does not plan for any of his negotiations.) Effective planning requires (a) a thorough understanding of the negotiation process so the negotiator has a general idea of what will happen and how things will evolve, (b) a clear formulation of goals and aspirations, (c) "homework" and research—putting together the information and arguments to support and defend the desired goals, and (d) knowing the adversary, understanding her goals, and using that information to design a strategy to reach an effective resolution. The chapter includes a series of diagnostic questions negotiators may use in planning for any negotiation.

Chapter 6 is a new chapter with the second edition, "Negotiation Breakdowns: Causes and Cures." As most negotiators discover, strategies do not always work the way they were intended to. Most commonly, negotiations break down because the conflict dynamics get out of control and inhibit the parties from reaching an agreement. (Recall Joe's problem with purchasing and Ed Laine, and with the budget process.) This may occur in a number of ways: parties dig in to their positions and refuse to yield, communication becomes unproductive, the parties cannot find a common ground or invent a solution to the problem, anger and frustration drive out effective reasoning and listening. In Chapter 6, we describe how negotiators can help put derailed negotiations back on track—most of these are tactics the negotiators can use themselves to keep conflict from becoming more destructive. We also specifically discuss cognitive traps negotiators sometimes lay for themselves and ways that negotiators can deal with difficult processes and opponents. And we present a basic plan for building and maintaining productive negotiating relationships.

Having considered the basic differences between two major strategic approaches to negotiation, the strategizing and planning processes to approach them, and ways to rescue them from the brink of disaster, we turn our attention to focusing on key subprocesses in negotiation. In calling them *subprocesses,* we simplify the more complex negotiation dynamics to understand them more clearly. Chapters 7 through 11 present five major subprocesses that are all parts of the larger and more complex negotiation process and that can dramatically influence a negotiation outcome. These subprocesses include communications between the parties (Chapter 7), the nature of persuasion used to influence the other party (Chapter 8), the social context in which negotiation occurs (Chapter 9), the types of power and influence used by negotiators (Chapter 10), and the impact of individual differences on negotiation outcomes (Chapter 11).

Chapter 7 examines the key roles played by communication, perception, cognition, and judgment in negotiation. Using a basic model of communication, we break negotiation into its key communication elements and show how each may lead to successful negotiations or negotiation breakdowns. We also examine the key roles played by perception, cognition, and judgment. In recent years, a great deal of work has shown that how negotiators perceive events, process information, and make judgments about a conflict is highly susceptible to some very predictable (and powerful) biases and distortions. Understanding these biases and distortions can help a negotiator know what types of perception and judgment errors may occur and how to correct for them in negotiation.

Successful persuasion is an important key to effective negotiation. In the Joe Carter case, Joe has a number of important people to persuade in several different disputes. The parties may spend a great deal of time assembling information to support their viewpoints, but effectively structuring and presenting a persuasive argument is equally critical. The world of advertising has taught us a great deal about what works and what does not work in getting the message across, and many of these lessons also apply to negotiation. Chapter 8 reviews important research findings about persuasion and the attitude change process and shows how that research may be used to most effectively construct persuasive tactics.

Through Chapter 8, this book approaches the negotiation process as a dialogue between two solitary individuals, dealing with their own and the other party's objectives. In fact, a great deal of negotiation involves more than two parties. In the Joe Carter case, Joe must deal with others who are representing their own department, organization, or political constituency. Sometimes negotiators argue not for their own interests, but as a representative of someone else's. A lawyer advocates for a client; a salesperson makes a deal for the company that must be approved by senior management; a labor leader negotiates for the union rank and file. When parties represent the interests of others and are accountable to those others, a whole new dimension of complexity is added to negotiation. In addition, some negotiations occur among small groups of people who are representing larger groups—as a negotiating team represents the larger labor union or a steering committee represents a larger association or assembly. Chapter 9 examines the impact of more than two parties on the negotiation process—either advocates or groups representing constituencies. The chapter also explores the role played by audiences to negotiation (observers, third parties, and the media), and shows how they affect the behavior of the negotiators and fundamentally change the nature of negotiation dynamics. Finally, we explore the special dynamics that occur when more than two interests are represented at the negotiation table, such as in a task force or committee where three or more parties have different concerns, but must reach a common agreement.

In Chapter 10, we take a closer look at the nature of power and influence strategies in negotiation. Power is an elusive concept. A number of authors in the social sciences have written extensively on the nature of power and its use, yet it is not always clear that they have captured the essence of power or the ways that it is used. This chapter attempts to define the different sources of power that negotiators have—the tools they can potentially use to get what they want—and strategies and tactics of influence—how these tools are put to use to achieve their desired ends. As we shall see, some of these power sources and influence strategies are fairly obvious, but other less obvious strategies are nonetheless very effective.

In Chapter 11, we address the role individual differences among negotiators may play in enhancing or diminishing their effectiveness. Our earlier models imply that the negotiation process occurs between two relatively rational, strategic, goal-oriented people (who are also subject to some systematic biases, distortions, and breakdowns). We have also consistently implied that with planning and practice, anyone can negotiate effectively. The question that experienced negotiators ask, then, is whether some individuals are *better* negotiators because of their personalities, or, conversely, whether anyone can be effective by following the right approach. Chapter 11 reviews the research on this question and explores several individual differences that appear likely to affect someone's predisposition to negotiation.

In Chapter 6, we discussed ways that negotiations may get off track and what negotiators themselves can do to get the process moving again. Chapter 12 shows how negotiations can use others—third parties—to bring parties back together. We encourage negotiators to seek out third parties when efforts to put things back on track are not fruitful. We explore the different types of third-party strategies that can be used to resolve breakdowns in negotiation: arbitration, mediation, process facilitation, and some additional hybrid forms. In the Joe Carter case, Joe is explicitly called on to help the Conservation Commission "resolve" the zoning issue.

As our discussion will show, negotiation is a process in which each party engages in all manner of tactics to persuade the other. Sometimes these tactics lead negotiators over the line of appropriate, proper, or even ethical behavior to unfair, inappropriate, unethical, or even illegal activities. They conceal information, bluff, or tell outright lies. They spy on the other to learn about his strategy. Negotiators may decide that it is worth doing something unethical or illegal in order to achieve their goals. All these tactics fall within the category of unethical behavior. Very little attention has been given to ethical and unethical behavior in negotiation. Chapter 13 indicates what types of conduct are generally viewed as unethical and explores the dimensions of these behaviors in negotiation. This chapter also describes the factors that affect ethical decision making in negotiation and outlines some of the research that has been done in this area.

Finally, Chapter 14, a new chapter to this revised edition, discusses the role that international and cultural differences play in negotiation. In many ways, international and cultural factors operate much like the social structure dimensions we describe in Chapter 9; that is, they are a context that tempers, modifies, or even changes negotiation dynamics. Because this book is being written by four white, upper-middle-class American authors, much of what we describe as typical and atypical is affected by the cultural biases we bring to negotiation. If the book were being written by four Asian Chinese or four Latin American Argentineans, our definitions of typical and atypical behavior might be quite different. Effective research on international differences in negotiation has only begun to occur in the past five to eight years. This research attempts to determine what factors are central to all negotiations regardless of culture and which factors and dimensions are strongly shaped by national and cultural style. We will present a current perspective on this emerging and evolving area of negotiation research.

# CHAPTER 2

# Interdependence

In negotiation, both parties need the other. A buyer cannot buy unless someone else sells and vice versa; each is dependent upon the other. This situation of mutual dependency is called *interdependence*. Interdependent relations are complex and have their own special challenge. They are more complex than situations in which we are independent of another person or in which we are dependent on another. When we are independent of another person we can, if we choose, have a relatively detached, indifferent, uninvolved outlook. When we are dependent on another, we have to accept and accommodate the demands of another. For example, if an employee is totally dependent on an employer for a job, he will have to do the job as instructed or quit. When we are interdependent, however, we have an opportunity to influence the other party, and many options are open to us. Managing those options can be difficult, however, because of the complexity of the interdependent relationship.

Interdependent relationships are characterized by interlocking goals—both parties need each other to accomplish their goals. For instance, in a business project management team, no single person could complete a complex project alone within the time limit required by the organization. Each person needs to rely upon the other project team members for the group to accomplish its goals. In that sense, the goals of the project team members are interdependent. Note that having interdependent goals does not mean that everyone wants exactly the same thing. Different project team members may want different things, but for the group to achieve its goals, they must work together. This mix of personal and group goals is typical of interdependent situations. Another example of interdependence is two people playing a competitive game of squash. Each person wants to win the game, so their goals are in conflict (only one person can win). On the other hand, each wants to play the game, so their goals converge (one cannot play squash alone). This mix of convergent and conflicting goals characterizes many interdependent relationships.

Interdependent goals are an important aspect of negotiation. The structure of the interdependence between different negotiating parties determines the range of possible outcomes of the negotiation and suggests the appropriate strategies and tactics that the negotiators should use. For instance, if the interdependence is a "win-lose" situation—that is, the more that one party gains, the more the other party loses—then the negotiation will focus on how to divide a fixed amount of outcomes. An example of this type of negotiation is determining the price of a major appliance or capital purchase (these distributive bargaining situations are discussed in detail in Chapter 3). Another type of interdependence occurs in a "win-win" situation—that is, solutions promote mutual gains. An example of this type of negotiation is determining the relationship between two companies in a joint venture (these integrative negotiation situations are discussed in detail in Chapter 4). The type of interdependence between the negotiating parties will determine both the range of possible negotiation solutions and the type of strategies the negotiators should use.

In this chapter, we will clarify some of the key aspects of interdependent relationships. First, we discuss how people evaluate interdependent relationships and possible courses of action. Next, we discuss how the type of interdependence between parties can lead to cooperation or competition. In the following section we discuss the dynamic nature of interdependence—people adjust their behavior based both on how they expect the other party to behave and on how the other party actually behaves. We then focus on the role of perceptions in interdependence, stressing that the way people perceive interdependent relationships may become as important as the objective structure of the interdependence. Finally, we discuss laboratory game research—a rich history of research into interdependence from a game theory perspective—and discuss the strengths and weaknesses of this research.

## COOPERATION AND COMPETITION

The interconnectedness (interdependence) of people's goals is the basis for much social interaction. Can it help us to estimate what type of social action will occur? The answer is frequently "yes," and by determining something about the way in which people's goals are interdependent, we can estimate what type of behavior is most likely to emerge. When the goals of two or more people are interconnected so that only one can achieve the goal—such as winning a gold medal in a race and therefore making the others losers of the race—we have a competitive situation. Deutsch (1962, 1973) defined this as *contrient interdependence* (also known as a zero-sum or distributive situation), in which "individuals are so linked together that there is a negative correlation between their goal attainments" (1962, p. 276). To the degree that one person achieves her goal, the other's goal attainment is blocked. In contrast, when parties' goals are linked so one person's goal achievement helps others to achieve their goals (a positive correlation between their goal attainments), we have a *promotive interdependence* situation (also known as a nonzero-sum or integrative situation). Deutsch's research has shown that promotive interdependence situations are usually characterized by trusting relations among the parties, a successful division of labor on the tasks to be performed, and successful efforts at mutually influencing one another. In contrast, contrient interdependence situations are characterized by mistrust and suspicion, significant efforts to block the other's goal attainment rather than to help it, and the use of coercive power and force to exercise influence. Needless to say, therefore, the nature of the interdependence will have a major impact on the nature of the relationship, the way negotiations are conducted, and the outcomes of a negotiation (Neslin and Greenhalgh, 1983; Raiffa, 1982).

## CHARACTERISTICS OF INTERPERSONAL RELATIONSHIPS

To better understand interdependence, we will use the analytical concepts developed by Thibaut and Kelley (1959). In a relationship, we usually have some idea of what kinds of outcomes to expect, and we can assess the desirability of these outcomes against some standard (see Figure 2.1). If we are buying a house, there is a limit above which we will not (or cannot) pay; if we are accepting a job, there is a limit in salary below which we will not work. These points beyond which we will not go act as a standard of comparison for an offered price. In a broader context, we can assess an entire negotiating relationship: how we feel about negotiation in general, how we feel about negotiating with this person, and what we feel to be an acceptable price or resistance point. Thibaut and Kelley call this stan-

**FIGURE 2.1**    Standards for Evaluating Relationship Outcomes

---

*Definitions*

---

**Anticipated Outcome:** What we expect to receive from this relationship

**Comparison Level:** The standard against which a person evaluates a relationship—what we could receive from other relationships

**Comparison Level for Alternatives (CLalt):** The lowest level of outcome that would be accepted from this relationship before changing to another relationship

---

*Example*

---

Laura has been employed by an organization for six months and is making $31,000 per year. When hired, the average salary of Laura's college classmates who were accepting new jobs was $30,000. Recently, the organization where Laura works was downsized and Laura's job was eliminated. Her boss offered her another job in the organization at $28,000. Laura realizes that most other companies are not currently hiring because it is not the end of the school year, and she believes that it would be difficult to find a new job for more than $25,000.

**Anticipated Outcome:** The salary for the new job in the organization, $28,000

**Comparison Level:** The average starting salary of Laura's classmates, $30,000

**Comparison Level for Alternatives (CLalt):** The perceived salary of a readily available alternate job, $25,000

---

dard the Comparison Level (CL); it is the standard against which a person "evaluates the attractiveness of a relationship or how satisfactory it is" (Thibaut and Kelley, p. 21). A relationship or anticipated outcome (O) that is above the CL is desirable; one below the CL is unattractive or unsatisfactory. The greater the distance between O and CL, the greater the attractiveness or unattractiveness of the relationship. In the job example, if we have determined that our minimally acceptable salary is $30,000 per year, this becomes our comparison level for jobs. Anticipated salaries above $30,000 will be viewed as more attractive, whereas salaries below $30,000 will be viewed as unattractive and will probably be rejected.

When a relationship is unattractive, we may think of leaving, but whether we do depends upon our options. We may not like our current job, but if we are relatively unskilled, we may find it difficult to get another job. If we have many skills, on the other hand, we may know of several jobs to which we can easily move. Another standard by which we judge outcomes, then, is the lowest level of outcomes (experienced or anticipated) a person will accept in light of the alternatives available. This is called the Comparison Level for Alternatives (CLalt). People leave relationships when outcomes fall below this CLalt. It is assumed that the more a person's actual outcome exceeds the CLalt, the more dependent upon the relationship she is. Thus, for example, let us assume that our job seeker took a job at $32,000 per year. Six months later her boss announced that because of major cutbacks in the business, her job had been eliminated; she could accept another job in the company at $28,000 or she would have to be laid off. Although $28,000 is considerably below the $30,000 limit our job seeker had set six months earlier, the prospects of being unemployed and seeking a new job (the CLalt) may appear to be much worse than the $28,000 job opportunity. The more dependent the job seeker is on the job, the more she will stay with a salary that is below the CL but above the CLalt.

Let us use these three concepts—comparison level (CL), comparison level for alternatives (CLalt), and anticipated outcome (O)—to clarify some aspects of interdependent relations. We will modify the example of the job seeker here, using $30,000 as the CL, not working at all or having another job opportunity as the CLalt, and the actual salary as the O. First consider the situation where a person's O exceeds both the CLalt, and the CL, respectively (Figure 2.2a). When the actual outcome exceeds the CL, this is an attractive, satisfactory relationship. However, because there are alternative jobs (CLalt) that would also have outcomes in excess of the CL, the individual is not very dependent upon this relationship. In this situation, assume that a person earning $32,000 a year was offered $31,000 a year to work elsewhere. Because $31,000 is also above the CL, the individual may feel that there are several good jobs around that pay well and hence feel less dependent on the current job as the only option available.

A second condition would be when a person's CL is below O but above CLalt (Figure 2.2b). Again the relationship is satisfactory, but the individual's dependence upon the relationship has *increased*. Thus, a person working for $32,000 who needs $30,000 to live and knows that other available jobs pay $27,000 will stay in the job and feel dependent on it as the best source of income.

**FIGURE 2.2**

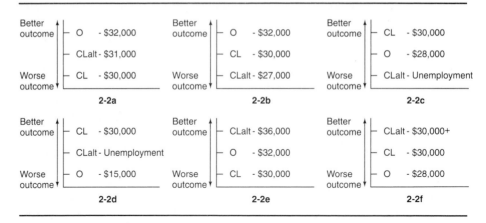

The third situation is where a person's CL exceeds the O, which in turn exceeds the CLalt (Figure 2.2c). This is clearly an unattractive, unsatisfactory relationship, but the outcome still exceeds the next most attractive possibility. Hence the individual is dependent upon the relationship and can be expected to stay, although unsatisfied. If our job seeker needs $30,000 minimum, has her salary cut to $28,000, and has a choice between that and unemployment, she is likely to stay in the $28,000 job but be unsatisfied. A fourth situation is where the CL and CLalt both exceed O (Figure 2.2d). In this situation the individual is both not satisfied and not dependent and thus will leave. If our job seeker is offered a clerk's job at $15,000 a year and has the choice between that and unemployment, she may well decide that the job or salary is so inadequate that she would rather be unemployed, and hence quit.

In a fifth situation, CLalt exceeds the outcome, which in turn exceeds the CL (Figure 2.2e). This is the bittersweet situation where an individual is satisfied with the relationship, but will leave because of a better opportunity. If there are other attractive jobs on the market for up to $36,000, the person is likely to see these as more attractive than the current salary of $32,000 and be tempted to move. A sixth possibility, in which the CLalt and CL both exceed the O is conceptually possible (Figure 2.2f), but because it would be both unsatisfying and lacking either dependency or desirable alternatives, it would not exist long if it ever came into being. Thus, according to this theory, it would be hard to imagine a person staying in a job at $28,000 when the CL is $30,000 and other jobs are readily available at better than $30,000 (assuming salary is the *only* basis for staying).

This mode of analysis permits us to draw a distinction between attractiveness and satisfaction on one hand and dependency on the other. A person can dislike a relationship and stay, or like a relationship and leave. In clarifying our own situation and understanding the situation of the other party, these distinctions are important. In negotiation, the other party may dislike dealing with us, but since we have "the best deal in town," he will hang in and negotiate with us. Alternately, the other party may like us, but nonetheless break off negotiations because of more attractive possibilities elsewhere.

Fisher, Ury, and Patton (1991), in their popular book *Getting to Yes,* stress the importance of understanding the nature of your interdependence with the other party. They suggest that knowing and developing alternatives to reaching an agreement with the other party in a negotiation is an important source of power in negotiation. They write, "whether you should or should not agree on something in a negotiation depends entirely upon the attractiveness to you of the best available alternative" (p. 105). They call this concept BATNA (an acronym for *B*est *A*lternative *T*o a *N*egotiated *A*greement) and suggest that negotiators need to understand the BATNA when they negotiate.

Interdependence is a critical aspect of a BATNA. Someone with a low CLalt also has a low BATNA, and the other party has more bargaining power. Returning to our employment example, if few jobs are available for $30,000 (and unemployment is high) then the person will be more likely to accept no raise in salary for the upcoming year compared to the situation where many jobs are available for $30,000 or more. Someone with a high CLalt, such as someone returning to school, changing careers, or finding many jobs available at $30,000, also has a high BATNA, and the likelihood that this person will accept no raise for the upcoming year is much lower.

CLalt and BATNA are very similar concepts, but they are not the same thing. A BATNA is one type of CLalt used to evaluate the worth of a negotiation outcome by comparing it to outcomes that could be gained by negotiating with other parties. CLalt is a broader concept that is not limited to evaluating the outcome of a negotiation, but that may be used to make comparisons about the value of anything.

## INTERDEPENDENCE

Interdependent relationships—those in which people are mutually dependent—are complex. Both parties know that they can influence the other's outcomes and that their outcomes can, in turn, be influenced by the other (Goffman, 1969; Pruitt and Rubin, 1986; Raven and Rubin, 1973). Let us explore a situation in which Bob is applying for a job and is being interviewed by Mary, an employer. Their discussion has revealed that Bob would like to have the job that is available, and Mary sees Bob as a desirable employee for the position. They are now attempting to establish Bob's salary. The job description announces the salary as "competitive." Bob has identified a salary below which he will not work ($30,000) but suspects he may be able to get considerably more. Mary's company has a reputation for running "hard and lean," and he suspects that means they will pay no more than necessary. For this reason, Bob has decided not to state his minimally acceptable salary because he suspects it would be accepted immediately. Moreover, he knows that it would be difficult to raise the level if it should turn out that $30,000 was considerably below what Mary could pay. Bob has thought of stating his ideal salary ($38,000), but suspects that Mary will view him as either presumptuous or rude for asking that much. The interview would probably end with Mary viewing him negatively and making it harder for him to get the best possible salary.

Let's take a closer look at what is happening here. Bob is making his decision based on how he *anticipates* Mary will react to his actions. Bob recognizes that his actions will affect Mary. Bob also recognizes that the way Mary acts in the future toward him will be influenced by the way his actions affect Mary now. As a result, Bob is assessing the *indirect* impact of his behavior on himself. Further, he also knows that Mary is alert to all this and will look upon any statement by Bob as reflecting a preliminary position on salary rather than a final one. To counter this expected view, Bob will probably try to find some way to state a number as close to his desired final salary as possible. For example, he could refer to salaries he knows others with similar qualifications have received in other companies. Bob is choosing among behavioral options with a thought not only to how they will affect Mary, but also to how they will then lead Mary to act towards Bob. Further, Bob knows that Mary believes he will act in this way and acts on the basis of this belief.

One may wonder if people really pay attention to all this complexity in their relationships with others. Certainly people don't do this most of the time, or we would all be frozen in inactivity while we tried to think through the possibilities. However, when people face complex, important, or novel situations, they are more likely to think in this way. Given that many negotiations are complex, important, and novel, the effective negotiator needs to understand that people will adjust and readjust what they say during negotiations based on what the other party does and is expected to do.

Behavior in an interdependent relationship is frequently calculated behavior—calculated on the premise that the more information one has about the other person, the better. There is the possibility, however, that too much knowledge only confuses (Beisecker, Walker, and Bart, 1989; Raven and Rubin, 1973, p. 158). For example, let us suppose that Bob knows Mary needs to get a project underway and needs to fill this job opening promptly. Mary has just had a performance review with her boss, during which her superior claimed that she was not controlling costs—particularly labor costs. In addition, other people working for Mary are complaining that they need additional talents in the organization, such as those possessed by Bob, but that they also resent new personnel being brought in at salaries higher than their own. Does all this help Bob determine his actions or only confuse things? In fact, given all these complexities, Mary may not have reached a decision about what salary should be paid, other than a maximum figure above which she will not go. This is the classic bargaining situation. Both parties have their outer limits for an acceptable settlement (how high or low they can afford to go), but within that range, neither has determined what the exact salary will or should be. It is a solution to be worked toward. The parties have to exchange information and make an effort at influencing the other and at problem solving. They must work toward a solution that takes into account each person's requirements and, hopefully, optimizes the outcomes for both (Fisher, Ury, and

Patton, 1991; Follett, 1940; Nash, 1950; Sebenius, 1992; Sen, 1970; Walton and McKersie, 1965).

Problem solving is essentially a process of specifying the elements of a desired outcome, examining the components available to produce the outcome, and searching for a way to fit them together. A person can approach problem solving in negotiation from his own perspective and attempt to solve the problem by considering only the components that affect his own desired outcome. For instance, Mary could decide what was best for her and her department and ignore Bob's needs. When approaching the situation as a joint problem-solving effort, however, the outcomes desired by the other party must be taken into account. For instance, Bob cannot determine his own salary without input from the employer about her preferences and limits (Pruitt, 1981). One difficulty is that opposing parties may not be open about their desired outcomes, or they may not be clear in their own minds about what they actually want. Hence, *a necessary step in all negotiation is to clarify and share information about what both parties really want as outcomes.*

As negotiations evolve, some knowledge of the combined set of desired outcomes becomes known (be they stated as bargaining positions or needs). If the suggested outcomes don't immediately fit, negotiation continues as a series of proposals. These proposals usually suggest alterations in the other party's position, and perhaps contain alterations in the proposer's own position. When one party accepts an alteration in its position, a concession has been made (Pruitt, 1981). Concessions restrict the range of options within which a solution or agreement will be reached; when a party makes a concession, the bargaining range is *confined closer* to one or both sides' limits or resistance point. Our job seeker would like to get a starting salary of $38,000, but scales his request down to $35,000, thereby eliminating all possible salary options above $35,000. People may recognize that concessions are necessary for a settlement, but they will obviously be reluctant to make all or most of them. For our job seeker to make further concessions below $35,000, he probably will want to see some willingness on the part of the company to increase its offer or add other attractive benefits to its salary package.

Making and interpreting concessions is no easy task, especially when there is little trust between negotiators. Two of the dilemmas that all negotiators face, identified by Harold Kelley (1966), help explain why this is so. The first dilemma, the Dilemma of Honesty, concerns how much of the truth to tell the other party (the ethical considerations of these dilemmas are discussed in Chapter 13). Telling the other party everything about your situation may give that person the opportunity to take advantage of you. On the other hand, not telling the other person anything about your needs, wants, and desires may lead to a stalemate. Just how much of the truth should you tell the other party? If our job seeker told Mary that he would work for as little as $30,000 but would like to start at $38,000 it is quite possible that Mary would hire him for $30,000 and keep the extra money that she might have paid him. We are not suggesting that Mary should do this; rather, because the long-term relationship is important in this situation, Mary should ensure that both parties' needs are met (see Chapter 4 for an expanded discussion of this point). If, on the other hand, our job seeker did not tell Mary any information about his salary needs, then Mary would have a much more difficult time knowing how to satisfy his needs.

The second dilemma that every negotiator faces, the Dilemma of Trust, concerns how much to believe what the other party tells you. If you believe everything that the other party says, then she could take advantage of you. On the other hand, if you believe nothing that the other party says, then you will have a great deal of difficulty in reaching an agreement. Exactly how much to believe of what the other party tells you depends on many factors, including the reputation of the other party, how he treated you in the past, the present circumstances, and so on. If Mary told our job seeker that $28,000 was the maximum she was allowed to pay him for the job without seeking approval "from above," should Bob believe her or not? As you can see, sharing and clarifying information is not as easy as it first appears!

To find an optimal solution through the processes of giving information and making concessions requires trust and a belief that you're being treated honestly and fairly. Two efforts in negotiation help to create this trust and belief—one is based on perceptions of outcomes and the other on perceptions of the process. The former attempts to change a party's estimation of the perceived importance or value of something. In the illustration above, if Mary convinces Bob that the low salary for the job is relatively unimportant given the high bonuses that people in the firm typically earn, then he can feel comfortable making a concession on this point. In contrast, efforts based on the negotiating process help convey images of equity, fairness, and reciprocity in proposals and concessions. When one party makes several proposals that are rejected by the other party and the other party makes no alternate proposal, the first party often feels improperly treated and may break off negotiations. When one party makes a concession, he will feel much more comfortable and be more trusting if the other party responds with a concession. In fact, the belief that concessions will occur in negotiations appears to be almost universal. During training seminars, we have asked negotiators from more than 50 countries if they expect give-and-take to occur during negotiations in their culture; all have said they do. This pattern of give-and-take is not just a characteristic of negotiation; it is also essential to joint problem solving in most interdependent relationships (Kimmel, Pruitt, Magenau, Konar-Goldband, and Carnevale, 1980; Putnam and Jones, 1982; Weingart, Thompson, Bazerman, and Carroll, 1990). Parties' satisfaction with a negotiation is as much determined by the process through which an agreement is reached as with the actual outcome obtained. To eliminate or even deliberately attempt to reduce this give-and-take, as some labor-management negotiating strategies have attempted (Raiffa, 1982; Selekman, Fuller, Kennedy, and Baitsell, 1964), is to short-circuit the process, eliminating both the basis for trust and any possibility of joint decision making. Even if the strategy results in maximizing joint outcomes, the other party will dislike the process by which these outcomes are reached.

Negotiators must recognize that negotiation should be a process of problem solving in which both parties work toward a maximum joint return. This process, which requires trust and security for each party, is critical to successful interdependent relationships. This trust can be developed by including the other party in the negotiation process and by ensuring that her needs are met as well as your own. Following a fair process will contribute to feelings of satisfaction and success for both parties.

## INTERDEPENDENCE AND PERCEPTIONS

We have been treating interdependence as a more or less objective phenomenon. That is, the structure of the negotiation itself plays an important part in determining how two negotiating parties should interact. At times, the situation will be structured as win-lose: the more one party gains, the more the other party loses. People frequently perceive economic exchanges, such as the purchase of a new car or a commodity, as examples of this type of situation (appropriate strategies and tactics for these situations are discussed in Chapter 3). At other times, however, the situation may be structured as win-win: there are opportunities for both parties to gain. A classic example of this situation, attributed to Mary Parker Follett (1940), is the story of two sisters deciding how to divide an orange. Both sisters wanted the same orange, one sister for the peel and the other for the juice. Both demanded the whole orange, however, and neither considered asking for only the part of the orange she needed. The sisters can reach a decision by each asking for only the part of the orange she needs; the challenge when negotiating is to find that solution (appropriate strategies and tactics for these situations are discussed in Chapter 4).

Understanding the nature of the interdependence between parties in a negotiation is critical to optimally concluding negotiations. Unfortunately, negotiation situations do not typically present themselves with neat labels describing the nature of the interdependence between parties. Rather, negotiators make judgments about the nature of the interdependence in their negotiation situations, and negotiator *perceptions* about interdependence become as important as the actual structure of the interdependence (Bazerman, Magliozzi and Neale, 1985; Neale and Bazerman, 1985; Neale and Northcraft, 1991; Pinkley, 1992; Thompson, 1990).

To examine how perception and structure are critically linked, let us return to Follett's example of the two sisters with the orange. Remember, the actual structure of the situation is that each sister needs only part of the orange (the juice or the peel), and each has stated that she wants the whole orange. The objective structure of the situation is that there is an opportunity for mutual gain. Assume for a moment that the sisters have negotiated frequently in the past and each is concerned about the other's needs and interests. A series of questions would allow them each to learn that they have different needs for the orange and each could take only that part of the orange that she needs. Now assume a different situation. Perhaps the sisters have negotiated frequently in the past and perceive that most of their disagreements are win-lose situations. They would then approach this as a win-lose negotiation and use distributive strategies to divide the orange. Perhaps they would split the difference and each take half of the orange—and neither would have enough juice or peel to be satisfied. The use of distributive strategies would decrease the likelihood that they would identify that each needs only part of the orange. Assume a third scenario. Perhaps one of the sisters realizes that the other is unhappy today and needs something to brighten her day. The first sister could simply give the orange to the other and allow her to use it as she wanted. A fourth scenario might be that one of the sisters could avoid the discussion by going out; the other sister would then have to decide how (whether) to divide the orange herself.

The point here is that people bring much baggage with them to a negotiation, including past history, personality characteristics, moods, habits, beliefs about how to negotiate, and the like. These factors will influence how people perceive an interdependent situation, and this perception will in turn have a strong effect on the subsequent negotiation.

Considerable research has been conducted on the role of perception and cognition in negotiation (see Bazerman and Neale, 1992; Neale and Bazerman, 1991, 1992b; Thompson and Hastie, 1990a, 1990b). This research suggests strongly that the way that people perceive interdependent situations has an important effect on how they will negotiate. Leigh Thompson and Reid Hastie (1990a) suggest that negotiator perceptions and judgments can have important influences on judgments that negotiators make about (a) the other party; (b) themselves; (c) the utilities of both parties; (d) offers and counter-offers; (e) negotiation outcomes; and (f) the negotiation process.

A classic treatise by Harold Kelley and Anthony Stahelski (1970), carefully reviewing research on the Prisoner's Dilemma game, suggests that negotiator perceptions have a critical influence on how negotiators evaluate the situation and how they subsequently behave. Kelley and Stahelski propose that there are two general types of negotiators: cooperators and competitors. Competitors enter negotiations expecting the other party to compete, and to compete with everyone. Cooperators will cooperate with other cooperators and compete with competitors. The consequences of these expectations are fascinating. Competitors believe that all negotiations are competitive, and that the world contains only competitors— because all the people they negotiate with compete (natural competitors or cooperators who have adapted and compete rather than being taken advantage of). Cooperators, on the other hand, understand that negotiations may be cooperative or competitive and recognize that there are both cooperators and competitors in the world; they view the task while negotiating as identifying the predisposition of the other party. In addition, their experiences continue to reinforce their beliefs about others who are competitors and cooperators, thus making these beliefs highly resistant to change.

Another line of research has sought to identify systematic biases in negotiators' initial perceptions of the nature of the interdependence between the negotiating parties. Max Bazerman, Thomas Magliozzi, and Margaret Neale (1985) labeled one such systematic bias as the "mythical fixed-pie" in negotiation. Bazerman and his colleagues suggest that most negotiators in mixed-motive situations (negotiations containing both cooperative and competitive elements) will assume that there is a fixed pie; that is, the more I get, the less you have. In a laboratory study of negotiation that investigated this hypothesis, Leigh Thompson and Reid Hastie (1990a) found that more than twice as many negotiators (68 percent) assumed their upcoming negotiations were win-lose situations rather than win-win situations (32 percent). Additionally, Thompson and Hastie found that the degree to which negotiators adjusted to the situation during the first five minutes of the negotiation had an important effect on the outcome of the negotiation. Negotiators who better adjusted their assessments of the structure of the negotiation early in the process earned higher profits than those negotiators who did not adjust until later.

Researchers continue to identify other systematic perceptual biases that make negotiators less than ideal decision makers (see Bazerman and Neale, 1992, and Neale and Bazerman, 1991, for excellent reviews of this literature). However, it is no simple task to correct the biased perceptions that occur when negotiating. Most authors agree that *identifying* the systematic biases in negotiators' perceptions is an important first step. Whether the next step, reducing the effect of the biases, is best accomplished through the use of an unfreezing-change-refreezing model (Neale and Bazerman, 1991), systematic consideration of the other party's position (Thompson and Loewenstein, 1992), or other techniques remains an important unsolved issue.

## UNDERSTANDING NEGOTIATION THROUGH THE STUDY OF GAMES

Because interdependent relationships are complex, they are difficult to study. Ideally, we would study the structure and processes of interdependent relationships during actual negotiations. Sometimes we do. More commonly we study such relationships through simulations in laboratory settings. In proceeding this way, we obviously lose some of the richness of real experiences. On the other hand, by limiting our focus and controlling as many variables as possible, we can systematically probe what does happen. One of the principal ways to study interdependent relationships in a controlled setting is through games (see Murnighan, 1991, for an excellent discussion of game research).

When social scientists discuss studying "games," they mean something different from other common definitions. To use games means they are studying behavior in an artificial, or make-believe sense, rather than in real life. They also might use terms like *experiment* or *simulation.* Games are artificial, simplified, and reconstructed models of reality. Like all games, they have players and rules. Mathematicians and economists usually construct and study games to determine what players *should* do, based on certain principles and rules of rational economic behavior (see Raiffa, 1982). In contrast, behavioral scientists study games to determine what people *actually* do in these situations—behavior that may be at considerable variance with predictions based on economic rationality alone. Thus in the study of interdependent behavior, *games* usually means a particular type of simulation. These games are structured to lead the parties to behave cooperatively or competitively.

There are numerous similarities and parallels between games and the situations we have been discussing as examples of interdependence, particularly interdependent negotiating. In a game, what one person does influences the range of possible outcomes of the other party; this, in turn, will influence how the other party acts toward the first. In tennis, I hit the ball to make points, but I also consider where I place the ball to influence how my opponent will return it to me (see Follett, 1940 for a discussion of how anticipated responses influence behavior). A tennis game has limits of time, ball placement, and so on. In negotiations, the limits might be price (bottom line), or how much abusive behavior I will tolerate, or the length of the negotiation (time limit). There are rules in games, and parties win by achieving their goal within those rules. There are also rules in negotiation—often unstated—such as responding to a concession from the other party with one of your own, or making the best case for your side without actually lying.

The term *game* has been used in a variety of ways. Games used to study negotiations fall into four categories: game-theory games, distribution games, economic exchange games, and role-playing games. Behavioral scientists have learned a great deal about negotiation through the study of games; this knowledge can significantly help them understand the complexity of negotiation, if we keep in mind the limitations imposed by studying negotiation in this way. Our treatment of game-theory games will be somewhat more extensive because of the important role that they have played in research on bargaining (Raiffa, 1982; Sebenius, 1992).

### Game-Theory Games

The term *game theory* comes from the approach taken by the following form of analysis: two parties, each of whom has conflicting interests, can take action independently in choosing one of two alternatives. The outcomes or payoffs for both parties are displayed in a matrix, and represent all the possible combinations of their individual choices. Two types of games have received most attention: zero-sum games (in which one party wins and the other necessarily loses) and mixed-motive or nonzero-sum games (in which the interests and outcomes of the parties are both in conflict and congruent, so that it is possible for one to win, both to win, or neither to win). Since most negotiations are mixed-motive situations, the nonzero-sum game has been most widely used in research.

The first and probably most popular form of mixed-motive game is the Prisoner's Dilemma, described by Luce and Raiffa (1957):

> Two suspects are taken into custody and separated. The district attorney is certain that they are guilty of a specific crime, but he does not have adequate evidence to convict them at a trial. He points out to each prisoner that each has two alternatives: to confess to the crime the police are sure the suspects have committed or not to confess. If they both do not confess, then the district attorney states he will book them on some minor trumped-up charge such as petty larceny or illegal possession of a weapon, and they

both will receive minor punishment; if they both confess they will be prosecuted, but he will recommend less than the most severe sentence; but if one confesses and the other does not, then the confessor will receive lenient treatment for turning state's evidence whereas the latter will get "the book" slapped at him. In terms of years in a penitentiary, the strategic problem might reduce to the possibilities shown in Figure 2.3.

Admittedly the Prisoner's Dilemma presents a gloomy picture for both prisoners. The best they can hope for is 3 months in jail; and if things do not go well, they may spend 10 years reflecting on the rewards of a life of crime. What are they to do? Let us begin with the assumption that the prisoners are kept in separate cells and cannot talk to each other. Let us further assume that they will not be able to take revenge on each other after they are released.

For Prisoner A, the best alternative is to confess and hope that Prisoner B does not. However, Prisoner A probably assumes, correctly, that the other prisoner has the same information, and thinks the same way. There is a strong likelihood that Prisoner B looks at things the same way and will also confess. Then they both get eight years in jail. Prisoner A could note that if both do not confess they will each get a one-year sentence. Not the best for either as individuals, but it is the most favorable joint outcome. In fact, when either party makes a "not confess" choice, he takes a position most favorable to the other party since the payouts for the other will be either one year or three months. A choice that has considerable advantage to the other party is called a *cooperative* choice, whereas the "confess" choice, which may result in the other party receiving a 10-year sentence, is called *competitive.* Given this analysis, Prisoner A may conclude that Prisoner B will notice that the best joint choice is for them both to not confess and take that position. If Prisoner A is not too imaginative, she may act at this point. But if she has some imagination (and perhaps a tinge of paranoia), she may have a further thought. "Suppose Prisoner B suspects I will think this way and is selfish and confesses, getting a 3-month sentence while I get 10 years?" All sorts of questions follow. "How imaginative is Prisoner B? How trustworthy? How trustworthy does Prisoner B think I am?"

**FIGURE 2.3**

| Prisoner A | Prisoner B | |
|---|---|---|
| | *Not Confess* | *Confess* |
| *Not Confess* | 1 year each | 10 years for Prisoner A<br>3 months for Prisoner B |
| *Confess* | 3 months for Prisoner A<br>10 years for Prisoner B | 8 years each |

This game raises these strategic choice issues, among others. The underlying issues of trust, honesty, cooperation, and competition are consistently raised in actual negotiations. How people respond to these issues depends in part on how they see the situation. If the parties see their interests as different, conflicting, or divergent, they are likely to see more evidence of dishonesty and deception in the actions of the other and act as if the other party is not trustworthy. They may follow a line of thinking somewhat like this: "I don't trust him. If he says A, he probably really intends B, but because he may be smarter than I think he is, he may anticipate that I will see through his lies and hence manipulate me, so I had better . . ." This line of thinking can go through several more iterations, getting the person so confused that she does not know what to think or do. If the parties see their interests as the same (convergent), they are more likely to accept what the other says, especially if the other's first statements seem reliable and are further supported and confirmed by later ones.

Let us look at some of the major factors that shape patterns of cooperation among people playing the Prisoners' Dilemma game:

1. *Motivation.* One way to affect the amount of cooperation displayed in the Prisoner's Dilemma game is to shape the players' motivation in the game. Research has shown that this motivation can be shaped through the kind of instructions given to the players (Deutsch, 1973). When participants are told that they are in a competitive situation and are to play the game to get a better score (i.e., shorter sentence) than their opponent, both almost always confess and get an eight-year sentence. When participants are told that they are in a cooperative situation where they are to work together (against the district attorney), they generally both settle on the "not confess" position. When they were told to do the best they could for themselves (an individualistic position with no reference to beating or helping the other party), the outcomes are less heavily weighted toward the confess-confess position (Deutsch, 1958; Scodel, Minas, Ratoosh, and Lipetz, 1959). The concept of motivation in negotiation is discussed in more detail in Chapter 11.

2. *Length of interaction.* If the basic Prisoner's Dilemma game is played once, players make a move and the game is over. Negotiation, however, frequently occurs over a longer period of interaction. To make gaming interactions more like real negotiations, game situations have been varied in a number of ways so that the parties win (or lose) points (or money) rather than acquiring prison terms. This permits repeated decisions or rounds of decisions, which, in turn, permits parties to be affected by and respond to each other's choices. Typically, *no* communication between the parties is allowed, other than knowledge of the other party's choice on the previous turn. A simple illustration of this modification to the original Prisoner's Dilemma is a game between two parties, A and B, who can take either of two actions, Low and High. Their payouts for each combination of choices are shown in Figure 2.4, and their pattern of choices for 11 rounds is shown in Figure 2.5.

**FIGURE 2.4**

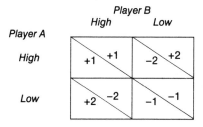

In this situation, parties typically develop a pattern of becoming more cooperative (i.e., choosing actions that will get the greatest joint return). That seems understandable because they quickly learn that the other party can cause them harm if they do not cooperate. What is surprising is that over time, one of the parties is frequently tempted to take an action that maximizes her return even though it costs the other dearly, as when B chooses Low on round 6 (Figure 2.5). Further, having done it once, B is likely to continue the competitive behavior, perhaps in the belief that A will look upon this as a mistake, not change the previously established pattern, and hence allow the exploitation to continue. Actually A responds quickly by taking a Low action; things frequently stabilize at Low-Low with both parties losing one point on each of the following rounds. Occasionally, pairs get out of this joint-loss situation when one of them takes a heroic action, choosing High and holding that position for two or more rounds. By this action, the player hopes to indicate to the other party that he is willing to accept a loss in order to get

**FIGURE 2.5**   A Sample Game

| | A | | B | |
|---|---|---|---|---|
| Round | Choice | Payout | Choice | Payout |
| 1 | High | −2 | Low | +2 |
| 2 | Low | −1 | Low | −1 |
| 3 | High | +1 | High | +1 |
| 4 | High | +1 | High | +1 |
| 5 | High | +1 | High | +1 |
| 6 | High | −2 | Low | +2 |
| 7 | Low | −1 | Low | −1 |
| 8 | Low | −1 | Low | −1 |
| 9 | High | −2 | Low | +2 |
| 10 | Low | −1 | Low | −1 |
| 11 | Low | −1 | Low | −1 |

them both to a winning position. Hopefully, the other party will respond; once cooperative choices are restored, they tend to be continued.

3. *Other party's strategy.* Another possible response to the heroic action by a party in choosing High for several rounds is that the other party will see this action as naive or stupid and choose Low to exploit the situation. It is therefore sensible for the first party to set a limit to how long she will be the hero. In general, the most rewarding strategy is for one party to mirror choices the other party makes, as A did in round 7 by mirroring B's Low choice on round 6 (Axelrod, 1984; Meeker and Shure, 1969). This, as we have seen, can lead to a cooperative but suboptimal joint solution. To break out of that cycle requires heroic action by one party, but that action should be guided by what is learned about the other party's strategy.

4. *Overt communication.* In the previous illustration, the parties are communicating through their actions. If additional spoken or written communication is permitted, it can help the parties move more quickly into a cooperative position. Hence, after round 6, if A had said, "If you continue to choose Low, I also will choose Low, but if you switch to High, I will do the same," B would most likely have chosen to cooperate. This verbalization contains both a promise and a threat. Research has found that communications containing promises are more effective than those containing threats (Tedeschi, Bonoma, and Brown, 1971).

5. *Personality characteristics of each decision maker.* Sometimes the strategy chosen reflects rational processes; at other times it reflects an individual's personality. Some people are strongly inclined to compete and others to cooperate (Kelley and Stahelski, 1970). Some are basically suspicious and distrustful and likely to think others are the same. Hence, they act accordingly (Deutsch, 1960; Loomis, 1959). Dogmatic people—those who are impatient with ambiguity and delay—make fewer concessions, take longer to reach an agreement, and make fewer agreements than less dogmatic people (Druckman, 1967). In general, however, the evidence concerning the role of personality on bargaining is not clear, because the results of one study often contradict others (Hermann and Kogan, 1977; Terhune, 1970). The effects of personality and individual differences in negotiation are discussed in more detail in Chapter 11.

How realistic is the situation constructed by the Prisoner's Dilemma game? One realistic example of a Prisoner's Dilemma–type situation is described in Box 2.1. For a second example, consider the problem of small businessmen—barbers, for example. Like most businesspeople, they want to maximize their income and therefore need to be open for business when customers want service. However, barbers are also human and would like to work only five, rather than six or possibly even seven days a week. Many states prohibit businesses to be open on Sunday. Saturday is likely to be a very busy day, whereas Monday might be a very

**BOX 2.1**
**Live-and-Let-Live in Trench Warfare**

Sometimes cooperation emerges where it is least expected. During World War I, the Western Front was the scene of horrible battles for a few yards of territory. But between these battles, and even during them at other places along the 500-mile line in France and Belgium, the enemy soldiers often exercised considerable restraint.

\* \* \*

The historical situation in the quiet sectors along the Western Front was an iterated Prisoner's Dilemma. In a given locality, the small units facing each other are the two players. At any time, the choices are to shoot to kill or deliberately to shoot to avoid causing damage. For both sides, weakening the enemy is an important value because it will promote survival if a major battle is ordered in the sector. Therefore, in the short run it is better to do damage now whether the enemy is shooting back or not. This establishes that mutual defection is preferred to unilateral restraint, and that unilateral restraint by the other side is even better than mutual cooperation. In addition, the reward for mutual restraint is preferred by the local units to the outcome of mutual punishment because mutual punishment would imply that both units would suffer for little or no relative gain. Moreover, both sides would prefer mutual restraint to the random alternation of serious hostilities.

\* \* \*

Locally, the dilemma persisted: At any given moment it was prudent to shoot to kill, whether the other side did so or not. What made trench warfare so different from most other combat was that the same small units faced each other in immobile sectors for extended periods of time. This changed the game from a one-move Prisoner's Dilemma in which defection is the dominant choice, to an iterated Prisoner's Dilemma in which conditional strategies are possible. The result accorded with the theory's predictions: with sustained interaction, the stable outcome could be mutual cooperation based upon reciprocity. In particular, both sides followed strategies that they would not be the first to defect, but that they would be provoked if the other defected.

\* \* \*

Once started, strategies based on reciprocity could spread in a variety of ways. A restraint undertaken in certain hours could be extended to longer hours. A particular kind of restraint could lead to attempting other kinds of restraint. And most importantly of all, the progress achieved in one small sector of the front could be imitated by the units in neighboring sectors.

\* \* \*

When a defection actually occurred, the retaliation was often more than would be called for by tit for tat. Two-for-one or three-for-one was a common response to an act that went beyond what was considered acceptable.

\* \* \*

BOX 2.1 continued

The live-and-let-live system that emerged in the bitter trench warfare of World War I demonstrates that friendship is not necessary for cooperation based upon reciprocity to get started. Under suitable circumstances, cooperation can develop even between antagonists.

Selected excerpts from *The Evolution of Cooperation* by Robert Axelrod. Copyright © 1984 by Robert Axelrod. Reprinted by permission of Basic Books, a division of HarperCollins Publishers, Inc.

slow day. A barber can easily reason that the few customers who want a haircut on Monday can easily wait until later in the week. The rub is that if one barber closes on Monday and others do not, the barber who closes may lose his customers to someone open on Mondays. Hence for barbers to really take Monday off, *all* the barbers in the area need to cooperate. On the other hand, if all the barbers but one close, that one could have a very large volume on Monday. Hence, this situation has the same mixed-motive structure as the Prisoner's Dilemma game.

Another illustration of this process is provided by the advertising problem confronting Goodyear and Sears several years ago in their promotion of radial tires. In their infancy, radial tires were mostly bought by men, and Goodyear decided that the best way to reach the male audience was to advertise during football games. For several years, only Goodyear advertised during the games; then Sears also began advertising during Monday night National Football League (NFL) games. After two years during which both companies advertised heavily, Goodyear dropped out (Marecki, 1974). How can we account for the behavior of these companies? Using a Prisoner's Dilemma analysis, we can get some insight into the relationship between the two companies and the reasons one was almost sure to drop out. Each year both Sears and Goodyear had to decide whether or not to advertise (Y = yes; N = no) during the NFL games. Some hypothetical payoffs reflecting income changes and costs are shown in Figure 2.6. If there is more than one advertiser for the same product in a short time period, like a football game, brand recognition gets lost, although the overall demand for radial tires is increased. The best outcome for each company is for one to advertise and for their competitor *not* to advertise; in this situation, the company that advertises gains while the nonadvertiser loses. However, if both companies advertise, then they *both* end up losing (because brand identity is lost and the advertising is expensive). In fact, when all four possible outcomes are considered, both companies may be better off if *neither* advertises because then no loss occurs. Given that the law would stand in the way of Goodyear and Sears talking directly about a coordinated plan, they would nevertheless move toward a viable arrangement through a series of moves, as in the classic Prisoner's Dilemma game.

**FIGURE 2.6**

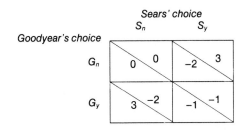

## Distribution Games

In this second type of game, players are given points or money to distribute between themselves through negotiation. The objective for each player is to get as much as possible above a minimum necessary level, or to share the pool. They win not on the basis of the absolute amount of money or points they make, but on how far the settlement is above their minimum level. The players do not know each other's minimum levels. During the simulation, players try to agree on how to distribute the points or money. Pressure on players can be created by setting a deadline for reaching agreement or by subtracting an amount from each party's profit for every minute (or some other unit of time) that passes (Kelley, Beckman, and Fisher, 1967; Fischer, 1970). Research shows that under pressure, parties become more interested in reaching any agreement than in the details of the agreement itself. One consequence is that the parties spend less time exchanging information about each other's minimum level, and hence reduce the amount of information available to determine their maximum joint return. Richer and more complex than the Prisoner's Dilemma game, distribution games permit an exchange of offers even though there is a limited range of what can be offered (Morley and Stephenson, 1977).

Raiffa (1982) discusses the results of many distribution game experiments. When subjects had equal power, a common outcome was for them to split the money (or poker chips) evenly. Surprisingly, however, when power was unequal, the person with more power frequently did *worse* than the weaker party (Raiffa, 1982). According to Raiffa, the uneven distribution of power seems to cause more conflict because the person with more power tries to use it to dominate the relationship, and this interferes with the parties finding a negotiated outcome. On the other hand, both parties seem to recognize when they have equal power, and they work together to find a negotiated agreement (the topic of power in negotiation is discussed in greater detail in Chapter 10). Distribution games have also been used to investigate the effects of increased information about the parties' interdependence on the outcomes of negotiation. Rather than always improving outcomes, increased information about reservation prices (the most a party will pay, or the least that they will accept) frequently leads to worse outcomes (Raiffa, 1982).

## Games of Economic Exchange

Games of economic exchange (Rapoport, 1963; Siegel and Fouraker, 1960; Kelley and Schenitzki, 1972) are more realistic than the games we just described. Exchange games involve "buyers" and "sellers" who work to reach an agreement on price and quantity; individual profits vary with the prices and quantities agreed on. Negotiators don't know the profit table of the other party. The structure of the two profit tables creates conditions of both competition and cooperation. In addition, the profit tables are constructed so that several possible price-quantity arrangements will yield one player the same profit, but disadvantage the other player to varying degrees. Some games offer a joint maximum return whereas others do not.

For example, suppose a purchaser (a manufacturing company) is buying 55-gallon drums of a chemical from a supplier. The chemical decays rapidly, so the purchaser can't buy a large amount and store it in the warehouse; instead, the purchaser has to determine (as closely as possible) the requirements for a given month. If the company buys too much, it decays and goes bad; if it buys too little, the manufacturing process stops. Similarly, the chemical company makes the most money when it produces the chemical in certain size batches; if it makes too little, the process is very costly, whereas if it makes too much, energy is wasted. Hence, for optimal results both buyer and seller must try to coordinate the amount purchased and manufactured. This kind of problem is a game of economic exchange.

This type of simulation has been used to study many aspects of negotiation, including the effects of negotiator personality, concession rate, and the size of opening offers on the outcomes of a negotiation (see Pruitt, 1981). An example of the type of payoff table developed by Kelley (1966) which has served as a prototype for much research is presented in Figure 2.7. These simulations have been most useful for examining the dynamics of both distributive and integrative negotiations, topics that will be discussed in greater detail in Chapters 3 and 4.

## Role-Playing Games

The games discussed earlier employed different payoff structures and different communication structures. Participants acted as they chose, in the context of the situation they faced. In role-playing games, however, participants enact a particular role in the game such as a union negotiator, a manager negotiating with another manager, or a job seeker. To make the role more realistic, several issues are usually on the table, each one with a number of possible outcome points. Hence a union-management negotiation will probably involve not only wages and hours but also working conditions, cost of living increases, contract length,

**FIGURE 2.7**    A Sample Preference Matrix for a Three-Issue Labor Management
Simulation

| Alternative Settlement Options | Management's Points* | | | Labor's Points | | |
|---|---|---|---|---|---|---|
| | Salary Package | Leave Policy | Health Benefits | Salary Package | Leave Policy | Health Benefits |
| A | 80 | 48 | 32 | 0 | 0 | 0 |
| B | 70 | 42 | 28 | 4 | 6 | 10 |
| C | 60 | 36 | 24 | 8 | 12 | 20 |
| D | 50 | 30 | 20 | 12 | 18 | 30 |
| E | 40 | 24 | 16 | 16 | 24 | 40 |
| F | 30 | 18 | 12 | 20 | 30 | 50 |
| G | 20 | 12 | 8 | 24 | 36 | 60 |
| H | 10 | 6 | 4 | 28 | 42 | 70 |
| I | 0 | 0 | 0 | 32 | 48 | 80 |

*Higher points represent a greater preference for that settlement option.

and other issues. Often the game is structured with a number of settlement points on each of these issues, each of which has different payouts for opposing parties.

Role-playing experiments have increased in popularity as both research and teaching tools in the last 10 years. As a research tool, role-playing games have been criticized because participants are playing the role of another person rather than being themselves. Hence, performance, in part, is influenced by participants' acting abilities and understanding of how an experienced person in that role would perform (Etzioni, 1969; Nicholson, 1970). Researchers can counter this disadvantage by carefully constructing the role-playing materials to mirror the aspects of actual negotiations that they want to examine and by using proper experimental techniques that ensure the success of the experience.

As a training tool, role playing has become the dominant method of teaching and learning about negotiation. The fact that participants have to take a perspective and argue that point of view can be very helpful. Participants are forced to ask, "What would I want if I were in this position; what would I be after? How would the arguments and proposals of the other party look?" Managers and union officials may simulate a labor negotiation in which they take the position of the other party. Managers playing the role of a union negotiator who is facing reelection by his constituency may see things from the union negotiator's perspective for the first time. Similarly, a union official, who is playing the role of a manager may see that some of the arguments the union was planning to use, although convincing to union members, are largely irrelevant to managers and that the union's position ignores issues that management is really concerned about. Discussing these discoveries with the union may help members plan a different strategy and negotiate more successfully.

## SUMMARY

In these first two chapters we have stressed that negotiation is a complex process and that negotiators must understand both the structure of the problem or situation and ways in which they can change it. People in negotiations have outcomes they would like to attain. Perhaps they can get what they really want, but perhaps they will have to settle for something less. Although they may adjust what they will accept, there are limits beyond which they will not go. The limits, however, are not always obvious. Some may be absolute, such as "I will not kill" or "I will not steal"; whereas others are relative, such as "What are my alternatives given this situation?" In negotiation, a party (either an individual or a group) needs to prioritize desired outcomes and the actions (strategies and tactics) that can be employed to get them.

The outcomes of one party are linked to those of the other party by the structure of the bargaining relationship. How outcomes are linked (or perceived to be linked) will have a fundamental influence on how negotiations proceed. Negotiators should clearly examine the objective structure of the issues in the negotiation and determine the implications for their strategies. Can both parties gain? Will there be a winner and a loser? What issues are most important to me? To the other party? Negotiators will not always be able to answer these questions before the negotiation begins. However, even a partial understanding and analysis of the interdependence will allow the negotiator to prepare better, set more realistic goals, and choose more appropriate strategy and tactics.

The second set of elements that must be considered in negotiation is ways to *change* the structural elements of the negotiation, the outcomes or actions available or preferences that the parties have. In this case, negotiators need to consider two sets of issues. The first involves what economists call "preference functions," or "the subjective nature of preferred outcomes" and the meanings we attach to them. Is an offered price on a house a good one? There is no absolute answer. It depends upon how much you like a house, how much money you have, how committed you are to buying a house for less than your brother did, and a host of other considerations. In this chapter, we acknowledged that individual personalities, values, social relationships, immediate needs, and the like actively shape outcome preferences and thereby influence negotiations. To negotiate, we need to know what the other party is really after—what her outcome preferences are. To do that effectively, we need data about outcomes and information about the negotiator's personality, values, and social environment.

Then a party in negotiation can attempt to *change* the other's goals, perceptions, or subjective evaluations. This involves processes of communication (Chapter 7), persuasion (Chapter 8), and power (Chapter 10) in interpersonal relations. These processes often occur in a broader social context (Chapter 9). Being interdependent, parties act knowing that their actions will affect the other and that these actions, in turn, will eventually affect themselves. Hence, people engage in anticipatory decision making. Given the interdependence, and the different (often conflicting) goals of negotiators, trust and distrust can become a significant factor in shaping both the nature of the interaction and the negotiation process.

All these elements are background components to a negotiation, which is the process of getting two people from the point where they have a problem or conflict to the point where they have a solution or agreement. Negotiation is a process of offer and counteroffer, of discussion and concession, through which the parties reach a point that both understand is the best (for them) that can be achieved. Although this process is the heart of negotiation, it cannot be understood or successfully carried out without a knowledge of how a wide array of other factors affect the process. The remainder of this book will be devoted to describing the possible effect of many of these factors.

# CHAPTER 3

# Strategy and Tactics of Distributive Bargaining

Eighteen months ago Larry decided to move closer to his place of employment. Following this decision to move, he put his house on the market and started to look for a new one. Fourteen months later, he had neither sold his house nor found another that he wanted to buy. He finally received the first offer to buy his house and, after a brief negotiation, settled on the selling price. Because he had not yet found a house to buy, he postponed closing the sale for six months to give himself additional time to look. The buyer, Barbara, was not happy to wait that long because of the inconvenience and the difficulty of getting a bank to guarantee an interest rate so far in advance. Larry adjusted the price so Barbara would accept this postponement, but it was clear that she would be much happier if the date could be moved closer.

There were relatively few houses on the market in the area where Larry wanted to live, and none of them was satisfactory. He jokingly said that unless something new came on the market, he would be sleeping in a tent on the town common when the leaves turned in the fall. Two months later a house came on the market that met his requirements. The seller, Monica, set the asking price at $145,000, which was $10,000 above what Larry hoped to pay but $5,000 below the most he would be willing to pay. Larry knew that the more he paid for the house, the less money he would have to make some very desirable alterations, buy draperies and some new furniture, and hire a moving company. There were attractive drapes already in Monica's house. She was moving to a new house; if she could not use the drapes in the new house, Larry might be able to purchase or include them with the house. The same might be true for several rugs, hall tables, and other items. Larry also learned that Monica's new home was supposed to be finished soon, about the time Larry was to close on the sale of his present house.

This illustration provides the basic elements of a distributive bargaining situation. Although there are a number of definitions of distributive bargaining, it is perhaps most useful to define it as *competitive,* or *win-lose,* bargaining. In a distributive bargaining situation, the goals of one party are usually in fundamental and direct conflict with the goals of the other party. Resources are fixed and limited, and each party wants to maximize his share of the resources. As a result, each party will use a set of strategies to maximize her share of the outcomes to be obtained. Most of these strategies and tactics guard information distribution carefully—information is given to the other party *only* when it provides a strategic advantage. On the other hand, it is highly desirable to *get* information from the other party to improve negotiation power. Distributive bargaining is basically a fight over who is going to get the most of a limited resource (often money). Whether or not one or both parties achieve their objectives will depend upon the strategy and tactics they employ (Walton and McKersie, 1965).

For many, the strategies and tactics of distributive bargaining are "what negotiation is all about." Images of smoke-filled rooms, packed with men arguing and fighting for their points of view, come to mind. Many people are attracted to this view of negotiation and look forward to learning and sharpening their hard bargaining skills; many others are repelled by this type of bargaining and would rather walk away than negotiate in this manner. They argue that this view of negotiation is old-fashioned, macho, and personally offensive.

Some people have suggested that by including this chapter in the book, we are promoting a dated, male-dominated view of negotiation. However, we have two reasons for presenting an extended discussion of distributive bargaining in this volume. First, some interdependent situations that negotiators face *are* distributive in nature, and negotiators need to understand these situations to do well in them. Second, because many people use distributive bargaining strategies and tactics almost exclusively, it is necessary to understand how these strategies and tactics work to counter their effects. We do not intend to glorify distributive bargaining techniques. Frequently they are counterproductive and costly to use. Often they cause negotiators to focus so much on the differences between negotiating parties that they ignore what the parties have in common. These negative effects notwithstanding, distributive bargaining strategies and tactics have their place, especially when a negotiator wants to maximize the value obtained in a single deal and when the relationship with the other party is not important. Some of the tactics discussed in this chapter will also generate ethical concerns (the topic of ethics and negotiation is discussed in detail in Chapter 13). Do not assume that the other party shares your ethical values when negotiating. Although you may not believe that it is ethical to use some of the tactics discussed in this chapter, other negotiators may be quite comfortable using them. Alternatively, you may be comfortable using some tactics that make other negotiators quite uneasy. Some of the tactics discussed are commonly accepted as ethical behavior when bargaining distributively (portraying your BATNA as more positive than it really is, for instance), whereas other tactics are considered unacceptable (see the discussion of typical hardball tactics later in this chapter).

## THE DISTRIBUTIVE BARGAINING SITUATION

To understand how the distributive bargaining process works, return to our opening example of the new house purchase. Several prices were mentioned: (1) Monica's asking price, (2) the price Larry would like to pay for a new house, and (3) the price above which he would not pay to buy the house. These prices represent key points in the analysis of any distributive bargaining situation. Larry's preferred price is the *target point,* the point at which a negotiator would like to conclude negotiations—his optimal goal. The price beyond which Larry will not go is the *resistance point,* a negotiator's bottom line—the most she will pay, the smallest amount she will settle for, and so on. Finally, the *asking price* is the initial price set by the seller; Larry might decide to counter this price with his *initial offer*—the first number he will quote to the seller. Using the house purchase as an example, we can treat the range of possible prices as a continuum, and Figure 3.1 shows the various points along that dimension.

How does Larry decide on his initial offer? There are many ways to answer this question. Fundamentally, however, to make a good initial offer Larry must understand something about the process of negotiation. In Chapter 2, we stated that people expect give-and-take when they negotiate, and Larry needs to factor this into the way he sets his initial offer. If Larry opened the negotiation at his target point ($135,000) and then had to make any concessions, with the first concession he would be moving *away* from his target point to a price closer to his resistance point. If he really wants to achieve his target, he should start at a price *lower* than his target point to create some room for making concessions. At the same time, the starting point cannot be too far from the target point. If Larry made the first offer too low, Monica might break off negotiations, believing him to be unreasonable or foolish. Although judgments about how to determine first offers can often be quite complex and can have a dramatic influence on the course of negotiation, let us stay with the simple case for the moment and assume that Larry decided to offer $133,000 as a "reasonable" first offer—less than his target point and well below his resistance point. In the meantime, remember that although this illustration concerns only price, *all* other issues or agenda items for the negotiation may also have starting, target, and resistance points.

Both parties to a negotiation have starting, target, and resistance points. Starting points are usually in the opening statements each makes (i.e., the seller's listing price and the buyer's first offer). The target point is usually learned or inferred as negotiations get under way. People typically give up the margin between their starting points and target points as they make concessions. The resistance point, the point beyond which a person will not go or break off negotiations, is not known to the other party and it is best kept secret (Raiffa, 1982). One party may not learn the other's resistance point even after the end of a successful negotiation.

**FIGURE 3.1**   The Buyer's View of the House Negotiation

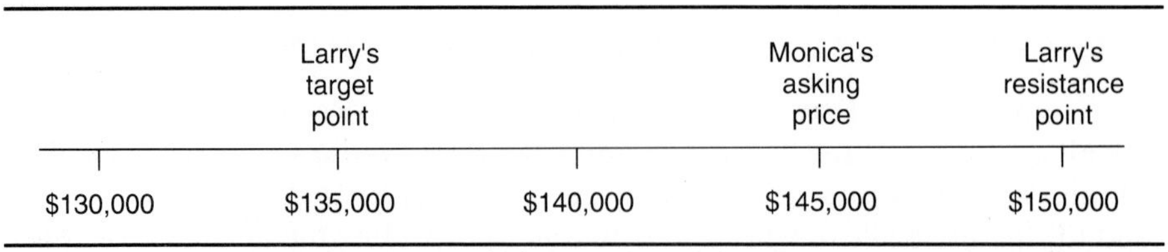

|  | Larry's<br>target<br>point |  | Monica's<br>asking<br>price | Larry's<br>resistance<br>point |
|---|---|---|---|---|
| $130,000 | $135,000 | $140,000 | $145,000 | $150,000 |

And, even after an unsuccessful negotiation, when the other party breaks off talks, one party may be able to infer the other's resistance point as the last offer the other was willing to consider before the negotiation ended.

Two parties' starting and resistance points are usually arranged in reverse order, with the resistance point being a high price for the buyer and a low price for the seller. Thus, continuing the illustration, Larry would have been willing to pay up to $150,000 for the house Monica listed for $145,000. Larry can speculate that she may be willing to accept something less than $145,000 and probably would think $140,000 a desirable (target) figure. What Larry does not know (but would dearly like to) is the *lowest* figure that Monica would accept. Is it $140,000? $135,000? Let us assume it is $130,000. Monica, on the other hand, initially knows nothing about Larry's position but soon learns his starting point when he offers $133,000. Monica may suspect that Larry's target point is not too far away (we know it was $135,000) but has no idea of his resistance point ($150,000). This information—what Larry knows or infers about Monica's positions—is represented in Figure 3.2.

The spread between the resistance points, called the *bargaining range, settlement range,* or *zone of potential agreement,* is particularly important. In this area the actual bargaining takes place, for anything outside these points will be summarily rejected by one of the negotiators. When the buyer's resistance point is above the seller's—he is minimally willing to pay more than she is minimally willing to sell for, as is true in the house example—there is a *positive bargaining range.* When the reverse is true—the seller's resistance point is above the buyer's, and the buyer won't pay more than the seller will minimally accept—there is a *negative bargaining range.* In the house example, if Monica would minimally accept $145,000 and Larry could maximally afford $140,000, then a negative bargaining range exists. Negotiations that begin with a negative bargaining range are likely to stalemate quickly. They can only be resolved if one or both parties are persuaded to change their resistance points, or if someone else forces a solution upon them that neither one likes. However, because negotiators don't begin their deliberations by talking about their resistance points (they're talking about initial offers and demands instead), it is often hard to know whether a positive settlement range really exists until the negotiators get deep into the process. Both parties may realize that there was no overlap in their resistance points only after protracted

**FIGURE 3.2**   The Buyer's View of the House Negotiation (extended)

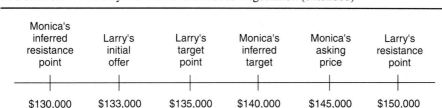

| Monica's inferred resistance point | Larry's initial offer | Larry's target point | Monica's inferred target | Monica's asking price | Larry's resistance point |
|---|---|---|---|---|---|
| $130,000 | $133,000 | $135,000 | $140,000 | $145,000 | $150,000 |

negotiations have been exhausted; at that point, they will have to decide whether to end negotiations or reevaluate their resistance points, a process to be described in more detail later on.

### The Role of Alternatives to a Negotiated Agreement

In addition to defining opening bids, target points, and resistance points, a fourth factor may enter the negotiations: the role played by an alternative outcome that can be obtained by completing a different deal with a different party. In some negotiations, the parties have only two fundamental choices: to reach a deal with the other party, or not to settle at all. In other negotiations, however, one or both parties may have the choice of completing an alternative deal. Thus, in the example of buying a house, there is probably more than one house for sale in the city where Larry wishes to buy. Similarly, if Monica waits long enough (or drops the price of the house far enough), she is sure to find another interested buyer. If Larry picks an alternative house to buy, talks to the owner of that house, and negotiates the best price that he can, that price represents his *alternative.* For the sake of argument, let us assume that Larry's alternative house costs $142,000, and Monica's alternative buyer will pay $134,000.

An alternative point can be identical to the resistance point, although the two do not necessarily have to be the same. If Larry's alternative is $142,000, then he should reject any price Monica asks above $142,000 because he could buy the second house above that amount. But Larry's alternative may not be all that desirable for reasons other than price—he likes the neighborhood less, it is 10 minutes farther away from where he works, or he likes the way Monica decorated the house and wants to enjoy that when he moves in. In this situation, therefore, Larry may maintain his resistance point at $150,000; he is therefore willing to pay Monica up to $8,000 more than his alternative, simply to buy her house.

Alternatives are important because they give the negotiator power to walk away from any negotiation when the emerging deal is not very good. In their discussion of distributive bargaining, Walton and McKersie (1965) did not elaborate on alternatives as a key point. We suspect that they neglected to give alternatives attention because their theory of distributive bargaining was derived from labor relations, in which labor and management had only two basic choices: come to a

**FIGURE 3.3** The Buyer's View of the House Negotiation (extended with alternatives)

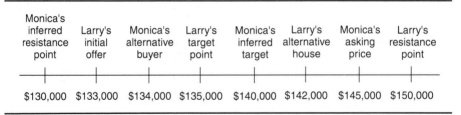

| Monica's inferred resistance point | Larry's initial offer | Monica's alternative buyer | Larry's target point | Monica's inferred target | Larry's alternative house | Monica's asking price | Larry's resistance point |
|---|---|---|---|---|---|---|---|
| $130,000 | $133,000 | $134,000 | $135,000 | $140,000 | $142,000 | $145,000 | $150,000 |

contract settlement or strike (lockout). That is, organized labor could not find another company to work for, and management could not go out and find a different union to hire. The power of alternatives has been described by Fisher, Ury, and Patton (1991), in their discussion of BATNAs. We will use the terms *alternatives* and *BATNA* interchangeably in our subsequent discussion.

### Settlement Point

The fundamental process of distributive bargaining is to reach a settlement within a positive bargaining range. The objective of both parties is to obtain as much of the bargaining range as possible—that is, to get the settlement as close to the other party's resistance point as possible.

Both parties in distributive bargaining know that they might have to settle for less than what they would prefer, but they hope that the settlement point will be better than their own resistance point. Thus both parties must believe that the settlement point, although less desirable than they would prefer, is the best that they can get. It is essential that each party believe the settlement point is the best she can get, both to reach agreement and to insure support for the agreement after the negotiations. Parties who do not think they got the best agreement possible, or who believe that they "lost," frequently try to get out of the agreement later or find other ways to recoup their losses. If Larry thinks he got the short end of the deal, he can make life miserable and expensive for Monica by making extraneous claims later on—claiming "hidden damages" to the house, or that fixtures that were supposed to come with the house were defective, and so on. Another factor that will affect satisfaction with the settlement point is whether the parties can "get even" in the future or whether they will ever see one another again. If Monica was moving out of the region, then Larry should ensure that he evaluates the current deal very carefully because he may be unable to contact her later for any adjustments.

### Bargaining Mix

In the house purchase illustration, as in almost all negotiations, agreement is necessary on several issues: the price, the closing date of the sale, renovations to the house, and the price of items that could remain in the house (such as drapes and appliances). This package of issues for negotiation is the *bargaining mix*. Each item in the mix can have its own starting, target, and resistance points. Some items are of obvious importance to both parties; others are of importance to only one party. Negotiators need to know what is important to them and to the other party, and they need to make sure they take these priorities into account during the planning process (see Chapter 5 for a detailed discussion of planning).

For example, in the negotiation that we are describing, a secondary issue that was important to both parties was the closing date of the sale—the date when the ownership of the house would actually be transferred. The date of sale was part of the bargaining mix. Larry learned when Monica's new house was going to be completed and anticipated that she would want to transfer ownership of the old house to Larry shortly after that point. Larry asked for a closing date very close to when Monica would probably want to close; thus the deal looked very attractive to her. As it turned out, Larry's closing date on his own house—his own target point—was close to this date as well, thus making the deal attractive for both Larry and Monica. If Larry and Monica had wanted different selling dates, then the closing date would have been a more contentious issue in the bargaining mix.

## FUNDAMENTAL STRATEGIES

The prime objective in distributive bargaining is to maximize the value of *this single deal.* In our example, the buyer has four fundamental strategies available:

1. To push for a settlement close to the seller's (as yet unknown) resistance point, thereby yielding for the buyer the largest part of the settlement range. The buyer may attempt to influence the seller's view of what settlements are possible by making very extreme offers and small concessions.

2. To get the seller to change her resistance point by influencing the seller's beliefs about the value of the house. The buyer may try to convince her to reduce her resistance point (e.g., by telling her that the house is very overpriced) and thereby increase the bargaining range.

3. If a negative settlement range exists, to get the seller to reduce her resistance point to create a positive settlement range or to modify one's own resistance point to create that overlap. Thus, Monica could be persuaded to accept a lower price, or Larry could decide he has to pay more than he wanted to.

4. To get the other party to think that this settlement is the best that is possible—not that it is *all* he can get, or that he is *incapable* of getting more, or that the other side is *winning* by getting more. The distinction between a party believing that an agreement is the *best possible* (and not these other interpretations) may appear subtle and semantic. However, in getting people to agree it is important they *feel* as though they got the best possible deal. Ego satisfaction is often as important as achieving tangible objectives (recall our discussion of tangibles and intangibles in Chapter 1).

In all these strategies, the buyer is attempting to influence the seller's perceptions of what is possible through the exchange of information and persuasion. Regardless of the general strategy taken, two tasks are important in all distributive bargaining situations: (1) discovering the other party's resistance point; and, (2) influencing the other party's resistance point.

### Discovering the Other Party's Resistance Point

Information is the life force of negotiation. The more you can learn about the other party's outcome values, resistance point, feelings of confidence, motivation, and so on, the more capable you will be to strike a favorable agreement. At the same time, you do not want the other party to have some kinds of information about you. Your real resistance point, some of the outcome values, and confidential information about a weak strategic position or an emotional vulnerability are best concealed. Alternatively, you *do* want the other party to have some information, some of it factual and correct; some of it contrived to lead the other party to believe things that are favorable to you. Because each side wants to get some information and to conceal other information, and because each side knows that the other also wants to conceal and get information, communication can become complex. Information is often conveyed in a "code" that evolves during negotiation. People answer questions with other questions or less-than-complete answers; yet, for either side to influence the other's perceptions, they must establish some points effectively and convincingly. We discuss the communication process in more detail in Chapter 7.

### Influences on the Other Party's Resistance Point

Central to planning the strategy and tactics for distributive bargaining is effectively locating the other party's resistance point and the relationship of that resistance points to your own. The resistance point is established by the value expected from a particular outcome, which in turn is the product of the worth and costs of an outcome. Larry sets a resistance point on the amount of money he would pay for a house based on the amount of money he can afford to pay (in total or in monthly mortgage payments), the estimated market value or worth of the house, and how other factors in his bargaining mix might be resolved (closing date, curtains, etc.). A resistance point will also be influenced by the cost an individual attaches to delay or difficulty in negotiation or in having the negotiations aborted. If Larry, who had set his resistance point at $150,000, were faced with the choice of paying $151,000 or living on the town common for a month, he might well reevaluate his resistance point. The following factors are important in attempting to influence the other person's resistance point: (1) the value the other attaches to a particular outcome; (2) the costs the other attaches to delay or difficulty in negotiations; and, (3) the cost the other attaches to having the negotiations aborted.

A significant factor in shaping the other person's understanding of what is possible—and therefore the value he places on particular outcomes—is the other's understanding of your own situation. Therefore, when influencing the other's viewpoint, you must *also deal with the other party's understanding* of your value for a particular outcome, the costs you attach to delay or difficulty in negotiation, and your cost of having the negotiations aborted.

To explain how these factors can affect the process of planning strategy and tactics in distributive bargaining, we will make four major propositions (refer to Walton and McKersie, 1965, pp. 59–82, for a more extensive treatment of this subject):

1. The other party's resistance point will vary directly with her estimate of the cost of delay or aborting negotiations. If the other party sees that you

need a settlement quickly and cannot defer it, he can seize this advantage and press for a better outcome. Therefore, expectations will rise and he will set a more demanding resistance point. The more you can convince the other that your costs of delay or aborting negotiations are *low* (we are in no hurry and can "wait forever"), the more modest will be the other's resistance point.

2. The other's resistance point will vary inversely with her cost of delay or aborting. The more a person needs a settlement, the more modest he will be in setting a resistance point. Therefore, the more you can do to convince the other party that delay or aborting negotiations will be costly to her, the more likely she is to establish a modest resistance point. In contrast, the more attractive the other party's alternatives—the better his BATNA (Fisher, Ury and Patton, 1991)—the more that person can "hang tough" with a high resistance point. If negotiations are unsuccessful, the other party can move to an attractive alternative. In the earlier example, both Larry and Monica have satisfactory alternatives.

3. A resistance point will vary directly with the values the other party attaches to that outcome. Therefore, the resistance point may become more modest as the person reduces the value for that outcome. If you can convince the other party that a present negotiating position will not have the desired outcome or that the present position is not as attractive because other positions are even more attractive, then he will adjust his resistance point.

4. The other's resistance point varies inversely with the perceived value the first party attaches to an outcome. Knowing that a position is important to the other party, you will expect the other to resist giving up on that issue; thus, there should be less possibility of a favorable settlement in that area. As a result, expectations will be lowered to a more modest resistance point. Hence, the more you can convince the other that you value a particular outcome outside the other's bargaining range, the more pressure you put on the other party to set a more modest resistance point.

## TACTICAL TASKS

From the above assessment of the fundamental strategies of distributive bargaining, four important tactical tasks emerge for a negotiator in a distributive bargaining situation:

1. Assess the other party's outcome values and the costs of terminating negotiations.
2. Manage the other party's impression of one's own outcome values.
3. Modify the other party's perception of her own outcome values.
4. Manipulate the actual costs of delaying or aborting negotiations.

We will now describe each of these tasks.

## Assess Outcome Values and the Costs of Termination

An important first step for a negotiator is to get information about the other party's outcome values and resistance point. The negotiator can pursue two general routes: getting more information indirectly about the background factors behind an issue (indirect assessment) or getting information directly from the other party about his outcome values and resistance points (direct assessment).

**Indirect Assessment.**    As pointed out earlier, the process by which an individual sets a resistance point may be based on many factors. How do we decide, for example, how much rent or mortgage payment we can afford each month? Or how do we decide what a house is minimally or maximally worth? There are lots of ways to go about doing this. Indirect assessment is aimed at determining what information an individual probably used to set her target and resistance points and how she interpreted this information. For example, in labor negotiations, management may infer whether or not a union is willing to strike by how hard the union bargains or by the size of its strike fund. Management decides whether or not the company can afford a strike based on size of inventories, market conditions for the company's product, and the percentage of workers who are members of the union. In a real estate negotiation, how long a piece of property has been on the market, how many other potential buyers actually exist, how soon a buyer needs the property for business or living, and the financial health of the seller will be important factors. An automobile buyer might view the number of new cars in inventory on the dealer's lot, refer to newspaper articles on automobile sales, read about the car's popularity in consumer buying guides, or consult reference guides to find out what a dealer pays for the car wholesale.

You can use a variety of information sources to assess the other party's resistance point. Making direct observations, consulting readily available documents and publications, or talking to knowledgeable experts are some ways to do so. It is important to note, however, that these are *indirect* indicators. How one person interprets this data could be very different from another person. A large inventory of automobiles may make a dealer willing to reduce the price of a car. However, the dealer may expect the market to change soon, may have just started a big promotional campaign that the buyer does not know about, or may see no real need to reduce prices and instead intends to wait for a market upturn. Thus, indirect measures provide valuable information that *may* reflect a reality the other person will eventually have to face. It is important to remember, however, that the same piece of information may mean different things to different people and hence may not tell us exactly what we want to know.

**Direct Assessment.**    In bargaining, one does not usually expect accurate and precise information about outcome values, resistance points, and expectations from the other party. Sometimes, however, the other party *will* give accurate information. When pushed to the absolute limit and when they require a quick settlement, the other party may explain the facts quite clearly. If management believes a wage settlement above a certain point would drive the company out of business, they may choose to state that absolute limit very clearly and go to considerable lengths to explain how it was determined. Similarly, a house buyer may tell the seller what his absolute maximum price is and support it with an explanation of income and other expenses. In these instances, of course, the party revealing the information believes that the settlement being proposed is within the settlement range—and that the other party will accept the offered information as true, rather than see it as a bargaining ploy. An industrial salesperson may tell the purchaser about product quality and service, alternative customers who want to buy the product, and the time required to manufacture special orders.

However, most of the time the other party is not so forthcoming, and the methods of getting direct information may become more complex. In international diplomacy, various means are used to gather information. Sources are cultivated, messages are intercepted, and codes broken. In labor negotiations, companies have been known to recruit informers or to bug the union's meeting rooms, and unions have had their members collect papers from executives' wastebaskets. In real estate negotiations, sellers have entertained prospective buyers with abundant alcoholic beverages in the hope that tongues will be loosened and information revealed. Other approaches involve provoking the other party into an angry outburst or putting negotiators under pressure to cause them to make a slip and reveal valuable information. One party may simulate exasperation and angrily stalk out of negotiations in the hope that the other, in an effort to avoid a deadlock, will reveal what is really wanted.

### Manage the Other Party's Impressions

Because each side attempts to get information about the other party through direct and indirect sources, an important tactical task may be to *keep* the other from getting accurate information about your position, while simultaneously guiding the other party to form a "preferred impression" of it. Your tasks, then, are to screen actual information about positions and to represent them as you would *like* the other to believe them.

**Screening Activities.**   Generally speaking, screening activities are more important at the beginning of negotiation, and representation is useful later on. This sequence gives more time to concentrate on gathering information from the other party, which will be useful in establishing your own resistance point, and on determining the best way to feed information to the other party about your own position. The simplest way to screen a position is to say and do as little as possible. Silence is golden when answering questions; words should be invested in asking them instead. This selective reticence reduces the likelihood of making verbal slips or presenting any clues that the other side could use to draw conclusions. A look of disappointment or boredom, fidgeting and restlessness, or probing with interest all can give clues about the importance of the points under discussion. Concealment is the most general screening activity.

Another approach, possible when group negotiations are carried on through a representative, is "calculated incompetence." Here, the negotiating agent is not given all the needed information, making it impossible for information to be leaked. Instead, the negotiator is sent with the task of simply gathering facts and bringing them back to the group. This strategy can make negotiations more complex and tedious, and it often causes the other party to protest vigorously at the negotiator's inability to divulge important data or to make agreements. Lawyers, real estate agents, and investigators are frequently used by others to perform this role. Representatives may also be limited (or limit themselves) in their authority to make decisions. For example, a man buying a car may claim that he must consult his wife before making a final decision.

When negotiation is carried out by a team—as is common in diplomacy, labor-management relations, and many business negotiations—channeling all communication through a team spokesperson reduces inadvertent revelation of information. In addition to reducing the number of people who can actively reveal information, this frees the other members of the negotiating team to observe and listen carefully to what the other party is saying so they can detect clues and pieces of information about the other party's position.

Still another approach to screening activities is to present a great many items for negotiation, only a few of which are truly important to the presenter. In this way, the other party has to gather so much information about so many different items that it becomes difficult to detect which items are really important. This tactic is frequently called the "snow job" or "kitchen sink,"—it raises so many demands that the negotiator's real priorities are disguised (Karrass, 1974).

**Direct Action to Alter Impressions.**   Negotiators can take many actions to present facts that will either directly enhance their position or make their position appear stronger to the other party. One of the most obvious methods is *selective presentation,* in which negotiators reveal only the facts necessary to support their case. Selective presentation can also be used to lead the other party to form the desired impression of your resistance point or to open up new possibilities for agreement that are more favorable to the presenter than those that currently exist. Another approach is to explain or interpret known facts to present a logical argument that shows the costs or risks to oneself if the other party's proposals were implemented. An alternative is to say, "If you were in my shoes, here is the way these facts would look in light of the proposal you have presented."

These arguments are most convincing when the facts used have been acquired from a neutral source because then they will not be seen as biased by a party's preferred outcome. However, even with facts that you provide, these interpretations can be helpful in managing the impression the other has of your preferences and priorities. It is not necessary for the other to agree that this is the way things would look if she were in your position. Nor must she agree that the facts lead only to the conclusion you have presented. As long as the other party understands how you see things, her or his thinking is likely to be influenced.

The *emotional* reaction a party displays to facts, proposals, and possible outcomes and conclusions provides the other party with information about what is important to him. Disappointment or enthusiasm usually suggests that an issue is important, whereas boredom or indifference suggest it is trivial or unimportant. A loud, angry outburst or an eager response suggests the topic is very important and may give it a prominence that will shape what is discussed. Clearly, however, emotional reactions can be real or feigned.

The length of time and amount of detail used in presenting a point or position can also convey importance. Carefully checking through the details the other side has presented about an item, or insisting on clarification and verification, all convey the impression of importance. Casually accepting the other party's arguments as true conveys the impression of disinterest in the topic being discussed.

Taking direct action to alter another's impression raises a number of hazards. It is one thing to select certain facts to present and to emphasize or de-emphasize their importance accurately, but it is a different matter to lie and fabricate. The former is expected and understood in distributive bargaining; the latter, even in hardball negotiations, is resented and often angrily attacked if discovered. Between the two extremes, however, what is said and done as skilful puffery by one may be perceived as dishonest distortion by the other (the ethical considerations are explored in detail in Chapter 13). Other problems can arise when trivial items are introduced as distractions or minor issues are magnified in importance. The purpose is to conceal the truly important and to direct the other's attention away from the significant, but there is a danger: the other person may become aware of this maneuver and, with great fanfare, concede on the minor points, thereby gaining the right to demand equally generous concessions on the central points. Thus the other party can defeat the maneuverer at his own game.

## Modify the Other Party's Perceptions

You can alter the other's impressions of his own objectives by making the outcomes appear less attractive or by making the cost of obtaining them appear higher. You may also try to make demands and positions appear more attractive or less unattractive to the other party.

There are several approaches to modifying the other party's perceptions. One approach is to interpret for the other party what the outcomes of her proposal will really be. You can explain logically how an undesirable outcome would result if the other party really did get what he is asking for. This may mean pointing out something that has been overlooked. For example, in union-management negotiations, management may point out that a union request for a six-hour work day would, on one hand, not increase the number of employees because it would not be worthwhile to hire people for two hours a day to make up the hours taken from the standard eight-hour day. On the other hand, if the company were to keep production at the present level, it would be necessary to use the present employees on overtime, thereby increasing the total labor cost and, subsequently, the price of the product. This rise in cost would reduce demand for the product and, ultimately, the number of hours worked or the number of workers.

Another approach to modifying the other's perceptions is by concealing information. An industrial seller may not reveal to a purchaser that certain technological changes are going to significantly reduce the cost of producing the products. A seller of real estate may not tell a prospective buyer that in three years a proposed highway will isolate property being sold from attractive portions of the city. Concealment strategies may enter into the same ethical hazards mentioned earlier (also see Chapter 13).

## Manipulate the Actual Costs of Delay or Termination

As noted previously, negotiators have deadlines. A contract will expire. Agreement has to be reached before a large meeting occurs. Someone has to catch a plane. Therefore, extending negotiations beyond a deadline can be costly, particularly to the person who has the deadline because that person has to either extend the deadline or go home empty-handed. At the same time, research (Roth, Murnighan, and Schoumaker, 1988) and practical experience (Walton and McKersie, 1965) suggest that a large majority of agreements in distributive bargaining are reached when the deadline is near. Manipulating a deadline or failing to agree by a particular deadline can be a powerful tool in the hands of the person who does not face deadline pressure. In some ways the ultimate weapon in negotiation is to threaten to terminate negotiations, denying both parties the possibility of a settlement. This pressure will usually be felt more acutely by one side than by the other, and thus it presents a potent weapon. There are three ways to manipulate the costs of delay in negotiation: (1) plan disruptive action; (2) ally with outsiders; and, (3) manipulate the scheduling of negotiations.

**Disruptive Action.**   One way to encourage agreement is to increase the costs of *not* reaching a negotiated agreement. In one instance, a group of unionized food service workers negotiating with a restaurant rounded up supporters, had them enter the restaurant just prior to lunch, and had each person order a cup of coffee and drink it leisurely. When regular customers came to lunch, they found every seat occupied (Jacobs, 1951). In another case, people dissatisfied with automobiles they purchased had their cars painted with large, bright yellow lemons and signs bearing the dealer's name, and then drove them around town in an effort to embarrass the dealer into making a settlement. Public picketing of a business, boycotting, and locking negotiators in a room until they reach agreement are all forms of disruptive action that increase the costs to negotiators for not settling and, hence, bring them back to the bargaining table. Such tactics can work, but they may also produce anger and escalation of the conflict.

**Ally with Outsiders.**   Another way to increase the costs of delay or terminating negotiations is to involve other parties in the process who can somehow influence the outcome. In many business transactions, a private party may profess that, if negotiations with a merchant are unsuccessful, they will go to the Better Business Bureau and protest the merchant's actions. Individuals protesting the practices and policies of businesses or government agencies form task forces, political action groups, and protest organizations to bring greater collective pressure on the target. For example, professional schools in universities often enhance their negotiation with higher management on budget matters by citing required compliance with external accreditation standards to substantiate their budget requests.

**Scheduling of Negotiations.** The negotiation scheduling process can often put one party at a considerable disadvantage. Businesspeople going overseas to negotiate with customers or suppliers often find negotiations are scheduled to begin immediately after their arrival, when they are still suffering from the fatigue of travel and jet lag. Alternatively, delay tactics can be used to squeeze negotiations into the last remaining minutes of their visit in order to extract concessions from the visiting party (Cohen, 1980). Automobile dealers will probably negotiate differently with the customer a half hour before quitting time than at the beginning of the work day. Industrial buyers have a much more difficult negotiation when they have a short "lead time" because their plants may have to sit idle if they cannot secure a new contract for raw materials in time.

The opportunities to increase or alter the timing of negotiation vary widely from field to field. In some industries it is possible to stockpile raw materials at relatively low cost or to buy in large bulk lots; in other industries, however, it is essential that materials arrive at regular intervals because they have a short shelf-life (as many manufacturing firms move to just-in-time inventory procedures, this becomes increasingly true). Thus, the opportunity to vary the scheduling of negotiations differs across industries. There are far fewer opportunities for an individual to create costly delays when negotiating a home purchase than when negotiating a huge bulk order of raw materials. Nonetheless, the tactics of increasing these costs by manipulating deadlines and time pressures are possible options, both to enhance your own position and to protect yourself from the other party's actions.

## POSITIONS TAKEN DURING NEGOTIATION

Effective distributive bargainers need to understand the process of taking a position during bargaining (the opening offer or opening stance) and the role of making concessions during the negotiation process. At the beginning of negotiations, each party takes a position. These positions may then change in response to information from the other party or in response to the other party's behavior. The other party's position will also typically change during bargaining. Changes in position are usually accompanied by new information concerning the other's intentions, the value of outcomes, and likely places for settlement. Negotiation is iterative. It provides an opportunity for both sides to communicate information about their positions that may lead to opportunities to change them.

## Opening Offer

When negotiations begin, the negotiator is faced with a perplexing problem. What should the opening offer be? Will the offer be seen as too high by the other and contemptuously rejected? An offer seen as modest by the other party could perhaps have been higher, either to leave more room to maneuver or to achieve a higher eventual settlement. Should the opening offer be somewhat closer to the resistance point, suggesting a more cooperative stance? These questions become less perplexing as the negotiator learns more about the other party and his limits and planned strategy. However, although knowledge about the other party helps negotiators set their opening offers, it does not tell them exactly what to do next. The fundamental question is whether the opening offer should be more extreme or modest. Studies indicate that negotiators who make more extreme opening offers get higher settlements than do those who make low or modest opening offers (Chertkoff and Conley, 1967; Donohue, 1981; Hinton, Hamner, and Pohlan, 1974; Komorita and Brenner, 1968; Liebert, Smith, and Hill, 1968; Pruitt and Syna, 1985; Weingart, Thompson, Bazerman, and Carroll, 1990). There are at least two reasons that an extreme opening offer is advantageous (see Pruitt, 1981, and Tutzauer, 1991, for further discussion of these points). First, it gives more room for movement in negotiation and therefore allows more time to learn about the other party's priorities in order to influence them. Second, an extreme opening offer acts as a "metamessage" and may create, in the other party's mind, the impression that (1) there is a long way to go before a reasonable settlement is achieved; and, (2) more concessions than originally intended may have to be made to bridge the difference between the two opening positions (Putnam and Jones, 1982; Yukl, 1974). The disadvantages of an extreme opening offer are these: (1) it may be summarily rejected by the other party; and, (2) it communicates an attitude of toughness that may be destructive to long-term relationships. Negotiators who make extreme opening offers should also have viable options or BATNAs that they can employ if the opposing negotiator refuses to deal with them; the higher these extreme offers, the more likely the offer will be summarily rejected by the other side.

## Opening Stance

A second decision to be made at the outset of negotiation is the stance or "attitude" to adopt. Will you be competitive—fighting to get the best on every point—or reasonable—willing to make concessions and compromises? Some negotiators take a belligerent stand, attacking the positions, offers, and even the character of the other party. In response, the other party may mirror the initial stance, meeting belligerence with belligerence. Even if the other party does not directly counter a belligerent stance, she is unlikely to respond with a reasonable stance of her own. Some negotiators adopt a position of reasonableness and understanding, seeming to say, "Let's be reasonable people who can solve this problem to our mutual satisfaction." Even if the attitude is not mirrored, the other's response is most likely to be constrained by this opening stance.

To communicate the most effective message, a negotiator should try to send a consistent message through both attitude and opening offer. A reasonable bargaining position is usually coupled with a friendly attitude, and an extreme bargaining position is usually coupled with a tougher, more competitive attitude. When the messages sent by position and attitude conflict, the other party will find them confusing to interpret and answer. Communication processes in negotiation are discussed in greater detail in Chapter 7.

### Initial Concessions

An opening offer is usually met with a counteroffer, and these two offers define the initial bargaining range. Sometimes the other party will not counteroffer but will simply state that the first offer (or set of demands) is unacceptable and ask the opener to come back with "a more reasonable set of proposals." In any event, after the first round of offers, the next question is "What movement or concessions are to be made?" You can choose to make none, hold firm, and insist on the original position, or you can make some concessions. Note that it is *not* an option to escalate one's opening offer; that is, to set an offer *higher* than the first. This would be uniformly met with disapproval from the other party. If concessions are to be made, the next question is "How large should they be?" It is important to note that the first concession conveys a message, frequently a symbolic one, to the other party about how you will proceed.

Opening offers, opening stances, and initial concessions are elements at the beginning of negotiations that parties can use to communicate how they intend to negotiate. An extreme original offer, a determined opening stance, a very small opening concession, or any combination signal a position of firmness; a more moderate opening offer, a reasonable, cooperative opening stance, and a more generous initial concession communicate a basic stance of flexibility. By taking a firm position, you attempt to capture most of the bargaining range for yourself to maximize the final outcome or to preserve maximum maneuvering room for later in the negotiations. Firmness also creates a climate in which the other side may decide that concessions are so meager that it is worthwhile to capitulate and settle quickly rather than to drag things out. Hence, firmness may be a way to shorten negotiations. There is also a possibility, however, that firmness will be reciprocated by the other. One or both parties may become either intransigent or disgusted and withdraw completely.

There are several reasons for adopting a flexible position. First, by taking different stances along the way, you can learn about the other party's outcome values and perceived possibilities from his responses. You may want to establish a cooperative rather than a combative relationship, hoping to get more concessions. In addition, flexibility keeps the negotiations going; the more flexible you seem, the more the other party will believe that a settlement is possible.

### Role of Concessions

Concessions are central to negotiation. Without them, in fact, negotiations would not exist. If one side is not prepared to make concessions, either the other must capitulate or negotiations will deadlock.

People enter negotiations expecting concessions. A good distributive bargainer will not begin negotiations with the other party with an opening offer too close to her own resistance point, but, rather, will ensure that there is enough room in the bargaining range to make some concessions. The other party usually resents a take-it-or-leave-it approach; an offer that may have been accepted had it emerged as a result of concession making may be rejected when it is thrown on the table and presented as a *fait accompli.* This approach, called Boulwarism, has been illustrated many times in labor relations. Management leaders have often in the past "objectively" analyzed what they could afford to give in their upcoming contract talks and made their *initial* offer at the point they intended for their *final* offer (i.e., they set the same opening offer, target point, and resistance point). They then insisted there were no concessions to be made because the initial offer was "fair" and "reasonable" based on their own analysis. Unions bitterly fought these positions and continued to resent them years after the companies abandoned this bargaining strategy (Northrup, 1964; Selekman, Selekman, and Fuller, 1958).

There is ample data that parties feel better about a settlement when negotiations involved a progression of concessions (Baranowski and Summers, 1972; Crumbaugh and Evans, 1967; Deutsch, 1958; Gruder and Duslak, 1973). Rubin and Brown (1975) suggest that "a bargainer wants to believe he is capable of shaping the other's behavior, of causing the other to choose as he (the other) does" (pp. 277–278). When you make concessions, you communicate that you will make adjustments to the other party.

Because concession making indicates an acknowledgment of the other party and a movement toward the other's position, it implies a recognition of that position and its legitimacy. Status and position are as much at stake as the substantive issues themselves. Concession making also exposes the concession maker to some risk. If the other party does not reciprocate, the concession maker may appear to be weaker by having given up something and received nothing in return. Thus, not reciprocating a concession sends a powerful message about firmness and leaves the concession maker open to feeling that his esteem has been damaged or reputation diminished.

A reciprocated concession cannot be haphazard. If the giver has made a major concession on a significant point, it is expected that the return offer will be on the same item or one of similar weight and somewhat comparable magnitude. To make an additional concession when none has been given (or when what was given was inadequate) can imply weakness and can squander valuable maneuvering room. When receiving an inadequate concession, a negotiator may explicitly state what is expected before offering further concessions: "That is not sufficient; you will have to go up X before I consider offering any further concessions."

To encourage further concessions from the other side, negotiators sometimes link their concessions to a prior concession made by the other. They may say, "Since you have given up on X, I am willing to concede on Y." More powerful concession making may be wrapped in a package, sometimes described as "log-rolling." For example, "If you will give A and B, I will give C and D." Packaging concessions also leads to better outcomes for a negotiator than making concessions singly on individual issues (Froman and Cohen, 1970; Neale and Bazerman, 1991; Pruitt, 1981). This tactic is discussed in more detail in Chapter 4.

### Pattern of Concession Making

The pattern of concessions a negotiator makes contains valuable information, but it is not always easy to interpret. When successive concessions get smaller, the most obvious message is that the concession maker's position is getting firmer and that the resistance point is being reached. This generalization needs to be tempered, however, by pointing out that a small concession late in negotiations may also indicate that there is little room left to move. When the opening offer is extreme, the negotiator has considerable room available for packaging new offers, making it relatively easy to give fairly substantial concessions. When the negotiation has moved closer to a negotiator's hoped-for settlement point, giving a concession the same size as the initial one may take a negotiator past her resistance point. Suppose a negotiator makes a first offer $100 below the other's target price; an initial concession of $10 would reduce the maneuvering room by 10 percent. When negotiations get to within $10 of the other's target price, a concession of $1 gives up 10 percent of the remaining maneuvering room. A negotiator cannot communicate such mechanical ratios in giving or interpreting concessions, but this example illustrates how the receiver might construe the meaning of concession size, depending on where it occurs in the negotiating sequence.

The pattern of concession making is also important. Consider the pattern of concessions made by two negotiators, Sandra and Linda, in Figure 3.4. Assume they are discussing the unit price of a shipment of computer parts, and each is dealing with a different client. Linda makes three concessions, each worth $4 per unit, for a total of $12. In contrast, Sandra makes five concessions, worth $4, $3, $2 and $1 per unit, for a total of $10. Both Linda and Sandra tell their counterparts that they have conceded "about all that they can." Sandra is more likely to be believed when she makes this assertion because she has signaled through the *pattern* of her concession making that there is not much left to concede. When Linda claims to have little left to concede, her counterpart is less likely to believe her because the pattern of Linda's concessions (three concessions worth the same amount) suggests that there is plenty left to concede (even though Linda has actually conceded more than Sandra in this example). Note that we have not emphasized the words spoken by the negotiators in this example. *Behaviors* are interpreted by the other party when we negotiate; it is important to signal to the other party with both our behavior and our words that the concessions are almost over.

**FIGURE 3.4**   Pattern of Concession Making for Two Negotiators

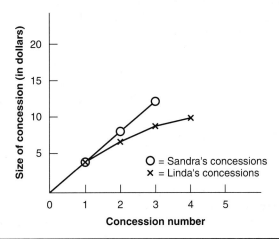

In multi-issue negotiations, skilled negotiators will also try out different forms of a potential settlement that are worth about the same to them. They recognize, however, that not all issues are worth the same amount to both parties. For example, a negotiator in a purchasing agreement may be interested solely in the total revenue of a package and not care whether it is paid in full without interest within one month or over six months with a financing fee at current interest rates. The time of the payment may be critical to the other party if he has a cash flow problem, and the other party may be willing to pay the financing fee for the right to spread the payments over a longer period of time. In fact, different combinations of principal, interest rate, and payback period may have the same value for one party but quite different value for the other. After trying out different proposals that are worth about the same to them, skilled distributive negotiators will frequently save a final small concession for near the end of the negotiation to "sweeten" the deal.

### Final Offer

Eventually a negotiator wants to convey the message that there is no further room for movement—that the present offer is final. A negotiator will probably make such statements as these: "This is all I can do." "This is as far as I can go." Sometimes, however, it is clear that no simple statement will suffice; an alternative is to use concessions to convey the point. A negotiator might simply let the absence of any further concessions convey the message in spite of urging from the other party. The other party may not recognize at first that the last offer was the final one and might volunteer a further concession to get the other to respond. Finding that no further concession results, the other party may feel betrayed and perceive that the pattern of concession-counterconcession was violated. The resulting bitterness may further complicate negotiations.

One way negotiators may convey the message that "this is the last offer" is by making the last concession substantial. This conveys the message that you are throwing in the remainder of the negotiating range. The final offer has to be large enough to be dramatic, yet not so large that it creates the suspicion that the negotiator has been holding back and that there is more to be had on other issues in the bargaining mix (Walton and McKersie, 1965). This final concession may be personalized to the other party ("I went to my boss and got a special deal just for you") and signals that this is the last concession the negotiator will make.

## COMMITMENT

A key concept in creating a bargaining position is that of commitment. One definition of commitment is "taking of a bargaining position with some explicit or implicit pledge regarding the future course of action" (Walton and McKersie, 1965, p. 82). An example would be a union official who, during negotiation, says to management, "If we do not get the salary increase asked for, I will resign from the union." Such an act identifies a position the negotiator insists on achieving and the threat of some future action if that position is not conceded. The purpose of a commitment is to remove ambiguity about the actor's intended course of action. By making a commitment, a negotiator signals the intention to take this course of action, make this decision, pursue this objective—it says, "If you pursue your goals as well, we are likely to come into direct conflict; and either one of us will win or neither of us will achieve her goals." Commitments also reduce the other party's options. They are designed to constrain the other party's choices to a reduced portfolio of options.

A commitment is often interpreted by the other as a threat—if the other doesn't comply or give in, some set of negative consequences will occur. Some commitments can be threats, but others are statements of intended action that leave the responsibility for avoiding mutual disaster in the hands of the other party. A nation that publicly states it is going to invade another country and that war can only be averted if no other nation tries to stop the action is taking a bold and dramatic commitment position. Commitments can also involve future promises such as, "If we get this salary increase, we'll agree to have all other points arbitrated as you request."

Returning to the management-union example, there are at least two possible messages in the union official's threat to resign. One is that if the present negotiator resigns, management will probably have to start all over with a new, and perhaps less cooperative, union negotiator. The other is based upon the premise that the union official does not want to resign but will *have* to resign if his terms are not met, simply to maintain the credibility of the threat. This premise leads to the conclusion that the official will fight long and hard before taking this ultimate step of resigning and that management should expect no further concessions on this point. Thus, management can decide either to go through long, difficult negotiations until the union negotiator resigns and the new party comes in, or to reconsider its own position and concede.

Because of their nature, commitments are statements that usually require a follow-through in action. A union official who threatens to resign, fails to get what he wanted with the threat, and then does not resign, is hardly going to be believed in the future. In addition, a person will suffer a loss of self-esteem after not following through on a publicly made commitment. Hence, once a negotiator makes a commitment, there is strong motivation to hold to it. Because the other party most likely will understand this, a commitment, once believed, will often have a powerful effect on what the other party believes to be possible (Pruitt, 1981).

### Tactical Considerations in Using Commitments

Like many tools, commitments are two-edged. They may be used to gain the advantages illustrated above, but they may also inextricably fix a negotiator to a particular position or point. Commitments exchange flexibility for certainty of action, but they create difficulties if you want to move to a new position. For example, suppose that after committing yourself to a course of action, additional information indicates that a different position is desirable. Later information shows an earlier estimate of the other party's resistance point to be inaccurate and that there is actually a negative negotiating range. It may be desirable, or even necessary, to shift positions after making a commitment. For these reasons, when you make commitments you should also make contingency plans that allow you to get out of them if necessary. The contingency plans must be secret for the original commitment to be effective. For example, the union leader might have planned to retire shortly after the expected completion of negotiations. By advancing retirement, the official can thereby cancel the commitment and leave the new negotiator unencumbered. A purchaser of a house may be able to back away from a commitment to buy by discovering the hitherto unnoticed "cracks in the plaster" in the living room or being unable to obtain financing from the bank.

Commitments may be a useful tool, but it is also advantageous to keep the other party from becoming committed. Further, if the other party should take a committed position, it is to the first party's advantage to keep open ways for the other to get out of the commitment. We now examine these tactical issues in more detail.

### Establishing a Commitment

Given that strong, passionate statements—some of which are pure bluff—are made during negotiation, how does a negotiator establish that a statement is to be understood as a commitment?

A commitment statement has three properties: a high degree of *finality,* a high degree of *specificity,* and a clear statement of *consequences* (Walton and McKersie, 1965). A buyer could say "We are going to get a volume discount, or there will be trouble." This statement is far less powerful than the same negotiator saying "We must have a 10 percent volume discount in the next contract, or we will sign with an alternative supplier next month." This latter statement communicates *finality,* how and when the volume discount must be granted; *specificity,* how much of a volume discount is expected; and a clear statement of *consequences,* exactly what will happen if the discount is not given. It is far stronger than the previous statement and much more difficult to get released from.

**Public Pronouncement.** A commitment statement increases in potency when more people know about it. The union leader's statement about resigning, if given at the bargaining table, will have a differing impact than one made at a meeting of a few union members. Some parties in negotiations have called press conferences or placed ads in newspapers or other publications stating what they want and what will or will not happen if they don't get it. In each of these situations, the larger the audience, the less likely the commitment will be changed. The effect of the broader social context on negotiations is also discussed in Chapter 9.

**Linking with an Outside Base.** Another way to strengthen a commitment is to link up with an ally. Employees who are dissatisfied with management can form a committee to express these concerns. Industry associations may coalesce to set standards for a product. A variation of this process is to create conditions that make it more difficult for the negotiator creating the commitment to move from her position. For example, by encouraging dedicated colonists to settle on the West Bank near Jerusalem, the Israeli government has made it more difficult to concede this land to Jordan, a point they wanted to reinforce all along.

**Increase the Prominence of Demands.** Many things can be done to increase the prominence of commitment statements. If most offers and concessions have been made orally, then writing out a commitment statement may draw attention to it. If prior statements have been written, then using a different size typeface or a different color paper will draw attention to them. Repetition is one of the most powerful ways of making a statement prominent. Using multiple means to convey a commitment hammers a point home. For example, tell the other party of a commitment; then hand him a written statement; then read the statement to him. Other persuasion tactics are discussed in Chapter 8.

**Reinforce the Threat or Promise.** When making a threat, there is the danger of going too far—stating a point so strongly that you look weak or foolish rather than threatening. Statements like "If I don't get this point, I'll see that you don't stay in business another day!" are more likely to be greeted with annoyance and dismissed than to evoke concern and compliance. Long, detailed statements—ones that are highly exaggerated—undermine credibility. In contrast, simple, direct statements of demands, conditions, and consequences are most effective.

Several things can be done to reinforce the implicit or explicit threat in a commitment. One is to review similar circumstances and what the consequences were; another is to make obvious preparations to carry out the threat. Facing the prospect of a strike, companies build up their inventories and move cots and food into their factories; unions build strike funds and give advice to their members on how to get by with less income should there be a strike. Another route is to create and fulfil minor threats in advance, thereby increasing credibility that major threats will be fulfilled. For example, a negotiator could say, "If the progress of these negotiations does not speed up, I am going to take a five-day weekend," and then do just that.

### Preventing the Other Party from Committing Prematurely

All the advantages of a committed position work against a negotiator when the other party becomes committed. Therefore, a general strategy is to try to keep the other from becoming committed. People often take committed positions when they become angry or feel pushed to the limit; these commitments are often unplanned and can work to the disadvantage of both parties. Consequently, negotiators should pay careful attention to the other party's level of irritation, anger, and impatience.

Good, sound, deliberate commitments take time to establish, for the reasons already discussed. One way to prevent the other party from establishing a committed position is to deny them the opportunity to take this time. In a real estate deal with an option about to run out, a negotiator may use up the time by being unavailable, or requiring extensive checking of deeds and boundaries, thereby denying time to the other party to make a case. Another approach to keep the other negotiator from taking a committed position is to ignore or downplay the threat by not acknowledging the other's commitment, or even by making a joke about it. A negotiator might lightheartedly say "You don't really mean that" or "I know you can't be serious about really going through with that" or simply move negotiations along as though the commitment statement was not heard or understood. If the negotiator can pretend that the other party's statement was not heard or was not understood to be significant, the statement can be ignored at a later point without incurring the consequences that would have occurred had it been taken seriously. Although the other side can still carry out the threat, the belief that it must be carried out (that control of the situation has been given up) may be reduced.

There are times when it is to a negotiator's advantage for the other to become committed. When the other party takes a position on an issue relatively early in a negotiation, it may be very much to a negotiator's advantage to pin down that position so it will not be changed as the negotiation on other issues progresses. A negotiator may handle this situation in two ways: by pointing out the significance of a commitment when it is made, or by taking notes and keeping track of the other's statements when it is to the negotiator's advantage to do so. An employee might be very upset about the way a particular problem was handled but may say that she will never get upset enough about it to resign. The manager might focus on this point when the statement is made or refer to it later when the employee is even more upset. Both actions are designed to keep the employee on the job in spite of her anger.

### Finding Ways to Abandon a Committed Position

Most of the time, a negotiator wants to get the other party out of a committed position, and many times that party may also want to get out of the committed position. How can this be done? One method has already been noted: when establishing a commitment, a negotiator should also plan a private way out. One way is by wording the commitment so that the conditions by which it applied have changed. Sometimes, information provided by the other party during negotiations can permit a negotiator to say, "Given what I've learned from you during this discussion, I see I am going to have to rethink my earlier position." The same could be done for the other party. A negotiator, wanting to make it possible for the other to move from a committed position and yet not lose credibility, might say "Given what I've told you about the facts of the situation (or given this new information), maybe I can help you see that your earlier position no longer holds." Needless to say, the last thing a negotiator wants to do is to embarrass the other party or make judgmental statements about the shift in position; rather, the other party should be given every opportunity to retreat with dignity (see our discussion of face-saving in Chapter 9).

A second way to abandon a commitment is to let the matter die silently. After a lapse of time, a negotiator can make a new proposal in the area of the commitment without mentioning the earlier one. A variation on this process is to make a tentative step in a direction previously excluded by the other's commitment. If the other party, in response to either of these moves, indicates through silence or verbal comment a willingness to let things move in that direction, progress should be pursued.

A third route to take is to restate the commitment in more general terms. The party that wants to move will make a new proposal, changing some of the details to be more in line with her needs, while ostensibly still living with the "general principles" of the earlier wording. For example, the purchasing agent who demanded a 10 percent volume discount may rephrase this statement later to say she needs a significant volume discount. The other party can then explore what level this discount could be.

Lastly, if the other party backs off from a committed position, it is important to help him minimize any possible damage. One strategy to use in this instance is to make a public attribution about the other party's move to some noble or higher outside cause. Diplomats can withdraw from a committed position because of their "deep concern for peace and humankind." A party can back off from a point during a real estate transaction to "support the economic well-being of the community." Managers can leave a committed position "for the good of the company."

A committed position is a powerful tool in negotiation; it is also a rigid tool. As such, it must be used with care; and as with any other tool, we must be as alert to ways of denying it to the other party as we are to ways we can use it for ourselves. Unfortunately, far more commitments are made as a result of anger and the desire to stop making concessions than as a result of clearly thought-out tactical planning. In either case, the essential property of a committed position is to arrange the consequences of an action so that some point is no longer an item of discussion or can only be negotiated at grave risk to one or both parties. The events or consequences are now inevitable unless stopped at serious risk to one or both sides. The committed position has to be believable, and what has to be believed is that nothing can be done to change the conditions—if X happens, Y is inevitable. Convincing the other party that fate is sealed on the matter at hand is demanding and requires preparation, time, and skill. Consequently, getting out of a committed position is not easy, but it is made simpler by planning a secret means of escape at the time the commitment is being established. Many of the steps a negotiator can use to get out of a commitment can also be used to help the other party get out of a committed position or, even better, to keep him from establishing one in the first place.

## TYPICAL HARDBALL TACTICS

Many popular books of negotiation emphasize the thrill of using hardball negotiation tactics to beat the other party (see Aaronson, 1989; Brooks and Odiorne, 1984; Cohen, 1980; Schatzki, 1981). Such tactics are designed to pressure targeted parties to do things they would not otherwise do, and their use usually disguises the user's adherence to a decidedly distributive bargaining approach. It is not clear how often these tactics work, but they work best against poorly prepared negotiators—and they *can* backfire. Many people find these tactics offensive and motivation for revenge when they are used against them. Many negotiators consider these tactics out-of-bounds for any negotiation situation. We do not recommend the use of any of the following techniques. In fact, it has been our experience that these tactics do more harm than good in negotiations. They are much more difficult to enact than they are to read about, and each tactic involves risk for the person using it, including harm to reputation, losing the deal, negative publicity, and dealing with the other party's revenge. But it is important that negotiators understand hardball tactics and how they work so they can recognize and understand them if they are the targeted recipients.

We will now discuss some of the more frequently described hardball tactics and their weaknesses. After we describe the tactics we will discuss the various options that negotiators have for dealing with others who use such tactics against them.

### Good Guy/Bad Guy

This tactic is named after a police interrogation technique where two officers (one kind, the other tough) take turns questioning a suspect. The use of this tactic in negotiations typically goes as follows: The first negotiator ("bad guy") presents a tough opening position, punctuated with threats, obnoxious behavior, and intransigence. She then leaves the room to make an important telephone call or to "cool off"—frequently at her partner's suggestion. While out of the room, the other negotiator ("good guy") tries to reach a quick agreement before the "bad guy" returns and makes life difficult for both negotiators. A more subtle form of this tactic is to assign the "bad guy" the role of speaking only when the negotiations are headed in a direction that the team does not want; as long as things are going well, the "good guy" does the talking. There are many weaknesses to using this tactic. It is relatively transparent and can be countered by the other party's willingness to discuss the tactic openly and describe what the negotiators are doing. It is also much harder to enact than it is to describe; it typically alienates the targeted party and frequently directs energy towards making the tactic work smoothly rather than toward accomplishing negotiation goals.

### Highball/Lowball

The negotiator using this tactic starts with a ridiculously high (or low) opening offer. The theory is that such an offer will cause the other party to reevaluate his own opening offer and move closer to his resistance point. An example of the use of this tactic was the Soviet Union's opening bid of $210 million for the sale of the U.S. television rights to the 1976 Olympic Games, expected to sell for about $75 million. Although the Soviets did not receive anywhere near their opening offer, they did succeed in having the American networks quickly reassess their bids. The real danger with this strategy is that the other party will halt negotiations because they think negotiating is a waste of time. Of course, in the Olympic example the Soviets held a monopoly on television rights, and the networks were collectively very unlikely to walk away. Even if the targeted person continues to negotiate after receiving a highball (lowball) offer, however, it takes a very skilled negotiator to be able to justify the high opening offer and to finesse the negotiation back to a point where the other side will be willing to make a major concession toward the outrageous bid.

### Bogey

Negotiators using this tactic pretend that an issue of little or no importance to them is quite important. Later in the negotiation this issue can then be "traded" for major concessions on issues that are actually important to the negotiator. This technique is most effective when the negotiator can identify an issue that is quite important to the other side but of little value to her. For example, a seller may have a product in the warehouse ready for delivery. When negotiating with a purchasing agent, however, the seller may ask for large concessions to process a "rush order" for the client. The seller can reduce the size of the concession demanded for the "rush order" in exchange for concessions on other issues, such as the price or the size of the order. Again, this is a difficult tactic to enact. Typically, the other party will take you seriously when you are trying to make a case for the issue that you want to bogey, and this can lead to a very awkward situation where both negotiators may be arguing against their true wishes (the other party is asking for large concessions on other issues to give you the bogey issue that you really don't want, and you are spending time evaluating offers and making arguments for an issue that you know you do not want).

### The Nibble

Negotiators using this tactic ask for a proportionally small concession (say 1 to 2 percent of the total profit of the deal) on an item that hasn't been discussed previously to close the deal. Herb Cohen (1980) describes the nibble as follows: After trying many different suits in a clothing store, tell the clerk that you will take a given suit if he throws in a tie for free. The tie is the nibble. Cohen claims that he usually gets the tie. In a business context, the tactic occurs like this: After negotiating a deal for a considerable amount of time with an agreement close, a negotiator asks that a clause that hasn't been discussed previously and that will cost the other party a proportionally small amount be included. This amount is too small to lose the deal over, but large enough to upset the other party. And that is the major weakness with the nibble. It is a great motivator for revenge because many people feel that the party using the nibble has not bargained in good faith (as part of a fair negotiation process, all items to be discussed during the negotiation should be placed on the agenda early). Even if the party claims to "be very embarrassed about forgetting this item until now" and that she "must have this item or lose my job," the party who has been nibbled will not feel good about the process and will often seek revenge in future negotiations.

### Chicken

This tactic is named after the 1950s recreation portrayed in the James Dean movie *Rebel Without a Cause* of driving cars at one another or towards a cliff until one person swerves to avoid disaster. The person who swerves is labeled a "chicken" and the other person is treated like a hero. Negotiators who use this tactic combine a large bluff with a threatened action to force the other party to "chicken out" and give them what they want. In labor-management negotiations, management may tell the union that if they do not agree to the current contract offer they will close the factory and go out of business (or move to another state or country). Clearly this is a high-stakes gamble. Management must be willing to follow through on their threat—if the union calls their bluff and they do not follow through, they will not be believed in the future. On the other hand, how can the union take the risk and call the bluff? If management is telling the truth, they may actually close and move elsewhere. If management is using the chicken tactic and the union calls their bluff, management may feel a great deal of pressure to follow through with it. The real weakness with this tactic is that negotiation is turned into a high-stakes game where reality and postured negotiation positions are difficult to distinguish from each other. For instance, in the mid-1970s the president of Eastern Airlines, Frank Borman, demanded givebacks from various unions. Was he using the chicken tactic, or would he really have closed the airline? We will never know for sure because he received the givebacks he requested from the unions.

### Intimidation

Many tactics can be gathered under the general label of intimidation. What they have in common is that they all attempt to force the other party to agree by employing various emotional ploys, usually anger and fear. For example, the other party may deliberately use anger to indicate the seriousness of a position. Once while I was negotiating with a car salesman, he lost his temper, destroyed his written notes, told me to sit down and listen to him, and explained in a loud voice that this was the best deal in the city and if I did not accept it that evening I should not bother returning to that dealership and wasting his time. I didn't buy the car and I haven't been back; nor do I suspect have any of the students in my negotiation classes, to whom I relate this story every year! I suspect that the salesman was trying to intimidate me into agreeing to the deal and realized that if I went elsewhere his deal would not look as good. What he didn't realize was that I had asked the accountant at the dealership for further information about the deal and had found that he had lied about the value of a trade-in; he really lost his cool when I exposed the lie!

Another form of intimidation includes increasing the appearance of legitimacy. When there is a high degree of legitimacy, there are set policies or procedures for resolving disputes. Negotiators who do not have such policies or procedures available may try to invent them and impose them on the other negotiator and make the process appear legitimate. For example, policies that are written in manuals or preprinted "official" forms and agreements are less likely to be questioned than those that are delivered verbally (Cohen, 1980); long and detailed loan contracts used by banks for consumer loans are seldom read completely (Hendon and Hendon, 1990). The higher the appearance of legitimacy, the less likely the other party will be to question the process being followed or the contract terms being proposed.

Finally, guilt can also be used as a form of intimidation. Negotiators can question the other party's integrity or the other's lack of trust in them. The purpose of this tactic is to place the other party on the defensive so they are dealing with the issues of guilt or trust rather than discussing the substance of the negotiation.

### Aggressive Behavior

A group of tactics similar to intimidation include various ways of being aggressive in pushing your position or attacking the other person's position. These tactics include the relentless push for further concessions ("You can do better than that"), asking for the best offer ("Let's not waste any more time. What is the most that you will pay?"), and asking the other party to explain and justify their proposals item by item or line by line ("What is your cost breakdown?"). The negotiator using these techniques is signaling a hard-nosed, intransigent position and trying to force the other side to make many concessions to reach an agreement.

### Other Hardball Tactics

We have discussed many of the hardball tactics that are typically used by distributive bargainers who are not afraid to use "dirty tricks" to get their own way. This is not an exhaustive list, however, and the interested reader can find more of this discussion in books by Cohen (1980), Schatzki (1981), Brooks and Odiorne (1984), and Aaronson (1989).

## DEALING WITH TYPICAL HARDBALL TACTICS

The negotiator dealing with another party who uses the hardball tactics described above has many choices about how to respond. A good strategic response to these tactics requires that the negotiator identify the tactic quickly and understand what it is and how it works. Most of the tactics are designed to either enhance the appearance of the bargaining position of the person using the tactic or to detract from the appearance of the options available to the other party. Choosing the best way to respond to a tactic depends on your goals and the broader context of the negotiation (who are you negotiating with; what is your BATNA?). No one response will work in all situations to meet your goals. We now discuss some options that negotiators have in responding to typical hardball tactics (see Fisher, Ury, and Patton, 1991; Ury, 1991 for extended discussion of these points).

### Ignore Them

Although ignoring a hardball tactic may appear to be a "weak" response, in fact it can be a very powerful way to deal with hardball tactics. It takes a lot of energy to use some of these hardball tactics (good guy/bad guy, for instance), and while the other side is using energy to play these games, you can be using your energy to work on satisfying your needs. Not responding to a threat is often the best way of dealing with it. Pretend you didn't hear. Change the subject and get your opponents involved in the new topic. Call a break, and upon returning, switch topics. All these options can deflate the effects of a threat and allow you to press on your agenda while the other party is trying to decide what trick to use next.

### Discuss Them

Fisher, Ury, and Patton, (1991; also see Ury, 1991) suggest that a good way to deal with hardball tactics is to negotiate the negotiation process (how you are to conduct the negotiations) before continuing the negotiation over the substance of the talks. Offer to change to less aggressive methods of negotiating. Explicitly acknowledge that they are tough negotiators and that you can be tough too. Then suggest that you both change and try more productive methods that can allow you both to gain. Fisher, Ury, and Patton suggest that negotiators separate people from the problem and then be "hard on the problem, soft on the people." It doesn't hurt to remind the other negotiator of this from time to time during the negotiation.

### Respond in Kind

It is always possible to respond to a hardball tactic with your own tactic. Although this response can frequently result in chaos and hard feelings, it is not an option that should be dismissed out of hand. Once the smoke clears both parties will realize that they are skilled in the use of hardball tactics and may recognize that it is time to try something different. This tactic may be most useful when dealing with another party who is testing your resolve or as a response to exaggerated positions taken in negotiations. A participant in a recent negotiation seminar told one of the authors the following story about bargaining for a carpet in a northern African country:

> I knew that the value of the carpet was about $2,000 because I had been looking at carpets throughout my trip. I found the carpet that I wanted and made sure not to appear too interested. I discussed some other carpets with the vendor before moving on to the carpet that I really wanted. When I asked him the price of this carpet, he replied $9,000. I replied that I would give him *negative* $7,000. We bargained for a while and I bought the carpet for $2,000.

The purchaser in this negotiation clearly responded to a hardball tactic with one of his own. When asked if he felt comfortable with his opening bid, he responded:

> Sure. Why not? The seller knew the value of the carpet was about $2,000. If anything, he seemed to respect me when I bargained this way. If I had opened with a positive number I would have ended up having to pay more than the carpet was worth. And I really wanted the carpet.

### Co-Opt the Other Party

One way to deal with negotiators who use aggressive hardball tactics is to try to befriend them before they use the tactics. This approach is built on the theory that it is much more difficult to attack a friend than an enemy. If you can stress what you have in common with the other party and find another element upon which to place the blame ("the system," "foreign competition") then you may be able to sidetrack the other party before he even begins.

# SUMMARY

In this chapter we examined the basic structure of competitive or distributive bargaining situations and some of the strategies and tactics used in distributive bargaining. The basic structure of distributive bargaining consists of setting your own opening, target, and resistance points. You soon learn the other party's starting points and find out her target points directly or through inference. Usually you won't know resistance points, the point beyond which a party will not go, until late in negotiation because the other party often carefully conceals them. All points are important, but understanding the resistance points is most critical. The spread between the parties' resistance points defines the bargaining range. If positive, it defines the area of negotiation, with each party working to get as much of the bargaining range for himself as possible. If negative, successful negotiation may be impossible.

It is rare that a negotiation includes only one item; more typically, there is a set of items referred to as a bargaining mix. Each item in a bargaining mix can have opening, target, and resistance points. The bargaining mix may provide opportunities for bundling issues together, logrolling, or mutually concessionary behavior.

Examining the structure of distributive bargaining reveals many options for a negotiator to achieve a successful resolution, most of which fall within two broad efforts: to influence the other party's belief in what is possible and to learn as much as possible about the other party's position, particularly about the resistance points. The negotiator's basic strategy is to conclude the final settlement as close to the other party's resistance point as possible. The tactics used to achieve this goal involve getting information about the opposition and its positions; convincing members of the other party to change their minds about their ability to achieve their own goals; and promoting your own objectives as desirable, necessary, or even inevitable.

Distributive bargaining is basically a conflict situation, wherein parties seek their own advantage—in part through concealing information, attempting to mislead, or using manipulative actions. All these tactics can easily escalate interaction from calm discussion to bitter hostility. Yet, negotiation is the attempt to resolve a conflict without force, without fighting. Further, to be successful, both parties to the negotiation must feel at the end that the outcome was the best that they could achieve and that it is worth accepting and supporting. Hence negotiation is a process that requires not only skill but also, and even more important, understanding and good planning.

# CHAPTER 4

# Strategy and Tactics of Integrative Negotiation

## INTRODUCTION

Periodically, we read of tragic fires in restaurants, night clubs, or theaters that kill large numbers of people. Often there is panic; in the rush to escape, exits are blocked, trapping many and causing unnecessary deaths. People seem to act as if their lives depended upon being first out of the building. In contrast, most of us are taught from our earliest school days that there is ample time for everyone to leave a burning building safely if people move out in an orderly fashion. As children, we were urged to have a shared concern to get everyone out of the building, to collaborate rather than to compete. The need for orderly, cooperative behavior comes not from ideals, but from reality.

The same principles are true for negotiation. In bargaining, there need not be winners and losers; everyone can be a winner. Rather than assume that all conflicts are win-lose events, negotiators can learn that win-win solutions are possible. These assumptions will lead them to search for the win-win options, and usually they will find them. This win-win approach to negotiation is called *integrative negotiation.*

In distributive bargaining, the goals of the parties are initially irreconcilable—or at least they appear that way to the parties. Central to the conflict is the belief that there is a limited, controlled amount of key resources available—a "fixed pie" situation (see Chapter 6 for a discussion of "fixed pie" beliefs). Both parties may want to be the winner; both may want more than half of what is available. For example, both management (on behalf of the stockholders) and labor (on behalf of the rank and file) believe that they deserve the larger share of the company's profits. Both may want to win on the same dimension, such as the financial package or control of certain policy decisions. In these situations, their goals are mutually exclusive, and hence lead to conflict.

In contrast, in integrative negotiation the goals of the parties are not mutually exclusive. If one side pursues its goals, that does not necessarily preclude the other from achieving its goals. One party's gain is not necessarily at the other party's expense. The fundamental structure of an integrative negotiation situation is that it is possible for both sides to achieve their objectives (Walton and McKersie,

1965). Although the conflict may appear initially to be win-lose to the parties—and may create the same kind of competitive panic we described in the fire example—discussion and mutual exploration will usually suggest win-win alternatives. The strategy by which negotiators discover these alternatives is the focus of this chapter. Our description will draw heavily from the writings of several authors who have written about the integrative process in great detail (Walton and McKersie, 1965; Filley, 1975; Fisher, Ury, and Patton, 1991; Pruitt, 1981, 1983; Carnevale and Pruitt, 1992; Pruitt and Carnevale, 1993). In addition, we will note recent research findings that have affirmed the validity of particular strategies and tactics.

## AN OVERVIEW OF THE INTEGRATIVE NEGOTIATION PROCESS

Past history, biased perceptions, and the truly distributive aspects of bargaining often make it remarkable that integrative agreements occur at all. But they do, largely because negotiators work hard to overcome the inhibiting factors and assertively search for common ground. The following processes tend to be central to achieving almost all integrative agreements.

### Creating a Free Flow of Information

Ample research evidence indicates that effective information exchange promotes the development of good integrative solutions (Pruitt, 1981; Thompson, 1991). For this open dialogue to occur, negotiators must be willing to reveal their true objectives and to listen to the other negotiator carefully. In short, negotiators must create the conditions for a free and open discussion of all related issues and concerns. This willingness to share information is significantly different from a distributive bargaining situation, in which the parties distrust one another, conceal and manipulate information, and attempt to learn information about the other for their own competitive advantage.

### Attempting to Understand the Other Negotiator's Real Needs and Objectives

As we noted earlier, negotiators differ in their values and preferences. What one side needs and wants may or may not be what the other side needs and wants. If you are to help satisfy another's needs, you must first understand them. Hence, throughout the process of sharing information about preferences and priorities, the parties must make a true effort to understand what the other side really wants to achieve. Again this is in contrast to distributive bargaining, where the negotiator either makes no effort to understand what the other side really wants or uses this information to challenge, undermine, or even deny the other the opportunity to have those needs and objectives met.

### Emphasizing the Commonalties Between the Parties and Minimizing the Differences

To sustain a free flow of information and an effort to truly understand the other's needs and objectives, negotiators may also require a different outlook or frame of reference. (We will address frame of reference later in this chapter.) In distributive bargaining, the parties focus on achieving their own individual objectives. However, in integrative negotiation, individual goals may need to be redefined as best achievable through collaborative efforts that achieve a broader collective goal. Sometimes the collective goal is clear and obvious. For example, politicians in the same party may recognize that their petty squabbles must be put aside to assure the party's victory at the polls. The phrase "politics makes strange bedfellows" suggests that the quest for victory can unite political enemies into larger coalitions that will be assured of political victory. Similarly, managers who are quarreling over cutbacks in their individual department budgets may need to recognize that unless all departments sustain budget cuts, they will be unable to change an unprofitable firm into a profitable one. At other times, the larger goal is not so clear, nor is it as easy to keep in sight. For example, one of the authors worked as a consultant to a company that was closing down a major manufacturing plant and, at the same time, opening several others in different parts of the country. The company was perfectly willing to transfer employees to new plants and let them take their seniority with them up to the time of the announced move; the union agreed to this arrangement. However, conflict developed because some employees were able to transfer immediately whereas others were needed to close and dismantle the old plant. Because workers acquired seniority in the new plant based on the date they arrived, those who stayed to close the old plant would have less seniority in the new plant compared to those who moved earlier. The union wanted everyone to go at the same time to avoid this inequity. Management was adamant that this was unworkable. In the argument that resulted, both parties lost sight of their larger goal—to transfer all employees who wanted to move to the new plant with their seniority intact. Only by constantly stressing this larger goal were the parties able to maintain a focus on commonalties that eventually led to a solution—transferred workers were allowed to select in advance the jobs they moved into, and their seniority was transferred to those jobs when the choice was made, not when the physical move actually occurred.

### Searching for Solutions that Meet the Goals and Objectives of Both Sides

Finally, successful integrative negotiation requires that the negotiators search for solutions that meet the objectives and needs of both (all) sides. In this process, negotiators must be firm but flexible (Fisher, Ury, and Patton, 1991; Pruitt and Rubin, 1986)—they must be firm about their primary interests and needs, but flexible about the manner in which these interests and needs are met through solutions. When the parties have traditionally held a combative, competitive orientation toward each other, they are more prone to be concerned only with their own objectives. In this competitive interaction, any concern with the other's objectives may be in one of two forms: first, to make sure that what the other obtains does not take away from one's own accomplishments; and second, to attempt to block the other from obtaining objectives because of a strong desire to win and even defeat the opponent. In contrast, successful integrative negotiation requires each negotiator not only to define and pursue her own goals, but also to be mindful of the other's goals and to search for solutions that will meet and satisfy the goals of both sides. Outcomes are measured by the degree to which they meet both negotiators' goals. They are *not* measured by determining whether one party is "doing better" than the other. If the objective of one party is to get more than the other, integrative negotiation is difficult at best; if both strive to get more than the other, integrative negotiation is impossible.

In summary, successful integrative negotiation requires a process fundamentally different from that of distributive negotiation. Negotiators must attempt to probe below the surface of their opponent's position to discover underlying needs. They must create a free and open flow of information, and they must use their desire to satisfy both sides as the perspective from which to structure their dialogue. If negotiators do not have this perspective—if they approach the problem and their opponent in win-lose terms—integrative negotiation cannot occur.

## KEY STAGES IN THE INTEGRATIVE NEGOTIATION PROCESS

There are four major steps in the integrative negotiation process: identifying and defining the problem, understanding the problem and bringing interests and needs to the surface, generating alternative solutions to the problem, and choosing a specific solution from among those alternatives.

### Identify and Define the Problem

The problem identification step is often the most difficult one; this is even more true when several parties are involved. Consider the following example:

In a large electronics plant, there was considerable difficulty with one of the subassemblies used in the final assembly department. Various pins and fittings that held the assembly in place were getting bent and distorted. When this happened to a unit, it would be laid aside as a reject. At the end of the month, these rejects would be returned to be reworked. The material to be reworked often arrived at the subassembly department at a time when workers there were under pressure to meet end-of-the-month schedules; in addition, they were often low on parts. As a result, the reworking effort had to be done in a rush and on overtime. The extra cost of overtime and expediting the rush work presented an additional problem because it did not fit into the standard cost allocation system. The manager of the subassembly department did not want the costs allocated to his overhead charge. The manager of the final assembly department insisted that he should not pay the additional cost because his unit did not cause the problem; he argued that subassembly should bear the cost because their poor work originally caused the problem. The subassembly department manager countered that the parts were in good condition when they left his area and that it was the poor workmanship in the final assembly area that created the damage. The immediate costs were relatively small. What really concerned both parties was setting a long-term precedent for paying the costs.

Eventually, an integrative solution was reached. During any given month, the subassembly department had a number of short slack time periods. Arrangements were made to return damaged subassemblies in small batches, allowing them to be worked on during the slack periods. It also became clear that many people in the final assembly department did not fully understand the parts they were handling, which may have contributed to some of the damage. Arrangements were made for some of these people to be temporarily transferred to the subassembly department during slack periods to learn more about that department and to pick up some of the rush orders in that department.

This example helps us identify a number of key aspects of the problem definition process (see Filley, 1975, and Shea, 1983, for fuller treatments of these points).

**Define the Problem in a Way that is Mutually Acceptable to Both Sides.** Ideally, parties should enter the integrative negotiation process with few if any preconceptions about the solution and with open minds about the other negotiator's needs. As a problem is defined jointly, it should accurately reflect both parties' needs and priorities. Regrettably, this is not what we usually encounter. An understandable and widely held fear about integrative negotiation is that during the problem definition process, the other party is manipulating information and discussion to state the problem for his own advantage. For positive problem solving to occur, both parties must be committed to stating the problem in neutral terms. The problem statement must be mutually acceptable to both sides and not stated so that it favors the preferences or priorities of one side over the other. The parties may be required to work the problem statement over several times until each side agrees upon its wording.

**Keep the Problem Statement Clean and Simple.** The major focus of an integrative agreement is to solve the primary problem. Secondary issues and concerns should be raised only if they are inextricably bound up with the primary problem. Discipline is required to identify the less important issues and keep them out of the picture. This approach is in stark contrast to the distributive bargaining process, in which the parties are encouraged to "beef up" their positions by bringing in a large number of secondary issues and concerns so they can trade these items off during the hard bargaining phase. If there are several issues on the table in an integrative negotiation, the parties may want to clearly identify the linkages among the issues and decide whether they will be approached as separate problems (which may be packaged together later) or redefined as one larger problem.

**State the Problem as a Goal and Identify the Obstacles to Attaining this Goal.**
The problem should be defined as a *specific* goal to be attained (*what* we want to
achieve) rather than as a solution process (*how* we are going to achieve it.) Moreover, problem definition should then proceed to specify what obstacles must be
overcome for the goal to be attained. For example, in the previous example, the
problem might be defined as "minimizing the number of rejects." This is not as
clear and explicit as "cutting the number of rejects in half." Moreover, although
this is a noble statement of a goal, greater progress may be made if the parties can
specify what they need to know about how the product is made, how defects occur,
what must be done to repair defects, and so on.

**Depersonalize the Problem.**    As we have pointed out earlier, when parties
are engaged in conflict, they tend to become evaluative and judgmental. They
view their own actions, strategies, and preferences in a positive light and the other
party's actions, strategies, and preferences in a negative light. As a result, when
negotiators attempt the integrative negotiation process, their evaluative judgments of the value or worth of the opponent's preferences can get in the way of
clear and dispassionate thinking simply because the other happens to own those
preferences (see Chapter 6 for a discussion of "reactive devaluation"). Viewing the
situation as "your point of view is wrong and mine is right" inhibits the integrative
negotiation process because we cannot attack the problem without attacking the
person who "owns" the problem. In contrast, by depersonalizing the definition of
the problem—stating, for example, that "there is a difference of viewpoints on this
problem"—both sides can approach the difference as a problem "out there,"
rather than as one they personally own.

**Separate the Problem Definition from the Search for Solutions.**    Finally, we
will repeat the maxim that every discussion of the problem-solving process
stresses: don't jump to solutions until the problem is fully defined. In distributive
bargaining, negotiators are encouraged to state the problem in terms of their preferred solution and to make concessions from this most desired alternative. In
contrast, the integrative negotiation process cannot work unless negotiators avoid
premature solutions (which probably favor one side or the other) until they have
fully defined the problem and examined all the possible alternative solutions.

## Understand the Problem Fully—Identify Interests and Needs

Many writers on negotiation—most particularly, Roger Fisher and William
Ury in their popular book, *Getting to Yes* (1981; also Fisher, Ury, and Patton,
1991)—have stressed that a key to achieving an integrative agreement is the ability
of the parties to get at each other's *interests.* Interests are different from positions
in that interests are the underlying concerns, needs, desires, or fears behind a negotiator's position, which motivate the negotiator to take that position. These writers argue that although negotiators may have difficulty satisfying each other's

specific positions, an understanding of underlying interests may permit them to invent solutions that meet those interests. In this section, we will first define interests more fully, and then discuss how understanding them may be critical to effective integrative negotiation.

An example reveals the essence of the difference between interests and positions:

> Consider the story of two men quarreling in a library. One wants the window open and the other wants it closed. They bicker back and forth about how much to leave it open: a crack, halfway, three quarters of the way. No solution satisfied them both.
>
> Enter the librarian. She asks one why he wants the window open. "To get some fresh air." She asks the other why he wants it closed. "To avoid the draft." After thinking a minute, she opens wide a window in the next room, bringing in fresh air without a draft (Fisher, Ury, and Patton, 1991, p. 40; originally told by Follett, 1940).

As Fisher, Ury, and Patton point out, this is a classic example of the parties' negotiating over positions and failing to understand underlying interests. Their positions are "window open" and "window closed." If they continue to pursue positional bargaining, the set of possible outcomes can either be a victory for the one who wants the window open, a victory for the one who wants it shut, or some form of a compromise in which *neither* gets what he wants. Note that a compromise here is more a form of lose-lose than win-win for these bargainers because one party believes that he won't get *enough* fresh air with the window open halfway, whereas the other views it as a loss because *any* opening is apparently unsatisfactory. The librarian's questions transform the dispute by focusing on *why* each man wants the window open or closed: to get fresh air or to avoid a draft. Understanding these interests enables the librarian to invent a solution that meets the interests of both sides—a solution that was not at all apparent when they continued to argue over their positions.

In this description, the key word is *why*—why they want what they want. Interests are motivators—the underlying needs, concerns, and desires that lead us to create a particular position. When we begin negotiation, we usually lay our position or demands on the table; and as we have pointed out, this position or these demands have emerged from a planning process in which we decided what we wanted and then specified opening bids, targets, and walkaway points. In distributive bargaining, we trade these points and positions back and forth, attempting to achieve a settlement as close to our target as possible. However, in integrative negotiation, we need to pursue the negotiator's thinking and logic to determine the factors that motivated her to arrive at those points. The presumption is that if both parties understand the motivating factors for the other, they may recognize possible compatibilities in interests that permit them to invent positions which both will endorse as an acceptable settlement. Consider the following dialogue between a company recruiter and a job applicant over starting salary:

*Recruiter:*

What were you thinking about as a starting salary?

*Applicant:*

I would like $40,000.

*Recruiter:*

We can only offer $35,000.

*Applicant:*

That's not acceptable.

Thus far, the parties have only laid positions on the table. They are $5,000 apart. Moreover, the applicant may be afraid to positionally bargain (Chapter 3) with the new employer, whereas the recruiter may be afraid that the applicant—who she very much wants to hire—will walk out. Now let us revise their dialogue to help them focus on interests.

*Recruiter:*

$40,000 is a problem for our company. Can you tell me why you decided you wanted $40,000?

*Applicant:*

Well, I have lots of education loans to pay off, and I will need to pay for a few more courses to finish my degree. I can't really afford to pay these bills and live comfortably for less than $40,000.

*Recruiter:*

Our company has a program to help new employees refinance their education loans. In addition, we also have a program to provide tuition assistance for new courses if the courses you need to take are related to your job. Would these programs help you with your problem?

*Applicant:*

Yes!

Thus, the recruiter was able to bring the applicant's interests—paying off education loans and future education costs—to the surface and offer a financial package that met the needs of both the recruiter's company and the applicant. Similarly, the applicant might have asked why the company could only pay $35,000 and discovered that it was company policy to not offer more than this to any applicant with the same qualifications. However, the question would also have revealed that the company can pay performance bonuses and would be willing to review the salary after six months on the job. This information may well enable the applicant to make $40,000 by the end of the first year, and thus have her financial goal met.

**Types of Interests.**    Lax and Sebenius (1986) have suggested that several types of interests may be at stake in a negotiation. Each type of interest may also be intrinsic—in that the parties value it for its essence—or instrumental—in that the parties value it because it helps them derive other outcomes in the future.

*Substantive interests* are the types of interests we have just been discussing. These are the interests that relate to the focal issues under negotiation—economic and financial issues such as price or rate, or the substance of a negotiation such as the division of resources. These interests may be intrinsic or instrumental; in the first case, we want something because it is intrinsically satisfying to us, whereas in the second case, it helps us achieve a longer range goal. Thus, the job applicant may want $40,000 both because the salary affirms her intrinsic sense of personal worth in the marketplace, and also because it instrumentally contributes toward paying off her education loans.

*Process interests* are related to the way we settle this dispute. One party may pursue distributive bargaining because he sees negotiation as a competition and enjoys the competitive game of wits that comes from nose-to-nose, hard-line bargaining. Another party may be negotiating because she believes she has not been consulted in the past, and she wants to have some say in how a key problem is resolved. In this latter case, the issues under discussion may be less important to the parties than the opportunity for them to be asked their views and invited to the negotiating table (see Chapter 5 of Sheppard, Lewicki, and Minton, 1992, for a more complete discussion of the role of "voice" in organizations). Process interests can also be both intrinsic and instrumental. Thus, in the voice example, having a say may be intrinsically important to a group to affirm their legitimacy and worth and the key role they play in the organization; it can also be instrumentally important, in that if they are successful in gaining voice in this negotiation, they may also be able to demonstrate that they should be invited back into the negotiation on a wide variety of other related issues in the future.

*Relationship interests* mean that one or both parties value their relationship with each other and do not want to take actions that will harm or damage the relationship. Intrinsic relationship interests value the relationship both for its existence and for the pleasure or fulfillment that sustaining the relationship creates. Instrumental relationship interests exist when the parties derive positive benefits from the relationship and do not wish to endanger future benefits by souring it.

Finally, Lax and Sebenius point out that the parties may have *interests in principles.* These principles—what is fair, what is right, what is acceptable, what is ethical, or what has been done in the past and should be done in the future—may be deeply held by the parties and serve as the dominant guides to their action. (These principles are often the "intangibles" we described in Chapter 1.) These interests can also be intrinsic—valued because of their inherent worth—or instrumental—valued because they can be applied instrumentally to a variety of future situations and scenarios. Bringing these interests in principles to the surface will lead the parties to explicitly discuss the principles at stake and to invent solutions consistent with it. For example, suppose three students (who are also good friends) collaborate on an essay and submit it for a major prize competition. Two of the students contributed equally, and together they did 90 percent of the work. The three students win the prize of $300. The issue is how to split the prize money. Obviously, one way to split it is for each to take $100. But if they split it based on what they each contributed, the two hard-working students would get $135 each and the third student would get $30. However, separately or together, they may also decide that it is not worth fighting over the workload—they don't want to alienate their third friend, or the difference in money is trivial—and simply decide to split the prize into $100 parts. Only by discussing the interests at stake—principles about what is fair in this situation and their relationship—can they arrive at a solution that divides the prize, minimizes animosity, and maintains their relationship.

**Some Observations on Interests.**    Based on this discussion, we may make several observations about interests and types of interests:

1. There may be more than one type of interest in a dispute. Parties can have more than substantive interests about the issues—they can also care deeply about process, the relationship, or the principles at stake. Note that "interests as principles" effectively cuts across substantive, procedural, and relationship interests as well, so that the categories are not necessarily exclusive.

2. Parties can differ on the type of interests at stake. One party may care deeply about the specific issues under discussion, whereas the other cares about how the issues are resolved—questions of principle or process. Bringing these different interests to the surface may enable the parties to see that in fact they care about very different things, and thus they can invent a solution that addresses the interests of both sides.

3. Interests are often based in more deeply rooted human needs or values. Several authors have suggested that frameworks for understanding basic human needs and values are most helpful for understanding interests. These frameworks suggest that needs are hierarchical and that satisfaction of the more basic or lower order needs will be more vigorously argued and defended in negotiation. For example, Nierenberg (1983) proposed a need theory of negotiation based on Maslow's well-known hierarchy of needs. In this hierarchy, basic needs to satisfy physiological and safety (security) requirements will take precedence over higher order needs such as recognition, respect, affirmation, and self-actualization. Similarly, Burton (1984) has suggested that the intensity of many international disputes reflects deep underlying needs for security, protection of ethnic and national identity, and other fundamental needs. Finally, Laue (1986) has also suggested a hierarchy of needs (see Figure 4.1). The more basic a need is, the more the parties will defend it, and the more the negotiated settlement must address it to satisfy the affected party.

4. Interests can change. Like positions on issues, interests can change over time. What was important to the parties last week—or even 20 minutes ago—may not be important now. Interaction between the parties can put some interests to rest, but it may raise others. Thus, the parties must continually be attentive to changes in their own interests and the interests of the other side. As we will point out, when parties begin to talk about things in a different way—when the language or emphasis changes—it may indicate a change in interests.

**FIGURE 4.1** Levels of Conflict Content

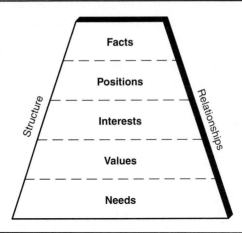

J. Laue, "Levels of Conflict Content," Remarks delivered at a conference on Guidelines for Newcomers to Track II, Washington, D.C., 1986.

5. Getting at interests. There are numerous ways to get at interests. Sometimes we are not even sure of our own interests. In these cases, we should be asking ourselves not only "What do I want (from this negotiation)?" but also "Why do I want that?" "Why is that important to me?" "What will achieving that help me do?" "What will happen if I don't achieve my objective?" Listening to your own inner voices—fears, aspirations, hopes, desires—is important to bring your own interests to the surface.

The same dialogue is essential in clarifying the other party's interests. Asking probing questions ("why" questions) and listening carefully to the other party's language, emotions, nonverbal behavior, and the like are the essential keys to the process. We might also want to distinguish between intrinsic interests—which need to be satisfied as ends in themselves—and instrumental interests—which help to get other outcomes. In both cases, once we understand these interests, we may then be able to invent a variety of ways to satisfy them through alternatives that are also acceptable to us. The result is a mutually satisfactory solution.

### Generate Alternative Solutions

The search for alternatives is the creative phase of integrative negotiations. Once the parties have agreed on a common definition of the problem and understood each other's interests, they generate a variety of alternative solutions in the next phase of negotiations. The objective is to create a list of options or possible solutions that solve the problem; selecting from among those options will be their task in the final phase.

A number of techniques have been suggested to help negotiators generate alternative solutions. These approaches fall into two general categories. The first approach requires the negotiators to redefine, recast, or reframe the problem (or problem set) so as to create win-win alternatives out of what earlier appeared to be a win-lose problem. In contrast, the second approach takes the problem as given and creates a long list of alternative options, from which they can choose a particular option. In integrative negotiation over a complex problem, both approaches may be used and intertwined.

**Generating Alternative Solutions by Redefining the Problem or Problem Set.** The approaches in this category recommend that the parties specifically define their underlying needs and develop alternatives to successfully meet them. At least five different methods for achieving integrative agreements have been proposed (see Pruitt, 1981, 1983; Pruitt and Lewis, 1975; Neale and Bazerman, 1991; Pruitt and Carnevale, 1993). Each of these approaches not only successfully refocuses the issues under dispute, but also requires progressively more information about the other side's true needs and hence moves from simpler, distributive solutions to more complex, integrative ones. Each approach will be illustrated by the example of a husband and wife attempting to decide where to spend their two-week vacation. The husband wants to go to the mountains for the entire two weeks, whereas the wife wants to go to the seashore for the entire two weeks. A compromise solution—to spend a week at each place—is possible, but the husband and wife want to determine whether other solutions are possible.

*Expand the Pie.*     Many conflicts begin with a shortage of resources. Each party believes that it is not possible for both sides to satisfy their interest because the available resources are limited and both parties cannot obtain their objectives under the current allocation. The simple solution is to add resources in such a way that both sides can achieve their objectives. If the married couple could persuade their employers to give them four weeks for their vacation they would expand the pie. *Expanding the pie* requires no information about the other party other than her interests, and it is a simple way to solve resource shortage problems. In addition, the approach assumes that simply enlarging the resources will solve the problem. Thus, four weeks would be a very satisfactory solution if the husband and wife both liked the mountains and the beach but each preferred one or the other. However, expanding the pie would not be a satisfactory solution if their conflict were based on other grounds, if for example, the husband couldn't stand the beach or the wife wouldn't go to the mountains under any conditions.

*Logroll.*     Successful logrolling requires that the parties establish (or find) more than one issue in conflict; the parties then agree to "trade off" these issues so one party achieves a highly preferred outcome on the first issue and the other person achieves a highly preferred outcome on the second issue. If the parties do in fact have different preferences on different issues, each party gets their most preferred outcome on their high priority issue and should be happy with the overall agreement. Thus, suppose that the husband and wife not only disagree about where to take their vacation, but also about the kind of accommodations. The husband prefers informal housekeeping cabins whereas the wife prefers a luxury hotel. If the wife decides that the formality of the accommodations is more important to her than the location, they may be able to agree on a luxury hotel in the mountains as a way to meet both their needs.

Logrolling is frequently done by trial and error, as the parties experiment with various packages of offers that will satisfy both the other person and themselves. The parties must first establish which issues are at stake and then decide their individual priorities on these issues. If there are already at least two issues on the table, then any combination of two or more issues may be suitable for logrolling. If it appears initially that only one issue is at stake, the parties may need to engage in "unbundling" (Lax and Sebenius, 1986) or "unlinking" (Pruitt, 1981) of a single issue into two or more issues, which may then permit the logrolling process to begin. Additional issues of concern may also be generated through the brainstorming processes that will be described below.

*Use Nonspecific Compensation.* A third way to resolve the conflict is to allow one person to obtain his objectives and "pay off" the other person for accommodating his interests. This payoff may be unrelated to the substantive negotiation, but the party who receives it nevertheless views it as adequate for acceding to the other party's preferences. In the vacation example, the wife could tell the husband that if he agrees to go to the seashore, she will buy him a new camera or set of golf clubs. For nonspecific compensation to work, the person doing the compensating needs to know what is valuable to the person and how seriously the other is inconvenienced (i.e., how much "compensation" is needed to make the other feel satisfied). She might need to test several different offers (types and amounts of compensation) to find out how much it will take to satisfy the other. This discovery process can turn into a distributive bargaining situation itself, as the husband may choose to set very high demands as the price for going along to the beach while the wife tries to minimize the compensation she will pay.

*Cut the Costs for Compliance.* Through cost cutting, one party achieves her objectives and the other's costs are minimized if he agrees to go along. In the vacation example, suppose that the husband really likes a quiet and peaceful vacation and dislikes the beach because of the crowds, whereas the wife really likes the beach because of all the activity. If peace and quiet is what the husband really wants, then he may be willing to go to the beach if the wife assures him that they will stay in a secluded place at the beach that is located far away from the other resorts. Unlike nonspecific compensation, where the compensated party simply receives "something" for going along, cost-cutting tactics are specifically designed to minimize the other party's costs and suffering. The technique is thus more sophisticated than logrolling or nonspecific compensation because it requires a more intimate knowledge of the other party's real needs and preference (the party's interests, what really matters to him, how his needs can be more specifically met).

*Find a Bridge Solution.* Finally, by "bridging," the parties are able to invent new options that meet each side's needs. Thus, if the husband reveals that he really wants to hunt and fish on his vacation, whereas the wife wants to swim, go shopping, and enjoy the night life, they may be able to discover a resort area that will satisfy all these desires. Successful bridging requires a fundamental reformulation of the problem such that the parties are no longer squabbling over their positions; instead, they are disclosing sufficient information to discover their interests and needs and then inventing options that will satisfy both parties' needs. Bridging solutions do not always remedy all concerns; the wife may not get the salt sea air at the resort, and the husband may spend more money than he wanted to. But both have agreed that taking their vacation together is more desirable than taking it separately (i.e., they have committed themselves to interdependence) and have worked to invent a solution that meets their most important needs. If negotiators fundamentally commit themselves to a win-win negotiation, bridging solutions are likely to be highly satisfactory to both sides.

As we stated earlier, the successful pursuit of these five strategies requires a high-quality information exchange between the parties. This information must either be volunteered or the parties must ask each other questions that will generate sufficient information to reveal possible win-win options. Table 4.1 presents a series of refocusing questions (Pruitt and Rubin, 1986; Pruitt and Carnevale, 1993) that may reveal these possibilities.

**Generating Alternative Solutions to the Problem as Given.**    In addition to the techniques mentioned above, there are a number of alternative approaches to generating possible solutions. These approaches can be used by the two negotiators or, alternatively, by involving a number of other parties (e.g. constituencies, audiences, bystanders, etc.). Several of these approaches are commonly used in small groups to facilitate group problem solving. The success of these approaches relies on the principle that groups of people are frequently better problem solvers than single individuals, particularly because groups provide a wider number of perspectives on the problem and hence can invent a greater variety of ways to solve it. However, as we noted, groups must also observe the procedures for defining the problem, defining interests, and generating options that we have just identified or the group process will quickly degenerate into a win-lose competition.

***Brainstorming.***    Individuals are asked to work in small groups, generating as many possible solutions to the problem as they can. Someone records the solutions, without comment, as they are identified. Parties are urged to be spontaneous, even impractical, and not to censor any idea because they think it is unworkable or too expensive. Moreover, parties are required not to discuss or evaluate any solution as it is proposed, since discussion and evaluation will criticize ideas and stop the free flow of new ideas. The success of the brainstorming approach depends upon the free flow of ideas and the intellectual stimulation that should occur as these ideas are tossed around. Therefore, successful brainstorming and group generation and discussion of alternatives requires that the following rules be observed:

1. Avoid judging or evaluating solutions. As we stated earlier, criticism inhibits creative thinking. In addition, some of the most creative solutions come from ideas that initially seemed wild and impractical. Parties should

**TABLE 4.1**   Refocusing Questions to Reveal Win-Win Options

---

*Expanding the Pie*

---

1. How can both parties get what they are demanding?
2. Is there a resource shortage?
3. How can resources be expanded to meet the demands of both sides?

---

*Logrolling*

---

1. What issues are of higher and lower priority to me?
2. What issues are of higher and lower priority to the other?
3. Are issues of high priority to me low for the other, and vice versa?
4. Can I "unbundle" an issue—i.e. make one larger issue into two or more smaller ones—that can then be logrolled?
5. What are things that would be inexpensive for me to give and valuable for the other to get that might be used in logrolling?

---

*Nonspecific Compensation*

---

1. What are the other party's goals and values?
2. What could I do for the other side that would make them happy and have them allow me to get my way on the key issue?
3. What are things that would be inexpensive for me to give and valuable for the other to get that might be used as nonspecific compensation?

---

*Cost Cutting*

---

1. What risks and costs does my proposal create for the other?
2. What can I do to minimize the other's risks and costs so that they would be more willing to go along?

---

*Bridging*

---

1. What are the other's real underlying interests and needs?
2. What are my own real underlying interests and needs?
3. What are the higher and lower priorities for each of us in our underlying interests and needs?
4. Can we invent a solution that meets both sides' relative priorities and their underlying interests and needs?

---

impose a clear rule that no idea will be evaluated or ruled out until the group is finished generating options.

2. "Separate the people from the problem." Fisher, Ury, and Patton (1991) and several other authors (e.g., Walton and McKersie, 1965; Filley, 1975) have noted that group discussion and brainstorming processes are often constrained because the parties take ownership of certain preferred solutions and alternatives. Since competitive negotiators assume an offensive posture toward the other negotiator, they are unlikely to see the merits of a

suggested alternative that appears to favor their opponent's position or that the opponent suggested. For effective problem solving to occur, negotiators must concentrate on attacking the problem and treat all possible solutions as equally viable, regardless of who initiated them. For example, if the parties try to depersonalize the suggestions by collectively listing them on a blackboard or flip charts, then they will be less likely to identify who originated any particular idea, and they will be in a better position to pick the solution that best solves the problem. Some other techniques for generating options may work better because they assure anonymity in suggesting ideas and minimize the likelihood that the interpersonal conflict will escalate.

3. Be exhaustive in the brainstorming process. Many times our best ideas come after a meeting is over or after a problem is solved. Sometimes, this happens because the parties were not persistent enough. Research has shown that when brainstormers work at the process for a long period of time, the best ideas are most likely to surface during the latter part of the activity. As Shea (1983) notes:

Generating a large number of superior ideas apparently increases the probability of developing superior ideas. Ideas, when expressed, tend to trigger other ideas. And since ideas can be built one upon the other, those that develop later in a session are often superior to those without refinement or elaboration. What difference does it make if a lot of impractical ideas are recorded? They can be evaluated and dismissed rapidly in the next step of the win-win process. The important thing is to ensure that few, if any, usable ideas are lost (p. 57).

4. Ask outsiders. Often, people who know nothing about the past history of the conflict, or even about the issues, can suggest options and possibilities that have not been considered. Outsiders can provide additional input to the list of alternatives, or they can help orchestrate the process and keep the parties on track.

*Nominal Groups.*    In the nominal group technique, negotiators must start with the problem as defined; each one then individually prepares a written list of possible solutions. Participants are encouraged to list as many solutions as they can. Then they meet in small groups and read their solutions aloud while a recorder writes them on flip charts or a blackboard. Particularly in a large group, this approach can generate a great number of possible options in a short period of time. These solutions can then be examined by all those working on the problem.

*Surveys.*    The disadvantage of nominal groups is that they usually do not solicit the ideas of those who are not present at the negotiation. In addition, the nominal group technique can be time consuming. A different approach is to distribute a written questionnaire to a large group of people, stating the problem and asking them to list all the possible solutions they can imagine. This process can be conducted in a very short period of time. The liability, however, is that the parties cannot benefit from seeing and hearing the other people's ideas, a key advantage of the nominal group technique.

**Summary.**   The two basic approaches to generating alternative solutions that we have discussed—generating options to the problem as given and generating options by redefining the problem—may give the impression that if bargainers simply invent enough different options, they will find a solution to solve their problem rather easily. Although identifying options sometimes leads to a solution, solutions are usually attained through hard work and pursuit of several related processes: information exchange, focusing on interests rather than positions, and firm flexibility (Fisher, Ury, and Patton, 1991; Pruitt, 1983). Information exchange will allow the parties to maximize the amount of information available. Focusing on interests will allow the parties to move beyond opening positions and demands to determine what the parties *really* want, what needs truly *must* be satisfied. Finally, firm flexibility means that the parties must be firm with regard to the ends they want to achieve (i.e., interests), while remaining flexible on the means by which they are achieved. Firm flexibility recognizes that negotiators have one or two fundamental interests or principles that must be achieved, although a wide variety of positions, possible solutions, or secondary issues may get drawn into the negotiations. Thus, although many viable alternative solutions will satisfy a negotiator, some are more important because they directly address the bottom line or most important priorities. Negotiators need to be able to signal to the other side the positions on which they are firm and the positions on which they are willing to be flexible. Pruitt (1983) and Fisher, Ury, and Patton (1991) suggest several tactics to communicate firm flexibility to an opponent:

1. Use contentious (competitive) tactics to defend and establish basic interests, rather than using them to demand a particular position or solution to the dispute. State what you want clearly.

2. At the same time, send signals of flexibility and concern about your willingness to address the other party's interests. Openly express concern for the other's welfare, and "acknowledge their interests as part of the problem" (Fisher and Ury, 1981, p. 55). In doing so, you communicate that you have your own interests at stake but are willing to try to address the other's as well.

3. Indicate a willingness to change your proposals if a way can be found to bridge the two parties' interests.

4. Demonstrate a problem-solving capacity. For example, use experts on a negotiating team or bring them in as consultants based on their expertise at generating new ideas.

5. Maintain open communication channels. Do not eliminate opportunities to communicate and work together, if only to demonstrate continually that you are willing to work with the other party.

6. Reaffirm what is most important to you through the use of deterrent statements—for example, "I need to attain this; this is a must; this cannot be touched or changed." These statements communicate to the other that a particular interest is fundamental to your position, but it does not necessarily mean that the other's interests can't be satisfied as well.

7. Reexamine any aspects of your interests that are clearly unacceptable to the other party and determine if they are still essential to your fundamental position. It is rare that negotiators will find that they truly disagree on basic interests.

8. Separate and isolate contentious tactics from problem-solving behavior to better manage the contentious behavior. This may be accomplished by clearly specifying a change in the negotiation process, by separating the two processes with a break or recess, or, in team negotiations, by having one party act contentiously and then having a second negotiator offer to engage in problem solving. This last approach is called a "good guy/bad guy" or "black hat/white hat" act and is also frequently used as a purely distributive bargaining tactic, as we discussed in Chapter 3. In this situation, however, we separate the competitive from the collaborative elements of the process by changing the individuals who represent those positions.

### Evaluation and Selection of Alternatives

The fourth stage in the integrative negotiation process is to evaluate the options generated during the previous phase and to select the best alternatives to implement them. When the problem is a reasonably simple one, the evaluation and selection steps may be effectively combined into a single step. When confronted with complex problems or a large number of alternative options, however, the evaluation stage may take considerably longer. Negotiators will need to determine criteria for judging the options and then rank order or weigh each option against the criteria. Finally, the parties will be required to engage in some form of decision-making process, in which they debate the relative merits of each side's preferred options and come to agreement on the best options. The following guidelines should be used in evaluating options and reaching a consensus (Filley, 1975; Pruitt and Carnevale, 1993; Shea, 1983; Walton and McKersie, 1965).

**Narrow the Range of Solution Options.**    Examine the list of options generated and focus on the options that are strongly supported by any negotiator. This approach is more positive than allowing people to focus on negative, unacceptable criteria and options. Solutions not strongly advocated by at least one negotiator should be eliminated.

**Evaluate Solutions on the Basis of Quality and Acceptability.**    Solutions should be judged on two major criteria: how good they are, and how acceptable will they be to those who have to implement them. These are the same two dimensions that research has revealed to be critical in effective participative decision making in organizations (Vroom and Yetton, 1973). Negotiators will evaluate the quality dimension by determining what is best, what is most rational, what is most logical. To the degree that parties can support their arguments with statements of hard fact, logical deduction, and appeals to rational criteria, their arguments will be more compelling in obtaining the support of others. Fisher, Ury, and Patton

(1991) suggest that the parties "appeal to objective standards" for making decisions. This suggests that the parties are more likely to accept a solution they perceive as fair and equitable to all concerned. Thus, the parties should search for past decisions, precedents, arbitration decisions, or other objectively fair outcomes and processes that can be used as benchmarks for legitimizing the fairness of the current settlement. These criteria may be different from what the negotiators judge to be most rational or the best solution. When a specific solution must meet the criteria of both quality and acceptability (fairness), those evaluating the solution options may have to be prepared to make trade-offs between the two to insure that both criteria are met.

**Agree to the Criteria in Advance of Evaluating Options.** Fisher, Ury, and Patton (1991) exhort negotiators to "insist on using objective criteria"—that is, to develop standards for deciding what is fair, correct, or "the right thing to do" in the situation. Groups often follow this process when they have to narrow the choice down to a single alternative—for example, to pick a candidate for a new job—or to select the option most likely to succeed. If the parties first debate their criteria and determine which ones are most important, they will be able to decide on criteria independent of the consideration of any particular candidate or option. Then, when they consider the individual candidates or options, they will pick the best one based on these criteria, not on the individual preferences of one side or the other. If the parties agree, they may revise their criteria later to improve their choice, but this should only be done by the agreement of all negotiators. In fact, it is not a bad idea to check criteria periodically and determine whether each negotiator places the same priority on them as before. Discussion of alternatives frequently leads negotiators to revise their preferences, as well as their estimates of the probability of success and the cost of particular options.

**Be Willing to Justify Personal Preferences.** Why someone likes what he likes, or dislikes what he dislikes, is often hard to publicly justify. "Why do you like that?" "I don't know, I just do," is usually the reply. Moreover, negotiators gain little by requiring opponents to justify themselves—that usually just makes them angry and defensive, that a simple statement of preference is not viewed as sufficient. For example, if the topic under negotiation is what to have for dinner, and one party states that she hates clam chowder, no amount of persuasive effort is likely to change that person's opinion of clam chowder. Instead, the parties would be more productive if they accepted this information and attempted to explore other options for dinner. Yet what we prefer often has a deeper seated rationale—as we pointed out how interests, values, and needs often underlie positions. Thus, inquiries from the other party about "why" we prefer what we want *may* be an effort to probe behind a position and identify underlying interests and needs. So when others ask us "why" questions, they may elicit a little defensiveness; but the questioner should explain that the intent is to probe for possible underlying interests that might facilitate a collaborative settlement, rather than to produce defensiveness.

**Be Alert to the Influence of Intangibles in Selecting Options.**    One side may favor some options because they help that negotiator satisfy some intangible—gaining recognition, looking strong or tough to a constituency, feeling like he has won, and so on. As we pointed out, intangibles or principles can serve as strong interests for a negotiator. Intangibles can lead the negotiator to fight harder to attain a particular solution option if that option satisfies both tangibles and intangibles. Help the other party identify those intangibles and make them public as part of the evaluation process; the other party is likely to prefer options that satisfy those intangibles, and to the degree that you can live with them, agreeing to those options may be important concessions.

**Use Subgroups to Evaluate Complex Options.**    Small groups may be particularly helpful when many complex options must be considered or when many people will be affected by the solution. Groups of six to eight people, composed of representatives from each faction, side, or subgroup, will be able to work more effectively than a large group. (See our earlier discussion of nominal groups for deciding on options.)

**Take Time Out to Cool Off.**    Even though the parties may have completed the hardest part of the process—generating a list of viable options—they may become upset if communication breaks down, they feel their preferences are not being acknowledged, or the other side pushes too hard for a particular option. If the parties become angry, take a break. Negotiators should make their dissatisfaction known and openly discuss the reasons for it. Make sure the parties are back on an even emotional keel before continuing to evaluate the options. Finally, work as hard as possible to keep discussions on the specifics of the proposals, not on the people advocating them. Keep the people advocating a point of view separate from the options for settlement, and depersonalize the discussion as much as possible.

**Explore Different Ways to Logroll.**    Earlier, we discussed a variety of ways to invent options. Logrolling as a strategy is effective not only in inventing options, but also as a mechanism to combine options into negotiated packages. In addition to simply combining several issues into a package, Neale and Bazerman (1991) point out several additional ways to logroll.

*Exploit Differences in Risk Preference.*    Suppose two business partners are discussing a future business venture. One has little to risk at the moment and everything to gain from the future; the other has a lot on the line now that he does not want to risk losing if the future is bad. If they simply agree to split profits in the future, the one with a large amount of current risk may feel very vulnerable. Logrolling around these interests can create a solution that protects one partner's current investment first and provides more long-term profits for the other partner.

*Exploit Differences in Expectations.*    In the same example, the person with a lot to lose may also have pessimistic expectations about the future of the joint venture, whereas the person with little to lose may be more optimistic about it.

The optimist may thus be willing to gamble more on the future profitability and payout, whereas the pessimist is willing to settle for a smaller but more assured payment. Like differences in risk, simple differences in expectations about what will happen can permit the parties to invent a solution that addresses the needs of both parties.

*Exploit Differences in Time Preferences.*    Negotiators may have different time preferences—one may be more concerned about meeting short-term needs, whereas the other may be more interested in the long-term rewards of their relationship. Parties with short-term interests will need immediate gratification, whereas parties who look for long-term rewards may be willing to make short-term sacrifices to assure the long-term payoff. Parties with different preferences can invent solutions that address both the short-term and long-term interests.

**Keep Decisions Tentative and Conditional until all Aspects of the Final Proposal Are Complete.**    Even though a rather clear consensus may emerge about the solution option(s) that will be selected, the parties should talk about the solution in conditional terms. This tentative tone allows any side to change or revise the final package at any time. Points agreed upon in earlier discussion are not firm until the entire package is determined. Parties do not have to feel that because they gave up on an earlier option, they have burned their bridges behind them; rather, nothing is final until everything is final.

**Minimize Formality and Record Keeping until Final Agreements Are Closed.**    Parties usually do not want to lock themselves into any specific language or written agreement until they are close to a consensus. They want to make sure that they will not be held to comments made and recorded in notes or transcripts. In general, the fewer the transcripts, minutes, or written records during the solution-generating phase, the better. In contrast, when the parties are close to consensus, one side should write down what they have agreed to. This document may then be used as a "single text" (Fisher Ury, and Patton 1991), passed around from party to party as often as necessary until all sides agree to the phrasing and wording of their agreement.

## FACTORS THAT FACILITATE SUCCESSFUL INTEGRATIVE NEGOTIATION

We have stressed that successful integrative negotiation can occur if the parties are predisposed to find that mutually acceptable joint solution. Many other factors contribute to a predisposition toward problem solving and a willingness to work with the other toward finding the best solution. These factors are also the preconditions necessary for the integrative negotiation process (Pruitt, 1981, 1983; Filley, 1975). In this section, we will review in greater detail these factors: the presence of a common goal, faith in one's own problem-solving ability, a belief in the validity of the other's position, the motivation and commitment to work together, trust, and clear and accurate communication.

## Some Common Objective or Goal

When the parties believe that they are likely to benefit more from working together than from competing or working separately, the situation offers greater potential for successful integrative negotiation. Three types of goals may facilitate the development of integrative agreements:

1. *A common goal,* by which all parties share the result equally, each one benefiting in a way that would not be possible if they did not work together. A town government and an industrial manufacturing plant may debate one another over the amount of taxes owed by the plant, but they are more likely to work together if the common goal is to keep the plant open and employ half the town's work force.

2. *A shared goal,* by which the parties work toward a common end but benefit differently. For example, partners can work together in a business but not divide the profits equally. One may get a larger share of the profit because he contributed more experience or capital investment. Inherent in the idea of a shared goal is that parties will work together to achieve some output that will be shared. The same result can also come from cost cutting, by which the parties can earn the same outcome as before by working together, but with less effort, expense, or risk. This is often described as an "expandable pie" as contrasted to the assumption of a "fixed pie" (Chapter 6).

3. *A joint goal,* by which individuals with different personal goals agree to combine them in a collective effort. For example, people joining a political campaign can have different goals: one wants to satisfy personal ambition to hold public office, a second wants to "serve the community," and a third wants to benefit from policies that will be implemented under the new administration. All will unite around the joint goal of helping the new administration get elected.

The key element of an integrative negotiation situation is the belief that all sides can benefit. Whether each side attains the same outcome or they achieve different outcomes, all sides must believe that they will be better off by working in cooperation than by competing or working independently.

## Faith in One's Own Problem-Solving Ability

Parties who believe they can work together usually are able to do so. Those who do not share this belief in themselves (and others) are less willing to invest the time and energy in the potential payoffs of a collaborative relationship and more likely to assume a contending or accommodating approach to conflict. Expertise in the focal problem area strengthens the negotiator's understanding of all the problem's complexity, nuances, and possible solutions. Neale and Northcraft (1986) have demonstrated that "expert" negotiators in a real estate problem— corporate real estate executives—achieved significantly better integrative agreements than amateurs. Expertise increases both the knowledge base and the self-confidence necessary to approach this problem with an open mind. Similarly, direct experience in negotiation increases the negotiator's sophistication in understanding the bargaining process and approaching it more creatively (Thompson, 1990a).

### A Belief in the Validity of the Other's Position

In distributive bargaining, negotiators invest time and energy in inflating and justifying the value of their own positions and debunking the value and importance of the other's position. In contrast, integrative negotiation requires negotiators to accept the other's attitudes, information, and desires as accurate and valid (Fisher, Ury, and Patton, 1991). If you challenge the other party's views she may become angry, defensive, and hence unproductive in the problem-solving process. The purpose of integrative negotiation is not to question or challenge the other's viewpoint, but to incorporate it into the definition of the problem and to attend to it as the parties search for mutually acceptable alternatives. In addition, these views are to be given equal value to one's own position and viewpoint.

### The Motivation and Commitment to Work Together

For integrative negotiation to succeed, the parties must be motivated to collaborate rather than to compete. They need to be committed to a goal that benefits both of them rather than to pursuing only their own ends. Finally, they must be willing to adopt interpersonal styles that are more congenial than combative, more open and trusting than evasive and defensive, more flexible (but firm) than stubborn (but yielding). Needs have to be made explicit, similarities have to be identified, and differences have to be recognized and accepted. Uncertainties have to be tolerated and inconsistencies unraveled.

It might seem that for successful integrative negotiation to occur, each party should be as interested in the objectives and problems of the other as each is in his own—each must assume responsibility for the other's needs and outcomes as well as for her own. This is an incorrect interpretation; in fact, such a position is more likely to be dysfunctional. Parties who are deeply committed to each other and each other's welfare often do not work out the best solution (Kelley and Schenitzki, 1972; Fry, Firestone and Williams, 1979) for several reasons. First, as close as the parties may feel to one another, they still may not fully understand one another's needs, objectives, and concerns, and thus they can fall into the trap of not meeting the other's objectives while thinking that they are (Rubin and Brown, 1975). Further, parties strongly committed to each other are likely to yield more than they would otherwise; the result is that they may arrive at a joint outcome that is less satisfactory than if they had remained firm in pursuing their own objectives. Parties in negotiation maximize their outcomes when they assume a healthy, active self-interest in achieving their own outcomes, yet also recognize that they are in a collaborative, problem-solving relationship (Kelley and Schenitzki, 1972).

Motivation and commitment to problem solving can be enhanced in several ways:

- The parties can come to believe that they share a common fate; to quote Ben Franklin, "If we do not hang together, we will surely hang separately."
- The parties can demonstrate to one another that there is more to be gained by working together (to increase the payoffs or reduce the costs) than by working separately.
- The parties can emphasize that they may have to work together after the negotiations are over or recognize that they may be able to work together and continue to benefit from the relationship they have created.

In spite of these efforts, competitive and contentious behavior may persist. In Chapter 6, we will elaborate upon approaches that may be used to enhance the parties' predisposition toward cooperation and problem solving.

### Trust

Although there is no guarantee that trust will lead to collaboration, there is plenty of evidence to suggest that mistrust inhibits collaboration. People who are interdependent but who do not trust each other will act defensively. Defensiveness usually means that they will not accept information at face value, but instead look for hidden, deceptive meanings. When people are defensive, they withdraw and withhold information. Defensive people also attack their opponent's statements and position, seeking to defeat their position rather than to work together. Either of these responses is likely to make the negotiator hesitant, cautious, and distrustful of the other, undermining the negotiation process (Gibb, 1961).

Generating trust is a complex, uncertain process; it depends in part on how the parties behave and in part on the parties' personal characteristics. When people trust one another, they are more likely to communicate accurately their needs, positions, and the facts of the situation. In contrast, when people do not trust one another, they are more likely to engage in positional bargaining, use threats, and commit themselves to tough positions (Kimmel et al., 1980). As with defensiveness, this behavior is likely to be reciprocated and to lead to unproductive negotiations. To develop trust effectively, each negotiator must believe that both he and the other party choose to behave in a cooperative manner; moreover, each must believe that this behavior is a signal of the other's honesty, openness, and a similar mutual commitment to a joint solution.

Trust in itself is not sufficient to create good problem solving; it must be linked to several other behaviors on the part of both negotiators. The first is a firm commitment to one's own position. If a negotiator is trustworthy but very willing to yield his own position to the other in negotiations, the other party will be likely to take advantage of it. Although trust may exist, the negotiator's willingness to yield leads the opponent to take a tough, firm position. In contrast, if the other party is firmly committed to the position, the negotiator must work hard to find alternatives that will meet both parties' needs. Thus, good problem solving is likely to come from a combination of trust and firmness (Michener et al., 1975; Wall, 1977). The second key behavior is support in the solution-exploration process. A person brainstorming about ways to solve a problem will respond differently if met with ridicule or silence than if met with interest and respect. A person who finds her ideas accepted and developed by someone will be encouraged to continue.

A number of key factors contribute to the development of trust between negotiators. First, we are more likely to trust someone we perceive as similar to us or holding a positive attitude toward us. Second, we often trust people who are dependent upon us because we are in a position to help or hurt them (and they frequently can do the same to us) (Solomon, 1960). Third, we are more likely to trust people who initiate cooperative, trusting behavior. Acting in a cooperative, trusting manner serves as an invitation to others, especially if the invitation is repeated despite initially contentious behavior from the opponent (Bonoma et al., 1969; Gahagan et al., 1969; Gruder and Duslak, 1973; Heller, 1967; Kleinke and Pohlan, 1971). Finally, we are more likely to trust negotiators who make concessions. The more other people's behavior communicates that they are holding firm in their fundamental commitment to their own needs at the same time as they are working toward a joint solution, the more we are likely to find their conduct trustworthy, in the spirit of the best joint agreement (Rubin and Brown, 1975).

Given that trust has to be built during the negotiation, opening moves are crucial. The more cooperative, open, and nonthreatening the opening statements and actions of a party are, the more trust and cooperation is engendered in the other party (Crumbaugh and Evans, 1967; Michelini, 1971; Oskamp, 1970; Sermat and Gregovich, 1966). Once a cooperative position is established, it is more likely to persist. If cooperative behavior can be established at the very beginning, there is a tendency for parties to lock in to this cycle and make it continue (Pilisuk and Skolnick, 1978). Finally, these opening moves not only set the tone for the negotiation, but also begin the momentum of the negotiation. The longer the cycle of trust and cooperation continues, the easier it is to restore should the cycle break down (Komorita and Mechling, 1967; Sermat, 1967; Swinth, 1967).

### Clear and Accurate Communication

The next precondition for high-quality integrative negotiation is clear and accurate communication. First, negotiators must be willing to share information about themselves (Neale and Bazerman, 1991). They must be willing to tell what they want—and, more importantly, they must be willing to state why they want it in specific, concrete terms, avoiding generalities and ambiguities. Second, the opponents must understand the communication. At a minimum, they must understand the meaning we attach to our statements; hopefully, they also attach the same meaning to the facts that we do. Others at the negotiating table can frequently identify ambiguities and breakdowns in communication. If someone on a bargaining team makes a confusing statement, others can try to clarify it. When one person on the other side does not grasp a difficult point, someone else from the same side will often be able to find the words or illustrations to bring out the meaning. This understanding is the responsibility of both sides. The communicator must be willing to test whether the other side has received the message that was intended. Similarly, the listener must engage in "active listening," testing to make sure that what they received and understood is the message that the sender intended.

If multiple communication channels are available (i.e., opportunities for the two sides to communicate in ways other than formally across the negotiation table), they will provide alternative ways to clarify the formal communication or to get information through if the formal channels break down. Conversations over coffee breaks, separate meetings between chief negotiators outside the formal sessions, or "off the record" contacts between key subordinates are all alternatives to the formal channel.

When there are strong negative feelings or when one or more parties are inclined to dominate, negotiators may create formal procedures for communication. Under these circumstances, negotiators should follow a procedure that gives everyone a chance to speak. For example, the rules of most debates limit statements to five minutes, and similar rules are often adopted in contentious open meetings or public hearings. In addition, the parties may agree to stick to a previously agreed-upon agenda so everyone can be heard and their contributions can be noted. Other ways to insure effective communication processes in negotiation are covered extensively in Chapter 7. In addition, in Chapter 12, we will describe ways that third parties can help facilitate disabled communication processes.

### Summary

We identified six major factors that are fundamental preconditions for successful integrative negotiation: some form of shared or common goal, faith in one's own ability to solve problems, a belief in the validity and importance of the other's position, the motivation and commitment to work together, trust in the opposing negotiator, and the ability to accurately exchange information in spite of conflict conditions. If the parties are not able to successfully meet all these preconditions, they will need to resolve these problems as the integrative negotiation process evolves.

## WHY INTEGRATIVE NEGOTIATION IS DIFFICULT TO ACHIEVE

Integrative negotiation is the process of identifying a common, shared, or joint goal and developing a process to achieve it. It is meant to be a collaborative process in which the parties define their common problem and pursue strategies to solve it. Unfortunately, negotiators do not always perceive situations as having integrative potential, or they are unable to sustain a productive integrative discussion. People frequently view conflict-laden situations (such as the example of escaping the fire at the beginning of this chapter) with a fundamentally more distrustful, win-lose attitude than is necessary or desirable. The approach that individuals take toward conflict and negotiation is essential to understanding the differences between distributive bargaining and integrative negotiation. We have stated that the primary reason negotiators do not pursue integrative agreements is that they fail to perceive a situation as having integrative potential and are primarily motivated to achieve outcomes that satisfy only their own needs. Three additional factors contribute to this difficulty: the history of the relationship between the parties, the tendency toward black-and-white thinking, and the mixed-motive nature of most bargaining situations.

### The History of the Relationship Between the Parties

The more competitive and conflict-laden their past relationship, the more negotiators are likely to approach the current negotiation with a defensive, win-lose attitude. Parties in this situation are unlikely to trust their opponents or to believe that a cooperative gesture is not some ruse or set-up for future exploitation. Since their opponent has never shown any genuine interest in cooperation in the past, why should the present be any different? Even if the parties have no past history with one another, the *expectation* of a competitive opponent is sufficient to create defensiveness. Research suggests that the majority of people enter negotiations expecting them to be win-lose, not win-win (Thompson and Hastie, 1990a). Although these perceptions are often loaded with self-serving rationalizations—negotiators expect competition from their opponents to justify their own strategies—the perceptions nevertheless deter them from initiating an integrative negotiation process.

### A Belief that an Issue Can Only Be Resolved Distributively

We have implied several times that conflict dynamics tend to lead negotiators to polarize issues or see them only in win-lose terms. In addition, negotiators may be prone to a number of cognitive biases or heuristic decision rules (Neale and Bazerman, 1985; 1991) that systematically allow them to bias their perception of the situation, the range of possible outcomes, and the likelihood of achieving possible outcomes, all of which tend to preclude negotiators from engaging in the behaviors necessary for integrative negotiation. We will extensively describe these biases in Chapter 6. For example, unions and management have historically clashed over the introduction of new technology that replaces workers with machines. Labor usually upholds job security, believing that the new machines will eliminate workers, whereas management takes the position that the new machines will increase efficiency, quality, and profit, and that it is management's right to make decisions regarding these issues. On the surface, the two positions seem irreconcilable: either the workers make the decisions to keep employees at the expense of machines, or management makes the decisions about how to introduce new technology. However, analysis of actual cases reveals that labor and management have devised a number of ways to solve the problem to both sides' satisfaction—such as retraining and reallocating employees, and reducing employees through attrition rather than layoff.

### The Mixed-Motive Nature of Most Negotiating Situations

Purely integrative or purely distributive negotiation situations are rare. Most situations are mixed-motive, containing some elements that require distributive bargaining processes, and others that require integrative negotiation. For example, when people become partners in a business, the common goal of making profit provides a basis for their collaboration. How to allocate the profits becomes a different matter, however, and is much more likely to create conflict. In this example, the parties must recognize that the integrative element is more important, that is, there must be a business before there can be profits to divide. Nevertheless, their competitiveness over profit distribution may make it hard for them to stay in business at all. As a general rule, conflict and competitiveness drive out cooperation and trust, making it more difficult for the parties to find common ground.

In summary, one of the most fundamental problems in integrative negotiation is that negotiation parties fail to recognize (or search for) the integrative potential in a negotiating problem. The primary cause of this failure is the negotiator's approach to conflict, motivated by the desire to satisfy her own concerns without regard to the other's concerns. Negotiators may also be led to this assumption when they are accountable to someone else for their performance, when the parties have had a conflictive history, and when the issues are too complex to disentangle and are interpreted more easily in simple win-lose terms. As a result, negotiators fail to invest the time and energy necessary to search for and find integrative options.

### SUMMARY

In this chapter, we have reviewed the strategy and tactics of integrative negotiation. The fundamental structure of integrative negotiation is that the parties are able to define goals that allow both sides to achieve their objectives. Integrative negotiation is the process of defining these goals and engaging in a set of procedures that permits both sides to maximize their objectives.

The chapter began with a discussion of a model of conflict management. This model allows us to describe differences in individual approaches to conflict according to the degree of concern an individual shows for attaining his own outcomes, helping the other party attain her outcomes, or both. It also shows that a collaborative, problem-solving approach is best represented by a high level of concern for both sides achieving their own objectives. Negotiators frequently fail at integrative negotiation because they fail to perceive the integrative potential of the negotiating problem. However, breakdowns also occur due to distributive assumptions about the negotiating problem, the mixed-motive nature of the issues, or the negotiators' previous relationship with one another.

Successful integrative negotiation requires several preconditions. First, the parties must be able to understand each other's true needs and objectives. Second, they must be able to create a free flow of information and an open exchange of ideas. Third, they should attempt to focus on their similarities, emphasizing their commonalities rather than their differences. Finally, they should engage in a search for solutions that meet the goals of both sides. This is a very different process from distributive bargaining, described in Chapter 3.

For this integrative negotiating process to occur successfully, several preconditions are necessary. First, the process will be greatly facilitated by some form of common goal or objective. This goal may be one that the parties both want to achieve, one they want to share, or one they could not possibly attain unless they worked together. Second, they must share a motivation and commitment to work together, to make their relationship a productive one. Third, the parties must be willing to believe that the other's needs are valid. Fourth, they must be able to trust one another and to work hard to establish and maintain that trust. Finally, there must be clear and accurate communication about what each one wants and an effort to understand the other's needs. Instead of talking the other out of his needs or failing to acknowledge them as important, negotiators must be willing to work for both their own needs and the other's needs to find the best joint arrangement. Given these preconditions, the integrative negotiating process is most likely to be successful.

The three major stages in the integrative negotiation process are problem identification, generating solutions, and choosing a specific solution. For each of these stages, we proposed a number of techniques and tactics to make the process successful. In spite of all of these suggestions, the process is not as easy as it seems for parties who are locked in conflict, defensiveness, and a hard-line position. Only by working to create the necessary conditions for integrative negotiation can the process occur with relative ease and success. In Chapters 6 and 12 we will discuss a number of ways that parties can defuse hostility, defensiveness, and the disposition toward hard-line negotiating to create the conditions for successful integrative negotiation.

# CHAPTER 5
# Negotiation Planning and Strategy

In this chapter, we discuss what negotiations should do before actually starting to bargain. Effective planning, preparation, and strategizing are the most critical precursors for achieving negotiation objectives. With effective planning and goal setting, most negotiators can achieve their objectives; without it, results occur more by chance than by negotiator effort. We begin with a brief, general overview of the strategy process. Those seeking more extensive coverage of business strategy and strategic planning should refer to one of the many available books on this topic (e.g., Ansoff, 1984; Fahey, 1989; Mintzberg and Quinn, 1991).

## STRATEGY: AN OVERVIEW

The word *strategy* comes from the Greek term for the art and activity of the military general and includes the attributes of vision, preparation, responsibility, and oversight. *Strategy* has been defined in many ways. Mintzberg and Quinn (1991) define strategy as "the pattern or plan that integrates an organization's major goals, policies, and action sequences into a cohesive whole" and state that "a well-formulated strategy helps to marshal and allocate an organization's resources into a unique and viable posture based on its relevant internal competencies and shortcomings, anticipated changes in the environment, and contingent moves by intelligent opponents" (p. 5). In *The Strategy of Conflict* (1960), Schelling states that strategy "is not concerned with the *application* of force, but with the *exploitation of potential force*" (p. 5; italics in the original).

Another definition of strategy, particularly useful for its applications to negotiation, comes from game theory (see Chapter 2). In game theoretic terms, a strategy is "a complete plan: a plan which specifies what choices (a game player) will make in every possible situation" (von Neumann and Morgenstern, 1944, p. 79). This definition presupposes that all players have *complete and perfect information* (i.e., everyone knows everything). Recognizing that these conditions occur rarely (if ever) in human behavior, a more pragmatic theory of games departs from the classical model to identify four elements typical to "real world" strategy formulation: *choice, chance, interdependence,* and *imperfect information* (McDonald, 1963). These conditions set the boundaries for a more accurate definition of the strategy processes that occurs in negotiation. For example, most definitions of negotiation characterize it as voluntary—a matter of *choice* (see Chapter 1).

Negotiation outcomes are rarely completely predictable, but are subject instead to the interplay of needs, interests, powers, skills, and applications between negotiators—the "play of the game"—the results of which are often a matter of *chance*. Many different motives usually affect the decision to enter this interplay; the entry itself recognizes, clarifies, and sometimes reinforces the *interdependence* between the parties (see Chapter 2). Finally, although each side in a negotiation may know its own interests, needs, strengths, and weaknesses, knowledge of these areas for the other side is usually *imperfect and incomplete* (as we will explain later in this chapter), and may or may not improve as the negotiation unfolds.

### Strategy, Tactics, and Planning

How are strategy and tactics related? Although the line between strategy and tactics may seem indistinct, one major difference is that of scale, perspective, or immediacy (see Quinn, 1991). Tactics are short-term, adaptive moves designed to enact or pursue broader (or higher level) strategies, which in turn provide stability, continuity, and direction for tactical behaviors. For example, one's negotiation *strategy* might be an integrative one, designed to build and maintain a productive relationship with another party while approaching issues with a joint problem-solving approach. In pursuing this strategy, appropriate tactics include building the other's trust in you based on your reliable, predictable behavior and conducting open communications by using open-ended questions and active listening. Tactics, then, are subordinate to strategy; they are structured, directed, and driven by strategic considerations.

How is strategy related to planning? Planning is an integral part of the strategy process—the "action" component, if you will. Using the example in the previous paragraph, *planning* encompasses the considerations and choices one makes about tactics, resource use, and contingent responses in pursuit of the overall *strategy*—how a party plans to proceed, to use what they have to get what they want, subject to their strategic guidelines.

### Types of Strategy

Strategies vary on a number of different dimensions. We will discuss four here: voluntariness, structure, informational locus, and opportunism.

**Voluntariness.**    A *voluntary* strategy is based on choice: what to pursue, how to pursue it, or even whether to have a strategy at all (see opportunism, below). Alternatively, a strategy may be *imposed* on the parties, who are charged with pursuing it by their superiors or by external forces, such as regulatory agencies. One example of an imposed strategy would be a public agency's strategic hiring plan, based on a court- or agency-imposed consent order, to recruit and retain specific numbers of minority applicants to correct a racial imbalance within its work force. Voluntary and imposed strategies differ primarily in the amount of involvement or discretion the directed party has in designing, pursuing, or amending the strategy.

**Structure.**    Strategies also may be more or less *structured.* When structure levels differ, the tradeoff is between control and adaptation. Highly structured strategies provide firm guidelines, controls, and a sense of direction and certainty; close adherence to such strategies, however, may prevent negotiators from responding and adapting to new information and opportunities that were unknown or undervalued when the original strategy was formulated. Still, a reasonable amount of structure helps to focus the strategy process; too little structure fails to provide the control necessary to guide decisions and direct the application of scarce resources. The dangers here, then, involve the extremes of too much structure or too little.

**Informational Locus.**    In many negotiations, strategy is based on incomplete or ambiguous information. Strategies prepared before negotiations begin are often *unilateral* or one-sided in that they reflect a certainty about one's own strategy, but only an educated guess (if that) about the other party's strategy. Improved information may emerge as the negotiation proceeds, making strategic corrections or adaptations advisable and possible. Changes may occur once the other party's interests and strategy are communicated or inferred, and the original strategy's *informational* locus changes from unilateral to *bilateral,* or two-sided (see, though, our discussion of Kelley's [1959] dilemmas of trust, honesty, and openness in Chapters 2 and 13). Negotiators who are able to adapt their intended strategies early in a negotiation appear to achieve better outcomes as a result (Thompson and Hastie, 1990a).

**Opportunism.**    For many, the essence of strategy is the definition and pursuit of a specific goal, or plan of action. However, *not* having a strategy is itself a form of strategy. When done intentionally, this may be called an *opportunistic,* adaptive, or emergent approach (Mintzberg, 1991), and it enables negotiators to evaluate and exploit opportunities as they recognize them. Some researchers suggest that these adaptive strategies are necessary for negotiation success (see Savage, Blair, and Sorenson [1989] for an excellent description of this). However, once again, extreme forms of this strategy can be dangerous. Too little responsiveness to changing information and situations may bind negotiators to strategies that no longer work. Total opportunism (i.e., the absence of prenegotiation direction) raises the question, "if you don't know where you're going, how will you know when you get there?" Either extreme is, at best, a risky basis for a negotiation strategy. However, the strategy of not having a strategy occurs unintentionally more often than not; there is no strategy because the responsible people neglected to formulate one. In our view, this is a recipe for negotiation disaster, insofar as those parties who are even marginally prepared will tend to be more successful than those who are unprepared.

### Plan, Ploy, Pattern, Position, or Perspective?

Using the "Five Ps" developed by Mintzberg (1991), strategy can be defined functionally as a plan, a ploy, a pattern, a position, or a perspective. Each of these labels is a valid descriptor for the broader term *strategy* at various times and for various parties engaged in, or observing, the negotiation.

**Strategy as Structure or Intent.** The first three of these terms involve aspects of strategy as *structure,* or intended action—that is, strategy conceived in advance of the actual actions to be taken.

*Plan.* Perhaps the most familiar enactment of strategy is as a *plan,* or a consciously intended course of action; the measures discussed in the previous section of this chapter fit that perspective. There are two central characteristics of a strategy as a plan: preparation in advance of the actions to which they will apply, and purposeful (i.e., goal-directed) development. Later in this chapter, we will employ this perspective on negotiation strategy, detailing what negotiators need to do to effectively plan for upcoming deliberations.

*Ploy.* Strategies can be general or specific. One way that a strategy can be specific is as a *ploy,* that is, as an intentional effort to maneuver, manipulate, or mislead another party. Because they have a specific objective, ploys tend to focus more on specific tactics than broader strategic questions. In Chapter 3, we described a number of the tactical ploys that negotiators use in distributive bargaining.

*Pattern.* Strategy may also be defined as a *pattern,* as in being able to detect some pattern of similarity in strategic action, behavior, or direction (Mintzberg and Waters, 1985). Patterns have more to do with strategy as it is actually *realized* or achieved than as it is *intended.* From this perspective, two things tend to happen: First, a pattern of behavior that was not intended to be strategic is inferred as a strategy, either when we or others look back on it. In negotiation, as in many other areas, hindsight tends to be "20/20"—that is, we think we see more than is really there. It is tempting (but often incorrect) to be able to say "we (or they) *intended* all along for things to turn out the way they did." This bias in hindsight leads us to seeing patterns in past behaviors or decisions that may not actually exist at the time the behavior was first performed. Second, because negotiation is interactive and perceptions of the others' actions are highly prone to bias and misinterpretation (see Chapter 6), it is rare that realized strategies are the same ones as those originally planned. When any particular pattern of behavior is intended, it also must be subject to revision and adaptation as the actual behavior sequence evolves. Depending on *intention* is strategically *proactive*—we plan and follow through—but if we adhere to our intentions too strictly, particularly when good cause tells us we should reexamine them, we may miss important opportunities to change and modify what we do. If we intend to follow a pattern of distributive bargaining and do not attend to cues from our opponent that they would like to negotiate integratively, we may miss opportunities for a win-win agreement and anger our opponent with our distributive tactics. Conversely, we may decide that we will choose a strategy based on what emerges in the negotiation (being strategically *reactive* to the other party). This may be a smart thing to do if you have little or no reliable information about the other side or if you have sufficient options and resources to afford developing a strategy once negotiations commence and the other's interests and strategies become more apparent. But it may also create problems if the failure to plan in advance allows the other's strategy to dominate. Achieving a successful pattern entails maintaining a balance between the two extremes of complete intention and complete emergence.

**Strategy as Focus.**   The last two functional definitions of strategy address not the structure or intent of strategy, but the *focus* (i.e., strategies *about* what, as opposed to strategies *to do* what).

*Position.*   Strategy as *position* involves locating an organization or its negotiating interests within some larger context. *Position* here means an *outward* orientation: a niche or unique opportunity, a situation to be defended, or a situation from which to attack or expand. As we discussed in Chapter 3, positional bargaining (and its related defensive behaviors) are key elements of the distributive model. Whether a strategic position is pursued in negotiation (to achieve a financial target point or protect larger interests) or in the broader scope of organizational behavior (to achieve a particular market position on a product line) strategy as position is contextually defined and cannot be understood without examining the specific context in which it is taken.

*Perspective.*   Strategy as *perspective* requires an *inward* orientation; it establishes and defines the frames and values that help us interpret "the play of the game." Strategy as perspective involves perceiving and dealing with strategic interaction as it evolves; it is the way we make sense of the evolving exchanges between ourselves and other players. In this respect, strategy "is to the organization what personality is to the individual"; it is its "collective intuition about how the world works" (Mintzberg, 1991, p. 17). In the context of negotiation, distributive or integrative strategies may also be "perspectives," arising from basic competitive or cooperative orientations of the parties to each other and to achieving their objectives. We say more about these personal perspectives when we discuss individual differences in Chapter 11.

When taken together, these labels—plan, ploy, pattern, position, and perspective—begin to capture the broadest meaning of strategy. The concept of strategy in negotiation, to different parties, in different settings, and at different times, subsumes all these descriptions and labels.

## A Choice Model of Negotiation Strategy

Although the forgoing descriptions capture some of the richness of the strategy concept, they do not provide procedural advice or operational guidance. To address these concerns, we propose a model based on the choices parties face when preparing a negotiation strategy. A general model of the process of choice of negotiation strategy includes at least five elements (see Figure 5.1):

1. Driving factors.
2. Principles and standards.
3. The role of trust.
4. Assumptions about the episodic nature of the process.
5. Negotiation goals.

We begin our discussion of the model by focusing on some of the dimensions of choosing a negotiation strategy (the right side of Figure 5.1). Next, we discuss four key factors that influence strategy choice: principles and standards, trust, assumptions about the process, and negotiation goals. Finally, we describe the driving factors that impact on principles and standards.

**Negotiation Strategy Choices.**   Our focus here is on the *unilateral* choice of a strategy (see our earlier discussion of strategy as a plan, ploy, or pattern). In its strictest sense, a unilateral strategy could be wholly one-sided and intentionally ignorant of any information about the other negotiator. This is *not* our intended meaning. By unilateral, we mean making a choice without the active *involvement* of the other party. A reasonable effort to find out about the other party and to incorporate that information into the choice of a negotiation strategy is *always* useful. We will now discuss this information-gathering process in more detail.

In Chapter 1, we used a framework called the dual concerns model (Pruitt and Rubin, 1986) to describe the basic orientation that people take toward con-

**FIGURE 5.1**   A Model of Negotiation Strategy Choice

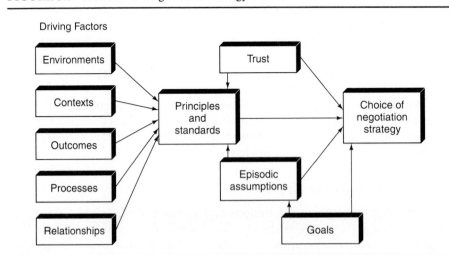

flict. This model proposes that individuals in conflict have two types of related concerns: a level of concern for their own outcomes, and a level of concern for the other's outcomes (refer back to Figure 1.3). Savage, Blair, and Sorenson (1989) propose a similar model for the choice of a negotiation strategy. According to this model, a negotiator's unilateral choice of strategy is reflected in the answers to two simple questions: how much concern does the actor have for achieving the *substantive* outcomes at stake in this negotiation, and how much concern does the negotiator have for the current and future quality of the *relationship* with the other party? The answers to these questions result in the mix of strategic alternatives presented in Figure 5.2.

***Situational Strategies.*** The power of this framework lies in requiring the negotiator to first determine the relative importance and priority of the two dimensions in the desired settlement. As Figure 5.2 shows, answers to these two simple questions suggest at least *four* types of initial strategies for negotiators: competition, collaboration, accommodation, and avoidance. A strong interest in achieving *only substantive outcomes*—getting *this* deal, winning *this* negotiation, with little or no regard for the effect on the relationship and subsequent exchanges with the other party—tends to support a competitive (distributive) strategy. A strong interest in achieving *only the relationship outcomes*—preserving or enhancing a good relationship with the opponent—suggests an accommodation strategy. If *both* substance and relationship are important, the negotiator should pursue a collaborative (integrative) strategy. Finally, if neither achieving substantive outcomes nor an enhanced relationship is important, the negotiator might be best to avoid negotiation. Each of these different strategic approaches also has different implications for negotiation planning and preparation (see also Johnston, 1982). We will briefly discuss avoidance and accommodation strategies below; competitive (distributive) and collaborative (integrative) strategies have been extensively addressed in Chapters 3 and 4.

*Avoidance* is by definition non-negotiation; however, it may serve a number

**FIGURE 5.2**    Choosing an Initial Negotiation Strategy

| | | Substantive outcome important? | |
|---|---|---|---|
| | | Yes | No |
| **Relational outcome important?** | **Yes** | Collaboration | Accommodation |
| | **No** | Competition | Avoidance |

Adapted from G.T. Savage, J.D. Blair, and R.J. Sorenson, "Consider Both Relationship and Substance When Negotiating Strategically," *Academy of Management Executive,* (vol. 3, 1989, pp. 37–48).

of strategic negotiation purposes. In fact, there are many reasons why potential negotiators might choose *not* to negotiate (similar to the reasons we mentioned for conflict avoidance in Chapter 1). First, if you are able to meet your needs without negotiating at all, it may make sense to use an avoidance strategy. Others in the negotiation may be willing to "cut you in" based on a simple request, or the relationship with the other may be so poor that it is not even worth asking for anything. Second, it simply may not be worth the time and effort to negotiate (although there *are* sometimes reasons to negotiate in such situations; see the section on accommodation below). Third, the decision to negotiate is closely related to the desirability of available alternatives or BATNA (Best Alternative to a Negotiated Agreement, Fisher, Ury, and Patton, 1991; see Chapter 3). Alternatives are a source of power in negotiation. A strong BATNA strengthens a negotiator's efforts—he doesn't need the negotiation to achieve at least a satisfactory outcome—but a weak BATNA (or no BATNA at all) puts negotiators at a strong disadvantage. Thus, the presence of an alternative can cut both ways in deciding whether to avoid negotiation. First, if you have a strong alternative, you may wish to avoid negotiation strictly on efficiency grounds—that is, it is simply quicker and easier to take the alternative than get involved in negotiation. But having a weak alternative may also suggest that you should avoid negotiation—once negotiations begin, the pressure of the negotiation process may lead you to a poor outcome, but you may feel obligated to accept it because your alternative is also very poor. Finally, avoidance may be appropriate when the negotiator is responsible for developing others (such as subordinates) into becoming better negotiators. Negotiating, like any other skill, is built by *doing* it. Although an active negotiation strategy may be called for, a negotiator may choose not to engage in it *personally,* but instead to turn it over to another individual who needs the exposure and experience. In such situations, though, it is usually appropriate to assist the novice negotiator in strategy preparation and to provide some level of advisory support as the negotiation unfolds.

   *Active-Engagement Strategies: Competition, Collaboration, and Accommodation.*    As noted above, the first two of these strategies have been extensively described in Chapters 3 and 4, respectively. Competition has been described as distributive or win-lose bargaining, and collaboration has been described as integrative or win-win negotiation. *Accommodation* is as much a win-lose strategy as competition, although it has a decidedly different image—it involves an imbalance of outcomes but in the opposite direction ("I lose, you win" as opposed to "I win, you lose"). As Figure 5.2 shows, an accommodative strategy may be appropriate when the relationship outcome is relatively more important to the strategizer than the substantive outcome. We want to let the other win, keep the other happy, or not endanger the relationship by pushing hard to achieve some goal on the substantive issues. This strategy is often used when the major goal of the exchange is to build or strengthen the relationship (or the opponent), and the negotiator is willing to make a major sacrifice on the outcome. An accommodative strategy may also be necessary if you envision that the negotiation relationship will extend past a single negotiation episode, so if "I lose and you win" this time, over multiple negotiations in the relationship the win-lose accounts will balance. In any long-term social exchange (see, for example, Homans, 1961), it is probably healthy for one negotiator or the other to accept a suboptimal outcome in the current negotiation in favor of expecting "tit-for-tat," reciprocal accommodation from the other negotiator in the future. Such reciprocity has, in fact, been called the glue that binds social groups together (e.g., Cialdini, 1993).

How do these three negotiation engagement strategies differ? Table 5.1 summarizes the three types of strategies (distributive, integrative, and accommodative), comparing and contrasting them across a number of different dimensions (adapted from Johnston, 1982).

In addition to the positive characteristics of these strategies, as described in the table, each of these three types of negotiations strategies, *if applied blindly, thoughtlessly, or inflexibly,* also has certain predictable drawbacks. Distributive strategies tend to create "we-they" or "superiority-inferiority" patterns, which often lead to distortions in judgment regarding the other side's contributions and efforts, and to distortions in perceptions of the other side's values, needs, and positions (see Chapter 6). Integrative strategies can also be problematic, if used blindly or exclusively. If the opponent believes that the negotiator is going to pursue a collaborative strategy without regard to the opponent's behavior, then the opponent can manipulate and exploit the collaborator and take advantage of the good faith and good will being demonstrated. Excessive integration can also lead negotiators to cease being accountable to their constituencies in favor of pursuit of the negotiation process for its own sake (see Chapter 9 for a discussion of negotiator-constituency dynamics). For example, negotiators who approach the process with an aggressive "we can solve it" attitude may produce an agreement that is unacceptable to the constituency (e.g., their companies). Finally, accommodative strategies also may have drawbacks. They may generate a pattern of constantly giving in to the opponent to keep them happy or avoid a fight. This pattern establishes a precedent that is hard to break. It could also lead to a false sense of well-being due to the satisfaction that comes with the "harmony" of a good relationship, which may completely ignore all the give-aways on substance.

It is also useful to remember that our description of these strategies represents *pure* forms, typically at odds with the mixture of issues and motivations that actually characterize the evolution of most negotiation strategies (Lax and Sebenius, 1986). Just as most conflicts are neither purely competitive or cooperative, neither are negotiation strategies. Actual strategies should reflect the mixture and diversity created by the driving factors and other components of the choice model (see Figure 5.1). As we pointed out when we discussed the "Ps" of strategy, negotiation strategy should be both intended and emergent; therefore, the pure strategic forms we just described will be modified both by our own specific needs and by the interactive dynamics that occur as the parties deliberate.

**Principles and Standards.**    The second major component in our model (see Figure 5.1) is *principles and standards.* These are the guidelines for desires and expectations about how the negotiation relationship will be established,

**TABLE 5.1**   Characteristics of Different Negotiation Engagement Strategies

| Aspect | Competition (Distributive Bargaining) | Collaboration (Integrative Negotiation) | Accommodative Negotiation |
|---|---|---|---|
| **Payoff Structure** | Usually a fixed amount of resources to be divided | Usually a variable amount of resources to be divided | Usually a fixed amount of resources to be divided |
| **Goal Pursuit** | Pursuit of own goals at the expense of those of others | Pursuit of goals held jointly with others | Subordination of own goals in favor of those of others |
| **Relationships** | Short-term focus; parties do not expect to work together in the future | Long-term focus; parties expect to work together in the future | May be short term (let the other win to keep them happy) or long term (let the other win to encourage reciprocity in the future) |
| **Primary Motivation** | Maximize own outcome | Maximize joint outcome | Maximize others' outcome or let them gain to enhance relationship |
| **Trust and Openness** | Secrecy and defensiveness; high trust in self, low trust in others | Trust and openness, active listening, joint exploration of alternatives | One party relatively open, exposing own vulnerabilities to the other |

| | | | |
|---|---|---|---|
| **Knowledge of Needs** | Parties know own needs, but conceal or misrepresent them; neither party lets the other know real needs | Parties know and convey real needs while seeking and responding to needs of the other | One party is over-responsive to other's needs so as to repress own needs |
| **Predictability** | Parties use unpredictability and surprise to confuse other side | Parties are predictable and flexible when appropriate, trying not to surprise | One party's actions totally predictable, always catering to other side |
| **Aggressiveness** | Parties use threats and bluffs, trying to keep the upper hand | Parties share information honestly, treat each other with understanding and respect | One party gives up on own position to mollify the other |
| **Solution Search Behavior** | Parties make effort to appear committed to position, using argumentation and manipulation of the other | Parties make effort to find mutually satisfying solutions, using logic, creativity, and constructiveness | One party makes effort to find ways to accommodate the other |
| **Success Measures** | Success enhanced by creating bad image of the other; increased levels of hostility and strong in-group loyalty | Success demands abandonment of bad images and consideration of ideas on their merit | Success determined by minimizing or avoiding conflict and soothing all hostility; own feelings ignored in favor of harmony |

**TABLE 5.1** *(continued)*

| Aspect | Competition (Distributive Bargaining) | Collaboration (Integrative Negotiation) | Accommodative Negotiation |
|---|---|---|---|
| **Evidence of Unhealthy Extreme** | Unhealthy extreme reached when one party assumes total zero-sum game; defeating the other becomes a goal in itself | Unhealthy extreme reached when one subsumes all self-interest in the common good, losing self-identity and self-responsibility | Unhealthy extreme reached when abdication to other is complete, at expense of personal and/or constituent goals |
| **Key Attitude** | Key attitude is "I win, you lose" | Key attitude is "What's the best way to address the needs of all parties?" | Key attitude is "You win, I lose" |
| **Remedy for Breakdown** | If impasse occurs, mediator or arbitrator may be needed | If difficulties occur, a group dynamics facilitator may be needed | If behavior becomes chronic, party becomes negotiationally bankrupt |

Adapted and expanded from Johnston, Robert W., "Negotiation Strategies: Different Strokes for Different Folks," *Personnel* (vol. 59, March–April 1982, pp. 38–39). Used with permission of the author.

conducted, and continued. Principles and standards have a major effect on the choice of negotiation strategy in that they help classify behaviors, procedures, and outcomes as acceptable or not. Examples of principles include these:

- A commitment to tell the truth and maintain integrity.

- A commitment to be polite and civil to each other (control our temper, respect each other's intelligence and capabilities).

- Beliefs about when competition or collaboration is appropriate to pursue.

- A belief that each side ought to "take care of itself" and not be concerned with how the other side is doing in the negotiation.

Principles help determine what approaches negotiators choose, avoid, or ignore; they are often personal values related to cooperation or competition and the way people "should" be treated. In contrast, standards help set boundaries for negotiation outcomes, processes, and behaviors by providing ways to choose among the various options that make up the broader, more basic personal principles. For example, negotiators frequently talk about "fairness" as a standard, using it either to decide what outcomes are fair or to decide what processes should be used to achieve those outcomes. Yet the real standards are the ways that "fairness" can be determined. For example, in distributing outcomes, the standard may be that everyone gets the same outcome (an equality standard), that people should get different outcomes if they work harder or contribute more (an equity standard), or that outcomes should be based on what people "need" (a need standard). (See Sheppard, Lewicki, and Minton, 1992, for a comprehensive discussion of fairness standards and Chapter 13 of this book for a discussion of fairness in negotiation.) "Objective" standards may also be used to decide how to divide or allocate outcomes (see Fisher, Ury, and Patton, 1991), but deciding on which "objective" standard will be used or how it will be applied can also be a critical part of the negotiation itself.

**Negotiation Goals.**    As shown in Figure 5.1, negotiators must anticipate the major events that are likely to occur during negotiation and prepare for these events in advance. This preparation must include attention to substantive items such as *goals, priorities,* and *multigoal packages,* as well as to procedural concerns dealing with *agendas* and *bargaining histories.* Effective preparation requires a thorough, thoughtful approach to these items; negotiators should specify their goals and objectives clearly. This includes stating all the goals that are to be achieved in the negotiation, determining their priority, identifying potential multigoal packages, and evaluating the possible tradeoffs among them. Goals may also include intangibles (see Chapter 1) such as maintaining a certain precedent or getting an agreement that is satisfactory to both sides.

Negotiation goals also have a major effect on the choice of negotiation strategy (see Figure 5.1). This effect occurs both directly and indirectly[1] (through "episodic assumptions"). We will address each of these effects in turn.

*Direct Effects of Goals on Choice of Strategy.*     When entering a bargaining relationship, we all have some idea of what we would like the outcome to be. We often say, "I'd be happy if . . ." and then state something we would really like to have; for example, ". . . I could buy this car at a price that wouldn't require all of my paycheck as the loan payment." Not bad as a *wish,* but not too good as a goal for negotiation. Four aspects of the impact of goals on negotiation are important to understand. First, *wishes are not goals,* especially in negotiation. Wishes may be closer to interests or needs that motivate goals (see Chapter 4), but they are not goals themselves. Second, *our goals are linked to the other's goals;* the linkage between the two parties' goals defines an *issue* to be settled (see below). My goal is to get the car cheaply, the dealer's goal is to sell it at the highest price, and thus the "issue" is the price I will pay for the car. Third, *there are boundaries or limits to what our goals can be* (see below). If what we want exceeds these limits (i.e., what the other party is capable of or willing to give), we must either change our goals or end the negotiation—goals must be reasonably attainable. If my goal— "to buy this car at a cheap price"—isn't possible because the dealer won't sell the car that cheaply, I'm going to either change my goal or find a cheaper car to buy. Fourth, *effective goals must be concrete or specific,* and preferably *measurable.* The less concrete and measurable they are, the harder it is to communicate to the other party what we want, to understand what she wants, and to determine whether any particular outcome satisfies our goals. To want "a price on a car so that the loan payment does not use all of my paycheck" is not very clear. Are we talking about every week's paycheck, or only one check a month? Do we mean 100 percent of a paycheck, or about 50 percent, or perhaps even 25 percent? Today's paycheck, or the ones we expect to receive over the life of the loan? We can't negotiate well by talking about portions of paychecks. Instead we have to determine exactly how much money we can comfortably take from our paychecks at present interest rates, add to that what we have available for a down payment, and thus be able to talk in terms of what we actually will pay every week or month. Even this figure is not totally clear. Is this number the largest amount we think we can possibly pay? Is it the amount we could pay with little or no inconvenience? Or is it the amount we arrived at after recalling that one shouldn't pay more than a stated amount (say 15 percent) of one's monthly salary for a car payment? (These goals can also be the same if we are expecting a more integrative negotiation for the car.)

The goals we just outlined are all quite tangible, and they directly address the questions of the purchase price and our cash flow. No less important are the many

---

[1] In referring to Figure 5.1, we will describe a *direct* effect as a relationship between two boxes, represented by an arrow from one box in the figure directly to another. An *indirect* effect will be described by arrows that pass through another box to get to the specified target. Thus, goals have a direct effect on strategic choice, but they can also have an indirect effect because goals can be modified by episodic assumptions before they impact the choice of a negotiation strategy.

*intangible* goals that typically accompany tangible goals in any negotiation. In the example of the car purchase, intangible goals might include enhancing my reputation with my friends from owning and driving an expensive, powerful car, or maintaining my friends' image of me as a shrewd, penny-wise negotiator. In other negotiations, intangible goals might include maintaining my reputation as a tough, but principled negotiator, or establishing a precedent for future negotiations (refer back to Chapters 1 and 2 for more discussion of intangible goals).

Which of these many criteria should we use? The answer is that *all* are probably important, for different reasons, and defining them is essential to effective planning.

***Indirect Effects of Goals on Choice of Strategy.***    Some goals (often the most simple and direct) can be attained in the short term, in a single negotiation session. However, because such goals are also pursued *infrequently* (such as when we make a major expenditure for a car or a home), we tend to view the negotiation as a single episode—a single defined event, without future consequences. This "episodic assumption" has, in turn, a *distributive* effect on negotiation strategy choice; the relationship with the other party tends to be ignored completely in favor of a simplistic concern for achieving *only* the substantive outcome. This pursuit of only a substantive goal often tends to support the choice of a distributive, or competitive, strategy.

Other negotiation goals, often more complex or more difficult to define, may require initiating a *sequence* of negotiation episodes. In these cases we expect that progress will be made incrementally, and that progress may depend on the prior establishment of a strong relationship with the other. Examples here might include a substantial increase in a line of credit with your bank or credit union, or the establishment of a most-favored nation status with an important trading partner. Such relationship-oriented goals should motivate the negotiator toward an integrative strategy choice; the relationship with the other party should be valued as much as (or even more than) the substantive outcome. Thus, relational goals tend to support the choice of an integrative, or collaborative, strategy.

**Trust.**    Trust is a complex concept in itself. In its most precise application to negotiation, trust "is the expectation that the other party will cooperate in the future" (Pruitt and Carnevale, 1993). Trust is sometimes viewed as a trait or state of personality; from this perspective, trust is a generalized orientation to other people that relates to one's belief that the "word, promise, verbal or written statement of another individual or group can be relied upon" (Rotter, 1971, p. 444; see also Sato, 1988). However, in negotiation, trust is more specifically derived from past experience with *this other person,* knowledge of *this other person's* actions with other opponents, and expectations that *this other* is likely to behave cooperatively in an upcoming interaction (see Pruitt and Carnevale, 1993, for a summary of negotiation research findings).

Trust acts on strategic negotiation choice both directly and indirectly (through the formation and consideration of principles and standards). The former, direct effect involves deciding how much the other party in a specific negotiation can be trusted to do (or not do). The effect on choice is direct in that it reflects beliefs about a particular, impending exchange. Trust also affects choice indirectly, through its direct effect on the negotiator's principles and standards. Beliefs and expectations about trust color and shape principles and standards in a global or general sense, and through them provide a filter, or test, that the negotiator applies to strategy choice. The difference between the direct and indirect effects of trust on strategy choice reflect what should or ought to happen (i.e., general beliefs about negotiation propriety and order), and what most likely will happen with a particular opponent, respectively. As most of us have experienced, it is possible to perceive a difference between beliefs and expectations ("I'd really *prefer* to be open and trusting, but I don't think I can afford to do that with this particular party"). It is also possible to face dilemmas between what we believe we should do and other, less admirable behaviors that violate our standards—but which we might be able to get away with at little or no cost.

The question of trust also relates to two aspects of dealing with other negotiators: the truthfulness of their information and statements, and the concern they will or will not have for the maintenance and enhancement of the negotiating relationship. The first aspect, that of truthfulness and credibility, is at the heart of what Kelley (1966) called the "dilemma of trust," in which we must decide how much to believe what the other tells us (see Chapters 2 and 13 for a fuller discussion). Kelley's second dilemma is the "dilemma of honesty and openness" (also see

---

**TRUST IN BUSINESS NEGOTIATIONS: A NEW TAXONOMY**

Shapiro, Sheppard, and Cheraskin (1992) have reconceptualized the role of trust in business relationships. Moving beyond the simple definitions of trust commonly used to describe cooperative relationships, they suggest that trust has different bases, depending on the level of the relationship between the parties. The three bases of trust are:

    Deterrence.

    Knowledge.

    Identification.

Trust based on deterrence is the lowest level of the three, and is the trust one acts on when one knows the other least well. It is quite compatible with the assumptions and behaviors usually associated with distributive negotiation (see Chapter 3). Higher levels of trust, based initially on knowledge and ultimately on identification, are achieved as the relationship between the parties develops and matures. These levels tend to reflect the assumptions and behaviors usually associated with integrative negotiation (see Chapter 4). Beliefs and desires associated with lower-level (deterrence-based) trust will tend to drive strategies in a distributive direction; beliefs and desires associated with higher-level (knowledge-based, identification-based, or both) trust will tend to put integrative strategies in a more favorable light.

Chapters 2 and 13), in which we must decide how open and candid to be with others. The trust one invests in the exchange of information that is necessary to the conduct of negotiations, then, will reflect how we address these two dilemmas. Negotiators "must learn to make attributions about the other's true intentions," attributions "in which [they] can have some minimal level of confidence" (Rubin and Brown, 1975, p. 15). The second aspect of trust relates to assumptions about the negotiating relationship and to the likely amount of care the parties are willing to invest (on their part) or expect (on the other's part). This question takes us back to the factors driving strategic choice that we discussed earlier.

**Episodic Assumptions.**    Episodic assumptions are assumptions negotiators make about what will happen in the next negotiation transaction (or series of transactions). Episodic assumptions are driven by goals. A focus on substantive goal success—getting *this* deal, winning *this* negotiation, with little or no regard for the effect on the relationship and subsequent exchanges—typically involves the assumption that this single negotiation is important enough to pursue substantive outcomes and ignore the possible impacts on relationships. In addition, if a negotiator is reasonably sure that he will never have to deal with this other party in the future, then beyond the observation of basic social convention, no particular care need be given to nurturing a strong, long-term relationship. This tends to support a competitive, or distributive, strategy. However, if the relational outcomes of the impending negotiation *are* important, interest should increase in pursuing a more integrative (or collaborative) strategy.

Episodic assumptions affect the choice of negotiation strategy directly and indirectly (through their direct effect on principles and standards). The direct effect reflects the negotiator's assumptions about the actual impending negotiation—the focus is on what most likely *will* happen or what we would prefer to happen to further our interests. As we described in our discussion of trust dynamics, the indirect effect reflects what we feel or believe should or ought to happen. Tension can arise in this case from conflicting beliefs and expectations, or between standards and short-term, low-cost benefits.

**Driving Factors.**    As shown in Figure 5.1, driving factors are the observed, inferred, or assumed elements of the negotiating arena. Five types of factors exist: *environments, contexts, outcomes, processes,* and *relationships.* How negotiators interpret, act on, or react to these elements generates the principles or standards that drive their choice of negotiation strategy.

*Environments* are the general settings within which events take place. In negotiation, environments include communities, industries, family groups, corporations, and so forth. Environments differ in the cultural and behavioral norms that shape the conduct of negotiations and determine what is appropriate and inappropriate conduct and action. They can affect the climate or ambiance of negotiations.

*Contexts* are the various situational settings that mark actual negotiation episodes within any given environment. For instance, within a given industry, management may negotiate frequently with suppliers, customers, regulatory agencies, and labor organizations. Each of these represents a different context within this single environment, and they may differ from each other in ways that affect norms and expectations of outcomes, processes, and relationships.

*Outcomes* are the effect that results from past negotiations have on subsequent exchanges. These include the results of a given negotiation on both the *current substantive issues* (e.g., "we gave up more on price last time than we should have, so we intend to do better on price next time"), and on the *current relationship* between the negotiating parties ("they really gouged us on price last time; I don't think they really care about us as valued customers").

*Processes* are the vehicles, methodologies, and behaviors by which the negotiation takes place—the "how" of the activity or the play of the game (as opposed to the results). Processes can have both an environmental and a historical effect. Environmentally, processes reflect and predict the negotiation climate and norms that are generally expected (e.g., whether the negotiation involves formality and reserved manners, or informality and easy-going behavior). Historically, specific past processes have an effect on future exchanges in much the same way as goals, as mentioned above.

Finally, *relationships* are the connections and associations among the negotiating parties, as well as those among the parties and their various constituencies (see the discussion of social structures in Chapter 9 for a more detailed treatment). This dual, "both ends against the middle" aspect of relationships as a driving factor is often particularly bothersome to negotiators. On the one hand, the general tenor of the relationship with the other side in the negotiation may tend to drive strategic choice in a distributive direction (see Chapter 3) or in an integrative direction (see Chapter 4). Prior experiences within a relationship operate similarly to the effect of historical outcomes; other things being equal, future relationships tend to mirror and perpetuate relationships experienced in the past. Thus, for example, a customer may have trouble expecting anything different out of a supplier who has been very powerful in the past and who has always dictated the price and product availability to the customer. On the other hand, negotiators must often be concerned with their relationships "back home," considering expected norms and appearances, or "constituency effects." Constituency expectations and accountability often drive negotiators to do (or not do) things in dealing with other negotiators that would not be issues if the constituencies did not exist or made no demands (e.g., "you'd better bargain *tough* for us with management this time; no contract, no work!").

### Summary

In this section, we have described a model that presents the key factors in selecting a negotiation strategy. Strategy choice is affected by four key elements: the trust level, principles and standards at stake, negotiating goals, and episodic assumptions about what will happen in the upcoming negotiation. Several of these elements also have an impact on each other. Principles and standards are also affected by five key driving factors: environmental factors, negotiation contexts, prior outcomes, prior processes employed to achieve those outcomes, and the status of the relationship with the opponent and with other key parties (e.g., a constituency). Thus, strategy choice is the result of a complex number of interrelated factors. In the next section, we will turn to strategy as the development of a plan, and articulate the key elements that must be described in preparing an effective plan.

## MANAGING THE PLANNING PROCESS

On the surface, the drama and theatrics of face-to-face confrontation can easily create the impression that negotiation success lies in persuasiveness, eloquence, clever maneuvers, and occasional histrionics. Although these tactics make the process interesting (and at times even entertaining), *the foundation for success in negotiation is the planning that takes place prior to the actual interaction process.*

### Many Negotiators are Not Good Planners!

Regrettably, systematic planning is not something that most of us do willingly. Managers, for example, are much more inclined to take action than to spend time reflecting about conditions and planning (Mintzberg, 1973; Sheppard, Blumenfeld–Jones, Minton, and Hyder, 1994). Time constraints and work pressures make it difficult to set aside the time to plan adequately. For many of us, planning is boring and tedious, easily put off in favor of "getting into the action" quickly. In addition to devoting insufficient time to planning negotiators frequently fail because of several weaknesses in their planning processes:

   • Negotiators *fail to set clear objectives* that can serve as standards by which to evaluate offers and packages. When something has to give, or when the other party makes a proposal that rearranges the component elements of a settlement, a negotiator who does not have clear objectives is not in a position to evaluate the new possibilities quickly and accurately. As a result, she may agree to something she later finds is not to her advantage. Alternatively, the negotiator may become confused and defensive and delay the process, causing the other party to lose patience.

   • If negotiators have not done their homework, they may not understand the strengths and weaknesses of their positions or recognize weaknesses in other parties' arguments. As a result, they *may not be able to formulate convincing arguments to support their own position or rebut their opponent's arguments.*

   • Negotiators *cannot simply depend upon being quick and clever* during the give and take of negotiation. Should the other party plan to win by stalling and delaying, holding to a position to wear you down, other approaches will be necessary. Being glib and eloquent in presenting your position is not helpful when the other party assails that position as illegal, inefficient, or ineffective.

Guarding against potential shortcomings in the planning process is necessary, but it's not enough. Effective planning also requires hard work on a number of specific steps:

- Defining issues.
- Assembling issues and defining agendas.
- Defining interests.
- Consulting with others.
- Managing goal-setting.
- Identifying your own limits.
- Developing supporting arguments.
- Analyzing the other party.

The remainder of this chapter discusses each of these steps in detail. The list represents the collective wisdom of several sources, including Richardson (1977), Asherman and Asherman (1990), and the reference manual for a negotiation planning software package, Negotiator Pro (Beacon Expert Systems, 1992). In this discussion, we assume that a single planning process can be followed for both a distributive and an integrative process. Although we have continually highlighted the differences between the processes, we believe that with the exception of the specific tactics the negotiators intend to pursue, one comprehensive planning process can suffice for either form of negotiation. We also assume that the planning process can proceed linearly, in the order in which these steps are presented. Yet information often cannot be obtained and accumulated quite this simply and straightforwardly; moreover, information discovered in some of the later steps may force one back to reconsider and reevaluate earlier steps. As a result, the first iteration through the planning process should be tentative, and the negotiator should be flexible enough to modify and adjust previous steps as new information becomes available.

### Defining the Issues

The first step in negotiation planning is to define the issues to be deliberated. An analysis of the conflict situation will usually be the first step in identifying the issues at stake. Usually, a negotiation involves one or two major issues (e.g., price or rate) and several minor issues. Hence, in buying a house (our example in Chapter 3), we immediately recognize that the central issues would be price, date of sale, and date of occupancy. We might quickly identify other issues, such as appliances to be included or payment for the fuel oil left in the storage tank. During the purchase process, our lawyer, banker, or real estate agent might hand us a list of other things to consider: taxes to pay, escrow amounts for undiscovered problems, or a written statement that the house must be "broom clean" before we move into it. Note that it does not take long to generate a fairly detailed list. In addition, experts (lawyers, agents, etc.) who have negotiated similar deals helped develop our list. In any negotiation, a complete list of the issues at stake is best derived from these sources:

1. An analysis of the conflict problem.
2. Our own past experience in similar conflicts.
3. Gathering information through research (e.g., reading a book on "how to buy a house").
4. Consultation with experts (real estate agents, bankers, attorneys, accountants, or friends who have bought a house recently).

Before considering ways to manage our list of issues, a word of caution is necessary. Note that we have used a simple, traditional example here—the purchase of a house. Many negotiations will differ markedly from this example, falling outside of traditional contracts and agreements. In addition, many negotiations are not over quantitatively defined issues (like the price of a house). In these situations, defining the key issues may be much more complex and elusive. For example, suppose a manager gets signals from his boss that his performance is not up to par, yet whenever he tries to confront the boss to discuss the problem and secure a realistic performance appraisal, the boss won't talk directly about the problem (which raises the manager's anxiety even further). Although the conflict in this situation is evident, the "issues" are elusive and complex. The central issue for the employee is the performance appraisal and why the boss won't give it. Maybe the boss is uncomfortable with doing the performance appraisal process or has a problem confronting other people about their behavior. Perhaps the boss is so preoccupied with her own job security that she doesn't even realize the impact she is having on her subordinate. In a situation like this one, where the issues are important but somewhat elusive, the manager needs to be clear about both what the issue is (in this case, getting a clear performance evaluation *and* getting the manager to talk about it) and how to initiate a productive discussion.

### Assembling Issues and Defining the "Bargaining Mix"

The next step in planning is to assemble all the issues we have defined into a comprehensive list. The combination of lists from each side in the negotiation determines the *bargaining mix* (see Chapter 3). In generating a list of issues, there may be a tendency to put too much on the table at once, to raise too many issues. This may happen if the parties do not talk frequently or if they have lots of business to transact. However, provided that all the issues are real, it often turns out that a longer list of issues makes success more, rather than less, likely. Larger bargaining mixes give us more possible components and arrangements for settlement, thus increasing the likelihood that a particular package will meet both parties' needs and, therefore, increasing the likelihood of a successful settlement

(Rubin and Brown, 1975). At the same time, larger bargaining mixes can lengthen negotiations because there are more possible combinations of issues to consider, and combining and evaluating all these mixes makes things very complex.

Once issues are assembled on an agenda, the next step for the negotiator is to prioritize them. In assigning priorities to issues, the negotiator must do two things:

1. *Determine which of the issues are most important and which are lower in importance.* In our house example, the buyer may determine that the price is the most important issue, whereas the closing date is secondary.

2. *Determine whether the issues are connected (linked together) or separate.* If they are separate, they can be easily added or subtracted; if connected, then settlement on one will be linked to settlement on the others and making concessions on one issue will inevitably be tied to some other issue. The negotiator must decide whether issues are truly connected—for instance, that the price he will pay for the house is dependent on what the bank will loan him—as opposed to simply being connected in his own mind for the sake of achieving a good settlement.

### Defining Your Interests

After defining the issues, the negotiator must proceed to define the underlying interests and needs. Although defining interests is more important to integrative negotiation than to distributive bargaining, even distributive discussions can benefit from identifying the key interests. We discussed the nature of interests and ways to bring them to the surface in Chapter 4. If issues help us define what we want, then getting at interests requires us to ask *why* we want it. Asking these "why" questions usually brings critical values, needs, or principles that we want to achieve in the negotiation to the surface. As we pointed out, these interests can be

- Substantive, directly related to the focal issues under negotiation.
- Process-based, related to the manner in which we settle this dispute.
- Relationship-based, tied to the current or desired future relationship between the parties.
- Based in principles and standards, tied to the intangibles of negotiation (Chapter 1), or referring to the informal norms by which we will negotiate and the benchmarks we will use to guide us toward a settlement (refer back to Figure 5.1).

### Consulting With Others

Having determined the relative importance of the issues, evaluated the bargaining mix, and ascertained underlying interests and needs, negotiators at this stage frequently consult with others—particularly if the negotiator represents some constituent group or organization. This may seem premature to new negotiators, but experienced negotiators know that one negotiator alone cannot determine the issues on an agenda. Considerable consultation—and negotiation—must often occur between the negotiator and her constituents, and between the negotiator and the opponent, before formal deliberations begin.

**Consulting with Constituencies.**   If a negotiator is bargaining on behalf of others (a company, union, department, club, family, etc.), they must be consulted so their concerns and priorities are included in the mix. In the house-buying illustration, let us assume that one member of a couple is doing the negotiating. If that person fails to consider his partner's concerns about the condition in which the house is left, or their children's concern that the move not occur during the school year, the negotiated resolution may be rejected. A negotiator who is representing a constituency is accountable to that constituency and must include their wishes in proposals, subsequently either fulfilling those wishes for them through negotiation or explaining why their desires were not met. When negotiating for a large constituency, such as an entire company or union or a community, the process of consulting with the constituency can be elaborate and exhaustive. Richardson (1977) describes management's preparation for labor negotiations as consulting with both internal sources (talking to supervisors and rank-and-file members, and noting patterns of conflict or grievances during the term of the current agreement) and external sources (monitoring agreements by other similar groups in the community, industry, etc.). Many times the negotiator also recognizes that the constituency's wish list is unrealistic and unobtainable; negotiators will then be required to negotiate with their constituency over what should be put on the agenda and what is realistic to expect (we explore these problems in detail in Chapter 9).

**Consultation with the Other Side—Clarifying Issues, Discussing Agenda, Negotiating Ground Rules.**   Consultation with the other side prior to actual negotiation is all too frequently neglected. A bargainer may draw up a firm list of issues, and even establish specific goals, well before the initial negotiation meeting. This process is valuable because it forces the bargainer to think through her position and decide on objectives. However, there is also potential risk in this process: the bargainer may define new issues to bring to the table that the other party is unprepared to discuss, or she may define priorities that cannot realistically be achieved. Opposing negotiators do not welcome "off the wall" surprises or the embarrassment that may come when the other side raises an issue they are completely unprepared to discuss. In this situation, most experienced negotiators will ask for a recess to get information and prepare themselves on the new issue, thus creating unanticipated delays. They may even refuse to include the new item on the agenda because they haven't had time to prepare for it or they fear they cannot discuss it adequately. If the other party is also accountable to a constituency, he may not want to go back to reopen earlier consultations. For this reason, many professional negotiators (labor negotiators, diplomats, etc.) often exchange (and negotiate) the list of issues in advance, so they can first agree to *what* will be discussed (the agenda) before actually engaging the substance of those issues.

However, preliminary consultation with the opponent does not always happen. When it does not, one side can preemptively dictate the negotiating issues, or the agenda itself (what issues we are discussing) becomes intertwined with the actual discussion of some agenda items. In distributive bargaining, negotiators are more likely to force their agenda on the others, hoping the opponent will not directly challenge the proposed agenda (the issues on it and the order in which they are discussed). Bargainers who believe they are being forced to accept the other's agenda should object as early in the negotiation as possible and push to assure that both sides can affect the issue portfolio and the order of issue discussion. In integrative negotiation, the agenda should be developed through mutual agreement and consultation prior to the actual discussion of the issue.

In addition to negotiating the agenda, it may also be useful to prenegotiate other elements of the negotiation protocol—in effect, to negotiate about how we are about to negotiate. There are several key elements to this protocol; each can have a subtle effect on the negotiation process and outcome:

- The location of negotiation. Negotiators tend to do better on their home turf—their own office, building, and city. They know the space, they feel more comfortable and relaxed, they have direct access to all the amenities—secretary, research information, expert advice, computer, and so on. In cross-cultural negotiations (see Chapter 14), language and cultural differences may come into play, and the parties may have to travel across many time zones. If negotiators want to minimize the advantage that comes with home turf, then they need to select neutral territory in which neither party will have an advantage. In addition, negotiators can choose the degree of formality of the environment. More formal deliberations are often held in a conference room or even a hotel meeting room; more informal deliberations can be held in restaurants, cocktail lounges, or rooms that offer a more informal array of furniture such as that found in a typical living room.

- The time period of negotiation. If negotiators expect long, protracted deliberations they might want to negotiate the time and duration of sessions. When do we start? How long do we meet? When do we need to end? When can we call for coffee breaks or time to caucus with our team?

- Other parties who might be involved in the negotiation. Is the negotiation between the principals only? Does one or both sides want to bring experts or advisors with them? What role will these outsiders play? Does one or both sides want to be represented by an agent who will negotiate for them? If so, will the principal be there, or will the agent only consult her later? Is the media involved, and what role might they play?

- What might be done if negotiation fails. What will happen if we deadlock? Will we go to a third party neutral (see Chapter 12)? Might we try some other techniques (see Chapter 6 for many suggestions on getting negotiations back on track)?

In new bargaining relationships, discussions on these procedural issues are often used as tests to determine how the negotiation on the substantive issues will proceed. If the negotiator enjoys success in these procedural negotiations, he might expect that it may be easier to reach agreement later on the substantive issues.

## Prioritizing—Defining the Relative Importance of Our Issues

The next step in negotiation planning is to determine the relative importance of issues. Once negotiation begins, parties can easily be swept up in the rush of information, arguments, offers, counteroffers, tradeoffs, and concessions. For those who are not clear in advance about what they want (and what they can do without), it is easy to lose perspective and agree to suboptimal settlements, or to get hung up on points that are relatively unimportant. When negotiators do not have priorities, they may be more likely to yield on those points aggressively argued by the other side, rather than to yield on the issues that are less important to *them.*

Priorities can be set in a number of ways. One simple way is for the negotiator to rank order the issues by asking "What is most important?" "What is second most important?" and "What is least important?" An even simpler process is to group issues into categories of high, medium, or low importance. When the negotiator represents a constituency, it is important to involve that group in setting priorities. Priorities can be set for both interests and more specific issues.

Setting priorities is also important on both the tangible and intangible issues. Intangible issues are often difficult to discuss and rank order, yet if they remain subjective and quantified, negotiators may tend to overemphasize or underemphasize them. It is easy to push such issues aside in favor of more concrete, specific, numerical issues—and negotiators must be careful not to let the "hard bargaining" over numbers drive out more abstract discussion of intangible issues and interests. However, more than one negotiator has received a rude shock when her constituency has rejected a settlement because it ignored the intangibles or dealt with them suboptimally in the final agreement.

### Assessing the Other's Priorities

If we have had the opportunity to meet with the other side, we may have been able to learn what issues are important to them. We also may have used this opportunity to discuss their priorities on those issues—which ones are most important, least important, and soon. Finally, we also may have learned something about their interests—why they want what they want. Conversely, if we have not had the opportunity to meet with people on the other side, then we may want to do what we can to either "put ourselves in their shoes" or gather information that might help us learn about their issues, interests, and priorities. We might call them and interview them prior to our actual meeting. We might try to take their perspective and anticipate what it is that we would want if we were negotiating from that point of view. We might talk to others who know them or people who have been in their situation before. All this will give us a better idea of what they are likely to want. By comparing this assessment against our own, we can begin to define areas where there may be strong conflict (we both have a high priority for the same thing), simple tradeoffs (we want the same group of things but in differing priorities), or no conflict at all (we want very different things and can easily both have our objectives and interests met).

### Knowing Our Limits

What happens if the other party in a negotiation refuses to accept some proposed items for the agenda or states issues in such a way that they are far below our resistance point? Negotiators should reassess these issues and decide how important they really are. Can they be dropped? Can they be postponed and taken up later? If the answer is "no," then the other side has to consider whether or not to proceed. The decision may well be *not* to negotiate. Is that bad? Not necessarily. We can look at this situation as the first test of the question, "Is a negotiated agreement feasible?" The answer here is "no." At this point, at least one party is considering whether to opt for an alternative or BATNA. In our earlier house purchase example, "not to buy" would imply a continuation of the status quo, finding another buyer or seller, or finding a third party to bring buyer and seller together. Above all else, negotiation planning must be *realistic.* If our needs can be addressed adequately without negotiation, or if the likely costs of negotiation (including the investment of time) exceeds the likely gains, it may be appropriate to forego negotiation altogether.

### Goal-Setting

Once the issues have been defined, a tentative agenda has been assembled, and others have been consulted as appropriate and necessary, the next step is to define goals on the key issues in the bargaining mix.

**Where to Start—Optimistic, Realistic, or Pessimistic?**    In setting goals, we need to consider four key points (see Chapter 3): the *target point* (at which we realistically expect to achieve a settlement), the *resistance point* (the least acceptable settlement point, or the point below which we are likely to reject a deal), the alternative or BATNA (the point where we may have an alternative settlement with another negotiator, or where we may "go it alone"), and the *asking price or opening bid* (representing the best deal we can possibly hope to achieve). In goal setting, the question arises of where planning should start: at the most optimistic point, the likely target point, or the most pessimistic resistance point?

From a technical perspective, it really does not matter at which point the goal setting begins. From a personal perspective, however, the starting point may be another matter. Bargainers who know that they tend to be too optimistic about what can be achieved may want to start with a wish list, then systematically cut this list down to what is more realistic and what is minimally acceptable. Conversely, those who know themselves to be pessimistic about negotiated outcomes may want to start with identifying the minimally acceptable settlement, then widening the range by defining what is probably realistic, and then brainstorming about what might be optimistically possible. Alternatively, many people begin with the target—where they want to wind up—and then define the resistance point and opening bids on either side of it. It may be difficult to be dispassionate (and thereby realistic) in establishing these points. Open discussion, expert advice, or even asking those we consult to play devil's advocate and challenge our thinking may help create the necessary sense of balance. The important point to remember about goal setting is that the negotiator ought to start where she feels most comfortable or at starting points, target points, or resistance points clearly dictated by research and preparation. Next, the negotiator should deliberately and systematically move into an area he might be inclined to avoid (e.g., defining an alternative) or think about carelessly (e.g., where to begin). By defining one point and then determining the other two, the negotiator will also be better prepared to frame offers and evaluate counteroffers. The process described here forces the negotiator to identify a bargaining range so as to avoid the rigidity that often accompanies the tendency to focus on a single, desirable settlement point.

**Goal Setting Forces Positive Thinking about Objectives.**    In approaching negotiation, the negotiator attempts to become aware of the other party—how members may behave, what they will probably demand, and how the bargainer feels about dealing with them. However, it is possible to devote too much attention to the other party, spending too much time trying to figure out what the other side wants, how to meet those demands, and so forth. If negotiators focus attention *totally* on the other side to the exclusion of themselves, they may plan the entire strategy as a reaction to the other's anticipated conduct. Reactive strategies are likely to make negotiators feel threatened and defensive and to make them less flexible and less creative in their negotiating behavior. Reactive strategies can also lead to confusion, particularly if assumptions about the other's strategy and intentions turn out to be wrong. In contrast, by defining realistic, optimistic, and pessimistic goals for themselves as described here, negotiators become more proactive, aware of the range of possible outcomes. This permits them to be more flexible in what they will accept and creates better conditions for arriving at a mutually satisfactory outcome.

**Goal Setting Usually Requires Anticipation of Packaging Among Several Issues and Objectives.**    Because most negotiators have a mixture of bargaining objectives, they must consider the best way to achieve satisfaction across these multiple issues. This returns us to our earlier definition of the issues, the bargaining mix, and an understanding of the other's bargaining mix. Negotiators propose settlements that will help them achieve realistic or optimistic targets on the more important issues; they may then balance these areas by setting more conservative targets for items less important to them (see also our house sale example in Chapter 3).

When evaluating a bargaining mix with a number of different issues, most people find that anticipating different ways to package issues in the mix is a great help in evaluating those packages against one's goals. Some negotiators evaluate packages the same way we advocate evaluating individual issues—they define optimistic, realistic, and pessimistic packages to permit better planning of the negotiation and to be in a better position to evaluate the other party's proposals (Rubin and Brown, 1975). If packages involve intangible issues, or issues for which is difficult to specify definite goals, it will be harder to explicitly evaluate and compare the packages. Evaluating the bargaining mix may also eventually require us to invent new options that will permit both parties to achieve their objectives; this process was extensively described in Chapter 4.

**Goal Setting Requires an Understanding of Tradeoffs and Throwaways.** Our discussion of packaging raises another possible problem. What do we do if the other party proposes a package that puts issues A, B, and C in our optimistic range, puts item D in the realistic range, puts E at the pessimistic point, and does not even mention item F, which is part of our bargaining mix? Is item F a "throwaway" item that we can ignore? If it is not a throwaway item, is it relatively unimportant and worth giving up in order to lock in agreement on A, B, and C in the optimal range? Suppose the other party had given us two proposed packages, the one described above and a second one that places items A and E in the optimistic range, items B and F in the realistic range, and C at the pessimistic point but ignores D. Would the first or the second package be more attractive?

Bargainers may also want to consider "giving away something for nothing" if such item may be part of the transaction. Even if an issue is unimportant or inconsequential to you, it may be valuable or attractive to another. Awareness of the actual or likely value of such concessions to the parties can considerably enrich the value of what you offer to the other at little or no cost to yourself. Using the house example again, the seller may have eight months left on a parking lot sticker on the car for the same lot that the buyer wants to use. Because the sticker is nonrefundable, the seller could never get the money back from the parking lot owner, but the buyer has a valuable item that is worthwhile to him.

To evaluate these packages, a negotiator needs to have some idea of what each item in the bargaining mix is worth in terms that can be compared across issues. The bargainer needs some way of establishing *tradeoffs*. This is sometimes a difficult thing to do because different items or issues will be of different value to the bargainer and will often be measured in different terms. If we are buying a used car, we need to decide how important it is to get (1) the make of car we would like, (2) the color, (3) the approximate age of the car, and (4) a price that will assure us a certain monthly payment to the bank for financing the purchase.

Even though it may not be possible to find a common dimension (such as dollar value) to compare issues in the bargaining mix or to compare tangibles with intangibles, many negotiators have found it convenient to scale all items on some common dimension. The premise is that, even if the fit is not perfect, any guide is better than none. Moreover, particularly if intangibles are a key part of the bargaining mix, negotiators must know the point at which they are willing to abandon the pursuit of an intangible in favor of substantial gains on tangibles. Translating every issue into dollars is one way to facilitate these comparisons. In labor relations, for example, most issues included in the bargaining mix are converted into dollar equivalents for easier comparison and evaluation of alternative packages. However, not everything is easy to convert into money (or other concrete) terms. Accountants experience this problem when trying to establish a book value for a business's goodwill.

Negotiators who want an alternative way to compare items and issues may use a point or utility scale to evaluate them. For example, if the value of the entire target package of issues is worth 500 points, then smaller, proportionate numbers of points could be assigned to each issue in the mix reflecting relative priorities and totaling 500. Needless to say, such points are only meaningful to the party establishing them, and only for as long as the points reflect the basic values and goals of the negotiator in that situation. As long as they do, such scales are a useful tool for planning and assessing offers and counteroffers.

### Developing Supporting Arguments—Research

One important aspect of actual negotiations is to be able to present a case clearly and to marshal ample supporting facts and arguments; another is to be able to refute the other party's arguments with counterarguments. We will consider how to structure and present successful arguments in Chapters 7 and 8 (on communication and persuasion). For now, we will address the research process necessary to assemble facts and arguments pertinent to the issues on the agenda.

Because of the breadth and diversity of issues that can be included in negotiations, it is not possible to specify all the procedures that can be used to assemble information. There are, however, some good general guides that can be used. A negotiator can ask these questions:

1. What facts support my point of view? What substantiates or validates this information as factual?

2. Who may I consult or talk with to help me elaborate or clarify the facts? What records, files, or data sources exist that support my arguments?

3. Have these issues been negotiated before by others under similar circumstances? Can I consult those negotiators to determine what major arguments they used, which ones were successful, and which were not?

4. What is the other party's point of view likely to be? What are their interests? What arguments are they likely to make? How can I respond to those arguments and seek more creative positions that go further in addressing both sides' issues and interests?

5. How can I develop and present the facts so they are most convincing? What visual aids, pictures, charts, graphs, expert testimony, and the like can be helpful or make the best case?

### Analyzing the Other Party

In this discussion of the planning process, we made repeated references to the other party and the negotiator's past history with them. Gathering information about the other party is a critical step in preparing for negotiation. What information do we need about the other party to prepare effectively? Several key pieces of background information will be of great importance in aiding in our own preparation:

- The other party's current resources, interests, and needs.
- The other party's objectives.
- The other party's reputation and negotiation style.
- The other party's BATNA.
- The other party's authority to make an agreement.
- The other party's likely strategy and tactics.

Let us now explore each of these in more detail. In theory, it would be extremely useful to have as much of this information as possible before negotiations occur; however, in reality, it may not be possible to obtain this information through either direct contact with the negotiator or other research sources. If not, the negotiator should plan to collect as much of this information as possible during the opening stages of the actual deliberations.

**The Other Party's Current Resources, Interests, and Needs.**    A negotiator will learn much about the other party at the negotiating table, but he should gather as much information as possible in advance through research and homework. Which data are most relevant will depend on the negotiation and who the other party is. You might study the other party's business history. An analysis of that person's previous negotiations, successful and otherwise, will provide useful clues. Financial data about the organization might be obtained through channels such as Dun and Bradstreet, financial statements, newspapers, files, company biographies, stock reports, and public records of legal judgments. You might investigate the other party's inventories. Sometimes, you can learn a great deal simply by visiting the other party or talking to his friends and peers and asking questions. Another way to learn is to ask questions of people who have done business with the other party (Calero and Oskam, 1983).

In addition to gaining information about the other, we also need to get information about their interests and needs (see Chapter 4 and pages 133–134 in this chapter). We can get this information through a variety of routes:

- Conduct a preliminary interview or discussion, in which we talk about what the other party would like to achieve in the upcoming negotiations.

- Anticipate their interests by putting ourselves "in their shoes."
- Ask others who know them or have negotiated with them.
- Read what they say about themselves in the media.

The importance of the issues or interests, and the nature of our past relationship with the other party, will influence the depth to which we probe to get information. Although it does take some time and effort to get information, the results are usually more than worth the investment. It is all too easy to neglect this step, which is unfortunate because valuable information can be gathered through a few simple phone calls or a visit.

**The Other Party's Objectives.**   Once we have obtained information about the other side's resources and interests, we also need to understand their objectives, just as we identified our own. We are often surprised when we hear other people describe their impressions of our initial interests and objectives. People often think stereotypically about the other party's interests and goals; they use their own goals and values as a guide and assume that others are like themselves and want similar things. A manager who is always after a bigger paycheck is usually surprised that some of his subordinates are more interested in a challenging job, schedule flexibility, or increased leisure time than they are in maximizing their salary.

How do we understand and appraise the other party's goals? Although we may speculate about another's goals and objectives, most of us do not gather information systematically—although we should. One of the best ways to get this information is directly from the other party. Because information about the other party's goals is so important to the strategy formulation of both parties, professional negotiators will often exchange information about goals or initial proposals days or even weeks before negotiations begin. If this does not occur, then the negotiator should plan to collect this information at the parties' first meeting.

**The Other Party's Reputation and Style.**   As noted earlier, the other party's past negotiating behavior is a good indication of how they will behave in the future. Hence, even if a bargainer has had no previous experience with the other person, talking to those who have dealt with him in the past can be very valuable. There is a potential danger in drawing conclusions from this information, however. Assuming that the other party will act in the future the way they have been described as acting in the past is just that—an assumption. People can and do act differently in different circumstances at different times. Although past behavior is a reasonable starting point for making assumptions, people do change over time. One author on negotiation notes:

> Assumptions are potential hurdles that can move us in the wrong direction. . . . The reality of negotiation is that we must and should make assumptions about the opposing party. . . . The important thing to remember is that your assumptions are just that. They are no better than poorly educated guesses at best. Don't fall in love with your assumptions. Check them out; they are neither right nor wrong until proven so (Karrass, 1974, p. 11).

Our impression of the other party's reputation may be based upon several factors:

1. How their predecessors have negotiated with us in the past.
2. How they have negotiated with us in the past, either in the same or in different contexts.
3. How they have negotiated with others in the past.

These different bases for our assumptions have different degrees of relevance and, therefore, different degrees of usefulness for predicting future behavior. We can use the information to prepare, to alert ourselves to what might happen; but we should also act with caution and actively look for new information that *confirms or denies* the validity of our assumption. There is always the danger, however, that invalid assumptions will lead a negotiator into unfortunate self-fulfilling prophecies. That is, there is often a tendency to seek and recognize information *confirming* our desires and assumptions, while failing to seek or recognize information that *counters* them.

A negotiator who assumes the other party is going to be demanding and aggressive may decide that "the best defense is a good offense" and open with aggressive demands and belligerent behavior. The other party may accept this behavior in stride or they may then decide to reply in kind, even though they initially intended to be cooperative. Of course, when the other party does fight back, the first negotiator's assumptions seem to be confirmed. If this initial misunderstanding is all that occurs, the problem may be recognized and corrected before it escalates. However, particularly when negotiations occur in long-standing relationships, our expectations can trigger an escalating cycle of competitive mistrust and hostility. These cycles are common in relationships between nations and between labor and management groups (see Lewicki and Alderfer, 1973; Pruitt and Rubin, 1986).

The previous paragraphs speak to the opponent's reputation. You may assess her style by looking at the way she has negotiated in the past and by categorizing various aspects of her personality. We discuss ways to deal with problematic negotiator behavior in Chapters 3 and 6, and we describe personality factors that can affect negotiator behavior in Chapter 11.

**The Other Party's BATNA.**    As part of the preparation process, we have stressed that negotiators need to understand their own alternative or BATNA. The alternative offers the negotiator a viable option for agreement if the current negotiation does not yield an acceptable outcome. Similarly, we should attempt to understand the quality of the other party's BATNA. If he has a strong and viable BATNA, the other party will probably be confident in negotiation, set high objectives, and be willing to push hard for those objectives. In contrast, if he has a weak BATNA, then he will be more dependent on achieving a satisfactory agreement with us, and we may be able to drive a harder bargain because the other party's alternative is unsatisfactory.

**The Other Party's Authority.**    When negotiators represent others, their power to make agreements may be limited; in fact, their ability to carry out negotiations may be restricted in many ways. Sometimes a constituency tells negotiators that they cannot make any agreements; often they can only pass on proposals from the constituency or collect information and take it back to their superiors.

There are many reasons for limiting a negotiator's authority. Negotiators kept on a "short leash" cannot be won over by a persuasive presentation to commit their constituency to something that is not wanted. They cannot give out sensitive information carelessly. Although these limitations may actually be helpful to a negotiator, they can also be frustrating. You might ask, "Why should I talk with this person, if she cannot make a decision and may not even be well informed about what I want?" Negotiation under these circumstances can seem like an exercise in futility. When a negotiator always has to "check things out" with those he represents, the other party may refuse to continue until someone who has the power to answer questions and make decisions is brought to the table. Negotiating teams, therefore, should think seriously about sending a negotiator with limited authority. Although that person will not be able to make unauthorized decisions, the limited authority may frustrate an opponent and create an unproductive tension in the negotiating relationship (see Chapter 9). Before negotiations, it might be appropriate to ask the other party specifically about any limits to authority in the impending negotiation; the temptation to lie will be balanced against the likely personal costs and costs to the negotiation of doing so.

**The Other Party's Strategy and Tactics.**    Lastly, it would be most helpful if we were able to gain information about the other party's intended strategy and tactics. Although it is unlikely the other party will tell us their strategy outright—particularly if they are intending to use distributive tactics—you can infer this information from whatever data you collect to answer the previous inquiries in this list. Thus, reputation, style, BATNA, authority, and objectives (compared to ours) may tell us a great deal about what strategy the other party intends to pursue. As we have noted before, you will have to gather this information on an emergent basis (as the negotiation unfolds); if your expectations have been incorrect then it will be necessary to recalibrate your own strategic response.

## SUMMARY

We believe planning to be the most important activity in negotiation. We began with a basic understanding of the concept of a strategy; we then discussed various aspects of strategy and the strategy process and presented a model of negotiation strategy choice. In that model, we suggested that strategy choice is determined by the interplay of five components: goals, principles and standards, trust, episodic assumptions, and a list of driving factors that includes environments, contexts, outcomes, processes, and relationships.

Having described our model, we then discussed the various aspects of managing the planning process. We propose that negotiation success is largely a function of careful planning. A negotiator who carefully plans will make an effort to do the following:

1. Realize that different negotiation situations might call for different basic strategies, as well as varying levels of concern for the substantive and relational aspects of the negotiations.

2. Clarify the goals and objectives that he would like to achieve.

3. Understand and define the key issues and interests at stake in the negotiation and be able to specify which ones are important and which she would like to achieve.

4. Consult with others—constituents and possibly opponents—to shape and refine the agenda of issues, interests, and goals.

5. Understand the fundamental predictability of the negotiation process so he can strategically plan how to achieve his goals and objectives and how one's limits should be defined.

6. Understand the other party and how the other party's personality, history, and negotiating style are likely to affect the strategy.

7. Develop the key supporting arguments and information to build a persuasive case for achieving objectives.

If a negotiator is able to consider and evaluate each of these factors, the negotiator will know what he wants and will have a clear sense of direction on how to proceed. This sense of direction, and the confidence derived from it, will be the single most important factor in affecting negotiating outcomes.

# CHAPTER 6

# Negotiation Breakdowns: Causes and Cures

In this chapter, we review the alternatives available to negotiators when deliberations get in trouble. As we have noted several times, negotiation is a conflict management process, and all conflict situations have the potential for becoming derailed. The parties become angry or entrenched in their positions. Perceptions become distorted, and judgments are biased. Communication decreases in effectiveness, and is used instead to accuse and blame the other. The other party's negotiation style does not enable us to reach agreement. The parties cannot find a middle ground where agreement is possible. In short, destructive conflict processes override the negotiation, and the parties cannot proceed.

This chapter focuses on three key areas where negotiation breakdowns may occur. First, we focus on the techniques available to the parties themselves to get negotiations back on track. Second, we examine processes that can be used to convert a negotiation situation from a more distributive bargaining process to a more integrative negotiation process. Finally, we explore strategy and tactics that can be used to control or manage "difficult" behavior in an opponent.

## GENERAL CONFLICT MANAGEMENT BY THE PARTIES THEMSELVES

In this section, we will review five major types of conflict reduction strategy:

- Reducing tension and synchronizing de-escalation of hostility.
- Enhancing communication, particularly as to understanding the other party.
- Controlling the number and size of issues at stake.
- Establishing a common ground on which the parties can find a basis for agreement.
- Enhancing the desirability of the options and alternatives that each side presents to the other.

Each of these approaches will be described in some detail, but several preliminary comments about the various approaches may be helpful. First, there is nothing firm or rigid about the number of different techniques for resolving disputes. Research on the nature of conflict and its resolution (e.g., Brown, 1983; Deutsch, 1973; Sheppard, 1984; Wall 1981; Pruitt and Rubin, 1986; Walton, 1987) has suggested a wide array of different dispute resolution techniques that can be aggregated in several different ways. Second, these approaches to conflict de-escalation and control are based on the premise that a highly polarized, unproductive conflict is characterized by the following dynamics:

1. The atmosphere is charged with anger, frustration, and resentment. Mistrust and hostility are directed at the opposing negotiator.

2. Channels of communication, previously used to exchange information and supporting arguments for each side's position, are now closed or constrained. Each side attempts to use communication channels to criticize and blame the opponent, while simultaneously attempting to close off the same type of communication from her opponent.

3. The original issues at stake have become blurred and ill-defined, and perhaps new issues have been added. Negotiators have become identified with positions on issues, and the conflict has become personalized. Even if a negotiator were ready to make a concession to the other side, he would not make it due to a strong dislike for the other party.

4. The parties tend to perceive great differences in their respective positions. Conflict heightens the magnitude of these differences and minimizes areas of perceived commonality and agreement. The parties see themselves as further apart than they may actually be, and they do not recognize areas where they may be in agreement.

5. As anger and tension increase, the parties become more locked into their initial negotiating positions. Rather than searching for ways to make concessions and move toward agreement, the parties become firmer in stating their initial demands, and they resort to threats, lies, and distortions to force the other party to comply with those demands. The opponent usually meets these threats with counterthreats and retaliation.

6. If there is more than one person on a side, those on the same side tend to view each other more favorably. They see the best qualities in the people on their side and minimize whatever differences exist; yet they also demand more conformity from their team members and will accept a more militant, autocratic form of leadership. If there is dissension in the group, it is hidden from the opposing party; group members always attempt to present a united front to the other side (Blake and Mouton, 1961a, 1961b, 1961c; Corwin, 1969; Harvey, 1953).

The techniques for conflict reduction and resolution presented in this chapter are designed to respond to each of these dynamics. Moreover, we suggest that the most productive procedure for resolving a highly polarized dispute is to approach it using the steps for conflict management in the order presented. The first step should be some effort at reducing tension, followed by efforts to improve the accuracy of communication and to control the proliferation of issues. Finally, the parties should engage in techniques for establishing commonalities and enhancing the attractiveness of each other's preferred alternatives. This procedure is by no means firm and inflexible; many disputes have been successfully resolved by invoking the steps in a different order. However, the order in which we present these procedures is the one frequently used by third parties in resolving disputes (see Chapter 12), and hence we believe it will also be the most effective if employed by the negotiators themselves. If the conflict cannot be effectively controlled, third party intervention may become necessary (Chapter 12).

### Reducing Tension And Synchronizing De-Escalation

Unproductive deliberations usually become highly emotional. Parties are frustrated, angry, and upset. They are strongly committed to their viewpoints and have argued strenuously for their preferred alternatives, seeing themselves as firm, principled, or deserving. The other side, behaving the same way, is seen as stubborn, bullheaded, inflexible, and unreasonable. The longer the parties debate, the more likely emotions will overrule reason—name-calling and verbal assaults on the other replace logic and reason. When the dispute becomes personalized, turning into a win-lose feud between individuals, negotiation loses all hope of productivity. Several approaches for controlling conflict are specifically directed at defusing volatile emotions.

**Tension Release.**    Tension is a natural by-product of negotiations. Consequently, negotiators should be aware that it is bound to increase, and they should know how to act to address or diminish it. Some negotiators who are sensitive to increases in tension know how to make a witty remark or crack a joke that causes laughter and releases tension. Others know that it is sometimes appropriate to let the other become angry and ventilate the pent-up anger and frustration, without having to respond in kind. Skilled negotiators also know that by listening to the other person and allowing the expression of feelings, the catharsis will vent emotion and clear the air and may permit negotiations to return to a calmer pace.

**Acknowledgment of the Other's Feelings: Active Listening.**    When one party states her views and the other openly disagrees, the first negotiator often hears the disagreement as more than *just* disagreement. She may hear a challenge, a put-down, an assertion that the statement is wrong or not acceptable, an accusation of lying or distortion of the facts, or another form of personal attack. Whether or not this is the message that was intended is unimportant; the negotiator has to deal with the way it was received. Understandably, such misinterpretations escalate conflict.

There is a difference between accurately hearing what the other party has said and agreeing with those statements. When conflict escalates, accurate listening frequently becomes confused with agreeing and accepting. Situations like this may be effectively handled by letting the other person know that you have heard and understood both the content and the emotional strength of the message. This technique is called *active listening* (Rogers, 1961), and it is frequently used in interviews and therapy settings as a way of encouraging a person to speak more freely. Rather than challenging and confronting the other negotiator's statements by bolstering your own statements (and position), you respond with statements that probe for confirmation and elaboration on the other's first statements. Comments may include these: "You see the facts this way," "You feel very strongly about this point," or "I can see that if you saw things this way, you would feel threatened and upset by what I have said." These statements do not indicate that you *agree* with these statements; rather, they communicate only that you have accurately heard and understood the other person.

**Separation of the Parties.**    The most common approach to letting tempers cool down is to break off face-to-face relations. Declare a recess, call a caucus, agree to adjourn and come back together later when the parties have had a chance to unwind. The parties should acknowledge explicitly that the purpose of the caucus is to allow tempers to cool so the dialogue will become less emotional. Each party should also agree to return with a renewed effort to make deliberations more productive—either by simply regaining composure, or by attempting to address the issue that created the anger in a new or different way.

Separation of the parties may occur for short periods of time such as a few minutes or hours, or it may be planned to last for several days or weeks. Variations in the time period are related to the level of hostility, as well as to unique situational circumstances. Parties may use the time to check with their constituencies, gather new information, and reassess their position and commitments.

**Synchronized De-Escalation: GRIT.**    Conflict situations are dynamic; they are constantly changing. Occasionally, tension and emotion decrease as negotiation continues; more commonly, however, tension increases. The escalation process is rooted in the reciprocal nature of dialogue during conflict (see Pruitt and Rubin, 1986). Alice and Bill are discussing cleaning their apartment. Alice likes to have the apartment very clean; Bill isn't bothered by a bit of dirt and clutter. Alice starts by telling Bill that he didn't do a very good job cleaning the bathroom. Bill hates cleaning bathrooms and tells Alice that if she doesn't like the way he did it, she can go clean it again herself. Tension in this situation may escalate for several reasons. Bill may be trying to punish Alice for what she said. Bill, who hates cleaning bathrooms, thought he had done a pretty good job and is angry that Alice wasn't satisfied and thinks she can do better. Bill may even believe that housecleaning, particularly cleaning bathrooms, is a job Alice should do. Even if Bill thinks that all he is trying to do is counter Alice's criticisms, it is likely that Alice will take Bill's remarks as more punishing than Bill intended (due to a "magnification factor"). This magnification probably occurs because Bill, not understanding the tension and anxiety that made Alice criticize the bathroom cleaning to begin with, will probably also not understand the magnitude of Alice's reaction. In any event, Alice experiences Bill's response as hostile, punishing, negative, and threatening, and she replies in kind (telling Bill he is insensitive and a slob), thereby repeating the cycle and increasing the level of tension and hostility. Clearly, the parties must find some way to de-escalate this conflict cycle.

Charles Osgood (1962), writing about the Cold War and disarmament, suggested a unilateral strategy for conflict de-escalation called GRIT (*G*raduated and *R*eciprocated *I*nitiatives in *T*ension Reduction). The party who desires to de-escalate a conflict initiates the action. He decides on some small concession that each side could make that would signal both sides' good faith and desire to de-escalate. The concession should be large enough so it can be read as an unambiguous signal of a desire to change the relationship, but not so large that if only one side followed through, that side would make itself weak or vulnerable. The unilateral action should then be publicly announced to the other side,

1. Stating exactly what the concession is;
2. Stating that the concession is part of a deliberate strategic policy to reduce tension;
3. Stating that the other side is explicitly invited to reciprocate in some specified form;
4. Stating that the concession will be executed on some stated time schedule; and
5. Stating that each party commits to execute the concession without knowing whether the other will reciprocate.

The party that initiated the de-escalation then executes the concession. The specific concession should be something that is obvious, unambiguous, and subject to easy verification. Making it public and symbolic will help. In our example, Bill could apologize for his comments and for raising his voice.

If the opposing party does not respond, then the initiator goes through with the action and repeats the sequence again, selecting a simple, low-risk concession in an effort to attract the other into synchronized de-escalation. If the other does respond, then the initiator proposes a second action, slightly "riskier" than the first, and once again initiates the sequence. For example, Bill could agree to clean the bathroom again or have Alice show him where she is unsatisfied with his cleaning efforts. As the synchronized de-escalation takes hold, the parties can both propose larger and riskier concessions that will bring them back into a productive negotiating relationship.

GRIT strategies are efforts to change the nature of relationships—from hostile and mistrusting, with each side attempting to "punish" the other to more open and trusting, in which one side initiates a trusting gesture, and each side rewards the other's gestures with more cooperative efforts. This mutual reward sequence will help to de-escalate the conflict and often leads to a positive, productive climate for negotiation.

### Improving the Accuracy of Communication

The second step in conflict reduction is to insure that both parties accurately understand the other's position (for a broader treatment of communication processes in negotiation, see Chapter 7). As stated earlier, when conflict becomes more heated, communication efforts concentrate on managing emotions and directing the next assault at the other. Effective listening declines. We think we know what the other side is going to say, and we do not care to listen to it anymore. In intense conflict, listening becomes so diminished that the parties are frequently unaware that their positions may have much in common. Rapoport (1964) has termed this the "blindness of involvement," because it inhibits the development of trust and the problem-solving process. Several approaches can be used to rectify this situation.

**Role Reversal.**    Although it is often easy for outsiders to see the logic, rationale, and potential commonalities on both sides of a conflict, recognizing them when we are personally involved in a conflict is another matter. Role reversal is one way of helping each side see things from the other's perspective. One party attempts to put herself in the other's shoes, looking at the issue from the other's perspective. Hence, a manager can put himself in the position of an employee; a salesperson can take the position of a customer; a purchasing agent, that of a supplier. You can reverse roles simply by playing out scenarios in your imagination, by asking a friend or colleague to assume the other role and act out a dialogue, or, more effectively, by including role reversal as part of a unilateral strategy preparation process. Although role reversal will not tell a negotiator exactly how the other party thinks and feels about the issues, the process can provide useful and surprising insights about how the other party might see, feel, and think about things.

During negotiations, one side often tries to encourage the other negotiator to reverse roles. He may plead, "Look at this from my perspective. What you're saying (or doing) puts me in this position, and thus how could you expect. . . ." A variant on this occurs when one party tells the other "If I were in your shoes, I would. . . ." If role reversal gives the negotiator an accurate understanding of the other's position and shows that her previous view was incorrect, it gives her a chance to correct specific misperceptions. This corrected understanding gives the negotiator a broader, more integrated view of the possible options. Role reversal also gives the negotiator an opportunity to explore how some planned action may affect the relationship. Hence, a member of management taking labor's role may discover that some of management's arguments or tactics may have an ineffective or undesirable effect, permitting them to drop the tactics before they cause problems (Johnson and Dustin, 1970).

In negotiation, the purpose of role reversal is to highlight areas of commonality and overlap between positions; however, this purpose cannot be achieved unless such compatibilities actually exist and at least one party moves toward areas of commonality by proposing compromises. When no actual compatibility exists, role reversal may simply sharpen the differences between actual positions. Although some negotiators would find this to be undesirable information because it inhibits the search for common ground, others would prefer to be aware of this lack of compatibility so they can find other means to resolve the dispute. In attempting to create a win-win situation, where integrative negotiation is possible, both parties need accurate knowledge of the other's goals. Only this type of information will permit a productive effort to satisfy each party's objectives. If it becomes apparent that the parties' goals are actually incompatible, integrative negotiation is impossible, and the sooner that is discovered, the better. As we showed in Chapter 3, the existence of a negative settlement range also has severe consequences for the distributive bargaining process. Role reversal can be a powerful tool for uncovering the true goals of both parties.

**Imaging.**   Like role reversal, imaging is also a method for gaining insight into the other party's perspective. In the imaging process, parties in conflict are asked to engage in the following activities separately:

1. To describe how they see themselves.
2. To describe how the other party appears to them.
3. To state how they think the other party would describe them.
4. To state how they think the other party sees themselves.

The parties then exchange this information. Parties first compare how they described themselves, then how they would describe the other, how they think the other party would describe them, and lastly, how they think the other would describe themselves. The differences between the two sets of statements are frequently surprising because they reveal dissimilarities and inconsistencies. Imaging usually produces animated discussion as the parties clarify and substantiate what they have said or heard. A common result is that the parties recognize that many apparent differences and areas of conflict are not real and begin to better understand those that are real. An example of imaging can be found in negotiations between top executives who met to work out a new organizational structure for the combined firm resulting from a merger of two organizations. Executives from both sides were deeply concerned that they would be outmaneuvered by the other and would "lose" as a result of the merger. A consultant suggested having an imaging meeting prior to actual negotiations. This meeting sharply altered the perceptions of both parties, and successful integrative negotiations became possible (Alderfer, 1977).

When parties complete role reversal or imaging processes, they have usually accomplished several things. First, they have clarified and corrected misconceptions and misinterpretations. They have brought needs, goals, and priorities, as well as limitations, to the surface so they can be used in the problem-solving process. One side often gains an understanding of the other party's true needs. Perhaps even more importantly, the process sets a positive tone for the negotiation. Parties find that they can make their needs and concerns heard and not be interrupted. This reduces defensiveness and encourages people to listen. Most people begin the negotiation process with a rather clear idea of what they need from the other party; in this phase, they learn more about the other's needs. Joint problem solving moves from being an unattainable ideal to an achievable process.

## Controlling Issues

A third major difficulty that inhibits parties from resolving conflict is that as conflict intensifies, the size and number of the issues expand. As conflict escalates, it snowballs; bits and pieces of other issues accumulate into a large, unmanageable mass. Although smaller conflicts can be managed satisfactorily one at a time, larger conflicts become unwieldy and less amenable to easy resolution. The problem for negotiators in escalated disputes, therefore, is to develop strategies to contain issue proliferation and reduce the dispute to manageable proportions.

Roger Fisher (1964) has been a major advocate of strategies of issue control in negotiation, particularly in international affairs. In a well-known article, Fisher suggests six major approaches to "fractionating" conflict, or reducing a large conflict into smaller parts: reduce the number of parties on each side; control the number of substantive issues involved; state issues in concrete terms rather than as principles; restrict the precedents involved, both procedural and substantive; search for ways to "fractionate" the big issues; and depersonalize issues, separating them from the parties advocating them.

We will examine each of these approaches in more detail.

**1. Reduce the Number of Parties on Each Side.**    When conflict escalates, both parties seek to build alliances for strength or to bring their constituencies into the dispute; either they increase the number of parties at the negotiation or they bring more clout to the table. Additional parties, such as lawyers, experts, or parties with more formal authority are often brought into negotiations for the information or the clout they can provide. Because the sheer number of parties at the table can make negotiations considerably more complex (more parties equal more perspectives on the issues, more time needed to hear each side, more opportunities for disagreement, etc.), negotiation ground rules should provide ways to limit the number of parties. One way to control conflict size is to return the dispute to the original negotiating parties. The fewer the actors present, or the more the conflict can be limited to two individuals, the more likely the parties will be to reach a favorable settlement.

**2. Control the Number of Substantive Issues Involved.**    A second way to control the size of a conflict is to keep the number of issues small enough to manage. When conflict escalates, the size and number of issues proliferate. Some conflicts escalate to the point where there are too many issues to manage constructively. At the same time, limiting negotiations to a very few issues also raises problems. Single-issue conflicts are frequently harder to manage because they quickly lead to win-lose polarization over the issue. In such circumstances, it is often desirable to expand the number of issues so both sides can see themselves as having gained something and achieve a win-win solution. You can expand the number of issues by defining the issue more broadly so resolution can benefit both sides or by coupling the issue with another issue so each party can receive a preferred settlement on one of the issues. We discussed bundling and packaging issues, the bargaining mix, and inventing options in Chapters 3 and 4.

**3. State Issues in Concrete Terms Rather than as Principles.**   A third way that conflict issues become difficult to control is when events or issues are treated as matters of principle. Small conflicts can rapidly become intractable disputes when their resolution is not treated as an isolated event, but instead must be consistent with a broader policy or principle. Because any deviation from policy is viewed as a threat to that policy, and because it is far more difficult to change broad policy than to make a concession on a single issue, negotiations are immediately problematic. For example, an employee needs to take her child to the doctor during her work hours and requests an excused absence from the company. The company does not have a policy that permits employees to take time off for this reason, and the employee's supervisor tells her she has to take sick leave or vacation time instead. "It's a matter of principle," management asserts. Resorting to arguments of principle and policy is often a strategic defense by high-power parties against any change from the status quo; however, the longer discussion remains at the level of policy or principle, the less likely those disputes can be successfully resolved. There are, of course, times when a single event is properly seen as indicative of a new principle or policy. That being the case, negotiations should be arranged to address the policy or principle specifically. Many times, people are reluctant to address principles because they know negotiations over principles are difficult and lengthy. However, to attempt to negotiate a concrete issue when the negotiation really involves the hidden agenda of a major principle only results in frustration. If this occurs, it is wise to face the issue and raise it directly. There are at least two strategies to do so:

1.  Question whether the issue needs to be addressed at the principle or policy level. Inquire about the link between the specific issue and the broader policy or principle. If none exists, and one party wants to look at the matter from a policy or principle level, suggest that the immediate concrete issue be handled and discussed separately from the underlying principle or policy. If need be, the parties can agree that the concrete issue can be settled in this instance, with no expectation as to how the policy will later be established.

2.  Point out that expectations can be made to all policies, and that principles and policies can be maintained even if minor deviations are agreed to under special circumstances. The parties may be willing to agree that this specific negotiation might be one of those times.

**4. Restrict the Precedents Involved, Both Procedural and Substantive.**   The final type of issue magnification occurs when the parties treat concessions on a single issue as violations of some substantive or procedural precedent. When a substantive precedent is at stake, one party will imply that to concede on this issue at this time will render him vulnerable to conceding on the same issue, or a similar issue, in the future. To return to our previous example, the manager is likely to argue that if she grants the employee an excused absence in this case, when no policy exists, then she will be obligated to grant every other employee the same request. Belief in the domino theory is strong. The high-power party, who supports the precedent, believes that if she gives in to this request, rather than nipping the problem in the bud, there will be no end to the number and types of requests she may get for excused absences in the future. In contrast, procedural precedents are at stake when parties agree to follow a process they haven't followed before. For example, a procedural precedent may be set when the parties agree to negotiate in a relationship that previously has not been characterized by negotiation, or where one has more power than the other. In the same employment example, the manager may not want to give the employee the excused absence because the employee did not submit any proof that she was, in fact, taking a child to the doctor.

Issues of precedent are usually as thorny to control as issues of principle. Once again, a negotiator trying to move a conflict toward de-escalation and resolution should try to keep from translating single issues into major questions of precedent. Focus the dialogue on the key issue and persist in arguments that concessions on this issue at this time do not necessarily dictate any precedents—substantive or procedural—for the future.

**5. Search for Ways to "Fractionate" the Big Issues.**    Fisher (1964) calls these "salami tactics": ways to slice a large issue into smaller pieces. Issues that can be expressed in quantitative terms are easy to slice. For example, compensation demands can be cut up into pennies-per-hour increments, or lease rates can be reduced to pennies per square foot. When trying to fractionate issues of principle or precedent, use the time horizon—when the principle goes into effect or how long it lasts—as a way to fractionate the issue, or vary the number of different ways that the principle may be applied. Thus, for example, the company may devise a family emergency leave policy, under which a manager may allow a period of no longer than three hours (without a formal application process), and no more often than once a month, for illness in the employee's immediate family.

**6. "Depersonalize" Issues: Separating Them from the Parties Advocating Them.**    Positional bargaining tends to create conflict over both the issues and the relationship between negotiators. People become identified with positions on issues, and vice versa. Effective negotiation requires separating the issues from the parties, not only by working to establish a productive relationship between the parties (leaving only the issue conflict at stake), but also by trying to resolve the issues without regard to the people. Fisher, Ury, and Patton, (1991) extensively elaborate on this point, suggesting that effective integrative negotiation is "tough" on the negotiating problem but "soft" on the people.

### Establishing Commonalities

As we noted earlier, parties in escalated conflict tend to magnify perceived differences and to minimize perceived similarities (Pruitt and Rubin, 1986). The parties tend to see themselves as further apart and having less in common than may actually be the case. Therefore, a fourth major action that parties can take to de-escalate conflict is to establish commonalities or focus on common objectives. Several approaches are possible: establishing common goals, focusing on common enemies, agreeing to follow a common procedure, and establishing a common framework for approaching the negotiation problem.

**Superordinate Goals.**    Superordinate goals are common goals; both parties desire them, and both parties must cooperate to achieve them. In a corporation, for example, people do different jobs (e.g., marketing, manufacturing) that have different objectives, yet they must work together (e.g., to get the product to the customer) or the corporation will not survive. A local city council and community members may disagree about the ways to spend limited funds for community development; however, they may be able to agree if it is possible for them to write a joint grant proposal that will provide enough money to meet all objectives. Two entrepreneurs may be in a heated conflict over how to resolve a design problem in a new product, but if they share a common objective of resolving the problem in time to present their case to a group of venture capitalists who could fund the project, they may be more likely to find a solution.

To have significant impact on negotiations, superordinate goals must be jointly desired by both sides and must not be seen as benefiting one side more than the other. Johnson and Lewicki (1969) showed in a research study that superordinate goals that were closely related to the issues of the conflict and that were introduced by one party in the dispute often became caught up in the conflict dynamics and lost their effectiveness. Random events (under neither party's control) or events created by neutral third parties are frequently better superordinate goals than those that are sought out and planned by the parties involved. For example, natural disasters such as floods, storms, blackouts, fires, and the like bring people and communities together with a common purpose of survival; the same impact can be seen in negotiations.

**Common Enemies.**    A common enemy is a negative form of superordinate goal. The parties find new motivation to resolve their differences to avoid intervention by a third party, or to pool resources to defeat a common enemy. Political leaders of all persuasions often invoke outside enemies (the other political party) to bring their own constituencies together. Managers who are in conflict learn that if they don't resolve their differences themselves, someone else (their boss) will make the decision for them. Labor and management may behave more collaboratively when threatened with binding arbitration, foreign competition, or government intervention in their dispute.

**Agreement on the Rules and Procedures.**    A third way parties can establish commonalities is by mutual agreement about the rules by which negotiations will be conducted. (We discussed this as a core element of planning in the previous chapter). Escalated conflict tends to exceed its original bounds; as parties become more upset, they may be more likely to resort to any and all tactics to defeat the other. Efforts at effective conflict de-escalation and control may require that the parties rededicate themselves to basic ground rules for how they will manage their dispute. These ground rules include the following:

- Determining a site for a meeting (changing the site or finding a neutral location).
- Setting a formal agenda as to what may and may not be discussed, and agreeing to abide by that agenda.
- Determining who may attend the meetings (changing key negotiators or representatives may be a signal of the intention to change the negotiation approach).
- Setting time limits for the individual meeting and for the overall negotiation session (as we have pointed out, progress in negotiation is paced according to the time available; therefore, setting limits is likely to create more progress than if no limits are set).
- Setting procedural rules, such as who may speak, how long they may speak, how issues will be approached, what facts may be introduced, how records of the meeting will be kept, how agreements will be affirmed, and what clerical or support services are required.

Finally—and perhaps this may be a radical step for some negotiators—the parties may agree to set aside a short period of time during negotiations to critique *how they are doing.* This mechanism effectively designates a selected time for the parties to evaluate their own progress in negotiation. It provides time to reevaluate ground rules, change procedural mechanisms, or perhaps even change negotiator behavior. This process orientation may provide the opportunity for the parties to self-correct the procedural mechanisms that will allow them to make greater progress on their substantive disagreements (Walton, 1987).

**Integrative Frameworks.** Superordinate goals, common enemies, and mutual commitment to rules are factors outside the boundaries of the dispute; they transcend the specific issues and bring the parties together in unified action. However, superordinate goals and common enemies do not establish the foundation for long-term cooperation; when the common goal or common enemy is removed, the parties may find that they have no greater basis for resolving their dispute than they did before. Hence, other mechanisms must be pursued to establish a common ground for agreement.

There are two primary vehicles for developing commonalities in disputes: first, focusing on similarities between the parties rather than on differences; and second, searching for ways to cognitively redefine the dispute to accommodate all parties' interests.

Maximizing similarities is simply a process of refocusing the parties' attention on what they have in common, rather than where they disagree. As noted earlier, conflict processes tend to highlight perceived differences and magnify the importance of these differences. The longer the parties are in dispute, the more they quibble about the differences and the more they recognize other differences that are then drawn into the dispute. One way to control this escalation is to reemphasize what the parties have in common, such as objectives, purposes, overall philosophies and viewpoints, long-range goals, and styles of operation. Another is to review what they have accomplished together, either in the current negotiation or in prior engagements. Reemphasizing the commonalities tends to put the differences back into their proper perspective, and it de-emphasizes the importance of differences. This process either defuses the emotionality tied to the differences or creates a positive emotional bond based on similarities that will allow differences to be bridged.

Integrative frameworks are ways of redefining the issues to create a common perspective from which initial positions appear more compatible (Eiseman, 1978; Fisher, Ury, and Patton, 1991). Eiseman (1978) refers to this process as creating an integrative conceptual framework, and Fisher, Ury, and Patton explain that successful negotiators focus on *interests,* not positions. By defining negotiated issues in terms of positions—my position on this issue is X—parties tend to simplify complex phenomena by defining a single point and then refusing to move from it. To create movement, parties must establish ways of redefining the conflict so that they can explore compatible interests. Recall the classic example from Chapter 4, adapted from Follett 1940). Two men are quarreling in a library about whether a window should be open or shut. They bicker back and forth about how much to leave it open. Enter the librarian. She asks one why he wants the window open, and he responds that he wants some fresh air. She asks the other why he wants it closed, and he responds that he wants to avoid a draft. So she goes into the next room and opens a window, affording each what he wants.

Eiseman (1978) notes that there are several ways to create integrative frameworks out of polarized positions. We use the Follett example as illustration:

1. *Dimensionalize the problem.* Instead of treating the conflict as distinctly different categorical viewpoints, treat it as points along a continuum. In the example, the parties disputed whether the window would be open or closed. In fact, there are almost an infinite number of degrees that the window can be open, from very slightly to a great deal. Once the parties redefine the issue as the amount it will be open, they can then negotiate more easily over the size of the opening.

2. *Increase the number of dimensions.* The successful intervention of the librarian in the above example is predicated on her imaginative solution: that both fresh air and no draft can be provided if the solution is not restricted to opening a window in the same room. Multiple dimensions allow one party to "win" on one dimension and the other to "win" on another. Increasing the number of dimensions increases the possibility that the parties can identify a dimension on which they can more easily reconcile their differences. It may also provide an entirely new way of looking at the problem, so both sides can recognize degrees, shades, and variations that offer the possibility of satisfying all parties.

3. *Construct an "ideal case".* Sometimes parties are in dispute because each is proposing a solution that meets only her own needs, but not those of the other. One way to break this deadlock is to construct an ideal case that would meet the needs of both sides. In the above example, the librarian did this by saying to herself, "Ideally, how can one party get fresh air while the other avoids a draft?" Negotiating parties can construct ideal solutions by creatively devising ways that both parties could ideally have their needs met, and then determining how that ideal scenario might be attained.

4. *Search for semantic resolutions.* Particularly in conflicts where the parties are negotiating over words and ideas—contract language, setting policy, or establishing memoranda of agreement—conflict intensifies over key words, phrases, and expressions. Sometimes this conflict can be reduced to irrelevant linguistic hairsplitting, yet to the parties involved the wording is significant in both meaning and intent. Discovering how parties attach different meanings to some words, or exploring language that can accommodate both sides, is another alternative for achieving an integrative framework.

This discussion of the development of integrative frameworks is quite general in nature. You'll find more specific treatment of the integrative solution-building process in the next section, and in our discussion of inventing options in Chapter 4.

## Making Preferred Options More Desirable to the Opponent

A final alternative method that parties can use to increase the likelihood of agreement is to make their desires and preferences appear more palatable to the other. We have noted that as conflict escalates, the parties may lock into a rigid position on an issue. Moreover, as this position is interpreted and reinterpreted over time, negotiators try to remain consistent with the original position—that is, to establish a clear-cut policy that applies in all circumstances. Because these policies are designed to apply to a variety of circumstances, they become broader rather than more specific. If the other party does not readily comply with a negotiator's position or policy, the negotiator's tendency is to escalate his demands or increase the magnitude of his threat for noncompliance. These actions heighten conflict.

Roger Fisher (1969) suggests that most influence situations can be characterized by a demand (what we want) and offers and threats (the consequences of meeting or not meeting the demand). The "who, what, when, and why" of this influence process is depicted in Table 6.1.

Fisher suggests that in most negotiation situations, the parties tend to emphasize the demand and the threat, and he claims this emphasis is greatly misplaced and self-destructive. Rather, negotiators should direct their efforts to the following question: How can we get them (our opponents) to make a choice that is best for us, given that our interests diverge? This approach is largely a matter of focusing

**TABLE 6.1**    Fisher's "Demand" Dynamics

|  | Demand *(The Decision We Desire)* | Offer *(The Consequences of Making the Decision)* | Threat *(The Consequences of Not Making the Decision)* |
|---|---|---|---|
| **Who?** | Who is to make the decision? | Who benefits if the decision is made? | Who gets hurt if the decision is not made? |
| **What?** | Exactly what decision is desired? | If the decision is made, what benefits/costs can be expected? | If the decision is not made, what risks/potential benefits can be expected? |
| **When?** | By what time does the decision have to be made? | When, if ever, will the benefit of making the decision occur? | How soon will the consequences of not making the decision be felt? |
| **Why?** | What makes this a right, proper, and lawful decision? | What makes these consequences fair and legitimate? | What makes these consequences fair and legitimate? |

Every feature of an influence problem can be located somewhere on this schematic map. The nature of a given problem can be discovered through estimating how the presumed adversary would answer the above questions.

R. Fisher, *International Conflict for Beginners* (New York: Harper and Row, 1969), p. 48. Used with permission of the author.

on the other's interests rather than our own. Like role reversal, it requires negotiators to focus less on their own position, and more on clearly understanding the opponent's needs. Moreover, once those needs are understood, parties should invest their efforts not in getting the opponent to come to us, but in moving toward them—in most cases, making offers rather than demands and threats. Fisher suggests several alternative strategies:

• *Give them a "yesable" proposal.* Rather than emphasizing her own position and letting the other party suggest alternatives that she can approve or overrule, a negotiator should direct her efforts to understanding the other side's needs and devising a proposal that will meet those needs. Fisher terms this a "yesable" proposal, one to which the only answer can be "yes, it is acceptable." To succeed, however, this approach requires a negotiator to begin to think about what the other party would want or would agree with, rather than exclusively considering her own goals and needs.

• *Ask for a different decision.* Rather than making demands more general, to fit with their policy, negotiators should endeavor to make demands more specific. Negotiators must determine what specific elements of their demands are most palatable or offensive to the other party, then use this information to refine the demand. "Ask for a different decision," asserts Fisher. Reformulate, repackage, reorganize, rephrase. Fractionate, split, divide, make more specific. Making demands more specific is not making them more rigid; rather, specific demands can be reformulated to meet the other's needs. Fisher, Ury, and Patton (1991) recommend that successful negotiators be skilled at inventing options for mutual gain (see Chapter 4). By inventing and refining ways that both parties can succeed, and by providing a variety of these options to the other party, the likelihood that both parties can select a desirable option is greatly enhanced.

• *Sweeten the offer rather than intensifying the threat.* Negotiators can also make options more palatable by enhancing the attractiveness of accepting them. Again, this is a matter of placing the emphasis on the positive rather than the negative. In the traditional "carrot-and-stick" tactics of managerial motivation, it makes the carrot more attractive rather than enlarging the stick. Promises and offers can be made more attractive in a variety of ways: maximizing their attractive qualities and minimizing their negative ones, showing how they meet the other party's needs, reducing the disadvantages to them of accepting an offer, making offers more credible (i.e., we will do what we promise to do), or setting deadlines on offers so they expire if not accepted quickly. Many would argue that these are common sales tricks akin to rebates, two-for-the-price-of-one offers, today only sales, and extra added attraction elements. They are. The same techniques that salespeople use to move their products can and should be used by negotiators to get another party to accept their position. Many of these techniques are described more fully in Chapter 8.

• *Use legitimacy or objective criteria to evaluate solutions.* Finally, negotiators may insist that alternative solutions be evaluated by objective criteria that meet the test of fairness and legitimacy. Negotiators on both sides should be able to demonstrate that their demands are based on sound facts, calculations, and information, and that preferred solutions are consistent with those facts and information. This procedure will frequently require disclosing and sharing facts, rather than disguising and distorting them. "Here's how we arrived at our proposal. Here are the facts we used, the cost data we used in our estimates, the calculations we made. You can verify these by the following procedures." The more this data is open to public verification and demonstrated to be within the bounds of fairness and legitimacy, the more convincing it will be that the position is independent of the negotiator who advocates it, and the more persuasive the position will be in achieving a settlement.

## Summary

In this section, we reviewed five major strategies that negotiators can use to get derailed negotiations back on track and return to a more productive flow of events: reducing tension and synchronizing the de-escalation of conflict, enhancing the quality of communication between the parties, controlling and limiting the number of issues at stake, establishing commonalities (common goals, common enemies, or common procedures) that can bind the parties together, and enhancing the demands and offers we make to the other. Taken together, these strategies create a large portfolio of alternatives that negotiators can pursue to manage unproductive conflict, enhance deteriorating communications, and find ways to invent acceptable solution alternatives. We now turn to a discussion of other causes of breakdowns in negotiation and ways to manage them.

## SPECIFIC REMEDIES: TRAPS, CHALLENGES, AND PROCESSES

In this section, we address three other ways that negotiation can break down: "traps" that we often set for ourselves, challenges that occur when dealing with particularly difficult opponents, and processes for building more productive, resilient relationships.

### Negotiation "Traps"

Often, negotiators can become their own worst enemies. This is most likely to happen when they engage in behaviors and thought processes that make negotiation more difficult and less productive than it can be. Margaret Neale and Max Bazerman (1991; Bazerman and Neale, 1992) have extensively studied negotiator cognition and rationality, and they describe a number of specific mistakes or heuristics (i.e., cognitive processes) that tend to impair negotiator performance. These include the irrational escalation of commitment, the mythical belief that the issue under negotiation is a "fixed pie," the process of anchoring and adjustment in decision making, issue and problem framing, the availability of information, the "winner's curse," negotiator overconfidence, the law of small numbers, biased causal accounts, the tendency to ignore others' cognitions, and a process called "reactive devaluation." We will discuss each of these in more detail.

**Irrational Escalation of Commitment.** Negotiators sometimes maintain commitment to a course of action, even when that commitment constitutes irrational behavior on their part. One reason this occurs is due to biases in individual perception and judgment; once a course of action is decided, negotiators often seek supportive (confirming) evidence for that choice, while ignoring or failing to seek *dis*confirming evidence. Initial commitments become "set in stone" (see the section on anchoring and adjustment that follows), and a desire for consistency prevents a negotiator from changing that commitment. This desire for consistency is often exacerbated by a desire to save face, to maintain an impression of expertise or control in front of others (see Chapter 9). No one likes to admit error or failure, especially when doing so may be perceived as a weakness in front of the other party. Escalation of commitment is common when a union goes on strike and expects management to eventually capitulate, in competitive bidding or auction situations, or when negotiators make a threat in anger and then find that they have to follow through on it. One way to combat these tendencies is to have an advisor serve as a "reality checkpoint"—someone who is not consumed by the play of the game can warn negotiators when they inadvertently begin to behave irrationally.

**Mythical "Fixed-Pie" Beliefs.**    Although *some* negotiations are categorized correctly as distributive or win-lose, many negotiators tend to assume that *all* negotiations involve a fixed pie. Negotiators often approach negotiation opportunities that are actually integrative in nature as zero-sum games or win-lose, fixed-pie exchanges. The belief in this mythical fixed pie assumes that the possibility for integrative settlements and mutually beneficial trade-offs doesn't exist, and this belief suppresses any efforts to search for such settlements and trade-offs. In the salary negotiations we have frequently used as an example, the job applicant may assume that salary is the only issue and insist on $35,000 when the company is offering $32,000. Only when the two parties discuss the possibilities further do they discover that moving expenses and starting date can also be negotiated, which makes the resolution of the salary issue far easier. In Chapter 4 (on integrative negotiations), we provided advice on minimizing this fixed-pie belief through procedures for inventing options.

**Anchoring and Adjustment.**    Traps in this area are related to the effect of the standard (or anchor) against which subsequent adjustments (gains or losses) are measured during negotiation. The choice of an anchor (e.g., an initial offer or an intended goal) might well be based on faulty or incomplete information and thus be misleading in and of itself. However, once this initial anchor is defined, parties tend to treat it as real and valid and use it as a benchmark to adjust all other judgments relative to it. For example, Bazerman and Neale (1992) report a study in which real estate agents appraising the value of a house were very strongly affected by its asking price. The asking price served as a convenient anchor to use in appraising the value of that house. Goals in negotiation—whether set realistically or carelessly—can also serve as anchors. These anchors may be visible or invisible to the other party (a published market price versus an uncommunicated expectation), and similarly the person who holds them may do so consciously or unconsciously (a specific expectation versus an unexamined, unquestioned expectation or norm). Thorough preparation and the use of a devil's advocate or reality check can help prevent errors of anchoring and adjustment.

**Framing.**    By a frame, we mean the subjective mechanism through which we evaluate and make sense out of situations, leading us to pursue or avoid subsequent actions (Bateson, 1972; Goffman, 1974). In decision theory terms, a frame is a perspective or point of view that we use when gathering information and solving problems. The framing process can cause us to exhibit certain behaviors while ignoring or avoiding others; frames can particularly lead us to seek, avoid, or be neutral about risk in decision making and negotiation. It is in evaluating risk that framing most affects negotiators—framing can make negotiators more or less risk averse or risk seeking. If a negotiator is more risk averse, she may accept any viable offer put on the table simply because she is afraid of losing it. On the other hand, if the negotiator is more risk seeking, she should be willing to pass up an offer, choosing instead to wait for a better offer or for possible future concessions.

The tendency to risk aversion or risk seeking may be based on the reference point against which offers and concessions are judged (see the preceding section on anchoring and adjustment). In a typical salary negotiation, a number of reference points are possible (adapted from Bazerman and Neale, 1992):

1. Your current salary ($30,000).
2. Your potential employer's initial offer to you ($35,000).
3. The least you feel you are willing to accept ($38,000).
4. Your estimate of the most the company is willing to offer to you ($40,000).
5. Your initial salary request ($45,000).

As you consider each point in this list (from the first to the fifth), the frame suggested (through which you will evaluate negotiation progress and possible success) changes from positive to negative. A given settlement (let's say $35,000), which could be judged as a *gain* with regard to your current salary, becomes progressively framed as a *loss* as you move down the list because the settlement of $35,000 is less than your initial request of $45,000.

This positive/negative framing process is not inconsequential. Negotiations in which the outcomes are negatively framed tend to produce fewer concessions, reach fewer agreements, and perceive outcomes as less fair than positively framed negotiations (Bazerman and Neale, 1992, p. 39.) Remedies for framing effects are similar to those mentioned above (e.g., better information, thorough analysis, and reality checks) but are more difficult to achieve (and thus, more critical) because frames are often tied to deeply held matters of personal value and belief or other anchors that we cannot detect.

**Availability of Information.**    Negotiators must also be concerned with information availability or ease of retrievability—how easily it can be recalled and used to inform or evaluate a process or an option. In negotiation, the availability trap operates when information that is presented in more vivid, colorful, or attention-getting ways becomes easier to recall, and thus more central and critical in evaluating events and options. Information presented through a particularly clear chart, diagram, or formula (even if it is overly simplified) might be used more readily than data that is confusing, detailed, or hard to understand.

Availability of information also affects negotiation through the use of established "search patterns." If we have a favorite way of collecting information or key things we tend to look for, we will use these patterns repeatedly and perhaps overvalue the information that comes from them. In Chapter 5, we pointed out that many negotiators fail to plan, and that the planning they do may tend to focus on a limited subset of information that is easily available. In sum, negotiators run the risk of letting availability overwhelm the need for and benefits of thorough analysis.

**The "Winner's Curse."**   The *winner's curse* is a term that describes the discomfort and misgivings that typically accompany a negotiation "win" that comes too easily. Too quick a capitulation on the other party's part often leaves the winner wondering, "could I have gotten this for less?" or asking "What's wrong with the item/product/option?" Because a settlement was achieved so easily, the other side (must) know more or have insight into an unseen advantage; thus, either "I could have done better" or "this must be a bad deal." In the salary example, if we ask for $45,000 and the boss immediately says yes, we are likely to suffer the winner's curse, even if we got a great salary.

There are a variety of remedies for the winner's curse. First, the value of thorough investigation and analysis cannot be underestimated; they provide the negotiator with an independent verification of the worth of the settlement. Negotiators can also try to secure performance or quality guarantees from the other party to make sure the outcome is not faulty and defective.

**Overconfidence.**   Overconfidence in your own judgments—the tendency to believe in your ability to be correct or accurate more often than is really true—has a double-edged effect. First, overconfidence can solidify the degree to which you support a position or option that may actually be incorrect or inappropriate. Second, overconfidence in your own judgment can lead you to discount the worth or validity of others' judgment, in effect shutting down other parties as sources of information, interests, and options necessary for a successful integrative negotiation. Neale and Bazerman (1983) report that negotiators not made aware of the overconfidence heuristic tended to overestimate their probability of being successful, and they were significantly less likely to compromise or reach agreements than trained negotiators. An awareness of this tendency and a commitment to more thorough planning seem to be the appropriate remedies.

**The Law of Small Numbers.**   In decision theory, the law of small numbers has to do with the tendency to draw big conclusions from small sample sizes. In negotiation, the law of small numbers applies to the way negotiators learn (and extrapolate) from their own experience. If that experience is limited in time or in scope (e.g., all one's prior negotiations have been hard-fought and distributive), the tendency is to project those norms and behaviors on future negotiations—often with disastrous effect. The smaller the prior sample (i.e., the more limited the negotiation experience), the greater the possibility that past lessons will be erroneously used to imply what will happen in the future. Styles and strategies that worked in the past *may* not work in the future, and *will* not work if future negotiations differ significantly from past experiences. The remedy here is to broaden your experience and be cautious about using only your own experience to deduce the future. In addition, including expert negotiators in the planning process assures that we challenge the assumptions underlying our strategic and tactical planning.

**Biased Causal Accounts.**    This is the process by which bias creeps into our accounts of what caused the current situation, and it is frequently a problem when the purpose of the negotiation is to work out the current problem. For example, two managers from different divisions of a company are negotiating how to deal with a shipment of faulty computer chips and the cost of repairing or replacing them. Manager A claims the chips went out of his plant with 100 percent quality; Manager B claims that when they were installed in computers, 20 percent of the computers failed. Causal accounts will tend to affect the attributions the parties make about the following:

- How did Manager A know that the chips left his plant at 100 percent quality?
- Is there any way the workers in Plant A could ship defective chips, or did they become defective after they left their plant?
- Did the workers in Plant B do anything to harm the chips once they were received in Plant B?
- How were the chips transported, and did that affect the chips?
- If the workers in Plant A were truly at fault, did they make any attempt to apologize or to make amends or retribution?

Each of these questions affects the observing negotiator's causal accounting process and may affect how the parties frame the negotiation, what type of strategy they will choose (e.g., distributive or integrative), or even what outcomes to pursue (correction, repair, replacement, repayment, etc.). Research in this area is growing (e.g., Bies and Moag, 1986; Bies and Shapiro, 1987; Bies, Shapiro, and Cummings, 1988; Einhorn and Hogarth, 1986; Shapiro, 1991) and suggests that causal accounts can have strong effects on the choices involved in the planning and conduct of negotiations. As with other informational heuristics, better information (less biased and more objective) can help prevent and correct poor attributions of what causes what.

**Ignoring Others' Cognitions.**    Negotiators often just don't bother to ask the other party what they see and think, thus forcing themselves to work with faulty or incomplete information, and thus producing faulty results. Failure to consider others' cognitions allows negotiators to simplify their thinking about otherwise complex processes (usually leading to a more distributive strategy), causing a failure to recognize the contingent nature of their behaviors and responses. Although this "failure to consider" might be attributed to some basic, underlying bias toward the other party, research suggests that it is more often a way "to make decision making under uncertainty more manageable" (Carroll, Bazerman, and Maury, 1988). Research also suggests that training and awareness of this trap reduces this bias somewhat, but that the improvement is rather weak (Carroll, Delquie, Halpern, and Bazerman, 1990). The emotional drives at work here can be very deep-seated, and they can only be avoided if negotiators explicitly focus on accurately understanding the other party's interests, goals, and perspective.

**Reactive Devaluation.** Reactive devaluation is the process of devaluing the other party's concessions simply because your opponent made them (Stillenger, Epelbaum, Keltner, and Ross, 1990). This devaluation may be based in emotionality ("I just don't like that so-and-so") or on distrust fostered by past experience. Reactive devaluation leads us to minimize the magnitude of a concession made by a disliked other, reduce our willingness to respond with a concession of equal size, or motivate us to want to seek even more once a concession has been made (see Neale and Bazerman, 1992b). Reactive devaluation may be minimized by maintaining an *objective* view of the process (or charging someone on your side to do so and to remind you of it periodically); by clarifying each side's preferences on options and concessions before making any (Stillenger, Epelbaum, Keltner, and Ross 1990); or by using a third party to mediate or "filter" concession-making processes (see Chapter 12).

---

**Thinking Rationally about Negotiation**

Bazerman and Neale (1992) help poor negotiations by providing definitions and remedies for the most frequent types of cognitive "traps" negotiators set for themselves. They also offer more general prescriptive advice to negotiators; we can present their prescriptions as nine diagnostic questions:

1. What will you do if you don't reach agreement with the other party?
2. What will they do if they fail to reach an agreement with you?
3. What are the true issues at stake?
4. How important is each issue to you?
5. How important is each issue to them?
6. What is the likely bargaining zone?
7. Where do trade-offs exist?
8. What is the likely degree to which your perceptions and decision making processes are affected by (these) cognitive traps?
9. What is the likely degree to which the other party is affected by them?

## CHALLENGES WHEN DEALING WITH OTHER NEGOTIATORS

Whether or not negotiators lay traps for themselves, they always run the risk of encountering parties who, for any of a number of reasons, are "difficult" negotiators. This section addresses methods negotiators can use when meeting such challenges; discusses some of the difficult negotiator types one might come across; and explains the skills and behaviors needed to defend against such parties, convert them to a more productive negotiation process, or both.

In trying to move from win-lose to win-win negotiations, at least three challenges exist:

- What to do when the other side uses distributive tactics (i.e., dirty tricks).
- What to do if the other side is more powerful.
- What to do if the other side is just generally difficult to deal with.

### Responding to the Other Side When They Use Dirty Tricks

By *dirty tricks,* we mean the distributive tactics that one side applies in a negotiation to put pressure on the other side to do something that is probably not in their best interest to do. We presented a list of such tactics in Chapter 3 when we discussed distributive negotiation. In that chapter, we also discussed strategies for responding to or dealing with these tactics (pp. 77–78). To briefly summarize, a party can respond in any of these ways:

1. Ignore them. A tactic ignored is, essentially, a tactic "defanged"; if it is recognized, it has no power to bring undue pressure to bear. Unfortunately, some bargainers are slow learners; if you ignore them, they may simply not get the message that you want something different to happen.

2. "Call" them on it. Let your opponents know you see what they are trying to do when they use dirty tricks by pointing the tactic out and raising it to the level of open discussion. Do so tactfully, but firmly. Indicate your distress or displeasure with the tactic and explain why it is problematic for you. Sometimes, the embarrassment value of such an observation is sufficient to make negotiators disavow the tactic and abandon its future use, or even convert their behavior to more win-win negotiating.

3. Respond in kind. We also suggested this approach in Chapter 3. However, responding in kind is likely to escalate the conflict, and it is not consistent with the principles we are proposing here.

4. Offer to change to more productive methods. Announce that you have noted your opponent's behavior and suggest a better way to negotiate. Fisher, Ury, and Patton (1991), in advising well-intentioned bargainers not to let themselves be victimized, suggest a comprehensive strategy: "Recognize the tactic, raise the issue explicitly, and question the tactic's legitimacy and desirability—negotiate over it" (p. 130). The logic of this advice lies in the assumption that, once the "trickster" understands that (1) you know what

he is doing and (2) continuing this behavior will entail certain costs (including the possibility that you will walk away from the negotiation), he will respond to your suggestion for a more integrative exchange (see Chapter 4).

### Responding to the Other Side When They Are More Powerful

Relative power alone can be a good predictor of how a conflict will evolve. Other things being equal, when power is unequal, victory typically goes to the more powerful party. Power imbalances in negotiation can represent clear dangers to the satisfaction of personal needs and to the collaborative process. First, high-power parties tend to pay little heed to the needs of lower power parties, who either settle for such short shrift (and don't get their needs met) or use disruptive, attention-getting tactics that make collaboration very difficult (Donohue and Kolt, 1992). Second, lower power parties are not usually in a position to engender the integrative processes. Integrative negotiation requires a tolerance of change and flexibility, which often requires negotiators to give up some control over outcomes; lower power parties "have less to give, and thus less flexibility to offer the other party" (Donohue and Kolt, p. 107).

When dealing with an opponent with more power, negotiators have at least four alternatives:

1. Protect themselves.
2. Cultivate their BATNA.
3. Formulate a "trip wire alert system."
4. Correct the power imbalance.

Negotiators can *protect themselves* by keeping in mind their real interests, that negotiation may be the preferred approach to getting those interests met, and that excessive accommodation to the high-power party will not serve them well over the long term. A point of caution, though: knowing your resistance point may provide a clear measure of minimum acceptability (lowest price, maximum monthly payment, etc.). However, too strict an adherence to it may deprive you of creativity and flexibility, which are critical components to the design of an integrative arrangement. It may also limit your ability to use information that emerges during the exchange (Fisher, Ury, and Patton, 1991).

Alternatively, negotiators should know and *cultivate their BATNA,* which represents the best they can accomplish without negotiation or an alternative deal. Many negotiators bargain without a clear definition of their BATNA; we pointed out in Chapters 3 and 4 that the lack of such a critical reference point gives negotiators less power because they are limited to what they can achieve in the current negotiation (Fisher, Ury, and Patton, 1991).

A clear, strong BATNA may also be reinforced by additional safety measures. Low-power negotiators are also advised to *formulate a "trip wire" alert system,* which serves as an early warning signal when bargaining enters the safety zone close to the walk-away option or the BATNA (Fisher, Ury, and Patton, 1991). The trip wire tells the negotiator to exercise special caution and pay increased attention to the negotiation in progress, as his options are becoming more constrained. Given that negotiations often become intense and engrossing at such points, it might be appropriate to assign a friendly party, even a co-negotiator, to attend to the trip wire and to notify the involved negotiator at the critical time.

The foregoing options involve dealing with an extant power imbalance. A final option for dealing with more powerful parties is to *correct the imbalance.* Three approaches to this are possible: *lower power parties taking power, high-power parties giving power,* or *third parties managing the transfer* and balance of power. The first approach, power-taking, is typically not feasible in negotiations; as we already mentioned, the disruptive or attention-getting actions required for lower power parties to take power typically contribute to a distributive exchange, generating in-kind responses from the high-power party. However, as we will point out in Chapter 10, power in negotiation is multifaceted, and power may be gained on dimensions different from those currently held by the high-power party. The third approach *is* feasible, and it represents a strategy used often by mediators and other third parties (see Chapter 12).

The middle, remaining approach is for the high-power party to *give* power to the other party to achieve a power balance. Such actions include sharing resources; sharing control over certain processes or outcomes (e.g., agendas, decisions, etc.); focusing on common interests rather than solely on their (high-power) interests; or educating the lower power party as to the power they *do* have and how to use it more effectively (Donohue and Kolt, 1992). The immediate question is why high-power parties would ever choose to give power away. The answer is complex. First, sharing power may facilitate a better integrative process. Second, even if one party does have power over the other, the best the high-power party can hope for is compliance rather than enthusiastic cooperation. Finally, no power imbalance exists forever, and when the low-power party does gain a power base or a BATNA, they are likely to either sever the relationship or look for some form of "revenge."

## Responding When the Other Side Is Being Difficult

When the other side presents a clearly problematic pattern of difficult behavior, two possibilities exist: You may be dealing with a negotiator who does not know any other process by which to negotiate, but who might be responsive to suggestions for changing his behavior. The second possibility is that you are dealing with a type of difficult person whose behaviors are consistent both within and outside of the negotiation context. However, in most cases you won't know enough about the other to make the distinction. In the following section, we will review several approaches for dealing with difficult opponents. The first, proposed by Ury (1991), suggests a broad-based approach that may be used with any difficult opponent, including an opponent using dirty tricks. The second, based on the work of Bramson (1981), suggests different strategies for dealing with opponents with particularly difficult styles.

**Ury's "Breakthrough Approach."**    William Ury (1991) suggests a five-stage "breakthrough approach," which sees obstacles set by the opponent as challenges that you can address by specific strategies. Ury's plan involves

- Creating a favorable negotiation environment, by
- Regaining your "mental balance" and controlling your own behavior and
- Helping the other party achieve similar balance and control;
- Changing the game from a distributive one to an integrative one;
- Overcoming the other party's skepticism by jointly crafting a mutually satisfactory agreement, and
- Achieving closure through firm, even-handed use of your negotiating power.

Ury suggests that his approach operates on the principle of acting *counterintuitively:*

> It requires you to do the opposite of what you might naturally do in difficult situations. When your opponent stonewalls or attacks you, you feel like responding in kind. When he insists on his position, you want to reject it and assert your own. When he exerts pressure, you are inclined to retaliate with direct counterpressure. But in trying to break down your opponent's resistance, you usually only increase it.
>
> The essence of the breakthrough strategy is indirect action. You try to *go around* his resistance. Rather than pounding in a new idea from the outside, you encourage him to reach from within. Rather than telling him what to do, you let him figure it out. Rather than trying to break down his resistance, you make it easier for him to break through it himself. In short, breakthrough negotiation is the art of letting the other person have it *your* way" (Ury, 1991, p. 9, emphasis in original).

Ury proposes a five-step process for this counterintuitive pattern of responding (the titles of the steps are Ury's; see Table 6.2).

***Stage One: Don't React—Go to the Balcony.***    As the above quote pointed out, the natural reaction to difficulty is to strike back, give in, or break off negotiations. None of these behaviors serve the negotiator's legitimate interests, let alone move the process in an integrative direction. The resulting challenge to this obstacle is *to not react,* thereby avoiding the destructive effect reacting naturally would have on the process. Instead, Ury recommends that you "go to the balcony"—that is, psychologically remove yourself from the interaction so that you become an observer to your own interaction with the other. The advantages of this are that

- It gives you distance from the dispute, and from your emotions.
- It creates "breathing space," allowing you to cool off so your eventual response can be more reasoned.
- It creates an opportunity for you to see the situation in context and to remind yourself why you were there in the first place.

**TABLE 6.2**   Ury's Strategies for Managing Difficult Negotiators

| Steps | Barriers to Cooperation | Challenges | Strategies |
|---|---|---|---|
| **Step 1** | Your natural reaction to opponents' competitive behavior | Don't react | Go to the balcony |
| **Step 2** | Others' negative emotions | Disarm them | Step to their side |
| **Step 3** | Others' positional behavior | Change the game | Don't react, reframe |
| **Step 4** | Others' skepticism about benefits of agreement | Make it easy for them to say yes | Build them a "golden bridge" |
| **Step 5** | Others' perceived power | Make it hard to say no | Bring them to their senses, not their knees |

Adapted from "Strategy Table," from *Getting Past No* by William Ury. Copyright © 1991 by William Ury. Used by permission of Bantam Books, a division of Bantam Doubleday Dell Publishing Group, Inc.

***Stage Two: Disarm Them—Step to Their Side.***   As we have often pointed out, negativity and attack in negotiation tend to breed more of the same; tensions heighten, and damaging exchanges tend to escalate. Confrontation and impending impasse typically elicit negative emotions for both sides. The negotiator's challenge is to act counterintuitively—to deflect or side-step the other party's negativity, disarming them through positive, constructive communication. The strategy of *stepping to the other's side* conveys the compelling image of "coming around" the table to listen to and acknowledge the other party's legitimate points, needs, and concerns. This strategy of disarmament includes

- Active listening.
- Acknowledging the other's points, without necessarily conceding their truth or accuracy.
- Agreeing, wherever you can, to recognize points of understanding that might provide the foundation for subsequent agreement.
- Acknowledging the other party personally, as a mark of recognition of and respect for their authority, sensitivities, and competencies.
- Expressing *your* views clearly and considerately.

***Stage Three: Change the Game—Don't Reject . . . Reframe.***   Earlier in this chapter, we discussed how the framing of a problem can be a powerful "trap" for negotiators. Given the obstacle of the other party's positional behavior, the challenge at this stage is to change the game by proactively *reframing* their tactics. A reframing strategy includes the following *active* behaviors:

- Asking open-ended, problem-solving questions.

- Reframing their tactics (for example, if they present you with a stone wall, ignore it, test it, or reinterpret it as just a wish on their part; if they attack you, ignore it, deflect it from you to the problem, or recast it in less confrontational terms that highlight common goals and interests).
- Directly and openly negotiate the rules of the game.

***Stage Four: Make It Easy To Say Yes—Build Them a Golden Bridge.***   This is the persuasive stage of the process, wherein the challenge (and opportunity) for you is to make it easy for them to say yes to your offer (see, for example, Fisher, 1969). According to Ury (1991, p. 89), the four most common objections from the other party are these: (1) it's not their idea (i.e., "not invented here"); (2) it doesn't address one of their basic interests; (3) it might cause them to lose face or look bad to some important constituency; or (4) it requires too big an adjustment for them (i.e., "too much, too fast"). The proposed strategy is to close this gap by *building a golden bridge,* to entice them to "cross over" to agreement by

- Involving them in the actual design of an agreement that addresses both the interests and aversions of *all* parties.
- As much as possible, satisfying their unmet needs without jeopardizing the basic fabric of the agreement.
- Recognizing and being empathetic to the range of personal and organizational demands and expectations that they face.
- Helping them to save face and deal with their constituencies by providing justifications for the agreement—changed conditions, third-party advice or expertise, or some objective standard of fairness.
- "Going slow to go fast" (Ury, p. 105), walking them through complex agreements step by step and not rushing closure until they are ready.

***Stage Five: Make it Hard to Say No—Bring Them to Their Senses, Not Their Knees.***   Throughout the first four stages, the other party may maintain an abiding belief in the value of their superior power or wits. Having made it easy for them to say yes, you must now address the challenge of making it hard for them to say no. Confronting power plays with power plays will most likely return you to the competitive dynamics you have worked to change, so your strategy must be to *bring them to their senses without bringing them to their knees.* The components of this strategy are to

- Tend to your BATNA, strengthening it and making sure the other parties know what it is.
- Help them think about the consequences of no agreement.
- If necessary, actually use your BATNA, being careful to anticipate and defuse their reaction to what may seem (to them) to be a punitive move on your part.
- Keep sharpening their choice—refer back to the attractive terms that got them to "cross the bridge" and help them maintain their focus on the advantages of completing the deal.

- Fashion a *lasting* agreement, thinking through and planning for implementation.

**Responding to Difficult People.**    Sometimes, problems in negotiation can be traced to difficulties in the other's behavioral style. The subject of how to deal with difficult people in the workplace has received increasing attention in recent years (e.g., Bramson, 1981, 1992; Bernstein and Rosen, 1989; Solomon, 1990). These authors (and other books on the same theme) make several important points. First, *all of us* exhibit difficult behaviors or are difficult to deal with at times; these works address those characters who are *invariably* difficult and whose behaviors conform to predictable and identifiable patterns. Second, *what is difficult behavior to one person is not difficult to another.* "Difficult" behavior may say as much about the receiver as it does about the sender. Person A may have a great deal of difficulty contending with a very aggressive opponent, whereas Person B has no difficulty with that same opponent. Third, *difficult people do what they do because it "works" for them.* Their behavior gives them control, feels comfortable, and lets them get their way. We reinforce the difficult behavior by giving in to it, providing the difficult person ample reason to behave in the present and future in ways that were useful in the past. Difficult people also may continue their difficult ways because they honestly are not aware of the long-term costs to people and organizations who must contend with them. Finally, we provide advice for coping with these invariably difficult people—*contending with their behavior on equal behavioral terms*—as opposed to giving in to them, accepting their behavior, or getting them to change their values, beliefs, or attitudes. In short, we must effectively counterbalance the potential power these behaviors give those who use them. The nearby box offers a general framework for coping with a difficult opponent.

---

**Coping with Difficult Negotiators: A Summary.**

Bramson (1981) proposes three stages for coping effectively with a difficult opponent:

1. Recognize the behavior for what it is.
2. Understand why the behavior exists and tends to persist.
3. Cope to produce effective behavior—for you, and for them.

Once you go through these stages and decide to try to cope with difficult people, six basic steps are involved:

1. *Assess* the situation *realistically.* More specifically,
   - Is the difficult behavior "in character" for this opponent (if not, wait it out—perhaps the person is just having a bad day).
   - Is my reaction to the situation appropriate and proportional (am I overreacting; should I really try to take this person on)?
   - Was there an identifiable trigger for the behavior (did I do something to create this behavior in the opponent)?

---

**Coping with Difficult Negotiators: A Summary** *(Continued)*

- Will direct, open discussion solve the behavioral problem? If not, I need to formulate a coping plan.

2. *Stop wishing* difficult people were different.
   - Wishing people were different, or blaming them, may only exacerbate the problem rather than solving it.

3. *Get some distance* between you and the difficulty.
   - *Label* the problem—characterize it so you can identify a way to respond. Although this may oversimplify the problem, it does create a way to distance yourself from the problem and begin planning for action.
   - Understand the problem—determine what might have caused it, or what triggers it.

4. *Formulate* a relevant coping plan.

5. *Implement* the plan *assertively.*

6. *Monitor* your effectiveness and *modify* your plan accordingly.

Relating to difficult people in negotiation or other highly charged, results-oriented exchanges is a critically important skill. We encourage anyone wishing to go beyond the basics presented here to refer to Bramson (1981), on which we have primarily based this presentation, and to other sources (e.g., Solomon, 1990; Ury, 1991) to build their skills and insights.

## SUMMARY

Through any number of different avenues—breakdowns in communication, escalation of anger and mistrust, polarization of positions and refusal to compromise, or simply the inability to invent options that are satisfactory to both sides—negotiations often break down. Productive dialogue stops. The parties may continue talking, but the communication is usually characterized by trying to sell or force one's own position, talking about the other's unreasonable position and uncooperative behavior, or both. When these breakdowns occur, the parties may simply agree to recess, "cool off," and come back tomorrow. More commonly, however, the parties fail to agree and walk away angry and upset. Although they may privately wish there was some way to get back together, they usually don't know how to arrange a reconciliation.

This chapter reviewed actions that the parties can take to return to a productive dialogue, focusing on methods that parties can try without outside assistance. When so left to their own devices, the parties themselves might try these techniques:

- Reduce tension by separating themselves from one another through cooling-off periods, talking about emotions and feelings, or attempting to synchronize de-escalation of the conflict.

- Improve the accuracy of communication by mirroring the other's statements or role reversal.
- Keep the number of issues under control so new issues are not added and large issues are divided into smaller ones;
- Search for commonalities in positions, ways to define the issues so both parties can achieve their objectives (integrative frameworks), and superordinate goals that will unite parties toward a common objective.
- Make each one's own preferred options more desirable and palatable to the opponent by the way they state, propose, and package their proposals.

We also dealt with two problem areas that plague most negotiators at one time or another: self-laid "traps" and dealing with difficult negotiations and negotiators. The tools we suggest here are broad in function and in application and represent self-help for negotiators in dealing with stalled or problematic exchanges. None of these methods and remedies are panaceas, and they should be chosen and applied with a reasonable amount of sensitivity to the needs and limitations of the subject situations and of the negotiators involved in them.

# CHAPTER 7

# Communication Processes

Communication is at the heart of the negotiating process. Although planning, preparing for, evaluating, and strategizing are all key negotiation elements, communication is the central instrumental process. Even if negotiators deal with one another simply by trading bids and offers on slips of paper, communication processes, both verbal and nonverbal, are critical to achieving negotiation goals. According to a recent review,

> (T)he activity of having or managing a conflict occurs through communication. More specifically, communication undergirds the setting and reframing of goals; the defining and narrowing of conflict issues; the developing of relationships between disputants and among constituents; the selecting and implementing of strategies and tactics; the generating, attacking, and defending of alternative solutions; and the reaching and confirming of agreements. (Putman and Poole, 1987, p. 550)

This chapter and the next focus on the processes by which negotiators influence one another's understanding, beliefs, outlook, and, ultimately, behavior. The topics that we will review in these chapters frequently overlap. In this chapter on communication, we will discuss the basic structures and processes by which information and meaning are transmitted from one person to another. In Chapter 8, on persuasion, we continue our examination of the communication process, paying particular attention to how communication tools can be used to influence another in the desired manner. We will review the ways that we can use persuasion tactics to defend ourselves against another's influence attempts.

Many communication theorists have studied conflict and negotiation, aiming "to uncover insights about the way media, messages, and symbols function in the negotiation process" (Putnam and Roloff, 1992, p. 2). In a recent review of this research, Putnam and Poole (1987) list a variety of linkages between communication and four specific components of conflict situations: actors, issues, relationships, and contexts. Focusing on the "arena" of bargaining and negotiations, in particular, Putnam and Poole report significant findings for a number of variables studied in relation to these components. See Table 7.1 for their listing of components and variables of conflict.

Clearly, communication pervades the negotiation process, and "communication scholarship sets forth a perspective for understanding the negotiation process, for examining bargaining interaction as a *system,* and for exploring the *micro*

**TABLE 7.1**   Significant Variables in Studies of Communication and Negotiation

| Component | Variables |
|---|---|
| **Actors** | Perspective-taking ability<br>Credibility<br>Face-saving ability |
| **Issues** | Distributive/integrative goals and issues, specifically involving<br>    information exchange<br>    negotiation strategies<br>    issue development<br>    phase analysis |
| **Relationships** | Power dependency<br>Bargainer's organizational role<br>Bargainer/constituency relationship |
| **Contexts** | Economic, social, and political environment<br>Bargaining history<br>Normative rules |

Adapted from L. Putnam and M. Poole in F. Jablin, L. Putnam, K. Roberts, and L. Porter (eds.), *Handbook of Organizational Communication: An Interdisciplinary Perspective* (Newbury Park, CA: Sage, 1987), Table 16.1, p. 585.

*elements* and subtleties that frequently alter the course of negotiations" (Chatman, Putnam, and Sondak, 1991, p. 159; emphasis added).

In this chapter, we will view negotiation as a communicative process involving the exchange of views, ideas, and perspectives, and we will examine a variety of theoretical approaches to it. We will address negotiation communication through a review of research on phase models; these models propose that the negotiation process flows through specific phases or stages: a beginning stage, a middle stage, and an end stage. Following this review, we will focus more narrowly on a communication model of interpersonal exchange, emphasizing the mechanisms by which messages are encoded, sent, received, and decoded. This model will also be used in Chapter 8, where we use a communication model to examine the persuasion process in negotiation. In both chapters, we will draw from the wide variety of applied theory and research that is available from social psychological studies of opinion and attitude change so we can understand the negotiation process from this perspective.

## COMMUNICATION IN NEGOTIATION: PHASE MODELS

### Communication in Negotiation: The Analysis of Processes

One reason that communication processes in negotiation have received relatively little research attention is the high cost of studying this process. Many of the other elements that affect negotiation outcomes—the power of the parties, magnitude of the stakes, nature of the problem, and the like—can be approached in research through relatively simple manipulations. In contrast, studying live negotiation deliberations requires both an intensive analysis of a great wealth of free-flowing communication and effective mechanisms for reducing this information to meaningful categories, sequences, and generalizations. As a result, researchers have either reported detailed transcripts (Douglas, 1962) with very little precise analysis, or they have preferred to characterize the communication patterns in broad generalizations (e.g., competitive, defensive, supportive, antagonistic).

Morley and Stephenson (1977) proposed that a scheme for analyzing communication in small groups (Bales, 1950) might be modified to understand negotiation dialogue. Bales proposed a framework for analyzing dialogue from small group meetings, using categories representing two major dimensions of group activity: "task" activities, in which group members focused on the nature of the problem to be solved or job to be accomplished, and "process" activities, in which group members displayed various social-emotional reactions to one another as the activity progressed. Bales' analysis demonstrated that communication changed as the group worked on the task and that definite stages of group work could be identified.

Morley and Stephenson (1977) extended Bales' (1950) work by defining a content communication analysis mechanism (Conference Process Analysis) for assessing negotiation deliberations. They identified three dimensions of such communication: mode, resource, and reference. The *mode* dimension indicates how information is being exchanged, for example, by offers, acceptances, rejections, or seeking responses from the other side. The *resource* dimension refers to the function of the information being exchanged (i.e., structuring the negotiations, as when discussing procedures; focusing on outcomes, as when discussing settlement points or limits; acknowledging others' behaviors, as with praise or criticism; and exchanging information, such as facts or supporting data). Finally, the *reference* dimension indicates who is being talked about in the information: the negotiator, a person on his own team or someone on the other team, the negotiator's organization, the opposing organization, or some combination of the above.

By applying this coding scheme to transcripts of negotiations in a complex role play, the authors were able to confirm that negotiation, like communication in problem-solving groups, proceeds through distinct phases or stages. In the early stages, negotiators are engaged in behavior to state and defend their own position (and their group's position) to the opponent. The most important elements of this stage are building a strong case and demonstrating power. At some point, negotiators move to a second phase of communication. During this phase, negotiators become less competitive and protective of their original position; they move from a more expository mode to a problem-oriented mode, searching for possible solutions to the criteria or limits that were defined earlier. Finally, in the third stage, negotiators work to achieve a joint solution. At this point, they are trying to agree on a settlement point that will satisfy them and those they represent. As you can see, the analysis of communication patterns follows the stages or sequences model of negotiation that many researchers have proposed (see Chapter 3) and that research in the communication field seems to support.

## Phase Models of Negotiation

Holmes (1992), examining work by others (e.g., Douglas, 1962; Gulliver, 1979; Morley and Stephenson, 1977), states that "phase models provide a narrative explanation of negotiation process; that is, they identify sequences of events that constitute the story of a negotiation . . . (A) *phase* is a coherent period of interaction characterized by a dominant constellation of communicative acts" that "serves a set of related functions in the movement from initiation to resolution of a dispute" (Holmes, p. 83; italics in original). Phase research typically addresses three types of questions (Holmes and Poole, 1991):

How interaction between parties changes over time.

How interaction structures, over time, relate to inputs and outcomes.

How tactics or interventions (e.g., changing actors) affect the development of a negotiation.

These questions typically are studied from one of two "process" approaches: how negotiators create, modify, and maintain meaning through interaction (an "interpretive-symbolic" perspective) or how negotiators develop verbal and nonverbal messages in a sequential pattern (a "systems-interaction" perspective) (Chatman et al., 1991). Of these two, the latter contributes more directly to work on phase models of negotiation. Systems-interaction research typically involves analyzing communication exchanges using some sort of categorical coding scheme (e.g., Bales, 1950; Morley and Stephenson, 1977; Walcott & Hoppmann, 1975) to detect changes in interaction over time.

Recent years have seen a marked increased in interest in conflict/negotiation phase modeling. This work has been both descriptive and prescriptive—some authors describe what they have observed in natural settings, whereas others advise or prescribe certain activity sequences they feel will lead to more effective negotiation. Much of this work is summarized in Table 7.2.

As the table shows, the various models fit nicely into a general structure of three phases, or stages: a beginning (or initiation) phase, a middle (or problem-solving) phase, and an ending (or resolution) phase. All are compatible with the assumptions and advice we offered in Chapter 5, on negotiation strategy and planning. However, a cautionary note is in order here. As Holmes (1992) points out, the "descriptive models depict *successful* negotiations" in that "unsuccessful negotiations do not proceed through the orderly stages of phase models" but tend to *stall interminably in the intermediate phase or cycle within or between the beginning and middle stages,* without achieving successful closure (Holmes, p. 92, emphasis added).

Holmes proposes that the phase structure of a negotiation arises from three factors:

**TABLE 7.2**   Phase Models of Negotiation: Labels and Descriptions

| *Phases* | *Prescriptive Models* | *Descriptive Models* |
| --- | --- | --- |
| **Initiation** | Exploration;[1] Preliminaries;[2] Diagnostic;[3] Introduction and relationship development.[4] | Establishing the range;[5] Search for arena, agenda, and issue identification;[6] Agenda definition and problem formulation.[7] |
| **Problem Solving** | Expectation structuring, movement, and solution development;[1] Positioning, bargaining, exploration;[2] Formulation;[3] Problem clarification and relationship development, problem solving.[4] | Reconnoitering the range;[5] Exploring the range, narrowing the range, preliminaries to final bargaining;[6] Narrowing differences.[7] |
| **Resolution** | Conclusion;[1] Settlement;[2] Details;[3] Resolution structuring.[4] | Precipitating the decision-making crisis;[5] Final bargaining, ritualization, execution;[6] Testing, agreement, and implementation.[7] |

*Model Legend:* [1]Atkinson (1980); [2]Carlisle and Leary (1981); [3]Zartman and Berman (1982); [4]Donohue, Kaufman, Smith, and Ramesh (1990); [5]Douglas (1962); [6]Gulliver (1979); [7]Putnam, Wilson, and Turner (1990).

Adapted from M. Holmes, "Phase Structures in Negotiation," in L. Putnam and M. Roloff (eds.), *Communication and Negotiation* (Newbury Park, CA: Sage, 1992), Tables 4.1 and 4.2, pp. 87–88.

"*Local processes*" as parties react to each other and attempt to gain control over events.

"*Cultural expectations*" as parties enact or express what they believe to be appropriate negotiation behaviors.

"*Global processes*" as the parties attempt to move the negotiation through the phases from beginning to end.

An alternative (but compatible) model, developed by Poole and Doelger (1986), suggests that negotiation phase structure is caused by two underlying structures, one entailing the parties' shared "mental model" of the task to be accomplished (which may develop as the negotiation unfolds), and the other involving the recognized rules of conversational exchange (e.g., staying on topic, taking turns speaking, etc.). The joint influence of these two underlying structures, if both are compatible, will create an orderly progression toward successful closure. If they are incompatible, as when local conversational norms override global assumptions of phase structure (e.g., the conversation wanders off the topic or strays back and forth between topics involving initiation and problem-solving [see Table 7.2]), disorder and digression may occur (Wilson and Putnam, 1990).

Although phase modeling of negotiation offers much potential value in enhancing our understanding of negotiation, further research is necessary before it becomes a proactive tool for improving negotiation practice. In particular, Holmes' (1992) review suggests that more study must be done about the nature of the phases themselves and about the nature of the processes that enable or drive the movement from phase to phase. Simple descriptions, or even prescriptions of the order of events in a negotiation, are insufficient to improve negotiation practice.

## Key Issues Regarding Negotiation Phases

As the foregoing section suggests, negotiation phase research offers great promise for enhancing our understanding of the negotiation process. It is clear that most, if not all, of this work fits nicely within the three-stage model that traces back to the pioneering work of Ann Douglas (1957, 1962). For simplicity's sake, as we suggested earlier, we will call these three stages the beginning, middle, and end of the negotiation process. Within each stage, we will address some of the key issues of perception and communication that have not been addressed elsewhere in this book:

- *Beginning Stage:* perceptual error, attributions and biases, framing.
- *Middle Stage:* offering sequences and issue development, evolution of framework and detail, linguistics and the role of language, listening skills, the use of questions.
- *End Stage:* decision making, avoiding decision "traps", achieving closure.

## The Beginning Stage

As shown in Table 7.2, the beginning or initiation stage of negotiation is marked by the delineation and diagnosis of issues, agendas, and bargaining ranges, and by the social exchange necessary to develop the bargaining relationship. We covered these processes in some detail in Chapters 3 (on distributive negotiation), 4 (on integrative negotiation), and 5 (on negotiation planning and strategy). For the purposes of this chapter, we choose to focus, instead, on the problems of perceptual error and framing that precede and shape the exploration and diagnosis processes identified in phase model research. However, it is worth noting that, although we discuss these issues and their formative effect in the beginning stage of negotiations, problems of perception and attribution can and do occur throughout the negotiation process.

The beginning stage of a negotiation is the point at which the negotiator balances what was (and is) versus what might be (if things come out as hoped or planned). Parties approach the present tasks of negotiation guided, in large part, by their perception of past situations, attitudes, and behaviors. Expectations of future outcomes and other parties' future behaviors are based, in large part, on this perceptual baggage, gained through direct or vicarious experience and observations that negotiators bring with them. Two common pieces of baggage that can be problematic are attributional errors and frames. We will now discuss each of these in more detail.

**The Role of Perception.**    Perception is the process by which individuals "tune in" to their environment. We stated earlier that the process of ascribing meaning to received messages is likely to be strongly affected by the receiver's current state of mind or comprehension of earlier communications. Our perceptions of other parties and the environment we operate in, and our own dispositions, are likely to affect how we ascribe meanings. Moreover, these same perceptions are likely to affect our ability to accurately ascertain the other's message, to determine exactly what they are saying and what they mean. We will now examine how these perceptions are created and how they contribute to accurate or inaccurate communication.

Perception is a complex physical and psychological process. It is defined as "the process of screening, selecting, and interpreting stimuli so that they have meaning to the individual." (Steers, 1984, p. 98). Perception is a "sense-making" process; individuals interpret their environment so they can make appropriate responses to it (see Figure 7.1). The body's physical senses—sight, hearing, taste, touch, and smell—receive cues from various environmental stimuli.

Most environments are extremely complex—they present a large number and variety of stimuli, each having different properties such as magnitude, color, shape, texture, and relative novelty. The "sensing" task quickly becomes unmanageable, so perception becomes selective, focusing on some stimuli while tuning out others.

Once attention and recognition have occurred, the individual then translates recognition into reactive behavior. This part of the process is called *perceptual organization;* once we recognize stimuli, we must make appropriate responses to them. The message of a hot stove, transmitted from our fingertips to the brain, will lead us to quickly withdraw our finger before we are burned. The message of a verbal warning, "look out for the truck," transmitted from our ears to the brain, will quickly lead us to look for the truck and move out of its way.

**Factors that Shape and Distort Social Perception.**    The stimuli we just used as examples are rather simple—sounds, visual images of size and shape, and so on. We can see how variations in these stimuli can be applied to negotiation, particularly in positioning arguments, using visual media in presentation, and the like. However, the impact of perception on communication and negotiation outcomes is much more dramatic when we consider the perceptions of other people. We mentioned these processes earlier in this chapter, when we identified perceptual error as a key issue in the beginning stage of a negotiation. We return to them now to examine them in greater detail.

**FIGURE 7.1**   The Perceptual Process

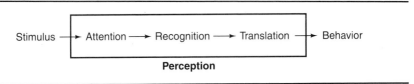

People as perceptual stimuli are more complex than simple sights, sounds, or colors. They have many physical characteristics—height, weight, age, sex, race, dress, and speech patterns (how articulate they are with words, whether they speak with an accent, what tone of voice they use) that affect our perception. People differ in their emotional expressiveness—how they communicate with facial gestures, body posture, hand movements, or even tone of voice.

Not only are people complex stimuli; the social context of the perceptual event can be a stimulus that affects perception as well. The nature of the negotiation issues or the previous experience of the parties can define the situation as a competitive or a cooperative one. On the basis of his research, Deutsch (1973) indicates that perceptions will vary as follows:

(a) A cooperative process tends to increase sensitivity to similarities and common interest, while minimizing the salience of differences. It stimulates a convergence and conformity of beliefs and values.

(b) A competitive process tends to increase sensitivity to differences and threats, while minimizing the awareness of similarities. It stimulates the sense of complete oppositeness: "You are bad, I am good." It seems likely that competition produces a stronger bias toward misperceiving the other's neutral or conciliatory actions as malevolently motivated than the bias induced by cooperation to see the other's actions as benevolently intended (p. 29–30).

Therefore, representing the relationship between the parties as competitive or cooperative based on issues such as whether the negotiation is zero-sum in nature, or on the previous history of the parties with one another, can lead the parties to judge their opposition's personal characteristics. They may also misdiagnose the degree of perceived similarity between them, and this misperception triggers assumptions about the other's behavior. These perceptions subsequently affect attitudes toward the other party, communication processes between the parties, and their strategic approach to the negotiating task.

**Perceptual Distortion in Negotiation.**   The perceiver's own needs, desires, motivations, and personal experiences may be likely to create a predisposition about the target in an upcoming negotiation. These predispositions are most problematic when they lead to biases and errors in perception and subsequent communication. Five major perceptual errors are typical: stereotyping, halo effects, selective perceptions, projections, and perceptual defenses. The first two—*stereotyping* and *halo effects*—are examples of perceptual distortion by *generalization:*

small amounts of perceptual information are used to draw large conclusions about individuals. The last three—*selective perception, projection,* and *perceptual defense*—are examples of perceptual distortion by the *anticipation* of encountering certain attributes and qualities in another person. In each case, the perceiver filters and distorts information to arrive at a consistent view.

*Stereotyping* is a very common distortion of the perceptual process. Stereotyping occurs when attributes are assigned to people solely on the basis of their membership in a particular social or demographic group. Stereotypes are formed about a wide variety of different groups: young people or old people, males or females, Italians or Germans, or people of different races, religions, or sexual orientations. In each case, stereotype formation generally happens the same way. We assign the individual to a group based on one piece of perceptual information (e.g., young or old); then we assign characteristics of some other group members to this individual (e.g., "old people are conservative, this person is old, therefore this person is conservative," or "young people are disrespectful, this person is young, therefore this person is disrespectful"). There is no factual basis for the conclusion—it is based on the generalization of qualities that have been ascribed to the larger group—and the error is compounded by applying traits we associate with the category to this single individual. In organizations, problems of age, race, and gender stereotyping have received much attention, yet they persist as major problems.

The simple process of using some criterion, even an arbitrary one, to divide people into groups allows group members to begin to define themselves as "we" and the other group as "they," and then to make evaluative comparisons and judgments between them. Direct competition for resources among groups, or conflicting values and ideologies, will significantly enhance the stereotyping process (Sherif, Harvey, White, Hood, and Sherif, 1988). In such cases, an individual's membership in one of these groups leads those from the other group to react stereotypically. In examining such "in-group/out-group mentality" dynamics, Haire (1955) showed photographs, labeled "manager" and "labor leader" to groups of managers and labor leaders. The managers attributed characteristics of honesty, dependability, and interpersonal competence to the individual in the "manager" photograph, whereas union leaders stereotyped the same individual in the "manager" photograph with the opposite characteristics. The findings were reversed for photos of "labor leaders." More recently, Kuhle and Ross (1990, 1992), studying a strike in the U.S. meat-packing industry, found evidence of similar perceptions and attributions that accompany, or even exacerbate, the miscommunication and escalation of conflict that mark serious organizational confrontations.

*Halo effects* in perception are similar to stereotypes. Rather than using a target individual's group membership as a basis for classification, halo effects occur when we generalize about a wide variety of attributes based on one attribute of an individual (Cooper, 1981). A smiling person is judged to be more honest than a frowning or scowling person, even though there is no necessary relationship between a smile and honesty. Halo effects can be positive or negative; negative halo effects have also been called "pitchfork" effects (e.g., Lowe, 1986.) A good attribute can be generalized so we see people in a very positive light, whereas a negative attribute has the reverse effect. The more prominent the attribute is in influencing the overall judgment of an individual, the more it will be used to cast further information into a perspective consistent with the initial judgment. Research shows that halo effects are most likely to occur in perception when (1) we have very little experience about a person along some dimension (and hence generalize about that person from our knowledge of him in other contexts), (2) when we know a person well, and (3) when the qualities have strong moral implications (Bruner and Tagiuri, 1954).

Halo effects are as common as stereotypes in negotiation—we are likely to form rapid impressions of new opponents based on very limited initial information, such as their appearance, group membership, or initial statements. We also maintain these judgments as we get to know people better, fitting each piece of new information into some consistent pattern. Finally, as Bruner and Tagiuri suggest, the mere suggestion that an adversary can be viewed in moral terms—honest or dishonest, ethical or unethical—is likely to affect our perception of a wide variety of other attributes.

*Selective perception* occurs when the perceiver singles out certain information that supports or reinforces a prior belief and filters out information that does not confirm that belief. Selective perception has the effect of perpetuating stereotypes or halo effects—we form quick judgments about individuals on the basis of limited information and filter out further evidence that might *dis*confirm the judgment. An initial smile from the opponent, which leads the perceiver to believe that the opponent is honest, might also lead him to ignore those statements by the opponent indicating that she intends to be competitive and aggressive. If the perceiver interprets the same smile as a smirk, the perceiver may ignore the opponent's statements that she wants to establish an honest and cooperative relationship. In both cases, the perceiver's own biases—the predisposition to view the smile as honest or dishonest—are likely to affect how he selects and interprets the other's cues.

*Projection* occurs when an individual ascribes to others characteristics or feelings he possesses himself. Projection usually arises out of a need to protect our own self-concept. People have a strong need to see themselves as consistent and in a positive light; therefore, if they perceive negative attributes, they tend to ascribe them to others. In negotiation, for example, it is extremely common for negotiators to claim that they want to be cooperative and develop a positive relationship with the other negotiator, but that the opponent is behaving uncooperatively and untrustingly. Such assertions often keep the negotiator from admitting to herself that she really wants to be deceptive and dishonest. American political leaders, fearful of "threats to national security," may project aggressive and militaristic motives on foreign heads of state and then argue that these motives justify our own military preparations. It is easy to see how such projection can lead to both self-fulfilling logic and highly destructive behavior.

*Perceptual defense* is the result of the same instinct for self-preservation, helping us to defend ourselves by screening out, distorting, or ignoring information that we find threatening or otherwise unacceptable. We are likely to deny, modify, distort, or redefine information that doesn't fit our self-image or our image of others to bring it into line with our earlier judgment. We refuse to believe that a person we respect may have committed a serious crime. We perceive ourselves as moral and therefore are likely to deny that we have ever done anything seriously wrong. We learn that a person we see as manipulative and dishonest has just contributed a great deal of money to a local charity; to rationalize this to ourselves, we decide that the donor must be using the contribution as a tax dodge or to manipulate the charity for malevolent ends, rather than as a true expression of benevolence and generosity.

**Framing.**   The second key issue in perception is *framing.* We covered this subject in some detail in Chapter 6, but we also mention it here because communications researchers have studied it extensively. In the communications context, framing helps explain "how bargainers conceive of ongoing sets of events in light of past experiences"; framing and reframing, or reevaluation of information and positions, "are tied to information processing, message patterns, linguistic cues, and socially constructed meanings" (Putnam and Holmer, 1992, p. 129). This concern with framing is captured by three approaches in the negotiation literature: cognitive heuristics, frame categories, and issue development. The first two belong in this section on the beginning stage of negotiation; the third, issue development, falls in the middle stage, and we will discuss it there.

The cognitive heuristics approach to framing derives from the literature on behavioral decision theory (BDT) and the "prospect theory" of judgment (e.g., Tversky and Kahneman, 1981). In this context, a *frame* denotes a decision maker's conception of the acts, outcomes, and contingencies associated with a particular outcome, involving perceptions of loss or gain, risk orientation, and the evaluative use of reference points. Neale and Bazerman (1991) have translated this into the idea of negotiator biases that limit negotiator effectiveness (see Chapter 6). Regarding the effect of frames on risk aversion in negotiation, Neale and Bazerman (1992a) suggest two things: first, negotiators are not usually *indifferent* to risk, but, second, they should not necessarily trust their *intuitions* regarding risk. In other words, negotiators may overreact to a perceived loss when they might react more positively to the same situation if it is framed as a perceived gain. Hence, negotiators must "avoid the pitfalls of being framed while, simultaneously, understanding positively and negatively framing your opponent" (Neale and Bazerman, 1992a, p. 50).

The second aspect of framing that fits in this stage is frame categories. Merging cognitive views of framing with linguistic analysis, the frame category approach is similar to "scripting" negotiations. Gray and Donnellon (1989) proposed six types of frames, based on their review of the bargaining literature:

*Substantive* (what the negotiation is about).

*Loss-gain* (the risks or benefits of various outcomes).

*Characterization* (different expectations and evaluations of others' behaviors and outcomes).

*Process* (how the negotiation will or should proceed).

*Aspiration* (regarding the parties' underlying needs and interests).

*Outcome* (the parties' preferred positions or solutions).

It is possible, even likely, that negotiators will have (and apply) multiple frames, as defined here. When different negotiators apply different or mismatched frames, they will find the bargaining process ambiguous and frustrating. In such situations, it may become necessary to reframe, to assist the other party in doing so, or (ideally) to establish a common frame or set of frames within which the negotiation communication and exchange may be conducted more productively. Reframing might involve any of a number of approaches. Rather than seeing something as a possibility for loss, it might be framed as an opportunity to win (e.g., Kahneman and Tversky, 1979), that is, a "bright side" alternative to approaching a given situation. Is the glass half empty, or half full? (How you answer that question probably depends on whether you like or dislike drinking what is in the glass, however!)

Negotiators can also reframe by trying to see the situation in a different way or from a different perspective. For instance, they can constructively reframe a problem by defining it in terms that are broader or narrower, bigger or smaller, riskier or less risky, or subject to a longer or shorter (i.e., looser or tighter) time constraint. We discussed ways this could be done in Chapter 4 when we reviewed ways in which the parties could creatively invent options to assure mutual gain.

**Attributional Error.**  In the most general sense, social perception is the process through which people come to understand each other. Starting with the "raw data" of other persons, a given situation, and their behavior therein, we apply or impose our own analyses and explanations of what they do. This information integrates the results into coherent (if impressionistic) "pictures" of others, which then subtly shape our understanding of reality. Similar processes lead to the production of "scripts" that guide us in anticipating the goals, behaviors, and outcomes likely to issue from particular situations (Ableson, 1981; Read, 1987). These scripts, based on prior perception, experience, and hearsay, are preconceptions of what is likely to occur in a situation, based on a process of classification and analogy. For example, we may expect to have to deal with tough, competitive bargaining accompanied by distributive tactics (such as the old "limited authority"/"I'll have to talk to the sales manager" ploy) when we buy a new automobile, based largely on our personal experience or experiences related to us by others. The advent of "one-price, no-haggle" auto sales by a growing number of dealers may not conform to our established schema, and we may be uncomfortable or unprepared when we encounter this new process for the first time (or we may be very comfortable if we really don't like to negotiate for a new car!). The attributions we make based on these perceptions and scripts are "correct" only insofar as we factor in new experiences as we encounter them, and as long as the base data remain undistorted. In particular, we are often guilty of distorting data through attribution error or bias.

Expectations of others are based on our perception and understanding of relatively stable aspects of their makeup, such as their personalities, attitudes, and abilities. Perceptual error can lead to biases in information processing and judgment, the "bloopers" of social perception (Brehm and Kassin, 1990). For example, we explain others' behaviors by making *attributions,* either *personal* (i.e., the behaviors were caused by factors *internal* to them, such as ability, mood, or effort) or *situational* (i.e., caused by factors *external* to them, such as the task, other people, fate, etc.) (Heider, 1958). In fact, in explaining others' behavior, the tendency is to *over*estimate the effect of personal or internal factors and *under*estimate the effect of situational or external factors—this perceptual error has come to be called the "fundamental attribution error" (Ross, 1977). A professional sports figure who seems competent, skilled, and aggressive when playing his sport may shock us by being shy, awkward, or docile when speaking to a group or being interviewed by writers or broadcast journalists. This error is often exacerbated by the *actor-observer effect,* in which we attribute our own behavior to situational factors, but attribute others' behaviors to personal factors (Jones and Nisbett, 1976), saying in effect "if *I* mess up, it's bad luck (the situation, someone else's fault, etc.); if *you* mess up, it's *your* fault!" Such attribution error can lead to faulty assumptions and inoperative scripts, with predictable effects on negotiation planning and conduct (see our discussion of unilateral planning in Chapter 5).

Perceptual error may also be expressed in the form of a bias, or distortion in the evaluation of data. For instance, the *false-consensus effect* is a tendency to overestimate the degree of support and consensus that exists for our own position, opinions, or behaviors (Ross, Greene, and House, 1977). If consensus information is available, but expressed in numerical probabilities (e.g., one chance in a hundred), many observers neglect to use the information, falling subject to a bias called the *base rate fallacy* (Bar-Hillel, 1980). Either of these biases could seriously damage a negotiation effort—negotiators subject to them would make faulty judgments regarding tactics or outcome probabilities.

**Perceptual Error: A Summary.** It cannot be stated strongly enough that perceptual distortions are frequently at the heart of breakdowns in communication between conflicting individuals. Stereotypes, halo effects, selective perceptions, and perceptual defenses bias and distort the information we receive. Perceptual biases tend to cast our own position and behavior in more favorable terms and the other person ("the opponent") in more negative terms. These biases affect expectations about an opponent and lead to assumptions about opponents (e.g., their position, their willingness to cooperate or make concessions, etc.). Finally, these assumptions may then cause us to assume a competitive, defensive stance early in a negotiation. The tragedy in this chain of events is that if these initial assumptions are incorrect, there may be no way for us to correct them—by the time we are in a position to accurately judge the predisposition of the other party, they may have interpreted our own competitive mood and defensive posture as offensive and antagonistic. This problem is likely to be most acute between groups that have had long-standing, hostile relationships: unions and management that have been plagued by bitter strikes, ethnic groups with long-standing disagreements (such as those in Northern Ireland, the Balkans, or the Middle East), or marital partners in divorce proceedings. To break this self-fulfilling perceptual spiral, individual negotiators (and their constituencies) must take clear-cut, specific, and public actions to signal to their adversaries a desire to change to cooperative behavior. Detailed approaches for engaging in this process were discussed in Chapter 6; third-party assistance, often of use in difficult negotiations, will be discussed in Chapter 12.

### The Middle Stage

The middle or problem-solving stage of negotiation is the most dynamic stage—it is marked by movement, process, interaction, and exchange. We will examine four key elements here: offer sequences, the evolution of framework and detail, the role of language, and the complementary processes of listening and questioning.

**Offer Sequences.**    According to Tutzauer (1992), "perhaps the most important communications in a bargaining session are those that convey the disputants' offers and counteroffers" (p. 67). Tutzauer assumes that bargainers have definite preferences and exhibit rational behavior by acting in accordance with those preferences, and that the preferences can be expressed according to some numerical scale, that is, that they have different degrees of utility or quantitative worth (see also Luce and Raiffa, 1957; also refer back to Chapter 3). A communicative framework for negotiation, in turn, is based on the assumptions that

The communication of offers is a *dynamic process* (the offers that are made change or shift over time).

The offer process is *interactive* (bargainers influence each other).

A variety of *internal* and *external factors* (e.g., time limitations, reciprocity norms, BATNAs, or constituency pressures) drive the interaction and "motivate a bargainer to change his or her offer" (Tutzauer, p. 73).

Another way of saying this is that the dynamic, interactive process of offer-counteroffer, similar in form to the "tit-for-tat" process of responding to the other's strategy choice (e.g., Axelrod, 1984) and subject to certain situational and environmental constraints, "herds" the negotiation exchange down a playing field, eventually narrowing the bargaining range (see Chapter 3) and funneling it toward an eventual settlement point. In short, offer sequences provide both direction and impetus during the middle stage of a negotiation.

Another process, that of *issue development* (Putnam and Holmer, 1992) is related conceptually to offer sequences. Issue development focuses on the way issues change during the negotiation process, which is related closely to the process of the transformation of disputes (e.g., Felstiner, Abel, and Sarat, 1980–81) in that the aim of a negotiation is to transform a disagreement, argument, or confrontation into a situation marked by peace, agreement, and joint success or gain.

"Disputes are transformed by shifting frames," and "framing occurs through the *process of shaping issues*" by determining "the importance and relevance of available facts in a case" (Putnam and Holmer, 1992, pp. 138–139; italics in the original). Issues are shaped by, among other things,

> Arguments attacking the significance or stability of problems or the workability of solutions.

> The ways parties "make cases" to others concerning the logic or propriety of needs or positions.

> The management and interaction (e.g., addition, deletion, packaging, etc.) of multiple issues on the negotiation agenda (Putnam and Holmer, 1992).

**Evolution of Framework and Detail.**   Ikle (1964), discussing diplomatic negotiations, suggested that successful bargaining results from a two-stage process called Framework/Detail. As described in a recent review,

> (P)arties first seek a compromise that establishes some framework of broad objectives and principles. Then they draw out a number of detailed points of agreement. The framework defines the subset of points that is debatable, while the detail phase permits the debate and "packaging" of specific issues to construct a settlement acceptable to both sides. (Lewicki, Weiss, and Lewin, 1992, p. 225)

Further elaboration of this model (Zartman, 1977; Zartman and Berman, 1982) resulted in a three-stage model:

> Diagnosis (in which the parties recognize the need for change or improvement, review relevant history, and prepare positions).

> Formula (in which they attempt to develop a shared perception of the conflict, including common terms, referents, and fairness criteria).

> Detail (in which they work out operational details consistent with the basic formula).

In actual use, the model may be more flexible than this description suggests; in some cultures, the stages may even be pursued in a different order. An excellent example of this approach would be the negotiations over Israeli and Palestinian rights and interests in the Mideast that led to the signing of a statement of mutual recognition in September 1993. Recent progress in this protracted confrontation was largely the result of a clear diagnosis (continued disagreement is in the interest of neither party), a shared formula (including complementary statements by each side regarding the other's right to existence, security, and autonomy) and the ability to work out all the complex details (i.e., given this shared vision, what must be done, specifically, to create and maintain an appropriate environment of rights, responsibilities, and assurances for all parties).

**Linguistics and the Role of Language.**   Does what a negotiator says and how she says it have an effect on the conduct of negotiation? Recent research in linguistics suggests that they do. Gibbons, Bradac, and Busch (1992) propose that "negotiation is essentially linguistic" in that it "represents the exchange of information through language that coordinates and manages meaning" (p. 156). In negotiations, language operates at two levels: the "logical" level (for proposals or offers) and the "pragmatic" level (semantics, syntax, and style). The meaning conveyed by a proposition or statement is a combination of a logical, surface message and other, pragmatic (i.e., hinted or inferred) messages. In other words, it is not only *what* is said that matters, but *how* it is said, and what additional, veiled, or subsurface information is intended, conveyed, or perceived in reception. By way of illustration, consider threats. We often react not only to the *substance* of a statement, but also (and possibly more strongly) to the unspoken messages. Gibbons, Bradoc, and Busch identify five linguistic dimensions of making threats:

1. The use of *polarized language,* in which a party uses positive words when speaking of his own position (e.g., *generous, reasonable,* or *even-handed*) and negative words when referring to the other party's position (e.g., *tight-fisted, unreasonable,* or *heavy-handed*).

2. The conveyance of *verbal immediacy* (a measure of intended immediacy, compellingness, or relative psychological distance), either *high* and intended to engage or compel the other party ("Okay, *here* is the deal" or "*I take* great care to . . .") or *low* and intended to create a sense of distance or aloofness ("Well, *there* it is" or "*One should take* great care to . . .").

3. The degree of *language intensity*—high to convey strong feelings in the recipient (as with statements of affirmation or the frequent use of profanity), or low to convey weak interest.

4. The degree of *lexical diversity* (or, more simply, the command of a broad, rich vocabulary)—high levels denote comfort and competence, and low levels denote discomfort, anxiety, or inexperience.

5. The extent of *high-power language style,* with low power denoted by the use of verbal hedges, hesitations, or politeness to the point of deference and subordination, and high power denoted by expressions of dominance, clarity and firmness of expression and self-assurance.

Using these dimensions, Gibbons, Bradoc, and Busch suggest that threats can be made more credible and more compelling by negatively polarized descriptions of the other party and their position, high immediacy, high intensity, high verbal diversity, and a distinctively high-power style.

Whether the intent is to command and compel or to sell, persuade, or gain commitment, middle-stage linguistics would seem to depend on adequate command of technique by the speaker, as well as on clear understanding and decoding of the intended message(s) by the listener (see Figure 7.2 later in this chapter). As it turns out, chances for miscommunication abound. Speakers may be untrained, incompetent, ineffective, or overwrought; they may simply be inarticulate. Furthermore, speakers' use of idioms or colloquialisms are often problematic, especially in cross-cultural negotiations (see Chapter 14). The meaning conveyed might be clear to the speaker, but confusing to the listener (e.g., "I'm willing to stay until the last dog is hung"—a statement of positive commitment on the part of some regional Americans, but probably confusing at best to those with different cultural backgrounds, even within the United States). Even if the meaning is clear, the choice of word or metaphor may convey a lack of sensitivity or create a sense of exclusion, as is often done when males convey strategic business concerns by using sports metaphors ("Well, it's fourth down and goal to go; this is no time to drop the ball"). Intentional or not, the message received or inferred by females may be that they're excluded from the "club." Deborah Tannen, in her aptly named book, *You Just Don't Understand,* states that "male-female miscommunication may be more dangerous (than cross-cultural miscommunication) because it is more pervasive in our lives, and we are less prepared for it" (Tannen, 1990, p. 281). The lack of awareness of the potential for such miscommunication with someone from our own culture may mean that, if miscommunication occurs, we are less well prepared to deal with it than we would be when dealing with someone with whom we *expect* to have difficulty communicating. We may be (excuse the expression) "blind-sided"—hit from an unexpected direction—and thereby damaged more than we might be if we had seen the blow coming.

Finally, one's choice of words may not only signal a position, but also shape and predict it. Using language and its relation to cognitive maps (Axelrod, 1976)—"the concepts and relations (a party) uses to understand organizational situations" (Weick and Bougon, 1986, pg. 106)—Simons (1993) examined the linguistic patterns of the communications in negotiations. Two findings were of interest. First, parties whose statements communicated interests in both the substance of the negotiation (i.e., "things") as well as the relationship with the other party (i.e., "people") achieved better, more integrative solutions than parties concerned solely with either substance or with relationship. Second, in support of Thompson and Hastie (1990a), "early discussion in negotiation may be critical in defining issues in a way that promotes or inhibits the discovery of integrative solutions" (Simons, 1993, p. 154). The "stage-setting" value of constructive communication is borne out by Simons' finding that "linguistic patterns from the first half of negotiation were better predictors of agreements than linguistic patterns from the second half of negotiation" (Simons, 1993, p. 139; see, also, issue definition earlier in this chapter).

**Listening Skills and the Use of Questions.**    Given the many ways communication can be disrupted and distorted, we can only marvel at the amount that actually gets accomplished. We contend that *failures and distortions in perception and communication are the single most dominant contributor to breakdowns and failures in negotiation.* Research cannot directly confirm this assertion because the processes of perception and communication are so intertwined with other major factors, including commitment to one's own position and objectives, the nature of the negotiating process, the use of power and power tactics, and the negotiators' personalities. Nevertheless, we have found in many simulated and actual negotiations that parties whose goals are compatible and whose overriding objectives are the same still may not reach agreement because of their misperceptions of the opponent or because of breakdowns in the communication process.

Research *is* available to support this proposition in a more limited way. For example, Deutsch and Krauss (1962) conducted a series of experiments on the impact of threat behavior in a simulated negotiation game. They first studied what impact the opportunity to threaten the opponent would have upon its use in negotiation. As might be predicted, when bargainers could threaten their opponents, they did; and the use of threats contributed to a significant decrease in each negotiator's outcome. The researchers predicted that the opportunity to communicate with the other party might improve bargaining efficiency and decrease the impact of the threat; however, they found that when communication was permitted, and even when it was required, it did not significantly affect outcomes. Parties *without* threats used communication to enhance their bargaining coordination, but not significantly so; parties *with* threats used communication to enhance the competitiveness between them. Only when the negotiators were *tutored* in how to communicate—how to make proposals that would improve their coordination in the bargaining game—did the participants use communication effectively (Krauss and Deutsch, 1966).

Since the Deutsch and Krauss experiments, a number of techniques have been suggested for improving the accuracy and efficiency of communications in negotiation. Either third parties or the parties to negotiation themselves can tutor communication—help the parties learn to communicate accurately and appropriately. These activities were reviewed in detail in Chapter 6. However, in this chapter, we review several techniques that the parties themselves can use to ensure that some of the typical perceptual and communication blocks are not confounding their ability to reach satisfactory agreement. Chief among these are the use of questions, active listening, and (as mentioned in Chapter 6), role reversal.

***The Use of Questions.*** One of the most common techniques for clarifying communications and eliminating noise and distortion is the use of questions. Nierenberg (1973) emphasized that questions are essential elements in negotiations for securing information; asking good questions enables a negotiator to secure a great deal of information about the opponent's position, supporting arguments, and needs.

Nierenberg proposes that questions can be divided into two basic classifications: those that are manageable, and those that cause difficulty (see Table 7-3). Manageable questions cause attention (e.g., prepare the other person's thinking for further questions, for example, "How are you?"), get information ("How much will this cost?"), and start thinking ("Do you have any suggestions for improving this?"). Unmanageable questions, or questions that cause difficulty, give information ("Didn't you know that we couldn't afford this?") and bring the discussion to a false conclusion ("Don't you think we've talked about this enough?"). As you can see in Table 7.3, most of these unmanageable questions are likely to produce defensiveness and anger in the opponent. Although they may yield information, they are likely to make the other party feel uncomfortable and less likely to provide more information in the future.

**TABLE 7.3**   Questions in Negotiation

| *Manageable Questions* | *Examples* |
| --- | --- |
| Open-ended questions—ones that cannot be answered with a simple yes or no. *Who, what, when, where,* and *why* questions. | "Why do you take that position in these deliberations?" |
| Open questions—invite the other's thinking. | "What do you think of our proposal?" |
| Leading questions—point toward an answer. | "Don't you think our proposal is a fair and reasonable offer?" |
| Cool questions—low emotionality. | "What is the additional rate that we will have to pay if you make the improvements on the property?" |
| Planned questions—part of an overall logical sequence of questions developed in advance. | "After you make the improvements to the property, when can we expect to take occupancy?" |
| Treat questions—flatter the opponent at the same time as you ask for information. | "Can you provide us with some of your excellent insight on this problem?" |
| Window questions—aid in looking into the other person's mind. | "Can you tell us how you came to that conclusion?" |
| Directive questions—focus on a specific point. | "How much is the rental rate per square foot with these improvements?" |
| Gauging questions—ascertain how the other person feels. | "How do you feel about our proposal?" |

| *Unmanageable Questions* | *Examples* |
| --- | --- |
| Close-out questions—force the other party into seeing things your way. | "You wouldn't try to take advantage of us here, would you?" |
| Loaded questions—put the other party on the spot regardless of her answer. | "Do you mean to tell me that these are the only terms that you will accept?" |
| Heated questions—high emotionality, trigger emotional responses. | "Don't you think we've spent enough time discussing this ridiculous proposal of yours?" |
| Impulse questions—occur "on the spur of the moment," without planning, and tend to get conversation off the track. | "As long as we're discussing this, what do you think we ought to tell other groups who have made similar demands on us?" |
| Trick questions—appear to require a frank answer, but really are "loaded" in their meaning. | "What are you going to do—give in to our demands, or take this to arbitration?" |

**TABLE 7.3**    (*Continued*)

| Unmanageable Questions | Examples |
|---|---|
| Reflective trick questions—reflects the other into agreeing with your point of view. | "Here's how I see the situation—don't you agree?" |

From Gerard Nierenberg, *Fundamentals of Negotiating* (New York: Hawthorn Books, 1973), pp. 125–126. Used with permission of the author.

Negotiators can also use questions to manage difficult or stalled negotiations. Aside from their typical uses for collecting and diagnosing information or assisting the other party in addressing and expressing needs and interests, questions can also be used tactically to pry or lever a negotiation out of a stall or an apparent dead end. Deep and Sussman (1993) identify a number of such situations and suggest specific questions for dealing with them (see Table 7.4).

The value of such questions seems to be in their power to assist or force the other party to face up to the effects or consequences of their behaviors, intended and anticipated or not.

***Active Listening.***    *Active listening* and *reflecting* are terms that are commonly used in the helping professions such as counseling and therapy (Rogers, 1957, 1961). Counselors recognize that communications are frequently loaded with multiple meanings and that the counselor must try to "tease out" these different meanings without making the communicator angry or defensive. In the decades since Carl Rogers advocated this key communication dynamic, interest in listening skills, and active listening in particular, has continued to grow both generally (e.g., Austin, 1989; Bostrom, 1990; Wolff, Marsnik, Tacey, and Nichols, 1983; Wolvin and Coakley, 1988) and with regard to business and organizational settings (e.g., Bone, 1988; Carnevale, Gainer, Meltzer, and Holland, 1988; Lewis and Reinsch, 1988; Rogers and Roethlisberger, 1991; Wolvin and Coakley, 1991).

One technique for gaining more information is to ask questions; however, as we pointed out in the previous section, frequent questions, particularly when the communication is emotionally charged, may contribute to defensiveness. The questioner should encourage the other party to voluntarily elaborate on his earlier statements, rather than making the communicator feel cross-examined by multiple questions. Another method of gaining more information is by listening. There are three major forms of listening: passive listening, acknowledgment, and active listening.

*Passive listening* is merely the reception of the message, providing no feedback to the sender about the accuracy or completeness of reception. As we will point out in the communication model presented later in this chapter (see Figure 7.2), listening is the key process in the reception and decoding stage of communication. Sometimes passive listening is enough in itself to keep a communicator sending information. Some people like to talk and can't handle long silences.

**TABLE 7.4**    Questions for Tough Situations

| The Situation | Possible Questions |
| --- | --- |
| *"Take it or leave it" ultimata.* | "If we can come up with a more attractive alternative than that, would you still want me to 'take or leave' your offer?" |
| | "Do I have to decide now, or do I have some time to think about it?" |
| | "Are you feeling pressure to bring the negotiation to a close?" |
| *Pressure to respond to an unreasonable deadline.* | "Why can't we negotiate about this deadline?" |
| | "If you're under pressure to meet this deadline, what can I do to help remove some of that pressure?" |
| | "What's magical about this afternoon? What about first thing in the morning?" |
| *The other party uses highball or lowball tactics.* | "What's your reasoning behind this position?" |
| | "What would *you* think I see as a fair offer?" |
| | "What standards do you think the final resolution should meet?" |
| *An impasse.* | "What else can either of us do to close the gap between our positions?" |
| | "Specifically what concession do you need from me to bring this to a close right now?" |
| | "If it were already six weeks from now and we were looking back at this negotiation, what might we wish we had 'brought to the table?'" |
| *The other party is torn between accepting and rejecting your proposal.* | "What's your best alternative to accepting my offer right now?" |
| | "If you reject this offer, what will take its place that's better than what you know you'll receive from me?" |
| | "How can you be sure that you will get a better deal elsewhere?" |
| *The other party asks if the offer you just made is the same as that offered to others.* | "What do you see as a fair offer, and given that, what do you think of my current offer to you?" |
| | "Do you believe that I think it's in my best interest to be unfair to you?" |
| | "Do you believe that people can be treated differently, but still all be treated fairly?" |
| *You are feeling pressured, controlled, or manipulated.* | "Shouldn't we both walk away from this negotiation feeling satisfied?" |
| | "How would you feel if our roles were reversed, and you were feeling the pressure I'm feeling right now?" |
| | "Are you experiencing outside pressures to conclude these negotiations?" |

Adapted from the book: *What to Ask When You Don't Know What to Say* by Sam Deep and Lyle Sussman © 1993. Used by permission of the publisher, Prentice Hall/A Division of Simon & Schuster, Englewood Cliffs, N.J.

Negotiators who have an opponent with this characteristic may find that their best strategy is to sit and listen and let the other party eventually talk himself into, or out of, a position on his own.

*Acknowledgment* is the second form of listening, slightly more active than complete passivity. When acknowledging, the receiver occasionally nods her head, maintains eye contact, or interjects responses like "I see," "mm-hmm," "interesting," "really," "sure," "go on," and the like. These responses are sufficient to keep the communicator sending messages, but the sender often misinterprets the acknowledgments as the receiver's agreeing with the position, rather than simply receiving the message.

*Active listening* is the third form of listening. When the receiver is actively listening, he restates or paraphrases the sender's message in his own language. Some examples include these (from Gordon, 1977):

*Sender:*

I don't know how I am going to untangle this messy problem.

*Receiver:*

You're really stumped on how to solve this one.

*Sender:*

Please, don't ask me about that now.

*Receiver:*

Sounds like you're awfully busy right now.

*Sender:*

I thought the meeting today accomplished nothing.

*Receiver:*

You were very disappointed with our session.

As Athos and Gabarro (1978) note, successful reflective responding (active listening) is characterized by the following:

A greater emphasis on *listening* than on talking.

Responding to personal rather than abstract points (personal feelings, beliefs, and positions rather than abstract ideas).

Following the other rather than leading him into areas we think we should be exploring (exploring his frame of reference rather than forcing ours upon him, at least until we fully understand his position).

Clarifying what the other has said about his own thoughts and feelings rather than close questioning or telling him what we believe he should be thinking or feeling.

Responding to the other's feelings in his communication.

This active listening technique has generally been recommended more for counseling communications such as employee counseling and performance improvement. In negotiation, it may appear initially that active listening is unsuitable because, unlike counseling sessions, the receiver does have a position of her own and usually *does* feel strongly about the issues. By recommending active listening, we are not suggesting that the receiver should automatically adopt or agree with her opponent's position and abandon her own. Rather, we are suggesting that active listening is a skill that encourages other parties to talk more fully about their frames of reference, that is, the position they are taking. When they do so, we may better understand the nature of their positions, the factors and information that support it, and the ways that the opponent's position can be compromised, reconciled, or negotiated in accordance with our own preferences and priorities.

*Role Reversal.*   We discussed the use of role reversal in some detail in Chapter 6, but it warrants mention in this chapter as well. Communication distortions may be eliminated through role reversal. Rapoport (1964) suggests that continually arguing our own position in debate leads to a "blindness of involvement," or a self-reinforcing cycle of argumentation that prohibits us from recognizing the possible compatibilities between our own position and the other party's. In the description of active listening, we suggested that one objective was to gain a better understanding of the other party's perspective or frame of reference, rather than only advocating our own. Active listening, however, is still a somewhat "passive" process. Role-reversal techniques allow us to understand others' positions by actively arguing them to *their* satisfaction. In doing so, negotiators more fully *understand* others' positions, perhaps come to accept their validity, and discover ways that both positions can be modified to make them more compatible.

A number of studies have examined the impact and success of the role-reversal technique (Johnson, 1971; Walcott, Hopmann, and King, 1977). In general, the research supports the following conclusions:

1. Role reversal is effective in producing cognitive changes (greater understanding of the opponent's position) and attitude changes (perceived similarities between the two positions).

2. When the parties' positions are fundamentally *compatible* with one another, role reversal is likely to produce better results (cognitive and attitudinal change); when the parties' positions are fundamentally *incompatible,* role reversal may sharpen the perceptions of incompatibility and inhibit positive attitude change.

3. Although role reversal may induce greater understanding of the opponent's position and highlight areas of possible similarity, it is not necessarily more effective overall as a means of inducing agreement between parties.

In sum, role reversal may be a useful tool for reducing the distortions in communication that prohibit accurate understanding of, and appreciation for, the other position in negotiation. However, such understanding may not necessarily lead to an easier resolution of the conflict, particularly when accurate communication reveals a fundamental incompatibility in the positions of the two sides.

### The End Stage

Ultimately, the end stage of negotiation is a function of what comes before it—the previous two stages (compare Thompson and Hastie, 1990a). But what the end stage lacks in a unique contribution to the flow of negotiation, it often makes up for in frustration. The successful completion of a negotiation often seems "so near, yet so far away." At this stage, negotiators must attend to two key issues simultaneously: the avoidance of fatal mistakes, and the achievement of a satisfactory closure constructive manner.

**The Avoidance of Fatal Mistakes.**    Achieving closure in a negotiation is, in large part, making decisions to accept offers, to compromise priorities, to trade off across issues with the other party, or some combination of these elements. Such decision-making processes can be broken down into four key elements: framing, gathering intelligence, coming to conclusions, and learning from feedback (Russo and Schoemaker, 1989). The first two of these elements are covered elsewhere: framing in Chapter 6 and earlier in this chapter, and gathering intelligence in Chapter 5. The process of coming to conclusions is specifically an end-stage element, but the dynamics of this process are not primarily communicative and have been specifically addressed in the chapters on distributive and integrative negotiation. The fourth element, that of learning (or failing to learn) from feedback, is largely communicative in nature, involving "keeping track of what you expected would happen, systematically guarding against self-serving expectations, and making sure you review the lessons your feedback has provided the next time a similar decision comes along" (Russo and Schoemaker, p. 3). Russo and Schoemaker warn of 10 decision traps that can ensnare decision makers, resulting in suboptimal decisions. Although some of these traps occur in earlier stages of the negotiation, we suspect that a number of them may occur at the end of a negotiation, when parties are in a hurry to wrap up loose ends and cement a deal. The traps include

1. *Plunging in*—reaching a conclusion to a problem before identifying the essence or crux of the problem (forcing negotiations into the end stage prematurely by pushing for a quantitative or substantive resolution to a problem that has been incompletely defined or is basically relational in nature).

2. *Overconfidence in one's own judgment*—blocking, ignoring, or failing to seek factual information that might contradict one's own assumptions and opinions (strictly adhering to a unilateral strategy, regardless of other information that emerges during the course of the negotiation).

3. *Frame blindness*—perceiving, then solving, the wrong problem, accompanied by overlooking options and losing sight of objectives because they do not fit the frame being used (forcing resolution of a complex, mixed-motive dispute into some simplistic, concrete measure of performance such as money).

4. *Lack of frame control*—failure to test different frames to determine if they fit, or being unduly influenced by the other party's frame (agreeing to a

suboptimal outcome ["being framed"] because the other party has taken advantage of our aversion to the risk of going home empty-handed") (Neale and Bazerman, 1992).

5. *Shortsighted shortcuts*—use of heuristics or rules of thumb, such as using convenient (but misleading) referent points (e.g., accepting the other party's commitment to turning over a new leaf when past experiences suggest that they are really unlikely to do so).

6. *Shooting from the hip*—managing a great deal of information in your head, rather than adopting and using a systematic process of evaluation and choice (proceeding on gut feelings or eye contact alone in deciding to accept a resolution, trusting that problems will not occur or that they will be easily worked out if they do).

7. *Group failure*—not managing the group process effectively; instead, assuming that smart and well-intentioned individuals can invariably produce a durable, high-quality group decision (see, for instance, the Janis' [1982] work on "groupthink"—to move stalled decisions, a group might take a vote on accepting a resolution, thereby disenfranchising the minority who do not vote for the resolution and stopping the deliberative process short of achieving its integrative possibilities).

8. *Fooling yourself about feedback*—failure to use feedback correctly, either to protect your ego or through the bias of hindsight (dealing with the embarrassment of being outmaneuvered by the other party because of a lack of good information or a failure to rigorously prepare).

9. *Not keeping track*—assuming that learning occurs automatically and thus not keeping systematic records of decisions and related outcomes (losing sight of the gains and deals "purchased" with concessions and trade-offs made during the negotiation, or not applying the lessons of one negotiation episode to future negotiations).

10. *Failure to "audit" one's own decisions processes*—failure to establish and use a plan to avoid the traps mentioned here or the inability or unwillingness to fully understand your own style, warts and all (thus, doggedly adhering to a flawed or inappropriate approach to negotiation, even in the face of frequent failures and suboptimal outcomes).

**Achieving Closure.** Gary Karrass (1985), focusing on sales negotiations in particular, advises about communication during the end stage. For instance, Karrass enjoins negotiators *to know when to shut up* to avoid surrendering important information needlessly or making "dumb remarks" that push a wavering party away from the agreement they may be *almost* ready to endorse. The other side of this is to "*beware of garbage and the garbage truck*" by recognizing the other party's faux pas and dumb remarks for what they are and refusing to respond to or be distracted by them. Karrass also reminds of the need to *watch out for last-minute hitches* (such as nit-picking or second guessing by parties who didn't partici-

---

**Do You Have A "Good" Agreement?**

Is there a preamble in which the intent of the agreement is spelled out clearly?

Are all the issues of interest to all parties addressed?

Are all the proposals workable?

Have all parties affected by the agreement been consulted?

For each point of agreement, is it crystal clear what you have agreed to, including what is to be done, by whom, by what time, and how?

Does the agreement *in total* make sense?

Is the agreement reasonable and equitable?

Have you considered the major barriers to fulfilling the agreement?

Do you have a vehicle for managing disagreements arising out of this agreement? Is it clear to all parties what this vehicle is and how to use it?

Used with permission of Blair Sheppard.

---

pate in the bargaining process, but who have the right or responsibility to review it) by *expecting* such hitches and being prepared to handle them with some aplomb. Finally, Karrass points out the importance of reducing the agreement to written form or *writing the contract*—the party that writes the contract is in a position to achieve clarity of purpose and conduct for the deal. As for the communicative quality of the final, written agreement, a reasonable checklist is presented in the box (Sheppard, 1993).

## COMMUNICATION IN NEGOTIATION: ANOTHER PERSPECTIVE

Most analyses of communication begin with a basic model of the process itself. Probably the most commonly cited model, and one that will serve our purposes well, was developed by Shannon and Weaver (1948) and is represented in Figure 7.2.

Although all the complexities of human communication cannot be captured in a single model, this diagram offers a reasonable beginning. A sender source has a message in mind. The source intends to encode the message into language that the receiver will understand. Perhaps it is a statement of the sender's preference for a particular outcome in a negotiation. The message may be encoded into verbal language (e.g., words and sentences), or it may be encoded into nonverbal expression (such as facial gestures, hand waving, and finger pointing.) Once encoded, the message is then transmitted (i.e., sent via voice, facial expression, or written statement) through a medium (e.g., face-to-face interaction, video, letter, telegram, etc.) to the receiver. The receiver's receptors—eyes and ears—pick up the transmission and decode it, giving it meaning to the receiver.

**FIGURE 7.2**    A Model of the Communication Process

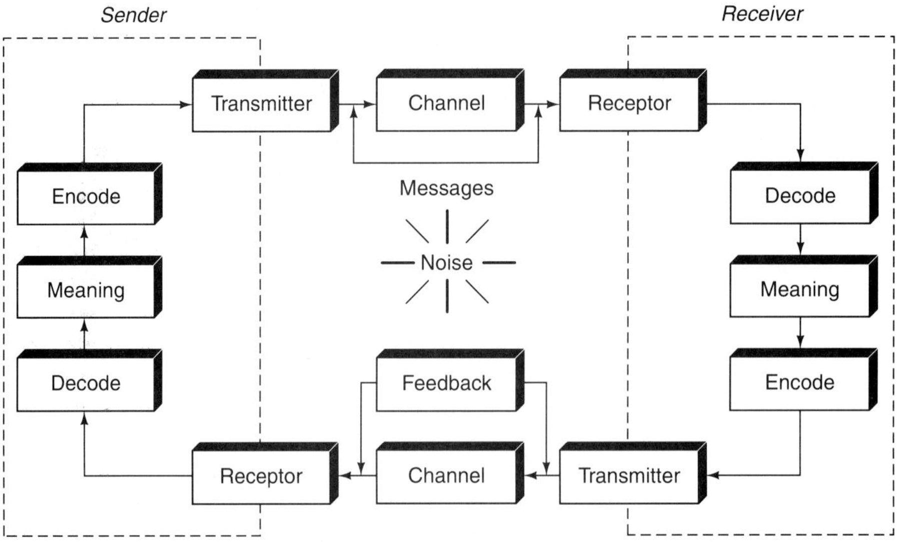

Adapted from E. Shannon and W. Weaver, *The Mathematical Theory of Communication* (Urbana, IL: University of Illinois Press, 1948). Reprinted by permission of the University of Illinois Press.

In a one-way communication event, from sender to receiver, this process would constitute a completed transmission. A source who puts a message in writing, reads it over to check its clarity, and sends it by mail to the receiver generally assumes that the message is received and understood. However, most communication—particularly in negotiation—involves continued dialogue and discussion between at least two parties. As a result, the receiver takes a more active role in the communication process, in two ways. First, the receiver provides information on how the message was received, and second, the receiver becomes a sender and responds to, or builds upon, the earlier message of the original sender. For the current discussion, we shall refer to both of these processes as *feedback.* In the feedback process, receivers decode the message—through reading or listening—to assure their own understanding and comprehension of what the sender said. They then ascribe meaning to the communication by comprehending the information content of the message as well as interpreting that content. Receivers then become senders of communication back to its original source. The encoded message may take multiple forms: questions or other communications to obtain clarification or a better understanding of the earlier message, emotional reactions to the information content of the message, or rebuttals to the content of the first message. All these forms of messages are encoded, transmitted through various channels, received, and decoded by the original source. The entire sequence may range from something as simple as a question by one employee, "Want to go for a cup of coffee?" and an affirmative head shake by another, to complex statements of fact and complex responses as negotiators shape an agreement.

This model of communication works to the degree that a wide variety of information—facts, opinions, feelings, preferences, and experiences—is completely and thoroughly shared among the parties. However, as most of us know from experience, human communication systems seldom perform with this high degree of efficiency and effectiveness. The elements of the model and the linkages among them are subject to external factors that distort messages and their meaning, keeping them from getting through accurately. We will first describe each element in the sequence and then more fully explore how distortions occur in communication.

1. *Senders* and *receivers* each have goals and objectives, things that they want to accomplish. The sender may want to change the receiver's mind or secure concessions toward a negotiated agreement. A receiver may not want to have her mind changed or to make concessions; moreover, the receiver may have the identical objective in mind as the other party. The more diverse the goals of the sender and receiver, or the more antagonistic they are in their relationship, the greater the likelihood of distortion and error in communication. Similarly, senders and receivers differ in their individual makeup— each is likely to have a different pattern of personal values, attitudes toward certain issues and objectives, previous experiences, life history, and personality characteristics. Each of these elements contributes to a different way of viewing the world.

2. *Transmitters* and *receptors* are simply the vehicle or mode by which information is sent and received. Information can be sent verbally—by speaking or by writing—and nonverbally—by body posture, hand and facial gestures, tone of voice, and the like. The choice of transmitter can affect outcomes, that is, some messages may be better spoken, whereas others need to be written. Moreover, when presenting information face-to-face, congruence or incongruence between multiple transmission channels is often a problem. Parent-to-child communications of "Don't do that!" accompanied by parental smiles or laughter highlight the incongruity of mixed messages that can be sent simultaneously through verbal and nonverbal channels, and the possible confusion ("Do I stop, or do I keep doing it?") introduced by these contradictory elements. On the receiver's end, poor eyesight, faulty hearing, or a distracted state may similarly diminish the ability to accurately receive a message.

3. *Messages* and *channels* are the vehicles by which information is communicated. As noted by many writers on communication, human beings are unique in their ability to use symbolic forms of communication—primarily written or spoken language—to transmit information. Some messages are direct expressions of meaning—I lean over the table and grab the pencil that

I want—whereas others are symbolic representations—I ask the person seated across the table, "Please pass me the pencil." The more prone we are to use symbolic communication, the more likely it is that the symbols we choose may not accurately communicate the meaning we intend. In the pencil example, if the other person does not understand English, or if there are several different pencils on the table, there is increased likelihood that the communication will be less than effective.

*Channels* are the vehicles by which messages are carried. If we speak directly, the channel is the airwaves; if we write, it is the paper and pen or the word processor; if we talk over the telephone, it is the telephone circuitry, cables, and microwaves. Both messages and channels are prone to distortion from *noise,* a broad term we will use to describe various forms of interference in the communication process. Messages can be transmitted more clearly in a quiet room than in a loud, distracting hotel ballroom. The greater the sources of distraction and confusion in the communication environment, the more that noise will interfere with accurate and complete message transmission.

4. *Decoding, meaning,* and *encoding* are the processes that individuals use to interpret the messages of others and to formulate messages themselves. *Decoding* is the process of translating messages from their symbolic form into interpretations that we can understand. If the parties speak the same language or use the same common nonverbal gestures to communicate messages, the process is reasonably simple and error-free; if they do not, decoding may involve a high degree of error. Although translators may help decode the other's messages, full translation may not be possible, that is, they may not capture the other's meaning or tone along with the words. In fact, translators may introduce additional error into the communications.

*Meanings* are the facts, ideas, feelings, reactions, or thoughts that exist within individuals and act as a set of filters for interpreting the decoded messages. If one person has asked the other to "please pass me that pencil," and the other person has said "no," the encoded "no" is likely to stimulate a variety of reactions in the first person's search for its exact "meaning." Did the other hear the message? Was the "no" a direct refusal to the request? Why did the other say "no"? Does he need the pencil too? Is he being obstinate and intentionally blocking me? Answers to these questions will vary depending upon a variety of other aspects of the communication sequence and the relationship between the parties, all of which leads us to ascribe different meanings to the word *no.*

Finally, *encoding* is the process by which messages are put into symbolic form. The encoding process will be affected by varying degrees of skill in encoding (e.g., fluency in language, skill at expression in written and verbal form, etc.). It will also be affected by earlier communication, including what we want to communicate and how we have reacted to earlier communications. Senders are likely to choose to encode messages in a preferred form;

this form may not be the same as that preferred by receivers. Consider two managers who want to negotiate an agreement. One may prefer to get together and discuss it over lunch, then shake hands on the deal and be done with it, whereas the other may prefer to prepare a written draft that they can exchange and revise until they can agree on the specific wording. Thus, *how* this contract will be prepared may, itself, be a subject of negotiation.

5. *Feedback* is the process by which the receiver reacts to the sender's message. Even in a one-way communication cycle, feedback is essential. It is necessary to let the sender know that the message was actually received, encoded, and ascribed with the same meaning that the sender intended. The absence of feedback can contribute to significant distortions in communication because senders never know whether their message is being received, much less understood. Those addressing a large audience may find themselves either talking into space or directing comments to the individual who is shaking her head to signify agreement, or smiling, or otherwise acknowledging that the communication is being received and appreciated. The sender is unlikely to direct comments to a receiver who is shaking his head to signify disagreement, scowling, or asleep, unless the comments are specifically designed to change the receiver's disposition.

## SUMMARY

In this chapter, we have taken a multifaceted look at the role of communication in negotiation. In particular, we examined three perspectives: the structural perspective, provided by phase and stage models of negotiation, the perceptual processes and phenomena that occur within these phases, and the "micro" processes that occur in message packaging, delivery, and reception.

The research on phase models of negotiation is quite consistent in proposing that negotiation can be partitioned into at least three stages: a beginning, a middle, and an end. These stages represent the initiation, exchange, and closure steps that mark a successful negotiation. Within each of the stages, negotiators engage in fairly predictable behaviors and processes, although in reality the process is rarely as neat and unidirectional as the models would suggest. More recently, researchers have suggested that this view of negotiation is inadequate and constraining, in that it doesn't describe what happens prior to the beginning stage (that is, as the parties build or create a relationship and decide whether to negotiate or not), and also what happens after the end stage (that is, as the parties implement their agreement or pursue other alternatives if they fail to agree). To date, stage models have not given sufficient consideration to the critical events that may occur in these pre-beginning and post-end stages.

In the beginning stage, the key behaviors and activities include the clarification of issues and agendas and the demarcation of the playing field—the bounded area of interests and potentials within which the negotiation will unfold. Critically important to this beginning stage is the process of social perception, including the potential for perceptual distortion (such as stereotyping, halo effects, selective perception, and projection.) Also important are the effects of framing and of the mistakes that can accrue from attributional biases.

The middle stage is marked by the exchange of offers and the evolution of a framework and the detail that fleshes out the negotiation and moves it toward closure. Interests and expectations are expressed, bargaining ranges are narrowed, and the parties move toward settlement. Communicative behaviors in this stage include providing clear information regarding one's own interests, proactively seeking information about the other's interests, and listening actively as those interests are expressed. This active listening requires a strong commitment to hearing the other party effectively and authentically, and it may be enhanced by empathic behaviors such as role reversal.

Finally, the end stage is marked by efforts to bring the negotiation to conclusion. At this stage, the parties must be careful to avoid a number of potential decision traps in their haste to reach a settlement and wrap up the details. Parties must also take care to write the agreement down and create a draft that contains language endorsed by both sides.

Finally, we presented a microlevel model of the communication process; we suggested that many of the elements of that model are also prone to error and distortion. Such distortions are very likely to occur when communicating parties have conflicting goals and objectives and strong feelings of dislike or disdain for one another. They may also be adversely affected by problems as information is encoded, transmitted, and decoded. The closure of the communication loop occurs through feedback, by which the success of the intended communication can be checked. During transmission and feedback, the problem of "noise" or interference might affect the clarity with which the message and response are sent and received.

We have explored communication from the perspective of both parties and the processes, channels, and mechanisms used by each. We shall now turn to a different approach to communication: articulating and emphasizing specific techniques one party can use to structure a message to be as persuasive as possible to the other in negotiations.

# CHAPTER 8

# The Persuasion Process

During negotiations, negotiators may need to convince the other party they have offered them something valuable, that their offer is reasonable, and that they cannot offer any more. Negotiators may also want to alter the other party's beliefs about the importance of their own objectives and convince them that their concessions are not as valuable as they first believed. Negotiators may portray themselves as likeable people who should be treated decently. They may also try to convince the other party that people will be watching them negotiate and will be evaluating them based on both the process and the outcome of the negotiation. All these efforts are designed to influence the other party's positions, perceptions, opinions, and attitudes, and they will be collectively called *persuasion.*

People differ widely in their ability to persuade. Some people think that the ability to persuade is something people are born with, something we either have or don't have. Although the natural persuasive abilities of people *do* differ, persuasion is as much a science as it is a native ability; it is possible for *everyone* to learn how to improve their persuasive skills.

There are three key components to the persuasion process: the *message,* the content that the sender wants the receiver to believe, accept, or understand; the *source,* the party attempting to persuade; and the *receiver,* the party to be persuaded (see Figure 8.1). Parts of each of these elements may be used singly or in combination to persuade someone successfully. Persuasion is an important subprocess of communication, and this chapter is a natural extension of the work on communication presented in Chapter 7.

Social scientists who study persuasion suggest that there are two general paths by which people are persuaded (see Chaiken, 1987; Petty and Cacioppo, 1986). One popular model of persuasion, the Elaboration Likelihood Model, is presented in Figure 8.2. The first route to persuasion occurs consciously and involves thought and integration ("sense-making") of the message into the individual's previously existing cognitive structures (thoughts, intellectual frameworks, etc.). Researchers Richard Petty and John Cacioppo have labeled this path to persuasion the central route; they argue that "the ultimate goal of this effort is to determine if the position taken by the source has any merit" (Petty, Cacioppo, Strathman and Priester, in press, p. 4). A great deal of research, especially in the 1950s and 1960s, has examined factors that influence persuasion via the central route. The other route to persuasion, the peripheral route, is characterized by less

**FIGURE 8.1**

cognitive effort by the receiver and a greater reliance on heuristics and cues (Chaiken, 1980; see Chapter 7 for a discussion of heuristics and negotiation). Persuasion via the peripheral route is thought to occur automatically (i.e., out of conscious awareness), and because information is not integrated into existing cognitive structures, persuasion occurring via this route will have effects that last a shorter time than persuasion that occurred via the central route (Petty and Cacioppo, 1986). Recent research has examined factors that influence persuasion on the peripheral route (see Chaiken, 1987; Cialdini, 1985).

Researchers disagree as to whether the two routes to persuasion are separate systems (e.g., Petty & Cacioppo, 1986) or compensatory systems (e.g., Chaiken, 1987). That is, it is not clear if the two routes to persuasion operate separately or if they work in conjunction with one another. There is also disagreement about what to label the two routes and which research findings fit more precisely into which route. For sake of clarity, we have adopted Petty and Cacioppo's labels for the two routes. It is also difficult to apply some of the concepts of persuasion a priori because of contradictory research findings and the complex relationships between variables. Despite these weaknesses, this model of persuasion is comprehensive and helps organize a great deal of conflicting research on persuasion. The model does *not* provide exact prescriptions about how to persuade everyone in all circumstances. It *does* provide a clear way to think about the variables that have been found to influence persuasion, and it helps clarify when persuasive tactics *can* work. This does not mean that these factors *will* work in all circumstances, however, and a skillful blend of many persuasive techniques carefully crafted to the situation at hand is always necessary.

In this chapter, we begin by examining the different aspects of message structure and content, address the credibility of the source of the message, and then review characteristics of the receiver of the message. Researchers think most of these factors have an influence on the central route to persuasion. We conclude the chapter with a discussion of six compliance strategies, factors that are thought to influence persuasion along the peripheral route.

## HOW TO CONSTRUCT A MESSAGE

Facts and ideas are clearly important in changing another person's opinions and perceptions. Facts can be selected, organized, and presented in many different ways, however. There are three major issues to consider when constructing a message: the *content* of the message (the facts and topics that should be covered), the

**FIGURE 8.2**   The Elaboration–Likelihood Model of Persuasion

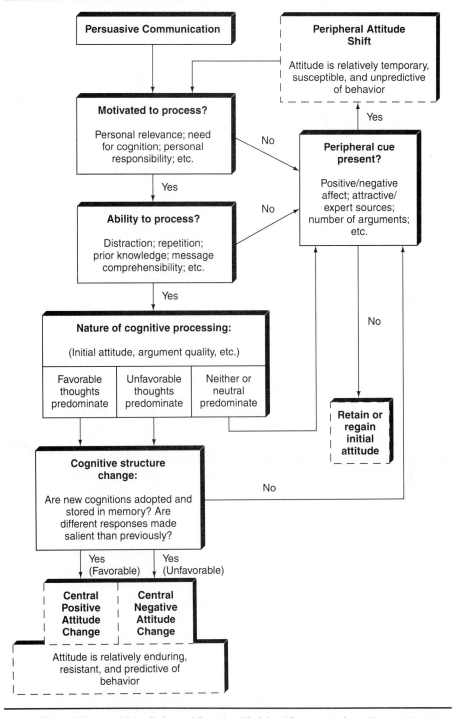

From Richard E. Petty and John Cacioppo, "Central and Peripheral Routes to Attitude Change." (New York: Springer Verlag, 1986). Used with permission of the authors.

message *structure* (how the topics and facts should be arranged), and the *delivery style* that should be used to present the message.

## Message Content

When constructing arguments to persuade the other party, negotiators need to decide what topics and facts they should include in their messages. In this section, we discuss four issues negotiators need to consider when constructing persuasive arguments: (1) the attractiveness of the offer to the other party, (2) getting them to "say yes," (3) obtaining agreements in principle, and (4) normative messages.

**Attractiveness of the Offer to the Receiver.**    One important thing to emphasize when negotiating is the advantage the other party gains from accepting our proposal (Michener and Suchner, 1971). Although this may seem obvious, it is surprising how many negotiators spend more time explaining and defending why their offer is attractive to themselves than identifying what aspects are likely to be attractive *to the other party.* Experienced negotiators ensure that the other party understands what they gain when they accept an offer. To do this well, negotiators need to understand the other party's needs. Salespeople often identify a customer's needs and requirements before they get down to the details of what a particular product or service can do. Labor negotiators will often have preliminary, unofficial meetings with management at which they can discuss the upcoming deliberations and sound each other out on the things that will be really important this year. With this information, offers can be constructed so they are more appealing to the other party.

When we are on the *receiving* end of a proposal, we frequently choose *not* to talk about the attractive features of an offer, but rather to discuss the undesirable features and why the things offered are not as valuable to us as the offerer tried to make us believe (Emerson, 1962). A strategy customers in foreign bazaars or antique shops often follow is to spend a considerable amount of time discussing something they do not want, dropping that topic, and then casually examining and inquiring about the thing they do want. The theory is that the trader will grab at the chance to make a sale before this apparently unsatisfied customer walks out and may accept a low price, one close to his resistance point. We suspect that even if professional traders had only a fraction of their reputed craftiness, they would have figured out this trick long ago. But then the customer is about to walk out . . . perhaps.

Thus, persuasion can be a struggle over how an attractive offer is evaluated. The negotiator making the offer stresses the attractive features of the offer to minimize further concessions. The receiver of the offer stresses unattractive features, hoping to receive more concessions. The more objective facts that either party can use in this exchange, the more likely they will create an agreement in their mutual favor.

**Getting Them to "Say Yes."**    Advertisers discovered long ago that people who agree with one statement or proposal, even though it may be minor, are likely to agree with a second, more significant statement or proposal from the same person or on the same topic (Fern, Monroe and Avila, 1986; Freedman and Fraser, 1966; Seligman, Bush, and Kirsch, 1976). Hence, if you can get the other party to agree about something, then you have laid the foundation for subsequent agreement. The task is to find something that the other party can agree with that has acceptable cost. A real estate salesperson who gets potential buyers to agree that the house they are visiting is in a nice neighborhood for their children has made the first step toward getting them to say "yes" to buying the house.

**Agreements in Principle.**    There are times when getting an agreement in principle may be a valuable step in a negotiation. For example, when there is bitter conflict between two parties who cannot seem to agree on anything, getting agreement on a general principle may be the first "yesable" statement that both parties can agree to. In the negotiations between Israel and Egypt over the Sinai, no details were settled about the fate of the Palestinians, but an agreement on the principle of Palestinian self-rule was reached. Although agreement in principle is desirable when other options are blocked, agreements based on principle only are less fruitful for a clear and implementable agreement than those containing specific action proposals. Principles sound good and most people may agree with what they advocate, but there is always uncertainty about how a principle applies to the specific situation. For example, if the parties agree that "honesty is the best policy," we are left with questions. Is honesty best all of the time? Some of the time? Most of the time? With colleagues, strangers, or both? Specific, concrete statements in negotiation eliminate errors in meaning and interpretation, thereby making them easier to implement.

**Normative Messages.**    It is easy to assume that people are driven by simple and direct self-interest. There is also plenty of evidence, however, that indicates that people are motivated to behave consistent with their values: religious, social, or ethical standards of behavior. These standards become part of people's self-image, a concept in their mind of what they are really like. People often go to considerable lengths to act or say things consistent with their self-image. At times, people are polite when they really want to tell another person to "drop dead." People can be generous when they are actually financially strained and feel like being greedy (Reardon, 1981). They behave this way to preserve their self-image and to convince others that they are nice people (see our discussion of face saving in Chapter 9).

A powerful argument in negotiation is to show the other person that by following a course of action (our proposal), they will be acting in accordance with their values and with some higher (more noble, moral, or ethical) code of conduct. Presidents use normative messages to justify fiscal policies to promote domestic purchases (e.g., "Buy American," "Protect American Jobs"), and interest groups use normative messages to promote their points of view (e.g., "Save a Tree," "Liberal Economics"). At times, the simple statement "this is the right (proper) thing to do," may carry considerable weight. People work hard to take responsibility for actions that lead to positive outcomes (Schlenker and Riess, 1979).

## Message Structure

People are influenced not only by what a negotiator says, but also by how a negotiator arranges his words. Any writer or speaker faces the question of whether to present material in the most logical, rational manner or to appeal to the receiver's emotions. Should the most important information or strongest arguments be placed at the beginning, the middle, or the end of a presentation? Should counterarguments or opposing ideas be mentioned at all? There has been a considerable amount of research on the persuasive power of these different aspects of message structure. Surprisingly, many things we might expect to have an important impact, such as the structure of logic in the message, have *not* been clearly shown to be important. Five aspects of message structure that *have* been shown to be significant are (1) message order, (2) one- and two-sided messages, (3) fractionating disputes, (4) repetition, and (5) drawing conclusions.

**Message Order.**   In preparing a persuasive argument, there is usually one major point, piece of information, or illustration that is particularly important or compelling. Where should it be placed in the message? At the beginning? In the middle? At the end? Research tells us one thing clearly—do not place the important point in the middle of the message (Bettinghaus, 1966). Should it be at the beginning or at the end? When the topics are familiar, interesting, or controversial to the receiver, the important points should be made early, exposing the receiver to the *primacy effect:* the first item in a long list of items is the one most likely to be remembered. Thus, we should state messages that are desirable to the receiver early, before we present something the receiver may not want to hear. In contrast, when the topic is uninteresting, unfamiliar, or not very important to the receiver, the most critical point should be placed at the end of the message to take advantage of the *recency effect:* the tendency for the last item presented to be the best remembered. The recency effect should be considered when the message is likely to be contrary to the receiver's current point of view (Rosnow and Robinson, 1967).

**One- and Two-Sided Messages.**   When we try to persuade another person, it is because we believe that she holds an opinion different from ours. Many people deal with this problem by completely ignoring arguments and opinions that might support the other party's position—a one-sided approach. Many politicians not only do not mention their opponent's point of view, they make a policy of never mentioning their opponent's name. Until recently, advertisements for consumer products would never mention the name of competing products or openly compare competitors' products.

An alternate approach to ignoring the competition is to mention and describe the opposing point of view and then show how and why it is less appropriate or desirable than the presenter's point of view—a two-sided approach. Which of these approaches is most effective? In general, two-sided messages are considered to be more effective (Jackson and Allen, 1987). Two-sided messages appear to be most effective (1) with better educated audiences, (2) when the other party initially *disagrees* with the position, (3) when the other party will be exposed to people who will argue points of view different from the position advocated, and (4) when the issue discussed is already familiar to the audience. In summary, when dealing with reasonably intelligent audiences, it is a mistake to ignore the impact of counter-arguments. The other party will be formulating them as you speak, and it is an advantage to refute them by using two-sided messages. In addition, when presenting two-sided arguments, it appears to be more effective to present the preferred argument *last* (Bettinghaus, 1966; Zimbardo, Ebbesen, and Maslach, 1977).

**Fractionating Disputes: Mountains into Molehills.**    Big ideas or large propositions are hard to grasp and accept, especially when they are significantly different from our own. You can help the other party understand and accept arguments by breaking them into smaller, more understandable pieces (Fisher, 1964; Ikle, 1964). It is even better if you can show that the ultimate objective contains component parts that the other party has already accepted or agreed with. For example, a company negotiating a change in work rules with a union might have trouble getting the whole package of rule changes accepted, but could break its presentation down into separate discussions of specific rules: transfers between departments within a plant, transfers between plants, permanent changes in work classifications, temporary changes in work classifications, and so on. In one case, for example, a union was very interested in interplant and interdepartmental changes in work rules to preserve job security; having already said "yes" to these changes, the union seemed more receptive to management's argument for other work rule changes. In addition, it is possible that the fractionation of complex arguments will lead to increased perceptions of possibilities to logroll, bundle, and trade off across issues because the issues in dispute will be seen in sharper focus.

**Repetition.**    We only have to think of typical television advertisements to realize that ad writers believe in the power of repetition to get their message across. Repeating a point is effective for the first few times. After that, additional repetition does not significantly change attitudes (McGuire, 1973), and it may become annoying.

**Drawing Conclusions.**    Sometimes writers or speakers will lay out a line of argument and then state the conclusion; other times, they will let the receivers draw their own conclusions. Letting the other party draw his own conclusion (as long as it is the conclusion *you* want drawn) can lead to a very effective presentation. Research suggests that for the intellectually inclined or for those who have not yet made up their minds, leaving the conclusion open is a good approach. In contrast, for people whose ideas are firm, leaving the conclusion implicit is to leave the most important part of the persuasive effort undone. In general, do not assume that the other party will use the same facts to reach the same conclusion as you; rather, draw explicit conclusions for the audience to ensure that they have understood the argument completely (Feingold and Knapp, 1977; Hovland and Mandell, 1952; McGuire, 1964).

### Delivery Style

When negotiators select a delivery style for the message they have constructed, they are setting the emotional tone and manner of their presentation. Some people are belligerent, others solicitous and accommodating. Some people make speeches, others start a dialogue. Some present detailed facts and draw specific conclusions, whereas others paint beautiful pictures with words and use metaphors. We will now consider six major elements of persuasive style and how they affect successful persuasion: (1) active participation versus passive responding, (2) metaphors, (3) fears and threats, (4) distractions, (5) language intensity, and (6) violation of the receiver's expectations.

**Active Participation versus Passive Responding.**     People learn better and are more likely to change their attitudes and beliefs for the long term when they are actively involved in the process of learning and understanding new material (Bettinghaus, 1966; Johnson and Eagly, 1989, 1990; Petty and Cacioppo, 1990). Good teachers know this—rather than lecture, they ask questions. Learning is even more effective when teachers can get people both intellectually and physically involved. The use of role plays and cases when teaching or learning about negotiation also recognizes the power of active participation when learning. In trying to persuade a car dealer that a trade-in is really worth a premium price, the customer could present facts and ask questions (a passive approach). On the other hand, the customer could have the dealer walk around the car with her, examine the car's exceptional points, take the car for a drive, and examine the repair records to note the frequent routine maintenance (an active approach). Active approaches generally result in more persuasion because they have the receiver exert effort, which leads to involvement, which leads to attitude change.

**Metaphors.**     Although facts and logical conclusions are important to persuasion, metaphors can be even more potent (Bowers and Osborn, 1966; Burgoon and King, 1974). An auto salesperson can give details about a car's carburetor, the miles per gallon of gasoline used at different speeds, and rates of acceleration, but these points can be made just as well by saying, "This car flies like the wind and is not a gas guzzler." The same salesperson could show a car's fine finish, point out the underside of the body, and draw attention to the immaculate condition of the engine, or he could say "this car is as sleek as a cat." An excessive use of metaphors may lead the other party to believe that you're "filled with hot air" (a metaphor itself for not having the facts to support arguments), but when used to summarize some facts or to establish clear visual impressions, metaphors are very valuable persuasion tools. Advertisers use metaphors frequently when they promote their products, like Allstate's "You're in Good Hands" or United Parcel Service's "We Run the Tightest Ship in the Shipping Business." Finally, we must be careful when using metaphors to choose the correct picture. This is especially difficult when negotiating across cultures, where the meanings of different metaphors can be quite different (see Chapter 14 for more discussion of culture and negotiation).

**Fears and Threats.**    Messages that contain threats—threats of strikes by unions or lockouts by management, threats to harm the other party's reputation, or threats to break off negotiations—can be useful when a negotiator needs to underscore the absolute importance of a point being made. In essence, threats are "if-then" statements with serious consequences: "If you do X, then I will be forced to do Y." Negotiators must be prepared to follow through with the consequences threatened, however, or they will be perceived as making empty threats and lose credibility. Because of their dramatic nature and the emotional response they evoke, we hear more about the use of threats than about many other negotiation tactics. In fact, threats are probably used less frequently than we might expect, for several reasons. One reason is that the other person's reaction to a threat is hard to predict. Some people respond by becoming belligerent and antagonistic, some by becoming defensive, cautious, or inflexible, and others by complying with the threat. The nature of the response depends upon the personality of the other person and the situation (Burgoon and Bettinghaus, 1980). A second reason is that it is hard to know how menacing the threat appears to the other party. Often our threats appear more powerful to us than to others. Third, threats put the other party in a position where she can "call our bluff," forcing us to carry out the threat. Often, to follow through with a threat may cost us more than we are willing to pay. Lastly, threats may produce compliance, but they do not usually produce commitment. As we have pointed out, negotiating parties want to reach an arrangement they can and will live with. People can find many ways to avoid arrangements they were forced to comply with, but to which they are not committed (see the last section of this chapter and Chapter 10 for further discussion of compliance).

Fear-arousing messages may be sent without issuing threats. One manager, negotiating with another about the flow of work between their two departments, may point out that if an agreement is not reached, the other manager will be portrayed to higher management as "uncooperative." Research suggests that fear-arousing messages can be effective if they increase the arousal level of the receiver (Boster and Mongeau, 1984; Sutton, 1982). To be most effective, this kind of message must be accompanied by a suggested alternative action that will reduce or eliminate the feared outcome and a reassurance that the action will work (Leventhal, 1970). For example, the manager could then propose that some of her employees be reassigned to help the other department speed up the work flow if the other manager will provide some additional storage space, and then show how these changes will eliminate their problem.

**Distractions.**    One factor that makes the persuasion process complex is that people start to defend themselves against being persuaded as soon as they suspect that someone is trying to persuade them. As they listen, part of their attention is devoted to what is being said, but a large portion is also devoted to developing counterarguments (Brock, 1963; Festinger and Maccoby, 1964). Negotiators can be more effective at persuasion if they can determine how to reduce the other party's efforts to develop counterarguments. One way to do this is to have a *distraction* occur at the same time the message is sent. Distractions apparently absorb the effort that normally would go into building counterarguments and the listener is ". . . left vulnerable to the message appeals" (Reardon, 1981, p. 192). For example, during an oral presentation of the economic advantages of an offer, negotiators could lay out papers with charts and graphs, hand them to the other party, and help them turn from one to another as the oral presentation continues. Presumably, the charts and graphs absorb that part of the person's attention that might normally go into formulating counterarguments. Distractions appear to work because they seem to inhibit the receiver's subvocalization (what you say to yourself as you hear the message). Sometimes these subvocalizations are counterarguments, which occur when we are opposed to or cautious about the message, but they can be supportive arguments as well. When we really *like* what is being said, such as when a friend is trying to persuade us to take a second helping of a high-calorie dessert, subvocalizations will encourage us to accept the offer. At that time, if we want to protect ourselves from temptation, *we* should create distractions. If the friend wants to successfully push the dessert, he should try to eliminate any distractions (Petty, Wells, and Brock, 1976).

**Language Intensity.**    The intensity of the language negotiators use has a major effect on their persuasiveness. Saying "This is certainly the best price you will get" is more intense than saying "This is quite a good price." Similarly, the statement "I don't feel like going out tonight" is not as intense as "You could not drag me out tonight with a team of elephants." The intensity of language can also be increased through the use of colorful metaphors, swear words, or even a change in intonation—from quiet to loud or loud to quiet (Bowers, 1964).

You might think that more intense language would also be more persuasive. To the contrary, language of relatively *low* intensity seems to be more effective than highly intense language (Bowers, 1964). Evidence indicates that people react negatively to persuasive attempts using language they perceive as too intense (Burgoon and King, 1974). People under stress seem to be particularly receptive to messages using low-intensity language and more inclined to reject those using high-intensity language (Jones and Burgoon, 1975). The impact of language intensity is even more complex, however: research has shown that the effect of intense language depends, in part, on who uses it. Sources with high credibility can use more intense language than those not seen as credible (Burgoon and Stewart, 1975). Hence, members of the clergy can speak with more intensity (and convincingness) about the characteristics of heaven and hell and the likelihood of someone going there than can the authors of this book. In conclusion, although there is a strong temptation to use intense language to make a point, it is typically better to moderate this impulse.

**Violation of Receiver's Expectations.**   In *All the King's Men,* Robert Penn Warren describes a scene in which Willy Stark, the demagogic, radical candidate for governor, is about to speak to a group of wealthy citizens to raise funds for his campaign. The citizens support neither his radical proposals, nor his violent manner of speech. When he arrives, he is conservatively dressed and greets them in a quiet, relaxed manner. In a conversational tone, he proceeds to describe some modest proposals for social change, along with some sensible ways of financing them. His audience is at first surprised, then impressed, and finally won over. Stark is employing the technique of "violating expectations." People who argue positions that are thought to be counter to their self-interest are generally more persuasive because they violate the receiver's expectation about what the sender "should" be arguing for. For instance, an automobile mechanic recently suggested that one of the author's of this book should use mid- or high-octane gas in his car to reduce fuel-injector maintenance and save money. This message was persuasive because the mechanic was arguing against his self-interest (future car repairs) when he suggested the change in gas (his business does not sell gasoline).

Another way that receivers' expectations can be violated occurs when they expect one style of delivery from the speaker and then experience a totally different style. For example, when you expect to be subjected to intense language (loud, volatile, provocative, etc.), you prepare defenses and counterarguments. If you instead find moderate, casual, reasonable language, you relax your defenses, listen to the message less critically, and are more likely to be persuaded (Miller and Burgoon, 1979). Great orators, such as Winston Churchill and Martin Luther King, have used this style, frequently changing the intensity of their voices to hold the audience's attention. Although this is not a stylistic tactic that everyone can use, strong orators have a valuable tool at their disposal. Clearly, the process may also work in reverse—audiences who are expecting a quiet, controlled, highly rational discourse may be equally persuaded by an emotionally intense speaker because they were unprepared to defend themselves against such passionate persuasion.

In summary, negotiators need to take care when they construct a message to persuade the other party to their point of view. Aspects of the message content, message structure, and the delivery style can all influence the extent to which a message is persuasive. In other words, *how* you say something can be as important as *what* you have to say, and if the other party is not persuaded by your arguments, then perhaps you did not construct the message effectively.

## CHARACTERISTICS OF SOURCES

The second major component in the persuasion process that has received considerable research attention is the source of the persuasive effort: who is attempting to do the persuasion. Research has generally addressed two aspects of sources: (1) source credibility and (2) source attractiveness. Although it is difficult to research the effects of source credibility and attractiveness separately (O'Keefe, 1990), we will discuss them separately in this chapter.

### Source Credibility

During a negotiation, both parties exchange information, opinions, and interpretations. What should be believed? Negotiations present incentives for the parties to attempt to mislead each other. At the same time, we have to accept and believe some of the information we are given, or successful negotiation and agreement is impossible (Kelley, 1966). We cannot check every fact and statement. The more information we are willing to accept without independent verification, the more persuaded we will be. The reverse is also true—the more credible you are to the other party, the more persuasive you will be.

The degree to which a person is willing to accept what another person says depends upon three things: the perceived *trustworthiness* of the source, how *qualified* the source is seen to be, and what *type of person* the source appears to be. Let us assume we are buying a house. The seller tells us that she has three other parties coming to look at the house in the afternoon; two of them are being transferred to this area and have only one day to locate a house. If this is true, and we like the house, it would be to our advantage to make an offer now rather than to delay our decision and possibly find that one of the afternoon visitors has bought the house. But are the seller's statements true? No doubt the seller knows whether or not there are other potential buyers coming that same day; hence there is no question that she is competent or qualified to have good information. The issue is whether or not the seller is telling the truth.

When people are determining how much to believe another person, the two most important things they take into account are these: (1) is this person in a position to possess the information she claims to have, that is, is she competent or qualified; and (2) is she reporting accurately what she knows, that is, is she personally believable or trustworthy (Berlo, Lemert, and Mertz, 1966). People appear more or less credible because of their "presence"—the way they present themselves to others. Three components of behavior are instrumental in creating a favorable presence: composure, sociability, and extroversion (McCroskey, Jensen, and Valencia, 1973). A person who seems hesitant, confused, or uncertain when giving information is not as convincing as a person who appears to know what he is talking about and is comfortable in talking about it. A friendly, open person is easier to talk to, to like, and therefore to believe than someone who is distant, abrasive, or haughty. A person with a dynamic vocal style and a confident delivery is often more persuasive than one without these attributes. Trustworthiness and how qualified the person appears seem to be more powerful characteristics in determining our perception of another's credibility than the type of person the source is, but all three play a critical role.

Many things about us influence others' perceptions of our credibility. We will now discuss the primary elements that have been found to influence a person's credibility. Each of these elements suggest things that negotiators can do to maximize their perceived credibility and persuasiveness.

**Personal Reputation.**    People with dishonest reputations have an extremely difficult time in negotiations—they tend not to be believed, even when they are telling the truth. Once you have a reputation of being dishonest it is very difficult to change. It is not surprising that professional negotiators work very hard to protect their reputations for honesty. As we noted in Chapter 3, negotiators are expected to engage in puffery and to present things in the best possible light for their side—but not to lie or misrepresent what they are offering. Although they may succeed at lying and deception in one negotiation, it is likely that few will believe them in later negotiations (see Chapter 13 for an expanded discussion of this point). A negotiator's reputation plays a critical role in how persuasive she will be: those with better reputations will be more persuasive, especially in the long term.

Frequently we enter negotiations with strangers, people whose reputations are unknown to us. If the substance of the discussion is important to us, it is sensible for us to check out the other party's reputation—and for them to check us out. We might want to help them check our reputations by identifying (perhaps during early discussions) other people who can vouch for our integrity.

**Position Bias of a Stranger.**    When meeting others they don't know, people generally tend to evaluate them positively rather than negatively (Greenberg and Miller, 1966). People are frequently open-minded when they first meet someone; if they do form a first impression, they often err toward the positive viewpoint. Although this bias may be an advantage in helping us persuade someone we've recently met, we should also keep in mind that this bias is probably working on us as well.

**Intention to Persuade.**    The statement, "First impressions are lasting impressions," has a great deal of validity. In the first few minutes after meeting a stranger, how we dress, behave, and speak can be enormously important. Do we initially come across as a huckster or as a persuasive promoter for our cause? Even appearing very confident can make people feel uncomfortable and guarded. Similarly, if we appear very cool, poised, polished, or calculating, we can also expect to put others on their guard. In short, the more prepared or rehearsed we appear to be in our persuasive efforts, the more suspicious others may be that they are about to have their attitudes changed, and the less receptive they may be. For instance, it is easy to identify telemarketers who try to involve the receiver in casual chit-chat ("How are you this evening?") while they ease into their prepared sales pitch script ("I'm glad you're well. Do you ever have problems with . . ."). In contrast, the ability to communicate natural enthusiasm, sincerity, and spontaneity may take the edge off persuasive communication and reduce defensive reactions. Many skillful negotiators and persuaders, therefore, may take on a mild-mannered or even slightly confused demeanor (such as Peter Falk in the television role of Lt. Columbo) to minimize the negative impact of a hard, persuasive style.

**Status Differential.**    Most people are aware of status and status differences. We assess status by a variety of criteria: occupation, age, sex, level of education, religion, the community where a person lives, dress, type of automobile, and the like. A president of a major corporation, for example, has more status than a university professor, but less than a Justice of the Supreme Court. A person's persuasiveness is influenced by her status—not in an absolute sense, but because the higher status person has more influence. Higher status plays several roles in increasing persuasiveness. It gives a person visibility, which allows him to get attention and be listened to. It also confers prestige on a person, lending the image that she is worth listening to or more believable (Bettinghaus, 1980). However, not everyone holds the same views on status. If I am concerned with my ability to influence another person, I need to understand what types of factors he views as high or low status. For example, corporation presidents are usually viewed as having higher status than union presidents, but union members might think the reverse is true.

**Appearance.**    It is not earth-shaking to observe that how we dress, speak, and behave will influence how credible we appear to others. What may not be as obvious is the way we should adjust our appearance to increase our credibility. Should we dress up and wear a tie and jacket for an interview, even if we usually wear jeans and a T-shirt? Should we adopt some of the local speech pronunciations and drop those that are native to us? In general, researchers have found that it is best to be "normal" (Bettinghaus, 1980), meaning to act appropriately, naturally, and unaffectedly. A Harvard-educated politician from New England who tries to spice his language with "aw, shucks" and "y'all" in the South will not appear normal; neither will a college student who drops in to buy a BMW dressed in cutoff jeans and dirty running shoes, with uncombed hair.

**Associates.**    Who we associate with also can influence how we are perceived, influencing our perceived status and perhaps our perceived expertise. Judicious name dropping, mentioning well-known references, even arranging for introductions by people who can add to our reputation, are all useful steps. (This is discussed in greater detail in Chapter 10.)

**Expertise.**    Sometimes our occupation, education, or past experiences will establish our expertise and therefore the perception of our competence (Swenson, Nash, and Roos, 1984). At other times, there are no obvious ways to make our expertise known; more unfortunately, there are still other times when one piece of knowledge about us diminishes the likelihood that we will be seen as an expert in certain areas. Stereotypes can lead us to see women as lacking knowledge about mechanical things or single men as ignorant about child care. In situations where our expertise is unknown or likely to be viewed stereotypically, we need to take extra efforts to establish our position. If people don't know our expertise, we can often find some way to mention our education or experiences: "When I went to college, we were taught that . . ." When our expertise is being stereotypically denied, we may need to prove our expertise as well as refer to its source. Asking questions or drawing quick conclusions that could only be derived from in-depth, firsthand knowledge or experience are subtle but effective ways to establish credibility. In one situation, a woman manager was representing her department at a committee meeting to plan a new office building. The other committee members, all men, were pointedly ignoring her until she started to ask questions about heat loss gradients through the walls and the number of foot candles of light falling on work surfaces.

In summary, many factors influence perceptions about the credibility of the source of a persuasive message, including personal reputation, the position bias of strangers, intention to persuade, status, appearance, associates, and expertise. Research suggests that more credible sources are more persuasive, so effective negotiators need to ensure that they have high credibility as sources of persuasive messages.

### Personal Attractiveness

People treat us differently when they like us (Eagly and Chaiken, 1975). They do nicer things for us. They are less likely to feel that we will be dishonest or attempt to coerce them (Tedeschi, Schlenker, and Bonoma, 1973). They are more likely to be influenced by us, to believe and trust us (Chaiken, 1986). Being nice and pleasant is a logical step to being more persuasive. It is not clear why personal attractiveness increases persuasiveness. More attractive people may receive more attention or they may cause others to imitate them in order to be more like them (Trenholm, 1989). In addition, people have a tendency to let their guard down and trust attractive people more readily.

Sometimes we can carry niceness to its extreme by using ingratiation tactics (Jones, 1964). Ingratiation involves flattering or enhancing the other's self-image or reputation through our statements or actions, and thus enhancing our own image in the same way. Ingratiation does not try to put the other person down, but to build her up. Handing out this flattery will presumably make others like us, and hence, others will be more prone to accept our persuasive arguments and point of view. The following tactics are frequently used as ways to enhance personal attractiveness or to make ingratiating strategies successful:

**Compliments.**    Flattering another person by giving compliments is perhaps the most obvious form of ingratiation. Because it is obvious, it is often used and abused. Recognition for what we have done well or for attributes we have is pleasant even when we think those qualities are not too important. Compliments have great impact when our qualities or actions have been overlooked or unappreciated previously but are now recognized favorably. But when people are complimented for attributes they do not have or actions they know they did not perform well, they are likely to become wary, wondering what the flatterer is after.

Nevertheless, compliments can be a potent means of ingratiation, not only because people like to receive them, but also because the norm of reciprocity leaves the other party with the obligation to return something for the compliment (Jones, 1964). Having paid us a compliment, the receiver faces some interesting pressures. Let us see why.

Human beings strive for cognitive consistency, that is, to have their various actions, opinions, attitudes, and statements about a topic be consistent with each other. We find it difficult to say nice things about people we dislike, not necessarily because we are mean or petty but because it does not seem consistent to us to recognize some quality we like in someone we dislike (e.g., "grudging respect"). In the same way, having said something positive about a person, we are likely to shape our impression about that person to fit that prior statement.

At times people act (sometimes under duress) in ways that are inconsistent with what they know about a person or situation. For example, people often object to giving money to umbrella charities like the United Way because they fear they will be contributing to some organization whose actions they disapprove of. When people have beliefs, thoughts, or opinions that are inconsistent with their actions, they experience *cognitive dissonance* (Festinger, 1957). Cognitive dissonance is an uncomfortable feeling that occurs when people's behavior and attitudes are inconsistent. Typically people do one of several things to reduce dissonance. First, they can *forget* or ignore the thought, attitude, or action that is causing dissonance; for example, they could forget that the offending charity is part of the United Way. Second, they can *change* one of their actions or opinions to make it more consistent with the other. For example, they might decide that the offending charity in the United Way is not too bad after all. Lastly, they can *rationalize* their actions or way of looking at the situation to make the dissonance understandable. For example, people could tell themselves that the offending charity gets such a small portion of their money that the impact is trivial compared to the importance of supporting the United Way as a whole.

The prospect of combining the norm of reciprocity with the effects of cognitive dissonance can make giving compliments, even to those who initially dislike us, a useful way of increasing our persuasiveness. If they return the compliment, the resultant cognitive dissonance may lead them to alter their initial attitude toward us into a more positive direction.

**Helping the Other Party.**    There are many ways one party can help the other in a negotiation: by doing them a favor, giving them time or information, or helping them with their constituency. Negotiators can help the other party avoid being caught by surprise. For example, an automobile salesperson may say, "In a moment I'm going to take you in to talk to the sales manager about the amount we are going to allow on your present car. You may hear me say some unfavorable things about your car. Don't let that bother you—we'll still get the figure you and I agreed on."

Frequently a negotiator represents other people. Lawyers represent clients. Union leaders negotiate for their members. Company executives negotiate for their firms. There are many ways one party can enhance the position of other negotiators with their constituencies. They can listen to them carefully and thereby enhance their appearance of being respected. They can be allow them to demand (and receive) concessions so their organizations will see them as having influence. For example, company management might agree to hold contract negotiations in a neutral location rather than on company property. In another example, one of the authors of this book once held an administrative position in a university. In my first few days in the job, I was confronted with a major problem concerning the shortage of office space for some new employees in one of my departments. I was able to get more space for this group without too much trouble, but I was considered a hero by the department because they had been fighting for more space for years without success! Naturally, I felt a great sense of debt to the person who helped me by giving up the space so willingly.

Finally, negotiators can give the other party important information that does not threaten their own position. For example, during negotiations on the sale of a large parcel of land to a major corporation, the seller privately told the company executive handling the negotiation about a forthcoming zoning change that would benefit the company. The executive got the credit for uncovering this inside information, and the seller was not materially affected one way or the other by sharing it.

**Perceived Similarity.**    When meeting someone new, people search for common experiences or characteristics. Perhaps they attended the same school, studied the same subjects, had the same type of job, traveled to the same places, or have friends in common. The possibilities are endless, and often so is the search. The more similarities we find, the more bonds we establish, the better both parties feel, and more importantly, the more receptive they will be to each other's messages and efforts at persuasion (O'Keefe, 1990). A useful negotiating tactic, therefore, is to search for experiences, characteristics, and opinions we hold in common with the other party. Pictures of a yacht on an office wall might suggest that we mention our own interest in sailing. The other party's February suntan might cue us to mention our own trips to the tropics or the ski slopes. Does the other party have some special views on foreign trade? International competition? The marketplace? We might mention some of our own views that are similar. The experiences, interests, and opinions that people may share are countless (sports, hobbies, politics, stock market, travel, etc.); thus, the opportunity to establish some common bonds almost always exists.

If it is to our advantage to find and explore commonalities in experience, attitude, and background with the other party, it is also to our *disadvantage* to highlight those areas where we differ or are in conflict but which are outside the realm of the dispute. Needless to say, differences about the substantive issues in the negotiation will come out; resolving them is the purpose of our negotiation. However, there is no point to exploring the experiences one of us had in public high school if the other went to an elite prep school, or arguing about the merits of a politically controversial topic when our attitudes might alienate the other party if this topic has no direct or important connection to the actual negotiations.

In summary, negotiators need to be aware that their personal characteristics as senders of persuasive messages will influence how persuasive they are. Research suggests that negotiators can do many things to increase their *credibility* and *attractiveness,* two key source factors that have important effects on how persuasive a person is.

## RECEIVER FACTORS

We have previously examined ways to construct a message to influence the other party as well as factors about the source of persuasion that influence the receiver's evaluation of a persuasive message. We now examine factors related to the receiver of persuasion. Not everyone responds to persuasive attempts in the same way. When trying to persuade people, it is important to monitor them, understand how they perceive our arguments, evaluate their positions and interests, and integrate their positions and interests with our views. Monitoring the receiver's perspective is important because negotiators frequently enter discussion combatively. The other party is probably prepared to defend themselves against our arguments, which makes it harder to get them to listen and accept our points. While the other party appears to be listening to us, they are often preparing counterarguments to refute our points and planning the points they want to make. When speaking, they may concentrate on what they want to say and resist questions, comments, or anything that would distract them. Our objective in dealing with the other party is to defuse this defensive/combative stance, to make the other party feel that he has been heard and understood, and to help them hear and understand us.

### Attending

Much of what we communicate to one another is through nonverbal body language. We communicate not only with words and sentences, but also with gestures: the way we position our body, the tone of our voice, the movement of our head. Many nonverbal acts, called *attending behaviors,* are very important in establishing and maintaining contact with another person. These behaviors let the other know that we are listening and prepare the other party to receive our message. We discuss three important attending behaviors: eye contact, body position, and encouraging.

**Eye Contact.**    Dishonest people and cowards are not supposed to be able to look people in the eye. Poets claim that the "eye is the lens that permits us to look into a person's soul." These and other maxims of conventional wisdom illustrate how important we believe eye contact to be. In general, making eye contact is one way that we show others we are paying attention and listening, and that we consider them important. If people do not look at us when we are speaking, we question whether they are listening. If someone is speaking and not looking at us, we wonder whether they are speaking to us or whether they consider us very important. Of course, we may listen very well even when we are not looking at the other person; the point is that we are not providing the other person with cues that we are listening.

In making eye contact, we generally do not keep our eyes fixed on the other person. In fact, if we did, we would be accused of staring, which usually leads to suspicion rather than trust. Instead, our eyes momentarily leave the other person. Generally, these breaks are fewer and shorter when we are listening actively than when we are speaking. When we are speaking, we will occasionally look away, especially when we search for a word or phrase or try to remember some detail. Averting the gaze briefly while speaking signals the other party that we are not finished.

When persuading someone, it is important to make eye contact when we deliver the most important part of our message. Having the verbal and nonverbal systems in parallel at this point emphasizes the importance of the message that is being sent. It is important to recognize that these patterns are characteristic of Western society. In other parts of the world, different patterns prevail. In the Far East, for example, to keep one's eyes down while the other is speaking is a sign of respect (Ivey and Simek-Downing, 1980).

**Body Position.**    Parents frequently advise their children about how to stand and sit, particularly when they are in formal settings such as school, church, dinner parties, or greeting strangers. "Sit up" is often accompanied by "pay attention." Here the parent is teaching the child another widely held belief—the way we hold our body indicates whether or not we are paying attention to the other party. If we want to make sure that others know we are attentive to them, we should hold our bodies erect, lean slightly forward, and face the other person directly (Ivey and Simek-Downing, 1980). We need to take care not to show *dis*respect with our body position by slouching, turning away while the other party is speaking, or placing our feet on the table.

**Encouraging.**    We can indicate our attention and interest in what another is saying by a variety of simple behaviors. A head nod, a simple hand gesture to "go on," or a murmured "uh huh" to indicate understanding all tell the other person to continue, that we are listening. In fact, we can encourage people to continue to talk about many subjects by simply nodding our heads when they talk about that subject, making it more likely that the discussion will continue. Brief eye contact or a smile and nod of the head will both provide encouraging cues.

## Exploring the Other Party's Position

Negotiators frequently give very little attention to the other party's opinions and point of view. This is unfortunate, because it is very much to our advantage to understand what the other party really wants, how things look to them, and how they developed their position. We can explore their perspective with questions (see Chapter 7 for further discussion about the use of questions in negotiation). In negotiation, we can use questions to explore the other party's needs and interests. For instance, "Why are those important objectives for you?" "What would happen if you did not get everything you have asked for?" "How did you arrive at your current position?" and "Have your needs changed since the last time we talked?" bring out more detailed information about the other party's position and interests. Exploring the other person's outlook not only gives us more information, which can lead us to designing solutions to meet both sides' needs, but further increases the other party's feeling of being listened to and makes them more receptive to meeting our needs. On the other hand, questions are often used as a weapon of attack. Questions such as "How in the world can you say that?" "What possible justification can you have for that position?" and "Who in their right mind would believe that?" are likely to make the other party feel tense and combative and may make the tone of the negotiations quite negative.

## Paraphrasing

Paraphrasing ensures that both parties have understood each other accurately. If we haven't understood the other party, then she has the opportunity to correct us. It is important to restate our understanding after being corrected, to make sure we *have* understood. We repeat in *our own words* what someone else has said. Do not literally repeat the other person's words; repeat their *message* in your own words. It is best not to wait until the end of a long message, because parts of it may be forgotten. Instead, it is best to paraphrase what has been said after several paragraphs or after each major point: "Let me see if I understand the point you just made." We should repeat this correction process until the other person is satisfied with the way we paraphrase what was said.

Paraphrasing tells the other person not only that we have heard his words, but also that we have understood what they meant. The importance of using our own words is clear because we can repeat another person's words and not understand what they meant, but stating the message in our own words demonstrates that we comprehend the intended message. In addition, vocalizing the other person's ideas helps us remember them better than simply hearing them. Finally, when people have an important message to get across, they will talk vigorously and at length, often reemphasizing the same point over and over. Once our paraphrasing indicates that they have been understood, they usually stop repeating the same point and move on; hence, paraphrasing can be very helpful in moving a discussion on to new topics.

When people find they are being listened to carefully, any feeling they may have had that they would need to fight for attention and the chance to make their case fades away. They not only will present their own points in a more reasonable way, but also they will be less defensive and more willing to listen to our points. When we speak and actively listen, the norm of reciprocity also encourages the other party to respond in kind.

We can also ask the other party to restate or paraphrase what we have said. We might say, "What I have said is very important to me, and I would appreciate it if you could restate what you understood to be my main points." This process accomplishes several things. First, it puts the other party in a position where they are being asked to listen closely and recall what we have said. Second, it gives us the opportunity to check out the accuracy of their understanding. Third, it emphasizes the most important points of our presentation. Finally, listening and paraphrasing may also validate the other party's participation in the process. If we have paraphrased some of the other party's statements earlier, it is not likely they will refuse or ignore our request.

### Reinforcing Points You Like in the Other Party's Proposals

Negotiators are frequently ineffective because they respond only to what they *dislike* in the other party's statement or proposal and ignore the things they like. Responding in this way ignores a powerful means of shaping and guiding what the other party is saying. Several behavioral science theories (e.g., exchange theory, learning and reinforcement theory, etc.) make the same basic point: people are more likely to repeat behavior that is rewarded than behavior that is not rewarded (Homans, 1961; Skinner, 1953). The simplest way to reward people for what they say during a negotiation is to *acknowledge* and *support* a point that they have made: "That is an interesting point." "I had not heard that before." Give a simple "mm-hmm" or a nod of the head. Statements and actions like these separate a key statement from other points the speaker has made. Second, we can compliment speakers when they make points we want emphasized, and we can express our appreciation to them for considering our interests and needs. In a labor negotiation, for example, management might say to the union, "You raised an important point when you said that if we develop a history of bad labor relations, customers will be much less likely to give us long-term contracts. We appreciate your being aware of some of our marketing and customer image problems." A third approach is to separate particular parts of a statement that we like from those parts we don't like and to encourage the other party to develop the favorable points. In negotiating a house sale, the buyer might say, "Let me focus on one of the points you made. I think making an adjustment in price for the necessary repairs is a good idea. Please go further and explain what type of repairs you have in mind and how we might handle this adjustment." A fourth approach is to return favors. If the other party makes a concession and offers us something we want, we can reward this behavior by making a concession or offering a favor in return. In summary, reinforcing the positive points in the other party's proposal is a powerful technique that receivers can use to shape what the other party is willing to offer; in addition, it validates their participation in the negotiation process.

## Making A Public Commitment

One of the most effective ways of getting a person to stand firm on a position is to have her make a public commitment to that position. Union leaders have said things to their rank and file like "I will resign before I settle for a penny less than . . ." Several pressures work on a union leader after making that statement. One is the potential loss of face with union members if the leader backs away from that position—the leader may be thrown out of office if he does not actually resign. A second pressure is that credibility with management will be sharply reduced in the future if the leader does not follow through on the commitment. Finally, the leader may have his own cognitive inconsistency to deal with because failing to resign will be inconsistent with his earlier commitment. On the other hand, negotiators want to prevent the other party from making public commitments to positions that counter their interests. They can do so by downplaying statements of commitment, not responding to them, or looking for a rationale to explain why the commitment does not apply at this time.

Negotiators can also use the process of public commitment to influence the other party. If we can get the other party to make a public statement that supports something we want, she will be very hard-pressed not to stand by the statement, even though she may later desire to abandon it. Sometimes negotiators make a statement such as "I'm committed to finding an agreement that we can both benefit from," and then invite the other party to make a similar statement. At other times the inviting statement may be more direct: "Are you interested in selling us this property or not?" or "Let's agree that we are going to work together, and then get down to work on the details of how to make it happen." Even better than eliciting statements of commitment is enticing the other party to make a behavioral commitment. For example, retail merchants use down payments and lay-away plans to get a behavioral commitment from customers when it is not possible to complete the total sale at that time.

## Inoculating Yourself against the Other Party's Arguments

One of the likely outcomes of listening carefully to the other party and exploring and understanding the other's point of view is that we may change some of our own positions. At times we may not want to change our position, and therefore we may want to "inoculate" ourselves against the other party's arguments to avoid being swayed by empathizing with her position (McGuire, 1964). For instance, managers who must support organizational policies with which they disagree may want to inoculate themselves against subordinates' arguments. Similarly, deans of MBA programs may inoculate themselves against the arguments of prospective students who have strong credentials but who do not meet the entrance requirements of the program.

Three approaches for inoculating against the arguments of other parties have been studied. The first approach is to prepare supporting arguments *for our position* only. The second approach is to develop arguments *against our position* and then to develop counterarguments, that is, find ways to refute them. The third approach is a *combination* of the previous two: develop arguments for our original position, then develop arguments against our position, and finally develop counterarguments to refute them. For example, a dean of an MBA program could (1) develop arguments about why the student should not be admitted (e.g., her grades are not high enough); (2) develop arguments in favor of the student's perspective (e.g., the student took difficult courses at a very scholarly university); and, (3) develop counterarguments to refute the student's arguments (e.g., the quality of the university and the courses were taken into account when the admission standards were set).

Research (McGuire, 1964; Tannenbaum and Norris, 1966) reveals the following about the three approaches to inoculation:

1. The combination approach, also called the "double defense" approach, works best to inoculate people against being influenced by the other side.
2. The second approach, when people are asked to develop arguments against their position and counterarguments to them, was the second-best approach.
3. The least effective, by a large margin, was the first approach—developing arguments only in support of our own position.
4. The best way to inoculate people against attacks on their position was to involve them in developing a defense.
5. The larger the number of arguments in any defense, the more effective it becomes.
6. Asking people to make public statements supporting their original position increases their resistance to counterarguments.

### Summary

Negotiators can do many things to reduce the other party's rigidity and defensiveness and to make them more willing to listen and understand statements and arguments. These approaches require negotiators to show the other party that he will be listened to and that negotiators will work to understand, but not necessarily agree with, their position. Negotiators should try to understand what the other party is after and how they are thinking, and also to decrease their defensiveness. These are powerful techniques, but there are also risks. In trying to understand the other side, negotiators may be persuaded by their arguments, be led to abandon some of their original positions, or be more willing to accept the other party's proposals. In fact, the other party's proposals may lead to a better agreement for all sides, particularly in integrative bargaining. However, there are times when negotiators want to preserve their own positions, and not be tempted or seduced by the other party's arguments. At times like these, negotiators need to inoculate themselves so they hear the other party and their arguments without the risk of being co-opted to their point of view.

In summary, we have reviewed many of the factors that can influence persuasion via the primary route (see Figure 8.2). These factors have been discussed under three broad areas: characteristics of the message, the sender, and the receiver. Negotiators can increase the degree to which their messages are persuasive by paying attention to the characteristics discussed. These are behaviors that *all* negotiators can use to increase their persuasiveness. Persuasion is not something that we are simply born with; rather, it is a set of behavioral skills that negotiators can learn. We now turn to a discussion of factors that can influence persuasion along the peripheral route (see Figure 8.2).

## COMPLIANCE STRATEGIES

Compliance strategies generally work on the peripheral route to persuasion, frequently with little or no apparent thought involved. In fact, Cialdini (1993) argues that this type of persuasion works almost automatically, like fixed-action patterns in animals. Although these strategies often will not result in long-term persuasion because they don't integrate information into existing cognitive structures, they can be very powerful in causing compliance in the short term.

Psychologist Robert Cialdini (1993) spent many years investigating why people comply with requests that, upon further reflection, they would rather not have complied with. Through a skillful blend of laboratory research and observation of "compliance experts" such as salespeople, fundraisers, and others, Cialdini identified six principles that explain many tactics compliance experts use to get people to comply. These strategies are reciprocity, commitment, social proof, liking, authority, and scarcity. In this section of the chapter we will discuss each of these principles, how they relate to negotiation situations, and how to deal with them. Consult Cialdini's books for more information on these strategies.

### Reciprocity

The norm of reciprocity has been studied for years by philosophers, anthropologists, sociologists, and other social scientists. This norm suggests that when we receive something from another person we should respond in the future with a favor for them (the "Golden Rule"). This norm is thought to be pan-cultural (Gouldner, 1960) in that all cultural groups appear to respect it. The norm of reciprocity plays an important role in negotiations. We give concessions and expect concessions in return. When we treat the other party politely we expect to be treated the same way in return. In negotiation, the norm can be also be used to obtain compliance from another negotiator. For instance, negotiator A does a small favor for negotiator B and later asks for a larger favor from B in return. Net advantage goes to A. Although we may think that the norm of reciprocity should only apply to favors of the same size, this does not appear to be the case. In fact, many sales pitches rely on giving the consumer a small gift early in an exchange in order to look for a large concession from them later. In parts of Africa, particularly Nigeria, there is a custom of giving a small gift, called *dash,* to a potential customer soon after he has walked into a shop—before there has been a chance for the customer to identify his needs. The shopkeeper will claim, legitimately, that it is a free gift, no strings, yours to keep even if you turn and walk out of the shop at this minute. However, knowing human nature, the shopkeeper does not really expect this to happen and is rarely disappointed. The shopkeeper knows that people like to receive gifts and will develop positive feelings toward those who give them. The shopkeeper also knows that an apparently universal norm of reciprocity impels people to do nice things in return. Having preconditioned the customer, the shopkeeper can begin to discuss the customer's needs with a higher expectation of making a sale and at a better price than might otherwise have been obtained.

Similar opportunities exist in other negotiation situations. A compliment, such as a reference to the other party's positive behavior in another negotiation, will make her feel good and set the scene for the other party to act positively. Giving a quick concession on an issue that the other party wants will both please them and create the implicit obligation for them to do the same. Too often, negotiators begin by holding every advantage close to their chest and give away things grudgingly, believing that this is the best way to succeed. Such rigid behavior is no more likely to lead to graceful and successful negotiation than it is to graceful and successful acting or public speaking. Flexibility and adaptability are necessary in all three.

Future research needs to explore the full extent of the power of the norm of reciprocity in negotiation settings. For instance, this norm suggests that a small concession made early in negotiation will lead to greater concessions later. Will the same hold true for a small favor, such as bringing coffee for the other party? Although research has not addressed this question directly, related research (Cialdini, 1993) suggests that small gifts (e.g., pamphlets or flowers) do lead to larger compliance in other circumstances (e.g., a donation to a religious group or charity).

Given the apparent powerfulness of the norm of reciprocity, how can the negotiator counter its effects? One possibility is to refuse all favors in a negotiation setting, but this would probably cause more problems than it resolves. For instance, refusing a glass of water from the other party may remove the effects of the norm of reciprocity but at the same time it may insult the other party, especially if five minutes later you go and get a glass of water yourself. Perhaps the other person was simply being polite. Perhaps he was setting a positive tone for the meeting. Or perhaps he was trying to use the norm of reciprocity to indebt you to him in the negotiation.[1] How should the negotiator respond to such favors? Cialdini suggests that you should respond politely to a favor and accept what is offered if it is something that you want. If it becomes apparent that the favor was an attempt at manipulation, however, then you should redefine the event as a trick rather than a favor. This will remove the obligation of the rule of reciprocity because "The rule says that favors are to be met with favors; it does not require that tricks be met with favors" (Cialdini, 1993, pp. 46).

## Commitment

Researchers have long recognized that once people have decided something, they can be remarkably persistent in their beliefs. This process has been labeled "commitment to a position," and it relies heavily on the common need that people have to appear consistent, both to themselves and others. Most of us are familiar with the "bait and switch" sales technique. Unscrupulous organizations advertise a piece of merchandise for sale at an incredibly low price but "run out" of stock by the time you arrive at the store. They then try to sell you an alternate piece of merchandise at a higher price. Why does this technique work? After people make the decision to purchase a product (commitment), they almost automatically follow through and make the purchase (even at a higher price).

In his youth, one of the authors of this book decided to purchase a used MG sports car. After searching the city where I lived and finding only one car within my price range ($2,400), I test drove the car, discussed the price with the salesman, made an offer to buy the car, completed most of the paperwork, was loaned the car overnight, and came back to sign the deal the next day. At this time the salesman embarrassedly told me that he was unaware the car had "electric overdrive" until his manager had told him, and that he could not sell the car for the agreed-upon price. Rather, the salesman would have to charge an additional $350 for the overdrive. Of course, he would allow me to change my mind and not buy the car. I bought the car, but after driving away I was convinced that the salesman's bargaining strategy had been a manipulation to induce compliance. I could have confronted the dealer, but there was no proof that the dealer was dishonest (and who would believe a young consumer versus an established car dealer?). The consequences of this decision cost the dealer much more than the extra $350 paid for the car. I told many of my friends to stay away from the dealer because of the way they did business. I didn't have any repairs done at the dealer after the warranty on the car expired. If you think that an honest mistake occurred and the salesman really had forgotten the overdrive, his behavior during the warranty period should convince you that wasn't the case. The only repair needed under warranty was to replace the tachometer. The warranty stated that the dealer would pay for the

---

[1] Note that many public sector bargaining laws prohibit negotiators from even buying a cup of coffee for each other. Negotiators need to be aware of the laws and norms that may have implications for compliance strategies. In addition, there are cross-cultural differences in refusing a gift, and negotiators need to prepare carefully for such instances when they negotiate across borders (see Chapter 14 for more discussion of culture and negotiation).

parts and 50 percent of the labor. The salesman told me that replacing the tachometer in an MG was very difficult: the dashboard had to be removed, and many pieces under the dashboard had to be removed in order to pass the wires. He advised me that it would take six hours to install the part, and suggested that I leave the car with them for the day. I didn't believe a word the salesman said. I diligently followed the mechanic around the car until he went into the service manager's office for a brief discussion. When he returned he replaced the tachometer in 15 minutes. After paying for half of the labor cost, I drove away, never to return.

Commitment strategies are very powerful devices for making people comply. One way to increase commitment is to write things down. Cialdini (1993) notes that encyclopedia companies that have customers complete their own order forms have a far lower cancellation rate than those companies where salespeople write out the form. Why? Writing it oneself seems to increase the commitment that we feel. It is as if we say to ourselves, "I wouldn't have written it down if I didn't want it, would I?" (see Bem, 1972 for more on this point). Many consumer product companies have people write testimonials about their products to enter a drawing for a prize. Why? Apparently writing testimonials increases the commitment to buy the product (Cialdini, 1993). Research has shown that even signing a petition can increase your compliance with a request to do something more intrusive several days later (Freedman and Fraser, 1966).

How can commitment work in a negotiation? When the other party is skilled at using the commitment strategy, agreement to innocuous statements early in the negotiation may be used as a foundation for further and further concessions. Frequently, our own words and behaviors are used to extract further concessions. In the MG example, I was more than pleased to pay the extra $350 because I had shown the car to many friends and told them about the purchase. The *fair* thing to do was to let the salesman off the hook for his mistake. After all, he had been nice enough to let me take the car overnight even before signing a contract!

Commitment strategies are very difficult to combat. Frequently, you have been influenced and already agreed to something before you even realize that the manipulation has taken place. To some extent, being forewarned about these techniques is being forearmed. Cialdini (1993) suggests that your body will send two types of warning signals when these techniques are in use. You will either feel uncomfortable when they are present, or something in the deal will just not seem quite right. If you encounter these thoughts or feelings when negotiating, look for use of a commitment strategy by the other party. At the very least, be aware of all the agreements you strike during a negotiation, even those small, innocuous ones. They may be the set-up for the next move.

### Social Proof

The principle of social proof suggests that people look to others to determine the correct response in many situations. This principle suggests that we often behave the way that we do "because everyone else is doing so." Cialdini (1993) suggests that this is the principle that makes laugh tracks so effective on television comedies (see Fuller and Sheehy-Skeffington, 1974). It also explains why some influence agents like to tell you the names of previously satisfied customers; if they used the product and liked it, then it must be good. Celebrities are hired to endorse products for similar reasons.

In negotiation situations, the principle of social proof can act as a powerful influence strategy. Salespeople will show lists of satisfied customers knowing that few people will take the time to verify the list (if it wasn't true, why would the salesperson show me the list?). Sweepstakes advertisements highlight previous winners, and celebrities often promote them. Negotiators will talk about how popular their new product is and how sales have really increased this year. Real estate agents will be sure that you are aware that many other people are interested in the house that you are considering buying.

The principle of social proof works because false information ("everyone thinks this product is good") is given weight in decisions. The person providing the false information has influence over us. Cialdini (1993) suggests that the way to reduce this influence is to identify the false information and give it the weight it deserves. In negotiations, this means careful preparation and being aware of "facts" about the others' advocated views that do not seem to match your preparation. When the other party offers "evidence" about the popularity of an item, do not automatically trust that the other party is being completely honest; rather, ask them to substantiate their claims. Even when there is a shortage of an item, be sure that you are behaving in your own best interests. Frequently, a planned delay ("let me sleep on it") will be enough to separate the influence of social proof from your own needs and interests.

## Liking

The liking principle is quite straightforward: people that we like have more influence over us (although there are exceptions—see Chapter 10). Many factors have been found to be related to liking, including physical attractiveness, familiarity, and repeated association. Marketers have used these factors for years. Attractive people sell beer and cigarettes in magazines and on television (lifestyle advertising). Salespeople seek to find things that we have in common with them so that they will seem more familiar to us (and thus have more influence over us). And advertisements are repeated *ad nauseam* to drive a point home through repeated association.

In negotiation, selecting members of a negotiation team that the other party will like is one way to use liking as an influence strategy. Some organizations, like IBM, had all employees who were in contact with the public dress in similar styles (very conservative business dress). As a result, an IBM representative would seem familiar based on appearance alone. Association is used as an influence tactic by negotiators who ensure that they are present when good news is delivered (and absent when there is bad news). Association with the good news is expected to rub off on the negotiator who expects to reap the long-term benefits of this association.

The effects of the liking principle are insidious. Liking can occur through many different approaches, and defending against them all would be impossible (Cialdini, 1993). Anyway, people enjoy being liked by others, and to remove it would be a cost itself. Cialdini suggests that it would be useless to try to prevent ourselves from liking others. Rather, we should let the liking occur and then explore *why* we like the other person. If we find that we like the person more than we would typically like another person under similar circumstances, then it is time to be wary. Separating our liking for the other party from our evaluation of the deal should be enough to moderate the influence of the liking principle in our negotiations.

### Authority

The principle of authority is quite simple: People in authority have more influence than those without authority. Researchers have long been interested in the effects of authority figures on human behavior. Stanley Milgram's (1974) classic studies of obedience to authority figures suggest that people will go to great lengths when their behavior is legitimized by an authority figure. Most people will obey the orders of a person wearing a uniform, even if there is no war or apparent emergency. This, too, is an effect of the principle of authority.

In negotiation, the principle of authority can be used in many ways (see also Chapter 10). Herb Cohen (1980) suggests that rules that are written down carry more weight than those given verbally. Cialdini suggests that the use of a title, such as Doctor or Professor, gives the user more authority and thus more influence. A friend of one of the authors uses the title Doctor whenever ordering airline tickets. He found out early in his career that airlines would telephone doctors when there was a flight delay but would ignore the other passengers. This simple illustration shows the esteem with which some titles (positions) are held in our society. Cialdini (1993) suggests that authority is more than position; it can also be expertise. He tells the story of a waiter who, regardless of what you order, recommends something else on the menu that is cheaper because the original dish "is not very good tonight." Not only does this maneuver call the principle of reciprocity into play when it is time to leave a tip, but the waiter also establishes his authority for later (more expensive) advice about the meal.

Cialdini (1993) offers the following advice about dealing with authority figures who may have influence over us. He suggests that we should ask two questions: "Is this authority truly an expert?" and "How truthful can we expect this expert to be?". The first question forces us to verify that the person really does have expertise in the situation and not just the appearance (title, attire) of expertise. The second question suggests that we examine the motive of the expert who is offering advice. If she acts like the waiter described above and gives us some negative information before another suggestion, she may in fact be manipulating us into thinking that she is honest when she is not (the ethical implications are discussed in Chapter 13).

## Scarcity

The principle of scarcity suggests that when things are less available, they will have more influence over us. Cialdini (1993) describes how common sales strategies rely upon the scarcity principle. Frequently, salespeople will tell us that they are not sure if the product we would like to purchase is currently in stock. Before making the trip to the stockroom they ask us if they should "grab one" for us before another salesperson gets it. Typically shoppers will say yes when they think the resource is limited and will feel relieved (lucky) when the salesperson returns with the "last one" in the store. This is the scarcity principle at work; people are easier to influence when they feel that they are obtaining a scarce resource. This principle can have extreme effects. Some people in China, for instance, have a penchant for eating rare animals; the rarer the species, the more attractive the delicacy. Two zoo workers in Beijing were recently arrested for eating the only two known members of a rare bird species at a wedding ceremony.

In negotiation situations, the scarcity influence strategy may be operating whenever there appears to be a great demand for a product. Some organizations deliberately keep their products in short supply to give the appearance that they are very popular. Car dealers will suggest that you not wait too long before deciding on the color car you want because they have very few cars left and they are selling fast. Any time that negotiators talk about "exclusive opportunities" and "time-limited offers," they are using the scarcity principle. Censorship also results in scarcity, with banned issues of magazines leading to increased popularity (see Brehm, 1972, for further discussion of this phenomenon, known as psychological reactance). Finally, auctions also rely on the principle of scarcity, selling off unique (one-of-a-kind) pieces to the highest bidder—the more scarce the item, the higher the bids.

The scarcity principle is very difficult to combat when used effectively. It creates in the victim an activity trap that is focused on obtaining the item and effectively suspends cognitive evaluation of the broader situation (Cialdini, 1993). Cialdini suggests that we need to be aware of the emotional trappings that this principle arouses; when confronted with a strong emotional response to obtain a scarce good, we should carefully evaluate our reasons for wanting the item in the first place.

## Summary

Social scientists have recently shifted their focus in research on persuasion to examining factors that work on the peripheral route. This research area began as a reaction against the purely cognitive reasoning that occurs in the central route to persuasion. Petty and Cacioppo (1990) suggest that the following factors will make persuasion on the peripheral route more likely: low personal relevance, responsibility for the final decision spread among many parties, persuasion from a single source, and less cognitively oriented people. Negotiation researchers have yet to explore the implications of persuasion on the peripheral route in much detail. It appears that this is an especially fertile ground for future research on a critical aspect of negotiation.

## CHAPTER SUMMARY

In this chapter, we discussed the central and peripheral routes to persuasion. On the central route, there are three major elements in the persuasion process: the semantic and logical structure of the message being sent, characteristics of the source sending the message, and characteristics of the receiver. Each of these elements will affect the reception of the message and its effectiveness in changing the receiver's viewpoint or attitude toward the issues.

Three major topics about the nature of the message were covered: which facts or topics to consider when constructing a persuasive message, how to structure and arrange that information, and what style to use in presenting the information. In general, information should be presented that highlights the attractive features to the other party or appeals to the other's sense of what is fair, right, and principled. Messages that contain fear appeals and threats or try to distract the other may have limited effectiveness—they are only likely to work when used selectively. Messages should be structured so that the most important points are repeated, particularly at both the beginning and end of the presentation. Either one-sided or two-sided messages may be used, depending upon the circumstances. The presenter should also find ways to break large demands or requests into smaller packages and help the receiver use the information presented to draw the conclusions the speaker desires. Finally, messages are likely to be more effective when the receiver takes an active role, when language intensity is frequently varied, when metaphor and graphic imagery is used, and when the receiver's expectations are occasionally violated so that her defenses are not allowed to build.

This chapter also proposed several factors that relate to the source presenting the message. One major source factor is credibility. Sources are more credible when they appear to be trustworthy, qualified to discuss their subject, of higher status, professional and well dressed, and of high integrity. A second factor is the source's intent to persuade. Sources who are less forthright about their desire to change our minds and use less of the "hard sell" are often more persuasive. Finally, sources are more persuasive when they treat us better. Use of compliments, identification of similar personal characteristics, or genuine offers to assist us lead us to like the source and hence to be more willing to accept his message.

This chapter then examined factors that distinguish among the receivers of persuasive messages. Receivers can vary their attending behaviors—eye contact, body position, head nodding, and the like—to encourage or discourage a speaker. Receivers can also engage in a variety of behaviors to let the speaker know that the message was both received and understood: paraphrasing, asking questions, and reinforcing desirable elements. Finally, receivers who want to resist having their position changed can engage in two tactics: making public commitments about their own position and inoculating themselves against persuasive communications by developing counterarguments.

In the final section of this chapter we discussed six compliance strategies that are thought to work on the peripheral route to persuasion—the route that we're unaware of. Although the effects of persuasion on the peripheral route tend to be short term, they can still have a remarkable influence on behavior. Little research on these factors in negotiation settings has been conducted, but we looked at research findings from other influence situations and suggested links to negotiation settings. We also discussed ways to recognize and respond to the other party's use of these tactics.

This chapter has only touched on some of the more important and well-documented aspects of persuasive communication that can be used in bargaining. Negotiators usually spend a great deal of time devising ways to support and document their positions; they devote less time to considering *how* the information is presented or *how* to use qualities of the source and receiver to increase the likelihood that persuasion will be successful. More careful attention to these factors is likely to have a very positive impact on negotiator effectiveness.

# CHAPTER 9

# The Social Structure of Negotiation

Probably one of the most influential factors in negotiations—and yet one that is the most poorly understood—is the nature of the negotiator's social environment. The social environment includes all parties who are present at the negotiation, those who help to plan it in advance or are affected by the outcome of negotiation (even though they are not actually negotiating), and different types of observers to the negotiation.

The major theme of this chapter is that the number of parties in a negotiation dramatically affects the negotiation process. Much of what we have said in the previous eight chapters has implied that two negotiators are acting alone and on their own, in a rather limited time frame, to arrive at an agreement. However, we will show in this chapter that a negotiator who is only representing her own interests will behave very differently from one who is negotiating as the representative of others. Moreover, negotiation occurs in a larger social context, which means that the negotiation process will be affected by social and cultural norms, the rules and customs of the society in which the negotiation takes place.

In this chapter we describe the impact of the social structure on bargaining orientation. As the social settings increase in participants—from two individuals to two groups to multiple groups and organizations—negotiation becomes more dynamically complex. This chapter describes the parameters of this larger social context and the ways that they affect what happens in the more limited, finite, bounded, "formal" negotiation event.

We will begin this chapter with the description of a socially complex negotiation: the deliberations following a prison riot in a maximum security penitentiary in Lucasville, Ohio. We will use this example to demonstrate how the number of different parties and the roles these parties play change the negotiation dynamics among the key negotiators and create processes that we have not yet identified in more simple two-party deliberations. This chapter also describes the manner in which negotiation changes when there are multiple parties at the negotiation table. Thus, we will describe group negotiations as an extension of the two-person, bilateral negotiation dynamic.

## An Example of the Complex Social Structure of Negotiation: The Lucasville Prison Riot

In Lucasville, Ohio, on Easter Sunday, April 11, 1993, at 3:15 P.M., the longest prison riot in U.S. history began. The Southern Ohio Correctional Facility in Lucasville was opened in 1972; it is a maximum security prison located in the southern part of the state. The demographics of the region are largely rural, Appalachian white, and poor, whereas the demographics of the prison inmates are disproportionately black, urban, and poor. Like many prisons in the United States, Lucasville suffered from serious overcrowding. The persistent overcrowding and underfunding of the prison system created a number of strong tensions. At the time of the riot, 1,850 prisoners were housed in a prison with a capacity of 1,100. Racial tensions persisted between white and black prisoners and between the white guards and black prisoners. Overcrowding forced prisoners to have cell mates, often with people of a different race and without regard to the ability of the prisoners to get along. Inadequate care was provided for the mentally ill prisoners. Mandatory testing for tuberculosis offended many prisoners. Finally, the underfunding of the prison system also led to weakened security and an inadequate number of guards—at the time of the riot, there was one corrections officer for every 12 prisoners at Lucasville (the highest—and worst—guard-to-prisoner ratio in the United States).

The violence actually started with a fight among inmates who were returning to their cells in L Block from the prison's recreation yard. Within minutes, a bloody and deadly battle broke out in two major sections of the prison, Blocks K and L. The prisoners seized guards as hostages. According to prison warden Arthur Tate, Jr., "it was difficult trying to get a fix on how many hostages they had. [Corrections] officers in L Block literally fought hand-to-hand combat with prisoners. Some of them literally fought their way out. 300 prisoners were still in the recreation yard and accessible to L Block, while another 400 inmates were rioting inside. The main gates into L Block were both secured by the inmates. They used bed sheets, wire cables, ice machine and footlockers to barricade the two gates" (*Columbus Dispatch,*[1] April 24, 1993).

Within an hour, the prison had hostage negotiators in place. The rioting prisoners had taken 11 guards hostage, but they soon released 3 injured guards voluntarily. At this time, prison officials were unsure if the fight that precipitated the riot had been staged to create a distraction, and they could not identify the key groups who might have organized and led the disturbance. Later that same evening, the bodies of six white prisoners were dumped into the recreation yard; the deceased had been badly beaten. Racial antagonisms had been a problem at the prison, but prison officials denied that they were the cause of the riot. The killings of the six inmates appeared to have taken place early in the disturbance, said Shar-

---

[1] Unless otherwise noted, all subsequent quotes comes from the *Columbus Dispatch.*

ron Kornegay, a prison spokeswoman. With the death toll rising, prison officials increased the pressure to negotiate and win the release of the hostages.

During the first afternoon of the riot, more than 300 inmates from L Block, seeking to avoid trouble, remained in the recreation yard rather than joining the other prisoners in the barricaded L Block. These inmates were later escorted into K Block by corrections officers.

**Monday, April 12th.**   The prisoners remained calm and reasonable. FBI negotiators arrived to offer expert advice to prison officials and to maintain the continuity of the negotiations. Despite the prisoners' demands to talk to the FBI, the FBI never had direct contact with the inmates. Reginald Wilkinson, director of the Department of Rehabilitation and Corrections for the State of Ohio, said the state and the prison officials were going by "textbook guidelines for negotiations." (All Departments of Corrections have specific guidelines for handling prison disturbances; Ohio was simply following these procedures at this time.) Also on Monday, in an effort to create an uncomfortable environment for the prisoners and advance negotiations, officials cut off all electricity, water, and food supplies to L Block. In response, prisoners asked to talk to a news media reporter to air their gripes. This was the first request by inmates to draw in the media as an active party in the negotiations process.

**Tuesday, April 13th.**   With the airspace over the prison full of small private aircraft and news media helicopters, the Federal Aviation Authority issued an order to ban nonemergency aircraft flights over the facility. A two-mile no-flight zone was established to minimize further disturbances or interference with the negotiations process. At 4:00 P.M., State Highway Patrol and medical emergency workers arrived. Their arrival prompted rumors that officials might storm the prison to free the hostages. Prisoners, however, continued their demand for media attention and hung bed sheets out L Block windows, stating "we want news."

During the first few days, preliminary negotiations were conducted by telephone between prison officials, who met in a small office behind the warden's office, and the prisoners in L Block. Warden Tate never talked directly to the prisoners; all communication was left to trained hostage negotiators. "I had to bite down hard during the negotiations. I was committed to making the negotiations work. I really had to give those guys things from time to time without getting anything in return," Tate said (April 24, 1993).

**Wednesday, April 14th.**   Tate told his boss, Reginald Wilkinson, director of the Department of Corrections of the State of Ohio, that the National Guard would be needed. Wilkinson relayed this request to Governor George Voinovich, who approved their use and sent 500 National Guard troops to Lucasville. At that time, no one knew whether the hostages were still alive. The negotiators and inmates held a 90-minute telephone negotiating session, which left authorities hopeful.

**Thursday, April 15th.**    The Lucasville siege took a turn for the worse. On Thursday night, convicts in L Block dropped the body of a guard from a prison window. The guard, Robert R. Vallandingham, age 40, had worked at the prison since 1991 and was a guard in cellblock L when the riot began. Prison officials later said he had been hanged. The hanging of Vallandingham was later attributed to public statements made by Tessa Unwin, a state corrections department spokesperson. When asked by the media about prisoner threats to kill the hostages if their demands were not met, Unwin stated to the press that "prisoners make those kinds of threats all the time in this type of situation," and that the threat did not need to be taken seriously.

Despite the death of Vallandingham, negotiations continued. Prison officials allowed inmates to air their grievances over a live radio broadcast. "Inmate George" listed five demands during a 10-minute broadcast over WPAY of Portsmouth, a local radio station. Inmate George appeared to take responsibility for the murder of the corrections officer, calling it something "that just had to be done" (the *New York Times,* April 22, page 10). George also stated that another hostage would be released after a telecast of inmates' demands on WBNS-TV, a Columbus station. "From the outset of this, we have tried desperately, desperately, desperately to get in contact with the news media," he said (April 16, 1993). Prisoner attorney Niki Schwartz added, "The ability to speak to the media and the public is very important to the inmates. Although the state claims that reporters and the media are hindering negotiations, inmates regard them as crucial to successful talks. Inmates believe that the interest and spotlight of media attention is protection for them, it is one of the things that helps to allay their fears of retaliation" (prisoner attorney Niki Schwartz, April 21, 1993).

Inmate George conducted the radio broadcast from the middle of the prison recreation yard where the riot had started. He entered the yard with hostage-guard Darrold Clark, whose head was covered by a sheet. As the two moved to a table where a microphone was set up, the inmate took off his shirt to show that he didn't have any weapons. He then removed the sheet from Clark. Three members of the prison's negotiating team were also at the table.

The inmate spoke nervously. He admitted that he had a lot on his shoulders and couldn't possibly remember all the prisoners' demands. He had no written notes or prepared text. He did, however, assert that the uprising was race related and that the rioting inmates "are prepared to die if need be." The prisoners' demands included live television news coverage of negotiations; an opportunity to present their views of the day-to-day living conditions in L Block to the news media and to push for reform of these conditions; the firing of Warden Arthur Tate, Jr.; and the restoration of electricity and running water in the occupied areas of the prison.

**Friday, April 16th.**    Inmates' demand for live TV coverage was granted. Prison spokeswoman Tessa Unwin told reporters that "we have made significant progress in negotiations in the last 36 hours. We're pulling together the necessary elements to achieve a successful negotiated conclusion" (April 17, 1993).

In the afternoon, prison hostage negotiators met with inmate Abdul Samad Mulin and guard-hostage James Anthony Demons. Once again, the meeting took place at a table in the center of the recreation yard. The two hostage negotiators sat across from Mulin and Demons. The inmate and guard were dressed in traditional Black Muslim clothing. Their entry into the yard and the entire negotiation process was carried live by a Cincinnati television station and picked up live by many other state and national television networks.

Mulin stated the prisoners' demands. These demands had expanded since Inmate George's earlier, more informal statement. They now included the following major demands:

No reprisals against any inmate involved in the uprising.

The right to practice Islam.

A revision or elimination of the unit manager system (for managing different cell blocks in the prison).

The abolition of forced integration and forced cell-mate policies.

No singling out any inmate or group as leaders of the riot.

A full-time Islamic imam (minister).

A clerk, office supplies, office space, and copier service.

Right to outside guests.

Kosher diets for Muslims.

Right to practice all tenets of the Muslim religion.

The right to have religious leaders and media present when any statement is made concerning surrender.

New phone call program.

Increase in prisoner pay.

A federal negotiator.

Hostage-guard Demons then made a statement. He addressed the reasons why some prisoners had been killed in the riot the first day and why Vallandinghan had been killed. "First of all, the Muslims did not kill those seven hostages. Those boys were killed because they were snitches . . . Now, I knew Vallandingham. He was a good friend of mine. The only reason that man is dead (is) 'cause he stayed in there so long, 'cause they went to cut off water and turn off electricity [in the occupied cellblock], which had me scared for my life in there."

After the broadcast, guard-hostage Demons was released by the inmates. Demons assured officials that the five remaining guard-hostages were being well taken care of.

**Saturday, April 17th.**    Prison officials continued talks with inmates and provided them with food and water. Officials believed that negotiations were proceeding productively and the inmates would eventually surrender. However, much to everyone's dismay, the surrender did not occur on Saturday because it would have conflicted with the Black Muslims' observance of their religion and their prayer service.

Outside interest groups were become increasingly vocal and critical of the situation:

- The small community of Lucasville, where most of the guards and employees lived, was impatient with the slow pace of the negotiations and very disturbed by the death of Vallandingham. Some citizens and protesters blamed Governor Voinovich for the stalemate. They believed that force rather than negotiations should be use to retake control. "Who is in charge here?" shouted an angry protester.

- Justice Watch, a prisoners' rights advocacy group, believed that state officials had made a fatal mistake by not involving people from prisoners' rights advocacy groups in the negotiations.

- the Ku Klux Klan and its local chaplain, Donald "Goose" Gesaman, offered to help negotiate. Gesaman declared that the riot was a holy war between the white supremacist Aryans and the Black Muslims.

- the founder of the Progressive Prisons Movement and a former inmate, Carl Upchurch, declared that the state officials should negotiate in good faith with the prisoners. He was not surprised that the riot started. Upchurch had received many letters from prisoners at Lucasville. The letters had discussed suspicious deaths of inmates, alleged brutality, and inadequate medical treatment. According to Upchurch, conditions at Lucasville were a symptom of the larger problem of prison injustice.

**Sunday, April 18th.**    Negotiations continued. Prison officials were confident that hostages were still alive because they had received audiotapes including the voices and identifying remarks from each one of the hostages. The turning point in the negotiations occurred when Niki A. Schwartz, a Cleveland criminal defense attorney, and Frank Navarre, a Dayton police sergeant, arrived in Lucasville to join in the negotiations. Schwartz was selected by the Ohio Association of Criminal Defense Lawyers to represent the inmates in the negotiations with prison officials. He had been involved in several prior prisoners' rights cases and the inmates themselves had requested him. Frank Navarre became the chief negotiator for the Department of Corrections and Rehabilitation in the standoff. Navarre had trained many people in hostage negotiations, was very familiar with the prison layout, and had worked often with corrections personnel in Ohio.

**Monday, April 19th.**    Prison authorities played a tape over the loudspeakers outside L Block at about 11:00 P.M., acknowledging the prisoners' list of 21 demands and asking them to negotiate. Officials said that the demands were being reviewed by the administration, and they would issue a statement indicating that they heard them and agreed to discuss the concerns. "We ask leaders to come to the bargaining table with a hostage, so we can resolve the matter safely for all involved," the tape said. The prisoners gave no response.

At 12:45 A.M., officials again played the tape, to make sure all the prisoners heard it. Cell Block L continued to be silent.

The demands considered by the officials were as follows (which omitted several of the original demands made by the prisoners):

- No retaliation against the 450 prisoners who had seized cellblock L.
- An impartial party to witness the surrender.
- Transfer of prisoners who feared for their safety after order was restored.
- A review of food and sundries prices in the commissary.
- A review of general discipline procedures to assure their fairness and impartiality.
- Complete medical attention to all involved in the riot.
- A reduction of the prison population to relieve overcrowding.
- A new telephone system.
- Adequate medical treatment for those suffering from tuberculosis.
- Improved communication between prisoners and employees.
- Legal representation for every inmate who requested it.

At 4:00 P.M. on Monday, the prisoners hung out a bed sheet, asking for a face-to-face meeting with Niki Schwartz. Officials replied that Schwartz would act as an adviser, not a negotiator. They believed that Schwartz's low-key style would help to lessen the tension. Schwartz, an expert in prisoner rights, would discuss the initial list of demands with the prisoners, informing them if some of the demands were either non-negotiable or could not be met. For example, the prisoners had demanded that the State guarantee no reprisals against inmates. The State would not agree to this demand because 10 people—inmates and guards—had already been killed.

Schwartz met with inmates at tables set up on opposite sides of a security fence in the recreation yard. This meeting was not covered by the media. He talked with the inmates for 90 minutes and then was joined by the State's hostage negotiators. The two groups negotiated for an hour while Schwartz observed. Both sides later reported that the discussions were very positive and responsible; they had made good progress toward a peaceful resolution. The inmates continued to assure the officials that the hostages were alive and well, and they provided new audiotapes from the guards as evidence.

**Tuesday, April 20th.**    The atmosphere around the prison and in the town of Lucasville was filled with grief, tension, and a dire sense of urgency. Tuesday evening, the community of Lucasville marched in a candlelight vigil in support of the guards being held hostage. The angry crowd demanded more action from prison officials and Governor Voinovich. (The governor's role in the negotiations had been intentionally minimal, although he serves as the Commander in Chief and Chief Law Enforcement Officer of the State. The demonstrators either wanted him to get visibly involved immediately or to direct the State Police and National Guard to end the rebellion. Voinovich, on the other hand, preferred to let his negotiation experts from the Department of Corrections handle the riot, and he chose to participate in a team making consensus decisions about the situation from a low-visibility position.)

On this day, Day 10 of the riot, it was still unclear whether the inmates would respond to the State's counteroffer. Therefore, the authorities' tape was played 12 times throughout the morning. The recording started with a telephone ringing, and then listed the concessions that had already been made by the two sides. In addition, prisoners were asked to bring another hostage to the negotiation table. The tape reiterated the State's desire for a peaceful end to the riot.

Niki Schwartz believed that rioting inmates and State negotiators were on the verge of an agreement. After his face-to-face meeting with the inmates, he was very optimistic. At 7:45 P.M., Schwartz commented: "I just talked to the lead inmate negotiator on the phone and he indicated that he is optimistic that they will be in a position to reach some agreement. If not tonight, then tomorrow."

**Wednesday April 21st.**    The inmates agreed to surrender. The surrender took place very slowly and was witnessed by a religious leader, as the inmates had requested. By agreement, the full surrender was broadcast live by many of the state's major television networks—a seven-hour process. At 4:00 P.M., five seriously injured inmates were carried out on stretchers, the first to leave L Block; the "walking wounded" followed. Then small groups of inmates peacefully left L Block. They emerged into the prison yard with their hands on their heads and were then processed by prison officials and escorted into waiting vans. At 10:30 P.M., the approximately 40 remaining prisoners emerged with the five guard-hostages. The hostages were immediately taken to a local hospital for check-ups and observation. Earlier in the day, prison officials had moved more than 600 inmates from the other blocks to other prisons in Ohio to make room for the prisoners who were released. Block L had been completely destroyed during the riot, and it would not be recoupable for many months.

The 21-item list of demands that Warden Tate signed (Exhibit 9.1) represents the commitment made by State and prison officials to respond to the issues. These 21 points address many of the prisoners' initial demands; in most cases, the officials merely committed to "look into" and "study" the complaints. Inmates had asked attorney Schwartz whether the document was legally binding. He replied that it was not, because contracts signed by law enforcement officers under duress in a hostage crisis are not binding. Schwartz said, "they assured me that they did intend to keep their word, that the things that they had agreed to were things that they felt should be done anyway and that they wouldn't agree to do anything that they didn't intend to follow though on."

**EXHIBIT 9.1**    Demands Agreed to by Department of Corrections

(1) SOCF is committed to following all administrative rules of the Ohio Department of Rehabilitation and Correction.

(2) Administrative discipline and criminal proceedings will be fairly and impartially administered without bias against individuals or groups.

(3) All injured parties will receive prompt and complete medical care and follow-up.

(4) The surrender will be witnessed by religious leaders and news media.

(5) The Unit Management system will be reviewed with attempts to improve in areas requiring changes.

(6) SOCF will contact the Federal Court for a review of the White v. Morris consent decree which requires integrated celling.

(7) All close security inmates have already been transferred (on K-side) from SOCF. L-side close inmates will be evaluated.

(8) Procedures will be implemented to thoroughly review inmate files pertaining to early release matters and changes will be made where warranted.

(9) Over 600 inmates have already been transferred from SOCF, greatly reducing previous population numbers.

(10) Current policies regarding inappropriate supervision will be rigidly enforced.

(11) Medical staffing levels will be reviewed to ensure compliance with ACA standards for medical care.

(12) Attempts will be made to expedite current plans to install a new phone system.

(13) We will work to evaluate and improve work and programmatic opportunities.

(14) There will be no retaliating actions taken toward any inmate or groups of inmates or their property.

(15) A complete review of all SOCF mail and visiting policies will be undertaken.

(16) Transfers from SOCF are coordinated through the Bureau of Classification. Efforts will be increased to ensure prompt transfers of those inmates who meet eligibility requirements.

(17) Efforts will be undertaken to upgrade the channels of communication between employees and inmates involving "quality of life" issues.

(18) The current commissary pricing system will be reviewed.

(19) We will consult the Ohio Department of Health regarding any future tuberculosis testing.

(20) The Federal Bureau of Investigation will monitor processing and ensure that civil rights will be upheld.

(21) The Ohio Department of Rehabilitation and Correction will consider on a case by case basis inter-state transfer for any inmate, if there is reasonable basis to believe that the Department is unable to provide a secure environment for that inmate. Any inmate denied a transfer, the Federal Bureau of Prisons will review their case.

**Subsequent Events.**    In a follow-up to signing the 21-point document, Warden Tate distributed copies of a memo to all guards, warning against future overreaction or retribution toward prisoners after the riot. "Employees who overreact in use-of-force situations will subject both themselves and our facility to negative consequences . . ." the memo said.

In describing the negotiation process at Lucasville, hostage negotiator Dave Michael of the Dayton Police Force later said that "we threw away the book on hostage negotiations and wrote a new one." The prison negotiators broke the conventional rules of hostage negotiations when they provided food and water on Day 4; this action was not in keeping with any of the normal rules of hostage negotiations, both because prison officials made the move *without* any requests from inmates and because they did not trade it for any specific concession from them. Officials later said that they took this action because Cell Block L was a fragmented community. There were several groups among the rioters, including various prison gangs, black and white militant groups, and inmates who did not want to be part of the riot and had been taken hostage along with the guards. The tactic of offering food worked—it helped to build some community among the rioters and thus enabled the prison negotiators to talk with a more cohesive group. In the past, experts have recommended that negotiators be put in a sterile environment—a room at the institution specifically set aside for negotiations.

As this chapter is being completed, almost six months after the riot, few changes have been made. The prisoners have periodically accused the State of reneging on its commitments and have threatened to riot again. Cell Block L is still being repaired for use. Finally, the Ohio Civil Service Employees Association (the union representing the prison guards) released a report in late August 1993, stating that continued overcrowding, understaffing, and tensions between guards and cellblock supervisors are so severe that another riot is almost certain. The union proposed 32 recommendations to make Ohio prisons safer.

## An Example of the Complex Social Structure of Negotiation

**The "Social Structure" of the Conflict.**    In contrast to many negotiations, which only involve two negotiating parties, this conflict was characterized by interactions among many parties. In addition, although these negotiators occasionally acted on their own individual preferences and priorities, they more commonly acted as formal representatives of larger groups—prisoners, the Department of Corrections, and so on. The following individuals and groups played a key role during the 11-day siege:

Governor George Voinovich, governor of the State of Ohio

Arthur Tate, warden of the Lucasville Prison

Reginald Wilkinson, director of the Department of Rehabilitation and Corrections

Sharron Kornegay and Tessa Unwin, spokespersons for the Department of Rehabilitation and Corrections

Col. Thomas Rice of the Ohio National Guard

Frank Navarre, Dayton police sergeant and an expert in hostage negotiations

Niki Schwartz, attorney representing the rioting prisoners (also served as a third-party facilitator)

"Inmate George" and Samad Mulin, spokespersons for the rioting prisoners

Prison guards who were taken as hostages

Families, friends, and neighbors of the guards living in the Lucasville area

Families and friends of the inmates

Groups and organizations that had a political stake in Lucasville and the way the riot would be handled: Justice Watch, the Ku Klux Klan, the Black Muslims, and others

Representatives of local, state, and national newspapers, magazines, local television stations, and four major television networks (CBS, NBC, ABC, and CNN)

Figure 9.1 portrays all these groups. In addition to the parties listed above, a large number of other parties—residents of Lucasville, residents of surrounding towns and counties, state legislators, government officials, and prisoners who were not rioting but were either at Lucasville or in other prisons around Ohio—all became involved in the dispute. At various times, these groups interacted with each other in open forums such as town meetings and legislative gatherings. There were also many private gatherings between key individuals, working on their own, representing the views of their groups or organizations, or debating the desired course of action. In short, what began as a rather focused confrontation—the riot in the prison yard escalating to an occupation of L Block—turned into a major negotiation among a constantly shifting array of parties and interests.

## THE SOCIAL STRUCTURE OF NEGOTIATION

The major theme of this chapter is that the number of parties in a negotiation dramatically affects the negotiation process. Social structure may be represented in relatively simple structural situations—two individual negotiators, each with their own needs and desires—or relatively complex situations—multiple negotiators, negotiators representing other parties, or negotiators representing groups and organizations. The greater the number of individuals, groups, and organizations that have a stake or interest in a conflict and its outcomes, the greater the number of possible interactions between the parties, and thus the more complex the flow of interaction becomes. In addition, within this larger context, individuals and groups will attempt to exert both direct and indirect pressures on the

**248**

**FIGURE 9.1** Key Figures in the Lucasville Prison Negotiation

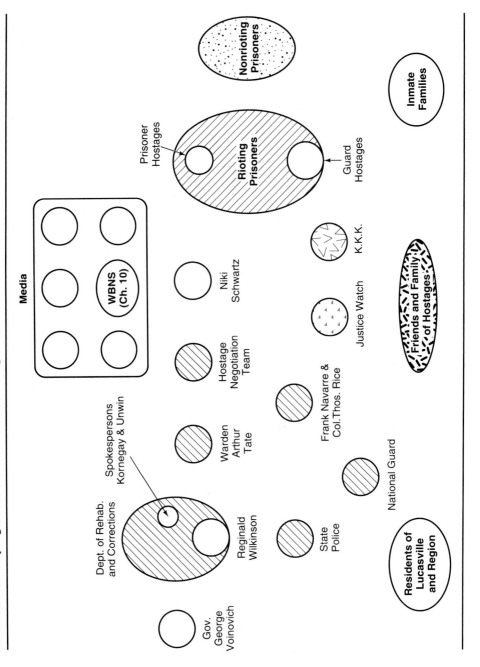

negotiators to advocate their interests and "win" the conflict. A second dimension of complexity, therefore, is the type of influence strategies that negotiators use in the bargaining arena and outside of it, and the different types of influence attempts that occur as the number of parties increases.

To begin, we will delineate the several levels of social structure that may exist in any given negotiation. These include:

- *A Negotiating Dyad.* The simplest form of social structure in a negotiation is two isolated individuals negotiating for their own needs and interests. Each is responsible only for stating and defending her own positions and needs and working with the opposing negotiator to arrive at an agreement.

- *Additional Negotiators.* Some disputes involve more than two negotiators. If a family is trying to decide where to spend summer vacation, each party—mom, dad, the two children and grandma—has his or her own preferences and priorities. Although each is only responsible for stating his or her own positions and needs, the agreement has to reflect the views of all parties (some parties with lower power may be "forced" to go along with the agreement by the others). As we will point out, when there are more than two negotiators, there is a strong possibility that some parties will form alliances, searching for strength in numbers or in the coincidence of their interests. In addition, as the number of negotiators increases, the likelihood of finding common ground to satisfy all interests usually decreases, thus making group negotiations even more difficult.

- *Negotiating Teams.* Negotiation can also occur between teams of negotiators. A *team* will be defined as two or more parties on the same side who are working together and collectively advocating the same positions and interests. Intrateam dynamics (e.g., whether some members have more power or status than others) will also affect the interteam negotiation process.

- *Constituencies and Representatives.* Often a negotiator (or team of negotiators) is acting not for himself, but for a constituency. A constituency is one or more parties that have designated someone else to represent their positions and interests in a negotiation. The most common examples of a representative and constituent are an attorney and her client, or a salesperson negotiating on behalf of his boss and the company. Constituencies may be present for all or part of the deliberations, but are usually absent from the discussions and trust their representatives to both advocate their interests and accurately report what has transpired during the deliberations.

- *Unrepresented Bystanders.* Bystanders are those who may have some stake in a negotiation and who care about the substantive issues, the process, or how the dispute gets resolved. Negotiators at the table do not formally represent bystanders. But bystanders frequently follow the negotiation, express public or private views to the negotiators about the potential outcomes or the process, and in some way are affected by what happens.

• *Audiences.* An audience is any individual or group of people who are not directly involved in or affected by a negotiation, but who have a chance to observe and react to the ongoing events and who may be drawn into the negotiation by offering input, advice, or criticism to the negotiators. Bystanders and constituencies can also serve as audiences. So, too, can members of negotiating teams who are not actively engaged in dialogue with the other side.

• *Third Parties.* Third parties are bystanders who may be drawn into the dispute to help resolve it. Third parties play key roles when their efforts reshape a polarized dispute into a constructive agreement. Bystanders can be effective as third parties if they have the necessary skills and are seen as neutral. We will say more about the key roles played by third parties in Chapter 12.

It is important to understand that, although we have attempted to clearly delineate these different roles, in fact, negotiating parties may take on more than one role during the course of a negotiation. We will now explore the structural dynamics of the different roles, first examining the simplest form (two individual negotiators) and then describing how the social structure becomes more complex as additional parties and roles are added.

### Two Individual Negotiators

In social structure terms, the simplest form of negotiation occurs when only two individuals are involved. Each individual is responsible for representing only her own needs and interests in the negotiation (see Figure 9.2). For example, consider a student who sets off to purchase a stereo system from another student on campus. The preferences of each party (asking price of the seller, amount the buyer can afford to pay, condition of the equipment, strength of the desire to buy or sell the system, and so on) will be determined wholly by the two individuals themselves. The price that they agree on—and any other terms and conditions of the sale, such as whether a few CDs are thrown in free—will be determined solely by the parties themselves through their deliberations. In the Lucasville dispute, none of the major negotiations were simply between two individuals, without the preferences and interests of others intruding.

**FIGURE 9.2**   A Negotiation Dyad

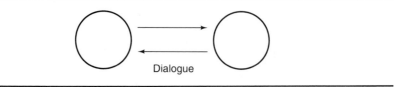

Dialogue

**FIGURE 9.3**    A Seller and Two Buyers

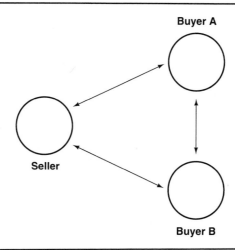

## Additional Negotiators

The first way that a negotiation situation becomes more complex is by adding more negotiators. In the previous example, if two students want to buy the stereo and they both show up at the seller's door at the same time, then the seller must decide how to deal with them—separately or together. The buyers may get into a bidding war with each other or the seller might get greedy because his stereo seems to be very attractive, raise his price, and then have both of the buyers walk away. If the situation were different—if, for example, the two buyers were roommates who were going to share the stereo—different negotiating dynamics might occur. As we will describe later in this chapter, when there are more than two negotiators in the event, negotiations instantly become more complex, and the likelihood of various subgroups getting together in some form of coalition increases.

## Group Negotiations

In the above example, the negotiating parties were primarily engaged in a bilateral negotiation—that is, one or more buyers were negotiating with a seller for the stereo system. However, there is another form of multiparty negotiation, in which *more than two* parties with separate interests are all present in the negotiation (see Figure 9.4). For example, let us assume that four roommates had bought the stereo system; they have now decided to sell it, possibly to split the profit or possibly to invest in a more advanced system. Each has a different preference for what they should do: Andy wants to sell it and simply split up the money because he wants to buy a new bike for himself; Aaron wants to sell it and

**FIGURE 9.4**   A Multiparty Negotiation

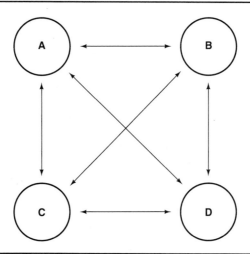

buy a newer but inexpensive stereo system; Chuck wants to sell it and buy a super high-quality system that will require each of them to chip in a lot more money; and Dan doesn't want to sell it at all and thinks the whole thing is a dumb idea. Each party has his own preferences and priorities, and the parties must figure out how to satisfy enough of the parties to make a decision. We will explore these group negotiations as a separate process in the second half of this chapter.

### Constituencies, Bystanders, and Audiences—Forms and Types

In the above situations, all parties were at the negotiating table. We shall now turn to consider the roles played by those parties who are *not* at the table, but whose interests are represented by someone else (their delegate, representative, or agent), who will be affected by the outcome in some way, or who are observing the negotiating process and perhaps offering comments, critique, or evaluation of the process or outcome. Under these conditions, the negotiators at the table will begin to redirect their behavior away from the opponent to pay some attention to these "outsiders" as well. We will broadly describe the attention paid to these additional parties—regardless of who they are—as *audience effects.*

There are many different kinds of audiences and audience effects. Initially, we will include *all* the roles we delineated above—negotiating team members, constituencies, bystanders, and even neutrals (with the sole exception of the focal negotiators themselves)—as audiences because they all tend to serve the function of observers, commentators, or stakeholders relative to the focal negotiator's behavior. As we begin to delineate the different roles and functions that audiences play, we will make distinctions among these different roles.

One form of audience is *additional team members* who are present with the negotiator at the deliberations. Members of a negotiating team may take on one or more important roles: chief spokesman, expert or resource person on a specific issue, advocate for a particular subgroup with a stake in the outcome, legal or financial counsel, statistician or cost analyst, recorder, or observer. For example, in the Lucasville case, the prisoners brought Attorney Niki Schwartz and guard hostages to the table, and the prison officials brought various police units and hostage negotiation experts. Team members agree to play a special role in negotiation, but they may change into another role as the negotiation evolves. The most frequent role shift is from being a negotiator (a person doing the talking) to being a more passive observer who is silent while others are talking. The observer may be taking notes, listening to the discussion, preparing for comments to be introduced later on, or simply evaluating and judging the actions of those who currently hold the floor. Negotiators also direct their comments toward observers on the other side. So, for example, while a member of one team (chief spokesperson) may appear to be talking directly to one member of the other team (the other chief spokesperson), she in fact may be trying to influence the other team's legal expert on some point. It is important to recognize these multiple roles that team members can play because their audience role can do as much to influence and shape a spokesperson's behavior as what the opposing negotiator says or does. Figure 9.5 represents a simple negotiation between two pairs of negotiators—on each side, one may be the primary spokesperson while the other assists, but they may change roles at any time. In Lucasville, although the negotiation began as a simple standoff between prison officials and prisoners, a number of external parties played multiple roles and made the dispute significantly more complex as it evolved.

Another type of audience is a *constituency*. A constituency is one or more parties whose interests, demands, or priorities are being represented by the focal negotiator at the table. The term *constituency* usually applies to politics; elected

**FIGURE 9.5**    Pairs of Negotiators in Teams

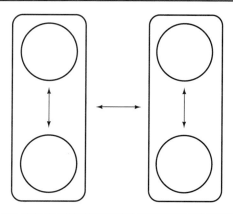

**FIGURE 9.6**    Negotiators Representing Constituents

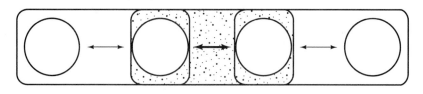

officials are usually accountable to the voters who elected them (their constituency). For an attorney, the constituent is his client. The social structure of this negotiation is represented in Figures 9.6 and 9.7. In the first figure, the negotiator has only one constituent; in the second figure, the negotiator represents a large group of constituents. At Lucasville, for example, Inmate George became the first spokesperson for his constituents—the rioting prisoners; later, attorney Niki Schwartz assumed this role.

As the figures suggest, negotiators with constituencies are involved in two distinctly different relationships—and often in two separate and distinct negotiations. The first relationship is with the constituency—the negotiator and constituency decide on their collective view of what they want to achieve in the negotiation and the strategy and tactics of how to get it. The constituency then delegates some power and authority to the negotiator to pursue the goals and strategy through negotiation. Constituents expect that the negotiator will accurately and enthusiastically represent their interests in the deliberations, periodically report back as negotiations evolve, and finally report the outcomes back at the end of the process. Constituents therefore expect to directly profit (or lose) as a result of the negotiator's effectiveness, and they often select their agent based on her ability to achieve the goals.

**FIGURE 9.7**    Negotiators Representing Larger Constituencies

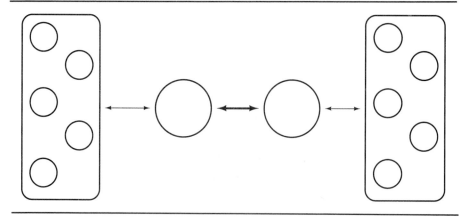

The second relationship is with the opponent—in this relationship, the negotiator and his opponent attempt to reach a viable and effective resolution of their differences. Reaching that resolution may require the negotiator to compromise on the goals set for him by his constituency and then to explain and justify those compromises back to the constituent. Therefore, representing a constituent creates unique pressures and conflicts for agents because they may be unable to both completely satisfy their constituent and achieve a resolution satisfactory to their opponent. We will have a great deal more to say about these pressures and conflicts later in this chapter.

A third type of audience is composed of *bystanders* and *observers*. Remember that negotiating team members themselves can act as bystanders and observers. In addition there are often many "pure" bystanders whose interests are not directly represented at the negotiating table, but who are affected by the negotiation outcome or have a vantage point from which to observe the negotiation and some strong need to comment on the process or the emerging outcome. In the Lucasville example, there were a large number of bystanders and observers: the media, local residents, various state and local government officials and departments, advocacy groups such as Justice Watch and the K.K.K., and "interested citizens." Figure 9.8 represents this most complex social environment for a negotiation. (This is what Lucasville ultimately became because it had all of these

**FIGURE 9.8**   Negotiators Representing Constituencies with Input from Audiences

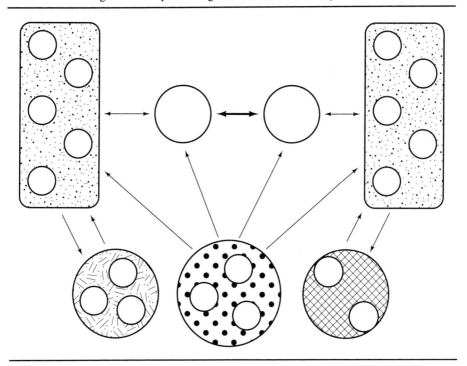

potential elements and grew more complex as the negotiations wore on.) A situation that includes bystanders and observers not only offers a context in which many parties are watching and evaluating the negotiation, but also offers a number of ways for the negotiator to use the audiences to bring indirect pressure to bear on the other negotiator. We will examine some of the most common tactics later in this chapter.

**Characteristics of Audiences and Bystanders.** There are a number of ways to describe the major characteristics of audiences (compare Rubin and Brown, 1975). First, audiences vary according to whether they are physically *present* at or *absent* from the negotiation event. Some observers may actually be at the negotiating table and directly witness the events that occur (e.g., attorney Niki Schwartz); others may be physically removed, and only learn about what happens through reports from the negotiators themselves or from other present observers (e.g., the governor of Ohio). Whether an audience is present or absent will affect how a negotiator behaves because she may say one thing with the audience present and another with the audience absent. In addition, when audiences are absent, negotiators must report what happened in the negotiations; when the audience has no real way of independently knowing what happened, these accounts may not be fully truthful and complete.

Second, audiences can also be *dependent* or *nondependent* on the negotiators for the outcomes derived from the negotiation process. Audiences who are *outcome-dependent* derive their payoffs as a direct result of the negotiator's behavior and effectiveness. In a labor contract, the amount of salary increase for each union member will be a direct result of the effectiveness of the chief negotiator and the negotiation team. In contrast, a *nondependent* audience is one that can observe the negotiation but will not be directly affected by the results. Although the general public may be interested in the contract arrived at by union and management, they may be minimally affected by the settlement.

A third major way that audiences affect negotiations is by the *degree of their involvement* in the process. Audiences may become *directly involved* in the negotiation process; when they do, the complexity of the interaction increases in a number of ways, depending on who the audience is, what is at stake, how much power the audience has, and what kind of a role the audience chooses to play. In international affairs, the United States has often become involved in some other country's or region's local negotiations and disputes—the Middle East, Eastern Europe, the former Yugoslavian republics, or Somalia. United States involvement has occurred in almost every form and variation—from expressing a preference for a particular strategy, process, or outcome, to attempting to facilitate negotiations and work out internal difficulties, to becoming militarily involved and either taking sides or keeping parties separate to help achieve a peaceful resolution. As the sole world superpower following the fall of the Soviet Union, the United States is a very powerful and directly involved third party in international affairs.

In contrast to this direct involvement, audiences may become *indirectly involved* in the negotiation. Indirect involvement occurs when audiences make their own wishes and desires known in an effort to influence the course of an ongoing negotiation (e.g., in Lucasville, the families of the hostages or Justice Watch.) Again, there are examples in international negotiations as well as labor and political disputes. Consumers often boycott a product (e.g., grapes, lettuce) to express their sympathy for a labor union and back its demands. Audiences also give periodic *feedback* to the negotiators, evaluating their effectiveness and letting them know how they are doing. Feedback may be written or verbal, such as notes, messages, letters, or personal conversations and advice; or it may even be in nonverbal form, such as smiles and nods of affirmation or scowls and frowns of disapproval. Feedback may be directed toward the positions that a negotiator has taken, concessions she has made, agreements she has arrived at, or the manner in which she has conducted herself in the deliberations.

Audiences may vary in a number of other ways:

1. Identity (who they are and what they stand for).
2. Composition (the number of different points of view represented, amount of power).
3. Size.
4. Relationship to the bargainer (emotional ties, amount of informal power and control they can exercise over the negotiator).
5. Role in the negotiation situation (readiness to try to directly affect the negotiator's behavior, style and content of communication).

In short, as soon as the negotiation setting is expanded to three or more parties, the nature and complexity of their interaction increases as audiences play a variety of different roles and attempt to shape the progress of negotiation in a variety of different ways.

Before we discuss audiences in more detail, it is important to summarize the most important principles about audiences and the significant ways that they influence the negotiator's choice of tactics.

**Negotiators Seek a Favorable Reaction from an Audience.**  The mere presence of an audience, particularly one that can easily observe the negotiator, motivates a negotiator to seek a favorable (positive) evaluation from that audience and to avoid an unfavorable (negative) evaluation. (These dynamics certainly affected the inmates' spokesmen during the occupation of the prison. If they did not forcefully state the prisoners' demands, the prisoners would have changed spokesman, and their former spokesman might be seriously harmed). The impact of a constituency that can exercise surveillance over a negotiator has been demonstrated in several research studies. First, merely being aware that they are under surveillance motivates negotiators to "act tough" (Benton and Druckman, 1974). In one experiment, Carnevale, Pruitt, and Britton (1979) told some subjects in an experimental negotiating situation that they were being watched by their constituents through a one-way window, while others believed they were not being watched. Negotiators who believed they were under surveillance were significantly more likely to conduct their negotiations in a distributive bargaining manner and to use threats, "commitment tactics" (refer to Chapter 3), and put-downs of their opponents to gain advantage. As a result, negotiators under surveillance were less likely to pursue integrative bargaining strategies and obtained lower joint outcomes than negotiators not under surveillance. When questioned later about their behavior, negotiators under surveillance felt that it was more important to look tough and strong, and as a result they were less likely to make concessions that would facilitate mutual gain.

In addition to the mere presence of an audience, the presence of a "salient" audience—one that the negotiator values for their opinions and supportive comments—affects a negotiator even more dramatically. A classic study by Brown (1968) reveals the power of feedback from a salient audience on a negotiator's subsequent behavior. In Brown's experiment, high school students played a competitive negotiation game with someone they thought was another student, but who was in fact an ally of the experimenter playing a preprogrammed strategy. In all cases, the preprogrammed strategy was aggressive and exploitative—thus, the students lost a lot in the early part of the game. The students then received contrived feedback messages from a group of their "peers" (whom they thought had been observing the first round), telling them either that they looked weak and foolish as a result of the way that they had been exploited in the first game, or that they looked good and strong in the first round because they had "played fair." Students then played a second round of the game, during which they were given the choice of using either a retaliatory strategy to "get back at" the opponent who took advantage of them (a strategy that would also cost them a great deal of money to execute), or a second strategy that did not involve retaliation, thus ignoring the "challenge" to their self-esteem created by the negative messages from the audience. The experiment, therefore, required the subjects to choose between pursuing a strategy that allowed them to make money but lose "face" (image and self-respect) in front of the audience or retaliating against the opponent and restoring their image with the important audience, but at great personal cost. As Brown summarized,

> The results were striking: Publicly humiliated subjects—those who received the derogatory feedback—were far more likely to retaliate, and with greater severity and self-sacrifice—than subjects who received the more favorable feedback. . . . Of special interest is the fact that when asked why they chose severe retaliation, 75 percent of the subjects who did so reported that they didn't want to look foolish and weak as a result of having been exploited, and that they retaliated in order to reassert their capability and strength (Rubin and Brown, 1975, p. 45).

In a follow-up study, Brown tested whether knowledge of the costs of retaliation was important in getting subjects to engage in this retaliatory behavior. In one variation, the audience knew how much personal cost the subject endured in order to retaliate. In a second variation, the audience did not know the costs. The results of these two variations demonstrated clearly that retaliation was greatest when the audience feedback had told the subject that he looked foolish *and* the audience did *not* know how much it cost the subject to retaliate. Thus, Brown has created the classic "face-saving" dilemma for negotiators: to preserve one's image to an audience at high costs or lose face but conserve resources. The research clearly shows that a bargainer is most aggressive when he needs to regain a positive image with his audience and no one knows how much it costs him to regain it.

Brown's study has several important implications for understanding the power of an audience over a negotiator. First, the student subjects in the study did not know the specific identity of anyone in the audience—only that they were from the same high school. The student negotiators never saw the audience, which was only vaguely identified as an "important" group. Moreover, the feedback message from the audience was not affected by *any actual events or any of the negotiator's behavior* in the bargaining game; the power of the audience feedback overshadowed everything that happened in the negotiation game. Thus, audiences that are only vaguely viewed as an important group to please can nevertheless exert powerful influences over a negotiator's behavior by simply telling the negotiator that she looks weak and foolish.

A second finding is that some students retaliated toward their opponent even when there was no audience present. This suggests that *the opposing negotiator may act as an audience as well.* Negotiators who believe that the opposing negotiator has caused them to look foolish or has evaluated their behavior as weak and ineffective may try to regain a positive evaluation, even from an adversary. Anyone who has ever played a "friendly" game of tennis, golf, ping pong, or basketball will recognize that much of the banter, teasing, and verbal harassment that occurs is designed to undermine the opponent's self-confidence or to challenge him to play better in the future. All of this is usually done with good-natured humor; yet the banter can quickly turn serious if a comment is made too sharply or taken wrong, and it can both seriously unsettle the opponent and hurt the relationship. One can thus imagine the impact of a message to a bargainer from his opponent that he was "easy to beat." Not only is the bargainer embarrassed by losing, but the embarrassment is doubled because, in his opponent's eyes, he was not even a worthy adversary. Such comments are the fuel for revenge and long-standing, deep-seated animosity.

Brown's research shows how important face-saving is to negotiators whose behavior is highly public, visible, and subject to a great deal of feedback from audiences. Numerous examples come to mind from the history of international relations, politics, and labor relations. Strong face-challenging language was used in late 1990 between President Saddam Hussein of Iraq and President George Bush, leading to Bush's escalation of the war with Iraq following its invasion of Saudi Arabia. Similarly, President Lyndon Johnson's characterization of the United States' early role in Vietnam as a "pitiful, helpless giant" soon led to the massive military buildup in Southeast Asia in order to "win" a war that humiliated American military capability at home and abroad. Not only was this effort to "free" South Vietnam ultimately unsuccessful—thus sustaining the actual loss of face that Johnson and others had dreaded—but also the loss was incurred at phenomenal costs in dollars, military equipment, and human lives that were only disclosed to the American public long after the war ended.

Finally, there is a tragic twist on face-saving dynamics in the Lucasville prison riot. Some observers have speculated that the comments made by Corrections Department spokesperson Tessa Unwin may have contributed directly to the murder of the guard Vallandingham. By publicly commenting to the media that "prisoners threaten to kill hostages all the time" and questioning the prisoners' credibility, Unwin may have prompted the prisoners to kill a guard to prove their threat was credible and save face with their own constituents.

***Audiences Hold the Negotiator Accountable.*** Audiences maintain control over a negotiator by holding her accountable for her performance and by administering rewards or punishments based on that performance. (At Lucasville, State officials and the families of the hostages maintained strong accountability over their negotiators. As a result of her comments, spokesperson Unwin was quickly relieved of her responsibilities). This accountability will occur under two dominant conditions: when a bargainer's performance is visible to the audience (so that the audience is able to judge how well the bargainer performs) and when the audience is dependent on the bargainer for their outcomes. An audience that is dependent upon a negotiator's performance for their outcomes will generally insist that she be tough, firm, demanding, and unyielding in her struggle to obtain the best possible outcome for her constituents. Failure to perform in this manner (in the eyes of the audience) may lead to public criticism of the negotiator, with the expectation that this criticism will embarrass her into performing in ways that guarantee a larger payoff for the constituency.

Continued characterizations of the negotiator as weak, soft, or someone who sells out may lead to unfortunate but predictable outcomes. First, the bargainer may become increasingly inflexible or retaliatory to demonstrate to her constituency that she is capable of defending their interests. Second, the bargainer may try to be a more loyal, committed, and dedicated advocate of the constituency's preferred outcomes and priorities, simply to attempt to regain their good favor and evaluation. Finally, she may find herself forced to resign, judged by herself or others as incapable of representing the constituency's best interests.

In addition to audience accountability, other aspects of a negotiator's relationship with his constituency can affect negotiation outcomes. Two aspects that have received recent research attention are the negotiator's *relative status* within the constituency and the amount of *accountability pressure* that the constituency can exert. Relative status does not appear to have the impact that might be expected—it does not appear that high-status members (e.g., senior level managers or formally designated leaders) negotiate more quickly, achieve fewer deadlocks in the negotiating process, or attain better solutions (Klimoski and Ash, 1974; Kogan, Lamm, and Trommsdorff, 1972). Folklore to the contrary, accountability pressure appears to have a more significant impact. Research simulations provide for accountability by having constituents watch the negotiation, having the negotiator formally report back to a constituency (perhaps allowing them to vote on the negotiated agreement), or letting the constituency decide how the negotiator will be compensated for services rendered. In general, this accountability makes the negotiator feel more pressure to respond to the constituency's desires and thus to act tougher in negotiations. Hence it leads to longer, more time-consuming negotiations than when accountability pressures are absent (Benton, 1972; Klimoski, 1972; Haccoun and Klimoski, 1975; Breaugh and Klimoski, 1977).

### Tactical Implications of Social Structure Dynamics: The Negotiator's Dilemma

The presence of an audience—particularly an outcome-dependent audience—creates a paradox for negotiators because of two sets of pressures. One set comes from the constituency, which communicates expectations that the agent should be tough, firm, unyielding, and supportive of the constituency's demands. The other set comes from the opposing negotiator and from the definition of negotiation itself: that the negotiator should be flexible, conciliatory, and willing to engage in give and take. (Visualize these pressures as depicted in Figure 9.7, simultaneously pushing the negotiator from opposite directions.) The basic dilemma, then, is to determine how a bargainer can satisfy both his constituency's demand for firmness (and a settlement favorable to their interests), and his opponent's demand for concessions (and a settlement favorable to the opponent or to their mutual gain).

The answer is that a negotiator must build relationships with both the constituency *and* the opponent. The relationship with the constituency must be cultivated on the basis of complete support for their demands and willingness to advocate these demands in negotiation. On the other hand, the relationship with the opponent must be developed by stressing the similarity and commonality of their collective goals or fate, and the desirability of establishing and maintaining a productive working relationship and a commitment to find a common goal. However, each of these relationships must be developed *privately, and without visibility to the other group.* This privacy assures that a negotiator can conduct deliberations with the opponent without accountability pressures. It may also require a certain degree of duplicity, with the negotiator promising utmost loyalty and dedication to each one, out of view of the others. Typically, negotiators first meet with the constituency to define their collective interests and objectives. They then meet with opposing negotiators, in privacy, so that they can openly state their constituent's expectations while also making necessary concessions without looking weak or foolish. Finally, a negotiator returns to the constituency to "sell" the concessions to them, persuading them that the achieved settlement was the best possible under the circumstances. Successful management of a constituency, therefore, requires that the negotiator have control over the visibility or invisibility of negotiating behavior to the constituency and to audiences. A negotiator who cannot control this visibility is going to be on public display all the time. Every statement, argument, concession, and mistake will be in full view of a critical audience that may pick it apart, critique it, and challenge it as possibly disloyal. These pressures are highly undesirable, and, as we have argued earlier, likely to lead to negotiator behavior that is more designed to appeal to the audience than to find an agreement.

**Manipulating Audience Visibility.**   A negotiator can control both the visibility of his behavior and the communication process with constituencies, audiences, and even the opponent by employing tactics that make them believe he is highly committed to the bargaining position they support. A few of the most common such tactics follow.

*Limit Concessions by Making Negotiations Visible to the Constituency.* Because negotiators who negotiate in full view of their constituencies are less likely to make concessions than negotiators who deliberate in private, negotiators can enhance their own visibility to limit making concessions. Negotiators typically "go public" when they want to remain firm in their positions. For example, the negotiator may insist on allowing his constituency to be present for all negotiations. At Lucasville, the prisoner who brought the guard to the negotiating session in the prison yard and announced the prisoners' demands to the prison officials in front of the national media was, in part, using the media to convince his constituency that their demands were receiving broad public attention. In contrast, most actual concessions in the negotiation were achieved when the parties deliberated in private.

*Use the Constituency to Show Militancy.*   A second way that a constituency can be used is to make the constituency visible and demonstrate that they are more extreme, radical, committed, and inflexible than the negotiator. At Lucasville, the prisoner negotiators could always point to the angry group holding the hostages as evidence of their militancy. The more angry and articulate prisoners are often the ones selected as spokespersons. Community groups that want to bring about change from public officials usually insist that the officials come to an "open meeting" of the community, in which community spokespersons confront the officials with their concerns or grievances. Those invited to speak at the meeting are often the most demanding or militant, who communicate a tough and demanding posture to the opponent. Militants may also be specifically invited in to let the other side know that concessions will not come easily and that the only way agreement is going to be reached (or disaster averted) is for the opponent to make concessions. In addition to intimidating the opponent, the tactic can have other side benefits. First, a barely-under-control militant constituency may not only intimidate an opponent, but also allow the negotiator to be a nice, pleasant, reasonable person in contrast. Opponents definitely prefer to deal with nice, pleasant negotiators rather than angry, militant ones. As a result, a negotiator can look more cool, calm and rational than her out-of-control constituency simply through the contrast effect (see Chapter 7 on negotiator biases). If the negotiator then implies that "either you deal with me and my demands or you work with someone else from my constituency who is far more irrational than me," the negotiator is likely to gain significant ground with an opponent. This is a variation of the classic "tough guy-nice guy" or "Mutt and Jeff" negotiating tactic.

*Limit a Negotiator's Authority.*    The third way a negotiator can use a constituency is by showing the opponent that the constituency has limited the negotiator's authority to make concessions—particularly "unauthorized" ones. This tactic may be used as a bluff or because of a genuine limit on authority. As a bluff, the negotiator misleads his opponent to believe that all concessions must be cleared with the constituency. As a genuine tactic, the negotiator's constituency has actually defined limits to what the negotiator can decide on his own. In banks, for example, new loan officers may have very limited authority to approve loans on their own signature, whereas the bank's senior loan officer probably has very wide latitude. Yet although the senior loan officer could easily approve the loan on her own authority, she uses the constituency (the bank's loan committee) both for protection (to make sure that the loan is not granted foolishly) and perhaps also to pressure the borrower into meeting certain terms and conditions.

Negotiators must be careful about revealing how much authority and autonomy they really have. On the one hand, it might seem that limiting authority would be a distinct advantage. Every minor deviation from the originally stated position would have to be approved, a process that is very tedious and time consuming. If the opponent is in a hurry, he may choose to make major concessions to avoid the delay. On the other hand, the tactic may backfire. Not only is it very tedious for the opponent to wait while every minor change and concession is reviewed and approved, but it also frustrates the negotiator, who feels like a powerless messenger. This mutual frustration eventually may lead to a complete breakdown in negotiations. Because negotiation is understood as the process of *making* concessions toward mutual agreement, encountering an opponent who cannot make any concessions on her own violates expectations and creates anger. Negotiators with severely limited authority can be effectively embarrassed by their opponents when they do not have the authority to make agreements on their own. This may lead the opponent to demand that the constituency "send someone to the table who has the power to negotiate and come to agreement."

*Use Great Caution in Exceeding Authority.*    The reverse side of this negotiating dilemma is that the negotiator who overextends her authority or exceeds the limits set by her constituency may be unable to persuade the constituency that the achieved settlement is a good one. This is often a problem in union-management relations, particularly when the union group is militant and has very high aspirations. After a long and arduous negotiation, a union negotiating team reaches a tentative settlement with management. But the union rank and file, who may have inflated expectations, reject the proposed contract offer. This rejection vote is tantamount to a vote of no confidence in their negotiators. Sometimes the negotiators resign; at other times they return to the table increasingly militant to prove their toughness to their constituency, which jeopardizes the possibility of any effective agreement with the opponent. In the extreme, the negotiators may be willing to endure extremely high personal costs—a long strike, personal fines, jail sentences, and negative public opinion—to restore their image with the constituency. For example, in the 1981 strike of the Professional Air Traffic Controllers Organization (PATCO) against the Federal Aviation Authority (FAA), the leader of PATCO, Robert Poli, spent several months negotiating a new package on behalf of his organization. When the deal was finally presented to the union for ratification, 90 percent of the membership rejected the tentative contract as inadequate. So Poli returned to the FAA and attempted to gain a better package, but the FAA wouldn't budge, and after two weeks of unsuccessful debate, PATCO called a strike. The strike (illegal under the terms of the government's contract with each union member) led the FAA and the Reagan administration to (1) fire all the striking controllers from their jobs, (2) obtain federal injunctions and impose fines of several million dollars per day against the union and its leadership, (3) jail some union members and officials, including Poli, (4) impound the union's strike fund, and (5) ban all striking controllers from any further employment with the U.S. government, either as controllers or in any other federal job. In the early days of this confrontation, ninety percent of the union supported Poli taking them out on strike and going to jail. Poli was put in the difficult position of either leading the union in its militant demands (and becoming a hero-martyr in going to jail for them) or affirming that the deal he struck with the FAA was a good one and be rejected by his union. It took until 1993 for President Bill Clinton to finally declare that fired air traffic controllers could be rehired.

**Increase the Possibility of Concessions by Cutting Off Visibility to Audiences.**    If increased audience visibility also increases the likelihood that negotiators will take tougher stands, be less flexible, and make fewer concessions, then a negotiator who wishes to be more flexible and conciliatory would want negotiations to be less visible. There are two approaches to accomplishing this objective.

*Establish "Privacy" Prior to the Beginning of Negotiations.*    In Chapter 5, we mentioned the importance of establishing negotiating ground rules before the actual process begins. One rule that should be considered is that the negotiations will be conducted in private, that no media or public interviews will be granted, and that contact with the other party's constituency (or visibility to audiences) will be strictly controlled. To enhance the privacy of the negotiations, parties may select a remote location in neutral territory, where their comings and goings will not be too obvious or visible. When the time comes for announcements about negotiating progress or achievements, both parties can make them jointly, coordinating their communications. Needless to say, if the other party wishes the negotiations to be held in a public environment—where communication with constituencies is easy and the constituencies may actually have a direct view—setting the terms and conditions for the visibility of the negotiation will be the first item for deliberations. Given the many ways that people can communicate with each other these days—telephones, fax machine, closed-circuit video, and electronic mail—finding and maintaining true privacy in a negotiation can be a real challenge, but it can be done. At Lucasville, the prisoners were permitted to publicize their demands in front of the news media—they wanted to make their demands well known—in exchange for a hostage, but once they were represented by Niki Schwartz, negotiations became private and public visibility was highly controlled.

***Screen Visibility during Negotiations.*** If negotiators have not agreed beforehand to a location that is private and secure, there are other options for screening out unwanted observers from sensitive discussions. One of the simplest ways is to have some discussions occur informally, on a strictly unofficial basis. These discussions can occur during coffee breaks, meal breaks, walks around the building, or even during a quick trip to the washroom. Key representatives may agree to meet for cocktails after formal deliberations or for breakfast before the day's formal deliberations begin. During such meetings, parties can speak more candidly "off the record," or they can hint as to their bottom-line position or their willingness to make certain concessions. "We've been sitting in that room for a long time, and you know, if your side were willing to name a proposal something like the following (insert the specific details here), my people would probably be willing to go along with it." In some cases, the meeting may be planned but very secretive. In one industry, for example, labor negotiations occurred every two years. Prior to the beginning of formal talks, the union president and the company president met for dinner in another city 500 miles away and broadly discussed the key issues that would be raised in the negotiations. Although the union president could lose his job if this meeting were ever announced to the rank and file, both presidents considered the meeting invaluable to keeping an informal communication channel open between them and permitting them to maintain a personal connection in the midst of the confrontational negotiations that would occur for the next few months.

Other kinds of information can also be privately exchanged in these informal venues. Negotiators can grumble and complain, brag about their constituency and its support, or even let conversations with their own constituents be "overheard" by an opponent. All these tactics give the other side information about what is really possible without saying it directly at the table. A union negotiator might say, "You know, Mike Moran is something else. He's been riding me about toughening up the work rules for the past six months. He's really campaigning to get my job." The management negotiator may well decide to give a little more on work rules to keep the present union negotiator in his job, rather than sustain a tough position, frustrate the union, push them to elect Mike Moran, and then have to face a much more difficult opponent in the future.

Contacts can also be made at dinners, parties, speeches, luncheons, or even church services. Heads of state who negotiate major arms and trade agreements are frequently photographed at dinners, receptions, or walks in the garden. (The play, "A Walk in the Woods" (Blessing, 1988) is an interesting recreation of the way President Jimmy Carter shaped the Camp David accords between Israel and Egypt.) Although a great deal of such functions is public and ceremonial, "private time" is frequently part of them as well. Before the fall of the Soviet Union several years ago, every major political event in either country—a funeral for a head of state, an inauguration, or the signing of a major international trade agreement— was seen as an opportunity for U.S. and Soviet leaders to informally meet with their political counterparts along with attending the required ceremonies.

**Communicating with the Constituency or with Audiences.**    A third technique that negotiators use in manipulating the social structure of negotiations is to communicate *indirectly.* Indirect communications are efforts by the negotiator to bring the opinions of audiences and constituents to bear on the opposing negotiator. Although the opponent may believe he is well defended against his adversary's arguments, he may not be able to defend himself against other people—his constituents, his friends, his superiors, or "public opinion"—when they appear to side with his opponent. This informal communication takes place in several ways.

***Communicate through Superiors.***    This technique is frequently used when negotiators are representatives of two hierarchically structured organizations (e.g., a company and a union, or two companies engaged in a business deal) and when one or both negotiators are dissatisfied with the progress of negotiations or the behavior of their opponent. To manage their frustration and dissatisfaction, they may go to their own superiors (who are probably not directly involved) and ask the superiors to either attend a negotiating session or, more commonly, to contact their counterpart in the opposing organization. The situation is represented in Figure 9.9. Consider the following example from labor relations. A union negotiator has presented a set of wage demands to the management negotiator. Management has examined the demands and is convinced that it will be financially impossible for the company to meet them. In spite of management's strong stance and documentation, the union negotiator refuses to believe the accuracy and validity of the arguments. In frustration, the management negotiator goes to one

**FIGURE 9.9**    Indirect Communication Between Negotiators through their Bosses

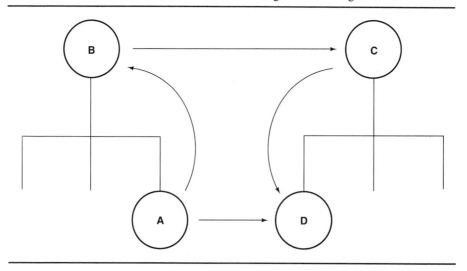

of his superiors, for example, the corporate treasurer, and asks her to contact the president of the local union. The corporate treasurer invites the union president out to lunch and provides sufficient financial data to convince the president that the company cannot meet the union's demands. The corporate treasurer then asks the union president to meet with his bargaining committee to scale back the union's wage demands (see Figure 9.10).

This indirect process works under several conditions. First, the tactic's effectiveness depends upon a social structure in which the negotiator represents an organization or group that has some formal hierarchy of power and authority—and the opponent represents a similar organization. Negotiations between formal private and public sector organizations fit this description. Second, the chief negotiator cannot be the most senior person with the most authority, the president, chairman, or official "leader." The reason the chief executive does not negotiate is *not necessarily* that she is too busy doing other things. Rather, conducting negotiations through an agent who is not the senior person allows the organization to limit its concessions by limiting the negotiator's power and authority to make decisions. Senior executives are only likely to become involved when negotiations are extremely delicate, critical, or symbolically significant to the well-being of the organization and its relationships with other organizations. In international relations, for example, contacts between nations occur on a number of diplomatic levels; the U.S. Secretary of State or the President may only become directly involved in the most delicate, symbolic, or politically important negotiations. Finally, the effectiveness of the tactic relies upon indirect communication originating from someone the opponent trusts more or is less well-defended against (as we described in Chapter 8). When the indirect communication comes from superiors, it may be even more effective because the communicator has high status, reputation, and visibility. Thus, in the previous illustration, confronted with a compelling case from the chief financial officer of the company (who, although she is still an agent of the company, is defined as a nonnegotiator), the union president may be more likely to accept and believe the financial information than if the same information were presented at the bargaining table.

*Communicate through "Intermediaries" and Constituency Members.* This approach (see Figure 9.11) is used when negotiators need to make informal contact with an opposing negotiator or constituency. Here the approach is made through any external contact who can serve as an intermediary or communication conduit. Those selected are usually chosen for some valid reason—trust, past experience in working together, a personal friendship or relationship, or a personal reputation for credibility, impartiality, and integrity. The tactic is most often used under two major circumstances: when a negotiator wants to "feel out" the opposing group to possibly gain inside information, or when deliberations are deadlocked and need to be unfrozen. In the Lucasville example, attorney Niki Schwartz served both as an attorney for the persons holding Block L, and as a conduit through which prison officials could communicate with both the rioting prisoners and the hostage-guards.

Similar to the tactic of communicating through superiors, the effectiveness

**FIGURE 9.10** Indirect Communication through Managers (union–management example)

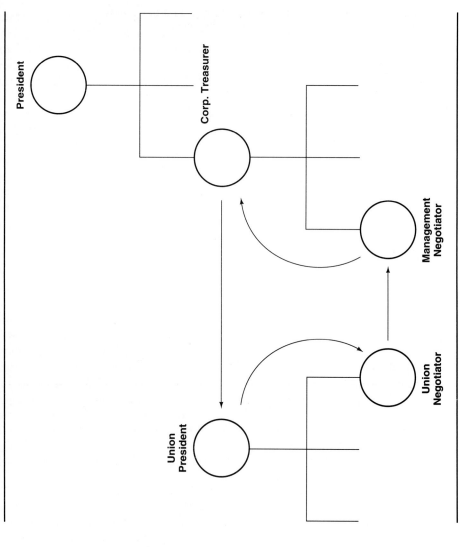

**FIGURE 9.11**   Indirect Communication through an Intermediary

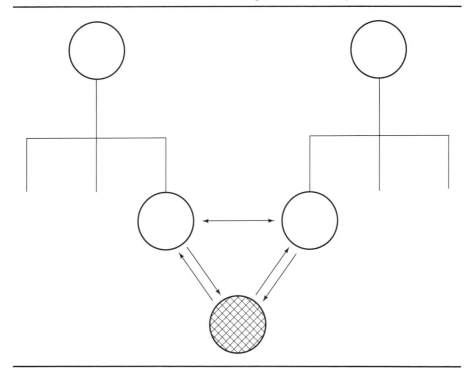

of informal contact depends upon employing the right individuals: ones who are not subject to the same accountability pressure that binds formal group representatives so they can use informal communication channels that may eventually clear blockages in the formal links.

*Communicate Directly to an Opponent's Constituency.*   In a third form of indirect communication (see Figure 9.12), one agent seeks to bypass the opposing negotiator and communicate *directly* with his constituency to persuade them to change their position or the instructions they are giving their representative. The agent himself may initiate this tactic, usually when he believes that negotiations are deadlocked or that the opposing agent is not communicating effectively with her constituency—when the opposing agent is either not representing her constituency's interests clearly and effectively at the table or not accurately reporting to his constituency. Thus, one agent attempts to "eliminate the middle man" and communicate directly with the opponent's constituency. In a union-management situation, for example, management representatives frequently prefer to speak or write directly to the rank and file rather than through the union leadership. The intent (and the impact) may not only be to insure that management's position is clearly heard and understood, but also to subtly undermine the credibility and effectiveness of the union leadership. By refusing to use the union leadership as

**FIGURE 9.12** Indirect Communication through a Constituency

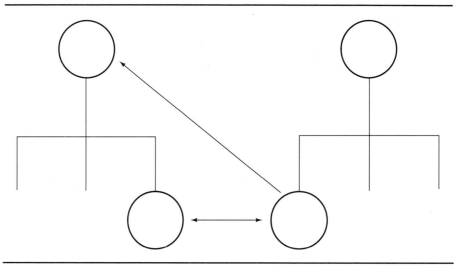

the sole channel of communication with the rank and file or by implying to the rank and file that their leadership is not doing a satisfactory job of representing their interests, may undermine union leadership. The tactic may also be initiated by the opposing negotiator. In this latter case, the opponent usually extends the invitation because she believes her credibility or integrity is being questioned and wants our agent to hear the message directly from her constituency.

However, it should be clear that direct communication with an opposing constituency—particularly without the sanction of the opposing negotiator—is likely to be viewed as an inflammatory tactic. If the negotiator is not consulted and does not grant permission, the act of going around her is usually interpreted as a lack of confidence in her communication skills. Negotiators who are undermined by their opponents in this way are likely to become more defensive and rigid. The immediate impact on the negotiator's constituency, however, is less clear. Sometimes, they may also perceive this direct communication from the opponent as a tactic to undermine their leadership's effectiveness and in response rally around their leadership more strongly. At other times, particularly when a constituency may already have doubts about the effectiveness of its own representation, direct, open, accurate communication from an opposing negotiator may undermine confidence in their representative even further.

***Communicating to Bystanders and Audiences.*** In this case, the agent's intent is to manipulate the opinion of bystanders (other than constituencies) and to mobilize their support, either to build support for her own position or to undermine the opponent's position (see Figure 9.13). Communication through bystanders may occur (1) as an explicit and conscious tactic to exert influence on the opponent, but through circuitous channels, (2) as an effort to build alliances and support for one's own position; or (3) as a result of the natural tendency for

**FIGURE 9.13**    Indirect Communication through Audiences and Bystanders

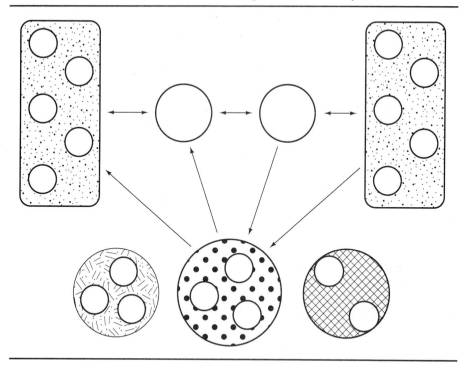

conflict to proliferate and envelop innocent bystanders. In all cases, negotiators are public about their own (or their organization's) demands. They will tell anyone who will listen how fair, legitimate, just, and appropriate their own side's position is, and how unfair, unjust, illegitimate, and inappropriate the opponent's position is. As a result, negotiators hope that third parties will openly side with them (hence lending strength and credence to their arguments), and that the third party will communicate their dissatisfaction and displeasure to the opponent (thus undermining the strength and credibility of the opponent's arguments).

Communication through audiences—particularly the media—is extremely common in major interorganizational negotiations such as intergovernmental, international, or labor-management relations. Most of these deliberations are well known for having a public phase in which the negotiators primarily address their arguments to audiences rather than to one another. In this phase, the media—radio, television, and newspaper—play an integral role by providing ready access to communication channels. The media serve as both an audience themselves and a communication vehicle to reach other audiences. Media relations and "image management" often become ends in themselves; the better negotiators can stage their performance before radio microphones or television cameras, the more likely they will be to win public opinion to their side, which will then put pressure on the opposing negotiators to concede their position. (As a parenthetical note, communication through the media can also be used to reach one's own constituency.) The quickest and most efficient way of letting one's own constituency know the exact elements of our negotiating posture and our personal commitment to this posture is to represent that position in the media—although, admittedly, many have learned that the media may not get it right either. This approach is more likely to be used when one wants to communicate firmness and toughness in a position. It is less likely to be used when one wants to communicate concession-making or defeat.

Communication may also be designed to "activate" and win over *interested audiences* who will communicate directly with the opponent. For example, in public-sector labor relations, such as a community's negotiations with school teachers or police, fire, or sanitation workers, it is not uncommon for the mayor or school board president to appear on television, state the union's salary demands, depict those demands as exorbitant, and point out how much those demands are likely to cost the taxpayers. The expectation is that the taxpayers will communicate their dissatisfaction to the union leadership, hence bringing strong social pressure on the union to modify its demands. Obviously, union leadership engages in similar tactics, attempting to win community support by stressing the wide variety of services they provide for minimal compensation and portraying the dire consequences that might occur if these services were not available. Leaders exhort taxpayers to call their local government representatives immediately and urge complete capitulation to the union's "fair and legitimate" requests. A comparable example can be found in the President's State of the Union address, in which the President of the United States lays out the agenda of legislation that will be submitted to Congress. Once the President delivers the State of the Union speech (to a fully assembled Congress as well as the American citizens through television and newspaper coverage), the President and Congress, Republicans and Democrats, and all forms of special interest groups who will be affected by the proposed legislation begin to compete for support from the American voters.

The effectiveness of communicating through audiences is determined by several factors. First, it depends upon the degree to which an audience's outcomes hinge directly on the negotiator's effectiveness and how severe the consequences are likely to be. This *degree and severity of effect* can vary from outcomes that directly affect the audience in a dramatic way to those that only minimally and indirectly affect the audience. If I live on the East Coast, a strike by farm workers in California will not affect me very strongly, particularly if I can purchase fruit and vegetables grown locally. On the other hand, a strike by the drivers of milk trucks in my local area is likely to affect me and my family very strongly. In addition, the California farm workers' strike would not affect me if I did not eat many fruits and vegetables; in contrast, I would be greatly affected by the milk strike if I had three small children.

The second factor in the effectiveness of communicating through audiences is the *degree to which the audience is organized* as a coherent unit. An audience may be directly and severely affected by the results of a particular negotiation, but unable to exert leverage on the negotiations because they are "unorganized": they have no means for polling opinions and determining their collective sentiments or communicating and making decisions among themselves. Community members who may be greatly inconvenienced by a bus or subway strike have no way to *collectively* express their dissatisfaction to strikers or management. Even when a very large group of people may be negatively affected, they are unlikely to have significant impact on the negotiations if their reaction cannot be brought to bear on the negotiators themselves. Interestingly enough, the media is increasingly providing opportunities for this "disorganized majority" to have a voice. The early 1990s saw a dramatic rise in radio talk shows, hosted by controversial journalists who provide airways access and "bait" their listening audiences with controversial topics. These talk-show formats have been credited with being one of the only vehicles by which average citizens can have a say in governmental and public affairs, and in many cases they have stirred significant public support or opposition for key political issues. Similarly, referring back to the Lucasville riot, the prisoners understood that, although they were dramatically divided along racial and political lines, they needed the media to communicate their message to prison officials, to win public support for the cause of prison reform, and to assure that the police did not repressively put down the riot.

Having stated the premise that audiences cannot have impact without some form of communication leverage, we must note that the reverse premise is also true: *well-organized audiences can have significant effect on the outcome of negotiations even if their total number is small.* The effectiveness of particular political lobbies in state and federal government (of all political persuasions and special interest orientations) is testimony to the positive effect of strong organization. For example, numerous public opinion polls in recent years have demonstrated strong popular support for limiting the sale of handguns. In spite of apparent widespread public support for this legislation, several national lobbies have effectively killed most legislation opposed to handgun control in Congress and in state legislatures. The success of these lobbies is based upon their ability to identify and contact audience members who support their position, to mobilize these members toward a common purpose, and to bring pressure on all legislators who might support a gun-control bill (through massive letter writing and telephone campaigns, promises of financial contributions to the legislator's campaign, and so on). This last tactic indicates that successful pressure through communication campaigns is significantly increased if actual financial resources can also be manipulated.

Finally, appeals to audiences will be effective to the degree that the negotiator is *sophisticated in his use of media relations.* To someone who is naive in dealing with and using the media as an effective but indirect negotiating tool, media relations may involve no more than appearing before a camera or microphone and reading a prepared statement. However, as we implied in Chapter 8, the content of one's message, particularly on television, is considerably less important than the visual presentation and the "performance." Portraying an image of confidence, control, and steadfast determination is essential. The negotiator needs to be well dressed, well spoken, and in control of the situation. She needs to be able to respond to hostile and "loaded" questions effectively. Finally, she may wish to be surrounded by her constituency—the rank and file, her supporters, her closest advisors—who will openly demonstrate their solidarity and support for their negotiator. Effective politicians in all industries and contexts have learned how to use the media to get their message across and win the "hearts and minds" of key audiences to buttress their own positions and agendas.

### Building Relationships with Opponents

Finally, rather than undermining an opponent's support, negotiators frequently try to develop personal relationships with the opponent. The negotiator's underlying assumption is that it is easier (and definitely more pleasant) to work with and persuade a friendly opponent than an unfriendly one. In addition, the assumption is that building a personal relationship will permit the agent to get his message across to a less defensive, less antagonistic adversary. These assumptions are based on many of the issues we raised as "source factors" in attitude change (see Chapter 8). Individuals who see themselves as similar to one another, who are attracted to one another, or who are likely to experience a common fate are more likely to change their attitudes toward one another. Because negotiation may be viewed as a mutual effort by both parties to change the other's attitudes (e.g., objectives, opening demands), the same principles apply.

Negotiators use a variety of techniques to make this tactic work (we have a lot more to say about this in Chapter 10, when we address a negotiator's power bases and power tactics). Some negotiators meet informally to get to know each other outside of the context of negotiations. Shared cocktails, a meal, or even an informal coffee break are well-known opportunities for promoting friendliness, easy conversation, and cordiality. The agenda for both sides is usually not to conduct formal deliberations, but to build a relationship that will alleviate the possible tension and conflict inherent in formal negotiations and keep negotiations from ending in deadlock or an angry walkout. Hence, the agents need to drop their formal negotiator roles and meet as individual people to create mutual bases of shared similarities, commonality, and liking for one another that will transfer over into developing a mutually acceptable negotiating agreement.

In addition to developing a relationship based on commonality of personal interests or genuine liking for one another, negotiators may also stress their "common fate"—namely, the accountability pressures put on them by their constituencies. If both negotiators feel strongly pressured by their constituencies, they are likely to stress their common fate as a way to build the relationship. Thus, "you and I are in this together," "we both have our constituencies to deal with," "we want to achieve the best for all of us," or "we want to develop an agreement based on mutual respect that we can live with successfully in the future," are all phrases that typify the opening stages of negotiation. Many experienced negotiators refer to these expressions of common fate as "the harmony and light speech"—they believe that such expressions are merely a tactical ploy to soften them up before the opposing negotiator presents tough demands. Although that allegation may be true, the "harmony and light speech" that opens many formal negotiations plays a critical role in negotiation. Even if the speech is ritualistic, it *does* communicate that the opposing negotiator is interested in building a personal relationship. Moreover, the absence of the speech may indicate that the parties are so adamant in their positions or so angry at one another that they cannot bring themselves to make the speech. This may be a clear sign that the negotiations will be tense and are likely to be deadlocked.

A further purpose of informal meetings is to permit each party to get a sense of each other's objectives. In many negotiations, chief negotiators meet before the formal deliberations, much like the chief executives we described earlier. The purpose of this meeting is usually twofold: to sense what the other side's major demands will be and to develop a relationship and an open channel of communication that can be used regardless of how tense the negotiations become. Such meetings are usually held without audience visibility (publicity) because publicizing the event might lead other management or union members to view the meeting as collusion. However, some negotiators may choose to publicize the event to demonstrate a "spirit of cooperation." When the President of the United States appears before the television cameras in the White House Rose Garden with some visiting foreign dignitary, the two are usually shown smiling, shaking hands, embracing, and demonstrating to their constituencies and audiences that they have developed a harmonious relationship that will lead to mutual agreement on substantive problems. The discussion between them, however, is private and we rarely know what was actually said.

### Summary

Sometimes negotiation is a private affair between two parties. Up until now we have talked about negotiation in this private context. However, at other times, there are audiences to a negotiation, and the presence of an audience has both a subtle and a direct impact on negotiations.

Three types of audiences may be encountered. First, when teams of people (rather than individuals) negotiate, the chief negotiators actually conduct much of the actual dialogue. Although these two usually talk directly to one another, they also use their own and opposing team members as an audience. A negotiator sends messages to members of the opposing team who she believes will be more receptive to the idea and able to influence the other chief negotiator.

A second type of audience is the constituency the negotiator represents. A wife negotiating for a new house represents her family, diplomats negotiate for their countries, and division heads on a companywide budget committee negotiate what portion of capital resources their departments will have for the coming year. These audiences have a stake in the outcome of the negotiation and benefit or suffer according to the skills of their representatives. The third type of audience is bystanders. Bystanders see or hear about the negotiations and, although they have little or no stake in the outcome, form opinions (favorable or unfavorable) of the settlement and the parties involved.

Audiences influence negotiators through two different routes. One way is that negotiators desire positive evaluations from those who are in a position to observe what they have done. The other is that audiences can (and do) hold negotiators responsible for the outcomes of negotiations. They can reward negotiators by publicly praising them and punish negotiators by firing them. They can intrude and change the course of negotiations—as when the public requires mandatory arbitration or fact-finding in some disputes. They can find ways of making their preferences known, for example, talking to the press, thereby putting pressure on one or both negotiators.

Audiences can have both favorable and unfavorable impacts on negotiations. Sometimes a negotiator tries to use an audience to his advantage, as when he thinks it will help pressure his opponent into a more flexible or desirable position; he may also try to prevent an audience from having influence effect when he thinks it might be undesirable for his position. Although there are many different ways of manipulating an audience, they all involve controlling the visibility of or the communication with that audience. In this chapter, we suggested four basic strategies to manipulate the effect an audience can have:

1. Limit concessions by making your actions visible to one's constituency, thereby putting yourself in a position that the opponent will recognize as difficult to change.
2. Increase the possibility of concessions by cutting off the visibility of negotiations from the audience.
3. Communicate indirectly with the other negotiator by communicating with her audiences.
4. Facilitate building a relationship with the other negotiator by reducing visibility and communication with both parties' audiences.

When negotiations move from a private to a public context, negotiations become more complex and more formal. In setting strategy, a negotiator needs to consider whether negotiations should be held privately or involve audiences in various ways. To ignore this social context is to ignore a potent factor in determining negotiation outcomes.

## MULTIPARTY NEGOTIATIONS

Thus far in the chapter, we have been focusing on negotiations in which there are *two* focal primary negotiators who are operating in a social context. In this context, the negotiators are primarily acting as *agents*—that is, as representatives of a larger group's negotiating issues and interests. As we have shown, agents face many different social pressures that are not usually experienced by negotiators in a simple dyad; these pressures come from their opponents (to give in and agree to the other's agenda), from their constituencies (to defend the constituencies' interests and issues zealously), and from audiences (to look "tough" and not look weak). We now move to another level of social complexity: three or more negotiators, each one representing either their own individual perspectives or acting as

**FIGURE 9.14**    A Within-Team Negotiation

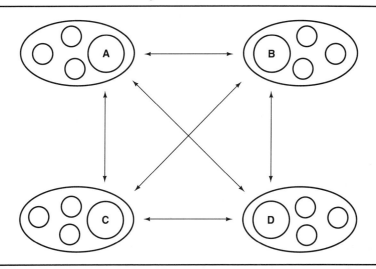

an agent for a constituency. We will describe this type of negotiations as *multiparty negotiations.* The general model for a multiparty negotiation is represented in Figure 9.14 (which is identical to Figure 9.4 except that each party has additional members). Although we have represented a multiparty negotiation in the diagram as a four-party deliberation (four agents representing four constituencies), multiparty dynamics will occur when there are *three or more* negotiators at the table. Most of the complexities that we describe next will increase linearly, if not exponentially, as more parties, constituencies, and audiences are added.

This section will be divided into several parts. In the first part, we will briefly comment on some of the different types and variations of multiparty negotiations. In the second part, we will note the factors that make multiparty negotiations more difficult to deal with than one-on-one negotiations. Finally, we will discuss strategies that can be used to manage multiparty negotiations. As we will consistently show, multiparty negotiations are very complex and highly susceptible to breakdown, and therefore they often require a commitment to manage the negotiation process to assure an effective multiparty agreement. The section draws heavily on the recent writings of Bazerman, Mannix, and Thompson (1988), Brett (1991), and Kramer (1991), who have done an excellent job of overviewing the problems and challenges of multiparty negotiations.

### Differences between Group Negotiations and Multiparty Negotiations

There are a number of important ways that multiparty negotiations differ from two-party deliberations. In every case, the differences are what make multiparty negotiations more complex, challenging, and difficult to manage.

**Number of Parties.**     The first difference is the most obvious one: multiparty negotiations put more negotiators at the table. Thus, negotiations simply become "bigger" because there are more agents in the negotiation. As we will see, this creates challenges for managing all the different perspectives and assuring that each party has adequate time to speak and be heard. Each of these parties may be acting as *principals*—that is, representing their own interests—or *agents*—representing the interests of at least one other party (their *constituency*). In addition, as we will point out, parties may have different social roles outside the negotiation (e.g., president, vice president, director, board chairman, etc.) that may lead to either equal or unequal levels of social hierarchy represented in the negotiation. If the parties are all equals (e.g., all vice presidents), the exchange within the negotiation should be more open than if one party has higher status or power than the others (e.g., one is president and the others are vice presidents, in which case we can expect the president to control and dominate the process more actively). We will have more to say about other roles that group members play later in this section.

**Informational and Computational Complexity.**     A second difference is that in multiparty negotiations, more issues, more perspectives on issues, and more total information (facts, figures, viewpoints, arguments, documentary support) are introduced. "One of the most fundamental consequences of increasing the number of parties is that the negotiation situation tends to become less lucid, more complex, and therefore, in some respects, more demanding. As size increases, there will be more values, interests, and perceptions to be integrated or accommodated" (Midgaard and Underal, 1977, p. 332, as quoted in Kramer, 1991). Keeping track of all this information, the perspective of each side, and the "parameters" into which a solution must fit becomes a major challenge for the negotiators.

**Social Complexity.**     A third difference is that as the number of parties increases, the social environment changes from a one-on-one dialogue to a small group. As a result, all the dynamics of small groups and group process begin to affect the way the negotiators operate. Social pressures develop to be cohesive, unified, and together; yet, the members are in conflict with each other and cannot be cohesive unless they can find an acceptable solution. Members compare themselves to each other, evaluate themselves against each other, and begin to try to use a variety of influence tactics to persuade each other toward their point of view (see Chapter 10 for a description of these tactics). Strong pressures for conformity develop as members pressure other members to adopt a common perspective or definition of the problem or to endorse a particular solution. In addition, the group can develop some of the more dysfunctional group dynamics that have been noted in other decision-making group processes. For example, if pressures to keep the group cohesive are strong, the group may attempt to avoid or minimize conflict by downplaying their differences or not working them through adequately to reach an effective solution. Janis' (1982, 1989) research on policy-making and decision-making groups has shown that these efforts to minimize and avoid conflict can frequently lead to group decision-making disasters. Fiascoes such as the U.S. invasion of the Bay of Pigs in Cuba during the Kennedy administration or NASA's decision to launch the Challenger space shuttle were caused by dynamics in the key decision-making groups in which group members were hesitant to create conflict and express their real reservations about going ahead with the project. This hesitancy led to an "illusion of consensus," in which all parties believed that they were the only dissenting member in a fairly strong emerging agreement about what actions to take. Afraid to express their dissent for fear of looking weak and foolish (note the face-saving dynamics), group members self-censored their reservations and concerns, thereby reinforcing the apparent surface consensus and leading to a decision with disastrous consequences.

**Procedural Complexity.**    A fourth way in which multiparty negotiations are more complex is that the process they have to follow is more complicated. In one-on-one negotiations, the parties simply "take turns" in either presenting their issues and perspectives, challenging the other's perspectives, or moving the negotiation along from its early stages to the later ones. When more parties are involved, the procedural rules become far less clear. Whose "turn" is it to do what? How do the parties coordinate where they are in the negotiations (e.g., opening statements, presentation of viewpoints, moving toward agreement)?

There are several results of this procedural complexity. First, negotiations will definitely take longer (Sebenius, 1983); more time must be allowed. Second, the greater the number of parties, the more complex and out of control the process can become—particularly if some parties choose to adopt a strategy of tough positional bargaining and dominate the process in an effort to railroad through their particular viewpoints (Bazerman, Mannix and Thompson, 1988). Third, as a result of these two elements, negotiators will probably have to explicitly devote discussion time to how they will manage the process to arrive at the type of solution or agreement they want. We will say more about this process management in following sections.

**Strategic Complexity.**    Finally, multiparty negotiations are more strategically complex. We hinted at this strategic complexity in the previous paragraph. In one-on-one negotiations, the negotiator need only attend to the behavior of the other negotiator; strategy is therefore driven by the objectives he wants to achieve, what the other negotiator is doing, and tactics to shape the other's behavior to reach the objective. The strategic and tactical options were discussed in Chapter 5.

Thus, in a group negotiation, complexity increases significantly. We must consider the strategies of *all* the other parties at the table and decide whether we are going to deal with each of them separately or as a group. The actual process of dealing with each of them usually evolves into a series of one-on-one negotiations, but conducted within the view of all of the other group members. These exchanges are thus subject to all the observability and audience dynamics that we described in the early part of this chapter. In this milieu, negotiators will be sensitive to being observed and will probably feel the need to be tough to show their firmness and resolve (both to the specific opponent and to other negotiators who are observing). As a result, the social milieu will lead negotiators to adopt more distributive strategies and tactics—even if they did not intend to do so—simply to show their toughness and resolve to others. The short-term result is that all negotiators in the group may become strongly positional unless specific actions are taken to manage the group beyond this competitive escalation and lock-in. A related dynamic is that once the parties have become strongly positional, negotiators will have to find satisfactory ways to explain modification of their positions—concession making or movement toward compromises and consensus—to their constituencies without the face-threatening dynamics we explained earlier.

There are two other ways in which multiparty negotiations increase in strategic complexity. First, negotiators who have some way to control the number of parties at the table (or even in the room) may begin to strategically manipulate this control to serve their objectives. The tactic used will be determined by the strategic interests to be served by adding other parties. Additional parties may be invited to add support or credence to the negotiator's position, to provide "independent" testimony or support to a point of view, or simply to present a show of force. For example, when communities are in dispute about whether to build a new shopping center or school, change a zoning law, or present a new tax package, it is not uncommon for the agents who will publicly speak to the issue to pack the audience with a large number of supporters who will occasionally show their enthusiasm and support (or opposition) for a position (recall our earlier discussions of enlisting audience support to pressure an opponent). Thus, a negotiator can strategically add parties to the negotiation to enhance her perceived power or to present some credible threat about consequences that will occur if the negotiator does not get her way.

A second strategic manipulation is to explicitly engage in coalition building as a way to marshal support. By coalitions, we mean here that parties explicitly (and sometimes implicitly) agree to support each other's positions in order to add collective weight to their combined view, and they use this coalition to either dominate the negotiation process or shape the desired settlement. These coalitions may emerge as a discussion proceeds (two or more parties begin to realize that they have compatible views and agree to help each other achieve their separate objectives as the group objective is attained), or they may be explicitly negotiated prior to negotiations or during negotiation recesses and breaks. Coalitions can exert greater strength in multiparty negotiations in a number of ways: by expressing solidarity with each other, by agreeing to help each other achieve their common or individual objectives, by dominating the air time, and by agreeing to support each other as particular solutions and negotiated agreements emerge. In fact, some authors (e.g., Murnighan, 1986) who have studied decision-making groups from a negotiation perspective have suggested that the emergence of consensus in these groups proceeds as a "snowballing coalition." In this process, as parties share information and then deliberate possible solutions, a few people emerge with a common perspective and then tacitly or explicitly agree to support each other's views. Other individuals then negotiate with the emerging coalition to incorporate their own views, and those who may be unwilling to negotiate or modify their views are eventually "rejected" and left out of the group decision. A number of coalition dynamics can be used in multiparty negotiations (see Murnighan, 1978, 1986, 1991 for reviews), and these dynamics definitely enter into multiparty negotiations as a way for individuals to enhance their power bases and shape the negotiation process and outcome toward their preferences.

**Summary.** In this section, we have examined five ways complexity increases as three or more parties simultaneously engage in negotiation. First, there are simply more parties involved in the negotiation, which increases the number of speakers, increases the demand for air time, and increases the number of different roles that parties may play. Second, more parties bring more issues and positions to the table, and thus more perspectives must be presented and discussed. Third, negotiations become socially more complex—social norms emerge that affect member participation, and there are stronger pressures for conformity and suppressing disagreement. Fourth, negotiations become procedurally more complex, and the parties may have to negotiate a new process that allows them to coordinate their actions more effectively. Finally, negotiations become more strategically complex, because the parties must monitor the moves and actions of several other parties in determining what each will do next. In addition, the possibility of subgroups coalescing together increases the likelihood that decisions will not be made by negotiated consensus, but by some subgroup that can dominate the discussion and decision-making processes.

## MANAGING MULTIPARTY NEGOTIATIONS

Given all the added complexity that occurs in a multiparty negotiation, what is the most effective way to cope with and manage this complexity? This section could actually be written from several different perspectives:

- What can a single agent do when she is simply one of the parties in a multiparty negotiation and wants to assure that her own issues and interests are clearly incorporated into the final agreement?
- What can a single agent can do when he wants to assure that the group reaches the highest quality and best possible final agreement?
- What can a single agent do when she is in charge of a multiparty negotiation process to assure that many of the strategic and procedural complexities are effectively managed?

We will incorporate all three perspectives into our recommendations, with a heavy emphasis on the second and third perspectives. Discussion of the key steps for managing multiparty negotiations follows.

## The Costs and Consequences of No-Agreement

Brett (1991) suggests that the first thing a negotiator needs to do is to understand the costs and consequences if the group fails to agree. This suggestion has been given repeatedly for negotiators in one-on-one negotiations. For example, suppose a group of vice presidents in a computer company is trying to decide which models of a new line of personal computers should be built next year and the quantities of each. First, what will happen if the parties fail to agree on what to do? Will someone else (i.e., the president) step in and decide for them? How will the president feel about the group if members can't agree? Second, are the costs for nonagreement the same for every negotiator? Usually this is *not* the case—agents have different costs for nonagreement. For example, if they cannot agree, the president may mandate the model line and quantities, which may have greater costs for engineering and manufacturing (which would have to change over) than for the marketing and sales departments (which would have to design a new marketing and ad campaign regardless of what was done). The group members with the better nonagreement alternatives are likely to have more "power" in the negotiation, because they care less about whether the group reaches a particular solution relative to no agreement. Finally, do group members perceive their agreement and nonagreement options accurately? There is much evidence that negotiators are prone to perceptual biases that lead them to believe that they are better than others, their options are better than others' options, they are more likely to achieve their outcomes than others, and they have more control over shaping an outcome than others (Taylor and Brown, 1988; Tyler and Hastie, 1991). In multiparty negotiations, these biases are likely to affect a negotiator by inflating his sense of power and ability to "win"—leading him to believe that the no-agreement alternative is much better than it really is. Reality checking with others will be important in keeping these biases under control.

## The Decision Rule

The second element in managing a multiparty negotiation is to understand how the other members of the group understand the decision rule—that is, how the parties are actually going to decide the final outcome. Is it possible that one member could push her entire preferences on the rest of the group, either because of that individual's formal status (e.g., the president) or her ability to be persistent and argue for her own views? Could a small group push their views on everyone else—for example, could a small coalition agree and dominate a split or fractured majority? Will the group vote? If so, will a majority rule? Or is the group aiming for true consensus in the form of a solution that incorporates everyone's views and represents all interests? These are not all the possible decision rules, but they do represent the most common ones. Understanding the decision rule allows individuals to shape the negotiation strategy they will pursue. If the current rule is unsatisfactory—for example, the president may dominate, everyone will acquiesce, but the quality of what the group agrees to may be inferior and create major problems for the company in the future—then it may be desirable (if possible) to challenge the rule early on and get the group to adopt a decision rule that permits greater opportunities to influence the final outcome and produce a higher quality solution.

### Strive for a "First Agreement"

If the objective is consensus or the best quality solution, do not strive to achieve it all at once. Rather, strive for a "first agreement" that can be revised, upgraded, and improved. As we have pointed out, the additional complexity of multiparty negotiations increases the complexity of the events, the likelihood of communication breakdown, and the likelihood that the parties will negotiate more positionally (either because of the competitive dynamics or the consequences of audience or constituency dynamics). Given these conditions, achieving true consensus among the parties becomes much more difficult, even if a true consensus solution exists. As a result, it is often better to set a more modest objective for these negotiations: to reach a preliminary agreement or a tentative consensus that can then be systematically improved through "renegotiation," using the first agreement as a plateau that can be modified, reshaped, and improved upon in a follow-up negotiation effort. As Brett (1991) notes:

> First agreements frequently reflect the views of the majority of group members, the position of a powerful group member, or an established norm (Nemeth, 1986, 1989). When the group's task is large, complex, political or under tight time constraints and group members have divergent interests, these approaches to group decision making may not be appropriate to the task.
>
> In contrast, dissent and minority views can foster the kinds of attention and thought processes that raise the quality of the decision, even when the dissenting views are wrong (Nemeth, 1986:28). Dissent stimulates consideration not just of the minority's views but of a host of alternatives.
>
> Majority and powerful individuals, however, are often intolerant of dissent. After all, why should they risk losing control over the group decision by providing an opportunity for dissent? A second agreement resolves this dilemma. It preserves the control of the powerful party—if no better agreement is forthcoming, the first agreement will stand. [It] also protects the interests of both the majority and the minority, letting them reveal information about their weaknesses and hidden agendas without fear that the group will use the information against them. At their best, second agreement deliberations encourage the sharing of minority points of view, the questioning of assumptions, the discussion of decision ramifications, the search for superior alternatives and the testing of consensus (1991, p. 294).

The drawback, of course, is that many group members may be satisfied with the first solution—either because it already incorporates their views or because the difficulty of achieving it may sap their enthusiasm to exert any more time and energy to improve it. This resistance may be overcome by taking a break after the first agreement is reached, encouraging the group to critique and evaluate the first agreement, and explicitly planning to come back with a commitment to try second-agreement negotiations (renegotiations). In addition, if the group has been through a great deal of divisive and unproductive conflict to reach the first agreement, then the renegotiations must specifically attend to changing and managing the conflict process. As Brett (1991) points out, effectively attending to this process may also allow a group to achieve a high-quality outcome in their first negotiation effort.

### Manage the Group Process and Outcome

The following approaches are likely to assure a high-quality group decision as the result of a multiparty negotiation:

**Appoint an Appropriate Chair.**    Appoint a chair who has little stake in the specific outcome but a strong stake in the process. If at all possible, multiparty negotiations will be greatly facilitated by the presence of a neutral chairperson who can implement many of the tactics we describe below. In this case, the chairperson functions as a third party who has no stake in any particular outcome but has a strong interest in assuring that the group works toward achieving the best possible outcome. If there is an individual who can serve as a chair within the organization, it will be useful to invite that individual to chair the meeting; if not, then it may be useful to invite a consultant or independent neutral to chair the meeting (see also Chapter 12). Note that if a chairperson is also advocating a particular position or preferred outcome, *it will be most difficult for that individual to act or be seen as "neutral,"* because the preferred solution he wants to obtain on the issues is likely to compromise his process activities.

**Assure a Diversity of Information and Perspectives.**    A second task is to assure that the group receives a wide variety of input from different perspectives on the task and different sources of information that may help in accomplishing the task. Because the nature of the information changes depending on the group's task—for example, designing and implementing a change, finding the best possible solution to a problem, or simply finding a solution that is "politically acceptable" to several constituencies—it is difficult to prescribe what information is critical and how to assure that the group is exposed to it. If there is a chair, the chair can assure that the group receives formal input from each group member, that various constituencies and stakeholders have an opportunity to make input (through written comments or opportunities for open testimony before the group), and that relevant reports, documents, or statistical analyses are circulated and discussed.

Ancona and Caldwell (1988) suggest four group member roles to help a group during this information management phase: scouts, ambassadors, coordinators, and guards. *Scouts* "patrol" the environment and bring in relevant external information that may be useful to the group—reports, statistics, findings, others' experience. *Ambassadors* represent a formal link to some important constituency— for example, senior management. They help to acquire resources the group needs to continue to operate and provide some limited information about the group's activities to constituencies (enough to give the constituency an idea about events and deliberations but not so much as to divulge private or confidential discussions). *Coordinators* provide a more formal link between the group members and the constituencies they represent—frequently, agents are themselves the coordinators of input from their constituency into the group deliberations. Finally, *guards* are specifically designated to keep some information inside the group and assure that there are no leaks or premature disclosures of key information or discussions. Clearly, agents can play more than one role and can rotate roles in the course of a multiparty negotiation.

**Assure Consideration of all the Available Information.**    Brett (1991) suggests two mechanisms that help to manage information in a multiparty negotiation: discussion norms and decision rules. Discussion norms reflect the way the group engages in sharing and evaluating the information introduced under the previous step. Decision rules reflect the manner in which the group will actually decide what it is going to do (as we discussed previously).

**Discussion Norms.**    Although it would be highly desirable to do so, groups seldom actually talk about what discussion norms and decision rules they are going to follow in advance of their deliberations. In most cases, this failure is probably due to a lack of understanding about how much deliberations can be improved by following norms and rules that will enhance discussion and decision quality. Several group norms can specifically undermine an effective discussion:

- Unwillingness to tolerate conflicting points of view and perspectives. There may be many reasons for this: one or more members dislike conflict, the group is afraid that conflict will be uncontrollable, or conflict is seen as destructive to group cohesiveness. But as we noted above, the absence of conflict can also lead to disastrous decisions.

- No means for diffusing an emotionally charged discussion, so anger, frustration, or resentment become mixed in with the issues and hamper the group's efforts. Although a great deal of negotiation literature suggests that parties should simply be calm and rational at all times, to do so is simply not human. The more the parties care about a particular issue and are invested in it, the more emotions will creep in. Vehicles must exist for the parties to vent emotions productively.

- Coming to a meeting unprepared. Usually, preparation for a meeting consists of either no preparation at all or simply preparing one's own position. Attention to the other's position or to assessing underlying interests and priorities requires more thorough preparation as well as effectively tuning in to what others want and are saying.

*Managing Discussion Norms.*    Several action strategies may be used for each of these three potentially destructive discussion norms. The parties must generate and exchange ideas in a manner that permits full exploration and allows everyone to have some input, yet avoids some of the destructive conflict and emotions that can creep in. Bazerman, Mannix, and Thompson (1988) suggest several group decision-making and brainstorming techniques that are frequently used to achieve this objective:

- **The Delphi Technique.** A moderator structures an initial questionnaire and sends it out to all parties, asking for input. Parties provide their input and send it back to the moderator. The moderator summarizes the input and sends it back to the parties. Parties then evaluate the report, make further input, and return it to the moderator. Over a number of rounds, through the questions and inquiries shaped by the moderator, the parties can exchange a great deal of information and share different perspectives. The advantages are that the group has little face-to-face interaction, does not get bogged down in personal hostility or inefficient communications, and can go through a number of iterations. The limitations are that the real priorities and preferences of group members may not get expressed, and the way the problem is defined and shaped early in the process will greatly determine the outcome achieved. The parties may miss opportunities to expand the pie of resources, redefine the problem in an important way, or truly evaluate important trade-offs. Thus, Delphi may tend to generate compromise settlements rather than truly creative, integrative solutions.

- **Brainstorming.** In brainstorming, the parties are instructed to define a problem and then to uncritically generate as many solutions as they can think of. Many of the suggestions may be unrealistic or impractical, but the purpose is to suggest as many solutions as possible and to be as creative as possible in suggesting them, and brainstorming accomplishes those goals. Brainstorming tends to generate a wider variety of solution options than might normally occur, particularly because it invites everyone to participate rather than just the small, vocal minority. By then inventing criteria to edit and modify the list, the parties can winnow down the solutions to two or three that appear feasible, effective, efficient, or easier to implement.

- **Nominal Group Technique.** This approach typically follows brainstorming. Once the brainstormed list of solution options is created, group members can rank, rate, or evaluate the alternatives in terms of the degree to which each alternative solves the problem. The leader collects, posts and records these ratings so all group members have an opportunity to formally evaluate the options and vote on the ones they consider to be most effective.

*Managing Decision Rules.*    The second element of the group decision process is to manage the decision rule—that is, the way the group will decide what to do. In decision-making groups, the dominant view is to assume that "majority rules" and, at some point, take a vote of all members, assuming that any settlement option that receives more than 50 percent of the votes will be the one adopted. Obviously, this is not the only option. As we indicated earlier, groups can make decisions by dictatorship (one person decides), oligarchy (a dominant minority coalition decides), simple majority (one more person than half the group), two-thirds majority, consensus (most of the group agrees, and those who dissent agree not to protest or raise objections) and true unanimity (everyone agrees). Understanding what decision rule a group will use before deliberations begin will also significantly affect the group process. For example, if a simple majority will make the decision in a five-person group, then only three people need to agree. Thus, any three people can get together and form a coalition—during the meeting or even prior to the meeting. In contrast, if the rule will be consensus and unanimity, then the group must meet and work hard enough to assure that all parties' interests are raised, discussed, and incorporated into the group decision. Whether a coalition-building strategy or a complete sharing of positions and interests and problem solving will be necessary requires significantly different approaches.

Table 9.1 presents a chart that summarizes the three different negotiating strategies and the related tactics, decision rules, goal orientations, and decision aids. Each of the three strategies—maximizing individual gain, entering into a

**TABLE 9.1**    Tactics, Decision Rules, Goal Orientations, and Decision Aids for Mutual, Coalition, and Individual Gain

| *Mutual* | *Coalition* | *Individual* |
|---|---|---|
| **Tactics** | | |
| 1. Share own and elicit others' interests | 1. Seek similar others and construct an alternative that meets your interests | 1. Open with a high, but not outrageously high, demand |
| 2. Consider many alternatives; be creative; look for ways to use available resources | 2. Recruit just enough members to control the group's decision | 2. Argue the merits of your alternative; do not reveal your interests |
| 3. Don't just compromise; make trade-offs | 3. Encourage interpersonal obligations among coalition members | 3. Appear unable or unwilling to concede |
| 4. Encourage positive relations | | 4. Encourage positive relations |
| | | 5. Use threats, time deadlines, and promises, if necessary |
| **Decision Rules** | | |
| Consensus | Oligarchy | Dictator |
| Unanimity | Majority | |
| **Goal Orientation** | | |
| Cooperative | Cooperative or individual | Individual |
| **Decision Aids** | | |
| Packaging | Packaging | |
| Search models | Search models | |

From J. Brett, "Negotiating Group Decisions," *Negotiation Journal,* July 1991, pp. 291–310.

coalition, or pursuing mutual gain (consensus or unanimity decision rules) is outlined, along with the tactics, decision rules, goal orientations, and decision aids that accompany each. As the chart reveals, any one set of elements can drive the others—decision rules or goals can drive the approaches, or vice versa. Thus, a negotiator would do well to understand the decision rules and goal orientations before selecting a strategy and set of tactics. Similarly, a negotiator would do well to understand the consequences of adopting an approach (strategy and tactics) that may not fit the related decision rules and goal orientations, because mismatches are likely to produce frustration, poor group process, and perhaps suboptimal outcomes.

**Structure and Use an Agenda.** Another way to control the flow and direction of negotiation is through an agenda. Either the chair or parties to the negotiation may introduce and coordinate the agenda. An agenda is an effective decision aid for the following reasons:

- It establishes the issues that will be discussed.
- Depending upon how the issues on the agenda are worded, it can also define how each issue is discussed.
- It defines the order in which issues are discussed.
- It can be used to introduce process issues (decision rules, discussion norms, member roles, discussion dynamics), as well as substantive issues, simply by including them.
- If time limits are assigned to agenda items, it will define the approximate time that is devoted to issues.

The advantage of an agenda is that it adds a high degree of structure, organization, and coordination to a discussion. For low-power or disadvantaged groups, agendas provide a vehicle for getting their issues heard and addressed, assuming that they can get them on the agenda. However, the manner in which an agenda is built (by collective consensus at the beginning of a meeting versus by one person prior to the meeting) and who builds it will have a great deal of impact on the flow of negotiation. Unless group members feel comfortable challenging the person who introduces a "preemptive" agenda, the agenda will go unquestioned, and hence the implicit discussion structure and format it suggests will prevail. Another disadvantage is that the construction of an agenda may artificially "partition" related issues so they are discussed separately rather than coupled or traded off to assure more integrative agreements. Once again, the parties using an agenda must be sensitive to the implicit structure it imposes, and they must be willing to challenge and reconfigure it if doing so will facilitate the emergence of a more integrative, consensus-based agreement.

**Manage the Process, not the Outcome.** Finally, chairpersons of multiparty negotiations must be sensitive to keeping tight control over the group process while not directly affecting the group's outcome. Particularly when the group wants to achieve a consensus or unanimous decision, the job of the chair is to be constantly attentive to group process. Some pointers for the chairperson follow (for another approach to this role, see the description of mediation in Chapter 12):

- Introduce yourself to the group and describe the nature of the role you will take. Be clear that you are there only to manage process and that the group will determine the outcome.

- Introduce the agenda or build one based on the group's issues, concerns, and priorities. If you introduce an agenda, make sure the group has an opportunity to discuss, modify, or challenge it before you begin.

- Introduce any necessary ground rules or let the parties suggest them. How long will the group meet? What is the expected output or final product? Will minutes be taken? Will the group take breaks? Where will negotiations take place? How and when can group members consult with their constituents?

- Review the decision rule—how will the group ultimately decide? Test for any concerns or questions.

- Assure that individual members have an opportunity to make opening statements or other ways of laying their individual concerns and issues on the table.

- "Gate keep"—make sure that people have a chance to speak and that the more vocal people do not dominate and the less vocal people become silent and drop out. Ask more vocal people to hold back and explicitly invite the more silent people to make comments and input.

- Listen for interests and commonalities. Encourage people to express interests, "mirror" them back if you hear them, and encourage people to identify not only what they want, but also why they want it. Listen for priorities and concerns.

- Introduce external information (studies, reports, statistics, fact finding, testimony from experts) that will shed further light on the issues and interests. Push for hard data to support assertions.

- Assure parties that once they are familiar with the issues, simultaneous discussion of several issues can take place. This will permit trade-offs among issues rather than forcing a compromise on each individual issue.

- Use a flip chart, blackboard, or overhead projector to write down issues and interests. Many negotiators have found that it is easier and produces less conflict to amass all information on a chart or blackboard "out there" rather than for group members to verbally confront each other face-to-face.

- Once issues and interests have been identified, explicitly set aside a time for inventing options. Use the brainstorming and other decision process techniques to generate options and evaluate them. Use the flip chart or blackboard as well.

- Summarize frequently, particularly when conversation becomes mired down, confused, or tense. State where you think the group is, what has been accomplished, what needs to be done. Paraphrasing and summarizing brings the group back to reality and back on task.

- Determine standards for what parties believe will be a fair or reasonable settlement. Determine the criteria that might be used to decide on whether a particular solution is fair, reasonable, and effective. Use the criteria to evaluate the solution options that are proposed.

- Move the group toward selecting one or more of the options. Use the process rules we mentioned earlier, as well as the wide variety of techniques for achieving an integrative agreement mentioned in Chapter 4. Listen for the emergence of the "snowballing coalition" among key members. Permit packaging, trade-offs, or modification of agreements. If the decision is particularly laden with conflict, pursue a first agreement, with the understanding that the group will take a break and come back to renegotiate the agreement at a later date.

- Shape a tentative agreement. Write it down. Work on language. Test to make sure all parties understand the agreement and its implications and consequences.

- Discuss whatever follow-up or "next steps" need to occur. Make sure individuals who have a role in this process understand what they need to do.

- Thank the group for their participation, their hard work, and their efforts. If it has been a particularly difficult discussion or required a large time commitment, a small group celebration and formal thank-yous may be in order.

- If desirable, conduct a post mortem. Have group members discuss the process and the outcome and evaluate what they might do better or differently next time. This will assure learning for both the group members and the chair.

### Summary on Multiparty Negotiations

Most negotiation theory has been developed under the assumption that negotiation is a bilateral process—that there are only two focal negotiators or teams of negotiators opposing each other. Yet many negotiations are multilateral deliberations—more than two negotiators are involved, each with his own interests and positions, and the group must arrive at a collective agreement as to a plan, decision, or course of action. In this section, we explored the dynamics of multiparty negotiations. We first discussed five ways that multiparty negotiations were significantly more complex than bilateral negotiations. We then described several ways that parties can manage this complexity more effectively to assure reaching a good outcome or decision. These included:

- Understanding the consequences of failing to agree due to the increased likelihood that the parties may not agree in complex multiparty negotiations.

- Understanding how the group will actually make a decision—what decision rules will be used?

- Understanding that if the decision rule is consensus or the best quality agreement, it may not be achievable in a single iteration.

- Understanding how the group process must be *managed* to assure the best quality decision. This management includes appointing a neutral chair, assuring that the group is exposed to a variety of information sources, managing the process to make sure that the group considers and discusses all available information thoroughly, and structuring the group's agenda with care.

If these procedures are followed carefully, the group is likely to feel considerably better about the process and make a far more effective decision than if these factors are left to chance.

## CHAPTER SUMMARY

In this chapter, we explored the social environment of negotiation. Much of negotiation theory is predicated on the assumption that two negotiating parties are dealing directly with each other, and no other parties are involved. Yet much of the professional negotiation conducted in business, law, communities, and international affairs occurs in an environment in which there a number of other parties are involved. These parties take on various roles—additional negotiators, constituencies, bystanders, audiences and third parties—who may or may not have a stake in the emerging outcome, care about the process, or wish to make comments and observations about events as they transpire. Depending on the number of additional parties and the roles they play, negotiations can be quickly transformed from a relatively quiet and calm dialogue to a three-ring circus. Understanding these dynamics is critical to learning how to better manage and control them to achieve your own negotiating objectives.

# CHAPTER 10

# Power in Negotiation

In this chapter, we will focus on the role of power in negotiation. *Power* has multiple, often overlapping, or even contradictory meanings. It is often used interchangeably with *leadership, influence,* and *persuasion.* And like these concepts, power is multidimensional and complex; thus, before going further, we need to clarify what we mean by the term and how we are going to use it.

## WHY IS POWER IMPORTANT TO NEGOTIATORS?

Most negotiators believe that power is important in negotiations. Yet when the question is pursued, it is often difficult to exactly answer why power should be important.

The primary reason that negotiators seek power is because power gives the negotiator some *advantage* or *leverage* over the other party. Negotiators usually use this advantage to secure a greater share of the outcomes or derive the preferred solution. Seeking power in negotiation usually arises from one of two perceptions:

- The negotiator believes she currently *has less* power than the other party. In this situation, she believes the other party already has some advantage that can and will be used in the negotiation process so she seeks power to balance or offset the power of the other.

- The negotiator believes he *needs more* power than the other party to increase the probability of controlling the process and securing a desired outcome. In this context, one negotiator believes that added power is necessary to gain or sustain an advantage in the upcoming negotiation.

The types of power negotiators seek in these two situations may well be the same, but the likely impact is different. The impact varies depending on whether the negotiator seeks power to create a power balance or imbalance relative to the other, and whether she does so for offensive or defensive strategic purposes. In the first situation, the negotiator who seeks power to equalize or *balance* the power of the two parties is doing so to increase the likelihood that each negotiator can achieve his goals. As an offensive strategy, balancing or equalization is likely to be more consistent with a desire to pursue an *integrative* strategy and achieve either a compromise or collaborative outcome. As a defensive strategy, a negotiator pursues equalization to assure that the other does not obtain an inappropriate or undeserved share of the outcome or settlement. Thus, as a general rule, power equalization is consistent with intentions either to pursue a collaborative outcome or to block the other from gaining a competitive advantage.

In contrast, the negotiator pursuing the power imbalance (enhancement) strategy seeks to gain more power than the other or even to increase the magnitude of a current power imbalance. As an offensive strategy, the negotiator may pursue this option to assure greater control over the outcome or division of resources— in short, to competitively "win" the negotiation. As a defensive strategy, the negotiator pursues this effort because of fears that the other is also trying to increase power—to beat the opponent at his own game. In both cases, negotiators pursue this type of power enhancement for distributive, win-lose purposes—to enhance the likelihood of achieving a preferred solution or to gain a disproportionate share of the negotiated outcomes.

As we discuss in this chapter, there are many forms of power in a negotiation context and hence many ways that negotiators can gain and use power. Moreover, as we will point out, having the potential for power does not necessarily mean that it is used, or used wisely. In general, negotiators who don't care about their power or who have matched power—equally high or low—will find that their deliberations proceed with greater ease and simplicity toward a mutually satisfying and acceptable outcome. In contrast, negotiators who *do* care about their power and who are seeking to match or exceed the other party's power, are probably seeking a solution in which they either do not lose the negotiation (a defensive posture) or that leads them to win the negotiation (an offensive posture).

Two brief comments are necessary before we begin our discussion of power. First, like some of the other areas covered in this text (e.g., communication and persuasion), there is remarkably little empirical research specifically on power tactics and power use in negotiation. We will try to cite that research where we can. However, much of the work discussed in this chapter has been drawn from broader studies on the use of power and influence in organizations, and we will apply that work to negotiation situations. Second, in order to provide some context for examples about power use and power tactics, we shall continue with the Lucasville prison negotiation example described in Chapter 9.

## A DEFINITION OF POWER

In a broad sense, people have power when they have "the ability to bring about outcomes they desire," or ". . . the ability to get things done the way one wants them to be done" (Salancik and Pfeffer, 1977). However, the same people could also be described as having influence, being persuasive, or being leaders. We need some way of separating power from other influence processes that are used in interpersonal relations.

One way of defining power builds on the observation that with power one party can get another to do what the latter normally would not do (Dahl, 1957; Kotter, 1979). This is often interpreted to mean that the other person is doing something she does not want to do; hence, that some sort of force is being used. When we mention force, it is common to think of *physical* force such as killing, beating, restraint in handcuffs, holding people in custody such as jail—the sort of things we associate with police power or military power.

We contend that this definition of power is not a particularly useful form of power to consider in negotiations. It focuses more on power as an absolute and on its more coercive aspects. We prefer what may be called a "relational" definition of power, as defined by Deutsch (1973):

> an actor . . . has power in a given situation (situational power) to the degree that he can satisfy the purposes (goals, desires, or wants) that he is attempting to fulfill in that situation. Power is a relational concept; it does not reside in the individual but rather in the relationship of the person to his environment. Thus, the power of an actor in a given situation is determined by the characteristics of the situation as well as by his own characteristics. (pp. 84–85)

In his discussion of power, Deutsch suggests that there has been a tendency to view power as an attribute of the actor only. This view would ignore that power is derived from the situation or context in which an actor operates. Rather, as Deutsch suggests, when considering the statement "A is more powerful than B," a discussion of power should view it from three distinct perspectives (which are often interrelated):

> *environmental power,* or "A is more usually more able to favorably influence his overall environment and/or to overcome its resistance than is B"; *relationship power,* or "A is usually more able to influence B favorably and/or to overcome B's resistance than B is able to do with A"; and *personal power,* or "A is usually more able to satisfy his desires than is B." (p. 85, italics in original)

Let us consider several examples of power that fit these views:

1. In recent years, union officials have been negotiating new labor contracts that *reduce* the wage package—giving back hard-fought concessions to management—hardly something union officials want to do. They have usually done so because the company officials have stated that unless wages go down, the firm will lay off thousands of employees, move its operations to another country, drop this line of business, or take some similar action. The union officials can be seen as making a rational or calculated decision to do something they ordinarily would not do (Dahl's definition), but in this case management is simply taking advantage of the shift in power within the economic environment as demand for product drops, costs rise, and cheap labor supplies become available in other areas.

2. In today's organizations, many individuals promoted from the ranks into managerial positions find they have to direct and control people who were (or still are) peers and, perhaps, close friends. Even though they may not want to direct and control these people because of a fear of losing a friendship, their role as a manager requires that they must exercise some control. In addition, given the many changes in the organizational structure of manufactur-

ing plants, service operations, or sales divisions, heads of projects, teams, and task forces find that they must effectively influence other people without the formal authority to give direct orders. As a result, managers are finding that they must be able to use "influence without authority" to get their jobs done and meet subunit goals. In short, managers must learn to use relationship and personal power because environmental power, derived from the formal organizational chart and lines of authority, is no longer available.

3. Not only must managers sometimes learn how to influence others successfully without the authority that comes from a formal title and office, but they also must successfully influence their bosses. An individual who approaches her superior with a list of grievances about the job and "what can't be done without the boss's help and intervention," will probably receive little or no attention. However, if the subordinate is able to use influence successfully to get the boss's help and assistance, she may earn the boss's respect *and* accomplish her goals as well. Once again, the need for strong relationship and personal power skills is demonstrated.

In these three illustrations, we confront the same problem: the individual who is responding to power—the target person—sees options and alternatives that are different from those that existed in the past. The union leader, who in the past found the strike to be the most effective tool of power, agrees to reduced wages because the alternative option, massive layoffs of union members or a totally closed plant, is even less desirable. The newly appointed supervisor recognizes that, as part of the new job, she must find successful ways to influence others. The boss, who now talks with a worker she may have ignored earlier, is doing so because that individual has found a way to attract the boss's attention and gain her cooperation.

Frederick Douglass, born a slave in Maryland, describes in his autobiography (1856) how he was regularly beaten by a slave breaker to force him to be more obedient. After one particularly severe beating, he decided that he would never be beaten again, even though he might be killed. The next time the slave breaker attempted to beat him, he fought back, not defeating the other man but also not letting him win. The draw established the point: Douglass was not beaten again. What changed was the way Douglass chose to respond to the situation—he redefined his options and the consequences he was willing to endure. Earlier, as would be true for most of us threatened with severe physical abuse, Douglass saw the situation as one of submitting or being killed—and he chose submission. Douglass changed this perspective and included being killed as an option—in fact, as an acceptable option—and that removed the power of the slave breaker. Douglass chose relational power rather than the submission he was "supposed" to show as a slave.

In this chapter, we organize our discussion of negotiator power into two stages: *power bases* or sources and *influence strategies.* We will refer to *power bases* as the repertoire of "tools" available to influence the environment, the other party, or our own desires. We will talk about a number of different bases of power, or types of tools, that are available to a negotiator. *The tools themselves are not power—power is the effective use of those tools in the right way in the appropriate situations.* In this chapter, as we consider the different bases of power, we shall essentially be looking at the way each base can be used to gain some advantage or leverage over the environment or the other party.

After discussing the dominant bases of power, we shall then turn to a discussion of *patterns (or strategies) of influence.* Influence strategies are the manner in which the tools are put into use, or enacted through a strategy, to accomplish a particular influence objective. We will describe several major influence strategies, each of which uses one or more of the power bases in a different way. In any given negotiation or influence situation, one or more influence strategies may be possible, depending upon the power sources available and the user's preference for using some influence strategies and not others.

It would be nice to be able to write a chapter on "power in negotiation" in which we could delineate all of the power sources available to negotiators, the major configurations of power that are put together as influence strategies, and a clean list of the times and conditions when each should be used. Unfortunately, such a task is not just daunting, it is impossible—and for several reasons. First, although negotiation researchers have learned a great deal about power and its use in recent years, much about power remains elusive. A number of ways that people exert power continue to defy clean, logical explanation. Second, the effective use of power requires a sensitive and deft touch—and thus some people use power much more successfully than others. In the hands of one user, the tools of power can create a magic kingdom, whereas in the hands of another, they may build a monster or a malfunctioning contraption. Third, not only do the key actors and targets change from situation to situation, but the context in which the tools of power operate changes as well. As a result, the best we can do is to point out the key sources of power and the major strategies of influence. Efforts to be more precise, such as how and when to use these tools, or in what combination, are beyond the scope of this book, although we shall mention several recent studies of influence tactics that have begun to address these questions (e.g., Schreisheim and Hinkin, 1990; Yukl and Tracey, 1992).

Before we begin, it is important to make three general statements about power:

1. Power is in the eye of the beholder and the recipient. What is important are the agent's *perceived* tools of power. For power to be effective, it need not necessarily be fully and completely possessed; rather, you must convey the appearance that you have power and *can* use it if you wish. As we will show, the effectiveness of power in many instances comes *not* from actually using it, but by making others (and yourself) *believe* you have it to use it if you desire. Power, therefore, is somewhat self-fulfilling. If you—and others—think you have it, you have it. If you—and others—don't think you have it, you don't have it. Perceived power is what creates leverage, and many power holders go out of their way to create the image of power as the critical element

of effective influence (see Sun Tsu, 1983, for an excellent exposition of this point).

2. Second, the effectiveness of power and influence is ultimately defined by the behavior of the target person. Does that individual comply, do what we want, or behave the way we want them to behave? Although we will spend most of this chapter defining the tools of power and influence strategies from the agent's (sender's) point of view, in fact, *what matters most is which tools and strategies actually work on the target (receiver).* Thus, when designing an influence strategy, the agent must pay attention to what he thinks will work with a particular target, while being sensitive to feedback that would suggest that alternative strategies would have more impact.

3. Finally, there is some indication that power is, in fact, corrupting—in Lord Acton's words, "Power tends to corrupt; absolute power corrupts absolutely." This may occur for several reasons. First, as just suggested, much of power is based on perception—creating the perception, or even the illusion, that you have it and can use it. In creating these illusions, it is not uncommon for actors to deceive themselves as much as they deceive the target. Second, power can be intoxicating. Although the most effective use of power is often to have it but not use it (as we will discuss later), the point is frequently lost on the naive and unskilled. Those who do not know how to use power effectively but gain a great deal of it through rapid career success and promotion, frequently overuse and abuse it. Power brings a large resource base, privileged information, and the ability to control the fates of many others. In the hands of the unskilled, power can be dramatically abused and destructive. (Lewis, 1990; Stewart, 1992.)

We now turn to a delineation of the major sources of power available to negotiators and the major commonly used influence strategies. Although a great deal has been written on power, we have drawn extensively from some of the best major sources on this subject: Boulding, 1989; Cialdini, 1993; Cohen and Bradford, 1990; French and Raven, 1959; Kipnis, 1976; Kipnis, Schmidt and Wilkinson, 1980; Kotter, 1977, 1985; Mintzberg, 1983; Pfeffer, 1992; Steward, 1989; and Zucker, 1991.

## SOURCES OF POWER

Understanding the different ways that power can be exercised is best accomplished by looking at the various sources (or bases) of power and the ways that they are typically exercised. In their seminal work on power, French and Raven (1959) identified five major bases of power: reward power, coercive power, legitimate power, expert power, and referent power. Although many contemporary discussions of power are still grounded in this typology, we will reclassify this list somewhat and add several new sources of power. A summary list of our major sources of power is shown in Table 10.1.

**TABLE 10.1**   Sources of Power

---

Information and expert power

Resource control

Legitimate power
   Authority
   Reputation
   Performance

Location in the structure
   Centrality
   Criticality, relevance
   Flexibility
   Visibility

Personal power
   Attractiveness and friendliness
   Integrity
   Patience and tenacity
   Emotion

---

## Information and Expert Power

Within the context of negotiation, information power is perhaps the most common source of power. Information power is derived from the ability to assemble information that can then be used to support the position we want to take, arguments we want to make, or outcomes we desire. This information may also be used as a tool to challenge the other's position or desired outcomes and hence undermine the effectiveness of his negotiating arguments.

Information power refers to the accumulation and presentation of information that will change the other's point of view or position on an issue. Information power and its sources is the basis of many of the "message" or "content" strategies that we described earlier in Chapter 8, on the persuasion process. Informational power (and the subsequent persuasiveness of information) may vary according to several factors. We list these below, using examples from the Lucasville negotiation described in the previous chapter.

1. The credibility and trustworthiness of the sender (source) of the message. As we have mentioned before in Chapter 8, the higher the credibility and trustworthiness of a source, the more powerful the information conveyed. At Lucasville, for example, the prisoners were aware that their own credibility would be highly suspect. As a result, they brought one of the guards to the negotiating session in the prison yard and later retained attorney Niki Schwartz to negotiate on their behalf. Similarly, Corrections Department spokesperson Tessa Unwin was quickly removed from her responsibilities

after her careless comments that may have contributed to the death of guard Robert Vallandingham.

2. The content of the message—for example, the type of information included. The more control we have over the content of the message and the more powerful the information contained within it, the more power it will have. At Lucasville, for example, key information included the condition of the hostages, the exact demands that the prisoners would make for the release of those hostages, and the State's response to those demands.

3. The structure of the message, particularly in the way that the information is presented. Again, refer back to Chapter 8 for a more complete discussion of these principles. At Lucasville, the prisoners eventually formulated their negotiating points as a formal, organized list of demands that was presented to the warden and other state officials. These authorities also made requests—for release of the hostages and surrender of the captured cell blocks—that were structured to be clear and unambiguous.

4. Scarcity of information can often be a source of power. Cialdini (1993) points out that banning certain types of information, as when information is censored, actually increases the demand for that information. Thus, we find a piece of information more persuasive if we do not think we can find it elsewhere. At Lucasville, in the hours immediately after the riot information was scarce, and all parties—state officials, the media, and the like—actively pursued any lead they could find to determine who was in charge and what the prisoners wanted.

5. The style and techniques used in presenting and delivering the message. At Lucasville, the prisoners insisted on having the media present for negotiations. At the first televised negotiations in the prison yard, the visual image of bringing in the guard with a blindfold over his head was a riveting and dramatic image. Prison officials similarly presented their position back to the prisoners by playing a tape recording over the public address system, using a ringing telephone to get their attention. Finally, the surrender shown on live television and recorded on videotape contained many images that got the message across most clearly.

Within the context of negotiation, information is the key source of power, at the heart of the process. In even the simplest negotiation, the parties take a position and then present facts, arguments, viewpoints, and data to support that position. I want to sell a used motorcycle for $1,000; you say it is only worth $500. I proceed to tell you how much I paid for it, point out what good condition it is in, what the attractive features are, and why it is worth $1,000. You point out the fact that it is five years old, emphasize the paint chips and rust spots, and comment that the tires are worn and really should be replaced. You also tell me that you can't afford to spend $1,000. After 20 minutes of discussion about the motorcycle, we have exchanged extensive information about its original cost and age, its depreciation and current condition, the benefits and drawbacks of this particular style and model, your financial situation and my need to raise cash, and we have settled on a price of $800, including a "loan" of $200 that I have given you to pay me back over six months.

The exchange of information in negotiation is also at the heart of the concession-making process. Through the information presented by each side, a common definition of the situation emerges. By the amount and kind of information shared and the way the negotiators about it, both parties derive a common (and hopefully realistic) picture of the current condition of the motorcycle, its market worth, and the preferences of each side with regard to buying and selling that motorcycle. (We have also discussed the powerful impact played by different strategies of information shaping, or "framing," earlier in Chapters 4 and 6.) This information need not be 100 percent true—bluffs, exaggerations, omissions, and distortions of information may occur. I may tell you I paid $1,800 for the bike when I only paid $1,500; I may not tell you that the clutch needs to be replaced. You may not tell me that you can actually pay $1,000 but that you simply don't want to spend that much. (We return to these issues in Chapter 13, when we discuss how lying and deception are used as power tactics.) Nevertheless, the information exchanged and the common definition of the situation that emerges, serve as a rationale for each side to modify their positions and, eventually, to accept a settlement. Both of us arrive at a mutually satisfactory price—we derive our feelings of satisfaction in part from the price itself and in part because we feel the price is justified because of our revised view of the cycle and of the other party in the negotiation. Thus, information exchange in negotiation serves as the primary medium for justifying our own and the other's position, and eventually for making concessions. We can see this same process occur at Lucasville, as the prisoners attempt to dictate the terms and conditions under which they will release the hostages and the captured cellblock, while state officials learned to accept that reality and decided what concessions they could make to regain control of the prison.

Expert power is a special form of informational power. The power that comes from information can be used by anyone who has assembled the facts and figures to support his arguments, but expert power is accorded to those who are seen as having achieved some level of command and mastery of that information. These individuals are often accorded respect and deference based on their achievements, and they are given a high level of credibility because of their acknowledged expertise. Because these people are recognized as experts, people give their arguments—either for or against a particular negotiation position—more credibility. Niki Schwartz served this role for the prisoners and experts in hostage negotiation, such as Frank Navarre of the Dayton Police Department, and other experts in riot control from the Department of Corrections and the National Guard served the same function.

You can establish yourself as an expert in a number of ways. One way is to show off your credentials: a university degree, a license, or an accomplishment that clearly displays your mastery of a body of information. Hence, physicians hang their degrees and licenses on their walls, accountants use the letters "C.P.A."

after their names and always appear in conservative business dress, and professionals of all types strive for the credentials and certification that will acknowledge them as "experts." Each of these is a way people can show that an outside party has tested and examined their qualifications and determined that they deserve certification as "experts."

A second approach to becoming an expert is to act like an expert; by showing the other party that you have a level of knowledge worthy of being deemed an expert, rattling off a mass of facts and figures, referencing relevant but obscure bits of critical information, or discussing the pros and cons of a strategy or argument at great length. Sometimes this same desired effect can be achieved by introducing a key piece of information at an opportune moment or even by asking a penetrating question that could only be asked if you knew a lot about the topic.

A third approach to being seen as an expert is by providing evidence that other people have acknowledged our expertise. We commonly provide references from high-prestige sources for previous work or experience. We "name drop" others whose expertise is well known and established. We note our publications—an article or a book on a topic suggests expert knowledge. Similarly, being able to show that others have referenced or quoted us in an article or being officially sought out or employed for our information or insight suggests expert status.

These findings suggest a number of techniques a negotiator can use to create the image of expertise. If credentials can be hung on the wall, why not have the negotiation in your office so they can see the evidence of your expertise? If you have had an article published recently or have been quoted by someone else, why not send a copy to the other party or use it as you make your negotiating arguments? This is not the time for modesty; this is the time to establish that you know what you are talking about, and the fact that others have acknowledged that expertise can be used to determine your credibility in this dialogue. You can make references or cite facts to convey the image of expert knowledge at many points during a negotiation. In fact, a common negotiation technique is "the snow job," in which the negotiator inundates the other party with so much information that the other party cannot process it all—he thus may be more likely to accept the expert's simplification of this information in a way that promotes the expert's preferred strategy or solution. The intent of providing all this information is to establish that you are an expert and better able than others to determine which options are possible and which are not. (At Lucasville, experts established themselves when the prisoners brought in attorney Schwartz and quickly demonstrated his expertise in dealing with the situation. Frank Navarre played a similar role for the State.) In a real estate negotiation, if the seller is able to establish that she is an expert in the zoning regulations of a particular area, she can more readily show the other party that some options are open (or closed as the case may be) to make the proposal more acceptable. In addition to mentioning the zoning regulation, the negotiator could reinforce her position by citing the particular section of the ordinance that validates her point or by showing a copy of the zoning ordinance itself.

Expert power is used for more than convincing the other party of the soundness of your statements in negotiation. People are less likely to argue with perceived experts in their areas of expertise. To really take on the challenge, the nonexpert would probably have to consult with another expert, which is costly, time consuming, and somewhat risky. Hence, when facing an expert in his area of expertise, the nonexpert often takes a less-expansive, less-aggressive posture and hence gives the expert a considerable advantage.

## Control over Resources

The second major source of power in negotiation is control over resources. People who control resources are powerful because they can allocate and dispense those resources to people who will do what they want and withhold (or take away) those resources from people who don't do what they want. Next to information, resource control is the second most important source of power in negotiation.

"Resources" can be of all types. As we have already discussed, the power that is most important is that which matters most to the target of the negotiation or influence effort. The same is true for resources as a power source. In an organizational context, some of the most important resources include these:

1. Money, in its various forms: cash, salary dollars, budget allocations, grants, bonus money, expense accounts, and so on.
2. Supplies: raw materials, parts and components, pieces and parts. (At Lucasville, the prisoners had hoarded food and water in preparation for a riot, and they stole more after the riot began. Prison officials cut off all food, water, and electricity to get the prisoners to negotiate.)
3. Time: if the other party is pressured to produce a quick settlement or meet a deadline, control over time can put extreme pressure on the other party.
4. Equipment: machines, tools, technology, hardware and software, vehicles, conveyor belts, and the like (at Lucasville, the prisoners seized an entire cell block and all the equipment in it).
5. Critical services: repair, maintenance, upkeep, installation and delivery, technical support, transportation, and so on.
6. Human capital: manpower, labor, work teams, staff (at Lucasville, the prisoners seized hostages as a way to get the State to negotiate prison reforms).
7. Interpersonal support—in short, the "resources" of verbal praise and encouragement for good performance or criticism for bad performance. This is an interesting resource, because it is really available to almost anyone without requiring significant efforts to create a resource base, and it is quite powerful on its own.

Pfeffer and Salancik (1974), among others, stress that the ability to control and dispense resources is one of the major power sources in organizations. Resource power comes not only from being able to control and dispense them, but also from the ability to create a resource base in an environment where resources appear to be scarce. (At Lucasville, this was done through prisoner-hostages and tight control over food, water, and weapons.) Pfeffer, in a major treatise on power (1992), effectively illustrates how a number of powerful political and corporate figures built powerful empires founded on resource control. Lyndon Johnson built a major power base during his early years in Congress by taking over the "Little Congress" (a speaker's bureau for clerical personnel and aides to Congressmen) and leveraging it into a major power base. Similarly, Robert Moses, beginning as Parks Commissioner of New York City, built a power empire that resulted in the successful construction of 12 bridges, 35 highways, 751 playgrounds, 13 golf courses, 18 swimming pools, and more than 2 million acres of park land in the New York metropolitan area, making him one of the major power brokers of New York in the 1960s, 1970s, and 1980s. Both Johnson and Moses

1. Chose a political backwater (an area or niche that was neglected and uncontested, but where the resources were plentiful and could be developed into something desirable) when they entered their organizations, and they used this backwater to build a power base. In marketing terms, they followed a key maxim for starting a new business: "Go where the competition ain't."

2. Obtained a position of influence in an organization—even a small organization can be used as a platform from which to operate (at Lucasville, note the power rise of some of the local groups that supported the prisoners, such as the KKK or Justice Watch, previously unknown and unrecognized in the region).

3. Figured out how to use that organization to obtain and gain control over desired resources—money, budgets, raw materials, or even information (at Lucasville, this occurred through gaining control over hostages and L Block).

4. Rationed the access of others to those resources by dispensing resources in exchange for reciprocal favors, other resources, and obedience and compliance to gain leverage and expand their power base (prisoners used the hostages and the L Block turf to negotiate for better prison conditions and prisoner freedoms, and prison officials used food, water, sanitation, and electricity to gain similar leverage).

Thus, to use resources as a basis for negotiation power, we must develop or maintain control over some scarce commodity that others—particularly the other party—wants. It may be physical space, such as desired offices, jobs, budget authorizations, or raw materials. Successful control over resources must also assure that the other party cannot get those same resources from someone else— in order to get what she wants, she must deal with you directly. Finally, in dispensing those resources, the power holder must be willing to give them out to others depending upon the other's compliance or cooperation with the power holder's request. Increasing scarcity of resources of all kinds has led to the New Golden Rule of Organizations: "Whoever has the gold makes the rules."

As we indicated earlier, almost any agent has is the power of interpersonal support—praise and encouragement for doing a job well or criticism for not doing a job well—available. Research in many disciplines of psychology has consistently shown that verbal encouragement, approval, and praise are frequently acceptable substitutes for tangible resources and rewards. In addition, given the choice between using praise for good performance and punishment or criticism for bad performance, research also shows that praise is far more effective than criticism (Luthans and Kreitner, 1985). Yet managers frequently do not follow this commonsense advice: they use praise and encouragement far less than they need to and criticism and punishment far more than they need to. They are also far more likely to try to influence behavior with more tangible resource tools (money, budgets, promotions, etc.) than with simple praise and affirmation for a job well done.

### Legitimate Power

Legitimate power is derived from occupying a particular job title, office, or position in an organizational hierarchy. There are times when people respond to directions from another, even directions they do not like, because they feel it is proper (legitimate) for the other to tell them and proper (obligatory) for them to obey, even though they do not like what they are being directed to do. This type of power is legitimate power.

Legitimate power is derived in several ways. Legitimate power is at the foundation of most of our social structure. When individuals and groups organize themselves into any form of social system—a small business, a combat unit, a union, a political action committee, a sports team, a school, and so on—they almost immediately create an organizational structure and hierarchy. They elect or appoint "leader" and may introduce formal rules about how decisions will be made, work divided, responsibilities allocated, and conflicts managed. Without this social ordering, chaos prevails. Group coordination takes forever. Either the group can take no coordinated action at all, or everyone is required to participate in every decision and action, a process that is extremely tedious, inefficient, and time consuming. The need for a social structure to enhance efficiency and effectiveness, then, creates the basis for legitimate power. People are willing to give up their own individual power to do any job or participate in every decision by vesting rights, responsibilities and power in an officer, title, or role who can act on their behalf (a president, chairperson, or spokesperson). By their very acceptance of the same social system that gives the power holder a power base, they are then *obligated* to obey directives and follow influence. At Lucasville, when the prisoners took the guards hostage, the guards lost their legitimate power and were at the mercy of those who directed the riot in the prison.

There are several ways to acquire legitimate power. First, it may be acquired by birth. Elizabeth II, as Queen of England, has the title of Queen and all of the stature this title commands in the structure of the British constitution and the history of the Empire. She also commands a great deal of the personal wealth of the monarchy; yet she has little actual power in terms of her ability to run the day-to-day affairs of Britain (which has created a great deal of controversy in recent years). Second, legitimate power may be acquired by election; the President of the United States has substantial legitimate power, derived from the legal structure of the American government. (At Lucasville, Governor George Voinovich had legitimate power by virtue of his election to the position of governor of the State of Ohio.) Finally, legitimate power is derived simply by being appointed or promoted to some office, job, rank, or organizational position. Thus, by holding the office or title of director or general manager (or warden, such as Arthur Tate at Lucasville), someone is therefore entitled to all the rights, responsibilities, and privileges that go with that position. In all these cases, power comes from a position in an organizational structure or hierarchy. Using that power means that the individual makes a request or demand, presumably because it is appropriate and necessary for a person occupying that position to make such a request or demand, and others comply.

Some legitimate authority also comes because an individual occupies a position for which we simply show respect. Such respect is derived because the organization or position performs some intrinsic social good or reinforces important social values. In many societies, the young listen to and obey elderly people. People listen to those who occupy highly respected public offices and certain occupations, like the clergy. They do what these people say because "it is proper to do so." Although these same power holders also have some reward and coercive power, they seldom, if ever, use it. Clergy, college presidents, and many others have precious little they can actually give as rewards or use as coercive punishments; yet they have considerable legitimate power (see Cialdini, 1993, on the "illusions of authority").

It should be clear from this discussion that the effectiveness of legitimacy and formal authority is derived from the willingness of followers to acknowledge the legitimacy of the organizational structure and system of rules and regulations that empowers its leaders (Barnard, 1938). In short, legitimate power cannot function without obedience, the "consent of the governed." If enough British citizens question the legitimacy of the Queen and her authority—even given the hundreds of years of tradition and law on which it is founded—her continued rule will be in serious jeopardy. If enough women challenge the Pope's rulings on abortion, birth control, or other social policy, the Pope's authority will erode. If the President's cabinet and key advisors are unwilling to act on and dispatch his orders, then his impact and effectiveness is nullified. Formal authority is only effective as a source of power to the degree that organizational members acknowledge the legitimacy of the authority and are willing to obey it. When enough people begin to distrust the authority or discredit its legitimacy, they will begin to defy it and undermine its potential as a power source.

Because legitimate power can be undermined if followers choose to no longer recognize its legitimacy, it is not uncommon for those who hold legitimate power to accumulate other power sources (such as resource control and information) to buttress their power base. Frequently, resource and information control accompanies a title, position, or job definition. With the title of vice president of a company also comes a great deal of privileged information and control over a large amount of financial and human resources—when that Vice President needs to implement an organizational decision, she may call on her title, information, and control over resources to get others to comply. Respect for legitimate power is often derived from manipulating these other sources of power. Military officers have known this for a long time. All military establishments still drill and march their personnel, even though military units never march into battle as they once did. Ages ago, when armies had to move large numbers of people with speed and precision during combat, drill practice had an obvious, useful place. From ancient Greece to the early 1800s, wars were fought by moving densely packed groups of soldiers around a battlefield. This military strategy began to change with the advent of cannons, and it disappeared when machine guns were introduced; but we still find that all armies spend vast amounts of time in close-order drill. There are several reasons for this: drill is an easy place to give instructions, teach discipline and obedience, closely monitor large numbers of people, and quickly punish or reward performance. It gets large numbers of people used to accepting, without question, orders from a specific person or class of persons. Those who follow orders are rewarded, whereas those who do not are quickly and publicly punished. After a while, the need to use reward and punishment drops off, and it seems natural or "legitimate" for the soldier to accept orders from an officer without asking why or inquiring about the consequences. It is exactly this compliance that the officer wants in battle conditions, when orders must be followed immediately rather than questioned and challenged.

In the context of extending legitimate authority, it is important to also discuss two other derivative sources of power: *reputation* and *performance.* The two are related to each other and to the success of legitimacy, and they also buttress formal authority just as information and resource control do. Whereas information and resources buttress the actual, tangible assets that a power holder has to work with, however, reputation and performance buttress the perception of the power holder's impact.

Reputation is the image one develops in an organization, the way people come to talk about and describe a particular individual. Reputation is shaped by what one has done before—performance. If you want to build a reputation for being powerful, then you have to use power, get things done, have an impact on others, and make sure that such events are made public so that others become aware of them. Niki Schwartz was quickly legitimized by the prisoners at Lucasville because of his prior reputation for defending prisoner rights. On the State side, the warden already had authority and reputation, and Frank Navarre gained it by virtue of his previous experience and good reputation for negotiating in similar circumstances. In short, with the acquisition of legitimacy comes resource control and information control. These three sources of power may be used to do a job well, get performance to occur, or have impact—in short, job performance. To the degree that you make this performance sufficiently public and visible, others will see it and comment on it. In this way, reputations are derived and employed as a power source—so much so that in any given incident, the power holder may not have to call on information, resources, or authority at all to gain compliance but may simply invoke a reputation for using any or all of those tools if necessary (see Tsui, 1983, 1984 for a discussion of reputational effectiveness).

For example, the reputations of Ghandi and Martin Luther King were derived from incidents in which they were willing to undergo great personal sacrifice for their causes early in their careers, a reputation that then served them well as they sought to mobilize larger groups of people to bring about broad societal change.

It is also worth noting some other facts about reputation and performance. Reputations go with the individual as well as the job title, and they need not be developed in the current job to be a source of power. Thus, they can also be a source of *personal* power (to be discussed shortly). If you have earned the reputation of being a tough negotiator from a previous assignment, the reputation may be all you need to exercise great power in this negotiation.

Reputations are also highly dependent on perceptions becoming reality—creating expectations in ourselves and others that will shape behavior. If others expect us to be powerful, then they may act deferentially toward us, thereby granting us more leeway to seize the initiative and push for the outcomes we prefer. Unless we specifically challenge their expectations by rejecting the power opportunity or encouraging them to take an active role in expressing their preferred outcome, their expectations create a power vacuum that we can fill. Similarly, expectations affect our own behavior. If we expect that we can have power, we probably invest more time, energy, and effort in pursuing our own outcomes, and thereby we may in fact be able to achieve them. If we do not expect to have any power, we either do not try very hard to achieve our objectives or we may even systematically undermine our own effectiveness, thereby reinforcing both the expectation and the actual outcome achieved. Pfeffer (1992) provides some excellent examples of senior corporate leaders—Roger Smith at General Motors, Frank Stanton at CBS, and Henry Kissinger in the State Department—whose reputations were greatly shaped by expectations, both their own and the expectations of others.

### Location in an Organizational Structure

In the previous discussion, power was derived from the legitimacy and authority that accompanied a particular organizational position, role, or title—governor or chairman or colonel or professor or warden. With this office or title comes access to privileged information and control over resources, both of which can be used to buttress positional authority and get things done (performance). As we noted, in most formal organizations, authority, information, and resource control are interrelated—even if we do not have a very formal or important organizational title, access to the resources and information that accompany it can be used to leverage the position and, over time, significantly enhance the power base.

We should note here that access to information, resources or both may also be sufficient to create a power base, even if no prestigious formal organizational title or role is assigned to that access position. Individuals who are exposed to a large amount of information, responsible for collecting vital information and passing it from one place to another, or do jobs the organization has deemed central to its organizational mission or success may become very powerful simply by virtue of being in a "key position" (see Kaplan, 1984 for one discussion).

Particularly as organizations change to meet the demands of changing markets, environmental conditions, economic turbulence, and worldwide competitive pressures, individuals find themselves in tasks, duties, and functions that become critical to the organization's ability to change or be successful. The job may not have a fancy title, a big budget, or a large corner office, but it can provide significant power by virtue of the information and resource control associated with it.

From an organizational perspective, understanding power in this way is derived from conceptualizing an organization not as a hierarchy, but as a network of interrelationships (see also Kotter, 1985). Networks represent key individuals as circles or nodes, and relationships between nodes as lines of transaction. (See Figure 10.1 for an example of a network, as compared to an organizational hierarchy.) Individuals who need to interact with each other (or who do interact with each other) in the organization are connected by these lines. Primarily information and resources are transacted, although personal relationships and authority may also be currencies transacted across the network lines. In hierarchy terms, position and formal authority are directly related to how high up the position is in the hierarchy and how many people report to that individual. In network terms, in contrast, power is determined by different ways of specifying power, according to the following criteria.

**Centrality.**   The more central a position (node) is in a network of exchanges and transactions, the more power that node occupant will have. Centrality may be determined by the amount of information that passes through a node, number of transactions that occur through the node, or degree to which the node is central to managing information flow. Research by Brass (1984) indicates that being in the center of information flows—the work flow network, the informal communication network, and the friendship network—was particularly important to being promoted. At Lucasville, the spokespersons and negotiators for both sides enjoyed very high centrality. Centrality may also simply relate to where one's office or parking space is located in the organization—in the hallway where the president walks to lunch, or near where she parks in the parking lot. Pfeffer (1992) relates a story about a new faculty colleague who became well known simply by the proximity of his office to one of the few men's rooms in the building—most colleagues got to know him on their periodic trips to the lavatory.

**Criticality and Relevance.**   A second source of network power is the criticality of the node. Although a great deal of information or resources may not flow through the node, what does flow through it is essential to the organization's mission, major task, or key product. Jobs that are high in their dependence on others may become critical to the degree that the key person is charged with assembling information from many locations, which brings them into frequent contact with many important people and requires them to integrate the information into a recommendation, action strategy, or decision. The more that recommendation or decision is relevant to the organization's goal or mission, the more critical the job. MBAs are frequently counseled to find jobs with high centrality and criticality in

**FIGURE 10.1A**    Formal Organizational Chart

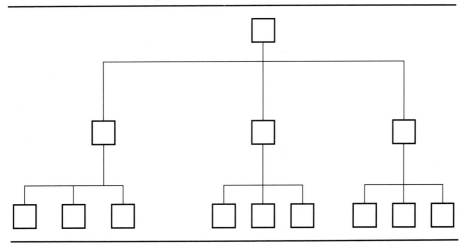

**FIGURE 10.1B**    Organizational Network

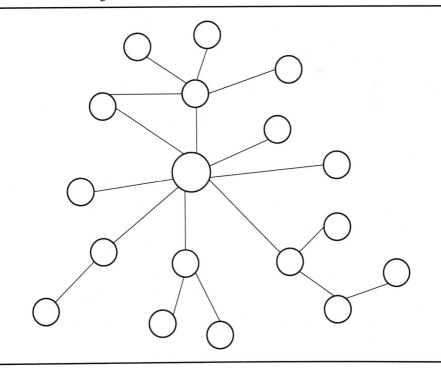

an organization so they can get the experience and visibility necessary for rapid promotion. Being critical—even irreplaceable—is a core part of getting and maintaining power.

**Flexibility.** A third source of network power lies in the position's flexibility, or the degree to which the key individual can exercise discretion in how certain decisions are made or who gains access. Flexibility is often related to criticality (see our preceding discussion). A classic example of "flexibility" is the role of gatekeeper, the person in a network who controls the access to a key figure or group. Anyone who wants to "get to" the key person has to go through the individual. If you want to see the boss, you have to get permission and access from the secretary. At Lucasville, prisoner spokespersons controlled access to the prisoners and State Police and Corrections personnel controlled access to the warden, governor, and other State officials.

**Visibility.** Finally, nodes differ in their degree of visibility—that is, how visible the task performance is to others in the organization. Visibility is not necessarily the same thing as centrality or criticality, but it is as important. A negotiator who negotiates with his constituency (or team) in the room has high visibility; if the negotiator gains significant concessions from the other party while being watched, the team will give him a great deal of affirmation. A node with high centrality and criticality may not be visible, but if not, it is much less likely to be recognized and rewarded.

In summary, the more traditional view of legitimacy as a source of power is that it is derived from the formal title, duties, and responsibilities that accompany an organizational position. The organization's structure, and the employees' endorsement of the validity of that structure, give particular jobs and positions authority and legitimacy by virtue of their location in the hierarchy. Those who occupy these positions can then assemble the information and resources that strengthen their power. However, other positions in an organization derive their power not from the formal organization structure, but from their location in the overall flow of information, goods and services, and personal relationships in that system. Acquisition of power, therefore, may not require formal appointment to an organizational office, but instead may simply require the savvy to understand which jobs and duties are central, critical, flexible, and visible, since occupants may also use them to accumulate information, resources, and personal relationships that may be leveraged into further power and influence.

## Personal Sources of Power

We come to the last category of sources of power: the personal qualities that an individual brings to the negotiator role, the personal attributes that individuals can convert into influence. Although a large number of personal qualities may contribute to a power base, we will mention four here: personal attractiveness, integrity, persistence, and emotion.

**Personal Attractiveness (Friendliness).**  A critically important attribute that a negotiator can bring is the ability to be friendly and outgoing and to establish a personal relationship with others—particularly the other parties in the negotiation. Warmth, empathy, caring about others, and simply the ability to show some direct, personal interest in the other helps to soften the harder edges of some of the other power sources. Friendliness also involves a strong emotional component, and therefore it appeals to the moods and feelings of the other party as well as the intellect. Rather than immediately getting down to business, the negotiator uses friendliness to get to know the other negotiator, talk about things that will put the other at ease, discover things that they may have personally in common, and establish a personal relationship with the other.

We also place the personal qualities of empathy and sensitivity to others within this category. Friendliness is the ability to show warmth and personal interest in the other individual. It is also related to the ability to perceive others accurately, know what they are about and how they are feeling, or to be aware of their personal preferences and circumstances that may dictate what we do and how we do it. This quality has been alluded to several times earlier in this text, particularly in Chapter 4, where we discussed integrative negotiation, Chapter 5 on planning and strategy, and Chapters 7 and 8, where we discussed communication processes and persuasion strategies. If a negotiator is to understand the other parties and their interests, then the negotiator must be able to establish some basis for communication to learn about them. Friendliness, empathy, and the ability to be sensitive to the other's needs, concerns, interests, and priorities are fundamental to effectiveness in this process.

Finally, although we discussed encouragement and praise as a resource that can be used, its effectiveness will be closely related to the interpersonal style of the power holder. It is likely that friendly, outgoing negotiators are far more likely to use reward and praise to encourage and support the target, whereas less friendly negotiators will be more likely to use criticism and verbal punishment. We will see how these sources come into play as we describe the various influence strategies.

**Integrity.**  A second personal quality is integrity. Integrity is character—the personal values and ethics that ground our behavior in high moral principles. Integrity is the quality that assures people we can be trusted. If people expose their vulnerabilities to us, we will not exploit those vulnerabilities when we are attempting to influence them. If people trust us with confidential information, we will not disclose that information to others. Finally, integrity is the quality that assures people that if we make an agreement, we can be trusted to keep that agreement, to abide by its terms and conditions and follow through on it. If people will trust us with confidential information and expose their vulnerabilities to us, we are likely to establish stronger personal relationships with them and to make stronger deals (Shapiro, Sheppard and Cheraskin, 1992). Similarly, if people believe that we can be trusted to follow through and implement our agreements, we are more likely to be able to complete agreements that will benefit us.

**Persistence and Tenacity.**    Persistence and tenacity are also valuable personal qualities in a negotiator. Children are often called great negotiators because they are so wonderfully persistent in pursuing what they want. Saying no to a child does not mean that the child gives up asking; usually, kids find all kinds of creative ways to persist in trying to achieve their objective (the cookie, the candy bar, watching the TV show). From watching children's persistence as negotiators, we can learn that part of persistence is doggedly pursuing the objective, but another part of success comes from finding new, unique, and creative ways to pursue the same request. Persistent people aren't necessarily doggedly committed to pursuing their goals blindly and rigidly; instead, they also display creativity in finding new ways to pursue the objective. Persistent people are comfortable being in a contentious mode with others—they don't fear conflict and try to escape simply because of a difference of opinion or views. They are persistent in pursuing their objectives, but they are also flexible, redefining strategy and approach as the times and conditions change. We will have more to say about these qualities as we begin to consider influence strategies.

**Emotion.**    Finally, we classify *emotion* as a personal source of power. Although emotion is clearly a component of friendliness, other emotions beside warmth, empathy, and compassion enter into negotiation. Fear, anger, or excitement can become an integral part of many negotiations—particularly over issues about which we feel strongly. Emotion combines with persistence to lead to assertiveness and determination.

Emotion is a power source because it offers a stark contrast to the expectation that negotiation should be a cool, calm, rational exchange of information and resources. As we have previously stated, most people expect negotiation to be a rational exchange process, driven by logical analysis of outcome maximization and economic valuation of alternatives. Yet we also know that negotiators frequently do not behave according to the principles of logic and economic rationality. In addition, when everyone else is being rational, it is frequently the person who expresses strong feelings, gets angry, or makes an impassioned speech in favor of her proposed solution that carries the day (Henderson, 1973). Emotion is a power source when it can be effectively used to win over the other party's heart by appealing to his emotions, his values, or his personal sense of what is right, fair, and just. Union organizers, political stump speakers, evangelists, and others whose aim is to organize and mobilize supporters all understand the importance of arousing emotion in their appeals. At Lucasville, for example, the radio broadcast by Inmate George and graphic descriptions of the conditions inside Lucasville attracted sympathy and attention from a number of prisoners around the State.

In summary, we have considered five major sources of power: information and expertise, resources, legitimacy and formal authority, location within a communication network, and personal sources such as personal attractiveness, friendliness, integrity, and persistence. We will now turn to the ways negotiators implement these power sources or "tools" through various strategies and tactics of interpersonal influence.

## THE APPLICATION OF POWER: STRATEGIES OF INFLUENCE

In the previous section, we looked at the sources people draw on when they want to use power in negotiation. In this section, we examine "power in action," which we will call *influence.*

Research and writing on the strategy and tactics of influence has boomed in the past 8 to 10 years. Several researchers have performed exhaustive surveys and inventories of the influence tactics managers use (e.g., Kipnis, Schmidt, and Wilkinson, 1980; Keys and Case, 1990; Yukl and Tracey, 1992) and others have written normative treatises on how and when to use these tactics (Cohen and Bradford, 1990; Falbe and Yukl, 1992; Zuker, 1991). These researchers have not reached a consensus on either the number of specifically different influence tactics used or the most meaningful groupings of these tactics. As a result, after reviewing a number of these studies, we propose 11 different influence strategies that may be used in negotiation. Each one draws on one or more sources of power, and each may be effective under specific conditions. Although we describe each one separately, in fact they may be used in various combinations to enhance their strength and impact or to suit the needs of the situation. Let us now consider each in detail. Table 10.2 presents a summary of these influence strategies and their power bases.

**TABLE 10.2**   Influence Strategies and the Power Tools They Use

| *Influence Strategy* | *Power Sources Used* |
| --- | --- |
| 1. Persuasion | Information and expertise—information may be derived from position in structure |
| 2. Exchange | Resources |
| 3. Legitimacy | Position in structure—may extend resources |
| 4. Friendliness | Friendliness, attractiveness, and emotion |
|    Ingratiation | More explicit use of friendliness for expedient purposes |
| 5. Praise | "Verbal" resources combined with friendliness |
| 6. Assertiveness | Information combined with persistence and emotion |
| 7. Inspirational appeal | Information combined with emotion |
| 8. Consultation | Information and resources combined with solicitation of others' information and resources |
| 9. Pressure | Information, negative resource control, and emotion |
| 10. Coalitions | Various power tools used to build support among a coalition (information, resources, friendliness) and then use group support as leverage |

## Persuasion

Persuasion is used when the negotiator wants to change the target's mind through information. The agent uses rational arguments, logic, facts, analyses, statistics, scientific studies, reports, data, and any other information that is available to construct a fact-based, logical case. Information and expertise are the primary sources of power used in this influence strategy. Use of the strategy assumes that the information and facts create a compelling logical argument, that the information and facts are not subject to bias or distortion, and that the other is seeking facts and logic and will make a decision based on high-quality information.

Persuasion is a very common form of influence, particularly in logical decision making and when exerting influence upward (to a boss). In Chapters 7 and 8, we addressed persuasion strategies in depth, showing how characteristics of the recipient of influence and the structure of the message (presentation approach, etc.) could affect the success of persuasive messages.

## Exchange

A second influence strategy is exchange, the process of explicitly or implicitly offering resources, or "favors" (promises and assistance), to secure the other's compliance and cooperation. Some authors have said that exchange is the same as *bargaining,* in that the user either directly or implicitly suggests reciprocity— in short, "If I do X for you, will you do Y for me?"

Exchange or bargaining relies on resources as the power base, particularly resources that can be translated into rewards for the other—favors, benefits, incentives, treats, perks, and the like. Thus, exchange frequently invokes the use of *promises* and *commitments* as persuasive tools—obligations that we are willing to make in exchange for the other's cooperation, compliance, or commitment to give us what we want. Finally, exchange transactions are often negotiated so that I complete my obligation now, but choose not to ask you to complete your obligation until some point in the future, either defined or undefined. By doing so, we leave a series of chits or obligations out in our interpersonal marketplace, which we can call back in when we need them. In his studies of successful managers and their use of power in organizations, Kotter (1977) emphasizes that a manager must recognize, create, and cultivate dependence among those around her—subordinates, peers, and even superiors—and to convert these dependencies into obligations. Obligations may be created in several ways (see also Chapter 8 on reciprocity). Doing favors for people, recognizing and praising them for their accomplishments, helping people out, paying them individual attention when the job demands do not require it or people do not expect it, and dispensing extra funds for special projects in a tight budget year are but a few examples of the way that resources can be controlled and measured to help people do their jobs better and to generate liking for the power holder.

Exchange transactions are extremely common in organizations. Pfeffer and Salancik (1974) stress that one of the major hallmarks of power in organizations is the ability to control and dispense desired resources. The power holder's ability to accumulate slack resources and to allocate them in exchange for reciprocal favors, obedience, or compliance is central to cultivating a power base. There are many different "currencies" of exchange, but the most common ones are organizational resources (money, budget increases, personnel, space, or raw materials), assistance (help getting a task accomplished or doing jobs others don't want to do), cooperation (providing exchanges more quickly, supportively, or innovatively than before) or even information. Cohen and Bradford (1990) advocate exchange as the medium by which we most successfully get things done in organizations, particularly when we lack formal position authority and titles, and they describe a wealth of other currencies that may be used in effective exchange transactions.

## Legitimacy

The third influence strategy is legitimacy, that is, using the power vested in the organizational position, title, and office and exerting influence by asking people to follow directives derived from that position or title. Legitimacy is effective to the extent that the target is convinced that the request is derived from the agent's formal authority base, is consistent with that authority, and is consistent with organizational rules, policies, practices, and procedures. Individuals using legitimacy styles may be more likely to give direct orders; to "pull rank" and refer to their higher status, title, or position; or to use the trappings of their position, such as a uniform, a title, or an office location (in the corner office suite) to reinforce their authority.

As we mentioned earlier when we discussed legitimacy as a source of power, the legitimacy tactic is often accompanied by other influence approaches, particularly information that is only available to the office holder or control of the rewards and punishments for compliance or noncompliance. Unlike exchange, where rewards are used as the sole medium of transaction, "authority" and "office" often combine both legitimacy and either rewards for compliance or punishment for noncompliance. In its most confrontational form, legitimacy and punishment (or threat of punishment) are combined to produce compliance. As Kipnis (1976) points out, all institutional roles have certain job specifications and requirements that may require the use of coercive power to exercise the duties of the job. The banker has an obligation, as a lending officer, to follow the bank's rules with regard to delinquent loans. The academic dean of a college has an obligation, as an academic administrator, to terminate students who do not meet minimum standards of academic performance. However, the existence of such role requirements frequently leads to abuse. Many times, the power holder will extend the use of coercive power beyond the scope and boundaries for which it was meant. The academic dean may let some athletes stay in school, even when they have failing grades, as a favor to the football coach. The banker may actually take a bribe from a businessman, and in exchange, fail to take action on the bad loan. Such behavior is not defined by the role, but occurs because the power enjoyed by the office holder is now being abused.

A variation on the use of legitimacy is to suggest that the target should comply not because the agent is directly using legitimate authority in the request, but because the organization or higher authorities are really the ones making the request. In this variation, the agent suggests that "the organization would like you to do this" or "those in higher authority in the organization" desire compliance (see Kipnis, Schmidt, and Wilkinson, 1980). In the former case, the organizational rules, regulations, policies, procedures, and practices are really requesting or mandating the desired behavior, and the agent is merely an innocent pawn in that larger process. In the second case, some vaguely defined higher authority (the president, the executive committee, "the dean's office," etc.) is making the request, so any anger or animosity will have to be directed at a source that is unlikely to be challenged directly. A final variation on the higher authority or higher legitimacy approach suggests that some ultimate value or ethical system should dictate what is done in a given situation. Thus, if the agent suggests that it is appropriate to comply with the request because "it is the right thing to do" (e.g., supporting a charity endorsed by higher management), some standard of higher moral authority and ethical values is being suggested as the appropriate framework to guide present actions.

## Friendliness

A fourth influence tactic is to use the power base of attractiveness and friendliness and to create a relationship with the other person. By establishing this relationship with the other person, we trust that the friendship that develops will lead the other to comply simply because friends like each other, help each other out, and do favors for each other. Some friendliness tactics include gaining rapport with others, showing genuine concern and interest for the other person, sharing feelings, expressing liking and appreciation for the other, working hard to understand the other's perspective and preferences, emotionally supporting the other, being loyal to her, and keeping confidences. Effective listening to others, eliciting contributions from others, and giving them credit for work done or contributions made are also effective interpersonal tactics for building friendships and strong interpersonal relationships.

Using friendliness is a less effective influence approach when there are time pressures or a decision is needed quickly. Developing a relationship takes time and must progress at its own pace. In fact, using friendliness as an influence tactic usually requires that the relationship between the agent and the target already be in place before the request is made so the relationship can be used effectively. If the agent tries to cultivate a relationship very quickly and to use it simply as a vehicle in which to lodge the influence request, it is likely that the target will see the friendliness gestures as superficial and insincere, a perception that will raise the target's defensiveness rather than lower it. We define this use of "expedient friendliness" as *ingratiation* (more colloquially referred to as "kissing up"). Some writers (e.g., Yukl and Tracey, 1992) specifically treat ingratiation as a separate influence strategy, but we see it as a variation on friendliness. Ingratiating behavior can be particularly irritating as the agent attempts to use flattery, emotion, and other friendliness tactics to "soften up" the target before making the request; yet people who are very accomplished at using ingratiation tactics are often good at winning over tough targets by softening them up through ingratiation, flattery, and emotional manipulation. In these cases, friendliness is combined with the expedient use of emotion to seduce an opponent into making a concession.

Friendliness is best used when the individual has taken the time to develop and cultivate a relationship. Part of the secret of such cultivation may be the ability to learn personal things about the other and then to use that information to provide help, assistance, or aid in times of need. To emphasize this point, consider the following example (Kotter, 1977), describing a manager who was particularly effective at building and cultivating relationships:

> Most of the people here would walk over hot coals on their bare feet if my boss asked them to. He has an incredible capacity to do little things that mean a lot to people. Today, for example, in his junk mail he came across an advertisement for something that one of my subordinates had in passing once mentioned that he was shopping for. So my boss routed it to him. That probably took 15 seconds of his time, and yet my subordinate really appreciated it. To give you another example, two weeks ago, he somehow learned that the purchasing manager's mother had died. On his way home that night, he stopped off at the funeral parlor. Our purchasing manager was, of course, there at the time. I bet he'll remember that brief visit for quite a while. (p. 130)

## Praise

A fifth influence tactic is the use of verbal praise, encouragement, and affirmation that the other is doing well. Praise may not seem to deserve a separate category as an influence tactic because it is often used in combination with exchange and friendliness approaches. Yet as we pointed out in our discussion of the use of verbal rewards as a component of resource power, we believe that the power of these verbal affirmations does deserve separate mention. Verbal reinforcement, approval, and praise are highly effective, perhaps as effective as tangible, economic resources in shaping behavior (Luthans and Kreitner, 1985). This same research has also shown that managers do not use positive reinforcement and praise enough. Too often, managers assume that praise is not necessary for people who are "just doing what they are supposed to do." Therefore, we need to specifically mention it here as a major way that negotiators can continue to shape the behavior of the other party simply by praising and verbally reinforcing the desired negotiation positions, attitudes, and postures that we want to see.

Not much more needs to be said beyond that it is important for the negotiator to use verbal reinforcement, praising language, and supportive words, gestures, and commentary to reward the target person for desired behaviors. If the other party expresses a view we like, show your approval of that view. If the party makes a favorable concession, express your appreciation for that concession. If he stops advocating a negotiating position that you did not like, affirm that behavior. You can use praise consistently and repeatedly throughout a negotiation, but you should particularly use it at the end, when the parties are summarizing and wrapping up their agreement. It is definitely important at that point to express support and appreciation to the other party for whatever she did that was consistent with our own objectives: cooperation, sharing information, willingness to make concessions, or whatever part she took in shaping the final deal.

### Assertiveness

A sixth influence tactic is assertiveness, which is to express what one wants in a strong, forceful style and manner. Assertiveness is information presented in clear, strong, compelling language—a combination of the personal quality of persistence and determination with emotional language that signals that determination. One way to express assertiveness is by making demands, clearly and emphatically stating what you want, assuming that if the other does not specifically and intentionally act to block them, your demands will be heeded. You can also demonstrate assertiveness by making unilateral decisions—who will attend a meeting, what the agenda will be, what the issues are, who gets to speak, and what alternatives will be considered. Demands, even threats, are also indicators of an assertiveness influence approach. Assertiveness is a style most often used by negotiators who have less power; with peers or bosses, assertiveness may work when used selectively but is unlikely to be effective in the long term because of the resistance and resentment it engenders in the other party (see Taetzsch and Benson, 1978, for one approach to the effective use of assertiveness).

### Inspirational Appeal

A seventh influence tactic is to create an inspirational appeal. This tactic successfully combines information with an emotional message that appeals to the target's idealism, personal values, or hopes and aspirations for the future. Inspirational appeals also increase the target's belief that he can accomplish a task through his own abilities and efforts. In short, inspirational appeals are motivational in the best sense of the term: they inspire people to perform, energize them, and build feelings of strength and confidence that will hopefully lead to superior performance.

Inspirational appeals are often called by other names: "pep talks," "sales pitches," or "motivational speeches." These influence appeals are a key staple of leadership in the modern organization. Leaders frequently invoke a vision of the future (a future task, goal, or objective to work for), of excellence (a standard of work or performance that all should strive to achieve), or of collective values and ethics (integrity, fairness, respect) that will serve as a rallying point for collective efforts and energy.

Inspirational appeals require several things to be successful. First, the agent must be able to present ideas powerfully, especially by invoking emotions. Speeches and pep talks are full of these emotional messages as well as the colorful language of symbols, metaphors, word pictures, and phrases that appeal to our values and ideals. Charismatic leaders, motivational speakers, and television evangelists understand these language principles well and know how to use them. Second, inspirational appeals must be able to articulate a future—a future state or condition that is significantly better than the present and a *future that the other party desires.* Finally, inspirational appeals must inspire people to action—that is, to outline a desired course of action that will supposedly lead to the attainment of the vision or values. Although the inspirational message may be strong on values and emotional content, it must also be translated into a specific course of action that will lead to the objective.

## Consultation

As an influence tactic, consultation is the process of involving others in planning a strategy, process, or outcome, or being willing to modify one's own position based on the other's ideas, suggestions, and input.

Consultation is not a strategy that is frequently mentioned as an influence tactic. In fact, in many ways, it is redundant with the concept of negotiation because by definition negotiation is the process of give and take to arrive at an outcome shaped by both sides. Therefore, by its very nature, negotiation—particularly integrative negotiation—is consultative because it seeks to incorporate the other's needs and interests into a joint solution. Yet it is important to recognize that a consultative influence strategy is empowering because it explicitly solicits and invites the other's input, as opposed to the strategies of persuasion or assertion, which unilaterally direct the other toward particular behaviors and outcomes. Consultation seeks to draw on the other's information, perspective, personal integrity, and self-respect by asking her advice and input. The power of participative decision making in management is drawn directly from the power of consulting others about their preferences rather than unilaterally directing their choices. (Fisher and Brown, 1988, develop the mnemonic, ACBD—Always Consult Before Deciding—as a key way to manage and strengthen an important relationship through consultation.)

## Pressure

We will use the term *pressure* to broadly define the tactical use of information plus sanctions, particularly punishment and threat of punishment, to accomplish objectives. By using pressure, an agent makes demands, suggests consequences about what will happen if the demands are not met, engages in frequent surveillance to determine whether the demands are carried out, reminds the other person frequently about what is expected, and eventually may follow through the actual punishment if the demand is not met or not met on time. A sales manager may cut her salesperson's pay for repeatedly failing to achieve sales target projections. An executive may fire her secretary for failing to improve her typing skills. A father may deny his son television privileges for a week because he didn't clean up his room. A supplier may put a late charge on an overdue bill to a customer. And, like reward power and the use of praise, coercive or punishment power can be as effective in verbal form as the withdrawal or denial of tangible resources. If the sales manager berates her salesperson for failing to make target sales quotas rather firing him, or if the father yells at his son rather than denying him television privileges, the impact may be just as great.

The conditions for the use of pressure are similar to those for the use of exchange and praise: the other party is dependent on the power holder in some way, the agent controls some form of resources which can be denied or taken away from the other party, and the punishment can be administered in a manner that will insure the other party person's compliance. The decision to use pressure is most likely related to the power holder's perception of the willingness of the other party to comply. Kipnis (1976) states that

> sanctions, whether positive or negative, are most likely to be involved when expectations of successful influence are lowest. Thus, [praise and rewards] appear to be preferred when the power holder wishes to retain the good will of the target person, or when the power holder anticipates that compliance is likely to drop off in the future. [Criticism and sanctions] appear to be preferred when the good will of the target is less involved, and the influence attempts are directed at changing some behavior rather than maintaining it. (p. 104, emphasis his)

Kipnis proposes a number of reasons why a power holder may decide to use pressure. First, pressure may be used as a way to *express anger, gain retribution,* or *get even* for something the target person has done. Research by Goodstadt and Hjelle (1973) has shown that the use of coercive power is likely to be greatest when the "other party's resistance or influence is attributed to *motivational causes* (I refuse) rather than to a lack of ability (I can't)" (Kipnis, p. 105, emphasis ours). Thus, if the son had said, "I can't clean my room; I've got to go to basketball practice this morning," the father might be more likely to accept the excuse as reasonable and less likely to resort to coercive influence. Second, pressure may be used as an expression of *role behavior*—the job (or role) requires it. For example, a banker forecloses on a loan "because bank rules mandate it," or a dean terminates a poorly performing student because "she didn't meet minimum standards." In these cases, pressure is tied to the use of the legitimacy influence strategy—in short, "I wouldn't ordinarily do this, but my job description or responsibilities say I must." Pressure is most likely to be used when we expect that the other party has little or no desire to meet our expectations, does not share the same deadline, or will not comply unless directly threatened with severe negative consequences.

The few empirical studies of power use in negotiation have tended to find that parties with higher power tend to use more pressure tactics, such as threats, and make fewer concessions (Hornstein, 1965; Michener, Vaske, Schleiffer, Plazewski, and Chapman, 1975). Interestingly, when the power distribution between the parties was relatively small, the low-power party also showed a high degree of threat use and power tactics, creating an escalation between the parties that usually destroyed the negotiation (see also Vitz and Kite, 1970).

At best, pressure tactics produce short-term compliance with requests, but they also are likely to produce high resistance from the other party. As a result, frequent use of pressure tactics leads to very high resistance, in which the agent must consistently escalate the severity of consequences for noncompliance and the willingness to invoke them. It should be clear, therefore, that frequent use of pressure tactics alienates the other party and requires a great deal of coercive pressure to sustain compliance. If possible, therefore, pressure tactics should be used sparingly and selectively because any use is likely to corrode the relationship between the parties, and any frequent use is likely to destroy it.

### Coalitions

The last influence tactic is the use of coalitions. In a coalition strategy, the agent enlists the aid or endorsement of a number of other people (who the agent knows, likes, or respects). The agent then either asks these other people to make direct requests to the other party or suggests to the other party that many people have already endorsed or supported the desired behavioral objective. Coalitions can be used in upward and lateral influence. In upward influence, the subordinate attempts to influence the boss and suggests that a number of other subordinates endorse the action. In lateral influence, the agent suggests that a number of the other party's peers already endorse the desired action and asks the other person to "get on board and be a team player." The agents can use these supporters by simply suggesting that they support the desired action or as go-betweens to approach the other party directly. In the latter case, go-betweens are usually selected because of already-strong friendship relationships with the other party that may now be exploited to change the other party's view or willingness to comply. Several researchers (Kipnis, Schmidt, and Wilkinson, 1980; Yukl and Tracey, 1992) have noted that this is an especially popular strategy for use with superiors and peers, over whom a manager may have no specific, direct authority.

### CHAPTER SUMMARY

A great deal has been written on power and its use in organizations, and this literature has been significantly enriched in the past 10 years. However, few of these works have been specifically directed at understanding power in negotiations. Unfortunately, therefore, we come to the same general conclusion we drew in our review of this literature almost 10 years ago: Although we know a great deal about power defined broadly, we do not know a great deal about power use in negotiating relationships. Nevertheless, we believe that much of the new work on power and influence strategies can be appropriately applied to negotiation dynamics, and we have attempted to do so in this chapter.

sons, depending on their intentions. If their intent is to gain some competitive advantage over the other party, then they will seek ways to enhance and use their power to achieve that objective. Thus, negotiators may use power to pursue a competitive objective. In contrast, they may also use power to pursue an integrative or cooperative objective; in this case, power will be sought to balance the power between the parties so they may pursue collaboration on an equal footing. We then discussed the different ways that power could be defined and the implications of these different definitions for a complete understanding of power use in negotiation.

In this chapter, we made an important distinction between power and influence: we described *power* as the repertoire of "tools" available to get another party to do something, whereas we described *influence tactics* as the manner in which the various tools are put into use to accomplish a particular influence objective. We spent the remainder of this chapter reviewing the basic power sources and the basic influence strategies.

With regard to power sources, we discussed

- Information and expert power.
- Resource control, such as raw materials, financial resources, and the like.
- Legitimate power, including authority, reputation, and performance.
- Location in an organizational structure, including centrality, criticality, flexibility, and visibility.
- Personal power, including attractiveness and friendliness, integrity, patience and tenacity, and use of emotion.

We devoted the second part of the chapter to a discussion of influence tactics. Each influence tactic draws upon one or more sources of power as its point of leverage. These influence strategies include

- Persuasion, the use of information and expertise.
- Exchange, the use of resources.
- Legitimacy, the use of legitimacy and related resources.
- Friendliness and ingratiation, the use of friendliness, attractiveness, and emotion.
- Praise, the use of verbal resources of recognition combined with friendliness.
- Assertiveness, the use of information combined with persistence and emotion.
- Inspirational appeal, the use of information and emotion.
- Consultation, the use of information and resources combined with soliciting these same resource contributions from others.
- Pressure, the use of information, threats of cutting off resources, and emotion.

- Coalitions, the use of information, resources, and friendliness to create a group with shared objectives and then to use the group pressure to attract other members to support the desired objective.

We encourage more research in how these tactics draw on power, when they are used, and under what conditions they are effective so we might enrich this discussion in the future.

# CHAPTER 11

# Individual Differences

Some people are better negotiators than others. How does the best negotiators' behavior differ from that of average negotiators? Researchers have been examining the effects of individual differences on the process and outcome of negotiations for years. An enormous amount of research has been conducted on this topic (for detailed reviews see Hermann and Kogan, 1977; Terhune, 1970; Rubin and Brown, 1975). Unfortunately many of the findings in this area are fragmented, contradictory, and difficult to apply in practical settings. Our goal in this chapter is to provide an overview of different aspects of individual differences and negotiation, and to discuss new research findings in this area that appear to be particularly promising.

We begin with a discussion of early research on personality and negotiation. Next, we discuss more recent research on individual differences and negotiation and outline some specific personality dimensions that appear to influence negotiations. We then turn to a discussion of the most frequently examined individual difference: the effects of sex and gender on negotiation.[1] The chapter then discusses the behavioral approach to studying individual differences in negotiations, and explores how superior negotiators behave differently than average negotiators when they negotiate. Finally, the chapter concludes with a critique of research on individual differences in negotiation and provides suggestions for future research in this area.

## EARLY RESEARCH ON PERSONALITY AND NEGOTIATION

Research efforts to define the effects of background, demographic, and personality factors in negotiations began in the late 1950s. Rubin and Brown, in their book *The Social Psychology of Bargaining and Negotiation* (1975), reviewed 200 empirical studies of background, demographic, and personality factors that might

---

[1] As noted later in this chapter, we will use the term *sex* to refer to the biological categories of male and female, and the term *gender* to refer to the psychological aspects associated with each category (Deaux, 1985).

contribute to differences in bargaining outcomes. Studies have examined the impact of differences in age, sex, race, cultural and national heritage, and socio-economic status on negotiation outcomes. Early research on the effect of person-ality examined risk-taking propensity, perceived locus of control, level of cogni-tive complexity, tolerance for ambiguity, level of self-concept, nature and strength of social motives (needs for achievement, power, or affiliation), attitudes (inter-personal trust, cooperativeness, authoritarianism), and normal or abnormal per-sonality structure, to name some of the more prominent variables studied.

The findings from these studies are widely disparate, inconclusive, and some-times directly contradictory. For example, Rubin and Brown review over 100 studies on sex differences and their impact on bargaining behavior. Of the 100 studies, approximately 30 studies report no difference in bargaining behavior between men and women, 20 studies report that males bargain more coopera-tively than females, and a large number of others report that females bargain more cooperatively than males. Similar contradictory results can be noted for many of the other personality variables mentioned previously. Explaining and coping with the reasons for these patterns of contradictory and nonsignificant findings became a major challenge in this area of research. At least three different explanations were proposed:

1. Differences in negotiation style and approach are too subtle and elusive to be identified and confirmed with current research methods. In effect, measuring instruments are too primitive to detect individual differences in negotiation that probably exist.

2. A great deal of the inconclusive and contradictory findings result from incon-sistent research methods. The variables examined and the methods by which they were examined consistently differ from one study to the next. Studies are designed and conducted in a disorganized and unsystematic manner. As a result, contradictory findings can be traced to the use of different research designs, methods, and experimental bargaining problems.

3. The inconclusive findings could reveal a great deal if they were properly con-ceptualized. In effect, the criticism is that we have been defining the key per-sonality factors in the wrong way.

These three perspectives are not mutually exclusive, nor necessarily contradic-tory. Each opens a different line of inquiry that throws light on a complex subject. We'll examine each of the three.

## Differences in Negotiation Style and Approach

The first perspective is that the effect of individual differences is too subtle and elusive to be revealed by contemporary research strategies and methods. Hamner (1980), in his review of the effect of individual differences on bargaining outcomes, noted that research has failed to find significant relationships between personality variables and negotiation outcomes (see Druckman, 1971; Hermann and Kogan, 1977; Terhune, 1968, 1970). He suggests several reasons for this repeated failure.

First, the impact of structural variables in negotiation may override the effects of personality variables. Although individual differences may predispose bargainers to particular behavior in the early rounds of negotiation, key structural factors such as the nature of the bargaining problem, the relative power between negotiators, pressures from constituencies, or simply the behavior of the other negotiator may quickly override the effect of any individual differences that may have existed at the start of bargaining. Moreover, these same structural variables may inhibit opportunities for individual differences to emerge and actually have an effect during negotiations. For example, much of the early research on demographic and personality differences employed a simple, two-choice Prisoner's Dilemma game (see Chapter 2 for a discussion of this game). Prisoner's Dilemma, and other similar games, are traditionally played by experimental subjects who cannot see one another, do not talk to one another, and whose "negotiating" consists of making simple choices between more cooperative and more competitive decision options. Limited and constrained interaction of this form is hardly comparable to the complex verbal and nonverbal communication and efforts at persuasion that occur in face-to-face negotiation. Hence, research scenarios and settings must be rich enough to allow the impact of personality variables to emerge, but not so dominated by major structural relationships that when personality factors do emerge, they are quickly obscured.

Second, personality variables may also interact with structural variables in complex and (perhaps) unpredictable ways. Not only do the structural variables—win-win versus win-lose, relative power, time pressure, accountability—dominate the prediction of likely outcomes, but if personality does have an effect, its impact may be in combination with structural elements. For example, Christie and Geis (1970), in their research on Machiavellianism (the tendency to manipulate others and to maneuver them to your point of view), conclude that individuals who measure high on Machiavellianism scales also require specific types of situations to be effective. If these specific situational factors are not present, or if the situation does not provide a Machiavellian individual with the opportunity to behave in his preferred way, then the impact of this personality factor is nullified. Research on Machiavellianism will be reviewed in more detail later in this chapter.

Finally, the effect of a particular personality predisposition may go undiscovered because previous research efforts have been limited to unique, homogeneous populations of research subjects who did not possess that predisposition. Most experimental negotiation studies have been conducted with volunteer college populations, usually students enrolled in introductory psychology or business administration courses. This particular population may be so homogeneous with respect to age, demographic background, and other personality characteristics that true differences in negotiation style may not be readily identified. Researchers can counter this problem when studying bargaining behavior by broadening the sample of subjects that are included in their studies of negotiation.

### Testing the Relationship between Personality Predispositions and Negotiation Outcomes

Responding to the deficiencies of the earlier, more chaotic approach to research in this field, several groups of researchers have conducted better controlled experimental studies to provide a "definitive" test of the effects of individual differences on negotiation. For example, building on earlier research, Hermann and Kogan (1977) proposed eight personality factors that should influence negotiation outcomes: level of manifest anxiety, authoritarianism, cognitive complexity, tendency to be conciliatory, dogmatism, propensity toward risk taking, level of self-esteem, and predisposition toward suspiciousness. Each of the factors was predicted to affect (1) a bargainer's predispositions toward the negotiating situation, influencing the individual's behavioral intentions and expectations about the other negotiator's behavior, (2) the behavior of the negotiator during negotiations, regardless of the conduct of the other party, and (3) the behavior of the negotiator during negotiations, given that the other party's personality dispositions were similar to, or the opposite of, the negotiator's. After administering a battery of personality instruments to 108 Princeton undergraduate males, pairs of these students were then asked to play a number of rounds of a Prisoner's Dilemma game.

Although the results are complex because of the number of variables studied and their effect on the negotiator's predispositions and actual behavior, they can be summarized as follows:

1.  Only four of the eight personality variables—level of anxiety, level of cognitive complexity, tendency to be conciliatory, and level of self-esteem—predicted a student's predisposed strategy toward the other party, and only two of the four—cognitive complexity and self-esteem—predicted at a statistically significant level.
2.  Only two of the eight personality variables—authoritarianism and self-esteem—differentiated the ways that students described their own actual strategy in the game.
3.  Only 3 of 32 analyses between personality variables and actual game-playing strategy reached acceptable levels of statistical significance.
4.  Certain personality variables, such as cognitive complexity, conciliatory tendency, dogmatism, risk-taking, and suspiciousness, emerged as important when bargainers were matched with a partner who scored similarly on the particular variable. Hence, pairing negotiators with similar styles allowed for the interactive effect of personality and behavior to come forth.

Thus, although selected results did emerge, they reveal no consistent pattern with regard to the clear effect of any one personality element across all three outcome measures. Many of the predicted results were not significant or were inconclusive. Moreover, the concerns raised by Hamner (1980) can be clearly applied to this research. First, although we know neither the demographic characteristics of Princeton undergraduate males, nor whether this sample of students represents a reasonable approximation of the general population, we can guess that the same arguments of homogeneity apply. Second, the constrained choice options of the Prisoner's Dilemma game may well minimize the subtlety and strength that these variables could have and that might emerge in a more complex negotiating scenario. Finally, Hermann and Kogan themselves note that once the gaming interaction has begun, personality elements are considerably less successful at predicting negotiating behavior. This supports the assertion that in the long run, structural and interactive factors may be likely to dominate initial personality differences.

## Reconceptualizing the Inconclusive Nature of Previous Findings

The third effort to deal with the inconclusive nature of personality variables proposes that the results can be explained more productively by different, underlying variables that have not yet been identified. The most significant effort in this regard was by Rubin and Brown (1975). In an effort to explain and organize the diverse and often contradictory findings their review revealed, Rubin and Brown propose a single dimension of personal style—Interpersonal Orientation (IO)—to explain the results.

Individuals may be classified as either high or low in their interpersonal orientation. A high IO is "responsive to the interpersonal aspects of his relationship with the other. He is both interested in, and reactive to, variations in the other's behavior" (Rubin and Brown, 1975, p. 158). High IOs determine their own behavior in a conflict setting by tuning in to the other's behavior—the other's cooperativeness or competitiveness, relative amount of power, use of power, and adherence to certain bargaining norms such as equity, exchange, and reciprocity.

High IOs use this information in one of two ways, depending upon whether they are cooperatively or competitively disposed. A cooperative high IO attends to the other's behavior to maximize cooperation. This type of individual seeks behavioral cues that the other can be trusted, and if he finds them, the high IO will act trustworthily and maximize the exchange and flow of information to enhance a cooperative, mutually satisfactory outcome. Faced with another party who is competitive or exploitative, however, a cooperative high IO will change strategies to defend against exploitation and will retaliate against the other party for behaving in an exploitative, hostile, and perhaps even unethical manner.

In contrast, a competitive high IO attends to the behavior of the other person to use this information to gain strategic advantage. Competitive high IOs are suspicious of others' motives and intentions (expecting to be exploited) and are often untrustworthy themselves (either to gain advantage or as a defense against expected exploitation). Information flow is either unilateral (to gain information about the other without divulging one's own intentions), or minimized (in order to beat the other). If the other party behaves cooperatively, this behavior is discounted ("what a fool" or "this is just an attempt to set me up"). If the other

**TABLE 11.1**  Summary of Individual Differences in Background and Personality That Appear to Lie at Opposite Ends of the "Sensitivity to the Other Party" Continuum

| *High Sensitivity to Other Party* | *Low Sensitivity to Other Party* |
| --- | --- |
| Older children and college students | Young children |
| Blacks | Whites |
| Females | Males |
| Low risk-takers | High risk-takers |
| Externals | Internals |
| Abstract thinkers | Concrete thinkers |
| Persons high in need for affiliation and power | Persons low in need for achievement |
| Cooperators | Competitors |
| Persons low in authoritarianism | Persons high in authoritarianism |
| Persons high in internationalism | Persons low in internationalism |
| Persons high in Machiavellianism | Persons low in Machiavellianism |
| Normal personalities (e.g., nonparanoids) | Abnormal personalities (e.g., paranoids) |

behaves competitively, the competitive high IO will see the other as similar ("we are both competitors") and will behave competitively to defend against the other party and gain an advantage.

In contrast to the high IO, a low IO is characterized by "a nonresponsiveness to the interpersonal aspects of his relationship with the other. His interest is neither in cooperating nor competing with the other, but rather in maximizing his own gain—pretty much regardless of how the other fares" (Rubin and Brown, 1975, p. 159). Low IOs determine their behavior in conflict situations on the basis of their own goals and preferred outcomes and an evaluation of the situation they are in. They are likely to attribute the other's behavior to variations in these same factors and therefore to attend more to the nature of the situation and their own goals than to variations in the other's behavior. In short, to achieve her own goals and preferred outcomes, a low IO is less concerned with the behavior of the other—either cooperative or competitive—than with the situational variations and complexities that might influence this outcome.

The major value of the IO construct is that it provides a single uniform dimension for organizing and explaining many of the discrepant, conflicting findings of earlier research. Rubin and Brown (1975) demonstrated that much of the conflicting research could be successfully explained if IO were considered to be the major element of differentiation between groups (see Table 11.1).

Swap and Rubin (1983) constructed a self-report measure of IO and conducted two experiments to test its usefulness. The first experiment was designed to compare the effect of sex differences with the effects of differences in IO on liking for another person (an important component of negotiation examined in Chapter 8). Earlier research had previously revealed contradictory findings. The results of the Swap and Rubin study indicate clearly that IO was a better predictor of liking for another person than were sex differences.

The second experiment was conducted to compare the effect of sex differences with the effects of differences in IO on a preference for equity versus equality in the distribution of outcomes. It has frequently been proposed that men demonstrate a greater preference for *equity* in outcomes (parties in the relationship receive outcomes in relation to their inputs), whereas women demonstrate a greater preference for *equality* in distribution (each party receives the same outcomes). In the Swap and Rubin experiment, IO and sex differences were systematically controlled in a resource-distribution task. The results indicate that males and low IOs tended to allocate rewards according to equity standards, whereas females and high IOs seemed more concerned with equality of outcomes.

As a measure of personal style, IO seems to offer more promise than other previously mentioned personality dimensions to predict predispositions toward negotiation. Little research, however, has been conducted with this construct since Swap and Rubin (1983).

## LATER RESEARCH ON PERSONALITY AND NEGOTIATION

Much of the earlier research on personality effects can be faulted for selecting personality variables more on the basis of convenience than on a strongly reasoned relationship between the variable and the negotiation process. For example, many of the earlier personality variables chosen for study seem to have been selected because well-established scales had already been developed for measuring the variable, rather than because of a clearly logical presumed influence on negotiation. Although this rationale makes sense for research reasons—it allows confidence in the reliability and validity of measurement—the dimensions themselves may be less important in negotiation settings than other, more meaningful personality distinctions. In this section, we review several more recent approaches to studying personality and negotiation that show promise as predictors of personal differences in negotiation.

### Conflict Management Style

Dealing with conflict is a central part of the negotiating process. In Chapter 1, we identified five modes of behavior that are commonly used to deal with conflict: competing, collaborating, avoiding, accommodating, and compromising. We also examined the effect on outcomes that would be created by choosing one style over another; what we did not examine were the *reasons* that one style is commonly chosen over another. A negotiator may make this choice based on rational criteria, such as selecting the style that is most likely to lead to the desired outcomes. However, everyday experience (and systematic research) indicates that the choice may also be an expression of a negotiator's personality. It is that personality predisposition that we will discuss here.

**FIGURE 11.1**    Kilmann-Thomas Conflict Orientations

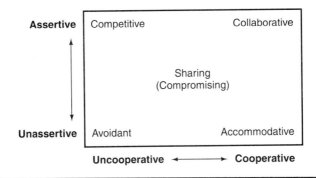

Adapted from Thomas, K. "Conflict and conflict management." In M. D. Dunnette, Ed. *Handbook of Industrial and Organizational Psychology* (Rand McNally, 1976). Used with permission of M. D. Dunnette.

Underlying the five conflict management styles are two levels of concern. One is the degree of concern a conflicting party shows for her own outcomes, and the second is the degree of concern shown for the other's outcomes. Thomas (1992) has proposed that two personality dimensions best represent these two levels of concern: the degree of *assertiveness* a conflicting party maintains for his own preferred solutions or outcomes, and the degree of *cooperativeness* a party shows toward working with the other party to achieve their goals. Analogous to the approaches we described in Chapter 4, Thomas' research identified five major conflict management styles (see Figure 11.1):

- A *competing* style, high on assertiveness and low on cooperativeness.
- An *accommodating* style, low on assertiveness and high on cooperativeness.
- An *avoiding* style, low on both assertiveness and cooperativeness.
- A *collaborative* style, high on both assertiveness and cooperativeness.
- A *compromising* style, moderate on both assertiveness and cooperativeness.

Research by Thomas and his colleagues (Thomas, 1977, 1992; Kilmann and Thomas, 1977) has supported the premise that individual conflict management styles vary according to two factors: the nature of the situation (i.e., negotiators make rational choices about which strategy to use), and individual biases to use certain styles regardless of the situation. In addition, individual differences in conflict management style have been correlated with other measures of personality. Using the Myers-Briggs measure of personality styles, Thomas (1976) reports a significant relationship between preference for: (1) integrative styles (a win-win perspective on conflict) and extroversion; (2) distributive styles (a win-lose perspective on conflict) and introversion; and (3) styles of conflict management and "thinking" as opposed to "feeling" individuals. A relationship between high scores on Machiavellianism (Christie and Geis, 1970) and a preference for a compromising style was also reported. Thomas (1976) suggests that individuals high in a competitive style would be lower in risk taking (higher in internal control), higher on needs for power and control, and lower on needs for affiliation. Similarly, individuals strong in collaboration would be more likely to be task oriented, creative, and capable of dealing with complexity. Each of these relationships is derived through inference, however, and is not a result of direct research with the Thomas-Kilmann instrument. Similar inferences are drawn between individuals with particular conflict orientations and their actual behavior in conflict situations. If the stakes for winning are high and outcomes are derived through individual effort, then individuals with strong competing modes should dominate the situation; if outcomes are derived from joint efforts, then individuals with a strong collaborative mode should dominate. In contrast, if the stakes are low for an individual, then that individual should be more likely to ignore the conflict (avoiding mode) or allow the other to reap what little resources are available (accommodating mode).

The Thomas-Kilmann model and subsequent research on the motivational potential of conflict management styles represent a simple and coherent model for viewing the effect of personality variables on bargaining and conflict management behavior. Research exploring the two dimensions has generally been supportive (Kabanoff, 1987; Rahim, 1983a; Pruitt and Rubin, 1986; Ruble and Thomas, 1976; van de Vliert and Kabanoff, 1988; van de Vliert and Prein, 1989). Although little research has explored the effects of negotiator choice of conflict management styles on actual negotiation behavior, four studies in which conflict styles were experimentally manipulated have generally supported the model (Carnevale and Keenan, 1990; Pruitt, Carnevale, Ben-Yoav, Nochajski, and Van Slyck, 1983; Ben-Yoav and Pruitt, 1984a, 1984b). Despite current debate about the extent of the usefulness of models of conflict styles (see Carnevale and Pruitt, 1992; Thompson, 1990b), the development of the measuring instruments, identification of common styles, and the relationship of these styles to conflict behavior has received considerably greater verification than that of the effects of personality variables studied in previous lines of research.

## Machiavellianism

A second stream of systematic research relating a personality predisposition to conflict and bargaining behavior was conducted by Christie, Geis, and their associates. After extensive study of the historical writings of Machiavelli and similar political philosophers, Christie and Geis (1970) developed an attitude scale based on Niccolo Machiavelli's classic writings. They conducted extensive research on the relationship between Machiavellianism and other personality variables. No significant relationships were discovered between Machiavellianism and measures of intelligence or political party preference, although there was a strong negative correlation between the Mach scale and the California F scale, a measure of authoritarian attitudes. Those scoring high in Machiavellianism (high Machs) tend to have a cynical view of people. As a result, they are much more candid about feelings of hostility and mistrust and much *less* likely to think or act in ways that others judge as socially desirable. Individuals scoring high in Machiavellianism also tend to be low in standards of conventional morality, honesty, and reliability, to behave selfishly and unsympathetically toward others, to be unwilling to change their convictions under social pressure, and to disagree that people have strong will power.

Christie and Geis have conducted several research studies on the relationship between a Machiavellian orientation and behavior in specific situations. We will describe several of these experiments here because of their applicability to many negotiation processes. You'll find a more detailed description of these and other studies of Machiavellianism in Christie and Geis (1970).

1. One experiment was designed to test differences in individual moral conduct (specifically, implication in cheating and the subsequent cover-up of that behavior). No differences were reported between high and low Machiavellians (Machs) in their willingness to resist becoming involved in a cheating situation. The structure of the situation created opportunities for subjects to dissuade another subject (an experimental confederate) from cheating, expose the confederate to the experimenter, refrain from using unethically obtained information, confess the behavior to the experimenter (either at the first opportunity, or after direct accusation by the experimenter), and lie with varying degrees of plausibility about their own behavior. High Machs initially tried harder to persuade the confederate not to cheat and initially resisted using the confederate's unethically obtained information in the experimental task. But high Machs were no different from low Machs in the frequency of lying before being directly accused by the experimenter. Once accused, however, high Machs maintained their ability to lie with far greater credibility. They confessed less, and were able to maintain more direct, convincing eye contact with the experimenter while lying than were low Machs.

2. A second experiment explored the willingness of experimental subjects to engage in manipulative behavior when they were in a high-power position. After experimentally creating the legitimacy for subjects to deceive and manipulate other subjects in a test-taking situation, subjects were placed in a role that allowed the manipulative behavior to occur. High Machs attempted significantly more manipulative behaviors than low Machs, both in the total number and variety of behaviors. They told bigger lies, used more verbally distracting behavior, and employed far more innovative manipulative techniques. Finally, high Machs enjoyed being manipulative and having a high-power role.

3. A third experiment reported on behavior in an experimental con game. A Parcheesi-like board game was created, and game rules were structured to allow players to enter into coalitions to win at the game. Coalitions could be formed or broken at will. In addition, players differed in the amount

of power they contributed to the coalition (point values assigned to their position). These power differences were either public knowledge to all players or privately known only to the player involved. The results indicate that high Machs won significantly more points than low Machs, regardless of the game variation; they also won significantly more when the amount of their power (point value contribution) was private. However, high Machs did not always increase their winnings more than low Machs when given more formal power. Follow-up research explored the game tactics most commonly used by high Machs. First, they were far more proactive in their game-playing strategies, particularly in testing the limits of the rules. Second, they displayed a more opportunistic sense of timing with regard to making or breaking a coalition. Third, high Machs more clearly controlled the initiation of bids and the structure of the coalition negotiations—they initiated more offers, decisively dissolved coalitions when they were not advantageous, and were constantly sought after by others to be in coalitions. As a result, compared to low Machs, they were usually members of the winning coalition and seldom lost the game or were shut out of points. Fourth, as reported earlier, they thrived more when their power was private; this allowed them to manipulate the structure of the negotiation. Finally, high Machs were less responsive to the personal or ethical concerns of others in the situation. They tended to treat both the game and other players with emotional detachment rather than becoming personally excited or involved with other people or outcomes. When there were differences in power, low Machs were more concerned with disclosure of their power and with determining the most appropriate ethical behavior consistent with their power. Such concerns did not trouble the high Machs, who showed a depersonalized, consistent manner of play regardless of their relative power or whether their power was publicly known.

4. An experiment similar to the Prisoner's Dilemma (see Chapter 2) was conducted with high Machs, to discover both their behavior in this situation and to investigate the effect of real money (as opposed to imaginary points) on behavior. Playing against a variety of preprogrammed strategies, high Machs did not perform significantly better, although they tended to become more exploitative over time. When real money was introduced into a game that had been previously played for points, high Machs became more *cooperative,* presumably because this behavior was more rational and would assure them a positive financial outcome. Thus, high Machs appear to be opportunistic, but only when the outcomes in a situation warrant it.

Little research has been conducted on the influence of Machiavellianism on negotiation since Christie and Geis's studies. In a distributive bargaining task, Greenhalgh and Neslin (1983) reported that high Machs tended to negotiate *lower* outcomes than low Machs. Greenhalgh and Neslin suggest that this counterintuitive finding may have been due to the fact that the negotiation task used in their research was quite rich and this reduces or moderates the influence of Machiavellianism; however, this hypothesis has yet to be examined empirically. A study by Fry (1985) suggests that the Machiavellianism of *both* negotiating parties may jointly influence negotiations. In a study of distributive negotiations with a sample of male college students, Fry reported that mixed-Machiavellianism dyads (a dyad containing one high and one low Mach negotiator) negotiated poorer outcomes than dyads containing negotiators with the same level of Machiavellianism (both negotiators were either high Mach or low Mach). Fry (1985) found that low Machs change their negotiation style as a function of the Machiavellianism of the other negotiator. When negotiating with a high Mach other party, low Mach negotiators make fewer offers and are less effective negotiators than when negotiating with low Mach other parties. High Mach negotiators did not change their negotiation style as a function of the other party's Machiavellianism.

### Interpersonal Trust

As we discussed in Chapter 2, one of the fundamental dilemmas in negotiation is the degree to which negotiators should trust the other party. Negotiators must gather information and determine how much the other party is likely to be deceptive or deceitful by misrepresenting true positions, distorting relevant facts, or introducing spurious information and positions. In addition, the trustworthiness of the other party may change over time, depending upon whether negotiations are beginning or near the end and whether the negotiation has proceeded cooperatively or competitively.

Rotter (1967, 1971, 1980) has proposed that interpersonal trust functions as a personality variable with important effects in social relationships. According to Rotter's research, individuals differ in their level of interpersonal trust, defined as "a generalized expectancy held by an individual that the word, promise, oral, or written statement of another individual or group can be relied upon" (1980, p. 1). Unlike a broad-based belief in the goodness of others and the benign nature of the world, Rotter argues that interpersonal trust is determined by the experiences that individuals have in dealing with others. If individuals have had experiences in which they have trusted others, and this trust has been rewarded by reciprocal trust and productive relationships, then generalized interpersonal trust should be high. In contrast, if individuals have experienced exploitation, deception, and dishonesty when they trusted someone, then interpersonal trust is likely to be low.

Rotter and his colleagues developed a test for diagnosing the level of interpersonal trust and used the scores to measure levels of interpersonal trustworthiness. First, individuals who act more trusting, or who say that they are willing to act more trustingly, are also less likely to lie or cheat. When placed in situations where the cost of being caught for cheating was perceived as low, individuals high in interpersonal trust are clearly less likely to resort to cheating than those low in interpersonal trust. High trusters believe that others will be trustworthy and that they need to be trustworthy themselves; hence, they are more likely to impose high moral standards on themselves and behave ethically. In contrast, low trusters believe that others cannot be trusted to observe the rules, and they therefore feel less pressure themselves to tell the truth. As a result, they believe that lying, cheating, and similar behaviors are necessary as a defensive reaction to protect themselves against others.

Second, high trusters are more liked by their peers. When individuals were asked to describe someone who scored high on the trust scale—either male or female—they tended to see the individual in a positive light. High trusters are perceived by others as happier, more ethical, more attractive to the opposite sex, having a happier childhood, and more desirable as a close friend than low trusters. In contrast, the low truster is seen as having more common sense, perhaps a cynical view about what the world is really about, and as having more interesting, varied, and unusual experiences than the high-trust individual.

Third—and surprisingly to some people—high trusters were not more gullible than low trusters. It might be assumed that high trusters would be more likely to believe communications from other people without questioning their validity, and therefore they would be more likely to be tricked. The studies summarized by Rotter (1980) indicate that the high-trust individual is not more prone to gullibility than the low trust individual. As Rotter states,

> it seems that high trusters can read the cues as well or as poorly as low trusters. They differ, however, in their willingness to trust the stranger when there are no clear-cut data about previous behavior. The high truster says to himself or herself, "I will trust the person until I have clear evidence that he or she can't be trusted." The low truster says, "I will not trust the person until there is clear evidence that he or she can be trusted." (1980, p. 6)

Both orientations are also prone to self-fulfilling prophecies. An individual with high interpersonal trust is likely to approach the other person, in attitude and style, in a way that communicates trust. Should the other be searching for cues as to appropriate behavior in this situation, she may respond with similarly high levels of trusting behavior. The other's behavior is thus likely to reward and reinforce the initial orientation of the high-trust individual, and lead to a high-trust (cooperative) relationship between the parties. In contrast, a low-trust individual is likely to approach the other, in attitude and style, in a way that communicates suspicion and mistrust of the other's motives and intentions. If the other is searching for cues as to the appropriate behavior, he may respond with low self-disclosure, dishonesty, and mistrust of the party. This behavior will thus reward and reinforce the initial low-trust orientation, and lead to a low-trust (competitive) relationship between the parties. In this way, levels of interpersonal trust can dramatically affect the cycle of trust and cooperation or mistrust and competition between negotiating parties, particularly if they have not had any significant prior interaction with one another. When there has been prior interaction, the parties would most likely pay more attention to the nature of the prior relationship to determine their initial orientation. In situations in which a high-trust individual is matched with a low-trust individual, we would again expect that each would be searching for cues as to the way that the other will behave and would adjust their behavior as a result of what the other does. Since the high truster's behavior may provide cues for the low truster to be exploitative at the same time as the low truster's behavior will put the high truster on guard, we would expect a competitive, low-trust relationship to evolve over time. Thus, over the long term, low trust and competition may drive out high trust and cooperation.

## Perspective-Taking Ability

Negotiators need to perceive, understand, and respond to arguments that the other party makes during negotiations. The ability to take the other person's perspective, especially during preparations for negotiation, should enable negotiators to prepare and respond to the arguments that the other party makes during negotiations (Neale and Bazerman, 1983). Neale and Northcraft define perspective-taking ability as "a negotiator's capacity to understand the other party's point of view during a negotiation and thereby to predict the other party's strategies and tactics" (1991, p. 174). Walton and McKersie (1965) suggest that distributive negotiators who better understand the resistance point of the other party will have a strategic advantage during negotiations. Negotiators who understand the other party's perspective will be more likely to form arguments that convince the other party and to find an agreement that satisfies the other party. Presumably, the ability to perceive the other party's perspective would also be important during integrative negotiations, as the negotiator strives to understand the other party's needs and interests and works to craft an agreement that satisfies the interests of both parties.

Neale and Bazerman (1983) investigated the importance of perspective-taking ability in a study of the effect of arbitration on distributive contract negotiations. They found that negotiators with higher perspective-taking ability successfully negotiated contracts of higher value than did negotiators with lower perspective-taking ability. The results of this study suggested that perspective-taking ability may influence the negotiation process by increasing the concession rate of the other negotiator. That is, negotiators who are high in perspective-taking ability appear to be able to increase the concessions that the other party is willing to make. In the only other published study to investigate the effects of perspective-taking ability, Greenhalgh and Neslin (1983) reported that perspective-taking ability was not correlated with settlement preferences or negotiated outcomes in a television advertisement negotiation simulation.

Perspective-taking ability would appear to be an important individual variable that may influence many different aspects of negotiations. No research has investigated the effects of perspective-taking ability on integrative negotiations, nor has research directly investigated how perspective-taking ability has an effect on the negotiation process.

## Self-Efficacy

Perceived self-efficacy is considered to be a critical aspect of mastering complex interpersonal skills, such as those involved in negotiation. Wood and Bandura (1989) define self-efficacy as "people's beliefs in their capabilities to mobilize the motivation, cognitive resources, and courses of action needed to exercise control over events in their lives" (p. 364). In essence, self-efficacy is a judgment about the ability to behave effectively in a given situation (Gist, Stevens, and Bavetta, 1991). People with high self-efficacy obtain higher outcomes in many organizational situations (Wood and Bandura, 1989). Self-efficacy influences performance directly and through setting higher goals and adopting more analytic strategies.

Gist, Stevens, and Bavetta (1991) suggest that self-efficacy may play an important role in negotiation. Their research used a salary negotiation simulation in which participants in an experiment played the role of an employee negotiating with her manager over the salary of a new job. Gist, Stevens, and Bavetta (1991; also see Stevens, Bavetta, and Gist, 1993) found that people with higher levels of self-efficacy obtained higher salaries in the simulation. Their research further suggested that self-efficacy leads to higher outcomes in the salary negotiation because people higher in self-efficacy were also more likely to set higher goals before the negotiation (see Chapter 3 for a discussion of the importance of goals).

Researchers have also investigated locus of control, a construct conceptually related to self-efficacy. Rotter (1967) defines locus of control as the extent to which people perceive that events are under their own control. Those who attribute the cause of events to external reasons (e.g., luck) are considered to have a high *external* locus of control whereas those who attribute the cause of events to internal reasons (e.g., ability) are considered to have a high *internal* locus of control (Rotter, 1967). In a distributive negotiation task, Ford (1983) found that Internals had higher resistance points than Externals. In addition, Ford found a tendency for teams composed of Internals to be more likely to stalemate during negotiations. In their television advertisement simulation study, Greenhalgh and Neslin (1983) found that Externals were more likely to prefer an impasse than a moderately favorable settlement. Although neither study found a direct effect of locus of control on negotiation outcomes, a study by Stolte (1983) of distributive negotiations in four-person networks made up of female college students suggests that Internals may negotiate higher outcomes than Externals, especially when they are in non-central positions in networks. Thus, the research findings suggest that locus of control may have an influence on negotiator aspirations, preferences, and negotiation outcomes.

### An Omnibus Approach

Rather than trying to identify a single personality dimension that influences negotiation outcomes, Greenhalgh, Neslin, and Gilkey (1985; see also Greenhalgh and Neslin, 1981, 1983; Gilkey and Greenhalgh, 1986) have conducted research that investigates the effects of numerous personality variables simultaneously. Over a period of five weeks, Greenhalgh and associates gathered 31 personality measures from 80 MBA students who participated in their study. These measures were then factor-analyzed, which resulted in 10 independent dimensions of negotiator personality: accommodating, outgoing, open-minded, assertive, driven, empathic, considerate, intelligent, people-oriented, and task-oriented. The students then participated in a simulation study in which they negotiated television commercial advertisements. Greenhalgh et al. measured the effects of personality on negotiator preferences for outcomes and the actual outcomes negotiated during the simulation. The results of the study showed that personality had a significant effect on preferences for negotiation outcomes, and these preferences in turn had a significant effect on the outcomes obtained in the negotiation. However, personality did not have a significant direct effect on the outcomes negotiated in the simulation.

## SEX, GENDER, AND NEGOTIATION: NEW APPROACHES[2]

We will use the term *sex* to refer to the biological categories of male and female, and the term *gender* to refer to the psychological aspects associated with each category (Deaux, 1985). Most of the empirical research on male-female differences in negotiation has examined sex differences and then posited theoretical aspects of gender to account for any differences found. For instance, a typical experiment may examine how males and females bargain differently in integrative negotiations. If differences are found, they are interpreted in reference to gender (e.g., men and women are socialized differently as children, and this explains an aspect of adult bargaining behavior). We agree with Deaux (1985) that there is more than just a semantic difference between the terms *sex* and *gender*. Investigators who study sex differences seem to implicitly believe that any differences found may be rooted in biological differences whereas investigators who examine gender lean more heavily toward the social causes of behavior (Deaux, 1985). Few investigators would support purely biological or purely social explanations of behavior; the difference is in the implicit assumptions underlying the research. One consequence of these different foci is that those studying biological causes of behavior will perceive that change in behavior is less possible than those who examine social causes. One weakness of the research in this area has been the use of sex rather than gender as the independent variable—we were unable to locate any study that directly compared subjects by gender (e.g., sex role) in the negotiation literature.

The most researched individual difference factor in negotiation has been the search for sex differences in negotiation. As a whole, this research has continued to yield contradictory findings, with some recent research suggesting little or no

---

[2] We follow the tradition of social psychology and treat gender as an individual difference variable. Feminist researchers have recently begun to investigate gender and negotiation (e.g., Kolb and Coolidge, 1991; Gray, in press). Their work suggests that the effects of gender on negotiation may be much broader than it has been conceptualized to date. For instance, negotiations occur in a gendered world. What factors cause gender to be an issue in negotiation? How do aspects of the setting influence how the same behavior may be interpreted differently if the source is a male or a female? How does our understanding about negotiation reflect a male point of view? Each of the questions takes a perspective on gender that is much broader than individual differences, and they are also beyond the scope of this chapter.

difference between male and female negotiators (Carnevale and Lawler, 1987; Pruitt, Carnevale, Forcey, and Van Slyck, 1986; Putnam and Jones, 1982) whereas other recent research documents significant differences between male and female negotiators (e.g., Kimmel, Pruitt, Magenau, Konar-Goldband, and Carnevale, 1980; Neu, Graham, and Gilly, 1988; Pruitt and Syna, 1985; Watson and Kasten, 1988). There is no simple answer to the question of how sex and gender influence negotiation, but there has been significant progress in *how* this question has been addressed. We turn now to a critique of previous research on the effects of sex and gender on negotiation and then conclude with a discussion of some new research that is beginning to provide some interesting findings on this topic.

### Theoretical Approaches to Understanding Male and Female Negotiators

Kolb and Coolidge (1991) suggest that there are differences in the way that males and females negotiate but that research on this topic has been so fundamentally flawed that it has been unable to detect these differences. One of the main problems with research on gender and negotiation has been "its very conception of gender as a stable set of characteristics that describe all women (or men) in negotiation situations" (Kolb and Coolidge, 1991, p. 273). That is, research has tended to treat sex and gender as factors that may affect many aspects of negotiations for all male and female negotiators. This ignores differences *among* women and men, and it makes the finding of stable differences difficult to detect in research. In addition, it is not clear *how* gender influences negotiation. Does it influence negotiator preferences? Strategies and tactics? Concessions? Direct outcomes? Situational factors combine with sex and gender to influence these variables in complex ways; thus, it is difficult to independently determine the precise effect that sex and gender have on negotiation behavior and outcomes.

Kolb and Coolidge argue that women approach negotiations in a way that is fundamentally different from men. They suggest that there are at least four ways that women conceptualize negotiations differently:

1. *Relational view of others.* Women are very aware of the relationships among the parties who are negotiating and the larger context within which negotiation takes place. A negotiation is not merely deciding how to resolve the content of the issues being discussed. Equally important to the needs and interests that are discussed during the negotiation is learning how the other party perceives the situation. According to Kolb and Coolidge, "(e)xpressions of emotion and feeling and learning how the other experiences the situation are as important, if not more important, than the substance of the discourse" (1991, p. 264). Contrast this way of perceiving negotiations with the stereotypical male who tends to be task oriented and wants to resolve the matter at hand, not to concentrate on the other party's feelings or perceptions except to understand them for their pragmatic value during the negotiation.

Women, on the other hand, are more likely to find value from the relationship itself, regardless of the issues being negotiated.

2. *Embedded view of agency.* Closely related to the importance of relationships, Kolb and Coolidge argue that women tend not to draw strict boundaries between negotiating and other aspects of their relationships with other people. Women are more likely to see negotiation as a behavior that occurs within relationships without large divisions marking when it begins and ends. Contrast this with the stereotypical male approach to negotiation, which tends to begin with a light discussion ("break the ice"), moves on to the negotiation phase ("talking turkey"), and concludes with another light discussion ("cement the deal"). In this way males tend to demarcate negotiating from other behaviors that occur in the relationship, and they signal the beginning and end of the negotiations behaviorally. Because women are more likely to see negotiations as flowing more naturally from the relationship, they may be less likely "to recognize that negotiations are occurring unless they are specifically demarcated [by an external power] from the background against which they occur" (Kolb and Coolidge, 1991, p. 265).

3. *Control through empowerment.* Women perceive and use power differently than men. According to Kolb and Coolidge, women are more likely to seek empowerment where there is "interaction among all parties in the relationship to build connection and enhance everyone's power" (1991, p. 265). This is a different way of perceiving power than the stereotypical male, who tends to use power to achieve his own goals or to force the other party to capitulate to his point of view. Although women's conceptualization of power may make them more comfortable with integrative than distributive negotiation, the fit is not perfect (Kolb and Coolidge, 1991).

4. *Problem solving through dialogue.* Women also tend to use dialogue during negotiations differently than men. Women "seek to engage the other in a joint exploration of ideas whereby understanding is progressively clarified through interaction" (Kolb and Coolidge, 1991, p. 266). Women alternatively listen and contribute, and this results in "the weaving of collective narratives that reflect newly-emerging understanding" (Kolb and Coolidge, 1991, p. 266). Contrast this with the stereotypical male view of communication during negotiation, in which the man uses dialogue to convince the other party that his position is correct, their position is incorrect, and various tactics and ploys are used to win points during the discussion.

## Empirical Approaches to Understanding Male and Female Negotiators

Empirical evidence also shows that males and females conceive of negotiations differently. Pinkley (1989, 1990, 1992; Pinkley and Northcraft, in press) has sought to identify how disputants interpret conflict situations. Her research used a critical incidents methodology where people remembered and described a recent dispute in which they were involved. Pinkley found that disputants use three dimensions to interpret conflicts: relationship versus task, emotional versus intellectual, and compromise versus win. She found that women were more likely to perceive conflict episodes in relationship terms, whereas males were more likely to perceive the task characteristics of conflict episodes. The focus on relationships and task characteristics was also related to better relationship outcomes and task outcomes, respectively (Pinkley, 1989). Pinkley found no differences between male and female perceptions of conflict on the other two dimensions. Watson and Kasten (1988) also reported differences in the way that males and females perceive negotiations. In simulated negotiation study with managers as participants, Watson and Kasten found that women perceived assertive male behavior as more assertive than males perceived the same behavior.

Not only do women perceive negotiations differently than men, there is growing evidence that they are often treated differently (worse) than men during negotiations. We will consider research findings from two different domains: negotiating the purchase of a new car and salary negotiations.

Ayres (1991; see also Siegelman and Ayres, 1991) has conducted a series of intriguing experiments documenting how men and women are treated during negotiations for a new car. Ayres assigned three different pairs of negotiators (black female/white male, black male/white male, white female/white male) to shop for a new car at 90 Chicago-area car dealerships. The same white male negotiator participated in all pairs. Each negotiator in the pair separately visited the same car dealership on different days and bargained for a new car (negotiators chose the particular car for each negotiation from a list; no cars were actually purchased). Negotiators received two days of training before visiting their first car dealer. They followed a set script during the negotiations, and they were similar in terms of age, education, dress, economic class, occupation, and attractiveness. The major dependent variables in the research were estimates of dealer profits from the initial and final offers that negotiators received. Dealer profits were calculated as the difference between published list prices of the cars and the offers received by the negotiators (dealer fixed costs were ignored in the study).

Ayres found that negotiators received very different offers from the car dealers included in the study, and that these offers differed significantly depending on the negotiators' gender and race (see Table 11.2). White males received the most favorable offers, followed in order by white females, black males, and black females. When the bargaining process (number of bids and counterbids) was examined, Ayres found that differences in the opening offers accounted for the majority of the differences in the final offers that the negotiators achieved. Concession rates and the length of the negotiation were *not* found to differ significantly across the gender and race of the negotiators.

The results of Ayres' study suggests that people are treated differently when they bargain for new cars—women and blacks may start negotiations at a less favorable position than white males. It is not clear why women and blacks are treated this way—it could be racism, sexism, or opportunistic behavior by the car dealers (dealers may believe that women and blacks are willing to pay more than

**TABLE 11.2**   Average Car Dealer Profit

| Experimenter | Initial Offer | Final Offer |
|---|---|---|
| White male | $ 818 | $ 362 |
| White female | 829 | 504 |
| Black male | 1,534 | 783 |
| Black female | 2,169 | 1,237 |

Note: Profit figures are estimates that Ayres calculated from published list prices of the new cars.

These figures are taken from I. Ayres, "Fair Driving: Gender and Race Discrimination in Retail Car Negotiations," *Harvard Law Review, 104,*1991, pp. 817–872.

white males for the same product). Note that there was *no* evidence that the negotiation *process* was different for women and blacks than white males; the differences in the final deals obtained were present in the opening offers made to the different negotiators, and these differences carried through to the final offers. Consider what this means to the typical negotiator in Ayres' study. Each negotiator received the *same* average concession from the car dealers during the negotiation, so in a relative sense, they believed that they negotiated a good deal. It is only when the results are compared across groups (which typically would not occur because most people simply don't know enough other people buying the same car to make these comparisons) that differences based on sex and race become clear. Finally, although Ayres controlled for many factors during the study, it is possible that an uncontrolled variable may have accounted for the results.

Research on salary negotiations by job seekers also documents how males and females may receive different treatment and outcomes during negotiations. In a study of recent MBA graduates, Gerhart and Rynes (1991) found that males received a higher monetary payoff for bargaining their salary than did females. Men and women were equally likely to bargain for their starting salary in the study. Although Gerhart and Rynes statistically controlled for the effects of industry, college major, grade point average, and business experience on the salaries received, it is possible that differences other than gender may still account for their results.

The results of a study by Dreher, Dougherty, and Whitely (1989) suggest that not only do males and females receive different outcomes during salary negotiations, but also that the same negotiation tactic may have opposite effects on salary negotiation outcomes depending upon whether is used by a male employee or a female employee (see also Kolb, 1992). Dreher, Dougherty, and Whitely (1989) found that the use of exchange tactics had a positive effect on the outcome of salary negotiations of male employees and a negative effect on the outcome of salary negotiations of female employees. That is, women using the *same* negotiation tactic (exchange) that males used successfully in their negotiations were less successful when they used it. Exchange tactics include reminding supervisors of previous favors and offers to make sacrifices for outcomes. These researchers suggest that women who use exchange tactics "may violate stereotypic expectations about appropriate female behavior," and therefore are penalized for using this tactic (p. 547). A possible alternative explanation, given these findings, is that women are less effective in their use of exchange tactics than men because women feel less comfortable in using them. This remains an open research question.

In conclusion, it is clear that women conceive of negotiations differently than men. More research and theory is required to understand the extent of the differences between males and females in their conceptualization of negotiation (see Gray, in press). A growing body of evidence suggests that women are treated differently before and during negotiations than men. To date, this research has been conducted only with distributive negotiations. The results of each of the studies reviewed above may be subject to an alternate explanation. Taken as a group, however, they suggest that women may be disadvantaged when they negotiate simply because they are women. The nature of this disadvantage may occur in receiving worse opening offers from the other party, receiving worse outcomes in similar negotiations than males, and in being penalized when they use the same negotiation tactic that males use successfully.

## THE BEHAVIORAL APPROACH

Some research has been conducted to try to identify how superior negotiators behave, rather than to identify the personality characteristics of better negotiators. The implicit assumption underlying this research is that negotiators who can copy or imitate the behavior of successful negotiators will become better negotiators themselves. Three approaches have been used to study the behavior of successful negotiators: (1) comparison of superior and average negotiators in actual negotiations, (2) comparison of expert and amateur negotiators in simulated negotiations, and (3) comparison of experienced and naive negotiators in simulated negotiations. Each of these approaches has strengths and weaknesses; none of them is ideal. However, this research does provide some interesting insights about how superior negotiators behave.

The most comprehensive study comparing superior and average negotiators in actual negotiations was conducted by Rackham (1992). Rackham compared the behavior of labor relations negotiators from a total of 102 actual negotiation sessions. He found important differences between superior and average negotiators during prenegotiation planning, face-to-face negotiations, and postnegotiation review. Table 11.3 summarizes the results of this study. Although the results of Rackham's study may not be fully applicable to relations negotiations outside of labor relations, many of the findings seem to be sensible advice for all negotiators.

Neale and Northcraft (1986) compared the performance of expert and amateur negotiators in a simulated negotiation market. This task allows buyers (sellers) the opportunity to negotiate with any other seller (buyer) in the market, but

**TABLE 11.3**    Behaviors of Superior Negotiators

---

**During Prenegotiation Planning:**
1. Considered more outcome options for the issues being discussed.
2. Spent more time looking for areas of common ground.
3. Thought more about the long-term consequences of different issues.
4. Prepared their goals around ranges rather than fixed points.
5. Did not form their plans into strict sequential order.

**During Face-to-Face Bargaining:**
1. Made fewer immediate counterproposals.
2. Were less likely to describe their offers in glowingly positive terms.
3. Avoided defend-attack cycles.
4. Used behavioral labeling, except when disagreeing.
5. Asked more questions, especially to test understanding.
6. Summarized compactly the progress made in the negotiation.
7. Did not dilute their arguments by including weak reasons when they were trying to persuade the other party.

**During Postnegotiation Review:**
1. Reserved time to review what they learned from the negotiation.

---

Adapted from N. Rackham, "The Behavior of Successful Negotiators," Huthwaite Research Group, 1980. Reprinted in R. J. Lewicki, J. A. Litterer, D. M. Saunders, and J. W. Minton (eds.), *Negotiation: Readings, Exercises and Cases,* 2nd ed. (Homewood, IL: Richard D. Irwin, 1992).

each buyer/seller pair may make only one deal. There is typically not enough time in market studies for all possible buyer and seller pairs to make a deal. The expert negotiators in the study were professional negotiators with over 10 years average experience in formal negotiations. The amateur negotiators were graduate and undergraduate college students. Neale and Northcraft found that although both experts and amateurs reached more integrative solutions as the market progressed, experts were more integrative at the beginning of the negotiations than amateurs. Experts also tended to receive higher average outcomes than amateurs, although this difference was not very strong.

Thompson (1990a) examined the effects of experience with integrative bargaining on judgment accuracy, behavior, and negotiation outcomes in a longitudinal simulation study. In a creatively designed study, Thompson formed two groups of negotiators. In the experienced negotiator group, negotiators bargained with a different person in seven different integrative negotiation simulations; these negotiators increased their experience in integrative negotiation during the study. In the naive negotiator group, negotiators had either no previous experiences or one experience with integrative negotiation in the simulation; these negotiators had only one opportunity to increase their experience in the study. Thompson found that negotiators made more accurate judgments about the other party's priorities as they gained experience, and that the likelihood of negotiating favorable agreements increased with experience, especially for a naive negotiator who had no previous experience with the simulation. However, experience with the simulation did not improve the experts' ability to identify issues where both parties had compatible interests.

In summary, research from the behavioral perspective suggests that there are many ways that superior negotiators behave differently than average negotiators. There is no ideal method for studying expert negotiators. Participant observation may change the process that is being observed, and frequently it is difficult for experimenters to gain access to actual negotiations (see Rackham, 1992). Although precision and control can be increased with laboratory simulations, simulations may lack the richness of actual negotiations. The most appropriate approach is a combination of the two, be it in the same study or across experiments as described in the three studies above. Unfortunately, few studies have been conducted that examine the behavior of expert or experienced negotiators. The existing studies need to be replicated and extended, and negotiator behavior appears to be a particularly fertile ground for further research on individual differences in negotiation.

## CLOSING COMMENTS

No single personality type or characteristic is directly and consistently linked to success in negotiation. Everyday experience and research suggests that personality does play an important role in negotiation processes and outcomes. Research in this area has been fragmented, however, and findings are often contradictory and complex. Our review of the research exploring individual differences and negotiation revealed two additional concerns that sorely need to be addressed by future research, in addition to those research ideas discussed throughout the chapter.

First, the majority of the research examining individual differences and negotiation has concentrated on distributive negotiations. The few studies that have examined individual differences and integrative negotiations have generally limited their study of integrative bargaining to log rolling (see Chapter 4). More detailed research on the individual difference factors related to integrative negotiating is clearly needed. Research identifying the personality and behavioral characteristics that distinguish superior from average integrative negotiators has yet to be conducted. By limiting the study of the effects of personality and other individual differences to distributive negotiations, researchers have inadvertently constrained the variance of the behaviors measured in their studies. Artificially constraining the variance makes it far less likely that significant effects due to individual differences will be found (see Johns, 1991). Future researchers need to study a wide range of negotiation situations in addition to the typical distributive negotiation task currently included in studies of the effects of individual differences on negotiation.

The second research concern that we have identified relates to *how* research on individual differences and negotiation has been conducted. Far more attention needs to be given to the design of studies that investigate individual differences and negotiation, especially to the negotiation part of the equation. In the past 10 years, researchers in this area have become far more sophisticated in identifying and measuring the individual difference characteristics that should influence negotiations. Greenhalgh and Neslin (1983; Greenhalgh, Neslin, and Gilkey, 1985) have been especially strong in identifying and measuring personality factors that could affect negotiations. What is missing from this field of research, however, is attention to the negotiation tasks used. Virtually all the research in this area includes one or more measures of personality variables, has subjects negotiate in a simulation, and then compares perceptual, behavioral, or outcome data as a function of personality. The flaw in this approach is that the research designs include only *one* instance of negotiation from which the dependent measures are collected. Most definitions of personality suggest that it is a generalized tendency for people to respond in a similar manner *across situations or time* (see Epstein, 1979, 1980). The appropriate way to study the effects of personality on negotiation is to gather data from many different negotiation situations and to investigate the effects of individual differences on the *average* negotiation outcome (perception, behavior, and so on). This method allows measurement and other errors to cancel each other out across negotiation situations and increases the probability that true individual differences will be found. Gathering behavioral data from multiple occurrences has become the standard method of assessing the personality-behavior relationship in other domains of behavioral research. *No study examining the effects of individual differences on negotiation has been conducted in this manner.* Thompson's (1990a) study of experienced and naive negotiators is close, but it did not examine the effects of existing individual differences on negotiation. Although much can and has been learned from studies that examine only one negotiation, it is time that researchers explored this area with a research method that more accurately assesses the full effects of individual differences on negotiation.

## SUMMARY

In this chapter, we reviewed the past and current research on the effects of individual differences on negotiation. This has been a very difficult question to address with controlled, systematic research. A wealth of research has shown that clear and simple effects do not exist. In many cases, the research methods have been inadequate to allow personality differences to emerge; in other cases, personality differences were obscured by major structural differences in the bargaining situation (e.g. the nature of the bargaining problem, relative power of negotiators, constituency pressures), or personality and structure have interacted to produce complex effects. Even comprehensive experiments that were designed to overcome many of these methodological problems have yielded inconclusive results.

Nevertheless, the search to understand the effect of individual differences on negotiation continues. We discussed several approaches to describing personality that may have some promise for characterizing differences among negotiators, including interpersonal orientation, conflict management style, Machiavellianism, interpersonal trust, perspective-taking ability, and self-efficacy. Each of these approaches appears to have good prima facie reasons for being directly related to individual differences in managing relationships with conflict and working competitively or collaboratively with others. Future research needs to explore the effect of these approaches in detail, particularly paying attention to how they affect both distributive and integrative negotiations. We also discussed research findings exploring the effects of gender on negotiation and the behavioral approach to studying individual differences. Both of these areas appear to be particularly fruitful for future research.

Many researchers believe that differences in a negotiator's personality play a far less important role in affecting negotiating outcomes than other key elements that we have discussed earlier in this book. It has become popular to believe that a negotiator is highly likely to succeed as long as he has a good understanding of the issues at stake, understands the dynamics of distributive and integrative bargaining, knows the role that likely will be played by differences in power and constituency pressures, has prepared for negotiation, and has worked out a plan to use effective persuasion. We suggest that researchers may have closed the book on the effects of individual differences on negotiation prematurely and that individual differences may have an important (and as yet undetermined) effect on the process and outcome of negotiations. Future researchers, however, must be careful to include many different negotiation situations in their studies so that the influence of individual differences on negotiations may be assessed appropriately.

# CHAPTER 12

# Third Party Interventions

In Chapter 6 we reviewed a number of techniques that negotiators themselves can use to break deadlocks, reduce unproductive tension and hostility, and return negotiations to a productive pace. However, frequently the parties cannot effectively implement these techniques by themselves. As we will explain, when the "heat of battle" overwhelms negotiators, mistrust and suspicion are high, or the parties cannot take actions toward defusing conflict without those actions being misinterpreted and mistrusted by others, third party involvement may become necessary. This chapter will describe the typical roles that third parties play and how those roles contribute to conflict resolution.

## ADDING THIRD PARTIES TO THE
## NEGOTIATION PROCESS

Third parties arise from a number of sources and situations, and they work to manage disputes in a wide variety of different styles and techniques. Often third parties need do no more than implement some of the dispute resolution techniques reviewed in Chapter 6, such as aiding in the reduction of tension, controlling the number of issues, enhancing communication, establishing a common ground, and highlighting certain decision options to make them more attractive to the parties. As we will point out, some of these techniques are more specific to certain styles of third-party negotiation than others.

The essence of negotiation entails parties working face-to-face, without the direct involvement of others. It is exactly this sort of direct, personal involvement that creates the understanding of the issues and the personal commitment necessary to manage conflict constructively. As long as this direct form of negotiation proves productive, it is best to allow it to proceed without the involvement of other parties. As we say throughout this book, however, negotiations are often tense, difficult, and generate more "heat" than "light." Negotiation over critical issues may also reach an impasse free of anger and resentment, but an impasse, nevertheless; the parties are unable to move the process beyond a particular sticking point. At these points, third party intervention may be a productive (if not the *only*) way to break deadlocks and get the negotiations back on track.

## Advantages and Disadvantages of Third-Party Intervention

At a minimum, third parties can provide (or even enforce) the stability, civility, and forward momentum necessary for the negotiators to readdress the problems at hand—problems central to the negotiation, and problems that have stalled or derailed it. Depending on the nature of the third party and the type of intervention involved, third-party interventions can provide a number of general advantages, including these:

Breathing space, or a cooling off period.

Reestablished or enhanced communications.

Refocus on the substantive issues.

Remedy or repair for strained relationships.

Establishment of or recommitment to time limits.

Salvaging the "sunk cost" of stalled negotiations.

Increased levels of negotiator satisfaction with and commitment to the conflict resolution process and its outcomes.

Even if the relationship between the parties is so damaged that future exchanges would be highly problematic, third parties may provide vehicles and processes that enable some degree of hostility abatement and closure on the issues at hand.

However, third party interventions may also present certain *dis*advantages. At a minimum, third party involvement represents a failure of the negotiation process, even if only temporarily. Third party intervention signals that parties have failed to grow, to build relationships, or to become more adept in managing their own lives and conflicts. This is especially true when parties turn to arbitration (which we will discuss later) since the parties lose (or abdicate) control over their own outcomes in the resolution. Arbitration hearings can be viewed as the result of negotiators' "agreement to disagree" (and nothing else). Other types of third-party interventions (especially process consultation, also discussed later) have as their express purpose the *enhancement* of parties' dispute resolution skills—their goal is to maintain the ultimate exercise of control by the parties themselves. Thus, as we will show, each type of third-party intervention presents its own particular advantages and disadvantages.

## Third-Party Interventions: When and Which Kind?

Our premise is that third-party intervention should be avoided as long as negotiations have a chance of proceeding unaided, that is, as long as progress is occurring or is likely to occur within reasonable limits of time and other resources. However, if intervention becomes advisable, it should be done in a timely and judicious manner. Third-party intervention may be sought by the negotiators themselves, or it may be imposed "from without" by choice, custom, or regulation. This outside imposition of third-party intervention, addressed later in this chapter in the section on informal third-party styles, may bring in the perspective of someone who is not party to the dispute per se, but is interested nonetheless in its resolution. Although we take a decidedly managerial view of these third-party processes (dispute resolution being a desirable managerial or supervisory skill in organizational settings), third parties who are friends or peers of the negotiators may also intervene. As a rule of thumb, uninvited interventions that are not sanctioned or reinforced by expertise, friendship, or the recognition of authority are unwelcome. Uninvited third parties may find themselves bearing the brunt of hostility from one (or even both) parties in a negotiation, regardless of the third party's intentions or motivations.

**When Is Third-Party Involvement Appropriate?**    Serious negotiators must make a realistic effort to resolve their own disputes. In labor/management negotiations, for example, failure to "bargain in good faith" has been codified as an unfair labor practice (ULP) under current U.S. labor law [N.L.R.A., Sections 8(a)(5) and 8(b)(3)]. In general, though, negotiators initiate third-party interventions when they believe they can no longer handle the dispute on their own. When one negotiator requests intervention, it must be acceptable to all the disputing parties. If only one party recognizes a need for third-party intervention, he must usually persuade the other party to go along. However, interventions may also be *imposed* by someone with power or authority over the negotiators when a failure to resolve the dispute threatens to lead to significant costs for the affected organization or for individuals affected by (but unable to act on) the dispute being negotiated. Moore (1986) provides a list of conditions that might create the need for mediation. Negotiators might seek third party involvement if they experience or observe any of these:

> Intense emotions that appear to be preventing a settlement.
>
> Poor quality or quantity of communication, beyond the ability of the negotiators to fix (see Chapter 7).
>
> Misperceptions or stereotypes that hinder productive exchanges.
>
> Repeated negative behaviors (e.g., anger, name-calling, blaming others, etc.) creating barriers between the parties.
>
> Serious disagreement over the importance, collection, or evaluation of data.
>
> Disagreement as to the number, order, and combinations of issues under dispute.
>
> Actual or perceived incompatible interests that the parties are unable to reconcile.
>
> Unnecessary (but perceived-as-necessary) value differences that divide the parties.
>
> Absence of a clear, common negotiation procedure or protocol, or not using established procedures (such as caucuses or cooling-off periods) to their best advantage.
>
> Severe difficulties initiating negotiations or "bargaining through" an impasse (Moore, Christopher W. *The Mediation Process: Practical Strategies for Resolving Conflict,* copyright 1986 by Christopher W. Moore and Jossey-Bass Inc., Publishers, pp. 11–12).

**FIGURE 12.1**    Categories of Third Party Intervention

Level of negotiator control over outcome

|  | Low | High |
|---|---|---|
| **Low** | Autocracy | Mediation |
| **High** | Arbitration | Negotiation |

**Level of negotiator control over procedure**

Adapted from B.H. Sheppard (1984), Third Party Conflict Intervention: A Procedural Framework. In B. M. Staw and L. L. Cummings (Eds), *Research in Organizational Behavior,* Vol. 6 (Greenwich, CT: JAI Publishing), pp. 141–190, and from J. Thibaut and L. Walker, *Procedural Justice: A Psychological Analysis* (Hillsdale, NJ: Lawrence Erlbaum Associates, 1975).

**Which Type of Intervention Is Appropriate?**    In third-party processes, negotiators typically surrender control over neither, either, or both dispute process (the *how*) and dispute outcome (the *what*) (see Figure 12.1).

Surrender of neither process nor outcome control constitutes negotiation as addressed by most of this book; surrender of both constitutes a complete withdrawal from negotiation and dependence on the peremptory involvement of an otherwise uninvolved person. Of the two mixed situations (arbitration and mediation, both discussed in detail later in this chapter), mediation is third-party involvement that is usually only *procedural* in nature. Many of the conditions listed by Moore (1986; see the preceding list) are also *procedural* in nature. Mediation, then, is less intrusive in that negotiators surrender control over process while maintaining control over outcomes. Third-party procedural control (i.e., mediation) can be highly effective in dispute resolution (compare Carnevale and Pruitt, 1992), while helping to preserve an important benefit of "unassisted" negotiation: control over, and thus commitment to, successful resolution. Negotiators in successfully mediated disputes tend to be "psychologically and structurally committed to (their) agreement" (Moore, 1986, p. 253). Our corollary to the rule "no third-party involvement unless necessary," then, is "if involvement is necessary, use a minimally intrusive intervention," such as mediation.

As for invited interventions, they support the needs of negotiators who desire guidance or procedural assistance but wish to maintain control over the choice and implementation of the ultimate outcome. Battle-weary negotiators may feel they just want an end to the dispute, but abdicating control completely to a third party will likely have a number of detrimental effects (see the discussion of arbitration later in this chapter). Choice of invited intervention may also be a function of what is available—what a community or organization offers, as well as what the negotiating parties know how to seek (and use). Failure to use third-party intervention when appropriate is just as wasteful and as damaging to the ultimate negotiation process as using the wrong intervention method (e.g., arbitration rather than mediation, when negotiator commitment to outcomes is critical for a lasting resolution), or even using the right method at the wrong time (e.g., before negotiators have exhausted unassisted methods [see Chapter 6] or after expressed anger and personal attacks have soured one or both parties on the entire process; see also Conlon and Fasolo, 1990).

The same measures of propriety and timeliness apply to uninvited interventions, as when a manager chooses to intervene in a dispute between two of her subordinates. The chooser (who, in this case, is usually the intervening third party) has the advantage of being potentially more objective than the disputants about the choices of whether and how to intervene.[1] The chooser must also keep in mind, however, the likely effect of the intervention on the negotiators, specifically on their ability to address and manage disputes more effectively in the future. Examples of this include the chilling and narcotic effects (described later when we discuss arbitration as a third-party process), or dependency of the disputants on the third party to continue to solve their problems for them, as often happens in therapeutic relations (compare Beckhard, 1978). Again, the operant rule is one of moderation (intervene and control only as deeply as appropriate), and—to borrow a medical dictum—"first, do no harm" to the negotiators or their willingness and ability to negotiate. In other words, use surgery when needed, but not when simple first aid would be sufficient. This advice assumes an overriding value in the negotiators' continued (or improved) ability to interact constructively; it also assumes that dispute resolution is not critically time dependent. To the extent that the disputants will have little or no interaction in the future or resolution timeliness is critical, relatively more invasive (i.e., controlling) interventions may be acceptable—even necessary. Quite often, neither of these conditions apply; we discuss choice processes in these less drastic situations in more detail later in this chapter.

---

[1] Two problems exist here. First, "naive" third parties may lack objectivity (i.e., impartiality) in that they have a feeling or value position about what is "right" as opposed to an interest in helping to resolve the dispute solely by working "to reconcile the competing interests of the two parties" (Moore, 1986, p. 17). Second, recent research by Conlon and Ross (1993) suggests that "partisan" third parties who lack impartiality (due to prior affiliation with one or both parties or to an overt bias as expressed by a lopsided imposed settlement) could have a significant effect on disputant satisfaction regarding the third-party intervention.

# AN OVERVIEW OF FORMAL INTERVENTION METHODS

Third-party interventions can be described as formal or informal. By *formal,* we mean roles and activities that are intentionally designed and recognized as third parties in a traditional sense, such as those taken by judges, labor arbitrators, divorce mediators, or process consultants such as psychologists or organization development (OD) practitioners. By *informal,* we mean roles and behaviors that are *incidental* to other, primary roles and behaviors such as those of managers, supervisors, or concerned friends. In this section, we describe three *formal* styles of third-party behavior: arbitration, mediation, and process consultation. In the next section of the chapter, we will address informal intervention techniques. We will review the objectives, style, and procedural impact of each approach and describe their impact on negotiation outcomes. As with many of the other areas of research that we have reviewed, the literature on third-party intervention in dispute resolution is large and growing rapidly. As a result, we can only hope to extract the most basic concepts and applications of each third-party style. Refer to the references to explore the research in greater detail or achieve a richer understanding of how to apply certain third-party models.

## Arbitration

Arbitration typically involves low or nonexistent levels of negotiator control over outcomes, but it retains high levels of negotiator control over process (see Figure 12.1). Even though arbitration represents loss of outcome control by negotiating parties, it is probably the most common and well-known form of third-party dispute resolution. The process is fairly clear-cut: parties in dispute, after having reached a deadlock or a time deadline without successful resolution of their differences, present their positions to a third party. The third party listens to both sides and then makes a ruling in regard to the outcome of the dispute (Elkouri and Elkouri, 1985; Prasow and Peters, 1983). Arbitration is used widely in disputes between businesses (Corley, Black, and Reed, 1977) and between business and their union-organized workers (e.g., Elkouri and Elkouri, 1985).

Arbitrators may hear and rule on a single issue under dispute or multiple issues in a total settlement package (Feigenbaum, 1975). Arbitration may be voluntary or binding. Under *voluntary* arbitration, the parties may submit their arguments to an arbitrator, but they are not required to comply with the arbitrator's decision. In contrast, *binding* arbitration requires the parties to comply with the decision, either by law or by their own previous commitment. A third variation in approaches to arbitration concerns the arbitrator's discretion. At one extreme, arbitrators are free to craft (and impose) any resolution they deem appropriate; at the other, their choice is severely constrained, as in "final offer" arbitration in which the arbitrator must approve *without amendment* one of the positions presented by the two disputing parties. (In labor management settings, management will frequently attempt to control the situation by charging the arbitrator to "neither add to nor detract from" the labor contract being interpreted; that is, the arbi-

---

**Arbitration with a Twist**

In an interesting variation, the Council of Better Business Bureaus, Inc., through its "Auto-Line" program, offers arbitration of consumer complaints on vehicles manufactured by participating corporations. Under the Auto-Line Program, local Better Business Bureaus offer arbitration by trained volunteers, with a twist: The arbitrator's decision is binding on the manufacturer, but not on the consumer-complainant, who is free to pursue other (chiefly litigational) remedies if they find the arbitration decision unacceptable.

---

trator's discretion to read into the contract or to rule outside of a strict interpretation of it is tightly curtailed.) The pros and cons of these variations will become evident as we critique arbitration.

Arbitration is most commonly used as a dispute resolution mechanism in labor relations. New contracts (chiefly in the public sector) that cannot be achieved through negotiation are frequently submitted for consideration (i.e., for "interest" arbitration), and disputes (grievances) about the coverage or interpretation of existing contracts are traditionally resolved by "grievance" arbitration.

Arbitration has come under increasing scrutiny and criticism as a dispute resolution mechanism, even in the labor relations area (e.g., Brett and Goldberg, 1983). Arbitration initially appears to have two distinct advantages as a resolution procedure: It imposes a clear-cut resolution to the dispute, and thereby the costs of prolonged, unresolved disputes can be avoided. However, as Kochan (1980) and others note, arbitration appears to have several negative consequences as well:

**The Chilling Effect.**   If the parties in negotiation anticipate that their own failure to agree will lead to a binding arbitrator's intervention, it may cool their incentive to work seriously for a negotiated settlement. This chilling effect occurs as "the parties avoid making compromises they might be otherwise willing to make, because they fear that the fact finder or arbitrator will split the difference between their stated positions" (Kochan, 1980, p. 291). If negotiators anticipate that the arbitrator will split the difference, then it is in their best interest to maintain an extreme, hard-line position because difference splitting is more likely to result in the hard-liner's favor. Research (Long and Feuille, 1974; Starke and Notz, 1981) supports this claim and suggests final offer arbitration (discussed below) as a better alternative. In final offer arbitration, the arbitrator must choose either one party's position or the other's—nothing in between, no splitting the difference. Given this constraint, it is believed that bargainers will be more motivated to settle, or to close the gap that will be arbitrated as much as possible, to minimize the loss that will occur if the arbitrator picks the other party's position as the basis for the arbitration award.

**The Narcotic Effect.**   When arbitration is anticipated as a result of the failure of parties to agree, negotiators may also lose interest in the process of negotiating. Because hard bargaining is costly in time and effort, there is no guarantee that agreement will be reached, and an imposed settlement is a guarantee under arbitration, negotiators may take the easy way out. Negotiator passivity, loss of initiative, and dependence on the third party are common results of recurring dispute arbitration. These results are even more likely when negotiators are accountable to constituencies because negotiators can take tough, unyielding stands on issues and blame compromise settlements on the arbitrator rather than on their own concessions.

**The Half-Life Effect.**   Parents are often aware that as the demand for arbitration from siblings increases, the sheer number of decisions required also increases and it becomes more likely that decisions will not please one or both sides. This is known as the half-life effect. For example, as one of the authors worked at home one Sunday afternoon, I was frequently subject to my children's demands to arbitrate disputes over sharing a home video game. After a series of decisions involving both my own children and half of the surrounding neighborhood, I was informed by my own child that my decisions were generally viewed as capricious, unfair, and without appropriate compassion for my own sons, and that my services were no longer desired. As the frequency of arbitration increases, disenchantment with the adequacy and fairness of the process develops (Anderson and Kochan, 1977), and the parties may resort to other means to resolve their disputes.

**The Biasing Effect.**   Arbitrators must be careful that their decisions do not systematically favor one side or the other and that they maintain an image of fairness and impartiality (compare Conlon and Ross, 1993). Even if each decision, taken separately, appears to be a fair settlement of the current conflict issue, perceived patterns of partiality toward one side may jeopardize the arbitrator's acceptability in future disputes. Parties to potential labor arbitrations frequently review published decisions of likely arbitrators in an effort to secure one likely to favor their own side or to avoid one who tends to make awards more consistently supportive of the other side.

**The Decision-Acceptance Effect.**   Finally, arbitrated disputes may engender less commitment to the settlement than alternative forms of dispute resolution. Research in the dynamics of group decision making (e.g., Vroom, 1973) has demonstrated that commitment to problem solutions and willingness to implement these solutions is significantly greater when group members participate in developing that solution than when it is imposed by a single member. Lasting dispute resolution requires timely and effective implementation, and "one of the most powerful drivers of effective implementation is the commitment to (a) decision that derives from *prior participation in making it*" (Leavitt and Bahrami, 1988, p. 173; emphasis added). For this reason, arbitration (as a procedure that minimizes disputants' choice of resolution or outcome) is likely to lead to situations in which disputants are less than fully committed to following through, especially if they feel dissatisfied with the arbitrator's decision.

## Mediation

In contrast to arbitration—and as a way to alleviate some of the problems with arbitration that we just discussed—mediation has developed increasing support (Kochan and Jick, 1978; Kochan, 1980), and it has been studied with increasing frequency (for literature reviews see Carnevale and Pruitt, 1992; Lewicki, Weiss and Lewin, 1992; and Wall and Lynn, 1993). Although the ultimate objective of mediation is the same as arbitration—to resolve the dispute—the major difference is that mediation seeks to achieve the objective by having the parties themselves develop and endorse the agreement. In fact, mediation has been called a form of "assisted negotiation" (Susskind and Cruikshank, 1987, p. 136) and "an extension and elaboration of the negotiation process" (Moore, 1986, p. 6), and "has always been an informal accompanist of negotiation" (Wall and Blum, 1991, p. 284). It is important to note that formal or contractual mediation is based on established and accepted rules and procedures; later in this chapter, when examining informal interventions, we will discuss emergent mediation, which is less well defined (Pruitt and Carnevale, 1993). Mediators have no formal power over *outcomes,* and they cannot resolve the dispute on their own or impose a solution. Instead, their effectiveness comes from their ability to meet with the parties individually, secure an understanding of the issues in dispute, identify areas of potential compromise in the positions of each side, and encourage the parties to make concessions toward agreement.

**Mediator Behaviors.**   Mediation generally proceeds in several stages (Folberg and Taylor, 1984; Kressel, 1972; Kochan, 1980; Lovenheim 1989; Moore, 1986; Wall, 1981). In the early stages of a dispute, a mediator will assume a reasonably passive role; he is most concerned with securing acceptance by the parties and with understanding the nature of the dispute. Mediator strategies may include separating the parties, questioning them about the issues, and actively listening to each side. The mediator must be able to separate rhetoric from true interest and to identify each side's priorities. Once this has been accomplished, the mediator will then begin managing the exchange of proposals and counterproposals, testing each side for areas where concessions may be possible.

As mediation progresses, mediators often become more active and take an aggressive role. They may bring the parties together for face-to-face deliberations, or they may keep them separate. They may press one or both sides to make concessions that the mediator judges to be essential. Mediators use many of the tactics we described in Chapter 6 at this stage. They may invent proposals and solutions that they think will be acceptable, testing them with each side or even announcing them publicly. The mediator will try to get the parties to agree in private. If the mediation effort has been successful, the mediator will ultimately bring the parties together to endorse a final agreement or to publicly announce their settlement. As Rubin (1980) notes, mediators primarily "facilitate concession-making without loss of face by the parties, and thereby promote more rapid and effective conflict resolution than would otherwise occur" (p. 380).

Several elements of the mediation process are integral to its success. The first is timing the mediation efforts based on the readiness of the parties. Because mediation is typically a voluntary process—the parties usually are not forced to enter into mediation except by their willingness to do so—mediation cannot be effective if the parties do not choose to cooperate. If they believe that they have more to gain by holding out or protracting the dispute, then mediation cannot work. Oddly enough, research suggests that when parties are pressured or required to enter mediation, they generally come away finding it to be a fair and satisfactory process (McEwen and Milburn, 1993). Mediators who judge that the parties are not ready for their intervention frequently tell them "call me when you're ready," and leave until the parties have achieved a greater willingness to participate in the process.[2]

Second, the mediator must be acceptable to the parties. The mediator is traditionally viewed as a neutral individual whom the parties recognize as impartial, experienced, and potentially helpful. An exception to this might be a friend, peer, or supervisor who chooses to intervene as a mediator; this is discussed in more detail later in this chapter. Mediators may be certified by an organization of third parties, such as the Federal Mediation and Conciliation Service of the U.S. Department of Labor, or a local mediation service or dispute settlement center, adding to their credibility. In addition, a variety of qualities such as integrity, impartiality and experience in comparable disputes may be required for a potential mediator to be viewed as acceptable by both sides. At times, however, the only (or most appropriate) mediator available is *not* without bias, to some degree. Although mediator bias has usually been thought to be incompatible with mediation effectiveness (Young, 1972), recent research has produced a less clear (if more complex) view of this problem (e.g., Smith, 1985; Touval and Zartman, 1985; Carnevale and Conlon, 1990; Conlon and Ross, 1993). Carnevale and Conlon (1990) suggest that mediator bias has two forms: that of general alignment or affiliation with parties prior to mediation, and that of greater support for one side than the other during mediation. However, disputants may overlook bias of the first sort if they are convinced that the mediator in question shows no bias of the second sort (i.e., actually mediates even-handedly).

As with arbitration, mediation's roots are in the field of labor relations, often

---

[2] Formal mediation in some settings (e.g., divorce, international hostilities, or certain types of organized labor strikes) may be *imposed* if doing so might prevent a situation from escalating or deteriorating beyond any hope of reclamation. This is usually a judgment call by an experienced mediator who is empowered by some external agency or authority to intervene (Donohue, 1991; Bercovitch, 1989).

as a preliminary step to arbitration in grievance and contractual negotiations. Mediation has also been described, though, as "the second oldest profession," having been around as long as conflict itself (Kolb, 1983a), and it is currently experiencing a dramatic rise in popularity as an alternative to the courts—particularly when the parties desire low-cost solutions that they can largely shape themselves (see Lovenheim, 1989). The Ford Foundation, in a 1978 report, documented many of the areas in which mediated settlements have occurred: malpractice suits, tort cases, small claims, pretrial diversions of alcohol and drug cases to treatment centers rather than criminal proceedings, consumer complaints, and liability claims, to name a few. Mediation has become an extremely popular alternative in divorce proceedings because the parties must be willing to abide by the terms of the settlement and therefore have the most influence in shaping its terms (Donohue, 1991; Kressel, Jaffe, Tuchman, Watson and Deutsch, 1977; Coogler, 1978). Mediation has also become a more common form of resolution for civil and community disputes (Duffy, Grosch, and Olczak, 1991; Kessler, 1978). Community mediation centers, staffed by trained volunteers, are springing up around the country (Duffy, Grosch and Olczak, 1991; Lovenheim, 1989; Singer, 1990). Mediation is also used increasingly to avoid costly litigation in business settings (Coulson, 1987) and to resolve business-government disputes, particularly in the area of environmental regulation (Drayton, 1981; Reich, 1981; Susskind and Cruikshank, 1987). Finally, mediation is being suggested more frequently as a mechanism for the resolution of international disputes. Fisher (1978) has prepared an extensive manual that offers an insightful array of analytical tools and action techniques for international mediation, and Rubin (1981) has documented Henry Kissinger's success as an extremely skilled international mediator.

**Is Mediation Effective?**    Kressel and Pruitt (1989) report that mediation was effective in about 60 percent of the cases studied, ranging from 20 percent to 80 percent across a variety of settings; greatest effectiveness occurred in situations marked by only moderate conflict. By *moderate* (an inexact term, to be sure), we mean situations in which tension is apparent and tempers are beginning to fray, but in which negotiations have not deteriorated to physical violence and irrevocably damaging threats and actions. Disputes beyond the moderate stage are often characterized by drastic actions, reactions, and "burning" relational (and perhaps other) bridges by one or both parties. Other research suggests that mediation is more effective when negotiators experience a "hurting stalemate" (Touval and Zartman, 1985). Several other studies have also shown that mediation is only effective in certain kinds of disputes. Kochan and Jick (1978), for example, in their review of mediation in the public sector, report that mediation was most successful in conflicts that involved a breakdown in negotiations, where bargainers were inexperienced or became overcommitted to their positions. In contrast, mediation was less effective when there was internal conflict within one or both of the negotiating parties, for example, when major differences exist between the demands of a union's rank and file and their chief negotiator's belief about what was attainable at the negotiating table. Mediation was also less effective as a strategy when the parties differed on major economic issues or had very strong differences in their expectations for a settlement.

In negotiating terms, if the resistance points of both sides don't overlap (Stevens, 1963), then mediators may have to exert greater direct and indirect pressure on the negotiators to create a "positive contract zone," an overlap of resistance points. Direct pressure occurs if the mediator uses tactics to encourage the parties to soften their positions; indirect pressure typically comes through the passage of time, wearing the parties down and increasing the cost of holding out. Some mediators achieve greater effectiveness by being aggressive (Johnson, 1993) and applying pressure on the negotiators to settle or to consider options (Kolb, 1983a, 1983b). It appears that mediation is less effective in more intense conflicts (Rubin, 1980), as when the conflict is large, many issues are at stake, or the parties disagree on major priorities. Again, under such conditions, mediation tactics may be insufficient to move the parties toward mutual agreement.

In a review of mediation research, Carnevale and Pruitt (1992) report that "mediation is effective in general—agreements are usually reached, participants are ordinarily satisfied, and compliance is high" (p. 562). In summary, Carnevale and Pruitt go on to report that mediation is more effective when

Conflict is moderate rather than intense.

The parties are highly motivated to settle.

Parties are committed to mediation.

The issues do not concern allocation of severely limited resources.

The issues do not involve broad, general principles.

The parties are essentially equal in power.

Greater intrusion (i.e., arbitration) is threatened as a next step (pp. 562–63).

Carnevale and Pruitt (1992) also suggest that mediation effectiveness can be viewed from a variety of perspectives, including the issues, the disputing parties, and the mediator's behaviors. Relating to the *issues,* effectiveness entails

Identifying the issues.

Uncovering underlying interests and concerns.

Setting agendas.

Packaging, sequencing, and prioritizing agenda items.

Interpreting and shaping proposals.

Making suggestions for possible settlements (p. 565).

Relating to the *parties,* mediation tended to be more effective if mediators assisted them in one or more of four ways:

Helping them to save face when making concessions.

Helping them resolve internal disagreements.

Helping them deal with constituents.

Applying positive incentives for agreement or concession making, or negative sanctions for noncooperation (p. 564).

Certain mediator behaviors, in particular, seem to lead to more effective mediation. These include creating and controlling the agenda, assisting the parties in establishing priorities, and maintaining calm, friendly, but firm control over the mediation process. Recognizing that mediators deal with a variety of situations and may choose their behaviors based on what they feel a given situation warrants, Carnevale (1986) developed a "strategic choice model" of mediator behavior (see Figure 12.2).

Carnevale proposes that the mixture of high or low levels of two variables—concern for the disputing parties' aspirations and perception of parties' "common ground" (i.e., areas of agreement)—will produce four basic mediation strategies: problem solving, compensation, pressure, or inaction (see Figure 12.2). *Problem solving* (*high* concern for parties' aspirations, *high* perception of common ground) takes the form of assisting the parties to engage in integrative exchange, as they would in win-win negotiation in the mediator's absence (see Chapter 4). *Compensation* (*high* concern for aspirations, *low* perception of common ground) involves mediator application of rewards and inducements to entice the parties into making concessions and agreements. *Pressure* (*low* concern for aspirations, *low* perception of common ground) involves trying to force the parties to reduce their levels of aspiration in the absence of perceived potential for an integrative

**FIGURE 12.2**   Carnevale's "Concern-Likelihood" Model of Mediator Behavior

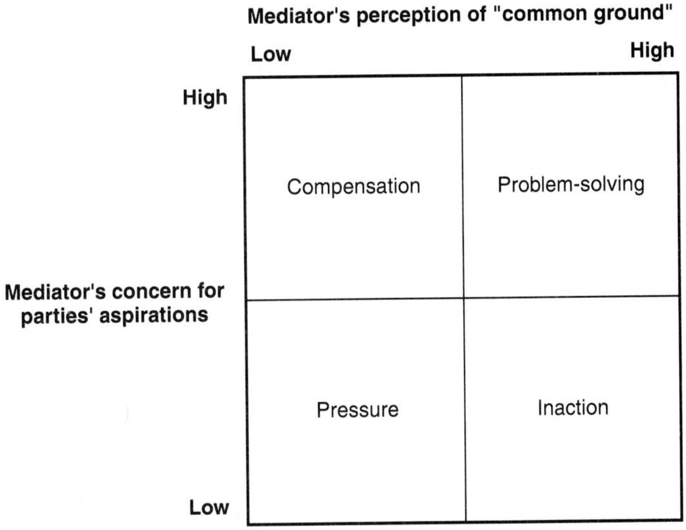

Adapted from P.J.D. Carnevale, "Strategic Choice in Negotiation," *Negotiation Journal, 2,* 1986, 41–56.

(win-win) resolution. Finally, *inaction* (*low* concern for aspirations, *high* perception of common ground) involves standing back from the dispute, leaving the parties to work things out on their own. Subsequent research has provided support and additional evidence for the model (e.g., Carnevale and Conlon, 1988; Chaudrhy and Ross, 1989; Harris and Carnevale, 1990).

Mediator-applied pressure, mentioned earlier, seems to interact with the type of situation being mediated. Success in mediations marked by intensity (e.g., major conflicts involving many issues and disagreement over major priorities) and high levels of interparty hostility tend to be positively related to more forceful, proactive mediation behaviors. Low-hostility situations tend to respond better to a less active, more facilitative approach (Donohue, 1989; Hiltrop, 1989; Lim and Carnevale, 1990). When high hostility was accompanied by high levels of problem-solving behavior by the negotiators, mediators assisted best by posing problems, challenging negotiators to solve them, and suggesting new ideas and soliciting negotiator responses to them (Zubek, Pruitt, Pierce, and Iocolano, 1989). Rubin (1980, 1981) proposes that these last findings also suggest that mediation may get in the way when negotiators are capable of solving their own problems, and that although forceful intervention and a high, proactive mediator profile may be appropriate in situations of high hostility, they may be counterproductive when hostility is lower, or even when high hostility is accompanied by high negotiator problem-solving skill. In such situations, process consultation (which we discuss later) may be a better intervention choice.

---

**How to Get Maximum Value from Mediation:**
**Advice from Veteran Mediators**

The decision to seek mediation is an important one for negotiators, and having made such a decision, it makes sense to get the most value possible from the intervention. One of the authors of this text is active in community mediation, and he interviewed Greg Squires and Shirley Eaton of Mediation Services of Forsyth, in Winston-Salem, North Carolina. These veteran mediators provided specific advice on disputants can get the best possible use from a mediator:

Key the mediator into the first-order issues (i.e., the primary topics or problems of the dispute); don't assume that the mediator will "just know."

Don't overinform the mediator by filling in the second-order issues (i.e., underlying or subordinate concerns that, while important, don't address the immediate focus of the dispute); a good mediator will be able to discover such underlying problems independently.

Don't tell the mediator your overall agenda or long-range plan with regard to the dispute or your relationship with the other party; this may distract the mediator or taint her approach to the dispute.

**How to Get Maximum Value from Mediation:**
**(continued)**

Be specific and realistic about the benefits to be gained through mediation and realize that it is necessary to surrender some process control to salvage and secure a better outcome, control over which you *do not* surrender.

If you are unsure about the nature or extent or the mediator's role, *say so;* your degree of benefit from the process is directly proportionate to your support for, and understanding of, the mediation process.

Don't be afraid to express your concerns or objections (the mediator has specific skills in addressing and clarifying positions and issues)—be prepared, though, to commit to the clarification once it is made.

Understand that a good mediator often functions as an "agent of reality," helping both parties manage their expectations of dispute resolution, as well as clarifying the likely contingencies of no agreement.

Understand that basic mediational skill involves seeing gaps and missing pieces, and that the mediator should introduce resolutions gently, by the skillful use of questions and specific language.

A thoughtful mediator may help you test a tentative agreement by helping you identify *all* potentially involved parties (whether present at the mediation or not) or by asking probing or "what if" questions, but that does not constitute imposing a resolution on you—the mediator is only acting as a quality control advisor.

Expect assistance, but don't expect miracles; mediators are process "mechanics" who can help you "tune up" your own dispute resolution "engine"—but they usually don't have the resources (chiefly time) to build you an entirely new engine!

Recognize that mediation often involves resolution development by a process of elimination; when parties specify what they *don't* want, what is left is usually the only viable resolution.

Remember, when all else is said and done, the problem is still between you and the other party; it is *not* the mediator's. Mediation reinforces *your* ultimate responsibility to identify, choose, and implement your own outcome.

## Liabilities of Arbitration and Mediation

It should be clear from this review that both mediation and arbitration have their liabilities. The liabilities of arbitration are these:

Negative consequences for negotiator behaviors in anticipation of third-party decisions (e.g., chilling and narcotic effects; see earlier discussion of arbitration).

Removal of outcome control from negotiators.

Possible lack of disputant commitment to implementing the imposed outcome.

In contrast, the liabilities of mediation include these:

Lack of impetus or initiative to adhere to any particular settlement or to settle at all.

Possible perpetuation of the dispute, perhaps indefinitely.

Possible extension or escalation of the dispute into more damaging, more costly forms and forums.

Several researchers have proposed that by combining mediation and arbitration into a two-stage dispute resolution model, the liabilities of each may be minimized (Starke and Notz, 1981; Grigsby, 1981; Grigsby and Bigoness, 1981). Starke and Notz proposed that mediation, as a preliminary step to arbitration, should have a complimentary and facilitating effect, but only when the arbitration is of the final offer format. Under conventional arbitration, the parties expect a compromise ruling by the arbitrator; because mediation also promises a compromise, the parties choose to wait for the arbitration ruling rather than make concessions during mediation. In contrast, under the expectation of final offer arbitration, mediation provides the parties with an incentive to evaluate the reasonableness of their current positions. As a result, they may be more willing to modify their positions prior to expected arbitration to improve their chances that the arbitrator will rule in favor of their side. Efforts to test these assertions have been mixed. Some research has produced only inclusive results (Grigsby, 1981; Grigsby and Bigoness, 1982). Other inquiries have suggested that final offer arbitration resulted in resolution of a larger number of issues than conventional arbitration and encouraged higher value concessions by the negotiators (Neale and Bazerman, 1983). Further research is necessary to explore the combined effects of mediation and type of arbitration on variables such as the speed of dispute resolution, satisfaction with the settlement, and willingness to live by and implement the solution.

### Process Consultation

A third formal approach to the resolution of disputes is process consultation (Walton, 1987), "a set of activities on the part of the consultant that helps the client to perceive, understand, and act upon the process events which occur in the client's environment" (Schein, 1987, p. 34). As used here, the objective of process consultation is to defuse the emotional aspect of conflict and improve communication between the parties, leaving them with renewed or enhanced abilities to manage future disputes. The difference between mediation and process consultation is that mediators are at least somewhat concerned with the *issues* in dispute (i.e., "deal making" per Kolb, 1983a), whereas process consultants focus only on *procedures* (similar to Kolb's "orchestration"). Process consultants assume that if they can teach the parties how to manage conflict more productively and effectively, these improved procedures will lead to productive outcomes. The purpose of the third party's intervention is to create the foundation for more productive dialogue over substantive issues and to teach the parties how to prevent conflicts from escalating destructively in the future.

**Process Consultation Behaviors.**    Process consultants usually employ a variety of tactics. Their first step is often to separate the parties and interview them individually, to determine each side's view of the other side, position, and a history of the relationship and its conflicts. Following this diagnostic phase, the consultant uses this information to structure a series of dialogues or confrontations between the parties (Beckhard, 1967, Walton, 1987). These meetings are designed specifically to address the causes of past conflicts and each side's perceptions of the other. Meetings are held on neutral turf, and who should attend and what issues should be discussed are planned ahead of time. The purpose of the third party is to encourage the parties to confront their differences and the reasons for them. The process consultant is referee, timekeeper, and gatekeeper of the process, working to keep the parties on track while also insuring that the conflict does not escalate. Finally, the third party directs all sides toward some type of problem solving and integration, assuming that by confronting and airing their differences, the parties can create a format for working on their substantive differences in the future and can pursue this agenda without a recurrence of unproductive escalation. Thus, changing the climate for conflict management, promoting constructive dialogue around differences of opinion, and creating the capacity for other people to act as their own "third parties" are major parts of the process consultant's agenda.

The description of successful process consultation suggests that process consultants should possess many of the same attributes that we have ascribed to other third parties. First, they should be perceived as experts in the technique, knowledgeable about conflict and its dynamics, able to be emotionally supportive while confronting the parties, and able to diagnose the dispute. Second, they should be perceived as clearly neutral, without bias toward one side or the other. Third, they should be authoritative—that is, able to establish power over the *process* that the conflicting parties are pursuing, thereby intervening and controlling it. Although they do not attempt to impose a particular solution or outcome, process consultants must be able to shape the manner in which the parties interact, separating them or bringing them together, and to control the agenda that they follow when interaction occurs. Without such control, the parties will resort to their earlier pattern of destructive hostility.

It should be apparent from this discussion of process consultation that the primary focus is not to resolve the substantive differences between the parties, but to teach them how to resolve those differences themselves. Thus, process consultation goes the farthest in putting the issues under dispute back in the hands of the disputing parties. To make process consultation work, however, the parties must put aside these substantive differences, something that is hard for them to do.

Process consultation has been used most commonly to improve long-standing relationships that the parties want to continue. Marital and family therapy are forms of process consultation, as are organizational development and team building among work groups. Process consultation has also been tried in labor-management relationships and in international conflict among ethnic, political, and cultural groups such as Protestants and Catholics in Northern Ireland and Arabs and Israelis in the Middle East. Many of the early efforts at process consultation in these environments were less than 100 percent successful (Lewicki and Alderfer, 1973; Brown, 1977; Boehringer, Zeruolis, Bayley and Boehringer, 1974; Cohen, Kelman, Miller, and Smith, 1977; Benjamin and Levi, 1979; Hill, 1982). However, these research studies have contributed to a better understanding of process consultation in the following ways:

1. Process consultation is less likely to work as an intervention technique when the parties are deeply locked in a dispute over one or more major unresolved issues. Because process consultation seeks to change the nature of the working relationship between the parties, it may only work before the parties are in open conflict, or between major outbreaks of hostility (Walton, 1987).

2. Process consultation may be an ineffective technique in short-term relationships. There is probably little need to teach parties to resolve disputes effectively when they will not be working together in the future.

3. Process consultation may be ineffective when the substantive issues in dispute are distributive, or zero-sum. The objectives of process consultation are to improve both the relationship and the skills for integrative bargaining. If the nature of their dispute or constituency pressures on the bargainers do not encourage and support the integrative process, then process consultation will not work. Efforts at process consultation will constantly be undermined by the divisive issues or constituency pressures to maintain a hard-line stance.

4. Process consultation may be ineffective when the level of conflict is so high that the parties are more intent on revenge or retribution than reconciliation. (See our discussion of forceful mediation intervention in the previous section.) In effect, process consultation may only work when sustained conflict has worn the parties out, making them want resolution more than continued warfare, or when the parties sincerely want to coexist but do not have the skills to do so. If the parties do not have sufficient incentive to work together, efforts at process consultation will be undermined. One side will exploit trust, cooperation, and honesty, and the dispute will quickly escalate.

## OTHER THIRD-PARTY STYLES: INFORMAL INTERVENTIONS

This far, we have reviewed several major approaches used by third parties to resolve disputes. These approaches—arbitration, mediation, and process consultation—represent formal or "textbook" approaches to the resolution of disputes, and they are the three most commonly described in the research on third-party behavior. However, a variety of other third-party approaches are possible, and many of them have only recently been investigated in research. Sheppard (1984) proposed a generic classification of third-party intervention procedures that spans a wide variety of different conflict environments (see Figure 12.1, presented earlier). Sheppard's model describes how managers actually intervene in conflict, rather than prescribing how they should intervene. His model was developed from an earlier model proposed by Thibaut and Walker (1975) to describe the psychological aspects of procedural justice systems (e.g., courts or tribunals). Thibaut and Walker conceived of dispute resolution as involving two stages: a procedural or process stage, in which evidence and arguments are gathered and presented, and an outcome or decision stage, in which the evidence is evaluated to determine which party the weight of evidence favors. They then distinguished among major conflict intervention styles based on the amount of process control, decision control, or both used by the third party. These two approaches to control may be thought of as independent dimensions of conflict intervention, and a third party may exert varying amounts of each in handling a dispute. For our current purposes, we shall simply refer to situations where a third party exerts high or low amounts of process or decision control and represent the possibilities in matrix form (Figure 12.1). Sheppard (1983) asked practicing managers to describe the last time they intervened in a dispute between their subordinates and then coded their responses according to the amount of process and decision control the third party used. He concluded that managers use one of three dominant styles when they intervened in a subordinate conflict (see Figure 12.3).

**FIGURE 12.3**    Managerial Third-Party Intervention Styles

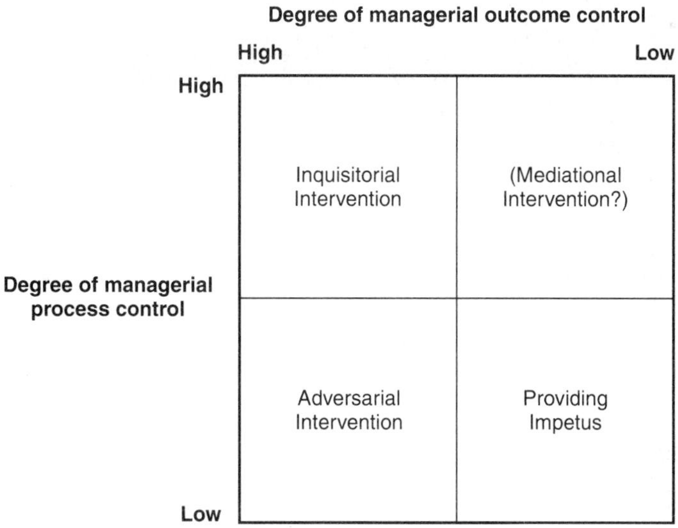

Adapted from B.H. Sheppard. (1983). Managers as Inquisitors: Some Lessons from the Law. In M. Bazerman and R.J. Lewicki (Eds.), *Negotiating in Organizations* (Beverly Hills: Sage Publications).

1. *Inquisitorial Intervention.* This was the most common style. A manager who uses this style exerts high control over both the process and the decision. She tells both sides to present their cases, asks lots of questions to probe into each side's position, and frequently controls who is allowed to speak and what they say. She then invents a solution that she thinks will meet both parties' needs, and usually enforces that solution on both parties. Inquisitorial intervention is a judicial style of handling conflicts that is found most commonly in European courtrooms.

2. *Adversarial Intervention.* Managers who use this style exert high control over the decision, but not the process. The manager does not control the process in that he does not ask questions, try to "get the whole story," or control the destructive aspects of the conflict between the parties. Instead, he passively listens to what each side chooses to tell him, and then makes a decision (tells the parties how to solve the conflict) based exclusively on the presentations. This style is most similar to the style used by most American courtroom judges.

3. *Providing Impetus.* Managers who use this style typically do not exert control over the decision, and they exert only a small amount of control over the process. The manager typically tries to make a quick diagnosis of what the conflict is about and then tells the parties that if they don't find a solution, she will impose one on them. In short, the manager first asks "What's going on here?" When she finds out what's going on, she says "You'd better solve this problem, or else I'll solve it for you, and neither of you will like the solution!"

### Which Approach Is More Effective?

Sheppard's research indicates that managers spontaneously tend to use styles that resemble acting like an arbitrator, acting like one of several forms of judges, or providing a common enemy by threatening to settle the dispute for the parties in an undesirable way if they can't settle it themselves. Note that the remaining cell in Figure 12.3, which we have labeled "Mediational Intervention," is *not* a style commonly observed among managers. Although subsequent research has shown that managers claim to prefer mediation as a third-party style (Lewicki and Sheppard, 1985), it is not clear that managers really understand how to mediate without training. When handling a conflict, managers seem prone to assume responsibility for having a major impact on the outcome of the conflict, that is, the specific decision or outcome arrived at by the disputing parties (see Sheppard, Blumenfeld-Jones, Minton, and Hyder, 1994). Therefore, managers may be very uncomfortable using a mediation strategy, which, by Sheppard's definition, requires that they control the process of conflict but leave the solution in the hands of the disputants.

There is evidence that the net benefit would be positive if mediation were used more often as an informal third-party intervention style. Karambayya and Brett (1989), studying classroom simulations, found that those filling managerial positions do assume a number of roles, depending on how they diagnose the situation. They found general support for Sheppard's (1983, 1984) research and reported that mediation in particular led to fairer outcomes and was perceived to be a fairer process by disputants, lending support to Brett and Rognes's (1986) advice that managers should act as mediators when acting as third parties. Later research (Karambayya, Brett, and Lytle, 1992), again using classroom subjects (but of greater age and experience than earlier studies), found that managers were most likely to intervene in autocratic or mediational manners, but that relative authority and experience had distinct effects. Experience aside, third parties in authority over the disputants were more likely to be autocratic, and peer interveners were no more likely to be mediational. More autocratic interventions tended to produce more one-sided outcomes and impasses, whereas mediational interventions tended to produce more compromises. Interveners with greater managerial experience, though, were significantly less likely to be autocratic, and third parties with both authority and more experience tended to exhibit the most mediational behavior in the study group. Finally, research by Conlon and Fasolo (1990) suggests that, although mediational interventions may be preferable to autocratic ones, timing may be critical. More specifically, the speed of intervention (i.e., earlier versus later in the dispute) was found to affect the disputants' perceptions of procedural fairness. Quick interventions tended to produce disputant feelings of lack of control and loss of voice—that is, their ability to have a say and lay out their cases to their satisfaction. Disputants also expressed lower satisfaction with third-party interventions that they felt to be inappropriate due to violation of disputant expectations of due process, meaning their beliefs that they were denied access to, and benefits of, normal procedural steps and safeguards.

Although these findings suggest strongly that mediation should be used more often for informal third party interventions than it is (Sheppard, Blumenfeld-Jones, Minton, and Hyder, 1994), further research is necessary. More attention needs to be focused on determining how managers can better identify mediational opportunities, how they can learn to mediate more effectively, and whether the managerial findings of recent research are true for third parties in other conflict situations (e.g., among peers or friends).

## SUMMARY

If negotiators are unable to engage in remedial dispute resolution activities when necessary, third-party intervention may be a way to help. In this chapter, we reviewed three prototypical styles of third party intervention: arbitration, mediation, and process consultation. Each of these styles has its strengths and weakness as an intervention and dispute resolution approach. The styles differ as to whether and the degree to which the disputants surrender control over the disputant interaction process or the choice of dispute resolution outcome to the third party. Arbitrators typically specify a structured process in which disputing parties have relatively free rein to present their stories, then decide the outcome, often imposing a resolution of the disputants. Mediators exert a great deal of control over how the parties interact, both physically and communicationally; although mediators may point the parties toward possible resolutions by suggestions and guidance, they typically do not choose the resolution for the disputants, who must then do so themselves. Finally, process consultants are less involved in the disputed issues than arbitrators or mediators, but they are heavily involved in helping to establish or enhance communication and dispute resolution skills disputants can then apply to both immediate and possible future disputes.

In addition, recent research has shown that there are other third-party roles and styles in common use (including informal versions of the three formal approaches we addressed) that have not been studied systematically to determine their application and impact. A great deal remains to be done in this area, both in determining the mastery and propriety of particular informal third-party styles and techniques for various types of conflict, as well as achieving a better understanding of the kinds of conflicts that third parties can effectively assist in resolving and the ways third parties go about deciding when and how to intervene in disputes.

# CHAPTER 13

# Ethics in Negotiation

In this chapter, we shall explore a subject not often addressed in writing on negotiation (particularly in management and business negotiations): the question of whether there are, or should be, ethical standards for negotiations. As we will indicate, the topic has received increased attention and research in recent years. It is our view that fundamental questions of ethical conduct arise *whenever* we negotiate. The effective negotiator must recognize when the questions are relevant and what factors must be considered to answer them.

## WHY DO NEGOTIATORS NEED TO KNOW ABOUT ETHICS?

Consider the following situations:

**Situation 1.** You are a manager badly in need of more clerical assistance for your office. Although work is getting done, a large and often unpredictable volume of work is creating periodic delays. Some of your staff are complaining that the work flow could be managed much more effectively if another clerk were added. However, you also know that your boss is not sympathetic; she thinks that the problem could be solved if all the current clerks simply agreed to work a bit harder or volunteer a few hours of overtime. Moreover, your department's budget is very tight, and to get a new clerical position approved, you will clearly have to demonstrate to senior management (particularly your boss) that you need additional personnel. You see the following options open to you:

1. Document the amount of work that each of your clerks is doing and the amount of work that is being delayed or not done properly, and make a complete report to your boss.

2. Give each of your clerks a lot of extra jobs to do now, particularly ones that could really be deferred for a few months (such as cleaning out and completely reorganizing the files). Thus, you will create an artificial backlog of incomplete work that can be used to argue for more help.

3. Talk to your clerks and stress that the most important standard by which they should do their jobs is to follow procedures exactly and to focus on high-quality work rather than getting all the work done. This will probably create a slow-down and a backlog that you can then use to argue for more help.

4. You've been watching the operation of the payroll office down the hall. Many of those clerks are standing around drinking coffee half the time. Talk to your boss about your observation and ask to have one of these clerks transferred to your department.

**Question:** Are some of these approaches more ethical than others? Which ones? Which ones would you try?

   **Situation 2.** You are an entrepreneur interested in acquiring a business that is currently owned by a competitor. The competitor, however, has not shown any interest in either selling the company or merging with your business. To gain inside knowledge of his firm, you instructed a consultant you know to call contacts in that company to determine if the company is having any serious problems that might threaten the viability of the business. If you can find out these problems, you might be able to use the information to either hire away their employees or find a way to get the competitor to sell.

**Question:** Is this ethical? Would you be likely to do it if you were the entrepreneur?

   **Situation 3.** You are a vice president of personnel, negotiating with a union representative for a new labor contract. The union has insisted that it will not sign a new contract until the company agrees to raise the number of paid holidays from four to six. Management has calculated that it will cost approximately $150,000 for each paid holiday, and has argued to the union that the company cannot afford to meet the demand. However, you know that in reality, money is not the issue— the company simply doesn't think the union's demand is justified. To convince the union that they should withdraw their demand, you have been considering the following alternatives:

1. Tell the union that their request is simply unacceptable to you because they haven't justified why they need six paid holidays.
2. Tell the union that the company simply can't afford it (without explanation).
3. Prepare some erroneous financial statements that show that it will cost about $300,000 per paid holiday, which you simply can't afford.
4. Offer the union leadership an all-expenses-paid trip to a Florida resort if they will simply drop the demand entirely.

**Question:** Do any of the strategies raise ethical concerns? Which ones? Why?

   The scenarios described are hypothetical; however, the problems they present are real ones for negotiators. Managers are frequently confronted with important decisions about the strategies and tactics that they will use to achieve important objectives, particularly when a variety of influence tactics are open to them. In this chapter, we will turn our attention to the major ethical questions that arise in negotiation. We will consider several questions:

1. What are ethics and how do they apply to negotiation?
2. What motivates ethically marginal behavior?
3. What are the principles of ethics that can be applied to negotiation?

4. What major types of ethical and unethical conduct are likely to occur in negotiation?
5. What personality and social context factors shape a negotiator's decision to use unethical tactics?

## What Are Ethics and Why Do They Apply to Negotiation?

First, we want to be clear that it is *not* our intention to advocate a specific ethical position for all negotiators or for the conduct of all negotiations. Many treatises on business ethics take a strongly perscriptive or normative position, advocating what a person *should* do. Instead, we intend to take a more descriptive stance, illustrating how a person *might* think about choices and options when confronted with strategies and tactics that fall in the realm of potentially unethical. We will identify the major dimensions of ethics that are relevant to the conduct of negotiation and suggest how those dimensions affect a negotiator's choice of strategies and tactics. We will provide negotiators with a framework for making more informed decisions about the strategies and tactics they select and the possible ethical consequences that will accrue. In doing so, we will be working in an area in which there has been considerably less systematic research than in other topics in this book, so some of our assertions will be speculative. We will also draw from some philosophical writings on the nature of ethics and from some psychological research on the way people make complex decisions involving ethical principles.

We also wish to distinguish among different criteria for judging and evaluating a manager's actions, particularly when questions of ethics might be involved. There are at least three standards for evaluating strategies and tactics in business and negotiation: ethics, prudence, and practicality (Missner, 1980). *Ethical* judgments evaluate strategies and tactics based on some standards of moral behavior, or of what is right and wrong. *Prudent* judgments are based on what is most effective—for example, what is beneficial or harmful for the people who perform those actions. Finally, *practical* judgments are based on what is the easiest, cheapest, or fastest way of getting something done to achieve an objective. For example, a salesperson preparing a presentation on a new product could use one or more of these standards in determining her strategy. The ethical salesperson would ask "What is the truth about this new product?" or "How can I compare this product fairly to its competitors on the market?" The prudent salesperson would ask "How can I best present this product?" "What can I say about it that will make it attractive to the buyer?" Finally, the practical salesperson will ask very pragmatic questions: "How should we lay out the advertisements?" How quickly can I do this?" "What is the cheapest or most cost-effective way to sell this product?"

Discussions of business ethics frequently confuse the ethical, prudent, and practical criteria for judging conduct—they try to determine what is wise or practical as distinct from what is ethical. In earlier chapters, we have extensively evaluated negotiation strategies and tactics by the prudence and practicality criteria;

in this chapter, we turn to ways by which we can judge negotiation strategies and tactics by ethical criteria. In addition, other criteria come into play. For example, Lax and Sebenius (1986) suggest that some people may want to be ethical for intrinsic reasons—it "feels better" because behaving ethically allows us to see ourselves as moral individuals or because certain principles of behavior are seen as moral absolutes. Other people may judge ethical behavior in more instrumental terms—good ethics make good business. As we will see, these criteria affect how negotiators tend to select tactics as well. But, similar to our evaluation of strategies and tactics by the other criteria, we will also show that people's judgments about what is ethical or unethical in negotiation are not crystal clear. On the one hand, some tactics are seen as marginal—defined in shades and degrees rather than in absolutes. Reasonable people will disagree as to exactly where they draw the line between what is ethical and what is unethical. On the other hand, there is remarkable agreement among negotiators on other tactics that are clearly ethical or clearly unethical. Thus, although it may be difficult to tell a negotiator exactly what is ethical and unethical to do in any circumstance, it does not make the subject of ethics any less important. Addressing the subject of ethics encourages negotiators to examine their own ethical decision-making processes. In addition, sharpening the questions we ask will create the opportunity for further research that can examine the complexity of these judgments in much more detail (Lewicki, 1983; Raiffa, 1982).

Having made these cautionary statements, we now consider the factors in a negotiation that may motivate unethical or ethically questionable conduct.

## WHAT MOTIVATES UNETHICAL CONDUCT?

Several major dimensions of individuals and the economic system motivate unethical conduct. Missner (1980) suggests four: profit, competition, justice, and generating wants (advertising). Questions and issues of profit, justice, and competition are common to the evaluation of negotiating behavior, and thus we will address them in depth. Questions and issues regarding advertising are less directly related because advertising is more of a one-way persuasion effort (as we described in Chapter 8) than the mutual exchange that characterizes negotiation. As a result, we will only deal with the first three dimensions: profit, competition, and justice. Issues related to generating wants will undoubtedly arise as we discuss these three. We will now turn to the major concerns about each dimension.

### Profit

The pursuit of profit is fundamental to our economic system. Whether it be the company president who is striving to maximize the profitability of the corporation, the stockholders who are looking for bigger dividends, or the salesperson who is pushing the customer to buy that new refrigerator, all are concerned both about the firm's profitability and its impact on them personally. In this context, we will avoid a number of technical definitions of profit and simply define the pursuit of profit as the pursuit of some "advantageous gain or return, or benefit" (Webster, 1990).

Profit is clearly a motive in negotiating. By its very nature, negotiating is a process by which individuals strive to maximize their outcomes, to get an advantageous gain or return. In addition, profit is the motive that turns individuals to negotiation. Individuals trying to maximize their profit frequently use negotiating strategies and tactics because they are recognized as techniques for improving on the outcome that the other party might otherwise give us if we did not negotiate. In short, the profit motive and the pursuit of negotiation as one strategy to improve profitability often go hand in hand.

Businesspeople frequently defend profit and the profit motive as ethically neutral, not inherently bad or good. In contrast, however, many ethical philosophers and political theorists have argued that *profit* is a "six-letter dirty word." Critics of the profit motive and its tendency to make businesspeople unethical—in particular, to be dishonest—have had more evidence than they could possibly use during the last decade. To take only the financial and investment sector as an illustration, incidents of fraud, deception, malfeasance, and other illegal and unethical practices have been chronicled in the front pages of major newspapers and such best-selling books as *Barbarians at the Gate* (Burrough and Helyar, 1990), *Liar's Poker* (Lewis, 1990), and *Den of Thieves* (Stewart, 1992). Although most of the specific events noted were efforts to cheat the market or another company rather than a specific other party, many others were much more personal in nature and are clearly part of an interpersonal negotiation process.

At the center of this debate between businesspeople and their critics are some fundamental questions: Is the motive to maximize our own outcome inherently unethical in itself, or does it lead to unethical behavior to attain it (because there are no limits to how profitable we can be or become)? Is the motive for profit innate or is it determined and shaped by the culture in which we grow up (and if it is culturally determined, can culture also shape how it is expressed and checked)? What standards should be used to judge the ethical integrity of an economic system? Has there been a decline or erosion in those standards in the past several decades? These are the questions that become relevant for judging the profit motive and the consequences it has for profit-maximizing (and negotiating) behavior.

### Competition

The pursuit of profit is a fundamental principle of both our overall economic system and individual economic behavior. This behavior occurs in a social context in which the total amount of resources available is insufficient to satisfy everyone's desires; therefore, competition occurs. As Missner points out, "as one embarks on one's journey to become a millionaire, one must face a salient, and perhaps disturbing fact: Others also want to become millionaires, and in the resulting competition, not everyone will be successful" (p. 69).

In the business system, there are several different types of competition. The fundamental differences between these types are (1) whether competitors know that they are in a competition at all, (2) whether they know the identity of their competitors, (3) whether they attain their goal by getting there first, or (4) whether they attain their goal by blocking the other party in their pursuit of the goal. An example of the first type is someone trying to set a record for pizza-eating to win recognition in the *Guinness Book of World Records;* an individual may simply be trying to gain recognition by doing something no one has done before, at least to a measurable level. The individual may not even know whether the Guinness Book recognizes pizza eating as an event, or whether anyone else may also be to achieve similar fame. The second case, knowing that others are competing but not knowing who the competitors are, may be exemplified by many scientists simultaneously searching for a cure for a disease such as cancer or AIDS. These scientists know that they are in a competition, but generally they don't know where they stand in the race until each scientist reports on research findings. An example of the third case might be two scientists in the same competition, each working in a major academic institution; in this case, each one knows the other well, each one knows approximately what the other's research plan and strategy is, and each is racing against the other to gain recognition for conclusively discovering a particular cure or treatment. Although both may ultimately achieve their goal, only one is likely to get most of the recognition. An example of the fourth case would be two athletic teams competing in a track meet. In most events, team members know who their competitors are, have probably competed against them in previous meets, and know which opponents they have to beat in their individual events. The key distinguishing aspect of this fourth type is that the competitor can only achieve his objective by directly beating (defeating) the opponent. If there were only one team in the track meet—and none of the team members was good enough to set world records—then the fundamental nature of the competition would be lost. They could compete against each other's times or distances, but this is not the same thing. Missner calls the first three types *incidental* competition and the last type *essential* competition.

Using Missner's terminology, much of the competition that occurs in the economic marketplace is incidental—auctions, bidding games, blind submission of proposals and bids, and the like—but what occurs in negotiation—particularly distributive—is largely essential competition. On the tangibles, bargainers are motivated to gain a favorable outcome, and even to maximize that outcome. Sometimes the pressure to achieve the best outcome on the tangibles leads negotiators to use either deception or dirty tricks to achieve their objective (we discussed this in depth in Chapters 3 and 6). In addition, a strongly competitive orientation can lead to intangibles that cause negotiators not only to seek to maximize gain but also to give specific attention to strategies and tactics that allow them to do better than the other person, beat the other, or even harm the other's ability to compete in the future. For example, if there is a history of acrimonious relations between a supplier and a purchaser, or evidence of past bad faith in their agreements, or a personal antagonism and vendetta between them, it may not take long for any given act of essential competition to quickly escalate and turn destructive.

These distinctions between various forms of incidental and essential competition raise some interesting research questions about the impact of competition on a negotiator's predisposition toward unethical action. On the one hand, it can be argued that the closer a negotiator comes to a situation of essential competition, where a specific adversary has to be defeated in order to achieve a goal, the more predisposed a party may be to use tactics that are ethically questionable. It can be argued that when the goal is to defeat another party, there may be considerably greater pressures to violate the rules to make sure we defeat the opponent (which often means a sound defeat or even complete defeat). For this reason, there are clear rules in most competitions—athletic, legal, and business—that limit what people can and cannot do. The competitions occur out in the open—that is, they are public displays in front of audiences, and audience visibility and referees who monitor and enforce the rules serve to keep them honest.

In contrast, however, it can also be argued that the greatest pressures to violate ethical standards arise instead during various forms of *incidental* competition. In these contexts, the rules may not be as clear-cut and the competitive behavior occurs in private. Hence it is more difficult to monitor the rules and the opportunities for unnoticed rule violation may be greater. Do more rule violations (instances of unethical conduct) occur when individuals compete in an international track meet or when scientists compete to win recognition for a major scientific discovery? Clearly, the question is not easily answered—we would have to know more about factors such as the ease of rule breaking, the amount and type of surveillance (monitoring), and the consequences for being caught at rule violation. Thus, in the track meet, rule violation may be less likely to occur in the public phase (e.g., actually running the race) than in the private phase (e.g., taking a drug that enhances the runner's performance and may not be detectable through normal blood, urine or breath testing). In the scientific example, there may be a great deal more opportunity to distort the scientific tests or falsify data in the seclusion of one's own research lab, but the ethical principles are strongly enforced and the costs of being discovered as a cheater are career-ending. In both cases, however, it is clear that competition may motivate parties toward more unethical conduct to win for themselves or for their organizations.

Ethics and business competition are not incompatible. John Akers, former chairman of the board of IBM, has stated that any competitive system requires ethical standards to remain viable over the long term. Akers (1989) argued that there are two ways to view competitiveness in the business system. One is through the quotation attributed to Vince Lombardi, the legendary coach of the Green Bay Packers: "Winning is not the most important thing; it's the *only* thing." Akers observes:

> That is a good quotation for firing up a team, but as a business philosophy, it is sheer nonsense. There is another, much better Lombardi quotation. He once said he expected his players to have three kinds of loyalty: to God, to their families, and to the Green Bay Packers, in that order. (p. 71)

The same may be said for negotiation. Although winning and competitiveness may be admirable motivators for energizing a negotiator in the short run, a failure to take ethics into consideration will only endanger effective long-term relations and the viability of the system in which negotiation occurs.

## Justice

The third major dimension of human conduct that motivates parties toward unethical action is a reaction against perceived injustice. Questions about fairness may be addressed to the outcomes being derived through a negotiation, the processes being used to lead to those outcomes, or the system (and its rules) in which a negotiation is taking place (Sheppard, Lewicki, and Minton, 1992). Questions of outcome justice relate to how we decide on a fair distribution of a negotiated outcome. This is a problem that often occurs when we need to divide up a scarce resource, such as a pool of money. Lax and Sebenius (1986) call this the problem of "distributive fairness," and they see it as a key ethical issue in negotiation. For example, suppose that three of us have worked hard at some joint project—let's say a new business—that has become very successful. Now we are negotiating over how to divide up the first year's profits. You believe the profit should be divided equally—we were all in this together, and should all get a one-third cut of the profit. I believe that I should get more than one third because the business was basically my idea and I should get some financial reward for that. Finally, our third partner believes that she should get more than one third because she is a poor, young, struggling student and really needs the money badly to pay off educational debts. Our negotiation, therefore, is over which common principle of outcome fairness—equality (we all get the same), equity (the person who contributes more gets more), or need (the person who needs more gets more)—we should use to divide the money. In addition, we could also debate the fairest procedure for making that decision, or turn to some dispute resolution system to help us out— a mediator, an arbitrator, a lawyer, or some other existing mechanism. How these issues are raised and resolved in negotiation are problems that have not been well researched. Although negotiators are often advised to use "objective criteria" to determine when outcomes and procedures are fair (Fisher, Ury, and Patton, 1991), not much work has been done on how the parties negotiate the criteria and procedures themselves (that is, negotiating over the criteria and processes we will use to decide what's fair, and by whose standards). Murnighan (1978, 1991), who studied the ways that various parties in coalitions decide how to allocate the resources available to them, has done the most authoritative work. The primary findings are that coalition members tend to argue for the norm (equity, equality, need, etc.) that will give them the best outcome—in short, their perceptions and arguments for particular norms are highly self-serving.

Interestingly enough, the pursuit of justice or fairness—which is, in itself, a strong ethical value—may lead negotiators to be unethical (dishonest) in the pursuit of a just end. When a negotiator believes that she has been treated unfairly— exploited, tricked, or taken advantage of by another party—the negotiator is likely to feel angry or duped or experience a loss of face, and she may be likely to seek revenge for the behavior. People can react to perceived injustice in a variety of ways (see Sheppard, Lewicki, and Minton, 1992, for one review). Among the options for redressing unfair outcomes or unfair treatment is to get back at the person, process, or system that created the unfairness by either seeking revenge, a redivision of wealth, or a restoration of what is rightfully yours. For example, employees who believe that they may have been unfairly treated by their companies may be more predisposed to pilferage, theft, work slowdowns, or other ways of "getting even" (Greenberg, 1990; Robinson, 1992). Although we do not have any direct evidence of this type of conduct in negotiation, it seems reasonable to speculate that a negotiator who believes she was unfairly treated in a previous negotiation—because the other party lied, withheld information, or used dirty tricks—might be more willing to use the same tactics to recover lost outcomes or to save face through the current negotiation.

### Summary

In this section we identified three major dimensions of individuals and the economic system that may lead to unethical conduct: the pursuit of profit, the nature of competition, and appropriate standards for assuring justice. Each of these dimensions is central to the evaluation of ethical issues in negotiations. When parties seek to maximize their profits, they may be more likely to use ethically questionable tactics than when they are not strongly profit-oriented. Similarly, when negotiators are strongly competitive, they are more likely to violate ethical standards to defeat their opponent or secure their goal. Finally, when parties disagree about what outcomes are deserved or the process by which outcomes will be decided upon, particularly when they think they have already been unfairly treated in some way, they may be more likely to be unethical (dishonest) to satisfy their perceived standards and criteria of fairness. We shall now turn to several ways of considering the major approaches to understanding unethical tactics in negotiation.

## HOW DO WE CLASSIFY THE MAJOR ETHICAL QUESTIONS?

Philosophers, theologians, and others who write about business ethics tend to approach questions of ethical behavior from the perspectives of the major philosophical and ethical theories. Based on a review of this literature, we propose that three major approaches to ethical conduct account for most of the ethical questions that arise in negotiations: means-ends, relativism-absolutism, and truth-telling (see Boatright, 1993; Donaldson and Werhane, 1993; and Rachels, 1986, for elaborations of these approaches).

### Means-Ends

Many of the ethically questionable incidents in business that upset the public are instances where people have argued that the ends justify the means—that is, it is deemed acceptable to break a rule or violate a procedure in the service of some greater good—for the individual, the organization, or even society at large. Several examples come to mind. Suppose a television network has convincing statistical evidence that a particular pickup truck was designed unsafely, so that in 1 test out of 10, it bursts into flame when hit in a side collision. To highlight this defect, the network decides to stage and videotape an accident to show the defect and have the truck burst into flame. But because a collision may only create a fire 1 time in 10, the producer does not want to destroy 10 (or more) trucks. So he decides to place detonators near the gas tank so the truck is sure to explode. Is this unethical, even if it was designed to warn the American people about the hazards of this truck model? Or take the case of a pharmaceutical company that is convinced, as a result of early tests, that it has developed a dramatic new miracle drug that will cure some forms of cancer. But it cannot release the drug because it has to comply with government regulation that controls drug testing prior to widespread distribution, and thousands of lives may be lost while the drug is in testing. Is it unethical to keep the drug off the market while all of this further testing goes on? These are means-ends questions. As applied to the negotiation context, when negotiators have very noble objectives to attain for themselves or their constituencies, can they use whatever strategies they want to obtain their goals? And what is the best way to approach and answer these questions?

Questions of means versus ends are best understood in the context of a theory of ethics known as *utilitarianism.* Utilitarianism holds that the moral value and worth of a particular action is judged on the basis of the consequences it produces. Since morality is measured by the goodness or badness of consequences, utilitarians believe that the way to maximize virtue is by maximizing the best consequences for the largest number of people. Debate then centers on several key questions about how this virtue is attained. First, how do we define (and who defines) what are good consequences, and how do we measure them? Second, should utilitarian acts be judged primarily on the virtues of the acts themselves (those acts that lead to the greatest good for the greatest number) or by complying with some specific set of correct and virtuous rules of conduct that will lead to good outcomes? *Act utilitarians* will argue that the best standard of moral conduct is to maximize the greatest good for the greatest number. *Rule utilitarians* will argue that a decision based on this criterion is not always that clear-cut, and could get a decision-maker into trouble; instead, she will argue that the best way to achieve the greatest good is to closely follow a set of rules and principles. For example, let us suppose that a militant subgroup within a union has called a wildcat strike over what it feels are critical questions of worker safety. Some other rank-and-file members support the strike because they think the questions are very important. The group has presented a series of safety demands to management—if these demands are met, the workers have agreed to end the strike. Management agrees to meet the demands, and the strike ends. Management then immediately dismisses all the wildcatters for participating in the illegal strike, and they take no action on the safety issues. The union leadership accuses management of unethical negotiating.

In this situation, *act utilitarians* would argue that management's tactic of agreeing to meet the worker's demands—even if that agreement was in bad faith—was necessary to end an illegal strike. It is management's job (not the workers') to determine conditions of worker safety, and it is also management's job to take action against illegal wildcat strikes; both of these job definitions justify, in management's mind, the tactic of falsely agreeing to meet the wildcatters' demands and then firing them. In contrast, *rule utilitarians* might argue that management has a responsibility to adhere to standards of credibility and integrity in conducting negotiations, because that behavior produces the best results and the best union-management relations. By lying to the strikers, management has compromised its integrity and its word, and no particular end can justify the costs of being dishonest. For example, in the truck fire scenario described above (a real series of events involving an NBC network news show in 1993), the decision to stage the collision cost NBC's news department a great deal of negative publicity and credibility, cost the producer his job, and eventually cost the head of the NBC News Division his job as well—consequences that are extremely serious and may or may not be equivalent to possible lives lost in the dangerous pickup trucks had the news media not tried to make a big event out of the story.

This scenario, and many others like it, constitute the "grist" by which act and rule utilitarians debate the virtues of their respective cases. These different approaches to utilitarianism are closely related to the motivation for profit that we discussed earlier in this chapter. Since we defined profit broadly—as the desire to get more—maximizing profit can be viewed as an end in itself, or it can be viewed as an objective that can only be legitimately attained by following some accepted rules and practices. These different views of maximizing profit are central to many debates about individual and societal economic values. For example, the continued debate between free market economists versus regulatory social economists reflects two different sets of values about how utilitarianism should be pursued in political, economic, and social policy. Similarly, when business students argue about the competing objectives of profit and social responsibility, they are debating utilitarian questions that usually have important means-ends issues attached to them.

When addressing means-ends questions in competition and negotiation, we usually focus the most attention on the question of what strategies and tactics may be seen as appropriate to achieve certain ends. Are exploitative, manipulative, or devious tactics ever justifiable? Under what circumstances? Even when such tactics are within the law, they still may be judged as unethical by two other standards: the ethical systems of the negotiators themselves, and the ethical norms of the social context (environment) in which they operate. We will address the ways these tactics are seen and interpreted later in this chapter.

### Relativism-Absolutism

The second major ethical dimension is relativism versus absolutism. Individuals who are *absolutists* are committed to the view that there are some ethical standards that hold in every situation. Whether absolutists hold these views as a result of religious teachings, moral upbringing, or serious philosophical study, they believe that there are some fundamental, uncompromisable rules in the world. For example, an absolutist who believes in the commandment "thou shalt not kill" argues that the commandment is the same, regardless of whether we are talking about murder, the death penalty for a convicted murderer, abortion (even to save the life of the mother), or euthanasia (mercy killing of terminally ill or suffering patients). Similarly, an absolutist committed to the Golden Rule ("Do unto others as you would have them do unto you") believes in kindness and generosity toward others even in the face of violence, abuse, and exploitation.

A *pure relativist,* in contrast, would argue that we cannot determine what is ethically good in any absolute sense because "everything is relative." Ethics are determined by an individual's personal values. Ethical judgments must be made by each individual; thus, there are no absolutes. Everyone must determine what is right and appropriate to do, on his own, and no one should impose his standards on others. An ethical relativist would believe it right to make up her own mind about whether sentencing a murderer to the death penalty differs from murder itself, and whether this is different from abortion on demand, abortion to save the life of the mother, or euthanasia of a suffering, terminally ill elderly patient. Many would find it acceptable to condemn actions that produce death in some of these cases and condone them in others. Similarly, relativists would argue that the Golden Rule is no rule at all, and that each individual should make up her own mind about how to respond to others who are hurting or harming her.

The distinctions we have just drawn are extremes. In reality, there are probably few pure absolutists or pure relativists in the world. Most people's views are probably within some middle range, varying slightly toward the relativistic or absolute sides of the scale. The mild absolutists generally adhere to a philosophy that one should try to "do good" whenever possible, and they usually believe that "doing good" is not hard to define. Similarly, the mild relativists usually believe, based on their own values, that they have a set of rules and standards that guide their lives, but that there is always the possibility of an exception to the rule—exceptions dictated largely by the social context. Finally, as we noted in our discussion of the means versus ends debate, dialogue between relativists and absolutists emphasizes different standards of conduct in business situations, even in negotiation. Relativists will argue that "when in Rome, do as the Romans do"; in other words, it is necessary to know something about your opponent and the cultural and social environment in which you are negotiating to know what tactics are most suitable and appropriate. (As we will see in Chapter 14, this orientation is absolutely necessary when negotiators begin to encounter international differences in negotiating style and approach.) The lesson regarding what is ethically appropriate in negotiation is that you cannot bargain with thieves the same way you bargain with principled people. In contrast, absolutists will argue that we must adhere to certain fundamental principles (integrity, trustworthiness, honor) or negotiating will quickly deteriorate into a free-for-all argument or even into the use of force. Thus, this relativism versus absolutism debate raises an intriguing question: Are there some basic and fundamental absolutes of principled (ethical) negotiation? We will directly address this question later in this chapter.

### Truth-Telling

Although we judge the "proper" orientation toward profit maximization and competition by standards of utilitarianism and questions of means versus ends, standards of truth-telling help to define what communication is ethical or unethical. The attention here is more on what we say (and how we say it) than what we do. Most negotiators would probably place some high value on a reputation for being truthful. Yet what does *truthfulness* mean? The questions about what constitutes truth-telling are quite straightforward, but once again the answers are not so clear. First, how does we define *truth?* Second, how do we define and classify any deviation away from the truth? Are all deviations "lies," no matter how small and minor they are? Finally, we can add a relativistic dimension to these questions. Should a person tell the truth all the time, or are there times when not telling the truth is an acceptable (or even necessary) form of conduct? These are definitely questions of major concern to negotiators as they decide what they can and cannot say and still remain ethical.

A number of articles in business journals have addressed the ethical question of truth-telling. For example, Carr (1968) argued in the *Harvard Business Review* that strategy in business is analogous to strategy in a game of poker. He advocated that, short of outright cheating (the equivalent of marking cards or hiding an ace up your sleeve), business ought to play its game as poker players do. Because good poker playing often involves concealing information and bluffing or deception (convincing others that you have the cards when you really don't), these rules ought to apply to business transactions. From time to time, most executives find themselves compelled, in their own interests or the interests of their companies, to practice some form of deception in their dealings with customers, suppliers, labor unions, government officials, or even other key managers in their companies. Through conscious misstatements, concealment of pertinent facts, or exaggeration—in short, bluffing—they seek to persuade others to agree with them. Carr argues that if an executive refuses to bluff periodically—if he feels obligated to tell the truth, the whole truth, and nothing but the truth all the time—he is probably ignoring opportunities permitted under the "rules" of business and is probably at a heavy disadvantage in business dealings (p. 144).

In making this assertion, therefore, Carr (1968) is advocating a modified ethical relativism for the standards of truth-telling, namely, that bluffing, exaggeration, and concealment or manipulation of information are legitimate ways for both individuals and corporations to maximize their self-interest. This strategy may be both advantageous and disadvantageous. Thus, an executive might plead poverty in a contract negotiation with a key employee and save significantly more money for the company than if he met all the employee's financial demands. However, the same philosophy might also lead that executive to condone the marketing and sale of a product known to be defective or hazardous, which could have severe long-term business consequences if the product defects lead to a major disaster or lawsuit. As you can well imagine, Carr's position sparked lively debate among *Harvard Business Review* readers. A number of critics argued that individual business people and corporations should be held to higher standards of ethical conduct, and they took Carr to task for his position.

Questions and debate regarding the ethical standards for truth-telling are central and fundamental in the negotiating process. As we pointed out when we discussed interdependence (Chapter 2), negotiation is based on "information dependence" (Kelley and Thibaut, 1969)—the exchange of information to learn the true preferences and priorities of the other negotiator. Arriving at a clear, precise, and effective negotiated agreement depends upon the negotiating parties and their willingness to share accurate information about their own preferences, priorities, and interests. At the same time, because negotiators may also be interested in maximizing their self-interest, they may want to disclose as little as possible of their positions—particularly if they think they can do better by manipulating the information they disclose to the other party. As Kelley (1966) has pointed out, this results in two fundamental negotiation dilemmas. First, negotiators must resolve the dilemma of trust—that is, they must infer the other's true intentions or preferences knowing that the other may be attempting to inflate, magnify, or justify those preferences. As Kelley writes, "to believe everything the other says is to place one's faith in his hands, and to jeopardize the full satisfaction of one's own interests. On the other hand, to believe nothing the other says is to eliminate the possibility of accepting any arrangement with him" (p. 60). In the second dilemma, negotiators must also resolve the dilemma of their own honesty and openness, that is, how frank and candid to be about their own true preferences and priorities. If you are completely honest and candid, you may be vulnerable to exploitation by the other party, commit to a position that allows no further concessions, or sacrifice gains that might have been successfully derived through less candid approaches. As Rubin and Brown (1975) note, "to sustain the bargaining relationship, each party must select a middle course between the extremes of complete openness toward, and deception of, the other. Each must be able to convince the other of his integrity while not at the same time endangering his bargaining position" (p. 15).

Deception and disguise may take several forms in negotiation (Lewicki, 1983):

**1. Misrepresentation of one's position to another party.** In misrepresentation, the negotiator lies about the preferred settlement point or resistance point. Negotiators may tell the other party that they want to settle for more than they really expect or threaten to walk away from a deal when they are actually ready to make further concessions and believe the parties are close to agreement. Misrepresentation is the most common form of deceit in negotiation.

**2. Bluffing.** Bluffing is also a common deceptive tactic. The negotiators state that they will commit some action that they don't actually intend to fulfill. The best examples of bluffs are false threats or promises. A false threat might be a negotiator's statement that she will walk out if her terms and conditions are not met (when she really doesn't intend to take that action); a false promise might be a negotiator's commitment to perform some personal favor for the opposing negotiator later on, when in fact she has no intention of ever performing that favor.

**3. Falsification.** Falsification is the introduction of factually erroneous information into a negotiation. Falsified financial information, false documents, or false statements of what other parties are doing, will do, or have done before are common examples.

**4. Deception.** The negotiator constructs a collection of true or untrue arguments that leads the other party to the wrong conclusion. For example, a negotiator may describe in detail what actions were taken in a similar circumstance in the past and lead the other party to believe he intends to take the same actions again in this context.

**5. Selective disclosure or misrepresentation to constituencies.** The negotiator does not accurately tell her constituency what has transpired in negotiation, does not tell the other party the true wishes, desires, or position of her constituency, or both. She may therefore play both sides (the constituency and the other party) against each other to engineer the agreement she wants most.

This is not meant to be an exhaustive list of the ways that lying and deceit can enter into negotiation, nor is it meant to create further confusion by trying to split semantic hairs over the different ways people can lie. It is meant, however, to show that various forms of lying and deceit can be an integral part of negotiation. Distinguishing the difference between "ethical" and "unethical" lying, or even between "necessary" and "unnecessary" lying in negotiation, is therefore not as easy as you might think. However, Anton (1990) reports the results of a study that lends some validity to this classification scheme. Anton selected four of the five types of untrue statements just listed—misrepresentation of the value of an outcome to the other party, deception, bluffing, and falsification—and constructed five brief negotiating scenarios for each type. Research participants from several different occupational groups rated each scenario from the perspective of the victim, evaluating the ethicality of the tactic on a 5-point scale. Findings show that the four categories were relatively distinct from each other, yet had moderate correlations; respondents clearly saw them as somewhat separate, but nevertheless related, categories.

### Summary

Three major ethical questions confront negotiators in evaluating strategy and tactics: means-ends, relativism-absolutism, and truth-telling. Means-ends questions arise when a negotiator must consider whether to use ethically marginal tactics to accomplish objectives. In other words, does the end justify the means? Such choices are more likely to be made when negotiators are strongly profit oriented, heavily competing with others, or attempting to redress situations of inequity and injustice. Truth-telling questions arise when a negotiator must consider whether to deviate from telling the truth, the whole truth, and nothing but the truth (in order to achieve objectives). Deviations from the truth—through bluffs, misrepresentations, distortions, or even outright falsification of facts—give negotiators temporary tactical advantage, but at the expense of their ethical integrity and reputation. Finally, questions of relativism arise when negotiators must determine the appropriate criteria for dictating ethical standards. The more negotiators lean toward ethical relativism, the more they will look to aspects of the specific situation or their personal values to dictate how they should behave or what is appropriate to do. In contrast, the more negotiators are prone toward an absolutist perspective, the more they will turn to established moral and ethical codes to direct their behavior. We shall now explore some of the factors that tend to influence and dictate how negotiators are disposed to deal with these ethical questions.

## A SIMPLE MODEL OF ETHICAL DECISION MAKING

Why do some negotiators choose to use tactics that may be unethical? The first answer that occurs to many of us is that these people are corrupt, degenerate, or immoral. In fact, that answer is much too simplistic. In addition, the answer reflects a more systematic bias in the way we tend to perceive other people and explain the reasons why they do what they do. Simply put, this bias encourages us to attribute the causes of other people's behavior to their personalities, whereas we attribute the causes of our own behavior to factors in the social environment around us (Miller and Ross, 1975). Thus, in attempting to explain why another negotiator used one or more ethically questionable negotiating tactics, we would probably say that this individual was somewhat unprincipled, profit-driven, and willing to use any tactic to get what she wanted. In contrast, when attempting to explain why we might use the same tactic, we would tend to say that we are highly principled and had very good reasons for deviating from those principles just this one time. Note that this may also be seen as another cast of the absolutist-relativist controversy: In general, we tend to perceive others in absolutist terms and attribute the causes of their behavior to a violation of some absolutist principles, whereas we tend to perceive our own behavior in more relativistic terms and permit ourselves an occasional minor transgression because we had "good reasons."

Building in part on the material already covered in this chapter, we propose a relatively simple model of decision making to help us understand the decision to employ ethically marginal tactics. This decision has three major components: the motivation to behave unethically, the functions served by this unethical conduct, and the consequences resulting from this decision.

### The Motivation to Behave Unethically

Earlier in this chapter, we identified three primary motivations that may lead to unethical conduct: profit-making, competition, and the restoration of justice. Although many ethical philosophers have questioned the ethical soundness of the motivations themselves, we will accept them as ethically legitimate objectives for negotiators to pursue. We propose that the more a negotiator desires these objectives, the more pressure he will feel to behave unethically. Thus, the stronger the desire to achieve a profit, compete with another party, or restore some standard of justice (or punish injustice), the more predisposed a negotiator is to select an unethical tactic.

## The Function of Unethical Conduct

Tactics can be primarily grouped into two categories: truth-telling tactics and means-ends tactics, reflecting two of the major ethical dimensions we described earlier. (The third dimension, relativism, will be introduced later as an important way to judge the situations in which a given tactic can be used.) The purpose of using either of these groups of tactics is to increase the negotiator's power in the bargaining environment.

Let us first examine unethical truth-telling tactics. As we discussed in Chapters 8 and 10 on persuasion and power, information is one of the major sources and strategies of power in negotiation. Information has power because negotiation is intended to be a rational activity of information and persuasion—my facts, arguments, and logic against your facts, arguments, and logic. In this exchange, we assume that the information is accurate and truthful. To assume otherwise— that it is not truthful—is to question the very assumptions on which daily social communication is based. So when violations of the truth—lies—are introduced into this social exchange, they manipulate information in favor of the dispenser of that misinformation. A lie enhances the power of the liar by changing the balance of "accurate" information in the negotiating relationship. Through the tactics we described earlier—bluffing, falsification, misrepresentation, deception, and selective disclosure—the liar gains advantage by controlling the apparent validity or accuracy of pertinent information. The receiver either accepts the information on its face or has to decide whether he has a basis for challenging the other person's accuracy, credibility, and intentions. Thus, a negotiator uses inaccurate or misleading information to change the other party's preferences or priorities toward the negotiator's own objectives.

In summary, negotiators use both lies and means-ends tactics to gain power. They derive power either by manipulating the information (through some form of truth distortion), gaining some form of tactical advantage over a competitor, or undermining the other party's negotiating position. Using these tactics frequently leads to consequences for the negotiator, the other party, and observers.

## The Consequences of Unethical Conduct

As a result of employing an unethical tactic, the negotiator will experience positive or negative consequences. The consequences are based on whether the tactic is effective, how the other person, constituencies, and audiences evaluate the tactic, and how the negotiator evaluates the tactic. First, consequences will

**FIGURE 13.1** Appropriateness Ratings Sorted by Means

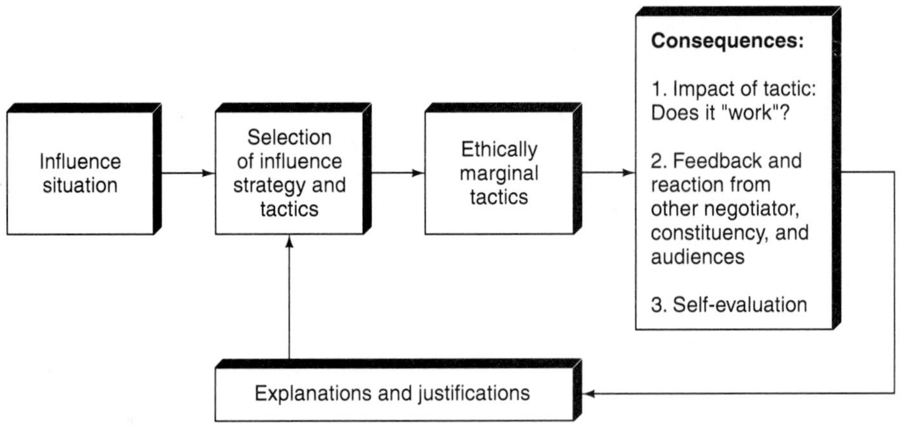

occur depending on whether the tactic "worked" or not—that is, whether the negotiator got what she wanted as a result of using the tactic. A second set of consequences may result from the judgments and evaluations that may come from the other negotiator, constituencies, or audiences that can observe the tactic. Depending on whether these parties recognize the tactic and whether they evaluate it as "proper" or "improper" to use, the negotiator may receive a great deal of feedback. Finally, a third set of consequences will occur depending on how the negotiator evaluates his own use of the tactic—whether using the tactic creates any discomfort, personal stress, or even guilt—or, in contrast, whether the actor sees no problem in using the tactic again and even begins to consider how to use it more effectively.

Figure 13.1 presents a simple model of this process—the decision to use an unethical tactic and its consequences. Let us first consider the consequences that occur based on whether the tactic is successful or not. It should be fairly clear that whether the tactic works—that is, leads to the outcome the negotiator hoped to achieve—should have some impact on whether the tactic is more or less likely to be used in the future (essentially, a simple learning and reinforcement process). If using the tactic allows a negotiator to attain rewarding outcomes that would be unavailable to him if he behaved ethically, and if the unethical conduct is not punished by others, we would expect the frequency of unethical conduct to increase because the negotiator believes he can "get away with it." Thus, real consequences—rewards and punishments that arise from using a tactic or not using it—should not only motivate a negotiator's present behavior, but also affect the negotiator's predisposition to use similar strategies in similar circumstances in the future. These propositions have not been tested in negotiating situations, but they have been extensively tested in other research studies on ethical decision making. For example, research by Hegarty and Sims (1978) appears to support both of these assertions. In their study, when research participants expected to be rewarded for making an unethical decision by participating in a laboratory-simulated kickback scheme, they not only participated, but also were willing to participate again when a second opportunity arose. Moreover, when there were also strong pressures on the research subjects to compete with others—by announcing how well each person had done on the task and giving one a prize for the highest score—the frequency of unethical conduct increased even further.

A second set of consequences occurs when the negotiator experiences the reaction of the target person. If the target person is unaware that a deceptive tactic has been used, then there is no reaction—other than the target being disappointed in having lost the negotiation. However, if the target discovers that deception has occurred, the reaction is likely to be far stronger. People who discover that they have been deceived or exploited are typically angry. In addition to having lost the negotiation, they feel manipulated and foolish for having allowed themselves be deceived by a clever ploy. As a result of both the actual loss they may have suffered in negotiations and the embarrassment they feel from having been deceived, most victims are likely to seek retaliation and revenge. Thus, although the use of unethical tactics may lead to short-term success for the negotiator, it may also create an adversary who is bent on revenge and retribution. The victim is unlikely to trust the other party again, may seek revenge from the negotiator in future dealings, and may also generalize this experience to negotiations with others. A strong experience of being exploited may thus sour a victim's perception of many other negotiators and negotiation contexts in the future (Miller and Vidmar, 1981; Bies and Moag, 1986; Werth and Flannery, 1986).

McCornack and Levine (1990) provide some research support for these assertions. In studying people's reactions to having been deceived (in many different types of relationships, not necessarily negotiating ones), these authors found that victims had strong emotional reactions to deception when they had a more intimate relationship with the subject, when the information at stake was very important, and when lying was seen as an unacceptable type of behavior for that relationship (i.e., expectations of truth-telling were strongly violated). In almost two thirds of the cases reported, discovery of the lie was instrumental in an eventual termination of the relationship with this other person, and in most cases the termination was initiated by the victim. Finally, the importance of the information that was lied about was the most significant predictor of whether the relationship would eventually terminate. If the information was about something that was serious, personal, and highly consequential for whether the parties could fundamentally trust one another or not, then discovered deception was most destructive to the relationship.

To our knowledge, no research has been performed on the negotiator's own reactions to the use of unethical tactics. Under some conditions—such as when the other party has truly suffered—a negotiator may feel some discomfort, guilt, or remorse. On the other hand, and particularly if the tactic has worked, the negotiator may also be able to rationalize and justify the tactic use. These processes will now be described more fully.

### Explanations and Justifications

From the negotiator's perspective, as we stated earlier, the primary motivation to use a deceptive tactic is to gain a temporary power advantage. The decision to use such a tactic may have been made casually and quickly in order to seize a tactical advantage or after long and careful evaluation of the possible options and their likely consequences. When a negotiator has used a tactic that may produce a reaction—such as the consequences we described above—the negotiator must prepare to defend the tactic's use. These defenses explain or justify the tactic's use—to one's self (e.g., "I see myself as a person of integrity, and yet I have decided to do something that might be viewed as unethical"), to the victim, or to constituencies and audiences who may express their concerns. The primary purpose of these explanations and justifications is to rationalize, explain, or excuse the behavior—there is some good, reasonable, legitimate reason why this tactic was necessary.

There is an increasing stream of research on the importance of various forms of explanations and justifications in accounting for undesirable social behavior. Although we could attempt to split linguistic hairs and make some distinction between these two, they are so similar and used so interchangeably that we will not attempt it. Some research has tended to focus on explanations and some has focused on justifications, and we shall simply review both here.

Those who employ unethical tactics are prone to use a number of explanations and justifications. As we will note, some of these have received some research attention. Most of these have been adapted from Bok (1978) and her excellent treatise on lying:

- **The tactic was unavoidable.** The negotiator was not in full control of her actions, and hence should not be held responsible. Perhaps she never intended to hurt anyone, her words were misinterpreted, it was a mistake, or she was pressured into using the tactic by someone else.

- **The tactic was harmless.** What the negotiator did was really trivial and not very significant. We tell "white lies" all the time. For example, we greet our neighbor with a cheery "good morning, nice to see you"; in fact, it may not be a good morning, we are in a bad mood, and we wish we hadn't even run into our neighbor at all. Exaggerations, bluffs, or peeking at the other party's private notes during negotiations can all be easily explained away as "harmless" actions. Note, however, that this particular justification interprets the harm from the actor's point of view; the victim may not agree and may have experienced significant harm or costs as a result.

- **The tactic will help to avoid negative consequences.** When using this justification, we are arguing that the ends justify the means. In this case, the justification is that the tactic helped to avoid greater harm. In a holdup, it is okay to lie to a gunman about where you have hidden your money because the consequences of telling the truth are that you will get robbed. Similarly, lying (or other similar means-ends tactics) may be seen as justifiable in negotiation if it protects the negotiator against even more undesirable consequences should the truth be known.

- **The tactic will produce good consequences,** or the tactic is altruistically motivated. Again, the end justifies the means, but in a positive sense. As we stated earlier, a negotiator who judges a tactic on the basis of its consequences is making judgments according to the tenets of utilitarianism—that the quality of any given action is judged by its consequences. Utilitarians will argue that certain kinds of lies or means-ends tactics are appropriate because they may provide for the larger good—for example, "Robin Hood" tactics in which we rob from the rich to make the poor better off. Another tack on this is the "I was only trying to help you . . ." explanation. In reality, most negotiators use these tactics for their own advantage, not for the general good. In this case, others are likely to view their actions as less excusable than tactics that avoid negative consequences.

- **"They had it coming," or "they deserve it," or "I'm just getting my due."** All these justifications are variations on the theme of using lying and deception against an individual who may have taken advantage of us in the past, "the system," or some generalized source of authority. The pollster Daniel Yankelovich (1982) noted the problem of a national erosion of honesty in the United States. Increasingly, people believed that it was appropriate to take advantage of "the system" in various ways—through tax evasion, petty theft, shoplifting, improper declaration of bankruptcy, journalistic excesses, and distortion in advertising. A decade later, newer statistical surveys show that the problem has increased dramatically on almost every front (Patterson and Kim, 1991).

- **The tactic is fair or appropriate to the situation.** This approach uses situational relativism as the rationale and justification. Negotiators frequently justify their actions by claiming that the situation made it necessary for them to act the way they did. Most social situations, including negotiations, are governed by a set of generally well-understood rules of proper conduct and behavior. These rules are sometimes suspended for two reasons: because it is believed that others have already violated the rules (therefore legitimizing the negotiator's right to violate them as well), and because it is anticipated that someone else will violate the rules (and therefore the other's actions should be preempted). The first case is an example of using unethical tactics in a tit-for-tat manner, to restore balance, to give others their due. Justifications such as "an eye for an eye," or "he started it and I'm going to finish it!" are commonly heard as a defense for resorting to unethical tactics in these cases. Anticipatory justification leading to preemptive behavior (the second case), usually occurs as a result of how you perceive the other party and usually is a self-fulfilling prophecy. For example, negotiators use an unethical tactic because they believe the other party is likely to use one; the other party retaliates with an unethical tactic of his own (because the first negotiator used one), which only goes to justify to the first negotiator that the other party was likely to behave unethically anyway.

Shapiro (1991) has conducted some important research on the role these explanations and justifications play in mitigating a victim's reactions to having been deceived. Shapiro created a laboratory simulation where experimental subjects were supposedly working together to apply for a loan to support a new business venture. In the course of the simulation, subjects were told that their "partner" had been caught by the loan officer falsifying information on the loan application. The experimenter then manipulated the severity of the consequences for being caught in the deception (how much the subject lost as a result of the partner's deception), as well as how adequately the partner explained why the deception had occurred (the deception was unintentional, or selfishly motivated, or ultruistically motivated). The findings indicate that the more a subject felt that the partner's explanation was adequate for the deception, the less subjects expressed feelings of injustice, disapproval, punitiveness, and unforgiveness toward the partner. If subjects were mildly upset, the explanations had more impact than if the subjects were strongly upset. Moreover, explanations had the most impact when the partner stated that the deception was unintentional, less impact when the deception was altruistic, and the least impact when the deception was selfishly motivated.

Explanations and justifications, therefore, are self-serving rationalizations for our own conduct. First, they allow the negotiator to convince others—particularly the victim—that conduct that would ordinarily be wrong in this situation is acceptable. As Shapiro's research shows, the adequacy of these explanations to others has a strong effect on mitigating the impact of deceptive behavior. In addition, explanations and justifications help us to rationalize the behavior to ourselves as well. We propose that the more frequently a negotiator engages in this self-serving justification process, the more her judgments about ethical standards and values will become biased, leading to a lessened ability to make accurate judgments about the truth. Moreover, although the tactics were initially used to gain power in a negotiation, we propose that the negotiator who uses them frequently will experience a loss of power over time. The negotiator is less likely to be trusted, will be seen as having less credibility and integrity, and will be treated as someone who will act exploitatively if the opportunity arises. Negotiators with these characteristics are probably less successful over time unless they are skillful at continually staying ahead of the negative reputation generated by their conduct.

In summary, we propose that the successful use of unethical tactics and their successful justification will be self-serving toward the negotiator's short-term goals, but they are also likely to distort the negotiator's perception of what is fair, necessary, and appropriate. Negotiators who use these tactics are likely to use them again in the future, but in using them, they will damage both their reputations and the long-term relationship with the other party.

## The Perception of Ethical Tactics

To determine how negotiators judged the "ethicality" of the truth-telling and means-ends negotiation tactics, Lewicki and Spencer (1990) asked a large sample of MBA students and executives to rate 18 tactics on two 7-point scales: how appropriate each tactic would be to use in a negotiation situation, and how likely the negotiator would be to use the tactics. The collection of 18 tactics was based on the truth-telling and means-ends principles that were described earlier. The following tactics are often perceived as violations of the truth, but they are used nevertheless by negotiators to gain advantage:

- Making an opening demand that is far greater than what you would really like to accomplish, even one so high that it is specifically designed to undermine the other party's confidence in their ability to achieve their objectives.
- Conveying a false impression that you are in no hurry to settle, even when you have such a deadline.
- Intentionally misrepresenting factual information to the other party, a constituency, or the media.
- Making false threats or false promises.
- Hiding your real bottom line from the other party.

Means-ends tactics constitute a second class of potentially unethical behavior. Means-ends tactics also give the negotiator additional power, but, unlike truth-telling, more than one basis of power may be manipulated: the negotiator's perceived expertise, reputation, legitimacy, position, or even the ability to reward or punish the other party. The following tactics often raise serious ethical concerns in the means they employ, but they are used by negotiators to gain advantage nevertheless:

- Using distractions such as gifts, entertainment, or even bribes to get the other party to soften their position.
- Using networks or spies to try to learn about another party's confidential information and resistance point.
- Undermining the other party in front of their constituency by persuading - or even bribing that constituency.
- Using electronic surveillance to bug the other party's office or constituency meetings.
- Theft of the other party's private files or confidential information.
- Trying to demean or humiliate the other party by making charges or accusations (either publicly or privately).
- Misrepresenting your own office, credentials, status, or reputation to fool the other party.
- In a competitive bidding environment, deliberately underpricing an offer to steal business from the other party.

The results are represented in Table 13.1. This table lists the tactics with those seen as most appropriate at the top of the list, and those seen at least appropriate at the bottom of the list. In addition, Figure 13.2 illustrates the tactics according to their mean appropriateness.

Several observations emerge from looking over this list. First, some tactics are seen as definitely appropriate: four tactics, on average, received a rating of 5 or above, which we judge to be in the appropriate range. These include gaining

**TABLE 13.1**  Mean Ratings of Appropriateness and Likelihood of Tactics, Ordered by Mean Appropriateness

| Tactic Number | Variables | Mean Appropriateness Ratings | Standard Deviation | Mean Likelihood Ratings | Standard Deviation |
|---|---|---|---|---|---|
| (6) | Gain information about an opponent's negotiating position and strategy by "asking around" in a network of your own friends, associates, and contacts. | 6.00 | 1.62 | 5.73 | 1.90 |
| (4) | Hide your real bottom line from your opponent. | 5.78 | 1.69 | 5.71 | 1.71 |
| (5) | Make an opening demand that is far greater than what you really hope to settle for. | 5.51 | 1.72 | 5.07 | 1.89 |
| (13) | Convey a false impression that you are in absolutely no hurry to come to a negotiation agreement, thereby putting more time pressure on your opponent to concede quickly. | 5.10 | 2.20 | 4.80 | 2.37 |
| (3) | Lead negotiators on the other side to believe that they can only get what they want by negotiating with you, when in fact they could go elsewhere and get what they want cheaper or faster. | 4.33 | 1.79 | 4.22 | 1.71 |
| (10) | Make an opening offer or demand so high (or low) that it seriously undermines your opponent's confidence in her own ability to negotiate a satisfactory settlement. | 4.38 | 2.11 | 4.01 | 2.10 |
| (16) | Intentionally misrepresent the nature of negotiations to the press or your constituency to protect delicate discussions that have occurred. | 3.20 | 1.97 | 3.15 | 2.03 |
| (18) | Intentionally misrepresent factual information to your opponent when you know that he has already done this to you. | 2.75 | 2.05 | 2.90 | 2.06 |
| (7) | Gain information about an opponent's negotiating position by paying friends, associates, and contacts to get this information for you. | 3.17 | 1.94 | 2.79 | 1.82 |

| | | | | |
|---|---|---|---|---|
| (12) | Talk directly to the people who your opponent reports to or is accountable to, and try to encourage them to defect to your side. | 2.91 | 1.84 | 2.72 | 1.75 |
| (9) | Gain information about an opponent's negotiating position by cultivating her friendship through expensive gifts, entertaining, or "personal favors." | 2.70 | 1.67 | 2.64 | 1.76 |
| (2) | Promise that good things will happen to your opponent if he gives you what you want, even if you know that you can't (or won't) deliver those good things when you have obtained the other's cooperation. | 2.58 | 1.69 | 2.58 | 1.69 |
| (1) | Threaten to harm your opponent if she doesn't give you what you want, even if you know you will never follow through with that threat. | 2.56 | 2.37 | 2.57 | 2.23 |
| (17) | Intentionally misrepresent the progress of negotiations to the press or your constituency to make your own position or point of view look better. | 2.49 | 1.75 | 2.55 | 1.84 |
| (14) | Threaten to make your opponent look weak or foolish in front of a boss or others to whom she is accountable. | 2.50 | 1.66 | 2.44 | 1.63 |
| (15) | Intentionally misrepresent factual information to your opponent to support your negotiating position. | 2.11 | 1.49 | 2.29 | 1.61 |
| (11) | Talk directly to the people your opponent reports to or is accountable to and tell them things that will undermine their confidence in your opponent as negotiator. | 2.22 | 1.49 | 2.14 | 1.47 |
| (8) | Gain information about an opponent's negotiating position by trying to recruit or hire one of your opponents' key subordinates (on the condition that the key subordinate bring confidential information with him). | 2.16 | 1.59 | 2.03 | 1.57 |

Mean correlation between individual appropriateness and likelihood ratings: .81, s.d. = .13.

**FIGURE 13.2**   A Simple Model of Ethical Decision Making

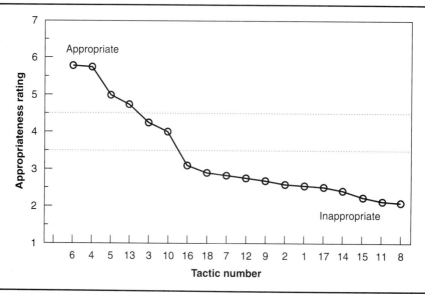

information about the other party by asking around among friends and associates, hiding your real bottom line, making a opening demand greater than what you really want to achieve, and stalling. Second, a large number of the tactics were judged as inappropriate: 12 of the 18 tactics received ratings of 3 or below. Third, ratings of appropriateness and likelihood of using the tactic are very strongly correlated, which suggests that whether we see a tactic as appropriate to use and whether we are likely to use it are very closely related phenomena. (What is still an open question is whether one causes the other.) Finally, although it would be inappropriate to infer one person's individual attitudes from a statistical summary of the data, it does appear that tactics like this can be "scaled"—some are clearly appropriate, some are clearly inappropriate, and some are in a middle range where what is appropriate is still unclear and debatable.

Anton's study (1990), reported earlier, revealed a comparable scaling of negotiating tactics. Respondents to a questionnaire evaluated the ethicality of four types of untrue statements (misrepresentation of value to the other party, bluffing, deception, and falsehood), as represented in negotiating scenarios. The results reveal that the ratings of ethicality decreased as one moved from misrepresentation of value to bluffing to deception to falsehood. The misrepresentation of one's preferred settlement to the other party was seen as generally acceptable (as judged by the mean rating for the category), although some raters took an absolutist position and said that even this kind of behavior constituted not telling the truth and was unethical. Anton had different occupational groups rate the statements and found that clergy rated misrepresentation most strictly, more so than

MBA students and alumni. Bluffs were where the groups tended to "draw the line" between ethical and unethical, whereas deception was seen as moderately unethical. Finally, all groups believed that outright falsification was highly unethical. Some variations in ratings were also a function of age: bluffing is seen as more acceptable and deception as less acceptable as one gets older.

Thus, both the Lewicki and Spencer (1990) and the Anton (1990) studies indicate that there are tacitly agreed-upon rules of the game in negotiation. In these rules, some minor forms of untruths—misrepresentation of one's true position to the other party and bluffs—may be seen as ethically acceptable and within the rules whereas deception and falsification are generally seen as outside of the rules. However, we must place some strong cautionary notes on these tentative conclusions. First, these statements are based on mean ratings by large groups of people; in no way can they predict how any one individual negotiator will perceive the tactics and use them or how any one target who experiences them will rate them. We will discuss reactions from the "victim's" perspective later in this chapter. Second, we are suggesting these conclusions on the basis of rating scales, not live negotiating experiences. Perceptions and reactions may be different when the parties are actually making decisions in a real negotiation rather than ranking the tactics on a questionnaire removed from any direct experience with another person in a meaningful social context. Third, we do not mean to suggest that it is appropriate or acceptable to draw the line where it is now drawn—that misrepresentation and bluffing are acceptable and deception and falsehoods are not. Our objective is to focus debate among negotiators on exactly these issues, rather than to suggest that this is where the line should be drawn.

## FACTORS CREATING A PREDISPOSITION TO CHOOSE UNETHICAL TACTICS

Thus far, we have talked about the use of ethically questionable tactics in terms of the simple model presented in Figure 13.1. This model describes a rational calculation process in which the negotiator selects a tactic, uses the tactic, evaluates the consequences and attempts to manage the consequences (if the tactic is detected) through explanations and justifications. A number of other factors can moderate the sequences described in the model. These factors include

- The background and demographic characteristics of the negotiators.
- The personality characteristics, motives, and moral development of the negotiators.
- The rewards and punishments derived from using a particular tactic.
- The social context that encourages or discourages unethical conduct.

In this section, we will briefly mention how each of these factors might influence the predisposition to use ethically questionable tactics. In many cases, the factors have been shown to influence unethical conduct in a variety of studies, although not necessarily a negotiation context. These factors are included in an expanded model, presented in Figure 13.3.

**FIGURE 13.3**   A More Complex Model of Ethical Decision Making

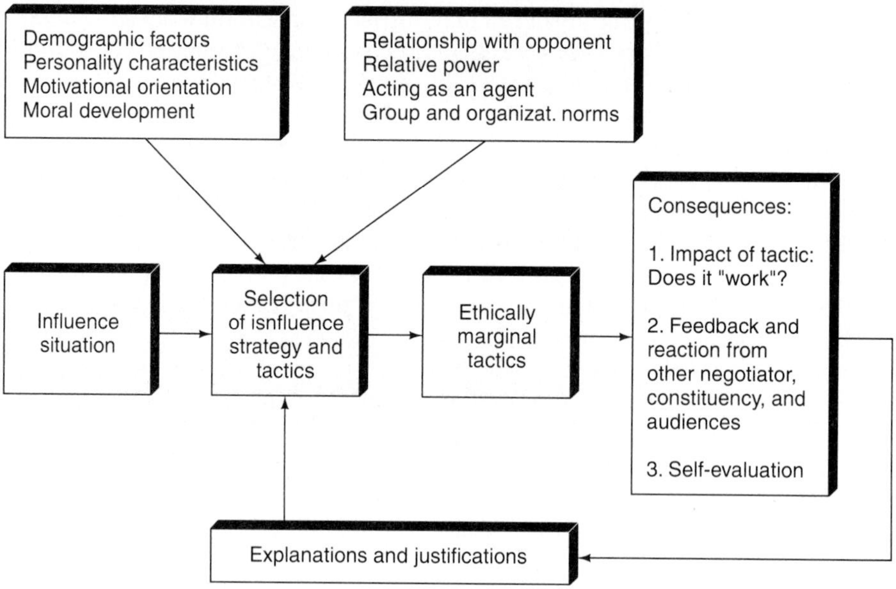

## Demographic Factors

Several survey-oriented research studies on ethical behavior have attempted to relate ethical conduct to differences in individual background, religious orientation, age, gender, nationality, and education. For example, Hassett (1981 June; 1981 November; 1982) reported in *Psychology Today* that individuals who were older or had a stronger commitment to some religious philosophy would be less likely to behave unethically. Others have shown that more ethical conduct was evident among individuals who have been educated in parochial schools or among those who claim a stronger personal and moral code (e.g., absolutists) (Maier and Lavrakas, 1976). Anton (1990) also reports some demographic differences in the perceived appropriateness of the categories of ethical tactics. For example, although there were no age or gender differences in viewing misrepresentation of the bottom line as ethically acceptable and outright falsehoods as unacceptable, there were differences in views of the appropriateness of bluffing and deception. Bluffing was more acceptable to middle-aged respondents (ages 30 to 60) than to either older or younger respondents, and females were significantly less tolerant of bluffing than males. Across occupational groups, clergy tended to be more ethically strict than other groups, whereas MBA students tended to see many of the tactic categories as more acceptable.

## Personality Characteristics, Motivational Orientation, and Moral Development

**Personality Characteristics.**    Researchers have sought to identify personality dimensions that would successfully predict the predisposition to behave unethically. We will mention two of them here.

*Machiavellianism.*    In Chapter 11, we noted that differences in Machiavellian orientation appeared to have a significant impact on negotiating behavior. Machiavellians adhere to a very pragmatic and expedient view of human nature—"the best way to handle people is to tell them what they want to hear" or "it is hard to get ahead without cutting corners here and there." A number of research studies have shown that individuals who are strongly Machiavellian are more willing and able con artists, more likely to lie when they need to, better able to tell bigger lies without feeling anxious about it, and more persuasive and effective in their lies (Braginsky, 1970; Christie and Geis, 1970; Exline, Thibaut, Hickey, and Gumpert, 1970; Geis and Moon, 1981). Machiavellianism thus appears to be a very important predictor of ethical conduct.

*Locus of Control.*    We also mentioned in Chapter 11 that individuals differ in their locus of control—that is, the degree to which they believe that the outcomes they obtain are largely a result of their own ability and effort (internal control) versus fate or chance (external control). Research studies have generally predicted that individuals who are high in internal control are more likely to do what they think is right (i.e., they have a stronger personal value system or ethical code), and that they had more control over producing the outcomes they wanted to achieve in a situation in which there were temptations to be less ethical. Research evidence from several different studies of cheating and ethical decision making has confirmed this prediction (Lefcourt, 1982; Trevino and Youngblood, 1990), although it is important to note that locus of control seems most important when individuals can also exert control over outcomes. Thus, locus of control appears to be a moderately powerful contributor to ethical decision making, although it has yet to be tested as a factor in tactic selection in negotiation.

**Motivational Orientation.**    Earlier in this chapter, we described research on how people perceive the ethicality and appropriateness of certain negotiation tactics (Table 13.1). In rating these tactics, the respondents were simply asked to imagine that they were in a negotiation situation where they wanted to maximize their outcome. In Chapter 11, we described how motivational orientation— whether the negotiator is motivated to be cooperative, competitive, or individualistic—can affect the strategies and tactics they pursue. In a follow-up study, Lewicki and Spencer (1991) explicitly told the respondents to assume either a competitive or cooperative motivational orientation of the negotiator, and also to assume that the other party would be taking either a competitive or cooperative motivational orientation. The authors predicted that if a negotiator were motivated to be competitive, the negotiator would see the ethically marginal tactics as more appropriate, and if a negotiator expected the other to be competitive, the negotiator would also see these ethically marginal tactics as more appropriate—when both parties were competitively motivated, it should produce the greatest tendency to employ the tactics.

The results revealed that differences in the negotiator's own motivational orientation—cooperative versus competitive—did not differentiate on the appropriateness of using the tactics, but the other's expected motivation did! Thus, negotiators were significantly more likely to see the marginally ethical tactics as appropriate to use if they anticipated that the other would be competitive than if the other were expected to be cooperative. Although these findings are preliminary, they do suggest that negotiators may rationalize the use of marginally ethical tactics in anticipated defense of the other's expected conduct, rather than take more personal ownership for using these tactics in the service of their own competitive orientation.

**Moral Development.**   Many researchers have explored the relationship of an individual's level of moral development to ethical decision making. Kohlberg (1969) proposed that an individual's moral and ethical judgments are a consequence of achieving a particular developmental level or stage of moral growth. Kohlberg proposed six stages of moral development, grouped into three levels:

1. A preconventional level (stages 1 and 2), where the individual is concerned with concrete outcomes that meet her own immediate needs, particularly external rewards and punishments.

2. A conventional level (stages 3 and 4), where the individual defines what is "right" on the basis of what his immediate social situation and peer group endorses or what "society in general" seems to want.

3. A principled level (stages 5 and 6), where the individual defines what is "right" on the basis of some broader set of universal values and principles.

The higher a stage people achieve, the more complex their moral reasoning should be and the more ethical their decisions should be. In addition, there may be gender-related differences in this ethical reasoning process (Gilligan, 1982). Many studies have demonstrated the power of measuring ethical orientation in this way (see Trevino, 1986, and Trevino and Youngblood, 1990, for two reviews). The results have indicated that higher levels of moral development are associated with more ethical decisions, less cheating behavior, more helping behavior, and more resistance to authority figures who are attempting to dictate unethical conduct.

## Situational Influences on Unethical Conduct

The last set of factors that should have an impact on a negotiator's willingness to act unethically are situational factors. We briefly examine three elements from this group: the negotiator's relationship with the other party, differences in power and status between the two negotiators, and the social or cultural norms that govern the negotiation process.

**Relationship Between the Negotiator and the Other Party.**    Two aspects of the negotiator's relationship with the other party affect the disposition to use certain tactics: what the relationship has been like in the past and what the parties would like it to be in the future. The negotiator's past relationship will affect current behavior if the parties have been previously competitive or cooperative, are friends or enemies, feel indebted to one another, or hold grudges toward one another. For example, research by Gruder (1971) showed that negotiators were more likely to make more deceptive arguments, negotiate for a longer period of time, and make fewer concessions to the counterpart they previously experienced as exploitative compared to one who had been cooperative. A similar argument can be made for a negotiator's expectations about how the counterpart will behave in the present or future. If you view the other party with suspicion—as exploitative, competitive, dishonest—you can then justify a relativistic approach to strategy and claim that anticipatory self-defense legitimizes your actions. We see this in the Lewicki and Spencer (1991) data reported earlier—when negotiators expected the other party to have a competitive motivational orientation, this expectation legitimized the use of more ethically marginal tactics. However, you can see how this form of rationalization may be easily distorted by fear and suspicion and hence create a self-fulfilling prophecy to justify pursuit of an unethical tactic. All a negotiator needs is to experience some mildly competitive or exploitative bit of behavior from the other party, or even to imagine that it is going to occur. Naturally, this will motivate the other party to seek revenge and act in exactly the ways that the negotiator anticipated.

A factor in the relationship that can balance this self-fulfilling dynamics is whether the negotiator expects the relationship to be short term or long term. Another variation in the Lewicki and Spencer (1991) study manipulated whether the negotiator expected to be in a short-term or long-term working relationship with the other party. Respondents who expected to be in a short-term relationship were more likely to see the ethically marginal tactics as appropriate than those expecting a long-term relationship, regardless of their own and the other party's motivations. This was the most powerful result of the study, and it appears to indicate that when a negotiator does not anticipate having to "live with" the consequences of using ethically marginal tactics, she is far more willing to use them. Anton (1990) reports some anecdotal results that also support this finding.

**Relative Power Between the Negotiators.**    A second situational factor is relative power—how much power one negotiator has relative to the other party. In general, negotiators with more power are more likely to abuse that power by using less ethical tactics. For example, in one research study, negotiators with more power bluffed more often and communicated less with their counterpart than those with less power (Crott, Kayser, and Lamm, 1980). This result will seem paradoxical to some people. Why should negotiators with more power, who can presumably get what they want by using their power legitimately, use unethical tactics that increase their power even more? The results seem to support the "intoxication" theories of power (see Chapter 10). These theories hold that power corrupts the thinking of the powerful; results confirming the theory have been consistently observed both in laboratory research and in the power dynamics between "haves" and "have nots" in society. A balance of power should lead to more stable, ethical conduct than an imbalance.

### Acting as an Agent versus Representing Our Own Views.

> Many negotiators fail to understand the nature of negotiation and so find themselves attempting to reconcile conflicts between the requirements of negotiation and their own sense of personal integrity. An individual who confuses private ethics with business morality does not make an effective negotiator. A negotiator must learn to be objective in his negotiations and to subordinate his own personal sense of ethics to the prime purpose of securing the best possible deal for his principals (Beckman, 1977, quoted in Lax and Sebenius, 1986, p. 363).

As we pointed out in Chapter 9, negotiators frequently find themselves representing others' views in negotiation, rather than negotiating for their own personal goals and interests. A number of authors have suggested that when we act as an agent for someone else—particularly when the goals for that agent are to get the best possible agreement—agents may be more willing to violate personal ethical standards (Bowie and Freeman, 1992). In essence, acting as an agent may release a person from his own personal ethical standards and code and allow him to create his own standards of legitimacy—that it is appropriate to do whatever is necessary to maximize the results for the constituent.

### Group and Organizational Norms and Pressures.

Finally, many negotiators look to the social norms of the particular situation to decide how to behave. Norms are the informal social rules—the "dos and don'ts"—that govern social behavior. In negotiation, the rules are defined in two ways: by what people believe is appropriate in negotiation, and by what other people say is appropriate in that situation. As an example of the first case, some negotiators may define negotiation as a game, and thus they feel that "gaming rules" apply to negotiation. For example, if negotiating is a game like poker, then it is very appropriate to play negotiation as we would play poker—to bluff, fake, or bet in order to try to drive others out of the game. Is it appropriate to do these things in negotiation? Do all people agree? (See Carr, 1968; McDonald, 1963.) What happens when some people believe these tactics are appropriate, and proceed to use bluffing tactics, while others don't believe they are?

Recent research suggests that group and organizational norms and pressures may play a key role in legitimizing inappropriate behavior (although, again, this research has not been directly performed on negotiating situations). First, research has shown that companies have distinctly different ethical climates or cultures (Jackall, 1988; Victor and Cullen, 1988). These climates differ in the ways that they value and endorse highly ethical conduct or, on the other hand, appear to condone and tolerate ethically marginal behavior in the service of achieving corporate objectives at any price. Second, whereas the company overall may have a very strong statement of corporate ethics and values, job-related pressures within particular work groups, departments, or divisions may be such that marginally ethical behavior is not only tolerated, but even condoned. The actions and practices of the key manager or supervisor in this work group or department probably play a large role in determining what people believe it is necessary and appropriate to do (see Murphy, 1992 for one review). In fact, authors have speculated that the more loyalty and commitment an individual feels toward an organization, the more that loyalty may be abused because the individual suspends her own ethical judgment and engages in any and all behavior—even unethical and illegal behavior—to demonstrate that loyalty (Charmichael, 1992). Finally, organizations may exert direct pressures on an individual to breach ethics or even break the law in the service of achieving some corporate or organizational goal. In these circumstances, the individuals have also suspended their best moral judgment—but in the service of obedience, following the rules, and doing what one is told—even if the actions are immoral and unethical. The pressures toward obedience in organizations are very strong, as anyone who has read about Milgram's famous experiments will recall (Milgram, 1974). These pressures are real in organizations, and many authors are beginning to document how thoroughly the pressures can undermine individual integrity (Brief, 1992; Kelman and Hamilton, 1989). In its most extreme forms, these pressures lead individuals to major crimes against humanity, such as the Holocaust or the infamous My Lai massacre in the Viet Nam war.

Summarizing this section briefly, research shows that a number of social forces can encourage negotiators to suspend their own personal and ethical standards and commit acts that are ethically questionable. These forces include

- Acting as an agent for someone else and responding to their pressures to achieve a very high goal, succeed at any price, or do whatever it takes to accomplish an objective.
- Viewing various forms of business dealings—such as negotiation—as a game (like poker or war), and therefore assuming that the rules of poker are the ones that should be applied to these business dealings.
- Being a member of a group, department, team, or organizational unit that values success and tolerates or even encourages bending or breaking the rules in order to achieve that success.
- Being so loyal to a group or organization that you can convince yourself that it is permissible to break the rules in order to be rewarded for your loyalty.
- Being willing to follow the direct or implied orders of more senior officials in the organization who tell us to get a job done and not worry about how it gets done.

*Any* of these forces appear to be sufficient, under the right circumstances, to permit individuals to suspend their own good moral judgment in the service of doing what the organization appears to need, want, or request. Combining them

---

**Ethical Persuasion: Another Perspective**

Thomas Rusk and Patrick Miller (1993) have recently proposed a framework for "getting to yes without drawing blood"—achieving successful resolution in "those high stakes conversations that are threatened by strong emotions and defensive reactions." Rusk and Miller argue that the destructive dynamics of conflict, the tendency to blame others and defend ourselves, the difficulty of acknowledging feelings as data, and the tendency to treat conflict in relationships as a "power struggle" lead to major communication breakdowns. To achieve successful resolution of these disputes without resorting to either destructive conflict escalation, unethical conflict practices, or both, Rusk and Miller outline a three-step framework:

1. A seven-step process for exploring the other person's viewpoint, including procedures for establishing a mutual goal of common understanding and efforts to understand the other through active listening and paraphrasing.

2. A five-step process for explaining your own viewpoint, including asking for a fair hearing in return, explaining how the other's thoughts and feelings affect you, stating your own thoughts, feelings, and desires and asking for restatements of your position until the other clearly understands.

3. A three-step process for creating resolutions, including affirming your mutual understanding of each other's thoughts, feelings, and desires; brainstorming options, and using other techniques for achieving a resolution if brainstorming does not produce quick results.

These principles of ethical persuasion are consistent with the framework and process of integrative negotiation that we described in Chapter 4.

From Thomas Rusk with D. Patrick Miller (1993). *The Power of Ethical Persuasion.* New York: Penguin Books.

---

together can produce an even more lethal concoction of social pressures that can permit an individual to rationalize his actions and do whatever is necessary, and that often leads to major breakdowns in ethical conduct and legal behavior.

## SUMMARY

In this chapter, we have discussed some of the primary factors that affect how a negotiator evaluates and decides to use negotiating strategy and tactics that may be ethically marginal. We began by considering several negotiation cases, showing how they were indicative of the ways that ethical questions can be critical to the selection of particular strategic and tactical options. We then reviewed some of the primary motivational factors that lead negotiators to consider using unethical tactics: the pursuit of profit, the desire to beat the other party in a competitive environment, and the need to insure or restore some standard of justice that may have been violated. Any of these motives may be sufficient to prompt a negotiator to move toward the use of marginally ethical and questionable behavior to accomplish his objectives.

We used three major approaches to understanding ethical conduct to describe the broad range of questionable negotiating strategies and tactics: means-ends, relativism, and truth-telling. Means-ends tactics are judged according to the philosophical tenets of utilitarianism—that one can achieve the greatest good by pursuing certain ends or by abiding by certain rules and procedures that will lead to those ends. The more we are committed to attain certain ends, the more we may be prone to believe that it is occasionally necessary to deviate from the rules to attain those ends. In contrast, the more we are committed to abide by certain rules and procedures, the more we believe that following the rules will eventually lead to the desired ends. The second group of tactics, relativistic versus absolute, forces us to deal with questions of whether there are truly absolute rules and principles of right and wrong or whether questions of ethics must be answered by each individual in her own personal, subjective view of the world. A negotiator who looks only to himself or to the dynamics of the immediate situation, rather than to broad principles of what is right and proper, would be more likely to espouse relativism as a standard for making his decisions. Lastly, truth-telling standards determine whether it is appropriate (or even necessary) to deviate from the truth to negotiate effectively. Many authors have suggested that bluffing, misrepresentation, or factual distortion is sometimes necessary to effectively negotiate; such behavior, however, may well be seen by others as unethical and inappropriate.

We have included this chapter because we believe that the negotiation process raises a host of ethical issues, more so than most other interpersonal transactions. Much of what has been written on negotiating behavior has been strongly normative about ethics and has prescribed "dos and don'ts." We do not believe that this approach facilitates the understanding of how negotiators actually decide to act unethically. In contrast, we argue that this process can best be presented within a decision-making framework. We proposed that a negotiator who chooses to use an unethical tactic usually decides to do so to increase her negotiating power. Power is gained by manipulating the perceived base of accurate information in the negotiation, getting better information about an opponent's plan, or undermining an opponent's ability to achieve his objectives. Using these tactics leads to two kinds of consequences: first, possible attainment of the goals the negotiator was seeking; and second, evaluation and criticism of the tactics by the negotiator herself, by the opponent, and by observers. As a result of the consequences and the evaluation, negotiators usually feel compelled to justify their actions—they know they have done something wrong and need to establish a good reason. The purpose of this justification is both to rationalize the action to themselves and to others and possibly to lead the negotiator to try it again in the future. In the context of this framework, we reported the results of research designed to understand how a collection of ethically marginal tactics is perceived and judged. The results of this research indicate that although several of these tactics are less than completely honest and truthful, they are considered ethically appropriate in negotiation to achieve a negotiator's objective. However, a large number of other tactics are also considered ethically inappropriate and outside the boundaries of acceptable practice. Finally, we suggested that the decision to use ethical or unethical tactics may be influenced by factors such as differences in individual backgrounds, personality, past rewards or punishments associated with ethical or unethical actions, the anticipated relationship with the other party, and the social and cultural norms that dictate what is appropriate or inappropriate in a given environment.

Research on negotiator ethics and on various aspects of this model lead us to suggest the following conclusions:

1. Individuals in negotiation may disagree as to what kinds of negotiating tactics are ethical and unethical. The research reported here suggests that there is much more convergence in the tactics that fall into these categories than might have been expected.

2. The decision to use an unethical tactic can probably best be understood through a decision-making model. It is clear that many personality and situational variables are also likely to affect that decision.

3. In deciding to use an unethical tactic, a negotiator is likely to be more heavily influenced by (a) her own motivations, (b) expectations of what the other negotiator will do, and (c) whether the negotiator expects to be negotiating with the other again in the future.

4. Negotiators who have used unethical tactics in the past or who are considering their use in the future should strongly consider three possible consequences of using unethical tactics:

   (a) Will they really help achieve objectives?

   (b) How will they affect the quality of the relationship with this opponent in the future?

   (c) How will they affect their reputation?

Negotiators frequently overlook the fact that, although unethical or expedient tactics may get them what they want in the short run, these same tactics typically lead to long-term problems and to diminished effectiveness.

# CHAPTER 14

# International Negotiation

The frequency of international negotiations is increasing rapidly as business becomes more international in scope and extent. Thus, international negotiations have become the norm for many organizations, rather than an exotic activity that occurs only occasionally. Numerous books and articles, from both academic and practitioner perspectives, have been written about the complexities of negotiating across borders, be it with a person from a different country, culture, or region. Although culture has many aspects, we will use the term to refer to the shared values and beliefs of a group of people. Culture describes group-level characteristics, which may or may not be good descriptors of any given individual within the group. (For example, countries can have more than one culture and cultures can span national borders.) With this caveat in mind, we will use the terms *culture* and *country* loosely in this chapter to refer to negotiation across borders (legal or cultural). As we discussed in Chapters 2 and 9, negotiating is a social process that is imbedded in a much larger context. This context becomes more complex when more than one culture is involved, making negotiation a much more complicated process when it occurs across borders. Far too much has been written on this topic to summarize in one chapter (for examples, see Binnendijk, 1987; Foster, 1992; Habeeb, 1988; Hendon and Hendon, 1990; Kremenyuk, 1991; Lukov, 1985; Mautner-Markhof, 1989; for earlier work, see Fayerweather and Kapoor, 1976; Hall, 1960; Van Zandt, 1970). Our goal is simply to highlight and discuss some of the most recent and interesting work that has been written on this topic.

It is important to recognize that this book has been written from an American perspective (United States and Canada),[1] and that this cultural filter has influenced how we think about negotiation, what we consider to be important aspects of negotiation, and our advice about how to become better negotiators. This chapter will also reflect our own cultural filter, both in our choices about what we discuss and because we will use Americans as the base from which to make comparisons to other cultures. That is not to say that all Americans reflect the same culture. In fact, there is evidence that people from countries as similar as the United States and Canada negotiate differently (see Adler and Graham, 1987;

---

[1] The primary author is a Canadian. We are not implying that Canadians should or do consider themselves "American." Rather, we will use the American standard as the basis by which comparisons can be drawn to all other cultures.

Adler, Graham, and Schwarz, 1987), and that within the United States and Canada, there are systematic regional and cultural differences (for example, English and French Canada; Hispanics, African Americans, the South, the Southwest, and other areas and populations in the United States). At some level, however, Americans do share (more or less) a common culture that is different from other cultures and countries. While recognizing the differences within America, we will use the common aspects of American culture to discuss the effects of culture on negotiating with people from other countries and cultures.

This chapter is organized in the following manner. First we will present the results of a program of research that has demonstrated that negotiators in different countries use different negotiation processes to reach the same negotiation outcomes. Then we will discuss some of the factors that make negotiations across borders more difficult, including political, economic, legal, and cultural considerations. The next section describes a model of international negotiation that can help organize the many aspects of cross-border negotiations and act as a guide in preparation for these negotiations. We then turn to a discussion of perhaps the most critical issue that negotiators face when they negotiate across borders: the effect of culture, be it national, regional, or organizational. We discuss how culture can be conceptualized in cross-border negotiations, how academics and practitioners use the concept of culture, and the influence of culture on negotiations. The next section of the chapter specifically examines the negotiating style of three countries in the Pacific Rim: Japan, China, and Korea. We decided to choose these three cultures because of the volume of business negotiations with these cultures and because we cannot possibly cover all possible cultures in a single chapter (for specific attention to negotiation processes in other cultures, see Acuff, 1993; Hendon and Hendon, 1990; Kennedy, 1985). Although there are similarities in negotiation styles across these three countries, there are also important differences of which the cross-border negotiator needs to be aware. The chapter concludes with a discussion of the options available to the international negotiator for managing these negotiations.

## NOT EVERYONE NEGOTIATES LIKE AMERICANS!

Graham and his colleagues (see Graham, 1993 for a review) have conducted a series of experiments comparing negotiators from the United States and 15 other countries, including Japan, China, Canada, Brazil, and Mexico. These studies each used the same research materials—a version of the buyer/seller negotiation simulation developed by Kelley (1966), in which negotiators have to decide on the prices of three products (televisions, typewriters, air conditioners). The participants in the studies were businesspeople who were either attending management seminars or graduate business courses. Participants in all these studies negotiated with people from their own countries (these were intracultural negotiations, not cross-cultural negotiations). The major dependent measures in these studies were (1) the individual profit level made by the two negotiators in the simulation and (2) the level of satisfaction that the negotiators had with the negotiation outcomes.

The results of this research have been quite consistent across studies. Graham and his colleagues found no differences in the profit levels obtained by negotiators in the simulation from the United States and the other countries studied, including: Japan (Graham, 1983, 1984), China (Adler, Brahm, and Graham, 1992), Canada (Adler and Graham, 1987; Adler, Graham, and Schwarz, 1987), Brazil (Graham, 1983), and Mexico (Adler, Graham, and Schwartz, 1987). Taken as a whole, these results suggest that negotiators from the different countries studied were equally effective in obtaining negotiation outcomes. One conclusion from this research, then, is that business negotiators from different countries appear to obtain similar negotiation outcomes when they negotiate with other people from their own country.

Graham and Adler did find, however, that there were significant differences in the negotiation *process* in the countries that they studied. In other words, although negotiators from different countries obtained the same outcome, *the way that they negotiated to obtain that outcome was quite different.* For instance, Graham (1983) concludes that "in American negotiations, higher profits are achieved by making opponents feel *un*comfortable, while in Japanese negotiations, higher profits are associated with making opponents feel comfortable" (p. 63). In addition, Graham (1983) reports that Brazilian negotiators who used powerful and deceptive strategies were more likely to receive higher outcomes; these strategies were not related to the outcomes attained by the American negotiators. Further, Adler, Graham, and Schwartz, (1987) report that representational strategies (gathering information) were negatively related to profits attained by Mexican and French-Canadian negotiators, whereas these strategies were unrelated to the profits that American negotiators received. Finally, although Adler, Brahm, and Graham (1992) found that Chinese and American negotiators used similar negotiation strategies when they negotiated, their communication patterns were quite different—the Chinese asked more questions, said "no" less frequently, and interrupted each other more frequently than did American negotiators.

Adler and Graham (1989) also conducted a study in which they compared intracultural and cross-cultural negotiation outcomes and processes. They found that Japanese and English-Canadian negotiators received lower profit levels when they negotiated cross-culturally than when they negotiated intraculturally; American and French-Canadian negotiators negotiated the same average outcomes in cross-cultural and intracultural negotiations. These results support Adler and Graham's hypothesis that cross-cultural negotiations will result in poorer outcomes, at least some of the time. In addition, Adler and Graham found some differences in the cross-cultural negotiation process. For instance, French-Canadian negotiators used more cooperative strategies in cross-cultural negotiations than in intracultural negotiations, and American negotiators reported higher levels of satisfaction with their cross-cultural negotiations (versus intracultural negotiations).

In summary, this program of research suggests that negotiators from different cultures (countries) use different negotiation strategies and communication patterns when they negotiate with other people from their own culture. Importantly, however, there was *no* difference in the negotiation outcomes attained by the negotiators across these studies. This suggests that there are many different ways to negotiate agreements that are, on average, worth the same value, and that a negotiator must employ the process that "fits" the culture they are in. Further, the culture of the negotiator appears to be an important predictor of the negotiation process that will occur and how negotiation strategies will influence negotiation outcomes in different cultures. In addition, this research suggests that cross-cultural negotiations may yield poorer outcomes than intracultural negotiations, at least on some occasions.

## WHAT MAKES CROSS-BORDER NEGOTIATIONS DIFFERENT?

Salacuse (1988) has suggested six factors that make cross-border negotiations more challenging than domestic negotiations. These factors can act to limit or constrain organizations that operate in the international arena, and it is important that negotiators who bargain across borders understand and appreciate their effects.

### Political and Legal Pluralism

When organizations make business deals that cross a national border, they come into contact with the legal and political system of another country. There may be implications for the taxes that the organization pays, the labor codes or standards that they must meet, and the different codes of contract law and standards of enforcement (e.g., case law versus common law versus no functioning legal system, for instance). In addition, political considerations may enhance or detract from the conduct of business negotiations in various countries at different times (compare the open business environment in the former Soviet bloc in the 1990s with the closed environment of the 1960s).

### International Economic Factors

The value of international currencies naturally fluctuates, and this factor must be considered when making deals across borders. Which currencies will the deal be made in? According to Salacuse (1988), the risk is typically greater for the party who must pay in the other country's currency. The less stable the currency, the greater the risk for both parties. In addition, any change in the value of a currency (upwards or downwards) can significantly affect the value of the deal for both parties, changing a mutually valuable deal into a windfall profit for one and a large loss for the other. Many countries also control the currency flowing across their borders. Frequently, purchases within these countries may only be made with "hard" currencies that are brought into the country by foreign parties, and domestic organizations are unable to purchase foreign products or negotiate outcomes that require payment in foreign currencies.

## Foreign Governments and Bureaucracies

Countries differ in the extent to which the government regulates industries and organizations. Organizations in the United States are relatively free from government intervention, although some industries are more heavily regulated (e.g., power generation, defense) and some states have tougher environmental regulations than others. Generally, however, business negotiations in the United States occur without government approval, and the parties to a negotiation decide whether to engage in a deal based on business reasons alone. Contrast this with the situation in many developing and (former) communist countries. Imports into these countries are closely supervised by the government, and frequently an agency of the government has a monopoly in dealing with foreign organizations (Salacuse, 1988). In addition, political considerations, such as the effect of the negotiations on the government treasury, the general economy of the country, and other social conditions, may influence the negotiations more heavily than what Western businesspeople would consider to be "legitimate" business reasons.

## Instability

Although the world continues to change at a rapid pace, businesspeople negotiating domestically in the United States are accustomed to a degree of stability that has not been present in many areas of the world. Instability may take many forms, including a lack of resources that Americans commonly expect during business negotiations (paper, electricity, computers), shortages of personal care products (e.g., food, reliable transportation, potable water), and political instability (coups, sudden shifts in government policy, major currency revaluations). The challenge for negotiators in these situations is to predict these changes accurately, and with enough lead time to adjust for their consequences if they occur. Salacuse suggests that negotiators faced with unstable circumstances should include clauses in their contracts that allow for easy cancellation or neutral arbitration, and they should investigate purchasing insurance policies to guarantee contract provisions. This advice presumes that contracts will be honored and that specific contract clauses like these are culturally acceptable to the other party.

## Ideology

Negotiators within the United States generally share a common ideology of individualism and capitalism. According to Salacuse, this includes a strong belief in individual rights, the superiority of private investment, and the importance of making a profit in business. Negotiators from other countries do not always share this ideology. The ideology in many other countries stresses group rights as more important than individual rights and public investment as a better allocation of resources than private investment, and it has different prescriptions for earning and sharing profit. Clashing ideologies increase the communication challenges in cross-border negotiations in the broadest sense because the parties may disagree on the most fundamental levels about what is being negotiated.

## Culture

People from different cultures appear to negotiate differently. In addition to behavioral differences in negotiation across borders, different cultures may also interpret the fundamental processes of negotiations differently (such as what factors are negotiable and the purpose of the negotiations). According to Salacuse, people in some cultures approach negotiations deductively (they move from the general to the specific) whereas people from other cultures are more inductive (they settle on a series of specific issues that become the area of general agreement). On a more fundamental level, cultures appear to differ on what is actually being negotiated. In some cultures, negotiation occurs over the content of what is discussed and the relationship between the parties is incidental. In other cultures, the relationship between the parties is the main focus of the negotiation, and the content of the deal itself is incidental. One does not have to leave the United States to see the influence of culture on negotiations. Contrast the negotiation described in Box 14.1 with the stereotypical business negotiator from Wall Street. Clearly there is a large challenge negotiating across borders when the fundamental beliefs about what negotiation is and how it occurs can be very different. We will spend most of the remainder of this chapter exploring different aspects of this issue in more detail.

---

**BOX 14.1**
**Cross-Cultural Negotiations within the United States**

I had a client in West Virginia who bought from me for several years. He had a family business that he'd started in a small town with his grandfather, and it had now grown to be the major employer in the town. We had developed quite a close relationship. Every few months, I would make a trip up from North Carolina to see him, knowing after a while that he would need to place an order with me as long as I spaced our visits out every few months. When we got together, at first we would talk about everything but business, catching up with each other. I would ask him about his life, the business, his family, the town, etc., and he would ask me about my work and the company and life in the big city in North Carolina where I lived and worked. Once we'd caught up with each other, we would get down to some business, and this was often after lunch. Each and every time, it would take a few hours of this and that, but I'd always leave with an order, and it was always a pleasant break, at least for me, from my usual hectic pace.

One day I phoned in preparation for my next trip, to see if he would be in, to arrange a convenient day, and he told me that he'd like me to meet a friend of his next time I was up there to visit him. His friend, he said, was interested in some of the things my company was selling, and he thought I should meet him. Of course I was delighted, and we arranged a convenient day for the three of us to meet.

When I arrived at my client's office, his friend, Carl, was already there. We were very casually introduced, and my client began explaining Carl's work, and how he

**Box 14.1 (continued)**

thought what my company sold could be useful to him. Carl then took over and spoke a little about what he did, and I thought for a moment that we were going to go straight into business talk. However, in just a few moments, the conversation between the three of us quickly turned back to discussions of life in town, North Carolina, our respective families, and personal interests. It turned out that Carl liked to hunt, and he and my client began regaling me with stories of their hunting adventures. I'd hunted a little, and shared my stories with them. One thing led to another, and soon we were talking about vacations, the economy, baseball—you name it.

Occasionally, we would make a brief journey back to the business at hand, but it always seemed to be in conjunction with the small talk, like how the tools we manufactured were or were not as precise as the mechanisms on the guns we used for hunting, things like that. I realized that quite a lot of information about our mutual work, my company, their needs, and their work, was being exchanged in all this, even though business was never directly addressed. I remember the first few meetings my client and I had had with each other many years ago—how we learned about each other this way then, too. I was struck with how quaint it felt now, how different it was from the way I usually had to sell, and yet how much I enjoyed working like this!

Well, our discussions went on this way through the rest of the morning, weaving some business back and forth through the larger context of informal chit-chat about each other and our lives. Just before lunch, my client leaned back and began what seemed to be a kind of informal summary of who I was and what I did, and how what I did seemed to him to be just the thing that Carl and his company could use. Carl agreed, and my client asked him, almost on my behalf, how much he wanted to order, and Carl thought for a moment and gave me the biggest order I ever got from West Virginia. "Now that that's done," my client said, "how about some lunch?" We all went to the same place we always go to when I'm in West Virginia, talking about life and things and some business. By midafternoon I said I had to be heading home. We all agreed to stay in touch. We've been in touch ever since, and now I've got two clients to visit whenever I'm in West Virginia.

D.A. Foster, *Bargaining Across Borders: How to Negotiate Business Successfully Anywhere in the World* (New York: McGraw-Hill, 1992), pp. 108–109. Reproduced with the permission of McGraw-Hill.

## THE RBC MODEL OF INTERNATIONAL NEGOTIATIONS

One of the challenges to understanding international negotiations is the sheer complexity of factors that can influence the process and outcome of negotiations across borders. Conducting research in this area is also complex. Researchers have many choices to make in their studies, including levels of analysis (individuals, groups, organizations), countries and cultures to be examined, and aspects of the negotiation process and outcome to study. Summarizing and organizing this information to make comparisons across studies has become a challenge in this area of research.

Weiss (1993) has proposed his "RBC" Model of International Negotiation to organize the wide variety of research findings in international negotiation and to facilitate future research and theory in a systematic manner. The RBC Model proposes that three aspects are necessary to understand international business negotiations: *relationships, behaviors,* and *conditions.*[2] Its strength is that it can organize fragments of research that examine only one or two of the many possible aspects of international negotiation and allow meaningful comparisons to be drawn across different studies. Figure 14.1 presents the RBC Model for a two-party case. Although the figure may be thought of as a snapshot of circumstances at one point in time, the model should be used in an iterative fashion—in other words, things that happen today may change the snapshot of the model tomorrow. Each of the three aspects of the model will now be described in more detail.

### Relationships

The *relationships* aspect of the model delineates the connections between the parties in the negotiation. These connections can occur on many levels between two organizations, and they may be positive, neutral, or negative. For instance, two organizations may be connected through a joint venture agreement. Two teams may be connected within an organization (e.g., the domestic and international marketing groups), or teams may be connected across organizations (e.g., two teams charged with making a joint venture work). And two individuals may be connected across the organizations, such as the heads of the production departments of a parent organization and its foreign subsidiary. These relationships may be parallel (e.g., CEO with CEO) or they may occur cross-level, such as between the CEO of one organization meeting with a team from the other.

### Behaviors

The *behaviors* of the parties to a negotiation may be examined as well, from the organizational, group, and individual level. They may also be intentional or unintentional. Weiss suggests that six types of behavior are important to understand:

1. *Independent*—undertaken by a party itself and relevant to the negotiation, but not communicated to the other primary party (e.g., planning).
2. *Horizontal*—action directed at the counterpart, typically at the negotiating table.
3. *Internal*—activity within a party, such as a negotiating team.
4. *Vertical*—a party's communications with its superior or subordinate.
5. *Lateral*—nonvertical, negotiation-relevant actions directed at a party's peers or colleagues.

---

[2] These aspects are important to understand any negotiation, but we will concentrate on their role in international negotiations in this chapter.

**FIGURE 14.1**   RBC Model of International Negotiation: The Bilateral (x-y) Case.

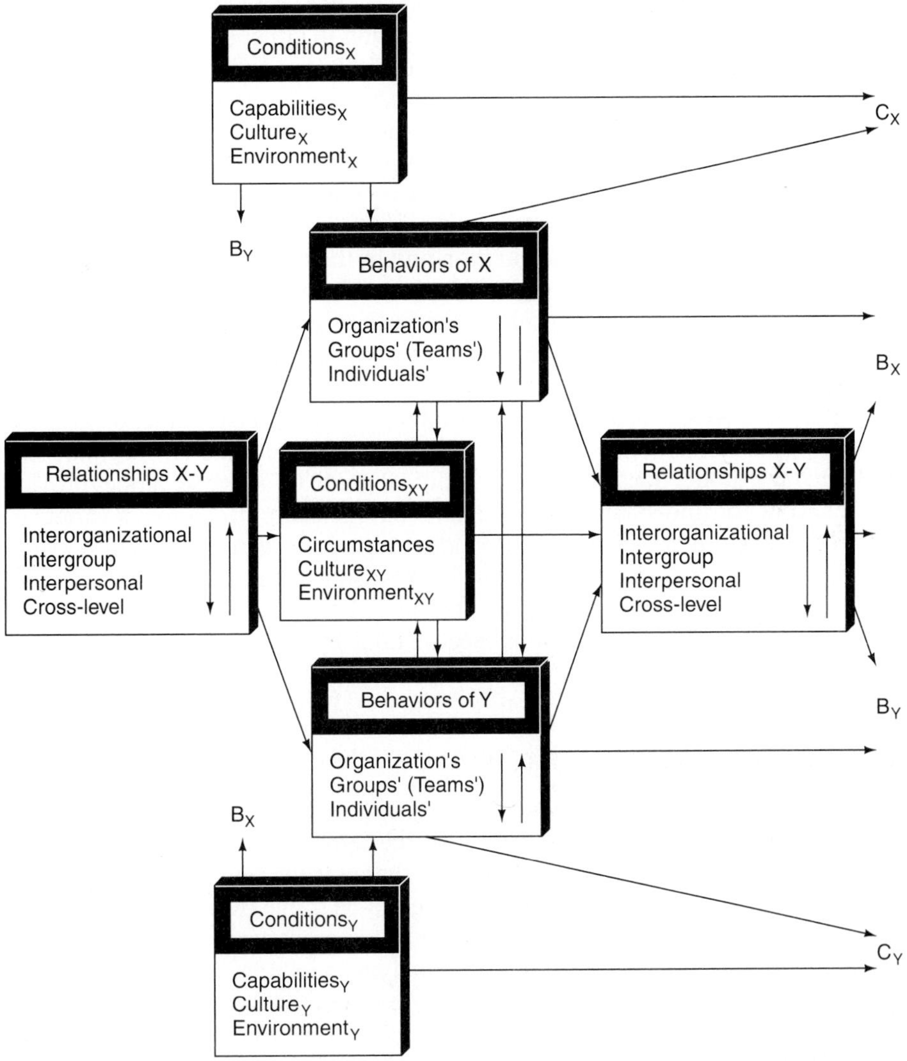

S.E. Weiss. (1993). Analysis of Complex Negotiations in International Business: The RBC Perspective. *Organizational Science, 4,* 269–300.

6. *External*—directed beyond the negotiation setting and the primary parties (e.g., to mass media) (Weiss, 1993, pp. 279–286).

Each of these behaviors can occur at each of three levels of analysis for a party (with the exception of internal behavior, which only occurs at the individual level), and each may also occur across relationship levels.

## Conditions

The final box in the RBC Model is *Conditions.* These are factors that affect the behaviors and relationships in the negotiation in either a positive or negative fashion. Four types of conditions are included in the model: circumstances, capabilities, culture, and environment. *Circumstances* refer to the structure of the negotiations themselves and include factors such as communication channels, the presence of third parties, media coverage, and the negotiation site. *Capabilities* refer to the skills, resources, and traits of a party that enable it to influence and be influenced by a counterpart. *Culture* refers to the way that a negotiation party interprets information in the negotiation and in the broader social context. Culture may be national, ethnic, regional, or organizational. Finally, *environment* refers to the broader sociopolitical factors, such as government policies, foreign exchange markets, and the general political environment that have an influence on the negotiations.

The RBC Model provides a rich framework for understanding, organizing, describing, and categorizing a wide variety of international negotiations. Although the model does not lead to empirical predictions per se, it does provide a framework for understanding the factors that are examined across a variety of international studies. The model also aids comparisons across different research projects by allowing a straightforward comparison of the factors included and excluded in different projects. Finally, the model offers practitioners a powerful guide for preparing for international negotiations by outlining numerous factors that should be considered during planning.

## CULTURE: A CRITICAL FACTOR

One construct that has frequently been used to explain differences in negotiation across borders is *culture.* Although the term *culture* has taken on many different meanings, we use it to refer to the shared values and beliefs held by the members of a group. Cultures are considered to be stable over time. Perhaps the most comprehensive and extensive program of research identifying and exploring different cultural dimensions in international business was conducted by Hofstede (1980a and 1980b, 1989, 1991). Hofstede examined data on values that had been gathered from over 100,000 IBM employees from around the world (to date, over 53 cultures and countries have been included in his study). Statistical analysis of this data suggests that four dimensions could describe the important differences among the cultures in the study. Table 14.1 lists the countries included in the study and their ranking on the four dimensions described below.

### Power Distance

This dimension describes "the extent to which the less powerful members of organizations and institutions (like the family) accept and expect that power is distributed unequally" (Hofstede, 1989, p. 195). According to Hofstede, cultures with greater power distance will be more likely to have decision making concen-

**TABLE 14.1**   Ranking of Countries/Cultures on Cultural Dimensions Reported by Hofstede (1991)

| Country | Rank Order On: | | | |
|---|---|---|---|---|
| | Power Distance | Individualism/ Collectivism | Masculinity/ Femininity | Uncertainty Avoidance |
| Arab Countries | 7 | 26/27 | 23 | 27 |
| Argentina | 35/36 | 22/23 | 20/21 | 10/15 |
| Australia | 41 | 2 | 16 | 37 |
| Austria | 53 | 18 | 2 | 24/25 |
| Belgium | 20 | 8 | 22 | 5/6 |
| Brazil | 14 | 26/27 | 27 | 21/22 |
| Canada | 39 | 4/5 | 24 | 41/42 |
| Chile | 24/25 | 38 | 46 | 10/15 |
| Colombia | 17 | 49 | 11/12 | 20 |
| Costa Rica | 42/44 | 46 | 48/49 | 10/15 |
| Denmark | 51 | 9 | 50 | 51 |
| East Africa | 21/23 | 33/35 | 39 | 36 |
| Ecuador | 8/9 | 52 | 13/14 | 28 |
| Finland | 46 | 17 | 47 | 31/32 |
| France | 15/16 | 10/11 | 35/36 | 10/15 |
| Germany F.R. | 42/44 | 15 | 9/10 | 29 |
| Great Britain | 42/44 | 3 | 9/10 | 47/48 |
| Greece | 27/28 | 30 | 18/19 | 1 |
| Guatemala | 2/3 | 53 | 43 | 3 |
| Hong Kong | 15/16 | 37 | 18/19 | 49/50 |
| India | 10/11 | 21 | 20/21 | 45 |
| Indonesia | 8/9 | 47/48 | 30/31 | 41/42 |
| Iran | 29/30 | 24 | 35/36 | 31/32 |
| Ireland (Rep.) | 49 | 12 | 7/8 | 47/48 |
| Israel | 52 | 19 | 29 | 19 |
| Italy | 34 | 7 | 4/5 | 23 |
| Jamaica | 37 | 25 | 7/8 | 52 |
| Japan | 33 | 22/23 | 1 | 7 |
| Malaysia | 1 | 36 | 25/26 | 46 |
| Mexico | 5/6 | 32 | 6 | 18 |
| Netherlands | 40 | 4/5 | 51 | 35 |
| New Zealand | 50 | 6 | 17 | 39/40 |
| Norway | 47/48 | 13 | 52 | 38 |
| Pakistan | 32 | 47/48 | 25/26 | 24/25 |
| Panama | 2/3 | 51 | 34 | 10/15 |
| Peru | 21/23 | 45 | 37/38 | 9 |
| Philippines | 4 | 31 | 11/12 | 44 |
| Portugal | 24/25 | 33/35 | 45 | 2 |
| Salvador | 18/19 | 42 | 40 | 5/6 |
| Singapore | 13 | 39/41 | 28 | 53 |
| South Africa | 35/36 | 16 | 13/14 | 39/40 |
| South Korea | 27/28 | 43 | 41 | 16/17 |
| Spain | 31 | 20 | 37/38 | 10/15 |

**TABLE 14.1**   Ranking of Countries/Cultures on Cultural Dimensions Reported by Hofstede (1991) *(continued)*

| Country | Power Distance | Individualism/ Collectivism | Masculinity/ Femininity | Uncertainty Avoidance |
|---|---|---|---|---|
| | | *Rank Order On:* | | |
| Sweden | 47/48 | 10/11 | 53 | 49/50 |
| Switzerland | 45 | 14 | 4/5 | 33 |
| Taiwan | 29/30 | 44 | 32/33 | 26 |
| Thailand | 21/23 | 39/41 | 44 | 30 |
| Turkey | 18/19 | 28 | 32/33 | 16/17 |
| Uruguay | 26 | 29 | 42 | 4 |
| U.S. | 38 | 1 | 15 | 43 |
| Venezuela | 5/6 | 50 | 3 | 21/22 |
| West Africa | 10/11 | 39/41 | 30/31 | 34 |
| Yugoslavia | 12 | 33/35 | 48/49 | 8 |

Based on G. Hofstede, *Culture and Organizations: Software of the Mind* (London, England: McGraw Hill, 1991).

trated at the top, and all of the important decisions will have to be finalized by the leader. The consequences for international negotiations are that negotiators from large power distance cultures may need to seek approval from their supervisors more frequently, and for more issues, leading to a slower negotiation process.

### Individualism/Collectivism

This dimension describes the extent to which the society is organized around individuals or the group. Individualistic societies encourage their young to be independent and to look after themselves. Collectivistic cultures, on the other hand, integrate individuals into very cohesive groups that take responsibility for the welfare of each individual. Hofstede suggests that the focus on relationships in collectivist societies plays a critical role in negotiations—negotiations with the same party can continue for years and changing a negotiator changes the relationship, which may take a long time to rebuild. Contrast this with more individualistic societies, in which negotiators are considered more interchangeable, and competency, rather than relationship, is a more important consideration when choosing negotiators. The consequences are that negotiators from collectivist cultures will strongly depend on cultivating and sustaining a long-term relationship, whereas negotiators from individualistic cultures may be more likely to "swap" negotiators, using whatever short-term criteria seem appropriate.

### Masculinity/Femininity

Hofstede found that cultures differed in the extent to which they held values that were traditionally perceived as masculine, such as "assertiveness, the acquisition of money and things, and *not* caring for others, the quality of life, or people" (Hofstede, 1980a, p. 46). According to Hofstede (1989), this dimension influences negotiating by increasing the competitiveness when negotiators from masculine cultures meet; negotiators from feminine cultures are more likely to have empathy for the other party and to seek compromise.

### Uncertainty Avoidance

The fourth dimension identified by Hofstede "indicates to what extent a culture programs its members to feel either uncomfortable or comfortable in unstructured situations" (1989, p. 196). Unstructured situations are characterized by rapid change and novelty whereas structured situations are stable, secure, and more absolutist. Negotiators from uncertainty avoidance cultures are not comfortable with ambiguous situations and are more likely to seek stable rules and procedures when they negotiate. Negotiators from cultures more comfortable with unstructured situations are more likely to adapt to quickly changing situations and will be less uncomfortable when the rules of the negotiation are ambiguous or shifting.

Hofstede's dimensions have received a great deal of attention in cross-cultural research and international business. Although the model is not without criticism (see, e.g., Kale and Barnes, 1992; Triandis, 1982), it is fair to say that it has become a dominating force in cross-cultural research in international business. Little research exploring the effects of Hofstede's dimensions on negotiation has been conducted, however, and the extent to which these dimensions influence cross-cultural and intracultural negotiations needs to be further explored (see Foster, 1992). At this point in time, our interpretations of the effects of these dimensions on negotiations should be considered tentative.

### Other Approaches to Cultural Differences

Although culture is considered by many international negotiation experts as the critical factor in negotiations across borders, there are in fact many different uses of the concept in this area. Janosik (1987) has identified four ways that culture has been used in international negotiation. Although there are similarities and differences among the four ways, each approach *does* stress the importance of understanding how culture effects negotiation.

**Culture as Learned Behavior.**   This approach to understanding the effects of culture concentrates on documenting the systematic negotiation behavior of people in different cultures. It is a pragmatic, nuts-and-bolts approach to understanding the effects of culture, and rather than focusing on why members of a given culture behave in certain ways, it concentrates upon creating a catalog of behaviors that the foreign negotiator should expect when entering a host culture (Janosik, 1987). Many of the books and articles in the popular press (e.g., Axtell, 1990, 1991, 1993) use the concept of culture as learned behavior in negotiations across borders, yielding lists of "do's and don'ts" to obey when negotiating with people from various cultures. For instance, Solomon (1987) suggests that people negotiating with the Chinese should recognize that they will begin negotiations with a search for broad principles and building a relationship. This will be followed by a long period of assessment where the boundaries of the relationship will be explored. A decision about whether or not to strike an agreement will eventually be made, and this agreement will form the foundation for further concessions and modifications.

**Culture as Shared Values.**    This approach concentrates on understanding the central values and norms of a culture and then building a model for how these norms and values influence negotiations within that culture. Cross-cultural comparisons are made by finding the important norms and values that distinguish one culture from another and then understanding how these differences will influence negotiation across borders. While the "culture as behavior" approach concentrates exclusively on behavior, the "culture as shared values" approach recognizes that thought precedes behavior and seeks to understand how culture influences those thought processes (Janosik, 1987). For example, a central value in American culture is individualism. Americans are expected to make individual decisions, defend their points of view, and take strong stands on issues that are important to them. Contrast this with a central value of the Chinese culture, collectivism. Chinese negotiators are expected to make group decisions, defend the group above the individual, and take strong stands on issues important to the group. When American and Chinese people negotiate, their differences in the individualism/collectivism cultural value may be expected to influence negotiations in many ways. For instance: (1) the Chinese will be likely to take more time when negotiating because they have to gain the consensus of their group before they strike a deal; (2) the Chinese use of multiple lines of authority will lead to mixed signals about the true needs of the group, and no single individual may understand all of the requirements; and (3) because power is shared by many different people and offices it may be difficult for foreigners to identify their appropriate counterpart in the Chinese bureaucracy (Pye, 1992).

**Culture as Dialectic.**    The third approach to using culture to understand negotiation across borders identified by Janosik (1987) recognizes that all cultures contain tensions, called *dialectics,* among their different values. These tensions are nicely illustrated in maxims from the Judeo-Christian (European) tradition. Consider the following examples: "Too many cooks spoil the broth" and "Two heads are better than one." These proverbs offer conflicting guidance for those considering whether to work on a task alone or in a group, reflecting a dialectic, or tension, within the Judeo-Christian tradition about the values of independence and teamwork. Neither total independence nor complete teamwork works all of the time; each has advantages and disadvantages that vary as a function of the circumstances (for instance, the type of decision to be made or task to be addressed). According to Janosik (1987), the "culture as dialectic" approach has advantages over the "culture as shared values" approach because it can explain variations within cultures (i.e., not every person in a culture shares the same values to the same extent). Although this may yield more accurate academic understanding of the effects of culture on international negotiations, it does not yet offer very clear guidelines for practitioners faced with negotiations across borders.

**Culture in Context.**    Proponents of the fourth approach to using culture to understand negotiations across borders recognize that no human behavior is determined by a single cause. Rather, all behavior may be understood at many different levels simultaneously, and a social behavior as complex as negotiation is determined by many different factors, one of which is culture. Other factors that may be important determinants of negotiation behavior include personality, social context, and environmental factors. In other words, proponents of the "culture in context" approach recognize that negotiation behavior is multiply determined, and using culture as the sole explanation of behavior is oversimplifying a complex social process. Many academic models of negotiation recognize the multiple determinants of negotiation behavior and are excellent guides for research and understanding negotiation. As the models become more complex, however, they may become less useful for practitioners of negotiation across borders because they are just too complex to put into practice (Janosik, 1987).

## How Do Cultural Differences Influence Negotiations?

Given that these cultural differences exist, can be measured, and operate on different levels, the issue becomes how they influence negotiations. Adopting work by Weiss and Stripp (1985), Foster (1992) suggests that culture can influence negotiations across borders in at least eight different ways.

**Definition of Negotiation.**    The fundamental definition of what negotiation is, or of what occurs when we negotiate, can differ greatly across cultures. For instance, "Americans tend to view negotiating as a competitive process of offers and counteroffers, while the Japanese tend to view the negotiation as an opportunity for information-sharing" (Foster, 1992, p. 272).

**Selection of Negotiators.**    The criteria used to select who will participate in the negotiations varies across cultures. These criteria can include knowledge of the subject manner being negotiated, seniority, family connections, gender, age, experience, and status. Different cultures weigh these criteria differently, leading to varying expectations about what is appropriate in different types of negotiations.

**Protocol.**    Cultures differ in the degree to which protocol, or the formality of the relations between the two negotiating parties, is important. American culture is among the least formal cultures in the world. The use of first names, ignoring titles, and a generally familiar communication style are quite common. Contrast this with the situation in other cultures. Many European countries (e.g.,

France, Germany, England) are very formal, and not using the proper title when addressing someone (e.g., Mr., Dr., Professor, Lord) is considered very insulting (see Braganti and Devine, 1992). Formal calling cards or business cards are always used in many countries in the Pacific Rim (e.g., China, Japan), and they are essential for introductions there. Negotiators who forget to bring business cards or who write messages on them are frequently breaching protocol and insulting their counterpart (Foster, 1992). Even the way that business cards are presented, hands are shaken, or people dress are subject to interpretation by negotiators and can be the foundation of attributions about a person's background and personality.

**Communication.**    Cultures influence the way that people communicate, both verbally and nonverbally. There are also differences in body language across cultures; the same behavior may be highly insulting in one culture and completely innocuous in another (Axtell, 1991). To avoid insulting the other party in negotiations across borders, the international negotiator needs to observe cultural rules of communication carefully. For example, the truly international negotiator needs to heed the following advice:

> Never touch a Malay on the top of the head, for that is where the soul resides. Never show the sole of your shoe to an Arab, for it is dirty and represents the bottom of the body, and never use your left hand in Muslim culture, for it is reserved for physical hygiene. Touch the side of your nose in Italy and it is a sign of distrust. Always look directly and intently into your French associate's eye when making an important point. Direct eye contact in Southeast Asia, however, should be avoided until the relationship is firmly established. If your Japanese associate has just sucked air in deeply through his teeth, that's a sign you've got real problems. Your Mexican associate will want to embrace you at the end of a long and successful negotiation; so will your Central and Eastern European associates, who may give you a bear hug *and* kiss you three times on alternating cheeks. Americans often stand farther apart than their Latin and Arab associates but closer than their Asian associates. In the United States people shake hands forcefully and enduringly; in Europe a handshake is usually quick and to the point; in Asia, it is often rather limp. Laughter and giggling in the West Indies indicates humor; in Asia, it more often indicates embarrassment and humility. Additionally, the public expression of deep emotion is considered ill-mannered in most countries of the Pacific Rim; there is an extreme separation between one's personal and public selves. The withholding of emotion in Latin America, however, is often cause for mistrust. (D. A. Foster, *Bargaining Across Borders: How to Negotiate Business Successfully Anywhere in the World* (New York: McGraw Hill, 1992), p. 281. Reproduced with the permission of McGraw Hill).

Clearly, there is a lot of information about how to communicate that an international negotiator must remember in order not to insult, anger, or embarrass the other party during negotiations. Many culture-specific books and articles have been written that provide considerable advice to international negotiators about how to communicate in various cultures, and this is an essential aspect of planning for negotiations that cross borders (Binnendijk, 1987; Graham and Sano, 1989; Pye, 1992; Tung, 1991).

**Time.**   Cultures have a large effect on defining what time means and how it affects negotiations. In the United States, people tend to respect time. This is shown by appearing for meetings on time, being sensitive to not wasting the time of other people, and a general belief that "faster" is better than "slower" because it symbolizes high productivity. Other cultures have quite different views about time. In more traditional societies, especially in hot climates, the pace is slower than in the United States. This tends to reduce the focus on time, at least in the short term. Americans are perceived by other cultures as enslaved by their clocks, because time is watched carefully and guarded as a valuable resource. In some cultures, such as China and Latin America, time per se is not important. The focus of negotiations is on the task, regardless of the amount of time that it takes. The opportunity for misunderstandings because of different perceptions of time is great during cross-cultural negotiations. Americans may be perceived as always being in a hurry and as flitting from one task to another. Chinese or Latin American negotiators, on the other hand, may appear to the American to be doing nothing and wasting the American's time.

**Risk Propensity.**   Cultures vary in the extent to which they are willing to take risks. Some cultures produce quite bureaucratic, conservative decision makers who want a great deal of information before making decisions. Other cultures produce negotiators who are more entrepreneurial and who are willing to act and take risks when they have incomplete information (e.g., "nothing ventured, nothing gained"). According to Foster (1992), Americans fall on the risk-taking end of the continuum, some Asians may be even more risk oriented, and some European cultures are quite conservative (such as Greece). The orientation of a culture toward risk will have a large effect on what is negotiated and the content of the negotiated outcome. Risk-oriented cultures will be more willing to move early on a deal and will generally take more chances. Risk-avoiding cultures will seek further information and will be more likely to take a wait-and-see stance.

**Groups versus Individuals.**   Cultures differ according to whether they emphasize the individual or the group. The United States is very much an individual-oriented culture, where being independent and assertive is valued and praised. Group-oriented cultures, on the other hand, favor the superiority of the group and the individual comes second to the group's needs. Group-oriented cultures value fitting in and reward loyal team players; those who dare to be different are socially ostracized, a large price to pay in a group-oriented society. This cultural difference can have a variety of effects on negotiation. Americans are more likely to have one individual who is responsible for the final decision, whereas group-oriented cultures like the Chinese are more likely to have a group responsible for the decision. Decision making in the group-oriented cultures involves consensus making and may take considerably more time than American negotiators are used to. In addition, because so many people can be involved in the negotiations in group-oriented cultures, and because their participation may be sequential rather than simultaneous, American negotiators may be faced with a series of discussions over the same issues and materials with many different people. In a negotiation in China, one of the authors of this book met with more than six different people on successive days, going over the same ground with different negotiators and interpreters, until the negotiation was concluded.

**Nature of Agreements.**   Culture also has an important effect both on concluding agreements and on what form the negotiated agreement takes. In the United States, agreements are typically based on logic (e.g., the low-cost producer gets the deal), are often formalized, and are enforced through the legal system if such standards are not honored. In other cultures, however, obtaining the deal may be based on who you are (e.g., your family or political connections) rather than what you can do. In addition, agreements do not mean the same thing in all cultures. Foster (1992) notes that the Chinese frequently use memorandums of agreement to formalize a relationship and to signal the *start* of negotiations (mutual favors and compromise). Frequently, however, Americans will interpret the *same* memorandum of agreement as the *completion* of the negotiations that is enforceable in a court of law. Again, cultural differences in how to close an agreement and what exactly that agreement means can lead to confusion and misunderstandings when we negotiate across borders.

In summary, a great deal has been written about the importance of culture in cross-border negotiations. Hofstede (1989) suggests that there are four important dimensions that can be used to describe cultural differences: power distance, individualism/collectivism, masculinity/femininity, and uncertainty avoidance. Academics and practitioners may use the term *culture* to mean different things, but they agree that it is a critical aspect of international negotiation that can have a broad influence on many aspects of the process and outcome of negotiations across borders.

## SOME SPECIFIC COUNTRY NEGOTIATION STYLES

Many books describing the negotiation styles of selected countries have been written. It is not possible for us to present in a single chapter on international negotiation the detail that these books contain. To give you a sample of this literature, we have included brief descriptions of the negotiation styles of three countries in the Pacific Rim. Each of the countries has an increasingly important relationship with the United States, and each is in the same geographic region. There are similarities and differences in the styles across the three countries, which make the comparison useful for our purposes. The international negotiator who is planning negotiations with counterparts from one of these countries (or any other country, for that matter) is well advised to consult more extensive materials on national negotiation styles than is presented here (see Graham and Sano, 1989; Pye, 1992; Thayer and Weiss, 1987; Tung, 1991; Acuff, 1993; Griffin and Daggatt, 1990; Harris and Moran, 1987; Hendon and Hendon, 1990).

## Negotiating with the Japanese

Japan and the United States have a special relationship, both historically and currently (Thayer and Weiss, 1987). Political, economic, and business relationships between the two countries are frequently in the news, and understanding how Japan has become an economic superpower is a frequent topic of conversation for Americans. Not surprisingly, how to negotiate with the Japanese has also been an important topic that has received attention from both academics and practitioners.

Graham and Sano (1989) have written one of the most comprehensive treatments of how to negotiate with the Japanese. They note that two critical values in Japan are the avoidance of conflict and the promotion of harmony. These cultural values have a pronounced effect on how Japanese negotiate. One way that they promote these values is through the presence of a strong social hierarchy, which has an important influence on business relationships. Larger organizations have an enormous amount of power and status, and the status relationship between the negotiating parties may be more important in determining the outcome of negotiations than the actions of the parties during negotiations (Graham and Sano, 1989). With the greater power comes more responsibility, however, and larger buyers must make sure that they consider the needs of smaller sellers when they negotiate.

Another aspect of negotiation in Japan that flows from their cultural values is a long-term time perspective on negotiation. Because relationships are expected to last a lifetime, Japanese are very cautious about entering a relationship and take care to evaluate the long-term implications of doing business together. The focus on relationships influences many aspects of negotiation. At the early stages, the two negotiating parties will spend a large proportion of their time in what may appear to an American as non-negotiation activities, including lavish entertainment, sporting and cultural events, and ceremonial gift-giving. The purpose of these activities is to get to know the other party and to build strong interconnections. The consequences of this relationship-building is that during later stages of negotiation the parties feel free to make large demands upon each other because they have a special relationship. As far as the process of negotiations is concerned, Japanese negotiators are very polite while negotiating and are very reluctant to say no (because it may hurt harmony). In addition, what is *not* said during negotiations is as important as what is spoken. Rather than saying no, Japanese negotiators may say nothing or may tell the other party that "it will be difficult to agree to the proposal." Frequently, expressions of agreement will simply indicate that the Japanese heard the other party correctly, but not that they agree with the substance of what was said (see Box 14.2).

Graham and Sano make many recommendations about how Americans can improve their negotiations with the Japanese. They suggest that choosing the negotiation team is critical—members of the team should be flexible and committed to the process. During preparations, the influence of time on the negotiation process needs to be considered explicitly. According to Graham and Sano, the negotiation itself may be viewed as having four stages: nontask discussions

**BOX 14.2**
**A Simple "Hai" Won't Do**

When a TV announcer here reported Bill Clinton's comment to Boris Yeltsin that when the Japanese say yes they often mean no, he gave the news with an expression of mild disbelief.

Having spent my life between East and West, I can sympathize with those who find the Japanese yes unfathomable. However, the fact that it sometimes fails to correspond precisely with the Occidental yes does not necessarily signal intended deception. This was probably why the announcer looked bewildered, and it marks a cultural gap that can have serious repercussions.

I once knew an American who worked in Tokyo. He was a very nice man, but he suffered a nervous breakdown and went back to the United States tearing his hair and exclaiming, "All Japanese businessmen are liars." I hope this is not true. If it were, all Japanese businessmen would be driving each other mad, which does not seem to be the case. Nevertheless, since tragedies often arise from misunderstandings, an attempt at some explanation might not be amiss.

A Japanese yes in its primary context simply means the other person has heard you and is contemplating a reply. This is because it would be rude to keep someone waiting for an answer without supplying him with an immediate response.

For example: A feudal warlord marries his sister to another warlord. (I am back to TV.) Then he decides to destroy his newly acquired brother-in-law and besieges the castle. Being human, though, the attacking warlord worries about his sister and sends a spy to look around. The spy returns and the lord inquires eagerly, "Well, is she safe?" The spy bows and answers, "*Hai*," which means yes. We sigh with relief, thinking, "Ah, the fair lady is still alive!" But then the spy continues, "To my regret she has fallen on her sword together with her husband."

Hai is also an expression of our willingness to comply with your intent even if your request is worded in the negative. This can cause complications. When I was at school, our English teacher, a British nun, would say, "Now children, you won't forget to do your homework, will you?" And we would all dutifully chorus, "Yes, mother," much to her consternation.

A variation of hai may mean, "I understand your wish and would like to make you happy but unfortunately . . ." Japanese being a language of implication, the latter part of this estimable thought is often left unsaid.

Is there, then, a Japanese yes that corresponds to the Western one? I think so, particularly when it is accompanied by phrases such as "*sodesu*" (it is so) and "*soshimasu*" (I will do so).

A word of caution against the statement, "I will think about it." Though in Tokyo this can mean a willingness to give one's proposal serious thought, in Osaka, another business center, it means a definite no. This attitude probably stems from the belief that a straightforward no would sound too brusque.

When talking to a Japanese person, it is perhaps best to remember that although he may be speaking English, he is reasoning in Japanese. And if he says, "I will think about it," you should inquire as to which district of Japan he hails from before going on with your negotiations.

where the relationship is explored, task-related information exchange, persuasion, and concessions and agreement. Finally, the negotiations will typically conclude with a signing ceremony that has important symbolic value.

### Negotiating with the Chinese

Since the normalization of relations with China began over 20 years ago, American-Sino business relationships have been growing at a rapid pace. Negotiations have often been a difficult process for both sides, for cultural and other reasons (Pye, 1992). Pye suggests that cultural differences between China and the United States present an enormous challenge for negotiations across this border. According to Pye, there are numerous cultural differences between the two countries, but two are particularly important. First, while Americans are a legalistic culture, the Chinese stress ethics and moral principles. Thus, Americans turn to the court system to resolve serious differences of opinion and to enforce contracts. The Chinese, on the other hand, would be more likely to apply ethical and moral principles in group discussion to resolve differences of opinion with harmony. The second critical cultural difference between the two cultures is the pervasive importance of politics in all aspects of Chinese life. No decision can be made without awareness of the political consequences, and the Chinese take a great deal of care to not make a mistake (not making a decision is safer than making a mistake).

Solomon (1987) notes that Chinese negotiators are very skilled at using pressure tactics to gain advantage during negotiations. These tactics include good guy-bad guy, extreme demands, creating competition among adversaries, pressuring third parties to influence the adversary, and sacrificing other negotiations to demonstrate resolve. Patience is a highly valued cultural virtue in China, and Chinese negotiators can delay years until they feel the time is right to conclude a deal.

Pye suggests many principles that American negotiators should follow when negotiating with the Chinese. A critical principle is *patience.* The Chinese bureaucracy is large and the political implications of all decisions must be understood before they are made. This can take a considerable amount of time, and the American negotiator needs patience to accept this. Pye labeled another principle "restrained steadfastness." When working towards building a relationship, the Chinese seek reliability, dignity, and reserve. They are not impressed by effusiveness, which can be misinterpreted as impatience. A third principle is to take agreements about general principles seriously. These agreements are critical to the Chinese who will use them later to enforce other aspects of the agreement. In addition, Pye points out that Americans need to avoid making exaggerated claims to the Chinese because they will be asked to deliver them at a later date (and nondelivery will result in attributions about the negotiator's degree of ethics and morality).

### Negotiating with Koreans

Korea has had one of the fastest growing economies in the last 20 years and is an increasingly important negotiating partner with the United States. While Koreans have a solid understanding of the American negotiating style, Americans are only just beginning to examine the Korean approach to business negotiation (Tung, 1991). Rosalie Tung has examined 18 U.S.-Korea joint business ventures in detail and has identified some important characteristics about the Korean negotiating style. Compared to other countries in the Pacific Rim, the Koreans can make decisions rapidly. Many Korean organizations are family run, and this tends to make determining the line of authority and source of decision-making power a clear task. On the other hand, Koreans will frequently send junior people (with limited authority) to the negotiation table as a delaying tactic to gain further concessions (Tung, 1991).

Although the relationship is important to Korean negotiators, they are not afraid to be direct and confrontational during negotiations. Perhaps more disturbing to the American negotiator is the fact that the Korean counterpart can occasionally appear somewhat irrational and inconsistent (Tung, 1991). Tung attributes this behavior to *kibun,* the personal feelings or inner voice the Korean negotiator listens to during negotiation. Finally, Tung argues that Korean negotiators are not blindly driven by profit. Rather, they seem to focus on long-term objectives like growth and increasing market share. Tung's advice for negotiating with Koreans is to be patient, understand and appreciate Korean culture and customs, and recognize that *who* you are will have an influence on the way that relationships are formed.

We have only briefly described some of the important aspects of the Japanese, Chinese, and Korean negotiation styles and the similarities and differences between them and the American negotiation style. The international negotiator needs to prepare carefully for negotiations that cross borders—the range of options open to the international negotiator for managing negotiations across borders is discussed in the next section of this chapter.

## CULTURALLY RESPONSIVE NEGOTIATION STRATEGIES

Although a great deal has been written about international negotiation and the extra challenges that occur when negotiating across borders, cultures, or nationalities, far less attention has been paid to what the individual negotiator should specifically *do* when faced with negotiating with someone from another culture. The advice by many theorists in this area, either explicitly or implicitly, has been, "when in Rome, act as the Romans do" (see Francis, 1991, and Weiss, in press, for reviews of the possible oversimplicity of this advice). In other words, negotiators are advised to be aware of the effects of cultural differences on negotiation and to take them into account when they negotiate. Much of the material discussed in this chapter reflects this tendency. Many theorists appear to assume implicitly that the best way to manage cross-border negotiations is to be sensitive to the cultural norms of the person with whom you are negotiating and to modify your strategy to be consistent with behaviors that occur in that culture (contrast this with the less culturally sensitive views that "business is business everywhere in the world" and the other party can adapt to your style of negotiating, that style is unimportant, or, more arrogantly, that my style should dictate what you do).

Although it is important to avoid cultural gaffes when negotiating, it is *not* clear that the best approach is to modify your strategy to match the other person's approach.

Several factors indicate that negotiators should *not* make large modifications to their approach when they negotiate across borders.

1. Negotiators may not be able to modify their approach *effectively*. It takes years to understand another culture deeply, and you may not have the time necessary to gain this understanding before beginning negotiations. Although a little understanding of another culture is clearly better than total ignorance, it may not be enough to make effective adjustments to your negotiation strategy. Attempting to match the strategies and tactics used by negotiators in another culture is a daunting task that requires fluency in their language as a precondition.

2. Even if negotiators can modify their approach effectively, it does not mean that this will translate automatically into a better negotiation outcome for their side. It is quite possible that the other side will modify their approach too. The results in this situation can be disaster, with each side trying to act like the other "should" be acting, and both sides not really understanding what the other party is doing. Consider the following example contrasting typical American and Japanese negotiation styles. Americans are more likely to start negotiations with an extreme offer in order to leave room for concessions. Japanese are more likely to start negotiations with gathering information in order to understand who they are dealing with and what the relationship will be. Assume that both parties understand their own and the other party's cultural tendencies (this is a large assumption that frequently is not met). Now assume that each party, acting out of respect for the other, decides to "act like the Romans do" and to adopt the approach of the other party. The possibilities for confusion are endless. When the Americans gather information about the Japanese are they truly interested or are they playing a role? It will be clear that they are not acting like Americans, but the strategy that they are using may not be readily identified. How will the Americans interpret the Japanese behavior? The Americans have prepared well for their negotiations and understand that the Japanese do not present extreme positions early in negotiations. When the Japanese *do* present an extreme position early in negotiations (in order to adapt to the American negotiation style), how should the Americans interpret this behavior? The Americans likely will think "that must be what they really want because they don't open with extreme offers." Adopting the other party's approach does not guarantee success, and in fact may lead to more confusion than acting like yourself (where at least your behavior is understood within your own cultural context).

3. Research suggests that negotiators may naturally negotiate differently when they are with people from their own culture than when they are with people from other cultures (Adler and Graham, 1989). The implications of

this research are that a deep understanding of how people in other cultures negotiate, such as two Japanese people negotiating with each other, may not help an American negotiating with a Japanese.

4. Research by Francis (1991) suggests that moderate adaptation may be more effective than "acting as the Romans do." In a simulation study of Americans' responses to negotiators from other countries, Francis found that negotiators from a familiar culture (Japan) who made moderate adaptations to American ways were perceived more positively than negotiators who made no changes or those that made large adaptations. Although these findings did not replicate for negotiators from a less familiar culture (Korea), more research needs to be conducted to understand why. At the very least, the results of this study suggest that large adaptations by international negotiators will not always be effective.

Recent theoretical work by Weiss (in press) has advanced our understanding of the options that people have when negotiating with someone from another culture. Weiss observes that a negotiator may be able to choose among up to eight different culturally responsive strategies. These strategies may be used individually or sequentially, and the strategies can be switched as the negotiations progress. According to Weiss, when choosing a strategy the negotiators should be aware of their own and the other party's culture in general, understand the specific factors in the current relationship, and predict or try to influence the other party's approach. Weiss's culturally responsive strategies may be arranged into three groups, based on the familiarity that a negotiator has with the other party's culture. Within each group there are some strategies that the negotiator may use individually (unilateral strategies) and others that involve the participation of the other party (joint strategies).

### Low Familiarity

**Employ Agents or Advisors (unilateral strategy).**    One approach for negotiators who have very low familiarity with the other party's culture is to hire an agent or advisor who is familiar with the cultures of both parties. This relationship may range from having the other party conduct the negotiations under your supervision (agent) to receiving regular or occasional advice during the negotiations (advisor). Although using an agent or advisor may create other problems (such as tensions between that person and yourself) they may be quite useful for negotiators who have little awareness of the other's culture and little time to become aware.

**Bring in a Mediator (joint strategy).**    Many types of mediators may be used in cross-cultural negotiations, ranging from someone who conducts introductions and then withdraws, to someone who is present throughout the negotiation and takes responsibility for orchestrating the negotiation process (compare Kolb,

1983a). Interpreters will often play this role, providing both parties with more information than the mere translation of words during negotiations. Mediators may encourage one side or the other to adopt one of the culture's approaches or a third cultural approach (the mediator's home culture). (Refer back to Chapter 12 for perspectives on third party actions.)

**Induce the Other Party to Use Your Approach (joint strategy).** The third option available to the negotiator with low familiarity with the other party's culture is to persuade the other party to use your approach. There are many ways to do this, ranging from a polite request to asserting rudely that your way is best. It can also be done with more subtlety by continuing to respond in your own language to their requests because you "cannot express yourself well enough in their language." Although this strategy has many advantages for the negotiator with low familiarity, there are also some disadvantages. For instance, the other party may become irritated or insulted at having to make the extra effort to deal with you on your own cultural terms. In addition, the other party may also have a strategic advantage because she may now attempt more extreme tactics, and if they don't work, excuse them on the basis of "cultural ignorance" (after all, you can't expect them to understand everything about how you conduct business).

## Moderate Familiarity

**Adapt to the Other Party's Approach (unilateral strategy).** This strategy involves making conscious changes to your approach so that it is more appealing to the other party. Rather than trying to act like the other party, negotiators using this strategy maintain a firm grasp on their own approach but make modifications to help relations with the other person. These modifications may include acting in a less extreme manner, eliminating some behaviors, and including some of the other party's behaviors. The challenge in using this strategy is to know which behaviors to modify, eliminate, or adopt. In addition, it is not clear that the other party will interpret your modifications in the way that you have intended.

**Coordinate Adjustment (joint strategy).** This strategy involves both parties making mutual adjustments to find a common process for negotiation. Although this can be done implicitly, it is more likely to occur explicitly ("How would you like to proceed?"), and it can be thought of as a special instance of negotiating the *process* of negotiation (refer back to Chapter 6). This strategy requires a moderate amount of knowledge about the other party's culture and at least some facility with their language (comprehension of their language, if not the ability to speak). Coordinating adjustment occurs on a daily basis in Montreal, the most bilingual city in North America (85 percent of Montrealers understand both English and French). It is standard practice for business people in Montreal to negotiate the process of negotiation before the substantive discussion begins. The outcomes of this discussion are variations on the theme of whether the negotiations will occur in English or French, with a typical outcome being that either party may speak either language. Negotiations often occur in both languages, and frequently the person with the superior second-language skills will switch languages to facilitate the discussion. Another outcome that occasionally occurs has both parties speaking in their second language (i.e., the French speaker will negotiate in English while the English speaker will negotiate in French) to demonstrate respect for the other party. Another type of coordinating adjustment occurs when the two negotiating parties adopt aspects of a third culture to facilitate their negotiations. For instance, during a recent trip to Latin America, one of the authors of this book conducted discussions in French with a Latin American colleague who spoke Spanish and French, but not English.

### High Familiarity

**Embrace the Other Party's Approach (unilateral strategy).** This strategy involves adopting completely the approach of the other party. To be used successfully, the negotiator needs to be completely bilingual and bicultural. In essence, the negotiator using this strategy doesn't "act like a Roman," he or she *is* "a Roman." This is a costly strategy to use (in preparation time and expense) and places the negotiator using it under considerable stress (it is difficult to switch back and forth rapidly between cultures). On the other hand, there is much to gain by using this strategy because the other party can be approached and understood completely on their own terms.

**Improvise an Approach (joint strategy).** This strategy involves crafting an approach that is specifically tailored to the negotiation situation, other party, and circumstances. Both parties to the negotiation need to have high familiarity with the other party's culture and a strong understanding of the individual characteristics of the other party to use this approach. The negotiation that emerges with this approach can be crafted with aspects from both cultures adopted when they will be useful. This approach is the most flexible of the eight strategies, which is both its strength and weakness. Flexibility is a strength because it allows the approach to be crafted to the circumstances at hand, but it is a weakness because there are few general prescriptive statements that can be made about how to use this strategy.

**Effect Symphony (joint strategy).** This strategy works to "transcend exclusive use of either home culture" (Weiss, 1993, p. 19) by the negotiation parties and instead has them create a new approach that may include aspects of either home culture or adopt practices from a third culture. Professional diplomats use such an approach when the customs, norms, and language that they use transcend national borders and form their own culture (diplomacy). Use of this strategy is complex and involves a great deal of time and effort. It works best when the parties are very familiar with each other, familiar with both home cultures, and have a common structure (like that of professional diplomats) for the negotiation. Risks of using this strategy include costs due to confusion, time lost, and the overall effort required to make it work.

## SUMMARY

This chapter examined various aspects of a growing field of negotiations that explores the complexities of negotiating across borders. We began the chapter with a discussion of a research program by John Graham and his colleagues (Graham, 1993) that compared American negotiators with negotiators from 15 other countries. Graham and his colleagues found that regardless of where negotiators were from, they negotiated the same level of outcomes on a standard negotiation task. The process of negotiation differed across countries, however, suggesting that there is more than one way to attain the same negotiation outcome. Finally, this research program also suggested that negotiators seem to use different strategies when negotiating with people domestically and internationally.

We then examined some of the factors that make cross-border negotiations different. Salacuse (1988) suggested six factors that increase the challenge of conducting negotiations across borders: (1) political and legal pluralism, (2) international economic factors, (3) foreign governments and bureaucracies, (4) instability, (5) ideology, and (6) culture. Each of these factors acts to make cross-border negotiations more difficult, and effective international negotiators need to understand how to manage these factors.

The chapter then discussed the RBC Model of International Negotiations (Weiss, 1993). This model provides a snapshot of the factors that influence negotiations at a given point in time and suggests that relationships, behaviors, and conditions are good organizing principles for comparing negotiations across borders. This model has great potential for both academics and practitioners. It can help organize the results of a fragmentary and somewhat opportunistic research area, while at the same time providing a strong guideline for preparing for negotiations.

We then turned to a discussion of culture, the factor that has been most frequently used to explain differences in negotiations across borders. We use the term *culture* to refer to the shared values and beliefs that are held by members of a group. The most comprehensive study of cultural dimensions in international business was conducted by Hofstede (1980a, 1980b, 1989, 1991). Hofstede concludes that four dimensions can summarize cultural differences: (1) power distance, (2) individualism/collectivism, (3) masculinity/femininity, and (4) uncertainty avoidance. Janosik (1987) maintains that culture is used in at least four different ways by researchers and practitioners in negotiations across borders: (1) culture as learned behavior, (2) culture as shared values, (3) culture as dialectics, and (4) culture in context. Each of these uses of the term *culture* has strengths and weaknesses, and occasionally there are communication breakdowns between researchers and practitioners when they use the same word in such different ways.

We then examined in more detail the negotiation styles of three different countries from the Pacific Rim: Japan, China, and Korea. Each of these countries has an increasingly important trade relationship with the United States, so it is important for the effective international negotiator to be aware of their negotiation styles. Although there are similarities among the negotiation styles from the three countries, there are also important differences.

The chapter concludes with a discussion of how to manage cultural differences when negotiating across borders. Weiss presents eight different culturally responsive strategies that negotiators can use with a negotiator from a different culture. Some of these strategies may be used individually, whereas others are used jointly with the other negotiator. Weiss indicates that one critical aspect of choosing the correct strategy for a given negotiation is the degree of familiarity that a negotiator has with the other culture. However, even those with high familiarity with another culture are faced with a daunting task if they want to modify their strategy completely when they deal with the other culture.

# Bibliography

Aaronson, K. (1989). *Selling on the fast track.* New York, NY: Putnam.

Abelson, R. P. (1981). Psychological status of the script concept. *American Psychologist, 36,* 715–729.

Acuff, F. L. (1993). *How to negotiate anything with anyone anywhere around the world.* New York, NY: AMACOM.

Adler, N. J., Brahm, R., & Graham, J. L. (1992). Strategy implementation: A comparison of face-to-face negotiations in the People's Republic of China and the United States. *Strategic Management Journal, 13,* 449–466.

Adler, N. J. & Graham, J. L. (1987). Business negotiations: Canadians are not just like Americans. *Canadian Journal of Administrative Sciences, 4,* 211–238.

Adler, N. J. & Graham, J. L. (1989). Cross-cultural interaction: The international comparison fallacy? *Journal of International Business Studies, 20,* 515–537.

Adler, N. J., Graham, J. L., & Schwarz, T. (1987). Business negotiations in Canada, Mexico, and the United States. *Journal of Business Research, 15,* 411–429.

Akers, J. (1989, Winter). Ethics and competitiveness: Putting first things first. *Sloan Management Review, 30,* 69–71.

Alderfer, C. P. (1977). Group and intergroup relations. In J. R. Hackman & J. L. Suttle, (Eds.), *Improving life at work: Behavioral science approaches to organizational change* (pp. 227–296). Santa Monica, CA: Goodyear.

Ancona, D. & Caldwell, D. F. (1988). Beyond task and maintenance: External roles in groups. *Group and Organizational Studies, 13,* 468–491.

Anderson, J. C. & Kochan, T. (1977). Impasse procedures in the Canadian Federal Service. *Industrial and Labor Relations Review, 30,* 283–301.

Ansoff, H. I. (1984). *Implanting strategic management.* Englewood Cliffs, NJ: Prentice Hall.

Anton, R. J. (1990). Drawing the line: An exploratory test of ethical behavior in negotiations. *The International Journal of Conflict Management, 1,* 265–280.

Asherman, I. G. & Asherman, S. V. (1990). *The negotiation sourcebook.* Amherst, MA: Human Resource Development Press.

Athos, A. G. & Gabarro, J. J. (1978). *Interpersonal behavior: Communication and understanding in relationships.* Englewood Cliffs, NJ: Prentice Hall.

Atkinson, G. (1980). *An introduction to negotiation.* London, UK; Industrial Relations Training Centre.

Austin, R. A. (1989). *Power listening: An empirical investigation of the effects of listening instruction on the listening skills of white collar business executives.* Unpublished master's thesis, University of Maryland, College Park, MD.

Axelrod, R. (1976). *The structure of decision: The cognitive maps of political elites.* Princeton, NJ: Princeton University Press.

Axelrod, R. (1984). *The evolution of cooperation.* New York, NY: Basic Books.

Axtell, R. E. (1990). *Do's and taboos of hosting international visitors.* New York, NY: John Wiley and Sons.

Axtell, R. E. (1991). *Gestures: The do's and taboos of body language around the world.* New York, NY: John Wiley and Sons.

Axtell, R. E. (1993). *Do's and taboos around the world.* (3rd ed.). New York, NY: John Wiley and Sons.

Ayres, I. (1991). Fair driving: Gender and race discrimination in retail car negotiations. *Harvard Law Review, 104,* 817–872.

Bales, R. F. (1950). *Interaction process analysis: A method for the study of small groups.* Cambridge, MA: Addison-Wesley.

Bar-Hillel, M. (1980). The base-rate fallacy in probability judgments. *Acta Psychologica, 44,* 211–213.

Baranowski, T. A. & Summers, D. A. (1972). Perceptions of response alternatives in a prisoner's dilemma game. *Journal of Personality and Social Psychology, 21,* 35–40.

Barnard, C. (1938). *The functions of the executive.* Cambridge, MA: Harvard University Press.

Bateson, B. (1972). *Steps to an ecology of mind.* New York, NY: Ballantine Books.

Bazerman, M. & Lewicki, R. (1985). Contemporary research directions in the study of negotiation in organizations: A selective overview. *Journal of Occupational Behavior, 6,* 1–17.

Bazerman, M. H., Lewicki, R. J., & Sheppard, B. H. (1991). *Research on negotiation in organizations* (Vol. 3). Greenwich, CT: JAI Press.

Bazerman, M. H., Magliozzi, T., & Neale, M. A. (1985). Integrative bargaining in a competitive market. *Organizational Behavior and Human Decision Processes, 35,* 294–313.

Bazerman, M. H., Mannix, E. A., and Thompson, L. L. (1988). Groups as mixed motive negotiations. In E. J. Lawler and B. Markovsky (Eds), *Advances in Group Processes* (Vol. 5, 195–216). Greenwich, CT: JAI Press.

Bazerman, M. H. & Neale, M. A. (1992). *Negotiating rationally.* New York, NY: Free Press.

Beckhard, R. (1978, July–September). The dependency dilemma. *Consultants' Communique, 6,* 1–3.

Beckman, N. (1977). *Negotiations.* Lexington, MA: Lexington Books.

Beisecker, T., Walker, G., & Bart, J. (1989). Knowledge versus ignorance in bargaining strategies: The impact of knowledge about other's information level. *The Social Science Journal, 26,* 161–172.

Bem, D. (1972). Self-perception theory. In L. Berkowitz (Ed.), *Advances in Experimental Social Psychology* (Vol. 6, pp. 1–62). New York, NY: Academic Press.

Ben-Yoav, O. & Pruitt, D. G. (1984a). Accountability to constituents: A two-edged sword. *Organizational Behavior and Human Performance, 34,* 283–295.

Ben-Yoav, O. & Pruitt, D. G. (1984b). Resistance to yielding and the expectation of cooperative future interaction in negotiation. *Journal of Experimental Social Psychology, 34,* 323–335.

Benjamin, A. J. & Levi, A. M. (1979). Process minefields in intergroup conflict resolution: The Sdot Yam workshop. *Journal of Applied Behavioral Science, 15,* 507–519.

Benton, A. A. (1972). Accountability and negotiations between representatives. *Proceedings, 80th Annual Convention, American Psychological Association,* Hawaii, 227–228.

Benton, A. A. & Druckman, D. (1974). Constituent's bargaining orientation and intergroup negotiations. *Journal of Applied Social Psychology, 4,* 141–150.

Bercovitch, J. (1984). *Social conflicts and third parties: Strategies of conflict resolution.* Boulder, CO: Westview Press.

Bercovitch, J. (1989). Mediation in international disputes. In K. Kressel & D. Pruitt (Eds.,), *Mediation research* (pp. 284–299). San Francisco, CA: Jossey-Bass.

Berlo, D. K., Lemert, J., & Mertz, R. (1966). *Dimensions for evaluating the acceptability of message sources.* East Lansing, MI: Michigan State University.

Bernstein, J. & Rosen, S. (1989). *Dinosaur brains: Dealing with all those impossible people at work.* New York, NY: John Wiley and Sons.

Bettinghaus, E. P. (1966). *Message preparation: The nature of proof.* Indianapolis: Bobbs-Merrill.

Bettinghaus, E.P. (1980). *Persuasive communication* (2nd ed). New York: Holt, Rinehart & Winston.

Bies, R. & Moag, J. (1986). Interactional justice: Communication criteria of fairness. In R. J. Lewicki, B. H. Sheppard, and M. H. Bazerman, (Eds), *Research on Negotiation in Organizations* (Vol. 1, pp. 43–55). Greenwich, CT: JAI Press.

Bies, R. & Shapiro, D. (1987). Interactional fairness judgments: The influence of causal accounts. *Social Justice Research, 1,* 199–218.

Bies, R., Shapiro, D., & Cummings, L. (1988). Causal accounts and managing organizational conflict: Is it enough to say it's not my fault? *Communication Research, 15,* 381–399.

Binnendijk, H. (1987). *National negotiating styles.* Washington, DC: Foreign Service Institute, Department of State.

Blake, R. R. & Mouton, J. S. (1961a). *Group dynamics: Key to decision making.* Houston, TX: Gulf Publications.

Blake, R. R. & Mouton, J. S. (1961b). Comprehension of own and outgroup positions under intergroup competition. *Journal of Conflict Resolution, 5,* 304–310.

Blake, R. R. & Mouton, J. S. (1961c). Loyalty of representatives to ingroup positions during intergroup competition. *Sociometry, 24,* 177–183.

Blessing, L. (1988). *A walk in the woods.* New York, NY: New American Library, Dutton.

Boatright, J. R. (1993). *Ethics and the conduct of business.* Englewood Cliffs, NJ: Prentice Hall.

Boehringer, G. H., Zeruolis, V., Bayley, J., & Boehringer, K. (1974). Stirling: The destructive application of group techniques to a conflict. *Journal of Conflict Resolution, 18,* 257–275.

Bok, S. (1978). *Lying: Moral choice in public and private life.* New York, NY: Pantheon.

Bone, D. (1988). *The business of listening.* Los Altos, CA: Crisp Publications.

Bonoma, T., Horai, J., Lindskold, S., Gahagan, J. P., & Tedeschi, J. T. (1969). Compliance to contingent threats. *Proceedings of the 77th Annual Convention of the American Psychological Association, 4,* 395–396.

Boster, F. J. & Mongeau, P. (1984). Fear-arousing persuasive messages. In R. N. Bostrom (Ed.), *Communication Yearbook* (Vol. 8, pp. 330–375). Beverly Hills, CA: Sage.

Bostrom, R. N. (1990). *Listening behavior: Measurement and application.* New York, NY: Guilford Publications.

Boulding, K. (1989). *The three faces of power.* Beverly Hills, CA: Sage Publications.

Bowers, J. W. (1964). Some correlates of language intensity. *Quarterly Journal of Speech, 50,* 415–420.

Bowers, J. W. & Osborn, M. M. (1966). Attitudinal effects of selected types of concluding metaphors in persuasive speeches. *Speech Monographs, 33,* 147–155.

Bowie, N. & Freeman, R. E. (1992). *Ethics and Agency Theory.* New York, NY: Oxford University Press.

Braganti, N. L. & Devine, E. (1992). *European customs and manners: How to make friends and do business in Europe* (Rev. ed.). New York, NY: Meadowbrook Press.

Braginsky, D. D. (1970). Machiavellianism and manipulative interpersonal behavior in children. *Journal of Experimental Social Psychology, 6,* 77–99.

Bramson, R. (1981). *Coping with difficult people.* New York, NY: Anchor Books.

Bramson, R. (1992). *Coping with difficult bosses.* New York, NY: Carol Publishing Group.

Brass, D. J. (1984). Being in the right place: A structural analysis of individual influence in an organization. *Administrative Science Quarterly, 29,* 518–539.

Breaugh, J. A. & Klimoski, R. J. (1977). Choice of group spokesman in bargaining member or outsider. *Organizational Behavior and Human Performance, 19,* 325–336.

Brehm, J. W. (1976). Responses to loss of freedom: A theory of psychological reactance. In J. W. Thibaut, J. T. Spence, & R. C. Carson (Eds.), *Contemporary topics in social psychology* (pp. 53–78). Morristown, NJ: General Learning Press.

Brehm, S. S. & Kassin, S. M. (1990). *Social psychology.* Boston, MA: Houghton Mifflin.

Brett, J. (1991). Negotiating group decisions. *Negotiation Journal, 7,* 291–310.

Brett, J. M. & Goldberg, S. B. (1983). Grievance mediation in the coal industry: A field experiment. *Industrial and Labor Relations Review, 37,* 3–17.

Brett, J. M. & Rognes, J. (1986). Intergroup relations in organizations: A negotiations perspective. In P. Goodman (Ed.), *Designing effective work groups* (pp. 202–236). San Francisco, CA: Jossey-Bass.

Brief, A. (1992). *Sanctioned corruption in the corporate world.* Unpublished manuscript.

Brock, T. C. (1963). Effects of prior dishonesty on post-decision dissonance. *Journal of Abnormal and Social Psychology, 66,* 325–331.

Brooks, E. & Odiorne, G. S. (1984). *Managing by negotiations.* New York, NY: Van Nostrand.

Brown, B. R. (1968). The effects of need to maintain face on interpersonal bargaining. *Journal of Experimental Social Psychology, 4,* 107–122.

Brown, L. D. (1977). Can "haves" and "have-nots" cooperate? Two efforts to bridge a social gap. *Journal of Applied Behavioral Science, 13,* 211–224.

Brown, L. D. (1983). *Managing conflict at organizational interfaces.* Reading, MA: Addison-Wesley.

Bruner, J. S. & Tagiuri, R. (1954). The perception of people. In G. Lindzey (Ed.), *The handbook of social psychology* (Vol. 2, pp. 634–654). Cambridge, MA: Addison-Wesley.

Burgoon, M. & Bettinghaus, E. P. (1980). Persuasive message strategies. In M. Roloff & G. R. Miller (Eds.), *Persuasion: New directions in theory and research* (pp. 141–169). Beverly Hills, CA: Sage Publications.

Burgoon, M. & King, L. B. (1974). The mediation of resistance to persuasion strategies by language variables and active-passive participation. *Human Communication Research, 1,* 30–41.

Burgoon, M. & Stewart, D. (1975). Empirical investigations of language: The effects of sex of source, receiver, and language intensity on attitude change. *Human Communication Research, 1,* 244–248.

Burrough, B. A. & Helyar, J. (1990). *Barbarians at the Gate.* New York, NY: Harper & Row.

Burton, J. (1984). *Global conflict.* Center for International Development, University of Maryland, College Park, MD.

Calero, H. H. & Oskam, B. (1983). *Negotiate the deal you want.* New York, NY: Dodd, Mead & Company.

Carlisle, J. & Leary, M. (1981). Negotiating groups. In R. Payne & C. Cooper (Eds.), *Groups at work* (pp. 165–188) New York, NY: John Wiley and Sons.

Carnevale, P. J. D. (1986). Strategic choice in negotiation. *Negotiation Journal, 2,* 41–56.

Carnevale, P. J. D. & Conlon, D. E. (1988). Time pressure and strategic choice in mediation. *Organizational Behavior and Human Decision Processes, 42,* 111–133.

Carnevale, P. J. D. & Conlon, D. E. (1990, June). *Effects of two forms of bias in mediation of disputes.* Paper presented at the third International Conference of the International Association for Conflict Management, Vancouver, B.C.

Carnevale, A., Gainer, L., Meltzer, A., & Holland, S. (1988). Workplace basics: The skills that employers want. *Training and Development Journal, 42,* 283–290.

Carnevale, P. J. D. & Keenan, P. A. (1990). *Decision frame and social goals in integrative bargaining: The likelihood of agreement versus the quality.* Paper presented at the annual meeting of the International Association of Conflict Management, Vancouver, B.C.

Carnevale, P. J. D. & Lawler, E. J. (1987). Time pressure and the development of integrative agreements in bilateral negotiations. *Journal of Conflict Resolution, 30,* 636–659.

Carnevale, P. J. D. & Pruitt, D. G. (1992). Negotiation and mediation. In M. Rosenberg & L. Porter (Eds.), *Annual Review of Psychology* (Vol. 43, pp. 531–582). Palo Alto, CA: Annual Reviews, Inc.

Carnevale, P. J. D., Pruitt, D. G., & Britton, S. D. (1979). Looking tough: The negotiator under constituent surveillance. *Personality and Social Psychology Bulletin, 5,* 118–121.

Carr, A. Z. (1968, January–February). Is business bluffing ethical? *Harvard Business Review, 46,* 143–153.

Carroll, J., Bazerman, M., & Maury, R. (1988). Negotiator cognitions: A descriptive approach to negotiators' understanding of their opponents. *Organizational Behavior and Human Decision Processes, 41,* 352–370.

Carroll, J., Delquie, P., Halpern, J., & Bazerman, M. (1990). *Improving negotiators' cognitive processes.* Working paper, MIT, Cambridge, MA.

Chaiken, S. (1980). Heuristic versus systematic information processing and the use of source versus message cues in persuasion. *Journal of Personality and Social Psychology, 39,* 752–766.

Chaiken, S. (1986). Physical appearance and social influence. In C.P. Herman, M.P. Zanna, & E.T. Higgins (Eds.), *Physical appearance, stigma, and social behavior: The Ontario symposium* (Vol. 3, pp. 143–177). Hillsdale, NJ: Lawrence Erlbaum Associates.

Chaiken, S. (1987). The heuristic model of persuasion. In M. Zanna, J. Olson, & C. Herman (Eds.), *Social influence: The Ontario symposium* (Vol. 5, pp. 3–39). Hillsdale, NJ: Lawrence Erlbaum Associates.

Charmichael, S. (1992). Focus: Countering employee crime. *Business Ethics, 1,* 180–184.

Chatman, J., Putnam, L., & Sondak, H. (1991). Integrating communication and negotiation research. In M. Bazerman, R. Lewicki, & B. Sheppard (Eds.), *Research on negotiation in organizations* (Vol. 3, pp. 139–164). Greenwich, CT: JAI Press.

Chaudrhy, S. S. & Ross, W. R. (1989). Relevance trees and mediation. *Negotiation Journal, 5,* 63–73.

Chertkoff, J. M. & Conley, M. (1967). Opening offer and frequency of concessions as bargaining strategies. *Journal of Personality and Social Psychology, 7,* 181–185.

Christie, R. & Geis, F. L. (Eds.). (1970). *Studies in Machiavellianism.* New York, NY: Academic Press.

Cialdini, R. B. (1993). *Influence: Science and practice* (3rd ed.). New York, NY: HarperCollins.

Cohen, A. & Bradford, D. (1990). *Influence without authority.* New York, NY: John Wiley and Sons.

Cohen, H. (1980). *You can negotiate anything.* Secaucus, NJ: Lyle Stuart.

Cohen, S. P., Kelman, H. C., Miller, F. D., & Smith, B. L. (1977). Evolving intergroup techniques for conflict resolution: An Israeli-Palestinian pilot workshop. *Journal of Social Issues, 33,* 165–189.

Conlon, D. E. & Fasolo, P. M. (1990). Influence of speed of third party intervention and outcome on negotiator and constituent fairness judgments. *Academy of Management Journal, 33,* 833–846.

Conlon, D. E. & Ross, W. H. (1993). The effects of partisan third parties on negotiator behavior and outcome perceptions. *Journal of Applied Psychology, 78,* 280–290.

Coogler, O. J. (1978). *Structural mediation in divorce settlement: A handbook for marital mediators.* Lexington, MA: Lexington Books.

Cooper, W. (1981). Ubiquitous halo. *Psychological Bulletin, 90,* 218–244.

Corley, R. N., Black, R. L., & Reed, O. L. (1977). *The legal environment of business* (4th ed.). New York, NY: McGraw-Hill.

Corwin, R. G. (1969). Patterns of organizational conflict. *Administrative Science Quarterly, 14,* 504–520.

Coser, L. (1956). *The functions of social conflict.* New York, NY: Free Press.

Coulson, R. (1987). *Business mediation: What you need to know.* New York, NY: American Arbitration Association.

Crott, H., Kayser, E., & Lamm, H. (1980). The effects of information exchange and communication in an asymmetrical negotiation situation. *European Journal of Social Psychology, 10,* 149–163.

Crumbaugh, C. M. & Evans, G. W. (1967). Presentation format, other persons' strategies and cooperative behavior in the prisoner's dilemma. *Psychological Reports, 20,* 895–902.

Dahl, R. A. (1957). The concept of power. *Behavioral Science, 2,* 201–215.

Dawson, R. (1986). *You can get anything you want (but you have to do more than ask).* New York: Simon & Schuster.

Deaux, K. (1985). Sex and gender. *Annual Review of Psychology, 36,* 49–81.

Deep, S. & Sussman, L. (1993). *What to ask when you don't know what to say: 555 powerful questions to use for getting your way at work.* Englewood Cliffs, NJ: Prentice Hall.

Deutsch, M. (1958). Trust and suspicion. *Journal of Conflict Resolution, 2,* 265–279.

Deutsch, M. (1960). Trust, trustworthiness, and the F scale. *Journal of Abnormal and Social Psychology, 61,* 138–140.

Deutsch, M. (1962). Cooperation and trust: Some theoretical notes. In M.R. Jones (Ed.), *Nebraska symposium on motivation* (pp. 275–318). Lincoln, NE: University of Nebraska Press.

Deutsch, M. (1973). *The resolution of conflict.* New Haven, CT: Yale University Press.

Deutsch, M. (1975). Equity, equality and need: What determines which value will be used as the basis for distributive justice? *Journal of Social Issues, 31,* 137–149.

Deutsch, M. & Krauss, R. M. (1962). Studies of interpersonal bargaining. *Journal of Conflict Resolution, 6,* 52–76.

Donaldson, T. & Werhane, P. (1993). *Ethical issues in business: A philosophical approach.* (4th ed.). Englewood Cliffs, NJ: Prentice Hall.

Donohue, W.A. (1981). Analyzing negotiation tactics: Development of a negotiation interact system. *Human Communication Research, 7,* 273–287.

Donohue, W. A. (1989). Communicative competence in mediators. In K. Kressel & D. Pruitt (Eds.), *Mediation research* (pp. 322–343). San Francisco, CA: Jossey-Bass.

Donohue, W. A. (1991). *Communication, marital dispute and divorce mediation.* Hillsdale, NJ: L. Erlbaum Assoc.

Donohue, W., Kaufman, G., Smith, R., & Ramesh, C. (1990, June). *Crisis bargaining: A framework for understanding intense conflict.* Paper presented at the annual conference of the International Communication Association, Dublin, Ireland.

Donohue, W. A. & Kolt, R. (1992). *Managing interpersonal conflict.* Newbury Park, CA: Sage.

Douglas, A. (1957). The peaceful settlement of industrial and intergroup disputes. *Journal of Conflict Resolution, 1,* 69–81.

Douglas, A. (1962). *Industrial peacemaking.* New York, NY: Columbia University Press.

Douglass, F. (1856). *My bondage and my freedom.* New York, NY: Miller, Orton and Michigan.

Drayton, W. (1981, July–August). Getting smarter about regulation. *Harvard Business Review, 59,* 38–52.

Dreher, G. F., Dougherty, T. W., & Whitely, W. (1989). Influence tactics and salary attainment: A gender specific analysis. *Sex Roles, 20,* 535–550.

Druckman D. (1967). Dogmatism, prenegotiation experience, and simulated group representation as determinants of dyadic behavior in a bargaining situation. *Journal of Personality and Social Psychology, 6,* 279–290.

Druckman, D. (1971). The influence of the situation in interparty conflict. *Journal of Conflict Resolution, 15,* 523–554.

Duffy, K., Grosch, J., & Olczak, P. (1991). *Community mediation: A handbook for practitioners and researchers.* New York, NY: Guilford.

Eagly, A. H. & Chaiken, S. (1975). An attribution analysis of the effect of communicator characteristics on opinion change: The case of communicator attractiveness. *Journal of Personality and Social Psychology, 32,* 136–144.

Einhorn, H. & Hogarth, R. (1986). Judging probable cause. *Psychological Bulletin, 99,* 3–19.

Eiseman, J. W. (1978). Reconciling incompatible positions. *Journal of Applied Behavioral Science, 14,* 133–150.

Elkouri, F. & Elkouri, E. (1985). *How arbitration works* (4th ed.). Washington, DC: BNA, Inc.

Emerson, R. M. (1962). Power-dependence relations. *American Sociological Review, 27,* 31–44.

Epstein, Y. (1979). The stability of behavior: I. On predicting most of the people much of the time. *Journal of Personality and Social Psychology, 37,* 1097–1126.

Epstein, Y. (1980). The stability of behavior: II. Implications for psychological research. *American Psychologist, 35,* 790–806.

Etzioni, A. (1969). Social psychological aspects of international relations. In G. Lindzey & E. Aronson (Eds.), *Handbook of Social Psychology* (Vol 5, pp. 538–601). New York: Addison-Wesley.

Exline, R., Thibaut J., Hickey, C., & Gumpert, P. (1970). Visual interaction in relation to Machiavellianism and an unethical act. In R. Christie & F. Geis (Eds.), *Studies in Machiavellianism* (pp. 53–75). New York: Academic Press.

Fahey, L. (1989). *The strategic planning management reader.* Englewood Cliffs, NJ: Prentice Hall.

Falbe, C. & Yukl, G. (1992). Consequences for managers of using single influence tactics and combinations of tactics. *Academy of Management Journal, 36,* 638–652.

Fayerweather, J. & Kapoor, A. (1976). *Strategy and negotiation for the international corporation.* Cambridge, MA: Ballinger.

Feigenbaum, C. (1975). Final-offer arbitration: Better theory than practice. *Industrial Relations, 14,* 311–317.

Feingold, P. C. & Knapp, M. L. (1977). Anti-drug abuse commercials. *Journal of Communication, 27,* 20–28.

Felstiner, W. L. F., Abel, R. L., & Sarat, A. (1980–81). The emergence and transformation of disputes: Naming, blaming, and claiming. *Law and Society Review, 15,* 631–654.

Fern, E. F., Monroe, K. B., & Avila, R. A. (1986). Effectiveness of multiple request strategies: A synthesis of research results. *Journal of Marketing Research, 23,* 144–152.

Festinger, L. A. (1957). *A theory of cognitive dissonance.* Stanford, CA: Stanford University Press.

Festinger, L. A. & Maccoby, N. (1964). On resistance to persuasive communication. *Journal of Abnormal and Social Psychology, 68,* 359–366.

Filley, A. C. (1975). *Interpersonal conflict resolution.* Glenview, IL: Scott, Foresman.

Fischer, C. (1970). The effects of threats in an incomplete information game. *Sociometry, 32,* 301–314.

Fisher, R. (1964). Fractionating conflict. In R. Fisher (Ed.), *International conflict and behavioral science: The Craigville papers.* New York: Basic Books.

Fisher, R. (1969). *International conflict for beginners.* New York: Harper & Row.

Fisher, R. (1978). *International mediation: A working guide.* New York: International Peace Academy.

Fisher, R. & Brown, S. (1988). *Getting together: Building a relationship that gets to yes.* Boston, MA: Houghton Mifflin.

Fisher, R., Ury, W., & Patton, B. (1991). *Getting to yes: Negotiating agreement without giving in* (2nd ed.). New York, NY: Penguin Books.

Folberg, J. & Taylor, A. (1984). *Mediation: A comprehensive guide to resolving conflicts without litigation.* San Francisco, CA: Jossey-Bass.

Folger, J. P., Poole, M. S., & Stutman, R. K. (1993). *Working through conflict: Strategies for relationships, groups and organizations* (2nd ed.). New York, NY: Harper Collins.

Ford, D. L., Jr. (1983). Effects of personal control beliefs: An explanatory analysis of bargaining outcomes in intergroup negotiation. *Group and Organization Studies, 8,* 113–125.

Foster, D. A. (1992). *Bargaining across borders: How to negotiate business successfully anywhere in the world.* New York, NY: McGraw-Hill.

Francis, J. N. P. (1991). When in Rome? The effects of cultural adaptation on intercultural business negotiations. *Journal of International Business Studies, 22,* 403–428.

Freedman, J. L. & Fraser, S. C. (1966). Compliance without pressure: The foot in the door technique. *Journal of Personality and Social Psychology, 4,* 195–202.

French, J. R. P. & Raven, B. (1959). The bases of social power. In D. Cartwright (Ed.), *Studies in social power.* Ann Arbor, MI: Institute for Social Research.

Froman, L. A. & Cohen, M. D. (1970). Compromise and logrolling: Comparing the efficiency of two bargaining processes. *Behavioral Sciences, 15,* 180–183.

Fry, W. R. (1985). The effect of dyad machiavellianism and visual access on integrative bargaining outcomes. *Personality and Social Psychology Bulletin, 11,* 51–62.

Fry, W. R., Firestone, I. J., & Williams, D. (1979, April). *Bargaining process in mixed-singles dyads: Loving and losing.* Paper presented at the Eastern Psychological Association meetings, Philadelphia, PA.

Fuller, R. G. C. & Sheehy-Skeffington, A. (1974). Effects of group laughter on responses to humorous materials: A replication and extension. *Psychological Reports, 35,* 531–534.

Gahagan, J. P., Long, H., & Horai, J. (1969). Race of experimenter and reactions to Black preadolescents. *Proceedings of the 77th Annual Meeting of the American Psychological Association, 4,* 397–398.

Geis, F. L. & Moon, T. H. (1981). Machiavellianism and deception. *Journal of Personality and Social Psychology, 41,* 766–775.

Gerhart, B. & Rynes, S. (1991). Determinants and consequences of salary negotiations by male and female MBA graduates. *Journal of Applied Psychology, 76,* 256–262.

Gibb, J. (1961). Defensive communication. *Journal of Communication, 3,* 141–148.

Gibbons, P., Bradac, J. J., & Busch, J. D. (1992). The role of language in negotiations: Threats and promises. In L. Putnam & M. Roloff (Eds.), *Communication and negotiation* (pp. 156–175). Newbury Park, CA: Sage.

Gilkey, R. W. & Greenhalgh, L. (1986). The role of personality in successful negotiating. *Negotiation Journal, 2,* 247–256.

Gilligan, C. (1982). *In a different voice.* Cambridge, MA: Harvard University Press.

Gist, M. E., Stevens, C. K., & Bavetta, A. G. (1991). Effects of self-efficacy and post-training intervention on the acquisition and maintenance of complex interpersonal skills. *Personnel Psychology, 44,* 837–861.

Goffman, E. (1969). *Strategic interaction.* Philadelphia, PA: University of Philadelphia Press.

Goffman, E. (1974). *Frame analysis.* New York, NY: Harper & Row.

Goodstadt, B. E. & Hjelle, L. A. (1973). Power to the powerless: Locus of control and the use of power. *Journal of Personality and Social Psychology, 27,* 191–196.

Gordon, T. (1977). *Leader effectiveness training.* New York: Wyden Books.

Gouldner, A. W. (1960). The norm of reciprocity: A preliminary statement. *American Sociological Review, 25,* 161–178.

Graham, J. L. (1983). Brazilian, Japanese, and American business negotiations. *Journal of International Business Studies, 14,* 47–61.

Graham, J. L. (1984). A comparison of Japanese and American business negotiations. *International Journal of Research in Marketing, 1,* 50–68.

Graham, J. L. (1993). The Japanese negotiation style: Characteristics of a distinct approach. *Negotiation Journal, 9,* 123–140.

Graham, J. L. & Sano, Y. (1989). *Smart bargaining.* New York, NY: Harper Business.

Gray, B. & Donnellon, A. (1989). *An interactive theory of reframing in negotiation.* Unpublished manuscript.

Gray, B. (In press). The gender-based foundation of negotiation theory. In B. H. Sheppard, R. J. Lewicki, & R. Bies (Eds.), *Research in Negotiation in Organizations,* (Vol. 4). Greenwich, CT: JAI Press.

Greenberg, B. S. & Miller, G. R. (1966). The effects of low-credible sources on message acceptance. *Speech Monographs, 33,* 135–136.

Greenberg, J. (1990). Employee theft as a reaction to underpayment inequity. The hidden cost of pay cuts. *Journal of Applied Psychology. 75,* 561–568.

Greenhalgh, L. (1986). Managing conflict. *Sloan Management Review, 27,* 45–51.

Greenhalgh, L. & Neslin, S. A. (1981). Conjoint analysis of negotiator preferences. *Journal of Conflict Resolution, 25,* 301–327.

Greenhalgh, L. & Neslin, S. A. (1983). Determining outcomes of negotiations. In M.H. Bazerman & R. J. Lewicki (Eds.), *Negotiating in organizations* (pp. 114–134). Beverly Hills, CA: Sage Publications.

Greenhalgh, L., Neslin, S. A., & Gilkey, R. W. (1985). The effects of negotiator preferences, situational power, and negotiator personality on outcomes of business negotiations. *Academy of Management Journal, 28,* 9–33.

Griffin, T. J. & Daggett, W. R. (1990). *The global negotiator: Building strong business relationships anywhere in the world.* New York, NY: Harper Business.

Grigsby, D. W. (1981, November). *The effects of intermediate mediation step on bargaining behavior under various forms of compulsory arbitration.* Paper presented to the Annual Meeting of the American Institute for Decision Sciences, Boston, MA.

Grigsby, D. W. & Bigoness, W. J. (1982). Effects of mediation and alternative forms of arbitration on bargaining behavior: A laboratory study. *Journal of Applied Psychology, 67,* 549–554.

Gruder, C. L. (1971). Relationships with opponent and partner in bargaining. *Journal of Conflict Resolution, 15,* 403–416.

Gruder, C. L. & Duslak, R. J. (1973). Elicitation of cooperation by retaliatory and nonretaliatory strategies in a mixed motive game. *Journal of Conflict Resolution, 17,* 162–174.

Gulliver, P. (1979). *Disputes and negotiations: A cross-cultural perspective.* New York, NY: Academic Press.

Habeeb, W. M. (1988). *Power and tactics in international negotiation.* Baltimore, MD: Johns Hopkins University Press.

Haccoun, R. R. & Klimoski, R. J. (1975). Negotiator status and source: A study of negotiation behavior. *Organizational Behavior and Human Performance, 14,* 342–359.

Haire, M. (1955). Role perceptions in labor-management relations: an experimental approach. *Industrial and Labor Relations Review, 8,* 204–216.

Hall, E. T. (1960 May–June). The silent language of overseas business. *Harvard Business Review, 38,* 87–96.

Hall, J. (1969). *Conflict management survey: A survey of one's characteristic reaction to and handling conflict between himself and others.* Conroe, TX: Teleometrics International.

Hamner, W. C. (1980). The influence of structural, individual, and strategic differences. In D. L. Harnett & L. L. Cummings (Eds.), *Bargaining behavior* (pp. 21–80). Houston, TX: Dame Publications.

Harris, K. L. & Carnevale, P. J. D. (1990). Chilling and hastening: The influence of third-party power and interests on negotiation. *Organizational Behavior and Human Decision Processes, 47,* 138–160.

Harris, P. R. & Moran, R. T. (1987). *Managing cultural differences: High-performance strategies for today's global manager* (2nd ed.). Houston, TX; Gulf Publishing.

Harvey, O. J. (1953). An experimental approach to the study status relations in informal groups. *Sociometry, 18,* 357–367.

Hassett, J. (1981, June). Is it right? An inquiry into everyday ethics. *Psychology Today,* 49–53.

Hassett, J. (1981, November). But that would be wrong. . . . *Psychology Today,* 34–53.

Hassett, J. (1982, August). Correlates of moral values and behavior. Paper presented at the annual meeting of the Academy of Management, New York, NY.

Hegarty, W. & Sims, H. P. (1978). Some determinants of unethical decision behavior: An experiment. *Journal of Applied Psychology, 63,* 451–457.

Heider, F. (1958). *The psychology of interpersonal relations.* New York, NY: John Wiley and Sons.

Heller, J. R. (1967). The effects of racial prejudice, feedback, strategy, and race on cooperative–competitive behavior. *Dissertation Abstracts International, 27,* 2507–2508b.

Henderson, B. (1973). *The nonlogical strategy.* Boston, MA: Boston Consulting Group.

Hendon, D.W. & Hendon, R.A. (1990). *World-class negotiating: Dealmaking in the global marketplace.* New York, NY: John Wiley and Sons.

Hermann, M. G. & Kogan, N. (1977). Effects of negotiators' personalities on negotiating behavior. In D. Druckman (Ed.), *Negotiations: Social-psychological perspectives* (pp. 247–274). Beverly Hills, CA: Sage.

Hill, B. J. (1982). An analysis of conflict resolution techniques: From problem solving workshops to theory. *Journal of Conflict Resolution, 26,* 109–138.

Hiltrop, J. (1989). Factors associated with successful labor mediation. In K. Kressel & D. Pruitt (Eds.), *Mediation research* (pp. 241–262). San Francisco, CA: Jossey-Bass.

Hinton, B. L., Hamner, W. C., & Pohlan, N. F. (1974). Influence and award of magnitude, opening bid and concession rate on profit earned in a managerial negotiating game. *Behavioral Science, 19,* 197–203.

Hocker, J. L. & Wilmot, W. W. (1985). *Interpersonal conflict* (2nd ed.). Dubuque, IA: Wm. C. Brown Publishers.

Hofstede, G. (1980a). Motivation, leadership, and organization: Do American theories apply abroad? *Organizational Dynamics, 9,* 42–63.

Hofstede, G. (1980b). *Culture's consequences: International differences in work related values.* Beverly Hills, CA: Sage.

Hofstede, G. (1989). Cultural predictors of national negotiation styles. In. F. Mautner-Markhof (Ed.), *Processes of International Negotiations* (pp. 193–201). Boulder, CO: Westview Press.

Hofstede, G. (1991). *Culture and organizations: Software of the mind.* London, UK: McGraw Hill.

Holmes, M. (1992). Phase structures in negotiation. In L. Putnam & M. Roloff (Eds.), *Communication and negotiation* (pp. 83–105). Newbury Park, CA: Sage.

Holmes, M. & Poole, M. S. (1991). Longitudinal analysis of interaction. In S. Duck & B. Montgomery (Eds.), *Studying interpersonal interaction* (pp. 286–302). New York, NY: Guilford.

Homans, G. C. (1961). *Social behavior: Its elementary forms.* New York, NY: Harcourt, Brace & World Co.

Hornstein, H. (1965). Effects of different magnitudes of threat upon interpersonal bargaining. *Journal of Experimental Social Psychology, 1,* 282–293.

Hovland, C. I. & Mandell, W. (1952). An experimental comparison of conclusion drawing by the communicator and by the audience. *Journal of Abnormal and Social Psychology, 47,* 581–588.

Ikle, F. C. (1964). *How nations negotiate.* New York: Harper & Row.

Ivey, A. E. & Simek-Downing, L. (1980). *Counselling and psychotherapy.* Englewood Cliffs, NJ: Prentice Hall.

Jackall, R. (1988). *Moral mazes.* New York, NY: Oxford University Press.

Jackson, S. & Allen, M. (1987). *Meta-analysis of the effectiveness of one-sided and two-sided argumentation.* Paper presented at the annual meeting of the International Communication Association, Montreal, Quebec.

Jacobs, A. T. (1951). *Some significant factors influencing the range of indeterminateness in collective bargaining negotiations.* Unpublished doctoral dissertation, University of Michigan, Ann Arbor, MI.

Janis, I. (1982). *Groupthink: Psychological studies of policy decisions and fiascoes.* Boston, MA: Houghton Mifflin.

Janis, I. (1989). *Crucial decisions: Leadership in policymaking and crisis management.* New York, NY: Free Press.

Janosik, R. J. (1987). Rethinking the culture-negotiation link. *Negotiation Journal, 3,* 385–395.

Johns, G. (1991). Substantive and methodological constraints on behavior and attitudes in organizational research. *Organizational Behavior and Human Decision Processes, 49,* 80–104.

Johnson, B. T. & Eagly, A. H. (1989). Effects of involvement on persuasion: A meta-analysis. *Psychological Bulletin, 106,* 290–314.

Johnson, B. T. & Eagly, A. H. (1990). Involvement and persuasion: Types, traditions, and the evidence. *Psychological Bulletin, 107,* 375–384.

Johnson, D. W. (1971). Role reversal: A summary and review of the research. *International Journal of Group Tensions, 1,* 318–334.

Johnson, D. W. & Dustin, R. (1970). The initiation of cooperation through role reversal. *Journal of Social Psychology, 82,* 193–203.

Johnson, D. W. & Lewicki, R. J. (1969). The initiation of superordinate goals. *Journal of Applied Behavioral Science, 5,* 9–24.

Johnson, R. (1993). *Negotiation basics: Concepts, skills, and exercises.* Newbury Park, CA: Sage.

Johnston, R. W. (1982, March–April). Negotiation strategies: Different strokes for different folks. *Personnel, 59,* 36–45.

Jones, E. E. (1964). *Ingratiation.* New York: Appleton-Century-Crofts.

Jones, E. E. & Nisbett, R. E. (1976). The actor and the observer: Divergent perceptions of causality. In J. W. Thibaut, J. T. Spence, & R. C. Carson (Eds.), *Contemporary topics in social psychology* (pp. 37–52). Morristown, NJ: General Learning Press.

Jones, S. B. & Burgoon, M. (1975). Empirical investigations of language intensity: 2. The effects of irrelevant fear and language intensity on attitude change. *Human Communication Research, 1,* 248–251.

Kabanoff, B. (1987). Predictive validity of the MODE conflict instrument. *Journal of Applied Psychology, 72,* 160–163.

Kahneman, D. & Tversky, A. (1979). Prospect theory: An analysis of decisions under risk. *Econometrica, 47,* 263–291.

Kale, S. H. & Barnes, J. W. (1992). Understanding the domain of cross-national buyer-seller interactions. *Journal of International Business Studies, 23,* 101–132.

Kaplan, Robert. (1984, Spring). Trade routes: The manager's network of relationships. *Organizational Dynamics, 12,* 37–52.

Karambayya, R. & Brett, J. M. (1989). Managers handling disputes: Third party roles and perceptions of fairness. *Academy of Management Journal, 32,* 263–291.

Karambayya, R., Brett, J. M., & Lytle, A. (1992). Effects of formal authority and experience on third-party roles, outcomes, and perceptions of fairness. *Academy of Management Journal, 35,* 426–438.

Karrass, C. (1974). *Give and take.* New York, NY: Thomas Y. Crowell.

Karrass, G. (1985). *Negotiate to close: how to make more successful deals.* New York, NY: Simon & Schuster.

Kelley, H. H. (1966). A classroom study of the dilemmas in interpersonal negotiation. In K. Archibald (Ed.), *Strategic interaction and conflict: Original papers and discussion* (pp. 49–73). Berkeley, CA: Institute of International Studies.

Kelley, H. H., Beckman, L. L., & Fisher, C. S. (1967). Negotiating the division of an award under incomplete information. *Journal of Experimental and Social Psychology, 3,* 361–398.

Kelley, H. H. & Stahelski, A. J. (1970). Social interaction basis of cooperators' and competitors' beliefs about others. *Journal of Personality and Social Psychology, 16,* 66–91.

Kelley, H. H. & Schenitzki, D. P. (1972). Bargaining. In C. G. McClintock (Ed.), *Experimental social psychology* (pp. 298–337). New York: Holt, Rinehart & Winston.

Kelley, H. H. & Thibaut, J. (1969). Group problem solving. In G. Lindzey & E. Aronson (Eds.), *Handbook of social psychology (2nd ed.),* (Vol. 4, pp. 1–101). Reading, MA: Addison-Wesley.

Kelman, H. & Hamilton, V. L. (1989). *Crimes of Obedience.* New Haven, CT:Yale University Press.

Kennedy, G. (1985). *Doing business abroad.* New York, NY: Simon & Schuster.

Kessler, S. (1978). *Creative conflict resolution: Mediation.* Atlanta, GA: NIPT.

Keys, B. & Case, T. (1990). How to become an influential manager. *Academy of Management Executive, 4* (4), 38–51.

Kilmann, R. H. & Thomas, K. W. (1977). Developing a forced-choice measure of conflict-handling behavior: The MODE instrument. *Educational and Psychological Measurement, 37,* 309–325.

Kimmel, M. J., Pruitt, D. G., Magenau, J. M., Konar-Goldband, E., & Carnevale, P. J. D. (1980). Effects of trust aspiration and gender on negotiation tactics. *Journal of Personality and Social Psychology, 38,* 9–23.

Kipnis, D. (1976). *The powerholders.* Chicago, IL: University of Chicago Press.

Kipnis, D., Schmidt, S. M., & Wilkinson, I. (1980). Intraorganizational influence tactics: Explorations in getting one's way. *Journal of Applied Psychology, 65,* 440–452.

Kleinke, C. L. & Pohlan, P. D. (1971). Effective and emotional responses as a function of other person's gaze and cooperativeness in two person games. *Journal of Personality and Social Psychology, 17,* 308–313.

Klimoski, R. J. (1972). The effects of intragroup forces on intergroup conflict resolution. *Organizational Behavior and Human Performance, 8,* 363–383.

Klimoski, R. J. & Ash, R. A. (1974). Accountability and negotiator behavior. *Organizational Behavior and Human Performance, 11,* 409–425.

Kochan, T. A. (1980). *Collective bargaining and industrial relations.* Homewood, IL: Richard D. Irwin.

Kochan, T. A. & Jick, T. (1978). The public sector mediation process: A theory and empirical examination. *Journal of Conflict Resolution, 22,* 209–240.

Kogan, N., Lamm, H., & Trommsdorf, G. (1972). Negotiation constraints in the risk taking domain: Effects of being observed by partners of higher or lower status. *Journal of Personality and Social Psychology, 23,* 143–156.

Kohlberg, L. (1969). Stage and sequence: The cognitive development approach to socialization. In D. Goslin (Ed.), *Handbook of socialization theory and research* (pp. 347–380). Chicago: Rand McNally.

Kolb, D. (1983a). *The mediators.* Cambridge, MA: MIT Press.

Kolb, D. (1983b). Strategy and the tactics of mediation. *Human Relations, 36*(3), 247–268.

Kolb, D. (1992, August). *Is it her voice or her place that makes a difference? A consideration of gender issues in negotiation.* Paper presented at the annual meeting of the Academy of Management, Las Vegas, Nevada.

Kolb, D. & Coolidge, G. G. (1991). Her place at the table: A consideration of gender issues in negotiation. In J. Z. Rubin and J. W. Breslin (Eds.), *Negotiation theory and practice* (pp. 261–277). Cambridge, MA: Harvard Program on Negotiation.

Komorita, S. S. & Brenner, A. R. (1968). Bargaining and concessions under bilateral monopoly. *Journal of Personality and Social Psychology, 9,* 15–20.

Komorita S. S. & Kravitz, D. A. (1979). The effects of alternatives in bargaining. *Journal of Experimental Social Psychology, 15,* 147–157.

Komorita, S. S. & Mechling, J. (1967). Betrayal and reconciliation in a two person game. *Journal of Personality and Social Psychology, 6,* 349–353.

Kotter, J. (1977, July–August). Power, dependence and effective management. *Harvard Business Review, 55,* 125–136.

Kotter, J. (1979). *Power in management.* New York: AMACOM.

Kotter, J. (1985). *Power and influence: Beyond formal authority.* New York, NY: Free Press.

Kramer, R. M. (1991). The more the merrier? Social psychological aspects of multiparty negotiations in organizations. In M. Bazerman, R. Lewicki, & B. H. Sheppard, *Research on Negotiation in Organizations* (Vol. 3, pp. 307–332). Greenwich, CT: JAI Press.

Krauss, R. M. & Deutsch, M. (1966). Communication in interpersonal bargaining. *Journal of Personality and Social Psychology, 4,* 572–577.

Kremenyuk, V. A. (Ed.) (1991). *International negotiation: Analysis, approaches, issues.* San Francisco, CA: Jossey-Bass.

Kressel, K. (1972). *Labor Mediation: An exploratory survey.* Albany, NY: Association of Labor Mediation Agencies.

Kressel, K., Jaffe, N., Tuchman, M., Watson, C., & Deutsch, M. (1977). Mediated negotiations in divorce and labor disputes: A comparison. *Conciliation Courts Review, 15,* 9–12.

Kressel, K. & Pruitt, D. (Eds.) (1989). *Mediation research.* San Francisco, CA: Jossey-Bass.

Kuhle, B. & Ross, W. H. (1990, June). *Us vs. them: A social psychological analysis of the Hormel meatpacking strike.* Paper presented at the third International Conference of the International Association for Conflict Management, Vancouver, B.C.

Kuhle, B. & Ross, W. H. (1992). The Hormel strike at Austin, Minnesota. *International Journal of Conflict Management, 3,* 45–68.

Landsberger, H. (1955). Interaction process analysis of the mediation of labor-management disputes. *Journal of Abnormal and Social Psychology, 51,* 552–558.

Laue, J. (1986). *Levels of conflict content.* Remarks delivered at a conference on Guidelines for Newcomers to Track II. Washington, DC.

Lawrence, P. R. & Lorsch, J. W. (1967 November–December). New management job: The integrator. *Harvard Business Review, 45,* 142–151.

Lax, D. & Sebenius, J. (1986). *The manager as negotiator: Bargaining for cooperation and competitive gain.* New York, NY: Free Press.

Leavitt, H. J. & Bahrami, H. (1988). *Managerial psychology: Managing behavior in organizations* (5th ed.). Chicago, IL: University of Chicago Press.

Lefcourt, H. M. (1982). *Locus of control: Current trends in theory and research* (2nd ed.). Hillsdale, NJ: Lawrence Erlbaum Associates.

Leming, J. S. (1978). Cheating behavior, situational influence and moral development. *Journal of Educational Research, 71,* 214–217.

Leventhal, G. S. (1976). Fairness in social relationships. In J. W. Thibaut, J. T. Spence, & R. C. Carson (Eds.), *Contemporary topics in social psychology* (pp. 211–239). Morristown, NJ: General Learning Press.

Leventhal, H. (1970). Findings and theory in the study of fear communications. In L. Berkowitz (Ed.), *Advances in experimental social psychology* (Vol. 5, pp. 120–186). New York: Academic Press.

Lewicki, R. J. (1970). The effects of cooperative and exploitative relationships on subsequent interpersonal relations. *Dissertation Abstracts International, 30,* 4550–A.

Lewicki, R. J. (1980, August). *Bad loan psychology: Entrapment in financial lending.* Paper presented at the annual meeting of the Academy of Management Meetings, Detroit, MI.

Lewicki, R. J. (1982a). Career style inventory: An assessment exercise. In D. T. Hall, D. D. Bowen, R. J. Lewicki, & F. S. Hall (Eds.), *Experiences in Management and Organizational Behavior* (2nd ed.), (pp. 188–201). New York, NY: John Wiley and Sons.

Lewicki, R. J. (1982b). Ethical concerns in conflict management. In G. B. J. Bomers & R. B. Peterson (Eds.), *Conflict management and industrial relations* (pp. 423–445). Boston, MA: Kluwer Nijhoff Publishing.

Lewicki, R. J. (1983). Lying and deception: A behavioral model. In M. H. Bazerman & R. J. Lewicki (Eds.), *Negotiating in organizations* (pp. 68–90). Beverly Hills, CA: Sage Publications.

Lewicki, R. J. (1992). Negotiating strategically. In A. Cohen, (Ed.), *The Portable MBA in Management* (pp. 147–189). New York, NY: John Wiley and Sons.

Lewicki, R. J. & Alderfer, C. P. (1973). The tensions between research and intervention in intergroup conflict. *Journal of Applied Behavioral Science, 9,* 424–468.

Lewicki, R. J. & Sheppard, B. H. (1985). Choosing how to intervee: Factors affecting the use of process and outcome control in third party dispute resolution. *Journal of Occupational Behavior, 6,* 49–64.

Lewicki, R. J., Sheppard, B. H., & Bazerman, M. H. (Eds.).(1986). *Research on negotiation in organizations* (Vol. 1). Greenwich, CT: JAI Press.

Lewicki, R. J. & Spencer, G. (1990, June). *Lies and dirty tricks.* Paper presented at the meeting of the International Association for Conflict Management, Vancouver, B.C.

Lewicki, R. J. & Spencer, G. (1991, August). *Ethical relativism and negotiating tactics: Factors affecting their perceived ethicality.* Paper presented at the meeting of the Academy of Management, Miami FL.

Lewicki, R. J., Weiss, S., & Lewin, D. (1992). Models of conflict, negotiation and third party intervention: A review and synthesis. *Journal of Organizational Behavior, 13,* 209–252.

Lewis, M. (1990). *Liar's Poker.* New York: Penguin Books.

Lewis, M. H. & Reinsch, N. L. (1988). Listening in organizational environments. *Journal of Business Communication, 25,* 49–67.

Liebert, R. M., Smith, W. P., & Hill, J. H. (1968). The effects of information and magnitude of initial offer on interpersonal negotiation. *Journal of Experimental Social Psychology, 4,* 431–441.

Lim, R. & Carnevale, P. J. D. (1990). Contingencies in the mediation of disputes. *Journal of Personality & Social Psychology, 58,* 259–272.

Long, G., & Feuille, P. (1974). Final offer arbitration: Sudden death in Eugene. *Industrial and Labor Relations Review, 27,* 186–203.

Loomis, J. L. (1959). Communication, the development of trust and cooperative behavior. *Human Relations, 12,* 305–315.

Lovenheim, P. (1989). *Mediate, don't litigate: How to resolve disputes quickly, privately, and inexpensively without going to court.* New York, NY: McGraw-Hill.

Lowe, T. (1986, January). Eight ways to ruin a performance appraisal. *Personnel Journal, 65,* 60–62.

Luce, R. D. & Raiffa, H. (1957). *Games and decisions: Introduction and critical survey.* New York, NY: John Wiley and Sons.

Lukov, V. (1985). International negotiations of the 1980s: Features, problems and prospects. *Negotiation Journal, 1,* 139–148.

Luthans, F. & Kreitner, R. (1985). *Organizational behavior modification and beyond.* Glenview, IL: Scott, Foresman.

Maier, R. A. & Lavrakas, P. J. (1976). Lying behavior and the evaluation of lies. *Perceptual and Motor Skills, 42,* 575–581.

Marecki, S. (1974). *Elements of competitive decision making: Non-zero sum games.* Cambridge, MA: Harvard University Press.

Mautner-Markhof, F. (Ed.). (1989). *Processes of international negotiations.* Boulder, CO: Westview Press.

McClelland, D. (1975). *Power: The inner experience.* New York, NY: Irvington Publishers.

McCornack, S. A. & Levine, T. R. (1990). When lies are uncovered: Emotional and relational outcomes of discovered deception. *Communication Monographs, 57,* 119–138.

McCroskey, J. C., Jensen, T., & Valencia, C. (1973, November). *Measurement of the credibility of mass media sources.* Paper presented at the Western Speech Communication Association, Albuquerque, NM.

McDonald, J. (1963). *Strategy in poker, business & war.* New York, NY: William Norton.

McEwen, C. A. & Milburn, T. W. (1993). Explaining a paradox of mediation. *Negotiation Journal, 9,* 23–36.

McGuire, W. J. (1964). Inducing resistance to persuasion: Some contemporary approaches. In L. Berkowitz (Ed.), *Advances in Experimental Social Psychology* (Vol. 1, pp. 191–229). New York: Academic Press.

McGuire, W. J. (1973). Persuasion, resistance and attitude change. In I. S. Poole, F. W. Frey, W. Schramm, N. Maccoby, & E. B. Parker (Eds.), *Handbook of Communication* (pp. 216–252). Skokie, IL: Rand McNally.

Meeker, R. J. & Shure, G. H. (1969). Pacifist bargaining tactics: Some "outsider" influences. *Journal of Conflict Resolution, 13,* 487–493.

Metcalf, H. & Urwick, L. (Eds.). (1940). *Dynamic administration: The collected papers of Mary Parker Follett.* New York, NY: Harper & Row.

Michelini, R. L. (1971). Effects of prior interaction, contact, strategy, and expectation of meeting on gain behavior and sentiment. *Journal of Conflict Resolution, 15,* 97–103.

Michener, H. A., Vaske, J. J., Schleiffer, S. L., Plazewski, J. G., & Chapman, L. J. (1975). Factors affecting concession rate and threat usage in bilateral conflict. *Sociometry, 38,* 62–80.

Michener, S. K. & Suchner, R. W. (1971). The tactical use of social power. In J. T. Tedeschi (Ed.), *The social influence process* (pp. 235–286). Chicago: AVC.

Midgaard, K. & Underal, A. (1977). Multiparty conferences. In D. Druckman (Ed.), *Negotiations: Social psychological perspectives* (pp. 329–345). Beverly Hills, CA: Sage.

Milgram, S. (1974). *Obedience to authority: An experimental view.* New York, NY: Harper & Row.

Miller, D. T. & Ross, M. (1975). Self-serving bias in the attribution of causality: Fact of fiction? *Psychological Bulletin, 82,* 213–225.

Miller, D. T. & Vidmar, N. (1981). The social psychology of punishment reactions. In M. J. Lerner (Ed.), *The justice motive in social behavior* (pp. 145–172). New York: Plenum Press.

Miller, S. K. & Burgoon, M. (1979). The relationship between violations of expectations and the induction of the resistance to persuasion. *Human Communication Research, 5,* 301–313.

Mintzberg, H. (1973). *The nature of managerial work.* New York, NY: Harper & Row.

Mintzberg, H. (1983). *Power in and around organizations.* Englewood Cliffs, NJ: Prentice Hall.

Mintzberg, H. (1991). Five Ps for strategy. In H. Mintzberg & J. B. Quinn (Eds.), *The strategy process: Concepts, contexts, cases* (2nd ed.) (pp. 12–19). Englewood Cliffs, NJ: Prentice Hall.

Mintzberg, H. & Quinn, J. B. (1991). *The strategy process: Concepts, contexts, cases* (2nd ed.). Englewood Cliffs, NJ: Prentice Hall.

Mintzberg, H. & Waters, J. (1985). Of strategies, deliberate and emergent. *Strategic Management Journal, 6,* 257–272.

Missner, M. (1980). *Ethics of the business system.* Sherman Oaks, CA: Alfred Publishing Company.

Moore, C. (1986). *The mediation process: Practical strategies for resolving conflict.* San Francisco, CA: Jossey-Bass.

Morley, I. & Stephenson, G. (1977). *The social psychology of bargaining.* London: Allen and Unwin.

Murnighan, K. (1978). Models of coalition behavior: Game theoretic, social psychological and political perspectives. *Psychological Bulletin, 85,* 1130–1153.

Murnighan, K. (1986). Organizational coalitions: Structural contingencies and the formation process. In R. J. Lewicki, B. H. Sheppard, & M. H. Bazerman (Eds.), *Research on Negotiation in Organizations* (Vol. 1, pp. 155–173). Greenwich, CT: JAI Press.

Murnighan, J. K. (1991). *The dynamics of bargaining games.* Englewood Cliffs, NJ: Prentice Hall.

Murnighan, J. K. (1992). *Bargaining games.* New York, NY: William Morrow.

Murphy, K. (1992). *Honesty in the workplace.* Pacific Grove, CA: Brooks Cole.

Nash, J. F. (1950). The bargaining problem. *Econometrica, 18,* 155–162.

Neale, M. & Bazerman, M. (1983). The role of perspective-taking ability in negotiating under different forms of arbitration. *Industrial and Labor Relations Review, 36,* 378–388.

Neale, M. & Bazerman, M. H. (1985). The effects of framing and negotiator overconfidence on bargaining behaviors and outcomes. *Academy of Management Journal, 28,* 34–49.

Neale, M. & Bazerman, M. H. (1991). *Cognition and rationality in negotiation.* New York, NY: Free Press.

Neale, M. & Bazerman, M. H. (1992a). Negotiating rationally: The power and impact of the negotiator's frame. *Academy of Management Executive, 6* (3), 42–51.

Neale, M. A. & Bazerman, M. H. (1992b). Negotiator cognition and rationality: A behavioral decision theory perspective. *Organizational Behavior and Human Decision Processes, 51,* 157–175.

Neale, M. A. & Northcraft, G. B. (1986). Experts, amateurs, and refrigerators: Comparing expert and amateur negotiators in a novel task. *Organizational Behavior and Human Decision Processes, 38,* 305–317.

Neale, M. A. & Northcraft, G. B. (1991). Behavioral negotiation theory: A framework for conceptualizing dyadic bargaining. In L. Cummings & B. Staw (Eds.), *Research in Organizational Behavior* (Vol. 13, pp. 147–190). Greenwich, CT: JAI Press, 147–190.

Nemeth, C. J. (1986). "Differential contributions to majority and minority influence. *Psychological Review, 93,* 23–32.

Nemeth, C. J. (1989). *The stimulating properties of dissent.* Paper presented at the first annual Conference on Group Process and Productivity, Texas A & M University, College Station, TX.

Neslin, S. A. & Greenhalgh, L. (1983). Nash's theory of cooperative games as a predictor of the outcomes of buyer-seller negotiations: An experiment in media purchasing. *Journal of Marketing Research, 20,* 368–379.

Neu, J., Graham, J. L., & Gilly, M. C. (1988). The influence of gender on behaviors and outcomes in a retail buyer-seller negotiation simulation. *Journal of Retailing, 64,* 427–451.

Nicholson, M. (1970). *Conflict analysis.* London: English University Press.

Nierenberg, G. (1976). *The complete negotiator.* New York, NY: Nierenberg & Zeif Publishers.

Northrup, H. R. (1964). *Boulwarism.* Ann Arbor, MI: Bureau of Industrial Relations, University of Michigan.

O'Keefe, D. J. (1990). *Persuasion: Theory and research.* Newbury Park, CA: Sage.

Osgood, C. E. (1962). *An alternative to war or surrender.* Urbana, IL: University of Illinois Press.

Oskamp, S. (1970). Effects of programmed initial strategies in a prisoner's dilemma game. *Psychometrics, 19,* 195–196.

Patterson, J. & Kim, P. (1991). *The day America told the truth.* New York, NY: Prentice Hall.

Petty, R. E. & Cacioppo, J. T. (1986a). *Communication and persuasion: Central and peripheral routes to attitude change.* New York, NY: Springer/Verlag.

Petty, R. E. & Cacioppo, J. T. (1986a). The elaboration likelihood model of persuasion. In L. Berkowitz (Ed.), *Advances in Experimental Social Psychology* (Vol. 19, pp. 123–205). New York: Academic Press.

Petty, R. E. & Cacioppo, J. T. (1990). Involvement and persuasion: Tradition versus integration. *Psychological Bulletin, 107,* 367–374.

Petty, R. E., Cacioppo, J. T., Strathman, A. J., & Priester, J. R. (In press). To think or not to think: Exploring two routes to persuasion. In T. Brock & S. Shavitt (Eds.), *Psychology of persuasion.* San Francisco, CA: Freeman.

Petty, R. E., Wells, G., & Brock, T. (1976). Distraction can enhance or reduce yielding to propaganda: Thought disruption versus effort justification. *Journal of Personality and Social Psychology, 34,* 874–884.

Pfeffer, J. (1992). *Managing with Power.* Boston, MA: Harvard Business School Press.

Pfeffer, J. & Salancik, G. R. (1974). Organizational decision making as a political process: The case of a university budget. *Administrative Science Quarterly, 19,* 135–151.

Pilisuk, N. & Skolnick, P. (1978). Inducing trust: A test of the Osgood proposal. *Journal of Personality and Social Psychology, 8,* 121–133.

Pinkley, R. L. (1989). *Dimensions of conflict frame: Disputant interpretations of conflict.* Unpublished dissertation, University of North Carolina at Chapel Hill, NC.

Pinkley, R. L. (1990). Dimensions of conflict frame: Disputant interpretations of conflict. *Journal of Applied Psychology, 75,* 117–126.

Pinkley, R. L. (1992). Dimensions of conflict frame: Relation to disputant perceptions and expectations. *The International Journal of Conflict Management, 3,* 95–113.

Pinkley, R. & Northcraft, G. B. (in press). Cognitive interpretations of conflict: Implications for dispute processes and outcomes. *Academy of Management Journal.*

Poole, M. & Doelger, J. (1986). Developmental processes in group decision-making. In R. Hirokawa & M. Poole (Eds.), *Communication in group decision-making* (pp. 35–62.). Beverly Hills, CA: Sage.

Prasow, P. & Peters, E. (1983). *Arbitration and collective bargaining: Conflict resolution in labor relations* (2nd ed.). New York, NY: McGraw-Hill.

Pruitt, D. G. (1981). *Negotiation behavior.* New York, NY: Academic Press.

Pruitt, D. G. (1983). Strategic choice in negotiation. *American Behavioral Scientist, 27,* 167–194.

Pruitt, D. G. & Carnevale, P. J. D. (1993). *Negotiation in social conflict.* Pacific Grove, CA: Brooks-Cole.

Pruitt, D. G., Carnevale, P. J. D., Ben-Yoav, O., Nochajski, T. H., & Van Slyck, M. (1983). Incentives for cooperation in integrative bargaining. In Tietz (Ed.), *Aspiration levels in bargaining and economic decision making* (pp. 22–34). Berlin: Springer.

Pruitt, D. G., Carnevale, P. J. D., Forcey, B., & Van Slyck, M. (1986). Gender effects in negotiation: Constituent surveillance and contentious behavior. *Journal of Experimental Social Psychology, 22,* 264–275.

Pruitt, D. G. & Lewis, S. A. (1975). Development of integrative solutions in bilateral negotiation. *Journal of Personality and Social Psychology, 31,* 621–633.

Pruitt, D. G. & Rubin, J. Z. (1986). *Social conflict: Escalation, stalemate and settlement.* New York: Random House.

Pruitt, D. G. & Syna, H. (1985). Mismatching the opponent's offers in negotiation. *Journal of Experimental Social Psychology, 21,* 103–113.

Putnam, L. & Holmer, M. (1992). Framing, reframing, and issue development. In L. Putnam & M. Roloff (Eds.), *Communication and negotiation* (pp. 128–155). Newbury Park, CA: Sage.

Putnam, L. & Jones, T. S. (1982). Reciprocity in negotiations: An analysis of bargaining interaction. *Communication Monographs, 49,* 171–191.

Putnam, L. & Poole, M. (1987). Conflict and negotiation. In F. Jablin, L. Putnam, K. Roberts, & L. Porter (Eds.), *Handbook of organizational communication: An interdisciplinary perspective* (pp. 549–599). Newbury Park, CA: Sage.

Putnam, L. & Roloff, M. (1992). Communication perspectives on negotiation. In L. Putnam & M. Roloff (Eds.), *Communication and negotiation* (pp. 1–17). Newbury Park, CA: Sage.

Putnam, L., Wilson, S., & Turner, D. (1990). The evolution of policy arguments in teachers' negotiations. *Argumentation, 4,* 129–152.

Pye, L. W. (1992). *Chinese negotiating style.* New York, NY: Quorum Books.

Quinn, J. B. (1991). Strategies for change. In H. Mintzberg & J. B. Quinn (Eds.), *The strategy process: Concepts, contexts, cases* (2nd ed.) (pp. 4–12). Englewood Cliffs, NJ: Prentice Hall.

Rachels, J. (1986) *The elements of moral philosophy.* New York, NY: McGraw Hill.

Rackham, N. (1992). The behavior of successful negotiators. Huthwaite Research Group. In R. J. Lewicki, J. A. Litterer, D. M. Saunders, & J. W. Minton (Eds.), *Negotiation: Readings, exercises and cases* (2nd ed.) (pp. 393–406). Homewood, IL: Richard D. Irwin.

Rahim, M. A. (1983a). A measure of styles of handling interpersonal conflict. *Academy of Management Journal, 26,* 368–376.

Rahim, M. A. (1983b). *Rahim Organizational Conflict Inventory-II, Forms A, B and C.* Palo Alto, CA: Consulting Psychologists Press.

Rahim, M. A. (1992). *Managing conflict in organizations.* (2nd ed.). Westport, CT: Praeger.

Raiffa, H. (1982). *The art and science of negotiation.* Cambridge, MA: Belknap Press of Harvard University Press.

Rapoport, A. (1963). Formal games as probing tools for investigating behavior motivated by trust and suspicion. *Journal of Conflict Resolution, 7,* 570–579.

Rapoport, A. (1964). *Strategy and conscience.* New York: Harper & Row.

Rapoport, A. (1966). *Two person game theory.* Ann Arbor, MI: University of Michigan Press.

Raven, B. H. & Rubin, J. Z. (1973). *Social psychology: People in groups.* New York: John Wiley and Sons.

Read, S. J. (1987). Constructing causal scenarios: A knowledge structure approach to causal reasoning. *Journal of Personality and Social Psychology, 52,* 288–302.

Reardon, K. K. (1981). *Persuasion theory and context.* Beverly Hills, CA: Sage Publications.

Reich, R. B. (1981, May–June). Regulation by confrontation or negotiation. *Harvard Business Review, 59,* 82–93.

Richardson, R. C. (1977). *Collective bargaining by objectives.* Englewood Cliffs, NJ: Prentice Hall.

Robinson, S. (1992). *Retreat, voice, silence and destruction: A typology of employees behavioral responses to dissatisfaction.* Unpublished manuscript.

Rogers, C. R. (1957). *Active listening.* Chicago, IL: University of Chicago Press.

Rogers, C. R. (1961). *On becoming a person: A therapist's view of psychotherapy.* Boston, MA: Houghton-Mifflin.

Rogers, C. R. & Roethlisberger, F. J. (1991). Barriers and gateways to communication. *Harvard Business Review, 69,* 105–111.

Rosnow, R. L. & Robinson, E. J. (1967). *Experiments in persuasion.* New York, NY: Academic Press.

Ross, L. (1977). The intuitive psychologist and his shortcomings: Distortions in the attributions proces. In L. Berkowitz (Ed.), *Advances in experimental social psychology* (Vol. 10, pp. 173–220). New York, NY: Academic Press.

Ross, L., Green, D., & House, P. (1977). The false consensus phenomenon: An attributional bias in self-perception and social-perception processes. *Journal of Experimental Social Psychology, 13,* 279–301.

Roth, A. E., Murnighan, J. K., & Schoumaker, F. (1988). The deadline effect in bargaining: Some empirical evidence. *American Economic Review, 78,* 806–823.

Rothman, J. (1992). *From confrontation to cooperation.* Newbury Park, CA: Sage.

Rotter, J. B. (1967). A new scale for the measurement of interpersonal trust. *Journal of Personality, 35,* 651–665.

Rotter, J. B. (1971). Generalized expectancies for interpersonal trust. *American Psychologist, 26,* 443–452.

Rotter, J. B. (1980). Interpersonal trust, trustworthiness, and gullibility. *American Psychologist, 35,* 1–7.

Rubin, J. Z. (1980). Experimental research on third party intervention in conflict: Toward some generalizations. *Psychological Bulletin, 87,* 379–391.

Rubin, J. Z. (Ed.) (1981). *Dynamics of third party intervention: Kissinger in the Middle East.* New York: Praeger.

Rubin, J. Z. & Brown, B. R. (1975). *The Social Psychology of Bargaining and Negotiation.* New York, NY: Academic Press.

Rubin, J. & Rubin, C. (1989). *When families fight.* New York: William. Morrow.

Ruble, T. L. & Thomas, K. W. (1976). Support for a two-dimensional model of conflict behavior. *Organizational Behavior and Human Performance, 16,* 143–155.

Rusk, T. with Miller, D. P. (1993). *The power of ethical persuasion.* New York, NY: Penguin Books.

Russo, J. E. & Schoemaker, P. J. H. (1989). *Decision traps: The ten barriers to brilliant decision-making and how to overcome them.* New York, NY: Simon & Schuster.

Salacuse, J. W. (1988). Making deals in strange places: A beginner's guide to international business negotiations. *Negotiation Journal, 4,* 5–13.

Salancik, G. R. & Pfeffer, J. (1977). Who gets power and how they hold on to it: A strategic–contingency model of power. *Organizational Dynamics, 5,* 3–21.

Sato, K. (1988). Trust and group size in a social dilemma. *Japanese Psychological Research, 30,* 88–93.

Savage, G. T., Blair, J. D., & Sorenson, R. L. (1989). Consider both relationships and substance when negotiating strategically. *Academy of Management Executive, 3*(1), 37–48.

Schatzski, M. (1981). *Negotiation: The art of getting what you want.* New York, NY: Signet Books.

Schein, E. (1987). *Process consultation Volume II: Lessons for managers and consultants.* Reading, MA: Addison-Wesley.

Schelling, T. C. (1960). *The strategy of conflict.* Cambridge, MA: Harvard University Press.

Schlenker, B. R. & Riess, M. (1979). Self-presentation of attitudes following commitment to proattitudinal behavior. *Journal of Human Communication Research, 5,* 325–334.

Schreisheim, C. & Hinkin, T. R. (1990). Influence strategies used by subordinates: A theoretical and empirical analysis and refinement of the Kipnis, Schmidt, and Wilkinson subscales. *Journal of Applied Psychology, 75,* 246–257.

Scodel, A., Minas, J. S., Ratoosh, P., & Lipetz, M. (1959). Some descriptive aspects of two-person, non-zero-sum games. *Journal of Conflict Resolution, 3,* 114–119.

Sebenius, J. K. (1983). Negotiation arithmetic: Adding and subtracting issues and parties. *International Organization, 37,* 1–34.

Sebenius, J. K. (1992). Negotiation analysis: A characterization and review. *Management Science, 38,* 18–38.

Selekman, B. M., Fuller, S. H., Kennedy, T., & Baitsel, J. M. (1964). *Problems in labor relations.* New York, NY: McGraw-Hill.

Selekman, B. M., Selekman, S. K., & Fuller, S. H. (1958). *Problems in labor relations.* New York, NY: McGraw-Hill.

Seligman, C., Bush, M., & Kirsch, K. (1976). Relationship between compliance in the foot in the door paradigm and size of first request. *Journal of Personality and Social Psychology, 33,* 517–520.

Seligman, M. (1975). *On depression, development, and death.* San Francisco, CA: Freeman.

Sen, A. K. (1970). *Collective choice and individual values.* San Francisco, CA: Holden-Day.

Sermat V. (1967). The effects of an initial cooperative or competitive treatment on a subject's response to conditional operation. *Behavioral Science, 12,* 301–313.

Sermat, V. & Gregovich, R. P. (1966). The effect of experimental manipulation on cooperative behavior in a checkers game. *Psychometric Science, 4,* 435–436.

Shannon, E. & Weaver, W. (1948). *The mathematical theory of communication.* Urbana, IL: University of Illinois Press.

Shapiro, D. (1991). The effects of explanations on negative reactions to deceit. *Administrative Science Quarterly, 36,* 614–630.

Shapiro, Debra. (In press). Threats, bluffs and disclaimers in negotiation. *Organizational Behavior and Human Decision Processes.*

Shapiro, D. L., Sheppard, B. H., & Cheraskin, L. (1992). Business on a handshake. *Negotiation Journal, 8,* 365–377.

Shea, G. F. (1983). *Creative Negotiating.* Boston, MA: CBI Publishing Co.

Shelling, T. G. (1966). *Arms and influence.* New Haven, CT: Yale University Press.

Sheppard, B. H. (1983). Managers as inquisitors: Some lessons from the law. In M. Bazerman & R. J. Lewicki (Eds.), *Negotiating in Organizations* (pp. 193–213). Beverly Hills, CA: Sage.

Sheppard, B. H. (1984). Third party conflict intervention: A procedural framework. In B. M. Staw & L. L. Cummings (Eds.), *Research in Organizational Behavior* (Vol. 6, pp. 141–190). Greenwich, CT: JAI Press.

Sheppard, B. H., Bazerman, M. H., & Lewicki, R. J. (1990). *Research on negotiation in organizations* (Vol. 2). Greenwich, CT: JAI Press.

Sheppard, B. H., Blumenfeld-Jones, K., Minton, J. W., & Hyder, E. (In press). Informal conflict intervention: Advice and dissent. *Employee Rights and Responsibilities Journal.*

Sheppard, B. H., Lewicki, R. J., & Minton, J. (1992). *Organizational justice: The search for fairness in the workplace.* New York: Lexington Books.

Sherif, M., Harvey, L., White, B., Hood, W., & Sherif, C. (1988). *The Robbers' Cave experiment: Intergroup conflict and cooperation.* Middletown, CT: Wesleyan University Press. (Original work published 1961.)

Siegel, S. & Fouraker, L. E. (1960). *Bargaining and group decision making: Experiments in bilateral monopoly.* New York, NY: McGraw-Hill.

Siegelman, P. & Ayres, I. (1991). *Price discrimination by race and gender in bargaining for new cars: Survey evidence.* Paper presented at the annual meeting of the Law and Society Association, Amsterdam, The Netherlands.

Simons, T. (1993). Speech patterns and the concept of utility in cognitive maps: The case of integrative bargaining. *Academy of Management Journal, 36,* 139–156.

Singer, L. (1990). *Settling disputes: Conflict resolution in business, families, and the legal system.* Boulder, CO: Westview Press.

Skinner, B. F. (1953). *Science and human behavior.* New York: Macmillan.

Smith, W. P. (1985). Effectiveness of the biased mediator. *Negotiation Journal, 1,* 363–372.

Solomon, L. (1960). The influence of some types of power relationships and game strategies upon the development of interpersonal trust. *Journal of Abnormal and Social Psychology, 61,* 223–230.

Solomon, M. (1990). *Working with difficult people.* Englewood Cliffs, NJ: Prentice Hall.

Solomon, R. H. (1987). China: Friendship and obligation in Chinese negotiating style. In H. Binnendijk (Ed.), *National negotiating styles* (pp. 1–16). Washington, DC: Foreign Service Institute.

Starke, F. A. & Notz, W. W. (1981). Pre- and postintervention effects of conventional vs. final-offer arbitration. *Academy of Management Journal, 24,* 832–850.

Steers, R. M. (1984). *Introduction to organizational behavior* (2nd ed.). Glenview, IL: Scott, Foresman.

Stevens, C. M. (1963). *Strategy and collective bargaining negotiations.* New York, NY: McGraw-Hill.

Stevens, C. K., Bavetta, A. G., & Gist, M. E. (1993). Gender differences in the acquisition of salary negotiation skills: The role of goals, self-efficacy, and perceived control. *Journal of Applied Psychology, 78* 723–735.

Steward, Thomas A. (1989, November 16). New ways to exercise power. *Fortune,* 52–66.

Stewart, J. B. (1992). *Den of Thieves.* New York: Touchstone Books.

Stillenger, C., Epelbaum, M., Keltner, D., & Ross, L. (1990). *The 'reactive devaluation' barrier to conflict resolution.* Working paper, Stanford University, Palo Alto, CA.

Stolte, J. F. (1983). Self-efficacy: Sources and consequences in negotiation networks. *Journal of Social Psychology, 119,* 69–75.

Sun, Tsu (1983). *The art of war.* New York, NY: Dellacorte Press.

Susskind, L. & Cruikshank, J. (1987). *Breaking the impasse: Consensual approaches to resolving public disputes.* New York, NY: Basic Books.

Sutton, S. R. (1982). Fear-arousing communications: A critical examination of theory and research. In J.R. Eiser (Ed.), *Social psychology and behavioral medicine* (pp. 303–337). New York: John Wiley and Sons.

Swap, W. L. & Rubin, J. Z. (1983). Measurement of interpersonal orientation. *Journal of Personality and Social Psychology, 44,* 208–219.

Swenson, R. A., Nash, D. L., & Roos, D. C. (1984). Source credibility and perceived expertness of testimony in a simulated child-custody case. *Professional Psychology, 15,* 891–898.

Swinth, R. L. (1967). [Review of *A behavioral theory of labor negotiations*]. *Contemporary Psychology, 12,* 183–184.

Taetzsch, L. & Benson, E. (1978). *Taking charge on the job: Techniques for assertive management.* New York, NY: Executive Enterprises Publications.

Tannen, D. (1990). *You just don't understand: Women and men in conversation.* New York, NY: Ballantine Books.

Tannenbaum, D. & Norris, E. (1966). Effects of combining congruity principle strategies for the reduction of persuasion. *Journal of Personality and Social Psychology, 3,* 233–238.

Taylor, S. E. & Brown, J. D. (1988). Illusion and well-being: A social-psychological perspective on mental health. *Psychological Bulletin, 103,* 193–210.

Tedeschi, J. T., Bonoma, T., & Brown, R. C. (1971). A paradigm for the study of coercive power. *Journal of Conflict Resolution, 15,* 197–223.

Tedeschi, J. T., Schlenker, B. R., & Bonoma, T. V. (1973). *Conflict, power and games: The experimental study of interpersonal relations.* Chicago: AVC.

Terhune, K. W. (1968). Motives, situation and interpersonal conflict within prisoner's dilemma. *Journal of Personality and Social Psychology, Monograph supplement, 8,* 1–24.

Terhune, K. W. (1970). The effects of personality in cooperation and conflict. In P. Swingle (Ed.), *The structure of conflict* (pp. 193–234). New York, NY: Academic Press.

Thayer, N. B. & Weiss, S. E. (1987). Japan: The changing logic of a former minor power. In H. Binnendijk (Ed.), *National negotiating styles* (pp. 45–74). Washington, DC: Foreign Service Institute.

Thibaut, J. & Kelley, H. H. (1959). *The social psychology of groups.* New York, NY: John Wiley and Sons.

Thibaut, J. & Walker, L. (1975). *Procedural justice: A psychological analysis.* Hillsdale, NJ: Lawrence Erlbaum Associates.

Thomas, K. W. (1976). Conflict and conflict management. In M. D. Dunnette (Ed.) *Handbook of Industrial & Organizational Psychology* (pp. 889–935). Chicago: Rand McNally, 889–935.

Thomas, K. W. (1977). Toward multidimensional values in teaching: The example of conflict behavior. *Academy of Management Review, 2,* 484–490.

Thomas, K. W. (1992). Conflict and negotiation processes in organizations. In M. D. Dunnette and L. H. Hough, *Handbook of Industrial & Organizational Psychology* (Vol. 3, pp. 651–718) (2nd ed.). Palo Alto, CA: Consulting Psychologists Press.

Thomas, K. W. & Kilmann, R. H. (1974). *Thomas-Kilmann conflict mode survey.* Tuxedo, NY: Xicom.

Thompson, L. (1990a). An examination of naive and experienced negotiators. *Journal of Personality and Social Psychology, 59,* 82–90.

Thompson, L. (1990b). Negotiation behavior and outcomes: Empirical evidence and theoretical issues. *Psychological Bulletin, 108,* 515–532.

Thompson, L. (1991). Information exchange in negotiation. *Journal of Experimental Social Psychology, 27,* 161–179.

Thompson, L. & Hastie, R. (1990a). Social perception in negotiation. *Organizational Behavior and Human Decision Processes, 47,* 98–123.

Thompson, L. & Hastie, R. (1990b). Judgment tasks and biases in negotiation. In B. H. Sheppard, M. H. Bazerman, & R. J. Lewicki (Eds.), *Research on Negotiation in Organizations* (Vol. 1, pp. 31–54). Greenwich, CT: JAI Press.

Thompson, L. & Loewenstein, G. (1992). Egocentric interpretations of fairness and interpersonal conflict. *Organizational Behavior and Human Decision Processes, 51,* 176–197.

Tjosvold, D. (1988). *Getting things done in organizations.* Lexington, MA: Lexington Books.

Touval, S. & Zartman, I. (1985). *International mediation in theory and practice.* Boulder, CO: Westview Press.

Trenholm, S. (1989). *Persuasion and social influence.* Englewood Cliffs, NJ: Prentice Hall.

Trevino, L. K. (1986). Ethical decision making in organizations: A person-situation interactionist model. *Academy of Management Review, 11,* 601–617.

Trevino, L. K. & Youngblood, S. (1990). Bad apples in bad barrels: A causal analysis of ethical decision-making behavior. *Journal of Applied Psychology, 75,* 378–385.

Triandis, H. C. (1982). [Review of *Culture's consequences: International differences in work values.*] *Human Organization, 41,* 86–90.

Tsui, A. S. (1983). An analysis of social structure and reputational effectiveness. *Proceedings of the 43rd Meeting of the Academy of Management,* 261–265.

Tsui, A. S. (1984). A role set analysis of managerial reputation. *Organizational Behavior and Human Performance, 34,* 64–96.

Tung, R. L. (1991, Winter). Handshakes across the sea: Cross-cultural negotiating for business success. *Organizational Dynamics, 19,* 30–40.

Tutzauer, F. (1991). Bargaining outcome, bargaining process, and the role of communication. *Progress in Communication Science, 10,* 257–300.

Tutzauer, F. (1992). The communication of offers in dyadic bargaining. In L. Putnam & M. Roloff (Eds.), *Communication and negotiation* (pp. 67–82). Newbury Park, CA: Sage.

Tversky, A. & Kahneman, D. (1981). The framing of decisions and the psychology of choice. *Science, 211,* 453–458.

Tyler, T. & Hastie, R. (1991). The social consequences of cognitive illusions. In M. Bazerman, R. Lewicki, and B. H. Sheppard (Eds.), *Research on Negotiation in Organizations* (Vol. 3, pp. 69–98). Greenwich, CT: JAI Press.

Ury, W. (1991). *Getting past no: Negotiating with difficult people.* New York, NY: Bantam Books.

Ury, W. L., Brett, J. M., & Goldberg, S. B. (1988). *Getting disputes resolved.* San Francisco: Jossey Bass.

van de Vliert, E. & Kabanoff, B. (1988). *Toward theory-based measures of conflict management.* Paper presented at the annual meeting of the Academy of Management, Anaheim, CA.

van de Vliert, E. & Prein, H. C. M. (1989). The difference in the meaning of forcing in the conflict management of actors and observers. In M. Rahim (Ed.), *Managing conflict: An interdisciplinary approach* (pp. 51–63). New York, NY: Praeger.

Van Zandt, H. F. (1970 November–December). How to negotiate in Japan. *Harvard Business Review, 48* (6), 45–56.

Victor, B. & Cullen, J. (1988). The organizational bases of ethical work climates. *Administrative Science Quarterly, 33,* 1010–1025.

Vitz, P. C. & Kite, W. A. R. (1970). Factors affecting conflict and negotiation within an alliance. *Journal of Experimental Social Psychology, 5,* 233–247.

von Neumann, J. & Morgenstern, O. (1944). *Theory of games and economic behavior.* Princeton, NJ: Princeton University Press.

Vroom, V. H. (1973). A new look at managerial decision making. *Organizational Dynamics, 4,* 66–80.

Vroom, V. H. & Yetton P. (1973). *Leadership and decision making.* Pittsburgh, PA: University of Pittsburgh Press.

Walcott, C. & Hoppmann, P. (1975). Interaction analysis and bargaining behavior. *Experimental Study of Politics, 4,* 1–19.

Walcott, C., Hopmann, P. T., & King, T. D. (1977). The role of debate in negotiation. In D. Druckman (Ed.), *Negotiations: Social Psychological Perspectives* (pp. 193–911). Beverly Hills, CA: Sage.

Wall, J. A. (1977). Intergroup bargaining: Effects of opposing constituent's stance' bargain opposing representative sing, and representative's locus of control. *Journal of Conflict Resolution, 21,* 459–474.

Wall, J. A. (1981). Mediation: An analysis, review and proposed research. *Journal of Conflict Resolution, 25,* 157–180.

Wall, J. A. & Blum, M. (1991). Negotiations. *Journal of Management, 17,* 273–303.

Wall, J. A. & Lynn, A. (1993). Mediation: A current review. *Journal of Conflict Resolution, 37,* 160–194.

Walton, R. (1987). *Managing conflict: Interpersonal dialogue and third-party roles* (2nd ed.). Reading, MA: Addison-Wesley.

Walton, R. E. & McKersie, R. B. (1965). *A behavioral theory of labor negotiations: An analysis of a social interaction system.* New York, NY: McGraw-Hill.

Watson, C. & Kasten, B. (1988). *Separate strengths? How men and women negotiate.* Newark, NJ: Center for Negotiation and Conflict Resolution, Rutgers University.

Weick, K. & Bougon, M. (1986). Organizations as cognitive maps: Charting ways to success and failure. In H. Sims, D. Gioia, and Associates (Eds.), *The thinking organization: Dynamics of organizational social cognition* (pp. 102–133). San Francisco, CA: Jossey-Bass.

Weingart, L. R., Thompson, L. L., Bazerman, M. H., & Carroll, J. S. (1990). Tactical behaviors and negotiation outcomes. *The International Journal of Conflict Management, 1,* 7–31.

Weiss, S. E. (1993). Analysis of complex negotiations in international business: The RBC perspective. *Organizational Science, 4,* 269–300.

Weiss, S. E. (in press). Negotiating with "Romans": A range of culturally-responsive strategies. *Sloan Management Review,*

Weiss, S. E. & Stripp, W. (1985). *Negotiating with foreign business persons: An introduction for Americans with propositions on six cultures.* New York, NY: New York University Graduate School of Business Administration, Working Paper #85–6.

Werth, L. F. & Flannery, J. (1986). A phenomenological approach to human deception. In R. W. Mitchell & N. S. Thompson (Eds), *Deception: Perspectives on human and non-human deceit* (pp. 293–311). Albany, NY: State University of New York Press.

Wilson, S. R. & Putnam, L. L. (1990). Interaction goals in negotiation. In J. Anderson (Ed.), *Communication yearbook* (Vol. 13, pp. 374–406.) Newbury Park, CA: Sage.

Wolff, F. I., Marsnik, N. C., Tacey, W. S., & Nichols, R. G. (1983). *Perceptive listening.* New York, NY: Holt, Rinehart & Winston.

Wolvin, A. D. & Coakley, C. G. (1988). *Listening* (3rd ed.). Dubuque, IA: Wm. C. Brown.

Wolvin, A. D. & Coakley, C. G. (1991). A survey of the status of listening training in some Fortune 500 corporations. *Communication education, 40,* 152–164.

Wood, R. & Bandura, A. (1989). Social cognitive theory of organizational management. *Academy of Management Review, 14,* 361–384.

Yankelovich, D. (1982, August). Lying well is the best revenge. *Psychology Today, 71,* 5–6, 71.

Young, O. (1972). Intermediaries: Additional thoughts on third parties. *Journal of Conflict Resolution, 16,* 51–65

Yukl, G. (1974). Effects of the opponent's initial offer, concession magnitude, and concession frequency on bargaining behavior. *Journal of Personality & Social Psychology, 30,* 323–335.

Yukl, G. & Tracey, J. A. B. (1992). Consequences of influence tactics used with subordinates, peers and the boss. *Journal of Applied Psychology, 77,* 525–535.

Zartman, I. W. (1977). Negotiation as a joint decision making process. In I. Zartman (Ed.), *The negotiation process: Theories and applications* (pp. 67–86). Beverly Hills, CA: Sage.

Zartman, W. & Berman, M. (1982). *The practical negotiator.* New Haven: Yale University Press.

Zimbardo, P. G., Ebbesen, E. B., & Maslach, C. (1977). *Influencing attitudes and changing behavior.* Reading, MA: Addison-Wesley.

Zubek, J., Pruitt, D., Pierce, R., & Iocolano, A. (1989, June). *Mediator and disputant characteristics and behavior as they affect the outcome of community mediation.* Paper presented at the Second Annual Meeting of the International Association for Conflict Management, Athens, GA.

Zuker, E. (1991). *The Seven Secrets of Influence.* New York, NY: McGraw Hill.

# Name Index

Aaronson, K., 73, 77
Abel, R. L., 187
Ableson, R. P., 185
Acuff, F. L., 408, 424
Adler, N. J., 407, 408, 409, 429
Akers, John, 377
Alderfer, C. P., 140, 149, 366
Allen, M., 211
Ancona, D., 284
Anderson, J. C., 356
Ansoff, H. I., 109
Anton, Ronald J., 385, 396, 397, 401
Asherman, Ira G., 128
Asherman, Sandra Vance, 128
Ash, R. A., 260
Athos, A. G., 195
Atkinson, G., 178n
Austin, R. A., 193
Avila, R. A., 209
Axelrod, R., 40, 41n, 187, 190
Axtell, R. E.420, 422
Ayres, I., 342, 343n

Bahrami, H., 356
Baitsel, J. M., 32
Bales, R. F., 176, 177
Bandura, A., 337, 338
Baranowski, T. A., 65
Bar-Hillel, M., 186
Barnard, C., 305
Barnes, J. W., 419
Bart, J., 30
Bateson, B., 161
Bavetta, A. G., 338
Bayley, J., 366
Bazerman, M., 15, 16, 32, 33, 34, 35, 63, 66, 91, 104, 106, 159
Beckhard, R., 353, 365
Beckman, N., 43, 402
Beisecker, T., 30
Bem, D., 231
Benjamin, A. J., 366
Benson, E., 318
Benton, A. A., 256, 261
Ben-Yoav, O., 332
Bercovitch, J., 358n

Berkowitz, L., 207n
Berlo, D. K., 216
Berman, M., 17, 178n, 188
Bernstein, J., 171
Bettinghaus, E. P., 210, 211, 212, 213, 218
Bies, R., 163, 389
Binnendijk, H., 407, 422
Blair, J. D., 17, 111, 115
Blake, R. R., 144, 149
Blumenfeld-Jones, T. S., 127, 368, 369
Blum, M., 357
Boatright, J. R., 379
Boehringer, G. H., 366
Bok, S., 390
Bone, D., 193
Bonoma, T., 40, 104, 219
Borman, Frank, 76
Boster, F. J., 213
Bostrom, R. N.193
Bougon, M., 190
Boulding, K., 297
Bowers, J. W., 212, 214
Bowie, N., 402
Bradac, J. J., 188, 189
Bradford, D., 297, 313, 315
Braganti, N. L., 422
Braginsky, D. D., 399
Brahm, R., 409
Bramson, R., 167, 171, 172
Brass, D. J., 308
Breaugh, J. A., 261
Brehm, J. W., 186, 234
Brenner, A. R., 63
Brett, J., 14, 277, 282, 283, 285, 287n, 355, 368, 369
Brief, A., 403
Britton, S. D., 257
Brock, T. C., 214
Brooks, E., 73, 77
Brown, B. R., 4, 65, 102, 104, 125, 130, 136, 256, 331n
Brown, L. D., 144
Brown, R. C., 40
Bruner, J. S., 183
Burgoon, M., 212, 213, 214, 215
Burrough, B. A., 375
Burton, J., 89

# General Index